LITERATURE AS ART: A READER

THE LIMBOURG BROTHERS: *August*, FROM *Les Tres Riches Heures du Duc de Berry*, MUSÉE CONDÉ, CHANTILLY, FRANCE.

LITERATURE AS ART: A READER

RALPH A. BRITSCH   TODD A. BRITSCH   GAIL W. BELL

BRIGHAM YOUNG UNIVERSITY PRESS

PN
6014
B734

Library of Congress Catalog Card Number: 70-161351
International Standard Book Number: 0-8425-1220-9
Brigham Young University Press, Provo, Utah 84601
© 1972 by Brigham Young University Press. All rights reserved
Printed in the United States of America. Previous edition: © 1965
1972 10M 94886

COPYRIGHTS AND ACKNOWLEDGMENTS

BANTAM BOOKS, INC. for "Babii Yar," by Yuvgeny Yevtushenko and "Parabolic Ballad" by Andrey Voznesensky, translated by George Reavey. From *Modern European Poetry*, edited by Willis Barnstone. Copyright © 1966 by Bantam Books, Inc.

MORRIS BISHOP for "Her Golden Hair," "On Hearing of Laura's Death," "He Sees Her Everywhere," and "Final Sonnet," of the Petrarch Sonnets, translated by Morris Bishop. Copyright by Morris Bishop.

DODD, MEAD & COMPANY, INC. for "The Obscure Night of the Soul," by St. John of the Cross from *Poems* by Arthur Symons. Copyright © 1927 by Dodd, Mead & Company, Inc.

DOUBLEDAY & COMPANY, INC. for "Elegy for Jane," copyright 1950 by Theodore Roethke, and "I Knew a Woman," copyright 1954 by Theodore Roethke from *Collected Poems of Theodore Roethke*. Reprinted by permissions of Doubleday & Company, Inc. For "The Sculpturing of the *David*," from the book *The Agony and the Ecstasy* by Irving Stone. Copyright © 1961 by Doubleday & Company, Inc. Reprinted by permission of Doubleday & Company, Inc.

E. P. DUTTON & COMPANY, INC. for Book II from the book *Of the Nature of Things* by Lucretius. Translated by William Ellery Leonard. Everyman's Library Edition. Published by E. P. Dutton & Company, Inc., and reprinted with their permission.

NORMA MILLAY ELLIS for "Euclid alone has looked on Beauty bare" and "On Hearing a Symphony of Beethoven." From *Collected Poems*, Harper & Row. Copyright 1923, 1928, 1951, 1955 by Edna St. Vincent Millay and Norma Millay Ellis. By permission of Norma Millay Ellis.

FARRAR, STRAUS & GIROUX, INC. for "Within and Without," by Hermann Hesse. Reprinted with the permission of Farrar, Straus & Giroux, Inc., from *Great Stories by Nobel Prize Winners*, edited by Leon Hamalian and Edmond L. Volpe, translated by T. K. Brown, copyright © 1959 by The Noonday Press.

JOHN GREEN of Brigham Young University for his translation of Moliere's "The Bourgeois Gentleman."

HARCOURT BRACE JOVANOVICH, INC. for "Journey of the Magi," from *Collected Poems* 1909-1962 by T. S. Eliot, copyright, 1936, by Harcourt Brace Jovanovich, Inc.; copyright © 1963, 1964, by T. S. Eliot. Reprinted by permission of the publisher. For "Wind Song," from *Smoke and Steel* by Carl Sandburg, copyright, 1920, by Harcourt Brace Jovanovich, Inc.; copyright, 1948, by Carl Sandburg. Reprinted by permission of the publisher. For "This is the garden," copyright, 1925, 1953, by E. E. Cummings. Reprinted from his volume *Poems* 1923-1954 by permission of Harcourt Brace Jovanovich, Inc. For "Jazz Fantasia," from *Smoke and Steel* by Carl Sandburg, copyright, 1920, by Harcourt Brace Jovanovich, Inc.; copyright, 1948, by Carl Sandburg. Reprinted by permission of the publisher. For "Falling Asleep over the Aeneid," copyright, 1951, by Robert Lowell. Reprinted from his volume *The Mills of the Kavanaughs* by permission of Harcourt Brace Jovanovich, Inc.

HARPER & ROW, PUBLISHERS, INC. for Act III, Scene I, and Act V from *Pelléas and Mélisande* by Maurice Maeterlinck, translated by Donald J. McGinn, as it appears in *Literature As a Fine Art*, edited by Donald J. McGinn and George Howerton. Copyright © 1959 by Row, Peterson and Company. Reprinted by permission of Harper & Row, Publishers, Inc. For "St. Teresa of Avila" from *The Flaming Heart or the Life of the Glorious St. Teresa*, trans. M. T., as it appears in *Literature As a Fine Art*, edited by Donald J. McGinn and George Howerton. Copyright © 1959 by Row, Peterson and Company. Reprinted by permission of Harper & Row, Publishers, Inc. For "L'Apres-Midi d'un Faune" (from the French of Stéphane Mallarmé) in *The Collected Poetry of Aldous Huxley*, edited by Donald Watt. Copyright © 1971 by Laura Huxley. Reprinted by permission of Harper & Row, Publishers, Inc.

HOLT, RINEHART AND WINSTON, INC. for "Fog" and "Nocturne in a Deserted Brickyard" from *Chicago Poems* by Carl Sandburg. Copyright 1916 by Holt, Rinehart and Winston, Inc. Copyright 1944 by

Carl Sandburg. Reprinted by permission of Holt, Rinehart and Winston, Inc. For "The Tuft of Flowers," "Acquainted with the Night," "Tree at My Window," and "The Onset" from *The Poetry of Robert Frost*, edited by Edward Connery Lathem. Copyright 1934, © 1969 by Holt, Rinehart and Winston, Inc. Copyright © 1962 by Robert Frost. Reprinted by permission of Holt, Rinehart and Winston, Inc. For "Loveliest of Trees" from "A Shropshire Lad" — Authorized Edition — from *The Collected Poems of A. E. Housman*. Copyright 1939, 1940, © 1959 by Holt, Rinehart and Winston, Inc. Copyright © 1967, 1968 by Robert E. Symons. Reprinted by permission of Holt, Rinehart and Winston, Inc.

HOUGHTON MIFFLIN COMPANY for "You, Andrew Marvell" from *Collected Poems of Archibald MacLeish, 1917-1952*. Reprinted by permission of the publisher, Houghton Mifflin Company.

THE MACMILLAN COMPANY for "Poetry" from *Collected Poems* by Marianne Moore. Copyright 1951 by Marianne Moore. Reprinted with permission of The Macmillan Company. For "The Lake Isle of Innisfree." Reprinted with permission of The Macmillan Company from *Collected Poems* by William Butler Yeats. Copyright 1906 by The Macmillan Company, renewed 1934 by William Butler Yeats. For "The Wild Swans at Coole." Reprinted with permission of The Macmillan Company from *Collected Poems* by William Butler Yeats. Copyright 1919 by The Macmillan Company, renewed 1947 by Bertha Georgie Yeats. For "On Growing Old." Reprinted with permission of The Macmillan Company from *Poems* by John Masefield. Copyright 1920 by John Masefield, renewed 1948 by John Masefield. For "When You Are Old." Reprinted with permission of The Macmillan Company from *Collected Poems* by William Butler Yeats. Copyright 1906 by The Macmillan Company, renewed 1934 by William Butler Yeats.

MACMILLAN SERVICES LTD. for excerpts from *Don Quixote* by Miguel de Cervantes, translated by Starkie. © 1957 by Macmillan Services Ltd.

DAVID MC KAY COMPANY, INC. for "The Prioress's Tale," from Chaucer's *The Canterbury Tales*, translated by Frank Ernest Hill. Copyright © 1964 by Frank Ernest Hill. (New York: David McKay Company, Inc.) Used by permission of the publisher.

METHUEN COMPANY, LTD. for Chapter XXI of "The Little Flowers of St. Francis," translated by W. Heywood. Reprinted by permission of Methuen Company, Ltd.

THE NEW AMERICAN LIBRARY, INC. for excerpts from "Medea and Jason's first exchange," "Chorale ode on moderation in love," and "Medea's farewell to her children," from *Three Great Plays of Euripides*, translated by Rex Warner. Copyright 1944 by Rex Warner. Reprinted by permission of The New American Library, Inc., New York.

NEW DIRECTIONS PUBLISHING CORPORATION for "Lament for Ignacio Sanchez Mejias." Federico García Lorca, *Selected Poems*. Copyright 1955 by New Directions Publishing Corporation. Reprinted by permission of New Directions Publishing Corporation. For "Do not go gentle...," "Fern Hill," and "In My Craft or Sullen Art." Dylan Thomas, *Collected Poems*. Copyright 1946 by New Directions Publishing Corporation, 1952 by Dylan Thomas. Reprinted by permission of New Directions Publishing Corporation. For "Dawn." William Carlos Williams, *Collected Earlier Poems*. Copyright 1938 by William Carlos Williams. Reprinted by permission of New Directions Publishing Corporation. For "A Virginal." Ezra Pound, *Personae*. Copyright 1926 by Ezra Pound. Reprinted by permission of New Directions Publishing Corporation. For No. 15, "Constantly risking absurdity...." Lawrence Ferlinghetti, *A Coney Island of the Mind*. Copyright 1958 by Lawrence Ferlinghetti. Reprinted by permission of New Directions Publishing Corporation.

HAROLD OBER ASSOCIATES INCORPORATED for "Saturday Night" by Langston Hughes from *Fine Clothes to the Jew*. Copyright 1927 by Alfred A. Knopf, Inc. Reprinted by permission of Harold Ober Associates Incorporated.

OXFORD UNIVERSITY PRESS, INC. for excerpts from *Beowulf: the Oldest English Epic*, translated by Charles W. Kennedy. Copyright © 1940 by Oxford University Press, Inc. Renewed 1968 by Charles W. Kennedy. Reprinted by permission. For "Morning Song of Senlin" and "At a Concert of Music" from *Collected Poems* by Conrad Aiken. Copyright © 1953 by Conrad Aiken. Reprinted by permission of Oxford University Press, Inc.

PENGUIN BOOKS, LTD. for excerpts from Philip Vellacott (tr): Aeschylus' *Agamemnon*. For. E. F. Watling (tr): Sophocles' *Antigone* (36 pp.). For E. F. Watling (tr): Sophocles' *Oedipus at Colonus*. For Cantos 1, 5, 13, 26, and 34 of *The Inferno* from Dante: *The Divine Comedy*, tr. Dorothy L. Sayers. Copyright Estate of Dorothy L. Sayers, 1949.

RANDOM HOUSE, INC. for excerpts from *The Plague*, by Albert Camus, trans. by Stuart Gilbert. Copyright 1948 by Stuart Gilbert. Reprinted by permission of Alfred A. Knopf, Inc. For "I think continually of those." Copyright 1934 and renewed 1962 by Stephen Spender. Reprinted from *Collected Poems 1928-1953*, by Stephen Spender, by permission of Random House, Inc. "Musée des Beaux Arts." Copyright 1940 and renewed 1968 by W. H. Auden. Reprinted from *Collected Shorter Poems 1927-1957*, by W. H. Auden, by permission of Random House, Inc. For "The Road from Colonus." Copyright 1947 by Alfred A. Knopf, Inc. Reprinted from *Collected Tales of E. M. Forster*, by permission of the publisher. For excerpts from *Eugene Onegin*, from *The Poems, Prose and Plays of Alexander Pushkin*. Copyright 1936 and renewed 1964 by Random House, Inc.

Reprinted by permission. For "Little Lizzie." Copyright 1936 and renewed 1964 by Alfred A. Knopf, Inc. Reprinted from *Stories of Three Decades,* by Thomas Mann, trans. by H. T. Lowe-Porter, by permission of the publisher. For excerpts from *Rembrandt,* by Gladys Schmitt. Copyright © 1961 by Gladys Schmitt. Reprinted by permission of Random House, Inc. For "Peter Quince at the Clavier." Copyright 1923 and renewed 1951 by Wallace Stevens. Reprinted from *Collected Poems of Wallace Stevens* by permission of Alfred A. Knopf, Inc. For "Velvet Shoes." Copyright 1921 by Alfred A. Knopf, Inc., and renewed 1949 by William Rose Benet. Reprinted from *Collected Poems of Elinor Wylie,* by permission of the publisher. For "Castilian." Copyright 1923 by Alfred A. Knopf, Inc. Reprinted from *Collected Poems of Elinor Wylie* by permission of the publisher. For "Paul's Case." Reprinted from *Youth and the Bright Medusa,* by Willa Cather, courtesy of Alfred A. Knopf, Inc. For "Homesick Blues." Copyright 1927 by Alfred A. Knopf, Inc., and renewed 1955 by Langston Hughes. Reprinted from *The Dream Keeper* by Langston Hughes, by permission of the publisher. For "Love the Wild Swan." Copyright 1935 and renewed 1963 by Donnan Jeffers and Garth Jeffers. Reprinted from *Selected Poetry of Robinson Jeffers* by permission of Random House, Inc. For "Hurt Hawks." Copyright 1928 and renewed 1956 by Robinson Jeffers. Reprinted from *Selected Poetry of Robinson Jeffers* by permission of Random House, Inc. For excerpts from *Faust I,* by Johann Wolfgang von Goethe, trans. by Bayard Taylor. Reprinted courtesy of Random House. For Chapters V, VI, VII, and XXX from *Candide and Other Writings,* translated by Richard Aldington and edited by Haskell M. Block. Reprinted courtesy of Random House.

JAMES L. ROSENBERG for stanzas 7-11 and 56-66 from *Sir Gawain and the Green Knight,* edited by J. R. Kreuzer and translated by J. L. Rosenberg. Copyright © 1959 by James L. Rosenberg.

SCHOCKEN BOOKS INC. for "A Hunger Artist," translated by Willa and Edwin Muir. Reprinted by permission of Schocken Books Inc. from *The Penal Colony* by Franz Kafka. Copyright © 1948 by Schocken Books Inc.

CHARLES SCRIBNER'S SONS for "A Clean, Well-Lighted Place" (Copyright 1933 Charles Scribner's Sons; renewal copyright © 1961 Ernest Hemingway); reprinted by permission of Charles Scribner's Sons from *Winner Take Nothing* by Ernest Hemingway. "Hunters in the Snow: Brueghel" is reprinted by permission of Charles Scribner's Sons from *The Green Town: Poems* by Joseph Langland. Copyright © 1956 Joseph Langland. (*Poets of Today III*). For Théophile Gautier's poem "Art" from *Poems* by George Santayana (Charles Scribner's Sons). For "Luke Havergal" from *The Children of the Night* by Edwin Arlington Robinson (Charles Scribner's Sons, 1897).

SIMON AND SCHUSTER, INC. for Book I from *The Odyssey: A Modern Sequel,* by Nikos Kazantzakis. Copyright © 1958, by Simon and Schuster, Inc. Reprinted by permission of Simon and Schuster, Inc.

IRENE SPEARS of Brigham Young University for her translations of Verlaine's "Song of Autumn" and "Thou Hast Wounded Me, Lord."

UNIVERSITY OF CALIFORNIA PRESS for "Autumn Day," "Autumn," and "Panther" from *Rainer Maria Rilke: Poems,* trans. by C. F. MacIntyre. Originally published by the University of California Press; reprinted by permission of The Regents of the University of California.

THE UNIVERSITY OF CHICAGO PRESS for excerpts from *The Iliad,* by Homer, translated by Richmond Lattimore. Copyright 1951 by The University of Chicago Press.

UNIVERSITY OF TEXAS PRESS for selections from *Platero and I,* by Juan Ramón Jiménez, translated by Eloise Roach. Copyright 1957 by University of Texas Press.

VERLAG DER ARCHE for "Ah, the Distant Land" ("Ach, das ferne Land"). Gottfried Benn: "Statische Gedichte," copyright Arche Verlag, Zurich, 1948.

THE VIKING PRESS, INC. for "In the Cart," from *The Portable Chekhov,* edited by Avrahm Yarmolinsky. Copyright 1947 by The Viking Press, Inc. Reprinted by permission of The Viking Press, Inc. For "Clay," from *Dubliners* by James Joyce. Originally published by B. W. Huebsch, Inc. in 1916. Copyright © 1967 by the Estate of James Joyce. All rights reserved. Reprinted by permission of The Viking Press, Inc. For "Piano," from *The Complete Poems of D. H. Lawrence,* Volume I, edited by Vivian Sola Pinto and F. Warren Roberts. Copyright 1920 by B. W. Huebsch, Inc., renewed 1948 by Frieda Lawrence. Reprinted by permission of The Viking Press, Inc. For "Orpheus and Eurydice," from *Ovid: The Metamorphoses,* translated by Horace Gregory. Copyright © 1958 by The Viking Press, Inc. Reprinted by permission of The Viking Press, Inc.

CONTENTS

Illustrations   xvii
Preface   xix

I.   CLASSICISM   1

Homer	from *The Iliad* 7
	from *The Odyssey* 24
Archilochus	On Losing His Shield 35
Sappho	Ode to Aphrodite 35
	Hesperus, the Bringer 36
	Mother, I Cannot Mind My Wheel 36
Anacreon	The Wounded Cupid 36
Pindar	First Olympian Ode 37
Empedocles	A Twofold Truth 40
Callimachus	Heraclitus 41
	Crethis 41
Aeschylus	from *Agamemnon* 43
Sophocles	Antigone 46
Euripides	from *Medea* 79
Plato	The Death of Socrates from *Phaedo* 85
Aristotle	The Nature of Tragedy from *On Tragedy* 87
Theocritus	The Incantation 95
Lucretius	from *Of the Nature of Things* 99
Virgil	from *Aeneid* 103
Catullus	On Lesbia 115
	Love Is Best 115
	After a Quarrel 115
	At the Grave of His Brother 115
Horace	To Postumus 116
Ovid	Orpheus and Eurydice 116
Pliny the Younger	The Tuscan Villa 121
	from *The Villas of Pliny the Younger*
Marcus Aurelius	from *The Meditations* 127

II.   CHRISTIANITY AND
THE MIDDLE AGES   131

Bible	The Creation 137
	The Messiah 138
	Psalms 139, 140

	The Annunciation 141
	The Birth of Christ 141
	The Last Supper 142
Saint Augustine	from *Confessions* 143
Anonymous	from *Beowulf* 148
Anonymous	from *The Song of Roland* 151
Anonymous	Te Deum 157
Saint Francis of Assisi	from *Little Flowers* 159
Thomas of Celano	Dies Irae 161
Dante Alighieri	five cantos from the Inferno 163
	from the *Divine Comedy*
Anonymous	from *Sir Gawain and the Green Knight* 187
Geoffrey Chaucer	The Prioress's Tale from *The Canterbury Tales* 198
John Ruskin	St. Mark's from *The Stones of Venice* 201
Henry Adams	The Virgin of Chartres 203
	from *Mont-Saint-Michel and Chartres*

III. RENAISSANCE 209

Edmund Spenser	from *An Hymn in Honour of Beauty* 213
Desiderius Erasmus	The Powers and Pleasures of Folly 216
	from *The Praise of Folly*
Giovanni Boccaccio	The Plague of 1348 219
	The Falcon of Federigo 223
	Chichibio and the Crane 226
	The Patient Griselda 227
	from the *Decameron*
Petrarch	If It Be Destined 233
	When I Reflect 233
	In Gratitude to Love 234
	Her Golden Hair 234
	On Hearing of Laura's Death 234
	He Sees Her Everywhere 235
	Final Sonnet 235
Niccolo Machiavelli	In What Way Faith Should Be Kept by Princes 235
	Fortune Is a Woman 237
	from *The Prince*
Benvenuto Cellini	The Casting of the Perseus 239
Sir Thomas Wyatt	Description of the Contrarious Passions in a Lover 247
Henry Howard, Earl of Surrey	Complaint of a Lover Rebuked 247
Pierre de Ronsard	To Marie 248
Edmund Spenser	Sonnet 15 (Ye Tradeful Merchants) 248
Sir Philip Sidney	With How Sad Steps 248
	Leave Me, O Love 248
Michael Drayton	Since There's No Help 249
William Shakespeare	Sonnet 8 (Music to Hear) 249
	Sonnet 18 (Shall I Compare Thee) 249
	Sonnet 30 (When to the Sessions) 250

	Sonnet 55 (Not Marble Nor the Gilded Monuments) 250
	Sonnet 73 (That Time of Year) 250
	Who Is Sylvia? 251
Orlando Gibbons	The Silver Swan 251
Walter Pater	La Gioconda 251
	from *The Renaissance*
Dmitri Merezhkovsky	Monna Lisa Gioconda 252
	from *The Romance of Leonardo da Vinci*
Irving Stone	The Sculpturing of the *David* 261
	from *The Agony and the Ecstasy*

IV. MANNERISM TO NEOCLASSICISM 267

Saint Teresa of Avila	from *The Flaming Heart or the Life of the Glorious Saint Teresa* 271
Miguel de Cervantes	from *Don Quixote* 273
Saint John of the Cross	The Obscure Night of the Soul 279
John Donne	Meditation 17 280
	Song 281
	Song 281
	from Holy Sonnets 282
	A Hymn to God the Father 282
George Herbert	The Altar 283
	Easter Wings 284
Calderón	The Dream Called Life 284
	from *Life Is a Dream*
John Milton	Lycidas 285
	from *Paradise Lost* 288
Andrew Marvell	To His Coy Mistress 301
Molière	from *The Bourgeois Gentleman* 303
John Dryden	A Song for St. Cecilia's Day 314
Edward Taylor	Housewifery 314
Jonathan Swift	A Voyage to Brobdingnag 315
	from *Gulliver's Travels*
Alexander Pope	from *An Essay on Man* 332
Voltaire	from *Candide* 337
Robert Herrick	To Daffodils 343
	Corinna's Going a-Maying 343
Gladys Schmitt	The Syndics from *Rembrandt* 344

V. ROMANTICISM 355

Continental 359

Heinrich Heine	Du Bist wie eine Blume 359
	The Two Grenadiers 359
Victor Hugo	The Djinns 360
Théophile Gautier	Art 363
Charles Baudelaire	Sois Sage O Ma Douleur 365

Jean-Jacques Rousseau	Correspondences 365
Johann Wolfgang von Goethe	from *The Confessions* 366
	from *Faust I* 368
	The Erl-King 420
Alexander Pushkin	from *Eugene Onegin* 421
Ivan Turgenev	The Singers 425

English   436

William Blake	Introduction 436
	The Divine Image 436
	from *Songs of Innocence*
	A Poison Tree 437
	London 437
	from *Songs of Experience*
Robert Burns	Ye Flowery Banks 437
	Afton Water 438
	A Red, Red Rose 439
William Wordsworth	Composed upon Westminster Bridge 439
	My Heart Leaps Up When I Behold 439
	I Wandered Lonely as a Cloud 439
	It Is a Beauteous Evening, Calm and Free 441
Samuel Taylor Coleridge	Kubla Khan: or, A Vision in a Dream 441
	The Eolian Harp 442
George Gordon, Lord Byron	Canto the Fourth 444
	from *Don Juan*
	Stanzas for Music 462
	She Walks in Beauty 462
	from *Hebrew Melodies*
Percy Bysshe Shelley	Ode to the West Wind 463
	Mutability 464
	Ozymandias 465
John Keats	La Belle Dame Sans Mercy 465
	Ode to a Nightingale 466
	Ode on a Grecian Urn 469
	The Last Sonnet 470
Alfred, Lord Tennyson	Mariana 471
	Ulysses 472
	Sweet and Low 474
	The Splendor Falls on Castle Walls 474
	Tears, Idle Tears 475
	Now Sleeps the Crimson Petal 475
	Songs from *The Princess*
Robert Browning	My Last Duchess 476
	The Bishop Orders His Tomb at Saint Praxed's Church 478
	Fra Lippo Lippi 481
	Meeting at Night 491
Matthew Arnold	The Forsaken Merman 492
	Dover Beach 493
Dante Gabriel Rossetti	Silent Noon 494

Christina Rossetti	A Birthday 494
Algernon Charles Swinburne	The Garden of Proserpine 495
	When the Hounds of Spring 496
	from *Atalanta in Calydon*
Thomas Hardy	The Oxen 498
	In Time of "The Breaking of Nations" 498
	The Darkling Thrush 498
Gerard Manley Hopkins	God's Grandeur 499
	The Windhover 499
	Pied Beauty 500
	Spring and Fall 500
A. E. Housman	To an Athlete Dying Young 501
	Loveliest of Trees, the Cherry Now 501
	American 502
Philip Freneau	The Wild Honeysuckle 502
William Cullen Bryant	To a Waterfowl 502
Ralph Waldo Emerson	The Rhodora 503
	Days 504
Henry Wadsworth Longfellow	Hymn to the Night 504
	from *Divina Commedia* 505
	translation of Michelangelo's *Dante* 506
Edgar Allan Poe	To Helen 506
	Ulalume 506
	Israfel 508
Walt Whitman	When I Heard the Learn'd Astronomer 508
	There Was a Child Went Forth 509
Emily Dickinson	To Hear an Oriole Sing 511
	There's a Certain Slant of Light 511
	There Is No Frigate like a Book 513
Sidney Lanier	Evening Song 513
	A Ballad of Trees and the Master 513
Edgar Allan Poe	The Masque of the Red Death 514
Nathaniel Hawthorne	The Wedding Knell 517

VI. REALISM AND IMPRESSIONISM   523

Henrik Ibsen	*The Master Builder* 526
Leo Tolstoy	Three Deaths: A Tale 572
Mark Twain	from *The Innocents Abroad* 580
Stéphane Mallarmé	Afternoon of a Faun 584
Paul Verlaine	Song of Autumn 588
	Thou Hast Wounded Me, Lord 588
Oscar Wilde	Preface to *The Picture of Dorian Gray* 590
George Bernard Shaw	Shaw on Music 590
	from *Androcles and the Lion* 594
Anton Pavlovich Chekhov	In the Cart 599
Maurice Maeterlinck	from *Pelléas and Mélisande* 605

VII. TWENTIETH CENTURY   615

William Butler Yeats	The Lake Isle of Innisfree 619
	The Wild Swans at Coole 619
	When You Are Old 620
Edwin Arlington Robinson	Luke Havergal 620
Paul Valéry	The Graveyard by the Sea 621
Robert Frost	Acquainted with the Night 625
	Tree at My Window 626
	The Onset 626
	The Tuft of Flowers 627
Rainer Maria Rilke	Autumn Day 628
	Autumn 629
	The Panther 629
Thomas Mann	Little Lizzy 631
Willa Cather	Paul's Case 639
Hermann Hesse	Within and Without 653
John Masefield	On Growing Old 661
Carl Sandburg	Fog 662
	Nocturne in a Deserted Brickyard 662
	Jazz Fantasia 663
	Wind Song 663
Wallace Stevens	Peter Quince at the Clavier 664
E. M. Forster	The Road from Colonus 665
Juan Ramón Jiménez	from *Platero and I* 672
James Joyce	Clay 675
	from *Dubliners*
Nikos Kazantzakis	from *The Odyssey: A Modern Sequel* 679
D. H. Lawrence	Piano 683
William Carlos Williams	Dawn 684
Elinor Wylie	Velvet Shoes 684
	Castilian 684
Ezra Pound	The River-Merchant's Wife: A Letter 685
	A Virginal 685
Robinson Jeffers	Hurt Hawks 686
	Love the Wild Swan 687
Marianne Moore	Poetry 687
T. S. Eliot	Journey of the Magi 688
	Sweeney among the Nightingales 689
	Morning Song of Senlin 690
Conrad Aiken	At a Concert of Music 692
Edna St. Vincent Millay	Euclid Alone Has Looked on Beauty Bare 693
	On Hearing a Symphony of Beethoven 693
Archibald MacLeish	You, Andrew Marvell 694
Franz Kafka	A Hunger Artist 694
Gottfried Benn	Ah, the Distant Land 700
E. E. Cummings	This Is the Garden 701
Federico García Lorca	Lament for Ignacio Sanchez Mejias 703
Ernest Hemingway	A Clean, Well-Lighted Place 708

Langston Hughes	Homesick Blues 711
	Saturday Night 711
W. H. Auden	Musée des Beaux Arts 712
Theodore Roethke	Elegy for Jane 712
	I Knew a Woman 713
Stephen Spender	I Think Continually of Those 714
Dylan Thomas	Do Not Go Gentle into That Good Night 714
	In My Craft or Sullen Art 715
	Fern Hill 715
Albert Camus	from *The Plague* 717
Joseph Langland	Hunters in the Snow: Brueghel 723
Robert Lowell	Falling Asleep over the Aeneid 725
Lawrence Ferlinghetti	Constantly Risking Absurdity . . . 727
	from *A Coney Island of the Mind*
Yuvgeny Yevtushenko	Babii Yar 728
Andrey Voznesensky	Parabolic Ballad 730

Index   733

ILLUSTRATIONS

Page
- iv frontispiece   The Limbourg Brothers: *August,* from *Les Très Riches Heures du Duc de Berry*
- 1 *Caryatids*
- 6 Bust of *Homer*
- 19 *Lapith and Centaur*
- 27 Dosso Dossi: *Circe and Her Lovers in a Landscape*
- 34 *Venus de Milo*
- 42 Greek Theater
- 46 Greek Temple to Athena
- 67 Lions at Delos
- 78 The Acropolis at Athens
- 98 Pont du Gard at Nîmes
- 122 Hadrian's Villa
- 126 Detail from Marcus Aurelius
- 131 (Robert Campin?): *Flemish Annunciation*
- 136 Gerard David: *The Rest on the Flight into Egypt*
- 140 The Good Shepherd
- 144 Christ the Way
- 152 Towers of Carcassonne
- 160 Giotto: *Saint Francis' Sermon to the Birds*
- 164 Auguste Rodin: *The Gates of Hell*
- 204 Chartres Cathedral
- 204 Mont-Saint-Michel
- 209 Leonardo da Vinci: *Ginevra de'Benci*
- 214 Bernardino Luini: *Venus*
- 220 Rogier van der Weyden: *Portrait of a Lady*
- 240 Benvenuto Cellini: *Perseus*
- 246 Botticelli: *The Adoration of the Magi*
- 254 Leonardo da Vinci: *Mona Lisa*
- 262 Michelangelo: *David*
- 267 Giovanni Battista Tiepolo: *Apollo Pursuing Daphne*
- 272 Bernini: *St. Teresa in Ecstasy*
- 276 El Greco: *Laocoön*
- 302 Peter Paul Rubens: *Marchesa Brigida Spinola Doria*
- 316 Jean-Honoré Fragonard: *A Young Girl Reading*
- 350 Rembrandt: *Young Girl at an Open Half Door*
- 355 John Constable: *Wivenhoe Park, Essex*
- 358 Gericault: *Officer of the Imperial Guard*
- 440 Joseph Mallord William Turner: *The Dogana and Santa Maria Della Salute, Venice*

460 John Singleton Copley: *Watson and the Shark*
468 Parthenon Frieze
486 Fra Filippo Lippi: *Madonna and Child*
510 John Constable: *The Hay-Wain*
512 Jean-Baptist Camille Corot: *Interrupted Reading*
523 Édouard Manet: *Gare Saint-Lazare*
581 Winslow Homer: *Breezing Up*
587 Georges Seurat: *Sunday Afternoon on the Island of La Grande Jatte*
598 Paul Cézanne: *La Gardanne*
615 Wassily Kandinsky: *La flèche*
618 Henri Matisse: *Back*
630 Giorgio de Chirico: *The Child's Brain*
648 Grant Wood: *American Gothic*
660 Andrew Wyeth: *Ground Hog Day 1959*
680 Henri Matisse: *Bathers*
702 Pablo Picasso: *Mandolin and Guitar*
724 Pieter Bruegel: *Hunters in the Snow*
732 Robert Rauschenberg: *Monogram*

PREFACE TO STUDENTS AND TEACHERS

This book of readings grows out of an earlier text called *A Humanities Reader*. The present volume, however, is markedly different from the earlier one. It includes many new selections and deletes a number of others; it has more long works given in their entirety and more generous excerpts from others; it has illustrations representative of periods and works; it has more numerous and extended introductions to individual works; and, perhaps most important, it has introductions to the various periods of literary history. This last feature makes the reader suitable for courses that briefly survey the literature of the Western world. Specifically, however, it is intended for humanities courses in which emphasis is placed on the artistic or aesthetic aspects of experience. We expect that the book will generally be used as a companion to a basic text concerned with the relationships of the major arts: architecture, painting, sculpture, music, and literature. Numerous experiences in the visual arts (architecture, painting, and sculpture) and in music should be provided for the student in the basic text and through the use of slides, films, recordings, and so forth. This anthology is designed to provide experiences in the fifth and, for this course, probably the central art — literature.

The selections that follow provide examples of the art of literature — specifically the literature of the Western world — from its beginnings in Homer's Greece to the literature of our century. Since the selections are chronologically arranged, the book can be used in courses which survey the arts historically or according to periods or movements. And since all the major types of literature are represented, at least by excerpts, the anthology should also be useful in courses concerned with form, style, and related matters.

We have tried to avoid adding one more to the large number of readers in which the selections, at least the nonfictional ones, are directed toward science or social problems or politics. As we have read and made selections for this book, we have tried to keep the arts constantly in mind. Thus the readings from Greek and Roman literature are meant to exemplify the artistic aspects of classical drama, epic, lyric, and idyl. The selections from the Bible, in addition to their literary merit, have inspired musicians, painters, and other artists through the ages. The lyrics, from the Greeks through the Renaissance to the present, are examples of the poetic art at its most refined — that is, of lyricism; and many of them are concerned in their subject matter with artistic experience. The short stories are based on artistic subject matter and themes. The excerpts from novels deal in fictionalized ways with important persons and events in the history of the arts. The first of the dramas, Sophocles' *Antigone,* is an example of the art of tragedy; another, Ibsen's *The Master Builder,* has as one of its themes the frustration of the artistic impulse. (The course should probably also include one of Shakespeare's plays; but since they are so readily available in libraries or in inexpensive reprints, we have felt it advisable to leave the choice to the teacher and his class.) Here, then, are examples of the art of literature from Homer to Yevtushenko.

                                              Ralph A. Britsch
                                              Todd A. Britsch
                                              Gail W. Bell

CLASSICISM

Caryatids ON THE ERECTHEUM, ACROPOLIS, ATHENS

CLASSICISM

Literature becomes the voice of a people and time. Though great literature outlives its historical milieu, its values are enhanced when the reader understands something of its origins.

The Greek Peoples

The study of Western literature begins with a consideration of the writings of the Greeks, from whom much of Western culture took its form. The name *Greek* was given to that people by the Romans. The Greek peoples referred to themselves as *Hellenes* and to their country as *Hellas.* In speaking of the *Hellenic* culture, scholars apply the term to Greek culture in general, but especially to the great period of their civilization from about 500 B.C. to 323 B.C., the death of Alexander the Great. The term *Hellenistic* (Greeklike) applies to the period from the death of Alexander to approximately the middle of the second century before Christ.

The Greek mind rose from the blending of many people, as does the character of great civilizations at any time. But time dims our abilities to depict accurately the strength of various influences, other than those we can reconstruct through noticeable evidences such as art styles or language similarities. And students and scholars tend to simplify centuries of experience in order to represent many different influences.

Primarily, then, there were two basic forces affecting the evolvement of the Greek temper: the vigorous Indo-European, a great influx of nomadic tribes that took place over several centuries around two thousand years before Christ; and the Mycenaean, a branch of the widespread Aegean culture that was strongly molded around Eastern concepts of grace, beauty, and religious mythos, but that, at this point in its history, was well into the final stages of decay.

The success of the Greeks lay in the unique way they combined these seemingly opposite traits into a recognizable whole—the Greek Mind or Spirit—over a tumultuous period of growth and intertribal struggle, emerging by the fifth century before Christ in the great Athenian (Periclean) Golden Age of Greece.

There are definite traits that distinguish the Greeks from the civilizations preceding them. True, aspects of each existed in the many cultures influencing Greek development, but it remained for the Greek peoples to give them that particular Greek imprint.

Probably one of the key points in understanding the Greek way of life is to recognize the importance Greeks gave to the individual and his potential. This respect for man opened the doors to complementary developments: a respect for the mind and a basically democratic form of government, both encouraging freedom and creativity. The Greek love of beauty and perfection is also important. This characteristic prompted the Greek peoples to seek excellence in all things; *arete* the Greeks called it, one of those elements traceable back to the Mycenaeans.

Greek religion is polytheistic. The Greek gods were higher than man at best, but they were capable of many petty conflicts and jealousies. To the Greeks the sin of *hubris,* overweening pride, was the cause of man's fall from favor with the gods. This sin motivates many of the Greek tragedies.

Greek Literature

Consideration of Greek literature begins with two of the earliest extant works of European literature, *The Iliad* and *The Odyssey*. Traditionally accredited to the poet Homer, these epic poems were probably dictated to a scribe. The oral tradition is evident in the stock figures of speech, epithets, and other devices such as descriptive tags and familiar selections from long-favorite myths and legends, a common source for a clever bard. Homer added the final touch of genius, however—the facile, understanding, and humorous touch of the true poet—that gives these works a unity and form which place them among the great written works of the world.

The Iliad has some basis in historical fact, but from the battles of Troy to Homer's time storytellers had four centuries in which to embellish reality with fantasy and legend. *The Odyssey*, on the other hand, becomes almost a prototype for the later developing romantic novel. Both exist as unified works of art.

Peoples change and so do poetic fashions. From 700 to 450 B.C. the composing of epics was largely replaced by the writing of shorter poems. These lyric poems, as they are generally classified, show the great ability of the Greeks to combine thought and feeling in a strong, recognizable form. Even in translation they have a directness and beauty that is often lacking in more modern lyric poetry. Lyrics, of course, were composed to be sung. The soloist, or chorus as the case might be, was accompanied by a lyre (or a flute); that is where we get the name *lyric*.

Another important development of Hellenic literature, Greek tragedy, had its birth about 490 to 405 B.C. Peculiar to the Golden Age and strongly affecting writers through the centuries, Greek tragedy has never been successfully imitated. Such tragedies were musical presentations, chanted and sung to instrumental accompaniment. Presented in conjunction with sacred festivals, they were religiously oriented. Originally Greek drama was performed by a chorus of about fifty members that carried on a dialogue with a chorus leader. Tradition has it that Thespis introduced the form during the sixth century. We know that Aeschylus (ca. 525) added a second actor, reduced the size of the chorus to twelve, and helped establish the basic form: (a) four plays produced by one playwright were part of the annual dramatic competition, three of them tragedies and the fourth a comedy or satyr play; and (b) in each play the prologue appeared first, with scenes then alternating between the actors' dialogue and the chorus's singing and dancing.

Sophocles increased the chorus to fifteen and added a third actor. The last member of this dramatic trio, Euripides, decreased the role of the chorus and increased that of the prologue.

The Greeks, who loved form, excellence, and beauty, also developed some of our earliest and most essential literary criticism. Plato and his pupil Aristotle represent this literary form, Plato with an excerpt from *Phaedo* and Aristotle with an excerpt from *On Tragedy*. Plato, with his deep belief in the metaphysical "ideal," and Aristotle, with his strong argument for the basic form or structure of an artistic work, have established the basis for much of all other criticism.

The Hellenistic Period

The Hellenistic period saw much of the Greek way of life disseminated by her conquerors (Athens surrendered to Philip of Macedonia in 338 B.C.). Philip's successor, Alexander the Great, defeated the Persians, conquered Egypt, and extended his empire into Russian Turkistan and India. During this period Alexander left his impress not only on the military rolls of history, but he became the primary catalyst for the widespread influence of Greek culture, promoting literature and art throughout the world he ruled. However it was not the culture of the Golden Age of Greece, for it reflected many of the patterns of a newer, ever-changing world.

During this period a remarkable development in the history of literature occurred with the establishment of schools and libraries to preserve the arts and provide means to study them. Callimachus was a scholar-poet who benefited from his connection with the library supported by contributions from the Ptolemies.

The Impact of Rome

Greece declines and Rome grows, and so goes the course of civilization. The Romans were pragmatists, developers, and consolidators. Legend says that Rome was established by the Trojan hero Aeneas somewhere around the eighth century before Christ; this story provides the content of the epic poem *Aeneid,* by Virgil. In 509 B.C. a republic was established, and the Republic's course was one of warfare. Invaders were many. But by the last battles, the three Punic wars, Rome had emerged the victor. In 146 B.C. the Roman Republic encompassed the entire Hellenic territory, and a new era had begun. In 27 B.C. Octavian became Caesar Augustus, the first emperor of the Roman Empire, a political force unlike any other in the history of the world.

Rome learned from others and borrowed freely, but the Roman spirit was as strong in its way as the Greek. Romans were dedicated to the state and to a sense of divine destiny. *Duty* and *discipline* were key words in their makeup.

Roman culture was identified with three strong influences: agriculture, military life, and politics. Roman religion was not the personal religion of the Greeks. Roman gods were spirits, not manlike. The gods did not play the primary role in the development of Roman art that they did in Greek art. Gradually, with the strong development of the state, religion, too, became a part of the large Roman "machine." The ritualistic and formal worship of Rome replaced the charm and imagination of the Greeks. Perhaps this explains the ease with which a weak state religion moved to emperor-worship.

Roman Literature

Roman writers freely adopted Greek forms. They openly admired what the Greeks had produced and just as openly imitated them. Yet, because of the Latin concern for duty, much of their writing is moralistic. Virgil purposefully utilizes the epic form in the *Aeneid* in order to accomplish his intent: to demonstrate to the Roman people their great past and equally promising future.

By the first century before Christ, poetry had become separated from music and existed as a distinct art form. One of the best of the lyric poets was Catullus (ca. 84-54 B.C.). His poetry demonstrates an intensity of feeling that is particularly evident in his love lyrics addressed to Lesbia, in reality an older woman named Clodia who evidently felt the whole affair was a simple flirtation. Catullus composed many other beautiful lyrics concerned with his homeland and family that reveal a strain of romanticism which appears throughout Roman literature.

Horace (born 65 B.C.) was one of Rome's best appreciated poets. He wrote 108 *Odes* reminding his fellow Romans about the beauty of life, the virtue of wisdom, and the value of contentment. His *Satires* served the same purpose but have a more amusing tone.

One final glimpse at Roman literature must include a brief encounter with the philosophical writings of a nation that would not listen to her own counselors. Marcus Aurelius composed his work *The Meditations* as a guide for personal living. He wrote his meditations, concise bits of moralistic philosophy ranging from short sentences to long paragraphs, in Greek. The work reflects his Stoic philosophy: the freedom that comes from obeying God; the brotherhood of man; the importance of the inner man; and the calm acceptance of pain.

Such words of advice, however, found few listeners in an empire that was already beginning to decay. For Rome felt the force of internal weakness and strangely ignored it. Her mighty empire was spoiling from the center out.

BUST OF *Homer* IN THE MUSEO ARCHEOLOGICO NAZIONALE IN NAPLES

Homer
(9th or 8th cent. B.C.)
from *The Iliad*

The Iliad and The Odyssey, *epic poems composed probably about eight hundred years before Christ, are the oldest extant works of European literature, and they still hold their places among the supreme masterworks of the Western world. Though scholars disagree as to the authorship of the poems, there is no strong reason not to believe that they were both the works of a Greek poet named Homer, who lived in Asia Minor or on one of the Aegean islands.*

In The Iliad—*the tale of Ilios or Troy—Homer does not tell the entire story of the siege of Troy. Instead, he limits himself to the last six weeks of the siege, and particularly to the theme of the wrath of Achilles, the great Greek warrior who has been offended by his leader Agamemnon and hence refuses to fight any further. Ultimately he returns to the battle, but only after his friend Patroclus has been slain, in armor borrowed from Achilles. In the meantime, deeds of valor are done by various other heroes, including the Greeks Ajax and Diomedes and the Trojan Hector, most valiant of the sons of King Priam of Troy.*

In Book Six of The Iliad, *Hector goes to the palace of his brother Paris or Alexander—whose taking of Helen from Greece started the whole conflict—and reproaches him for staying out of the fighting. Then Hector has a strangely moving encounter with his wife Andromache and his young son Astyanax, a moment that has been called one of the high points of Western literature. This passage and the other from* The Iliad *that follow are from what is probably the finest of modern verse translations, that of Richmond Lattimore. Incidentally, he uses the Greek rather than the more familiar Latinized spellings of names.*

But Hektor went away to the house of Alexandros,
a splendid place he had built himself, with the men who at that time
were the best men for craftsmanship in the generous Troad,
who had made him a sleeping room and a hall and a courtyard
near the houses of Hektor and Priam, on the peak of the citadel.
There entered Hektor beloved of Zeus, in his hand holding
the eleven-cubit-long spear, whose shaft was tipped with a shining
bronze spearhead, and a ring of gold was hooped to hold it.
He found the man in his chamber busy with his splendid armour,
the corselet and the shield, and turning in his hands the curved bow,
while Helen of Argos was sitting among her attendant women
directing the magnificent work done by her handmaidens.
But Hektor saw him, and in words of shame he rebuked him:
'Strange man! It is not fair to keep in your heart this coldness.
The people are dying around the city and around the steep wall
as they fight hard; and it is for you that this war with its clamour
has flared up about our city. You yourself would fight with another
whom you saw anywhere hanging back from the hateful encounter.
Up then, to keep our town from burning at once in the hot fire.'
Then in answer the godlike Alexandros spoke to him:
'Hektor, seeing you have scolded me rightly, not beyond measure,
therefore I will tell, and you in turn understand and listen.
It was not so much in coldness and bitter will toward the Trojans

that I sat in my room, but I wished to give myself over to sorrow.
But just now with soft words my wife was winning me over
and urging me into the fight, and that way seems to me also
the better one. Victory passes back and forth between men.
Come then, wait for me now while I put on my armour of battle,
or go, and I will follow, and I think I can overtake you.'
He spoke, but Hektor of the shining helm gave him no answer,
but Helen spoke to him in words of endearment:
'Brother
by marriage to me, who am a nasty bitch evil-intriguing,
how I wish that on that day when my mother first bore me
the foul whirlwind of the storm had caught me away and swept me
to the mountain, or into the wash of the sea deep-thundering
where the waves would have swept me away before all these things had happened.
Yet since the gods had brought it about that these vile things must be,
I wish I had been the wife of a better man than this is,
one who knew modesty and all things of shame that men say.
But this man's heart is no steadfast thing, nor yet will it be so
ever hereafter; for that I think he shall take the consequence.
But come now, come in and rest on this chair, my brother,
since it is on your heart beyond all that the hard work has fallen
for the sake of dishonoured me and the blind act of Alexandros,
us two, on whom Zeus set a vile destiny, so that hereafter
we shall be made into things of song for the men of the future.'
Then tall Hektor of the shining helm answered her: 'Do not, Helen,
make me sit with you, though you love me. You will not persuade me.
Already my heart within is hastening me to defend the Trojans, who when I am away long greatly to have me.
Rather rouse this man, and let himself also be swift to action
so he may overtake me while I am still in the city.
For I am going first to my own house, so I can visit
my own people, my beloved wife and my son, who is little,
since I do not know if ever again I shall come back this way,
or whether the gods will strike me down at the hands of the Achaians.'
So speaking Hektor of the shining helm departed and in speed made his way to his own well-established dwelling,
but failed to find in the house Andromache of the white arms;
for she, with the child, and followed by one fair-robed attendant,
had taken her place on the tower in lamentation, and tearful.
When he saw no sign of his perfect wife within the house, Hektor
stopped in his way on the threshold and spoke among the handmaidens:
'Come then, tell me truthfully as you may, handmaidens:
where has Andromache of the white arms gone? Is she
with any of the sisters of her lord or the wives of his brothers?
Or has she gone to the house of Athene, where all the other
lovely-haired women of Troy propitiate the grim goddess?'
Then in turn the hard-working housekeeper gave him an answer:

'Hektor, since you have urged me to tell you the truth, she is not
with any of the sisters of her lord or the wives of his brothers,
nor has she gone to the house of Athene, where all the other
lovely-haired women of Troy propitiate the grim goddess,
but she has gone to the great bastion of Ilion, because she heard that
the Trojans were losing, and great grew the strength of the Achaians.
Therefore she has gone in speed to the wall, like a woman
gone mad, and a nurse attending her carries the baby.'
So the housekeeper spoke, and Hektor hastened from his home
backward by the way he had come through the great city,
the Skaian gates, whereby he would issue into the plain, there
at last his own generous wife came running to meet him,
Andromache, the daughter of high-hearted Eetion;
Eetion, who had dwelt underneath wooded Plakos, in Thebe below Plakos, lord over the Kilikian people.
It was his daughter who was given to Hektor of the bronze helm.
She came to him there, and beside her went an attendant carrying
the boy in the fold of her bosom, a little child, only a baby,
Hektor's son, the admired, beautiful as a star shining,
whom Hektor called Skamandrios, but all of the others
Astyanax—lord of the city; since Hektor alone saved Ilion.
Hektor smiled in silence as he looked on his son, but she,
Andromache, stood close beside him, letting her tears fall,
and clung to his hand and called him by name and spoke to him: 'Dearest,
your own great strength will be your death, and you have no pity
on your little son, nor on me, ill-starred, who soon must be your widow;
for presently the Achaians, gathering together,
will set upon you and kill you; and for me it would be far better
to sink into the earth when I have lost you, for there is no other
consolation for me after you have gone to your destiny—
only grief; since I have no father, no honoured mother.
It was brilliant Achilleus who slew my father, Eetion,
when he stormed the strong-founded citadel of the Kilikians,
Thebe of the towering gates. He killed Eetion
but did not strip his armour, for his heart respected the dead man,
but burned the body in all its elaborate war-gear
and piled a grave mound over it, and the nymphs of the mountains,
daughters of Zeus of the aegis, planted elm trees about it.
And they who were my seven brothers in the great house all went
upon a single day down into the house of the death god,
for swift-footed brilliant Achilleus slaughtered all of them
as they were tending their white sheep and their lumbering oxen;
and when he had led my mother, who was queen under wooded Plakos,
here, along with all his other possessions, Achilleus
released her again, accepting ransom beyond count, but Artemis
of the showering arrows struck her down in the halls of her father.
Hektor, thus you are father to me, and

my honoured mother,
you are my brother, and you it is who are my young husband.
Please take pity upon me then, stay here on the rampart,
that you may not leave your child an orphan, your wife a widow,
but draw your people up by the fig tree, there where the city
is openest to attack, and where the wall may be mounted.
Three times their bravest came that way, and fought there to storm it
about the two Aiantes and renowned Idomeneus,
about the two Atreidai and the fighting son of Tydeus.
Either some man well skilled in prophetic arts had spoken,
or the very spirit within themselves had stirred them to the onslaught.'
Then tall Hektor of the shining helm answered her: 'All these
things are in my mind, also, lady; yet I would feel deep shame
before the Trojans, and the Trojan women with trailing garments,
if like a coward I were to shrink aside from the fighting;
and the spirit will not let me, since I have learned to be valiant
and to fight always among the foremost ranks of the Trojans,
winning for my own self great glory, and for my father.
For I know this thing well in my heart, and my mind knows it:
there will come a day when sacred Ilion shall perish,
and Priam, and the people of Priam of the strong ash spear.
But it is not so much the pain to come of the Trojans
that troubles me, not even of Priam the king nor Hekabe,
nor the thought of my brothers who in their numbers and valour
shall drop in the dust under the hands of men who hate them,
as troubles me the thought of you, when some bronze-armoured
Achaian leads you off, taking away your day of liberty,
in tears; and in Argos you must work at the loom of another,
and carry water from the spring Messeis or Hypereia,
all unwilling, but strong will be the necessity upon you;
and some day seeing you shedding tears a man will say of you:
"This is the wife of Hektor, who was ever the bravest fighter
of the Trojans, breakers of horses, in the days when they fought about Ilion."
So will one speak of you; and for you it will be yet a fresh grief,
to be widowed of such a man who could fight off the day of your slavery.
But may I be dead and the piled earth hide me under before I
hear you crying and know by this that they drag you captive.'
So speaking glorious Hektor held out his arms to his baby,
who shrank back to his fair-girdled nurse's bosom
screaming, and frightened at the aspect of his own father,
terrified as he saw the bronze and the crest with its horse-hair,
nodding dreadfully, as he thought, from the peak of the helmet.
Then his beloved father laughed out, and his honoured mother,
and at once glorious Hektor lifted from his head the helmet
and laid it in all its shining upon the ground. Then taking
up his dear son he tossed him about in his arms, and kissed him,
and lifted his voice in prayer to Zeus and

the other immortals:
'Zeus and you other immortals, grant that this boy, who is my son,
may be as I am, pre-eminent among the Trojans,
great in strength, as am I, and rule strongly over Ilion;
and some day let them say of him: "He is better by far than his father",
as he comes in from the fighting; and let him kill his enemy
and bring home the blooded spoils, and delight the heart of his mother.'
So speaking he set his child again in the arms of his beloved
wife, who took him back again to her fragrant bosom
smiling in her tears; and her husband saw, and took pity upon her,
and stroked her with his hand, and called her by name and spoke to her:
'Poor Andromache! Why does your heart sorrow so much for me?
No man is going to hurl me to Hades, unless it is fated,
but as for fate, I think that no man yet has escaped it
once it has taken its first form, neither brave man nor coward.
Go therefore back to our house, and take up your own work,
the loom and the distaff, and see to it that your handmaidens
ply their work also; but the men must see to the fighting,
all men who are the people of Ilion, but I beyond others.'
So glorious Hektor spoke and again took up the helmet
with its crest of horse-hair, while his beloved wife went homeward,
turning to look back on the way, letting the live tears fall.
And as she came in speed into the well-settled household
of Hektor the slayer of men, she found numbers of handmaidens
within, and her coming stirred all of them into lamentation.
So they mourned in his house over Hektor while he was living
still, for they thought he would never again come back from the fighting
alive, escaping the Achaian hands and their violence.
But Paris in turn did not linger long in his high house,
but when he had put on his glorious armour with bronze elaborate
he ran in the confidence of his quick feet through the city.
As when some stalled horse who has been corn-fed at the manger
breaking free of his rope gallops over the plain in thunder
to his accustomed bathing place in a sweet-running river
and in the pride of his strength holds high his head, and the mane floats
over his shoulders; sure of his glorious strength, the quick knees
carry him to the loved places and the pasture of horses;
so from uttermost Pergamos came Paris, the son of
Priam, shining in all his armour of war as the sun shines,
laughing aloud, and his quick feet carried him; suddenly thereafter
he came on brilliant Hektor, his brother, where he yet lingered
before turning away from the place where he had talked with his lady.
It was Alexandros the godlike who first spoke to him:
'Brother, I fear that I have held back your haste, by being
slow on the way, not coming in time, as you commanded me.'
Then tall Hektor of the shining helm spoke to him in answer:
'Strange man! There is no way that one,

giving judgments in fairness,
could dishonour your work in battle, since you are a strong man.
But of your own accord you hang back, unwilling. And my heart
is grieved in its thought, when I hear shameful things spoken about you
by the Trojans, who undergo hard fighting for your sake.
Let us go now; some day hereafter we will make all right
with the immortal gods in the sky, if Zeus ever grant it,
setting up to them in our houses the winebowl of liberty
after we have driven out of Troy the strong-greaved Achaians.

Much of the poetic tone of The Iliad *is provided by the poet's use of extended and often vivid figures of speech which have long been called Homeric similes. One of the best is found at the end of Book Eight.*

So with hearts made high these sat nightlong by the outworks
Of battle, and their watchfires blazed numerous about them.
As when in the sky the stars about the moon's shining
are seen in all their glory, when the air has fallen to stillness,
and all the high places of the hills are clear, and the shoulders out-jutting,
and the deep ravines, as endless bright air spills from the heavens
and all the stars are seen, to make glad the heart of the shepherd;
such in their numbers blazed the watchfires the Trojans were burning
between the waters of Xanthos and the ships, before Ilion.
A thousand fires were burning there in the plain, and beside each
one sat fifty men in the flare of the blazing firelight.
And standing each beside his chariot, champing white barley
and oats, the horses waited for the dawn to mount to her high place.

Achilles' friend Patroclus, wearing Achilles' armor, has been slain, and the armor has been kept by the Trojans. Bereaved and enraged, Achilles determines to return to battle. In order to supply him with new armor, his mother, the nymph Thetis, goes to Mount Olympus and there enlists the aid of Vulcan or Hephaestus, the craftsman god. The "renowned smith of the strong arms" makes a new suit of armor, beginning with a shield on which are pictured in relief most of the activities of Greek life and which is described in wonderful detail. The passage is found in Book Eighteen.

Now as these two were saying things like this to each other,
Thetis of the silver feet came to the house of Hephaistos,
imperishable, starry, and shining among the immortals,
built in bronze for himself by the god of the dragging footsteps.
She found him sweating as he turned here and there to his bellows
busily, since he was working on twenty tripods
which were to stand against the wall of his strongfounded dwelling.
And he had set golden wheels underneath the base of each one
so that of their own motion they could wheel into the immortal
gathering, and return to his house: a wonder to look at.
These were so far finished, but the elaborate ear handles

were not yet on. He was forging these, and
 beating the chains out.
As he was at work on this in his craftsmanship and his cunning
meanwhile the goddess Thetis the silver-
 footed drew near him.
Charis of the shining veil saw her as she
 came forward,
she, the lovely goddess the renowned
 strongarmed one had married.
She came, and caught her hand and called
 her by name and spoke to her;
'Why is it, Thetis of the light robes, you
 have come to our house now?
We honour you and love you; but you
 have not come much before this.
But come in with me, so I may put entertainment before you.'
She spoke, and, shining among divinities,
 led the way forward
and made Thetis sit down in a chair that
 was wrought elaborately
and splendid with silver nails, and under
 it was a footstool.
She called to Hephaistos the renowned
 smith and spoke a word to him:
'Hephaistos, come this way; here is Thetis,
 who has need of you.'
Hearing her the renowned smith of the
 strong arms answered her:
'Then there is a goddess we honour and
 respect in our house.
She saved me when I suffered much at the
 time of my great fall
through the will of my own brazen-faced
 mother, who wanted
to hide me, for being lame. Then my soul
 would have taken much suffering
had not Eurynome and Thetis caught me
 and held me,
Eurynome, daughter of Ocean, whose
 stream bends back in a circle.
With them I worked nine years as a smith,
 and wrought many intricate
things; pins that bend back, curved clasps,
 cups, necklaces, working
there in the hollow of the cave, and the
 stream of Ocean around us
went on forever with its foam and its murmur. No other
among the gods or among mortal men
 knew about us
except Eurynome and Thetis. They knew,
 since they saved me.
Now she has come into our house; so I
 must by all means
do everything to give recompense to lovely-haired Thetis
for my life. Therefore set out before her
 fair entertainment
while I am putting away my bellows and
 all my instruments.'
He spoke, and took the huge blower off
 from the block of the anvil
limping; and yet his shrunken legs moved
 lightly beneath him.
He set the bellows away from the fire, and
 gathered and put away
all the tools with which he worked in a
 silver strongbox.
Then with a sponge he wiped clean his
 forehead, and both hands,
and his massive neck and hairy chest, and
 put on a tunic,
and took up a heavy stick in his hand,
 and went to the doorway
limping. And in support of their master
 moved his attendants.
These are golden, and in appearance like
 living young women.
There is intelligence in their hearts, and
 there is speech in them
and strength, and from the immortal gods
 they have learned how to do things.
These stirred nimbly in support of their
 master, and moving
near to where Thetis sat in her shining
 chair, Hephaistos
caught her by the hand and called her by
 name and spoke a word to her:
'Why is it, Thetis of the light robes, you
 have come to our house now?

We honour you and love you; but you have not come much before this.
Speak forth what is in your mind. My heart is urgent to do it
if I can, and if it is a thing that can be accomplished.'
Then in turn Thetis answered him, letting the tears fall:
'Hephaistos, is there among all the goddesses on Olympos
one who in her heart has endured so many grim sorrows
as the griefs Zeus, son of Kronos, has given me beyond others?
Of all the other sisters of the sea he gave me to a mortal,
to Peleus, Aiakos' son, and I had to endure mortal marriage
though much against my will. And now he, broken by mournful
old age, lies away in his halls. Yet I have other troubles.
For since he has given me a son to bear and to raise up
conspicuous among heroes, and he shot up like a young tree,
I nurtured him, like a tree grown in the pride of the orchard.
I sent him away in the curved ships to the land of Ilion
to fight with the Trojans; but I shall never again receive him
won home again to his country and into the house of Peleus.
Yet while I see him live and he looks on the sunlight, he has
sorrows, and though I go to him I can do nothing to help him.
And the girl the sons of the Achaians chose out for his honour
powerful Agamemmon took her away again out of his hands.
For her his heart has been wasting in sorrow, but meanwhile the Trojans
pinned the Achaians against their grounded ships, and would not
let them win outside, and the elders of the Argives entreated
my son, and named the many glorious gifts they would give him.
But at that time he refused himself to fight the death from them;
nevertheless he put his own armour upon Patroklos
and sent him into the fighting, and gave many men to go with him.
All day they fought about the Skaian Gates, and on that day
they would have stormed the city, if only Phoibos Apollo
had not killed the fighting son of Menoitios there in the first ranks
after he had wrought much damage, and given the glory to Hektor.
Therefore now I come to your knees; so might you be willing
to give me for my short-lived son, a shield and a helmet
and two beautiful greaves fitted with clasps for the ankles
and a corselet. What he had was lost with his steadfast companion
when the Trojans killed him. Now my son lies on the ground, heart sorrowing.'
Hearing her the renowned smith of the strong arms answered her:
'Do not fear. Let not these things be a thought in your mind.
And I wish that I could hide him away from death and its sorrow
at that time when his hard fate comes upon him, as surely
as there shall be fine armour for him such as another
man out of many men shall wonder at, when he looks on it.'
So he spoke, and left her there, and went to his bellows.
He turned these toward the fire and gave them their orders for working.
And the bellows, all twenty of them, blew on the crucibles,

from all directions blasting forth wind to blow the flames high
now as he hurried to be at this place and now at another,
wherever Hephaistos might with them to blow, and the work went forward.
He cast on the fire bronze which is weariless, and tin with it
and valuable gold, and silver, and thereafter set forth
upon its standard the great anvil, and gripped in one hand
the ponderous hammer, while in the other he grasped the pincers.
First of all he forged a shield that was huge and heavy,
elaborating it about, and threw around it a shining
triple rim that glittered, and the shield strap was cast of silver.
There were five folds composing the shield itself, and upon it
he elaborated many things in his skill and craftsmanship.
He made the earth upon it, and the sky, and the sea's water,
and the tireless sun, and the moon waxing into her fullness,
and on it all the constellations that festoon the heavens,
the Pleiades and the Hyades and the strength of Orion
and the Bear, whom men give also the name of the Wagon,
who turns about in a fixed place and looks at Orion
and she alone is never plunged in the wash of the Ocean.
On it he wrought in all their beauty two cities of mortal
men. And there were marriages in one, and festivals.
They were leading the brides along the city from their maiden chambers
under the flaring of torches, and the loud bride song was arising.
The young men followed the circles of the dance, and among them
the flutes and lyres kept up their clamour as in the meantime
the women standing each at the door of her court admired them.
The people were assembled in the market place, where a quarrel
had arisen, and two men were disputing over the blood price
for a man who had been killed. One man promised full restitution
in a public statement, but the other refused, and would accept nothing.
Both then made for an arbitrator, to have a decision;
and people were speaking up on either side, to help both men.
But the heralds kept the people in hand, as meanwhile the elders
were in session on benches of polished stone in the sacred circle
and held in their hands the staves of the heralds who lift their voices.
The two men rushed before these, and took turns speaking their cases,
and between them lay on the ground two talents of gold, to be given
to that judge who in this case spoke the straightest opinion.
But around the other city were lying two forces of armed men
shining in their war gear. For one side counsel was divided
whether to storm and sack, or share between both sides the property
and all the possessions the lovely citadel held hard within it.
But the city's people were not giving way, and armed for an ambush.
Their beloved wives and their little children stood on the rampart
to hold it, and with them the men with age upon them, but meanwhile
the others went out. And Ares led them, and Pallas Athene.

These were gold, both, and golden raiment
    upon them, and they were
beautiful and huge in their armour, being
    divinities,
and conspicuous from afar, but the people
    around them were smaller.
These, when they were come to the place
    that was set for their ambush,
in a river, where there was a watering place
    for all animals,
there they sat down in a place shrouding
    themselves in the bright bronze.
But apart from these were sitting two men
    to watch for the rest of them
and waiting until they could see the sheep
    and the shambling cattle,
who appeared presently, and two herds-
    men went along with them
playing happily on pipes, and took no
    thought of the treachery.
Those others saw them, and made a rush,
    and quickly thereafter
cut off on both sides the herds of cattle
    and the beautiful
flocks of shining sheep, and killed the
    shepherds upon them.
But the other army, as soon as they heard
    the uproar arising
from the cattle, as they sat in their councils,
    suddenly mounted
behind their light-foot horses, and went
    after, and soon overtook them.
These stood their ground and fought a
    battle by the banks of the river,
and they were making casts at each other
    with their spears bronze-headed;
and Hate was there with Confusion among
    them, and Death the destructive;
she was holding a live man with a new
    wound, and another
one unhurt, and dragged a dead man by
    the feet through the carnage.
The clothing upon her shoulders showed
    strong red with the men's blood.
All closed together like living men and
    fought with each other
and dragged away from each other the
    corpses of those who had fallen.
He made upon it a soft field, the pride
    of the tilled land,
wide and triple-ploughed, with many
    ploughmen upon it
who wheeled their teams at the turn and
    drove them in either direction.
And as these making their turn would
    reach the end-strip of the field,
a man would come up to them at this point
    and hand them a flagon
of honey-sweet wine, and they would turn
    again to the furrows
in their haste to come again to the end-
    strip of the deep field.
The earth darkened behind them and
    looked like earth that has been ploughed
though it was gold. Such was the wonder
    of the shield's forging.
He made on it the precinct of a king, where
    the labourers
were reaping, with the sharp reaping hooks
    in their hands. Of the cut swathes
some fell along the lines of reaping, one
    after another,
While the sheaf-binders caught up others
    and tied them with bind-ropes.
There were the three sheaf-binders who
    stood by, and behind them
were children picking up the cut swathes,
    and filled their arms with them
and carried and gave them always; and
    by them the king in silence
and holding his staff stood near the line
    of the reapers, happily.
And apart and under a tree the heralds
    made a feast ready
and trimmed a great ox they had slaugh-
    tered. Meanwhile the women
scattered, for the workmen to eat, abun-
    dant white barley.
He made on it a great vineyard heavy with
    clusters,
lovely and in gold, but the grapes upon
    it were darkened

and the vines themselves stood out through poles of silver. About them
he made a field-ditch of dark metal, and drove all around this
a fence of tin; and there was only one path to the vineyard,
and along it ran the grape-bearers for the vineyard's stripping.
Young girls and young men, in all their lighthearted innocence,
carried the kind, sweet fruit away in their woven baskets,
and in their midst a youth with a singing lyre played charmingly
upon it for them, and sang the beautiful song for Linos
in a light voice, and they followed him, and with singing and whistling
and light dance-steps of their feet kept time to the music.
He made upon it a herd of horn-straight oxen. The cattle
were wrought of gold and of tin, and thronged in speed and with lowing
out of the dung of the farmyard to a pasturing place by a sounding
river, and beside the moving field of a reed bed.
The herdsmen were of gold who went along with the cattle,
four of them, and nine dogs shifting their feet followed them.
But among the foremost of the cattle two formidable lions
had caught hold of a bellowing bull, and he with loud lowings
was dragged away, as the dogs and the young men went in pursuit of him.
But the two lions, breaking open the hide of the great ox,
gulped the black blood and the inward guts, as meanwhile the herdsmen
were in the act of setting and urging the quick dogs on them.
But they, before they could get their teeth in, turned back from the lions,
but would come and take their stand very close, and bayed, and kept clear.
And the renowned smith of the strong arms made on it a meadow
large and in a lovely valley for the glimmering sheepflocks,
with dwelling places upon it, and covered shelters, and sheepfolds.
And the renowned smith of the strong arms made elaborate on it
a dancing floor, like that which once in the wide spaces of Knossos
Daidalos built for Ariadne of the lovely tresses.
And there were young men on it and young girls, sought for their beauty
with gifts of oxen, dancing, and holding hands at the wrist. These
wore, the maidens long light robes, but the men wore tunics
of finespun work and shining softly, touched with olive oil.
And the girls wore fair garlands on their heads, while the young men
carried golden knives that hung from sword-belts of silver.
At whiles on their understanding feet they would run very lightly,
as when a potter crouching makes trial of his wheel, holding
it close in his hands, to see if it will run smooth. At another
time they would form rows, and run, rows crossing each other.
And around the lovely chorus of dancers stood a great multitude
happily watching, while among the dancers two acrobats
led the measures of song and dance revolving among them.
He made on it the great strength of the Ocean River
which ran around the uttermost rim of the shield's strong structure.
Then after he had wrought this shield, which was huge and heavy,

he wrought for him a corselet brighter than fire in its shining,
and wrought him a helmet, massive and fitting close to his temples,
lovely and intricate work, and laid a gold topridge along it,
and out of pliable tin wrought him leg-armour. Thereafter
when the renowned smith of the strong arms had finished the armour
he lifted it and laid it before the mother of Achilleus.
And she like a hawk came sweeping down from the snows of Olympos
and carried with her the shining armour, the gift of Hephaistos.

The climax of the epic is reached in Book Twenty-two, when Achilles and Hector, greatest of Greek and Trojan heroes, meet at long last in single combat. Brave as he is, Hector finds that "the shivers" take hold of him when he sees Achilles, and he flees, frightened.

But swift Achilleus kept unremittingly after Hektor,
chasing him, as a dog in the mountains who has flushed from his covert
a deer's fawn follows him through the folding ways and the valleys,
and though the fawn crouched down under a bush and be hidden
he keeps running and noses him out until he comes on him;
so Hektor could not lose himself from swift-footed Peleion.
If ever he made a dash right on for the gates of Dardanos
to get quickly under the strong-built bastions, endeavouring
that they from above with missiles thrown might somehow defend him,
each time Achilleus would get in front and force him to turn back
into the plain, and himself kept his flying course next the city.
As in a dream a man is not able to follow one who runs
from him, nor can the runner escape, nor the other pursue him,
so he could not run him down in his speed, nor the other get clear.
How then could Hektor have escaped the death spirits, had not
Apollo, for this last and uttermost time, stood by him
close, and driven strength into him, and made his knees light?
But brilliant Achilleus kept shaking his head at his own people
and would not let them throw their bitter projectiles at Hektor
for fear the thrower might win the glory, and himself come second.
But when for the fourth time they had come around to the well springs
then the Father balanced his golden scales, and in them
he set two fateful portions of death, which lays men prostrate,
one for Achilleus, and one for Hektor, breaker of horses,
and balanced it by the middle; and Hektor's death-day was heavier
and dragged downward toward death, and Phoibos Apollo forsook him.
But the grey-eyed Athene came now to Peleion
and stood close beside him and addressed him in winged words: 'Beloved
of Zeus, shining Achilleus, I am hopeful now that you and I
will take back great glory to the ships of the Achaians, after
we have killed Hektor, for all his slakeless fury for battle.
Now there is no way for him to get clear away from us,
not though Apollo who strikes from afar should be willing to undergo

much, and wallow before our father Zeus of the aegis.
Stand you here then and get your wind again, while I go
to this man and persuade him to stand up to you in combat.'
So spoke Athene, and he was glad at heart, and obeyed her,
and stopped, and stood leaning on his bronze-barbed ash spear. Meanwhile
Athene left him there, and caught up with brilliant Hektor,
and likened herself in form and weariless voice to Deiphobos.
She came now and stood close to him and addressed him in winged words:
'Dear brother, indeed swift-footed Achilleus is using you roughly
and chasing you on swift feet around the city of Priam.
Come on, then; let us stand fast against him and beat him back from us.'
Then tall Hektor of the shining helm answered her: 'Deiphobos,
before now you were dearest to me by far of my brothers,
of all those who were sons of Priam and Hekabe, and now
I am minded all the more within my heart to honour you,
you who dared for my sake, when your eyes saw me, to come forth
from the fortifications, while the others stand fast inside them.'
Then in turn the goddess grey-eyed Athene answered him:
'My brother, it is true our father and the lady our mother, taking
my knees in turn, and my companions about me, entreated
that I stay within, such was the terror upon all of them.
But the heart within me was worn away by hard sorrow for you.
But now let us go straight on and fight hard, let there be no sparing
of our spears, so that we can find out whether Achilleus
will kill us both and carry our bloody war spoils back
to the hollow ships, or will himself go down under your spear.'

Lapith and Centaur, FROM THE PARTHENON FRIEZE IN THE BRITISH MUSEUM, COURTESY OF THE TRUSTEES OF THE BRITISH MUSEUM

So Athene spoke and led him on by beguilement.
Now as the two in their advance were come close together,
first of the two to speak was tall helm-glittering Hektor:
'Son of Peleus, I will no longer run from you, as before this
I fled three times around the great city of Priam, and dared not
stand to your onfall. But now my spirit in turn has driven me
to stand and face you. I must take you now, or I must be taken.
Come then, shall we swear before the gods? For these are the highest
who shall be witnesses and watch over our agreements.
Brutal as you are I will not defile you, if Zeus grants
to me that I can wear you out, and take the life from you.
But after I have stripped your glorious armour, Achilleus,
I will give your corpse back to the Achaians. Do you do likewise.'
Then looking darkly at him swift-footed Achilleus answered:
'Hektor, argue me no agreements. I cannot forgive you.
As there are no trustworthy oaths between men and lions,
nor wolves and lambs have spirit that can be brought to agreement
but forever these hold feelings of hate for each other,
so there can be no love between you and me, nor shall there be
oaths between us, but one or the other must fall before then
to glut with his blood Ares the god who fights under the shield's guard.
Remember every valour of yours, for now the need comes
hardest upon you to be a spearman and a bold warrior.
There shall be no more escape for you, but Pallas Athene
will kill you soon by my spear. You will pay in a lump for all those
sorrows of my companions you killed in your spear's fury.'
So he spoke, and balanced the spear far shadowed, and threw it;
but glorious Hektor kept his eyes on him, and avoided it,
for he dropped, watchful, to his knee, and the bronze spear flew over his shoulder
and stuck in the ground, but Pallas Athene snatched it, and gave it
back to Achilleus, unseen by Hektor shepherd of the people.
But now Hektor spoke out to the blameless son of Peleus:
'You missed; and it was not, o Achilleus like the immortals,
from Zeus that you knew my destiny; but you thought so; or rather
you are someone clever in speech and spoke to swindle me,
to make me afraid of you and forget my valour and war strength.
You will not stick your spear in my back as I run away from you
but drive it into my chest as I storm straight in against you;
if the god gives you that; and now look out for my brazen
spear. I wish it might be taken full length in your body.
And indeed the war would be a lighter thing for the Trojans
if you were dead, seeing that you are their greatest affliction.'
So he spoke, and balanced the spear far shadowed, and threw it,
and struck the middle of Peleides' shield, nor missed it,
but the spear was driven far back from the shield, and Hektor was angered
because his swift weapon had been loosed from his hand in a vain cast.

He stood discouraged and had no other ash spear; but lifting
his voice he called aloud on Deiphobos of the pale shield,
and asked him for a long spear, but Deiphobos was not near him.
And Hektor knew the truth inside his heart, and spoke aloud:
'No use. Here at last the gods have summoned me deathward.
I thought Deiphobos the hero was here close beside me,
but he is behind the wall and it was Athene cheating me,
and now evil death is close to me, and no longer far away,
and there is no way out. So it must long since have been pleasing
to Zeus, and Zeus' son who strikes from afar, this way; though before this
they defended me gladly. But now my death is upon me.
Let me at least not die without a struggle, inglorious,
but do some big thing first, that men to come shall know of it.'
So he spoke, and pulling out the sharp sword that was slung
at the hollow of his side, huge and heavy, and gathering
himself together, he made his swoop, like a high-flown eagle
who launches himself out of the murk of the clouds on the flat land
to catch away a tender lamb or a shivering hare; so
Hektor made his swoop, swinging his sharp sword, and Achilleus
charged, the heart within him loaded with savage fury.
In front of his chest the beautiful elaborate great shield
covered him, and with the glittering helm with four horns
he nodded; the lovely golden fringes were shaken about it
which Hephaistos had driven close along the horn of the helmet.
And as a star moves among stars in the night's darkening,
Hesper, who is the fairest star who stands in the sky, such
was the shining from the pointed spear Achilleus was shaking
in his right hand with evil intention toward brilliant Hektor.
He was eyeing Hektor's splendid body, to see where it might best
give way, but all the rest of the skin was held in the armour,
brazen and splendid, he stripped when he cut down the strength of Patroklos;
yet showed where the collar-bones hold the neck from the shoulders,
the throat, where death of the soul comes most swiftly; in this place
brilliant Achilleus drove the spear as he came on in fury,
and clean through the soft part of the neck the spearpoint was driven.
Yet the ash spear heavy with bronze did not sever the windpipe,
so that Hektor could still make exchange of words spoken.
But he dropped in the dust, and brilliant Achilleus vaunted above him:
'Hektor, surely you thought as you killed Patroklos you would be
safe, and since I was far away you thought nothing of me,
o fool, for an avenger was left, far greater than he was,
behind him and away by the hollow ships. And it was I;
and I have broken your strength; on you the dogs and the vultures
shall feed and foully rip you; the Achaians will bury Patroklos.'
In his weakness Hektor of the shining helm spoke to him:
'I entreat you, by your life, by your knees, by your parents,

do not let the dogs feed on me by the ships of the Achaians,
but take yourself the bronze and gold that are there in abundance,
those gifts that my father and the lady my mother will give you,
and give my body to be taken home again, so that the Trojans
and the wives of the Trojans may give me in death my rite of burning.'
But looking darkly at him swift-footed Achilleus answered:
'No more entreating of me, you dog, by knees or parents.
I wish only that my spirit and fury would drive me
to hack your meat away and eat it raw for the things that
you have done to me. So there is no one who can hold the dogs off
from your head, not if they bring here and set before me ten times
and twenty times the ransom, and promise more in addition,
not if Priam son of Dardanos should offer to weigh out
your bulk in gold; not even so shall the lady your mother
who herself bore you lay you on the death-bed and mourn you:
no, but the dogs and the birds will have you all for their feasting.'
Then, dying, Hektor of the shining helmet spoke to him:
'I know you well as I look upon you, I know that I could not
persuade you, since indeed in your breast is a heart of iron.
Be careful now; for I might be made into the gods' curse
upon you, on that day when Paris and Phoibus Apollo
destroy you in the Skaian gates, for all your valour.'
He spoke, and as he spoke the end of death closed in upon him,
and the soul fluttering free of the limbs went down into Death's house
mourning her destiny, leaving youth and manhood behind her.
Now though he was a dead man brilliant Achilleus spoke to him:
'Die: and I will take my own death at whatever time
Zeus and the rest of the immortals choose to accomplish it.'
He spoke, and pulled the brazen spear from the body, and laid it
on one side, and stripped away from the shoulders the bloody
armour. And the other sons of the Achaians came running about him,
and gazed upon the stature and on the imposing beauty
of Hektor; and none stood beside him who did not stab him;
and thus they would speak one to another, each looking at his neighbour:
'See now, Hektor is much softer to handle than he was
when he set the ships ablaze with the burning firebrand.'
So as they stood beside him they would speak, and stab him.
But now, when he had despoiled the body, swift-footed brilliant
Achilleus stood among the Achaians and addressed them in winged words:
'Friends, who are leaders of the Argives and keep their counsel:
since the gods have granted me the killing of this man
who has done us much damage, such as not all the others together
have done, come, let us go in armour about the city
to see if we can find out what purpose is in the Trojans,
whether they will abandon their high city, now that this man
has fallen, or are minded to stay, though Hektor lives no longer.

Yet still, why does the heart within me debate on these things?
There is a dead man who lies by the ships, unwept, unburied:
Patroklos: and I will not forget him, never so long as
I remain among the living and my knees have their spring beneath me.
And though the dead forget the dead in the house of Hades,
even there I shall still remember my beloved companion.
But now, you young men of the Achaians, let us go back, singing
a victory song, to our hollow ships; and take this with us.
We have won ourselves enormous fame; we have killed the great Hektor
whom the Trojans glorified as if he were a god in their city.'
He spoke, and now thought of shameful treatment for glorious Hektor.
In both of his feet at the back he made holes by the tendons
in the space between ankle and heel, and drew thongs of ox-hide through them,
and fastened them to the chariot so as to let the head drag,
and mounted the chariot, and lifted the glorious armour inside it,
then whipped the horses to a run, and they winged their way unreluctant.
A cloud of dust rose where Hektor was dragged, his dark hair was falling
about him, and all that head that was once so handsome was tumbled
in the dust; since by this time Zeus had given him over
to his enemies, to be defiled in the land of his fathers.
So all his head was dragged in the dust; and now his mother
tore out her hair, and threw the shining veil far from her
and raised a great wail as she looked upon her son; and his father
beloved groaned pitifully, and all his people about him
were taken with wailing and lamentation all through the city.
It was most like what would have happened, if all towering
Ilion had been burning top to bottom in fire.
His people could scarcely keep the old man in his impatience
from storming out of the Dardanian gates; he implored them
all, and wallowed in the muck before them calling each man
and naming him by his name: 'Give way, dear friends,
and let me alone though you care for me, leave me to go out
from the city and make my way to the ships of the Achaians.
I must be suppliant to this man, who is harsh and violent,
and he might have respect for my age and take pity upon it
since I am old, and his father also is old, as I am,
Peleus, who begot and reared him to be an affliction
on the Trojans. He has given us most sorrow, beyond all others,
such is the number of my flowering sons he has cut down.
But for all of these I mourn not so much, in spite of my sorrow,
as for one, Hektor, and the sharp grief for him will carry me downward
into Death's house. I wish he had died in my arms, for that way
we two, I myself and his mother who bore him unhappy,
might so have glutted ourselves with weeping for him and mourning.'

(Translated by Richmond Lattimore)

from *The Odyssey*

After the Greeks have successfully ended the ten-year siege of Troy, Odysseus (Ulysses) and his men set sail, with the intention of returning swiftly home to the island of Ithaca. But one adventure or misadventure after another delays them and takes from Odysseus his ships and his faithful followers. For seven years, after he has lost all of his men, he is a half-willing guest of the beautiful nymph Calypso on the isle of Ogygia. When Zeus (Jove) commands her to send him on his way, she shows him how to build a raft, and then she reluctantly dismisses him. But after he has floated for seventeen days, his old enemy Poseidon (Neptune) makes more trouble for him.

from Book v

     Upon him, from on high,
A huge and frightful billow broke; it whirled
The raft around, and far from it he fell.
His hands let go the rudder; a fierce rush
Of all the winds together snapped in twain
The mast; far off the yard and canvas flew
Into the deep; the billow held him long
Beneath the waters, and he strove in vain
Quickly to rise to air from that huge swell
Of ocean, for the garments weighed him down
Which fair Calypso gave him. But at length
Emerging, he rejected from his throat
The bitter brine that down his forehead streamed.
Even then, though hopeless with dismay, his thought
Was on the raft; and, struggling through the waves,
He seized it, sprang on board, and, seated there,
Escaped the threatened death. Still to and fro
The rolling billows drave it. As the wind
In autumn sweeps the thistles o'er the field,
Clinging together, so the blasts of heaven
Hither and thither drove it o'er the sea.
And now the south wind flung it to the north
To buffet; now the east wind to the west.
  Ino Leucothea saw him clinging there,—
The delicate-footed child of Cadmus, once
A mortal, speaking with a mortal voice,
Though now within the ocean gulfs she shares
The honors of the gods. With pity she
Beheld Ulysses struggling thus distressed,
And, rising from the abyss below, in form
A cormorant, the sea-nymph took her perch
On the well-banded raft, and thus she said:—
  "Ah luckless man! how hast thou angered thus
Earth-shaking Neptune, that he visits thee
With these disasters? Yet he cannot take,
Although he seek it earnestly, thy life.
Now do my bidding, for thou seemest wise.
Laying aside thy garments, let the raft
Drift with the winds, while thou, by strength of arm,
Makest thy way in swimming to the land
Of the Phaeacians, where thy safety lies.
Receive this veil, and bind its heavenly woof
Beneath thy breast, and have no further fear
Of hardship or of danger. But, as soon
As thou shalt touch the island, take it off,
And turn away thy face, and fling it far
From where thou standest into the black deep."
  The goddess gave the veil as thus she spoke,
And to the tossing deep went down, in form
A cormorant; the black wave covered her.

But still Ulysses, mighty sufferer,
Pondered, and thus to his great soul he
    said:—
  "Ah me! perhaps some god is planning
    here
Some other fraud against me, bidding me
Forsake my raft. I will not yet obey,
For still far off I see the land in which
'T is said my refuge lies. This will I do,
For this seems wisest. While the fastenings
    last
That hold these timbers, I will keep my
    place
And bide the tempest here; but when the
    waves
Shall dash my raft in pieces, I will swim,
For nothing better will remain to do."
  As he revolved this purpose in his mind,
Earth-shaking Neptune sent a mighty
    wave,
Horrid and huge and high, and where he
    sat
It smote him. As a violent wind uplifts
The dry chaff heaped upon a threshing-
    floor,
And sends it scattered through the air
    abroad,
So did that wave fling loose the ponderous
    beams.
To one of these, Ulysses, clinging fast,
Bestrode it, like a horseman on his steed;
And now he took the garments off, be-
    stowed
By fair Calypso, binding around his breast
The veil, and forward plunged into the
    deep,
With palms outspread, prepared to swim.
    Meanwhile
Neptune beheld him,—Neptune, mighty
    king,—
And shook his head, and said within him-
    self:—
  "Go thus, and laden with mischances
    roam
The waters till thou come among the race
Cherished by Jupiter, but well I deem
Thou wilt not find thy share of suffering
    light."
  Thus having said he urged his coursers
    on,
With their fair-flowing manes, until he
    came
To Aegae, where his glorious palace stands.
  But Pallas, child of Jove, had other
    thoughts.
She stayed the course of every wind beside,
And bade them rest, and lulled them into
    sleep,
But summoned the swift north to break
    the waves,
That so Ulysses, the high-born, escaped
From death and from the fates, might be
    the guest
Of the Phaeacians,—men who love the sea.
Two days and nights among the mighty
    waves
He floated, oft his heart foreboding death.
But when the bright-haired Eos had
    fulfilled
The third day's course, and all the winds
    were laid,
And calm was on the watery waste, he saw
That land was near, as, lifted on the crest
Of a huge swell, he looked with sharpened
    sight;
And as a father's life preserved makes glad
His children's hearts, when long time he
    has lain
Sick, wrung with pain, and wasting by the
    power
Of some malignant genius, till at length
The gracious gods bestow a welcome cure,
So welcome to Ulysses was the sight
Of woods and fields. By swimming on he
    thought
To climb and tread the shore; but when
    he drew
So near that one who shouted could be
    heard
From land, the sound of ocean on the rocks

Came to his ear,—for there huge breakers roared
And spouted fearfully, and all around
Was covered with the sea-foam. Haven here
Was none for ships, nor sheltering creek, but shores
Beetling from high, and crags and walls of rock.
Ulysses trembled both in knees and heart,
And thus to his great soul, lamenting, said:—

"Now woe is me! as soon as Jove has shown
What I had little hoped to see, the land,
And I through all these waves have ploughed my way,
I find no issue from the hoary deep.
For sharp rocks border it, and all around
Roar the wild surges; slippery cliffs arise
Close to deep gulfs, and footing there is none
Where I might plant my steps and thus escape.
All effort now were fruitless to resist
The mighty billow hurrying me away
To dash me on the pointed rocks. If yet
I strive, by swimming further, to descry
Some sloping shore or harbor of the isle,
I fear the tempest, lest it hurl me back,
Heavily groaning, to the fishy deep;
Or huge sea-monster, from the multitude
Which sovereign Amphitrite feeds, be sent
Against me by some god,—for well I know
the power who shakes the shores is wroth with me."

While he revolved these doubts within his mind,
A huge wave hurled him toward the rugged coast.
Then had his limbs been flayed, and all his bones
Broken at once, had not the blue-eyed maid,
Minerva, prompted him. Borne toward the rock,
He clutched it instantly with both his hands,
And panting clung till that huge wave rolled by,
And so escaped its fury. Back it came,
And smote him once again, and flung him far
Seaward. As to the claws of Polypus,
Plucked from its bed, the pebbles thickly cling,
So flakes of skin, from off his powerful hands,
Were left upon the rock. The mighty surge
O'erwhelmed him; he had perished ere his time,—
Hapless Ulysses!—but the blue-eyed maid,
Pallas, informed his mind with forecast. Straight
Emerging from the wave that shoreward rolled,
He swam along the coast and eyed it well,
In hope of sloping beach or sheltered creek.
But when, in swimming, he had reached the mouth
Of a soft-flowing river, here appeared
The spot he wished for, smooth, without a rock,
And here was shelter from the wind. He felt
The current's flow, and thus devoutly prayed:—

"Hear me, O sovereign power, whoe'er thou art!
To thee, the long-desired, I come. I seek
Escape from Neptune's threatenings on the sea.
The deathless gods respect the prayer of him
Who looks to them for help, a fugitive,
As I am now, when to thy stream I come,
And to thy knees, from many a hardship past.
O thou that here art ruler, I declare
Myself thy suppliant; be thou merciful."

He spoke; the river stayed his current, checked

DOSSO DOSSI: *Circe and Her Lovers in a Landscape*, SAMUEL H. KRESS COLLECTIONS, NATIONAL GALLERY OF ART, WASHINGTON, D.C.

The billows, smoothed them to a calm, and gave
The swimmer a safe landing at his mouth.
Then dropped his knees and sinewy arms at once,
Unstrung, for faint with struggling was his heart.
His body was all swoln; the brine gushed forth
From mouth and nostrils; all unnerved he lay,
Breathless and speechless; utter weariness
O'ermastered him. But when he breathed again,
And his flown senses had returned, he loosed
The veil that Ino gave him from his breast,
And to the salt flood cast it. A great wave
Bore it far down the stream; the goddess there
In her own hands received it. He, meanwhile,
Withdrawing from the brink, lay down among
The reeds, and kissed the harvest-bearing earth,
And thus to his great soul, lamenting, said:—
"Ah me! what must I suffer more? what yet
Will happen to me? If by the river's side
I pass the unfriendly watches of the night,
The cruel cold and dews that steep the bank
May, in this weakness, end me utterly.
For chilly blows this river-air at dawn;
But should I climb this hill, to sleep within
The shadowy wood, among thick shrubs, if cold
And weariness allow me, then I fear,
That, while the pleasant slumber o'er me steal,
I may become the prey of savage beasts."
    Yet, as he longer pondered, this seemed best.
He rose, and sought the wood, and found it near

The water, on a height, o'erlooking far
The region round. Between two shrubs that sprang
Both from one spot he entered,—olive-trees,
One wild, one fruitful. The damp-blowing wind
Ne'er pierced their covert; never blazing sun
Darted his beams within, nor pelting shower
Beat through, so closely intertwined they grew.
Here entering, Ulysses heaped a bed
Of leaves with his own hands; he made it broad
And high, for thick the leaves had fallen around.
Two men and three, in that abundant store,
Might bide the winter storm, though keen the cold.
Ulysses, the great sufferer, on his couch
Looked and rejoiced, and placed himself within,
And heaped the leaves high o'er him and around,
As one who, dwelling in the distant fields,
Without a neighbor near him, hides a brand
In the dark ashes, keeping carefully
The seeds of fire alive, lest he, perforce,
To light his hearth must bring them from afar;
So did Ulysses in that pile of leaves
Bury himself, while Pallas o'er his eyes
Poured sleep, and closed his lids, that he might take,
After his painful toils, the fitting rest.

from Book X

Odysseus (Ulysses) is awakened by sounds of merriment that come from a meadow where Nausicaa, lovely princess of Phaeacia, is at play with her maids. She befriends him and takes him to the palace of her father, King Alcinous. Here, after the proper formalities have been observed, he tells of the remarkable adventures that have befallen him since he and his men left Troy. One of them is his encounter with Circe, sorceress-goddess on the isle of Aeaea.

"Numbering my well-armed men, I made of them
Two equal parties, giving each its chief.
Myself commanded one; Eurylochus,
The hero, took the other in his charge.
   "Then in a brazen helm we shook the lots;
The lot of brave Eurylochus leaped forth,
And he with two-and-twenty of our men
Went forward with quick steps, and yet in tears,
While we as sorrowful were left behind.
   "They found the fair abode where Circe dwelt,
A palace of hewn stone within the vale,
Yet nobly seated. There were mountain wolves
And lions round it, which herself had tamed
With powerful drugs; yet these assaulted not
The visitors, but, wagging their long tails,
Stood on their hinder feet, and fawned on them,
Like mastiffs on their master when he comes
From banqueting and brings them food. So fawned
The strong-clawed wolves and lions on my men.
With fear my men beheld those beasts of prey,
Yet went, and, standing in the portico
Of the bright-haired divinity, they heard
Her sweet voice singing, as within she threw
The shuttle through the wide immortal web,

Such as is woven by the goddesses,—
Delicate, bright of hue, and beautiful.
  "Polites then, a chief the most beloved
And most discreet of all my comrades,
    spake:—
    "'Some one is here, my friends, who
      sweetly sings,
Weaving an ample web, and all the floor
Rings to her voice. Whoever she may be,
Woman or goddess, let us call to her.'
  "He spake; aloud they called, and forth
    she came
And threw at once the shining doors apart,
And bade my comrades enter. Without
    thought
They followed her. Eurylochus alone
Remained without, for he suspected guile.
She let them in and seated them on
    thrones.
Then mingling for them Pramnian wine
    with cheese,
Meal, and fresh honey, and infusing drugs
Into the mixture,—drugs which made
    them lose
The memory of their home,—she handed
    them
The beverage and they drank. Then in-
    stantly
She touched them with a wand, and shut
    them up
In sties, transformed to swine in head and
    voice,
Bristles and shape, though still the human
    mind
Remained to them. Thus sorrowing they
    were driven
Into their cells, where Circe flung to them
Acorns of oak and ilex and the fruit
Of cornel, such as nourish wallowing swine.
  "Back came Eurylochus to our good ship
With news of our poor comrades and their
    fate,
He strove to speak, but could not; he was
    stunned
By that calamity; his eyes were filled
With tears, and his whole soul was given
    to grief.
We marvelled greatly; long we questioned
    him,
And thus he spake of our lost friends at
    last:—
    "'Through yonder thickets, as thou
      gav'st command,
Illustrious chief! we went, until we reached
A stately palace of hewn stones, within
A vale, yet nobly seated. Some one there,
Goddess or woman, weaving busily
An ample web, sang sweetly as she
    wrought.
My comrades called aloud, and forth she
    came,
And threw at once the shining doors apart,
And bade us enter. Without thought the
    rest
Followed, while I alone, suspecting guile,
Remained without. My comrades, from
    that hour,
Were seen no more; not one of them again
Came forth, though long I sat and watched
    for them.'
  "He spake; I slung my silver-studded sword
Upon my shoulders,—a huge blade of
    brass,—
And my bow with it, and commanded him
To lead the way. He seized and clasped
    my knees
With both his hands in attitude of prayer,
And sorrowfully said these winged
    words:—
    "'Take me not thither; force me not
      to go,
O foster-child of Jove! but leave me here;
For thou wilt not return, I know, nor yet
Deliver one of our lost friends. Our part
Is to betake ourselves to instant flight
With these who yet remain, and so escape.'
  "He spake, and I replied: 'Eurylochus,
Remain thou here, beside our roomy ship,
Eating and drinking. I shall surely go.
A strong necessity is laid on me.'
  "I spake, and from the ship and shore
    went up

Into the isle; and when I found myself
Within that awful valley, and not far
From the great palace in which Circe dwelt,
The sorceress, there met me on my way
A youth; he seemed in manhood's early prime,
When youth has most of grace. He took my hand
And held it, and, accosting me, began:—
 " 'Rash mortal! whither art thou wandering thus
Alone among the hills, where every place
Is strange to thee? Thy comrades are shut up
In Circe's palace in close cells like swine.
Com'st thou to set them free? Nay, thou like them
Wilt rather find thyself constrained to stay.
Let me bestow the means to make thee safe
Against that mischief. Take this potent herb,
And bear it with thee to the palace-halls
Of Circe, and it shall avert from thee
The threatened evil. I will now reveal
The treacherous arts of Circe. She will bring
A mingled draught to thee, and drug the bowl,
But will not harm thee thus; the virtuous plant
I gave thee will prevent it. Hear yet more:
When she shall smite thee with her wand, draw forth
Thy good sword from thy thigh and rush at her
As if to take her life, and she will crouch
In fear, and will solicit thine embrace.
Refuse her not, that so she may release
Thy comrades, and may send thee also back
To thine own land; but first exact of her
The solemn oath which binds the blessed gods,
That she will meditate no other harm
To thee, nor strip thee of thy manly strength.'
 "The Argus-queller spake, and plucked from earth
The potent plant and handed it to me,
And taught me all its powers. The root is black,
The blossom white as milk. Among the gods
Its name is Moly; hard it is for men
To dig it up; the gods find nothing hard.
 "Back through the woody island Hermes went
Toward high Olympus, while I took my way
To Circe's halls, yet with a beating heart.
There, as I stood beneath the portico
Of that bright-haired divinity, I called
Aloud; the goddess heard my voice and came,
And threw at once the shining doors apart,
And prayed me to come in. I followed her,
Yet grieving still. She led me in and gave
A seat upon a silver-studded throne,
Beautiful, nobly wrought, and placed beneath
A footstool, and prepared a mingled draught
Within a golden chalice, and infused
A drug with mischievous intent. She gave
The cup; I drank it off; the charm wrought not,
And then she smote me with her wand and said:—
'Go to the sty, and with thy fellows sprawl.'
 "She spake; but drawing forth the trusty sword
Upon my thigh, I rushed at her as if
To take her life. She shrieked and, stooping low,
Ran underneath my arm and clasped my knees,
And uttered piteously these winged words:—
 " 'Who art thou? of what race and of what land,

And who thy parents? I am wonder-struck
To see that thou couldst drink that magic
   juice
And yield not to its power. No living man,
Whoever he might be, that tasted once
Those drugs, or passed them o'er his lips,
   has yet
Withstood them. In thy breast a spirit
   dwells
Not to be thus subdued. Art thou not then
Ulysses, master of wise stratagems,
Whose coming hither, on his way from
   Troy,
In his black galley, oft has been foretold
By Hermes of the golden wand? But
   sheathe
Thy sword and share my couch, that,
   joined in love,
Each may hereafter trust the other's faith.'
   "She spake, and I replied: 'How canst
      thou ask,
O Circe, that I gently deal with thee,
Since thou, in thine own palace, hast
   transformed
My friends to swine, and plottest even now
To keep me with thee, luring me to pass
Into thy chamber and to share thy couch,
That thou mayst strip me of my manly
   strength
I come not to thy couch till thou engage,
O goddess, by a solemn oath, that thou
Wilt never seek to do me further harm.'
   "I spake; she straightway took the oath
      required,
And, after it was uttered and confirmed,
Up to her sumptuous couch I went. Mean-
   while
Four diligent maidens ministered within
The palace,—servants of the household
   they,
Who had their birth from fountains and
   from groves,
And sacred rivers flowing to the sea.
One spread the thrones with gorgeous
   coverings;

Above was purple arras, and beneath
Were linen webs; another, setting forth
The silver tables just before the thrones,
Placed on them canisters of gold; a third
Mingled the rich wines in a silver bowl,
And placed the golden cups; and, last, the
   fourth
Brought water from the fountain, and be-
   neath
A massive tripod kindled a great fire
And warmed the water. When it boiled
   within
The shining brass, she led me to the bath,
And washed me from the tripod. On my
   head
And shoulders pleasantly she shed the
   streams
That from my members took away the
   sense
Of weariness, unmanning body and mind.
And when she thus had bathed me and
   with oil
Anointed me, she put a princely cloak
And tunic on me, led me in, and showed
My seat,—a stately silver-studded throne,
High-wrought,—and placed a footstool for
   my feet.
Then came a handmaid with a golden ewer,
And from it poured pure water for my
   hands
Into a silver laver. Next she placed
A polished table near to me, on which
The matron of the palace laid the feast,
With many delicacies from her store,
And bade me eat. The banquet pleased
   me not.
My thoughts were elsewhere; dark imagin-
   ings
Were in my mind. When Circe marked my
   mood,
As in a gloomy revery I sat,
And put not forth my hands to touch the
   feast,
She came to me and spake these winged
   words:—

"'Why sittest thou like one who has no power
Of speech, Ulysses, wrapt in thoughts that gnaw
Thy heart, and tasting neither food nor wine?
Still dost thou dream of fraud? It is not well
That thou shouldst fear it longer, since I pledged
Myself against it with a mighty oath.'
"She spake, and I replied: 'What man whose heart
Is faithful could endure to taste of food
Or wine till he should see his captive friends
Once more at large? If with a kind intent
Thou bidst me eat and drink, let me behold
With mine own eyes my dear companions free.'
"I spake; and Circe took her wand and went
Forth from her halls, and, opening the gate
That closed the sty, drove forth what seemed a herd
Of swine in their ninth year. They ranged themselves
Before her, and she went from each to each
And shed on them another drug. Forthwith
Fell from their limbs the bristles which had grown
All over them, when mighty Circe gave
At first the baleful potion. Now again
My friends were men, and younger than before,
And of a nobler mien and statelier growth.
They knew me all; and each one pressed my hand
In his, and there were tears and sobs of joy
That sounded through the palace. Circe too
Was moved, the mighty goddess; she drew near
And stood by me, and spake these winged words:—
"'Son of Laertes, nobly born and wise,
Ulysses! go to thy good ship beside
The sea and draw it up the beach, and hide
The goods and weapons in the caverns there,
And come thou back and bring with thee thy friends.'
"She spake, and easily my generous mind
Was moved by what she said. Forthwith I went
To my good ship beside the sea, and found
My friends in tears, lamenting bitterly.
As in some grange the calves come leaping round
A herd of kine returning to the stall
From grassy fields where they have grazed their fill,
Nor can the stall contain the young which spring
Around their mothers with continual bleat;
So when my comrades saw me through their tears,
They sprang to meet me, and their joy was such
As if they were in their own native land
And their own city, on the rugged coast
Of Ithaca, where they were born and reared;
And as they wept they spake these winged words:—
"'O foster-child of Jove! we welcome thee
On thy return with a delight as great
As if we all had reached again the land
That gave us birth, our Ithaca. And no
Tell by what death our other friends have died.'
"They spake; I answered with consoling words:—
'First draw our galley up the beach, and hide

Our goods and all our weapons in the caves,
And then let all make haste to follow me,
And see our friends in Circe's sacred halls,
Eating and drinking at the plenteous board.'
   "I spake; and cheerfully my men obeyed,
Save that Eurylochus alone essayed
To hold them back, and spake these winged words:—
   " 'Ah, whither are we going, wretched ones?
Are ye so eager for an evil fate,
That ye must go where Circe dwells, who waits
To turn us into lions, swine, or wolves,
Forced to remain and guard her spacious house?
So was it with the Cyclops, when our friends
Went with this daring chief to his abode,
And perished there through his foolhardiness.'
   "He spake; and then I thought to draw my sword
From my stout thigh, and with the trenchant blade
Strike off his head and let it fall to earth,
Though he were my near kinsman; yet the rest
Restrained me, each one speaking kindly words:—
   " 'Nay, foster-child of Jove! if thou consent,
This man shall stay behind and with the ship,
And he shall guard the ship, but lead us thou
To where the sacred halls of Circe stand.'
   "They spake, and from the ship and shore went up
Into the land, nor was Eurylochus
Left with the ship; he followed, for he feared
My terrible threat. Meantime had Circe bathed
My comrades at the palace, and with oil
Anointed them, and robed them in fair cloaks
And tunics. There we found them banqueting.
When they and those who came with me beheld
Each other, and the memory of the past
Came back to them, they wept abundantly,
And all the palace echoed with their sobs.
And then the mighty goddess came and said:—
   " 'Son of Laertes, nobly born and wise,
Prolong thou not these sorrows. Well I know
What ye have suffered on the fishy deep,
And all the evil that malignant men
Have done to you on land. Now take the food
Before you, drink the wine, till ye receive
Into your hearts the courage that was yours
When long ago ye left your fatherland,
The rugged Ithaca. Ye are unnerved
And spiritless with thinking constantly
On your long wanderings, and your minds allow
No space for mirth, for ye have suffered much.'
   "She spake; her words persuaded easily
Our generous minds, and there from day to day
We lingered a full year, and banqueted
Nobly on plenteous meats and delicate wines."

             (Translated by William Cullen Bryant)

Venus de Milo, IN THE MUSÉE DU LOUVRE IN PARIS

Archilochus
(ca. 648 B.C.)
On Losing His Shield

Some Thracian strutteth with my shield;
    For, being somewhat flurried,
I left it in a wayside bush,
    When from the field I hurried;
A right good targe, but I got off,
    The deuce may take the shield;
I'll get another just as good
    When next I go afield.
        (Translated by Paul Shorey)

Sappho
(ca. 610 B.C.)
Ode to Aphrodite

Throned in splendor, deathless, o Aphrodite
child of Zeus, charm-fashioner, I entreat you
not with griefs and bitternesses to break my
    spirit, o goddess;

standing by me rather, if once before now
far away you heard, when I called upon you,
left your father's dwelling place and descended
    yoking the golden

chariot to exquisite doves, who drew you
down in speed aslant the black world, the bright air
trembling at the heart to the pulse of countless
    fluttering wingbeats.

Swiftly then they came, and you, blessed lady,
smiling on me out of immortal beauty
asked me what affliction was on me, why I
    called thus upon you,

what beyond all else I would have befall my
tortured heart: "Whom then would you have Persuasion
force to serve desire in your heart? Who is it,
    Sappho, that hurt you?

Though she now escape you, she soon will follow;
though she take not gifts from you, she will give them:

though she love not, yet she will surely love you
    even unwilling."

In such guise come even again and set me
free from doubt and sorrow; accomplish all those
things my heart desires to be done; appear and
    stand at my shoulder.
      (Translated by Richmond Lattimore)

Hesperus, the Bringer

O Hesperus, thou bringest all good things—
    Home to the weary, to the hungry cheer,
To the young bird the parent's brooding wings,
    The welcome stall to the o'erlabored steer;
Whate'er of peace about our hearthstone clings,
    Whate'er our household gods protect of dear,
Are gathered round us by thy look of rest;
Thou bring'st the child too to its mother's breast.
      (Translated by Lord Byron)

Mother, I Cannot Mind My Wheel

Mother, I cannot mind my wheel;
    My fingers ache, my lips are dry;
Oh! if you felt the pain I feel!
    But oh, who ever felt as I!
      (Translated by Walter Savage Landor)

Anacreon
(ca. 6th century B.C.)
The Wounded Cupid

Cupid, as he lay among
Roses, by a bee was stung.
Whereupon, in anger flying
To his mother, said thus, crying,
"Help, oh help, your boy's a-dying!"
"And why, my pretty lad?" said she.
Then, blubbering, replied he,
"A winged snake has bitten me,
Which country people call a bee."
At which she smiled; then with her hairs

And kisses drying up his tears,
"Alas," said she, "my wag! if this
Such a pernicious torment is;
Come, tell me, then, how great's the smart
Of those thou woundest with thy dart!"
    (Translated by Robert Herrick)

Pindar
(ca. 522-442 B.C.)
First Olympian Ode

Best of all things is water; but gold, like a gleaming fire
by night, outshines all pride of wealth beside.
But, my heart, would you chant the glory of games,
look never beyond the sun
by day for any star shining brighter through the deserted air,
nor any contest than Olympia greater to sing.
It is thence that the song winds strands
in the hearts of the skilled to celebrate
the son of Kronos. They come their ways
to the magnificent board of Hieron,

who handles the scepter of dooms in Sicily, rich in flocks,
reaping the crested heads of every excellence.
There his fame is magnified
in the splendor of music, where
we delight at the friendly table. Then take the Dorian lyre
    from its peg,
if any glory of Pisa or Pherenikos
slide with delight beneath your heart,
when by Alpheus waters he sped
his bulk, with the lash laid never on,
and mixed in the arms of victory his lord,

king of Syracuse, delighting in horses; and his fame shines
among strong men where Lydian Pelops went to dwell.
Pelops that he who clips the earth in his great strength,
Poseidon, loved when Klotho lifted him out
of the clean cauldron, his shoulder gleaming ivory.
Great marvels in truth are these, but tales
told and overlaid with elaboration of lies
amaze men's wits against the true word.

Grace, who brings to fulfilment all things for men's delight,
granting honor again, many a time makes

things incredible seem true.
Days to come are the wisest witnesses.
It is better for a man to speak well of the gods; he is less to
    blame.
Son of Tantalos, against older men I will say
that when your father summoned the gods
to that stateliest feast at beloved Sipylos,
and gave them to eat and received in turn,
that he of the shining trident caught you up,

his heart to desire broken, and with his horses and car of gold
carried you up to the house of Zeus and his wide honor,
where Ganymede at a later time
came for the same desire in Zeus.
But when you were gone, and men from your mother looked,
    nor brought you back,
some man, a neighbor, spoke quietly for spite,
how they took you and with a knife
minced your limbs into bubbling water
and over the table divided and ate
flesh of your body, even to the last morsel.

I cannot understand how a god could gorge thus, I recoil.
Many a time disaster has come to the speakers of evil.
If they who watch on Olympos have honored
any man, that man was Tantalos; but he was not
able to swallow his great fortune, and for his high stomach
drew a surpassing doom when our father
hung the weight of the stone above him.
He waits ever the stroke at his head and is divided from joy.

That life is too much for his strength; he is buckled fast in
    torment,
agony fourth among three others, because he stole
and gave to his own fellowship
that ambrosia and nectar
wherewith the gods made him immortal. If any man thinks
    to swindle
God, he is wrong. Therefore, they sent his son
back to the fleeting destiny of man's race.
And when at the time of life's blossoming
the first beard came to darken his cheek,
he thought on winning a bride ready at hand,

Hippodameia, the glorious daughter of a king in Pisa.
He walked alone in the darkness by the gray sea,

invoking the lord of the heavy trident,
and he appeared clear at his feet.
He spoke: "Look you, Poseidon, if you have had any joy of
    my love
and the Kyprian's sweet gifts, block the brazen spear
of Oinomaos, and give me the fleeter chariot
by Elis' river, and clothe me about in strength.
Thirteen suitors he has killed now, and ever
puts aside the marriage of his daughter.

The great danger never descends upon a man without
    strength;
but if we are destined to die, why should one sit
to no purpose in darkness and find a nameless old age
without any part of glory his own? So my way
lies this hazard; yours to accomplish the end."
He spoke, with words not wide of the mark.
The god, increasing his fame, gave him
a golden chariot and horses never weary with wings.

Breaking the strength of Oinomaos, he took the maiden and
    brought her to bed.
She bore him six sons, lords of the people, blazing in valor.
Now he lies at the Alpheus
crossing, mixed with the mighty dead.
His tomb is thronged about at the altar where many strangers
    pass; but the glory
of Pelops looks afar from Olympia
in the courses where speed is matched with speed
and a man's force harsh at the height.
And the winner the rest of his lifetime
keeps happiness beside him sweeter than honey

as far as the games go; but the good that stays by day and
    abides with him
is best that can come to a man. Be at my work to crown
in the rider's rhythm and strain
of Aiolis that king. I believe
there is no man greater both ways, for wisdom in beautiful
    things and power's weight
we shall ever glorify by skill in the folds of song.
Some god stands ever about you, musing
in his mind over what you do,
Hieron. May he not leave you soon.
So shall I hope to find once more

even a sweeter word's way to sing and help the chariot
    fleeting,
coming again to the lifting hill of Kronos. For me
the Muse in her might is forging yet the strongest arrow.
One man is excellent one way, one in another; the highest
fulfils itself in kings. Oh, look no further.
Let it be yours to walk this time on the height.
Let it be mine to stand beside you
in victory, for my skill at the forefront of the Hellenes.
                    (Translated by Richmond Lattimore)

Empedocles
(ca. 444 B.C.)
A Twofold Truth

I will report a twofold truth. Now grows
The One from Many into being, now
Even from the One disparting come the Many.
Twofold the girth, twofold the death of things:
For, now, the meeting of the Many brings
To birth and death; and, now, whatever grew
From out their sundering, flies apart and dies.
And this long interchange shall never end.
Whiles into One do all through Love unite;
Whiles too the same are rent through hate of Strife.
And in so far as is the One still wont
To grow from Many, and the Many, again,
Spring from primeval scattering of the One,
So far have they a birth and mortal date;
And in so far as the long interchange
Ends not, so far forever established gods
Around the circle of the world they move.
But come! but hear my words! For knowledge gained
Makes strong thy soul. For as before I spake,
Naming the utter goal of these my words,
I will report a twofold truth. Now grows
The One from Many into being, now
Even from the One disparting come the Many,—
Fire, Water, Earth and awful heights of Air;
And shut from them apart, the deadly Strife
In equipoise, and Love within their midst
In all her being in length and breadth the same.
Behold her now with mind, and sit not there
With eyes astonished, for 'tis she inborn
Abides established in the limbs of men.

Through her they cherish thoughts of love, through her
Perfect the works of concord, calling her
By name Delight or Aphrodite clear.
She speeds revolving in the elements,
But this no mortal man hath ever learned—
Hear thou the undelusive course of proof:
Behold those elements own equal strength
And equal origin; each rules its task;
And unto each its primal mode; and each
Prevailing conquers with revolving time.
And more than these there is no birth nor end;
For were they wasted ever and evermore,
They were no longer, and the great All were then
How to be plenished and from what far coast?
And how, besides, might they to ruin come,
Since nothing lives that empty is of them?—
No, these are all, and, as they course along
Though one another, now this, now that is born—
And so forever down Eternity.

(Translated by W. E. Leonard)

Callimachus
(ca. 310 B.C.)

Heraclitus

They told me, Heraclitus, they told me you were dead;
They brought me bitter news to hear and bitter tears to shed.
I wept as I remembered how often you and I
Had tired the sun with talking and sent him down the sky.
And now that thou art lying, my dear old Carian guest,
A handful of gray ashes, long, long ago at rest,
Still are thy pleasant voices, thy nightingales, awake;
For Death, he taketh all away, but them he cannot take.

(Translated by William Cory)

Crethis

For Crethis' store of tales and pleasant chat
Oft sigh the Samian maidens, missing that
Which cheered their tasks, but she, beyond their call,
Sleeps here the sleep that must be slept by all.

(Translated by Richard Garnett)

GREEK THEATER AT EPIDAURUS

Aeschylus
(525-456 B.C.)
from *Agamemnon*

Thespis, a Greek poet who lived in the sixth century before Christ, is traditionally considered the originator of Greek tragedy. But Thespis (hence thespian, actor) is only a name. It was Aeschylus who gave to tragedy the essential dramatic form, the poetic intensity, and the intellectual and moral profundity that made it one of the glories of the Greek Golden Age and one of mankind's greatest artistic achievements.

*Of Aeschylus' seven remaining tragedies, three constitute the only extant group of plays meant to be produced in a single day as a dramatic unity—the Oresteian trilogy (*Agamemnon, Choephoroe *or* Libation-Bearers, *and* Eumenides*). They tell the story of the ill-fated House of Atreus—of King Agamemnon, who, after a series of crimes and other disasters that had plagued his ancestors, is murdered by his wife Clytemnestra; of their children Electra and Orestes, who resolved to avenge their father's murder; of Orestes' killing of his mother; and of the resulting moral dilemma, which can be solved only by the combined efforts of gods and men. The excerpt here is from the play* Agamemnon.

While Agamemnon has been serving as leader of the Greeks who are besieging Troy, his wife Clytemnestra has taken as her lover Agamemnon's cousin Aegisthus. A signal sent by means of a chain of beacons tells her that the war is over and her husband is returning. When the chorus of elders expresses doubts, she vividly describes both the chain of fire and—as she sees it in her mind's eye—the destruction of Troy.

CLYTEMNESTRA: The god of fire!
  Ida first launched his blazing beam;
    thence to this palace
  Beacon lit beacon in relays of flame.
    From Ida
  To Hermes' crag on Lemnos; from that
    island, third
  To receive the towering torch was Athos,
    rock of Zeus;
  There, as the blaze leapt the dark
    leagues, the watch in welcome
  Leapt too, and a twin tower of bright-
    ness speared the sky.
  Pointing athwart the former course; and
    in a stride
  Crossing the Aegean, like the whip-lash
    of lightning, flew
  The resinous dazzle, molten-gold, till the
    fish danced,
  As at sunrise, enraptured with the bea-
    con's glow,
  Which woke reflected sunrise on Ma-
    kistos' heights.
  The watchman there, proof against
    sleep, surprise or sloth,
  Rose faithful to the message; and his
    faggots' flame
  Swept the wide distance to Euripus'
    channel, where
  Its burning word was blazoned to the
    Messapian guards.
  They blazed in turn, kindling their pile
    of withered heath,
  And passed the signal on. The strong
    beam, still undimmed,
  Crossed at one bound Asopus' plain, and
    like the moon
  In brilliance, lighted on Cithaeron's
    crags, and woke
  Another watch, to speed the flying token
    on.
  On still the hot gleam hurtled, past Gor-
    gopis' lake;
  Made Aegiplanctus, stirred those watch-
    ing mountaineers
  Not to stint boughs and brushwood;
    generously they fed
  Their beacon, and up burst a monstrous
    beard of fire,
  Leapt the proud headland fronting the
    Saronic Gulf,
  To lofty Arachnaeus, neighbor to our
    streets;

Thence on this Atreid palace the triumphant fire
Flashed, lineal descendant of the flame of Ida.

Such, Elders, was the ritual race my torch-bearers,
Each at his faithful post succeeding each, fulfilled;
And first and last to run share equal victory.
Such, Elders, is my proof and token offered you,
A message sent to me from Troy by Agamemnon.

CHORUS: Madam, we will in due course offer thanks to Heaven;
But now we want to savour wonder to the fill,
And hear you speak at length: tell us your news again!

CLYTEMNESTRA: Today the Greeks hold Troy! Her walls echo with cries
That will not blend. Pour oil and vinegar in one vessel,
You'll see them part and swirl, and never mix: so, there,
I think, down narrow streets a discord grates the ear—
Screams of the captured, shouts of those who've captured them,
The unhappy and the happy. Women of Troy prostrate
Over dead husbands, brothers; aged grandfathers
Mourning dead sons and grandsons, and remembering
Their very cries are slave's cries now...
And then the victors:
After a night of fighting, roaming, plundering,
Hungry to breakfast, while their hosts lie quiet in dust;
No rules to keep, no order of place; each with the luck
That fell to him, quartered in captured homes of Troy,
Tonight, at least, rolled in dry blankets, safe from frost—
No going on guard—blissfully they'll sleep from dusk to dawn.

If in that captured town they are reverencing the gods
Whose home it was, and not profaning holy places,
The victors will avoid being vanquished in their turn.
Only, let no lust of unlawful plunder tempt
Our soldiers' hearts with wealth, to their own harm—there still
Remains the journey home: God grant we see them safe!
If the fleet sails free from the taint of sin, the gods
May grant them safely to retrace their outward course—
Those whom no wakeful anger of the forgotten dead
Waits to surprise with vengeance....
                These are a woman's words.
May good prevail beyond dispute, in sight of all!
My life holds many blessings; I would enjoy them now.

When Agamemnon reaches his home, Clytemnestra, who has already laid plans to kill him, greets her "dearest husband" with apparent warmth. She even urges him to walk from his chariot to the palace on a crimson or purple carpet, knowing that if he does so he will prove himself guilty of hubris—*of arrogance that the gods cannot forgive.*

CLYTEMNESTRA: Elders and citizens of Argos! In your presence now
I will speak, unashamed, a wife's love for her husband.
With time dies diffidence. What I shall tell I learnt

Untaught, from my own long endurance, these ten years
My husband spent under the walls of Ilion.
First, that a woman should sit forlorn at home, unmanned,
Is a crying grief. Then, travellers, one on other's heels,
Dismay the palace, each with worse news than the last.
Why, if my Lord received as many wounds as Rumour,
Plying from Troy to Argos, gave him, he is a net,
All holes! Or had he died each time report repeated
News of his death—see him, a second Geryon,
Boasting his monstrous right, his thrice-spread quilt of earth—
A grave for each death, each body! Many times despair
At a cruel message noosed my throat in a hung cord,
Which force against my will untied.

      These fears explain
Why our child is not here to give you fitting welcome,
Our true love's pledge, Orestes. Have no uneasiness.
He is in Phocis, a guest of Strophius your well-tried friend,
Who warned me of peril from two sources; first, the risk
Threatening your life at Troy; then, if conspiracy
Matured to popular revolt in Argos, fear
Of man's instinct to trample on his fallen lord.
Such was his reasoning—surely free from all suspicion.

For me—the springing torrents of my tears are all
Drawn dry, no drop left; and my sleepless eyes are sore
With weeping by the lamp long lit for you in vain.
In dreams, the tenuous tremors of the droning gnat
Roused me from dreadful visions of more deaths for you
Than could be compassed in the hour that slept with me.

There is no dearer sight than shelter after storm;
No escape sweeter than from siege of circumstance.
Now, after siege and storm endured, my happy heart
Welcomes my husband, faithful watch-dog of his home,
Our ship's firm anchor, towering pillar that upholds
This royal roof; as dear, as to a father's hope
His longed-for son, a spring to thirsty travellers,
Or sight of land unlooked-for to men long at sea.

Such praise I hold his due; and may Heaven's jealousy
Acquit us; our past suffering has been enough.

Now, dearest husband, come, step from your chariot.
But do not set to earth, my lord, the conquering foot
That trod down Troy. Servants, do as you have been bidden;
Make haste, carpet his way with crimson tapestries,
Spread silk before your master's feet; Justice herself
Shall lead him to a home he never hoped to see.
All other matters forethought, never lulled by sleep,
Shall order justly as the will of Heaven decrees.

    (Translated by Philip Vellacott)

Sophocles
(ca. 496-406 B.C.)
Antigone

We have only seven of the more than 120 plays of Sophocles, in his lifetime the most popular of Greek playwrights. Most celebrated of these is King Oedipus, *a play so artfully constructed and so dramatically intense that one almost overlooks the series of implausible plot elements on which is it based. Almost as intense and surely of more nearly universal concern in the moral and social issues it deals with is Sophocles'* Antigone. *The background is this: Following the exile and death of King Oedipus, it is understood that his two sons, Eteocles and Polynices, will take turns ruling the city of Thebes. But when Eteocles' turn expires, he refuses to relinquish the throne. Polynices assembles armies led by himself and six allies (the Seven against Thebes) and makes war on his native city. In a hand-to-hand combat the brothers Eteocles and Polynices kill each other. Their uncle Creon becomes ruler of Thebes. Creon decrees that since Polynices was an invader, his body should not be given the burial that would insure entry of his spirit into the abodes of the dead. But Polynices' sister Antigone resolves to defy the decree, in the name of love for her brother and of a high, god-ordained morality. Here arises one of the still-current issues of the drama: civil law in conflict with religious law and personal conviction. Whether Creon's edict was simply the self-willed act of a tyrant, and whether one should bow to such an act, is another issue.*

CHARACTERS

Ismene
Antigone } daughters of Oedipus
Creon, *King of Thebes*
Haemon, *son of Creon*
Teiresias, *a blind prophet*
A Sentry
A Messenger
Eurydice, *wife of Creon*
Chorus *of Theban elders*
King's attendants
Queen's attendants
A boy leading Teiresias
Soldiers

GREEK TEMPLE TO ATHENA AT RHODES

Scene: Before the Palace at Thebes

Enter ISMENE *from the central door of the Palace.* ANTIGONE *follows, anxious and urgent; she closes the door carefully, and comes to join her sister.*

ANTIGONE: O sister! Ismene dear, dear sister Ismene!
You know how heavy the hand of God is upon us;
How we who are left must suffer for our father, Oedipus.
There is no pain, no sorrow, no suffering, no dishonour
We have not shared together, you and I.
And now there is something more. Have you heard this order,
This latest order that the King has proclaimed to the city?
Have you heard how our dearest are being treated like enemies?
ISMENE: I have heard nothing about any of those we love,
Neither good nor evil—not, I mean, since the death
Of our two brothers, both fallen in a day.
The Argive army, I hear, was withdrawn last night.
I know no more to make me sad or glad.
ANTIGONE:
I thought you did not. That's why I brought you out here,
Where we shan't be heard, to tell you something alone.
ISMENE:
What is it, Antigone? Black news, I can see already.
ANTIGONE:
O Ismene, what do you think? Our two dear brothers...
Creon has given funeral honours to one,
And not to the other; nothing but shame and ignominy.
Eteocles has been buried, they tell me, in state,
With all honourable observances due to the dead.
But Polynices, just as unhappily fallen—the order
Says he is not to be buried, not to be mourned;
To be left unburied, unwept, a feast of flesh
For keen-eyed carrion birds. The noble Creon!
It is against you and me he has made this order.
Yes, against me. And soon he will be here himself
To make it plain to those that have not heard it,
And to enforce it. This is no idle threat;
The punishment for disobedience is death by stoning.
So now you know. And now is the time to show
Whether or not you are worthy of your high blood.
ISMENE: My poor Antigone, if this is really true,
What more can *I* do, or undo, to help you?

Antigone:
  Will you help me? Will you do something with me? Will you?
Ismene: Help you do what, Antigone? What do you mean?
Antigone:
  Would you help me lift the body . . . you and me?
Ismene:
  You cannot mean . . . to bury him? Against the order?
Antigone:
  Is he not my brother, and yours, whether you like it
  Or not? *I* shall never desert him, never.
Ismene:
  How could you dare, when Creon has expressly forbidden it?
Antigone: He has no right to keep me from my own.
Ismene: O sister, sister, do you forget how our father
  Perished in shame and misery, his awful sin
  Self-proved, blinded by his own self-mutilation?
  And then his mother, his wife—for she was both—
  Destroyed herself in a noose of her own making.
  And now our brothers, both in a single day
  Fallen in an awful exaction of death for death,
  Blood for blood, each slain by the other's hand.
  Now we two left; and what will be the end of us,
  If we transgress the law and defy our king?
  O think, Antigone; we are women; it is not for us
  To fight against men; our rulers are stronger than we,
  And we must obey in this, or in worse than this.
  May the dead forgive me, I can do no other
  But as I am commanded; to do more is madness.
Antigone: No; then I will not ask you for your help.
  Nor would I thank you for it, if you gave it.
  Go your own way; I will bury my brother;
  And if I die for it, what happiness!
  Convicted of reverence—I shall be content
  To lie beside a brother whom I love.
  We have only a little time to please the living,
  But all eternity to love the dead.
  There I shall lie for ever. Live, if you will;
  Live, and defy the holiest laws of heaven.
Ismene: I do not defy them; but I cannot act
  Against the State. I am not strong enough.
Antigone: Let that be your excuse, then. I will go
  And heap a mound of earth over my brother.
Ismene: I fear for you, Antigone; I fear—
Antigone: You need not fear for me. Fear for yourself.

ISMENE: At least be secret. Do not breathe a word.
   I'll not betray your secret.
ANTIGONE: Publish it
   To all the world! Else I shall hate you more.
ISMENE: Your heart burns! Mine is frozen at the thought.
ANTIGONE: I know my duty, where true duty lies.
ISMENE: If you can do it; but you're bound to fail.
ANTIGONE: When I have *tried* and failed, I shall have failed.
ISMENE: No sense in starting on a hopeless task.
ANTIGONE: Oh, I shall hate you if you talk like that!
   And *he* will hate you, rightly. Leave me alone
   With my own madness. There is no punishment
   Can rob me of my honourable death.
ISMENE: Go then, if you are determined, to your folly.
   But remember that those who love you . . . love you still.

> ISMENE *goes into the Palace.*
> ANTIGONE *leaves the stage by a side exit.*
> *Enter the* CHORUS *of Theban elders.*

CHORUS:
   Hail the sun! the brightest of all that ever
   Dawned on the City of Seven Gates, City of Thebes!
   Hail the golden dawn over Dirce's river
   Rising to speed the flight of the white invaders
      Homeward in full retreat!

   The army of Polynices was gathered against us,
   In angry dispute his voice was lifted against us,
   Like a ravening bird of prey he swooped around us
   With white wings flashing, with flying plumes,
      With armed hosts ranked in thousands.

   At the threshold of seven gates in a circle of blood
   His swords stood round us, his jaws were opened against us;
   But before he could taste our blood, or consume us with fire,
   He fled, fled wih the roar of the dragon behind him
      And thunder of war in his ears.

   The Father of Heaven abhors the proud tongue's
      boasting;
   He marked the oncoming torrent, the flashing stream
   Of their golden harness, the clash of their battle gear;
   He heard the invader cry Victory over our ramparts,
      And smote him with fire to the ground.

Down to the ground from the crest of his hurricane
    onslaught
He swung, with the fiery brands of his hate brought low:
Each and all to their doom of destruction appointed
    By the god that fighteth for us.

Seven invaders at seven gates, seven defenders
Spoiled of their bronze for a tribute to Zeus; save two
Luckless brothers in one fight matched together
    And in one death laid low.

Great is the victory, great be the joy
In the city of Thebes, the city of chariots.
Now is the time to fill the temples
With glad thanksgiving for warfare ended;
Shake the ground with the night-long dances,
Bacchus afoot and delight abounding.

But see, the King comes here,
Creon, the son of Menoeceus,
Whom the gods have appointed for us
In our recent change of fortune.
What matter is it, I wonder,
That has led him to call us together
By his special proclamation?

The central door is opened, and CREON *enters.*

CREON:
My councillors: now that the gods have brought our city
Safe through a storm of trouble to tranquillity,
I have called you especially out of all my people
To conference together, knowing that you
Were loyal subjects when King Laius reigned,
And when King Oedipus so wisely ruled us,
And again, upon his death, faithfully served
His sons, till they in turn fell—both slayers, both slain,
Both stained with brother-blood, dead in a day—
And I, their next of kin, inherited
The throne and kingdom which I now possess.
    No other touchstone can test the heart of a man,
The temper of his mind and spirit, till he be tried
In the practice of authority and rule.
For my part, I have always held the view,
And hold it still, that a king whose lips are sealed

By fear, unwilling to seek advice, is damned.
And no less damned is he who puts a friend
Above his country; I have no good word for him.
As God above is my witness, who sees all,
When I see any danger threatening my people,
Whatever it may be, I shall declare it.
No man who is his country's enemy
Shall call himself my friend. Of this I am sure—
Our country is our life; only when she
Rides safely, have we any friends at all.
Such is my policy for our common weal.
    In pursuance of this, I have made a proclamation
Concerning the sons of Oedipus, as follows:
Eteocles, who fell fighting in defence of the city,
Fighting gallantly, is to be honoured with burial
And with all the rites due to the noble dead.
The other—you know whom I mean—his brother Polynices,
Who came back from exile intending to burn and destroy
His fatherland and the gods of his fatherland,
To drink the blood of his kin, to make them slaves—
He is to have no grave, no burial,
No mourning from anyone; it is forbidden.
He is to be left unburied, left to be eaten
By dogs and vultures, a horror for all to see.
I am determined that never, if I can help it,
Shall evil triumph over good. Alive
Or dead, the faithful servant of his country
Shall be rewarded.
CHORUS: Creon, son of Menoeceus,
  You have given your judgment for the friend and for
    the enemy.
  As for those that are dead, so for us who remain,
  Your will is law.
CREON: See then that it be kept.
CHORUS: My lord, some younger would be fitter for that task.
CREON: Watchers are already set over the corpse.
CHORUS: What other duty then remains for us?
CREON: Not to connive at any disobedience.
CHORUS: If there were any so mad as to ask for death—
CREON: Ay, that is the penalty. There is always someone
  Ready to be lured to ruin by hope of gain.

He turns to go.
A SENTRY *enters from the side of the stage.*
CREON *pauses at the Palace door.*

SENTRY:
    My lord: if I am out of breath, it is not from haste.
    I have not been running. On the contrary, many a time
    I stopped to think and loitered on the way,
    Saying to myself 'Why hurry to your doom,
    Poor fool?' and then I said 'Hurry, you fool.
    If Creon hears this from another man,
    Your head's as good as off.' So here I am,
    As quick as my unwilling haste could bring me;
    In no great hurry, in fact. So now I am here . . .
    But I'll tell my story . . . though it may be nothing after all.
    And whatever I have to suffer, it can't be more
    Than what God wills, so I cling to that for my comfort.
CREON: Good heavens, man, whatever is the matter?
SENTRY: To speak of myself first—I never did it, sir;
    Nor saw who did; no one can punish me for that.
CREON: You tell your story with a deal of artful precaution.
    It's evidently something strange.
SENTRY: It is.
    So strange, it's very difficult to tell.
CREON: Well, out with it, and let's be done with you.
SENTRY: It's this, sir. The corpse . . . someone has just
    Buried it and gone. Dry dust over the body
    They scattered, in the manner of holy burial.
CREON: What! Who dared to do it?
SENTRY: I don't know, sir.
    There was no sign of a pick, no scratch of a shovel;
    The ground was hard and dry—no trace of a wheel;
    Whoever it was has left no clues behind him.
    When the sentry on the first watch showed it us,
    We were amazed. The corpse was covered from sight—
    Nor with a proper grave—just a layer of earth—
    As it might be, the act of some pious passer-by.
    There were no tracks of an animal either, a dog
    Or anything that might have come and mauled the body.
    Of course we all started pitching in to each other,
    Accusing each other, and might have come to blows,
    With no one to stop us; for anyone might have done it,
    But it couldn't be proved against him, and all denied it.
    We were all ready to take hot iron in hand
    And go through fire and swear by God and heaven
    We hadn't done it, nor knew of anyone
    That could have thought of doing it, much less done it.
        Well, we could make nothing of it. Then one of our men
    Said something that made all our blood run cold—

Something we could neither refuse to do, nor do,
But at our own risk. What he said was 'This
Must be reported to the king; we can't conceal it.'
So it was agreed. We drew lots for it, and I,
Such is my luck, was chosen. So here I am,
As much against my will as yours, I'm sure;
A bringer of bad news expects no welcome.

CHORUS: My lord, I fear—I feared it from the first—
That this may prove to be an act of the gods.

CREON: Enough of that! Or I shall lose my patience.
Don't talk like an old fool, old though you be.
Blasphemy, to say the gods could give a thought
To carrion flesh! Held him in high esteem,
I suppose, and buried him like a benefactor—
A man who came to burn their temples down,
Ransack their holy shrines, their land, their laws?
Is that the sort of man you think gods love?
Not they. No. There's a party of malcontents
In the city, rebels against my word and law,
Shakers of heads in secret, impatient of rule;
They are the people, I see it well enough,
Who have bribed their instruments to do this thing.
Money! Money's the curse of man, none greater.
That's what wrecks cities, banishes men from home,
Tempts and deludes the most well-meaning soul,
Pointing out the way to infamy and shame.
Well, they shall pay for their success.

(*To the* SENTRY)

See to!
See to it, you! Upon my oath, I swear,
As Zeus is my god above: either you find
The perpetrator of this burial
And bring him here into my sight, or death—
No, not your mere death shall pay the reckoning,
But, for a living lesson against such infamy,
You shall be racked and tortured till you tell
The whole truth of this outrage; so you may learn
To seek your gain where gain is yours to get,
Not try to grasp it everywhere. In wickedness
You'll find more loss than profit.

SENTRY: May I say more?
CREON: No more; each word you say but stings me more.
SENTRY: Stings in your ears, sir, or in your deeper feelings?
CREON: Don't bandy words, fellow, about my feelings.
SENTRY: Though I offend your ears, sir, it is not I

But he that's guilty that offends your soul.
CREON: Oh, born to argue, were you?
SENTRY: Maybe so;
　But still not guilty in this business.
CREON: Doubly so, if you have sold your soul for money.
SENTRY:
　To think that thinking men should think so wrongly!
CREON: Think what you will. But if you fail to find
　The doer of this deed, you'll learn one thing:
　Ill-gotten gain brings no one any good.

He goes into the Palace.

SENTRY: Well, heaven send they find him. But whether or no,
　They'll not find me again, that's sure. Once free,
　Who never thought to see another day,
　I'll thank my lucky stars, and keep away.

Exit.

CHORUS:
　Wonders are many on earth, and the greatest of these
　Is man, who rides the ocean and takes his way
　Through the deeps, through wind-swept valleys of perilous seas
　　That surge and sway.

　He is master of ageless Earth, to his own will bending
　The immortal mother of gods by the sweat of his brow,
　As year succeeds to year, with toil unending
　　Of mule and plough.

　He is lord of all things living; birds of the air,
　Beasts of the field, all creatures of sea and land
　He taketh, cunning to capture and ensnare
　　With sleight of hand;

　Hunting the savage beast from the upland rocks,
　Taming the mountain monarch in his lair,
　Teaching the wild horse and the roaming ox
　　His yoke to bear.

　The use of language, the wind-swift motion of brain
　He learnt; found out the laws of living together
　In cities, building him shelter against the rain
　　And wintry weather.

There is nothing beyond his power. His subtlety
Meeteth all chance, all danger conquereth.
For every ill he hath found its remedy,
    Save only death.

O wondrous subtlety of man, that draws
To good or evil ways! Great honour is given
And power to him who upholdeth his country's laws
    And the justice of heaven.

But he that, too rashly daring, walks in sin
In solitary pride to his life's end.
At door of mine shall never enter in
    To call me friend.

*(Severally, seeing some persons
approach from a distance)*

O gods! A wonder to see!
Surely it cannot be—
It is no other—
Antigone!
Unhappy maid—
Unhappy Oedipus' daughter; it is she they bring.
Can she have rashly disobeyed
The order of our King?

Enter the SENTRY, *bringing* ANTIGONE *guarded
by two more soldiers.*

SENTRY: We've got her. Here's the woman that did the deed.
  We found her in the act of burying him. Where's the King?
CHORUS: He is just coming out of the palace now.

Enter CREON.

CREON: What's this? What am I just in time to see?
SENTRY: My lord, an oath's a very dangerous thing.
  Second thoughts may prove us liars. Not long since
  I swore I wouldn't trust myself again
  To face your threats; you gave me a drubbing the first time.
  But there's no pleasure like an unexpected pleasure,
  Not by a long way. And so I've come again,
  Though against my solemn oath. And I've brought this
    lady,

Who's been caught in the act of setting that grave in order.
And no casting lots for it this time—the prize is mine
And no one else's. So take her; judge and convict her.
I'm free, I hope, and quit of the horrible business.
CREON:
How did you find her? Where have you brought her from?
SENTRY:
She was burying the man with her own hands, and that's
    the truth.
CREON: Are you in your senses? Do you know what you
    are saying?
SENTRY: I saw her myself, burying the body of the man
Whom you said not to bury. Don't I speak plain?
CREON: How did she come to be seen and taken in the act?
SENTRY: It was this way.
After I got back to the place,
With all your threats and curses ringing in my ears,
We swept off all the earth that covered the body,
And left it a sodden naked corpse again;
Then sat up on the hill, on the windward side,
Keeping clear of the stench of him, as far as we could;
All of us keeping each other up to the mark,
With pretty sharp speaking, not to be caught napping
    this time.
So this went on some hours, till the flaming sun
Was high in the top of the sky, and the heat was blazing.
Suddenly a storm of dust, like a plague from heaven,
Swept over the ground, stripping the trees stark bare,
Filling the sky; you had to shut your eyes
To stand against it. When at last it stopped,
There was the girl, screaming like an angry bird,
When it finds its nest left empty and little ones gone.
Just like that she screamed, seeing the body
Naked, crying and cursing the ones that had done it.
Then she picks up the dry earth in her hands,
And pouring out of a fine bronze urn she's brought
She makes her offering three times to the dead.
Soon as we saw it, down we came and caught her.
She wasn't at all frightened. And so we charged her
With what she'd done before, and this. She admitted it,
I'm glad to say—though sorry too, in a way.
It's good to save your own skin, but a pity
To have to see another get into trouble,
Whom you've no grudge against. However, I can't say
I've ever valued anyone else's life

More than my own, and that's the honest truth.
CREON (*to* ANTIGONE): Well, what do you say—you, hiding your head there:
Do you admit, or do you deny the deed?
ANTIGONE: I do admit it. I do not deny it.
CREON (*to the* SENTRY):
You—you may go. You are discharged from blame.

Exit SENTRY.

Now tell me, in as few words as you can,
Did you know the order forbidding such an act?
ANTIGONE: I knew it, naturally. It was plain enough.
CREON: And yet you dared to contravene it?
ANTIGONE: Yes.
That order did not come from God. Justice,
That dwells with the gods below, knows no such law.
I did not think your edicts strong enough
To overrule the unwritten unalterable laws
Of God and heaven, you being only a man.
They are not of yesterday or to-day, but everlasting,
Though where they came from, none of us can tell.
Guilty of their transgression before God
I cannot be, for any man on earth.
I knew that I should have to die, of course,
With or without your order. If it be soon,
So much the better. Living in daily torment
As I do, who would not be glad to die?
This punishment will not be any pain.
Only if I had let my mother's son
Lie there unburied, then I could not have borne it.
This I can bear. Does that seem foolish to you?
Or is it you that are foolish to judge me so?
CHORUS: She shows her father's stubborn spirit: foolish
Not to give way when everything's against her.
CREON: Ah, but you'll see. The over-obstinate spirit
Is soonest broken; as the strongest iron will snap
If over-tempered in the fire to brittleness.
A little halter is enough to break
The wildest horse. Proud thoughts do not sit well
Upon subordinates. This girl's proud spirit
Was first in evidence when she broke the law;
And now, to add insult to her injury,
She gloats over her deed. But, as I live,
She shall not flout my orders with impunity.

My sister's child—ay, were she even nearer,
　　　Nearest and dearest, she should not escape
　　　Full punishment—she, and her sister too,
　　　Her partner, doubtless, in this burying.
　　　　 Let her be fetched! She was in the house just now;
　　　I saw her, hardly in her right mind either.
　　　Often the thoughts of those who plan dark deeds
　　　Betray themselves before the deed is done.
　　　The criminal who being caught still tries
　　　To make a fair excuse, is damned indeed.
ANTIGONE:
　　　Now you have caught, will you do more than kill me?
CREON: No, nothing more; that is all I could wish.
ANTIGONE:
　　　Why then delay? There is nothing that you can say
　　　That I should wish to hear, as nothing I say
　　　Can weigh with you. I have given my brother burial.
　　　What greater honour could I wish? All these
　　　Would say that what I did was honourable,
　　　But fear locks up their lips. To speak and act
　　　Just as he likes is a king's prerogative.
CREON:
　　　You are wrong. None of my subjects thinks as you do.
ANTIGONE: Yes, sir, they do; but dare not tell you so.
CREON: And you are not only alone, but unashamed.
ANTIGONE: There is no shame in honouring my brother?
CREON:
　　　Was not his enemy, who died with him, your brother?
ANTIGONE:
　　　Yes, both were brothers, both of the same parents.
CREON: You honour one, and so insult the other.
ANTIGONE: He that is dead will not accuse me of that.
CREON: He will, if you honour him no more than the traitor.
ANTIGONE:
　　　It was not a slave, but his brother, that died with him.
CREON: Attacking his country, while the other defended it.
ANTIGONE: Even so, we have a duty to the dead.
CREON: Not to give equal honour to good and bad.
ANTIGONE: Who knows? In the country of the dead that
　　　　 may be the law.
CREON: An enemy can't be a friend, even when dead.
ANTIGONE: My way is to share my love, not share my hate.
CREON: Go then, and share your love among the dead.
　　　We'll have no woman's law here, while I live.

　　　　　　Enter ISMENE *from the Palace.*

CHORUS: Here comes Ismene, weeping
   In sisterly sorrow; a darkened brow,
   Flushed face, and the fair cheek marred
   With flooding rain.
CREON: You crawling viper! Lurking in my house
   To suck my blood! Two traitors unbeknown
   Plotting against my throne. Do you admit
   To a share in this burying, or deny all knowledge?
ISMENE: I did it—yes—if she will let me say so.
   I am as much to blame as she is.
ANTIGONE: No.
   That is not just. You would not lend a hand
   And I refused your help in what I did.
ISMENE: But I am not ashamed to stand beside you
   Now in your hour of trial, Antigone.
ANTIGONE:
   Whose was the deed, Death and the dead are witness.
   I love no friend whose love is only words.
ISMENE: O sister, sister, let me share your death,
   Share in the tribute of honour to him that is dead.
ANTIGONE: You shall not die with me. You shall not claim
   That which you would not touch. One death is enough.
ISMENE: How can I bear to live, if you must die?
ANTIGONE: Ask Creon. Is not he the one you care for?
ISMENE: You do yourself no good to taunt me so.
ANTIGONE: Indeed no: even my jests are bitter pains.
ISMENE: But how, O tell me, how can I still help you?
ANTIGONE: Help yourself. I shall not stand in your way.
ISMENE: For pity, Antigone—can I not die with you?
ANTIGONE:
   You chose; life was your choice, when mine was death.
ISMENE: Although I warned you that it would be so.
ANTIGONE: Your way seemed right to some, to others mine.
ISMENE: But now both in the wrong, and both condemned.
ANTIGONE: No, no. You live. My heart was long since dead,
   So it was right for me to help the dead.
CREON: I do believe the creatures both are mad;
   One lately crazed, the other from her birth.
ISMENE: Is it not likely sir? The strongest mind
   Cannot but break under misfortune's blows.
CREON: Yours did, when you threw in your lot with hers.
ISMENE: How could I wish to live without my sister?
CREON: You have no sister. Count her dead already.
ISMENE: You could not take her—kill your own son's bride?
CREON: Oh, there are other fields for him to plough.
ISMENE: No truer troth was ever made than theirs.

CREON: No son of mine shall wed so vile a creature.
ANTIGONE: O Haemon, can your father spite you so?
CREON: You and your paramour, I hate you both.
CHORUS:
   Sir, would you take her from your own son's arms?
CREON: Not I, but death shall take her.
CHORUS: Be it so.
   Her death, it seems, is certain.
CREON: Certain it is.
   No more delay. Take them, and keep them within—
   The proper place for women. None so brave
   As not to look for some way of escape
   When they see life stand face to face with death.

The women are taken away.

CHORUS:
   Happy are they who know not the taste of evil.
   From a house that heaven hath shaken
   The curse departs not
   But falls upon all of the blood,
   Like the restless surge of the sea when the dark storm drives
   The black sand hurled from the deeps
   And the Thracian gales boom down
   On the echoing shore.

   In life and in death is the house of Labdacus stricken.
   Generation to generation,
   With no atonement,
   It is scourged by the wrath of a god.
   And now for the dead dust's sake is the light of promise,
   The tree's last root, crushed out
   By pride of heart and the sin
   Of presumptuous tongue.

   For what presumption of man can match thy power,
   O Zeus, that art not subject to sleep or time
   Or age, living for ever in bright Olympus?
   To-morrow and for all time to come,
     As in the past,
     This law is immutable:
   For mortals greatly to live is greatly to suffer.

     Roving ambition helps many a man to good,
   And many it falsely lures to light desires,
   Till failure trips them unawares, and they fall

On the fire that consumes them. Well was it said,
Evil seems good
To him who is doomed to suffer;
And short is the time before that suffering comes.

But here comes Haemon,
Your youngest son.
Does he come to speak his sorrow
For the doom of his promised bride,
The loss of his marriage hopes?

CREON:
We shall know it soon, and need no prophet to tell us.

Enter HAEMON.

Son, you have heard, I think, our final judgment
On your late betrothed. No angry words, I hope?
Still friends, in spite of everything, my son?
HAEMON: I am your son, sir; by your wise decisions
My life is ruled, and them I shall always obey.
I cannot value any marriage-tie
Above your own good guidance.
CREON: Rightly said.
Your father's will should have your heart's first place.
Only for this do fathers pray for sons
Obedient, loyal, ready to strike down
Their fathers' foes, and love their fathers' friends.
To be the father of unprofitable sons
Is to be the father of sorrows, a laughing-stock
To all one's enemies. Do not be fooled, my son,
By lust and the wiles of a woman. You'll have bought
Cold comfort if your wife's a worthless one.
No wound strikes deeper than love that is turned to hate.
This girl's an enemy; away with her,
And let her go and find a mate in Hades.
Once having caught her in a flagrant act—
The one and only traitor in our State—
I cannot make myself a traitor too;
So she must die. Well may she pray to Zeus,
The God of Family Love. How, if I tolerate
A traitor at home, shall I rule those abroad?
He that is a righteous master of his house
Will be a righteous statesman. To trangress
Or twist the law to one's own pleasure, presume
To order where one should obey, is sinful,

And I will have none of it.
He whom the State appoints must be obeyed
To the smallest matter, be it right—or wrong.
And he that rules his household, without a doubt,
Will make the wisest king, or, for that matter,
The staunchest subject. He will be the man
You can depend on in the storm of war,
The faithfullest comrade in the day of battle.
There is no more deadly peril than disobedience;
States are devoured by it, homes laid in ruins,
Armies defeated, victory turned to rout.
While simple obedience saves the lives of hundreds
Of honest folk. Therefore, I hold to the law,
And will never betray it—least of all for a woman.
Better be beaten, if need be, by a man,
Than let a woman get the better of us.

CHORUS: To me, as far as an old man can tell,
It seems your Majesty has spoken well.

HAEMON: Father, man's wisdom is the gift of heaven,
The greatest gift of all. I neither am
Nor wish to be clever enough to prove you wrong,
Though all men might not think the same as you do.
Nevertheless, I have to be your watchdog,
To know what others say and what they do,
And what they find to praise and what to blame.
Your frown is a sufficient silencer
Of any word that is not for your ears.
But *I* hear whispers spoken in the dark;
On every side I hear voices of pity
For this poor girl, doomed to the cruellest death,
And most unjust, that ever woman suffered
For an honourable action—burying a brother
Who was killed in battle, rather than leave him naked
For dogs to maul and carrion birds to peck at.
Has she not rather earned a crown of gold?—
Such is the secret talk about the town.

    Father, there is nothing I can prize above
Your happiness and well-being. What greater good
Can any son desire? Can any father
Desire more from his son? Therefore I say,
Let not your first thought be your only thought.
Think if there cannot be some other way.
Surely, to think your own the only wisdom,
And yours the only word, the only will,
Betrays a shallow spirit, an empty heart.
It is no weakness for the wisest man

>   To learn when he is wrong, know when to yield.
>   So, on the margin of a flooded river
>   Trees bending to the torrent live unbroken,
>   While those that strain against it are snapped off.
>   A sailor has to tack and slacken sheets
>   Before the gale, or find himself capsized.
>   So, father, pause, and put aside your anger.
>   I think, for what my young opinion's worth,
>   That, good as it is to have infallible wisdom,
>   Since this is rarely found, the next best thing
>   Is to be willing to listen to wise advice.
> CHORUS:
>   There is something to be said, my lord, for his point of view,
>   And for yours as well; there is much to be said on both
>   sides.
> CREON: Indeed! Am I to take lessons at my time of life
>   From a fellow of his age?
> HAEMON: No lesson you need be ashamed of.
>   It isn't a question of age, but of right and wrong.
> CREON:
>   Would you call it right to admire an act of disobedience?
> HAEMON: Not if the act were also dishonourable.
> CREON: And was not this woman's action dishonourable?
> HAEMON: The people of Thebes think not.
> CREON: The people of Thebes!
>   Since when do I take my orders from the people of Thebes?
> HAEMON: Isn't that rather a childish thing to say?
> CREON: No. I am king, and responsible only to myself.
> HAEMON: A one-man state? What sort of a state is that?
> CREON: Why, does not every state belong to its ruler?
> HAEMON: You'd be an excellent king—on a desert island.
> CREON: Of course, if you're on the woman's side—
> HAEMON: No, no—
>   Unless you're the woman. It's you I'm fighting for.
> CREON:
>   What, villain, when every word you speak is against me?
> HAEMON: Only because I know you are wrong, wrong.
> CREON: Wrong? To respect my own authority?
> HAEMON: What sort of respect tramples on all that is holy?
> CREON: Despicable coward! No more will than a woman!
> HAEMON: I have nothing to be ashamed of.
> CREON: Yet you plead her cause.
> HAEMON:
>   No, *yours,* and mine, and that of the gods of the dead.
> CREON: You'll never marry her this side of death.
> HAEMON: Then, if she dies, she does not die alone.

CREON: Is that a threat, you impudent—
HAEMON: Is it a threat
  To try to argue against wrong-headedness?
CREON: You'll learn what wrong-headedness is, my friend,
    to your cost.
HAEMON:
  O father, I could call you mad, were you not my father.
CREON: Don't toady me, boy; keep that for your lady-love.
HAEMON: You mean to have the last word, then?
CREON: I do.
  And what is more, by all the gods in heaven,
  I'll make you sorry for your impudence.
  (*Calling to those within*)
  Bring out that she-devil, and let her die
  Now, with her bridegroom by to see it done!
HAEMON: That sight I'll never see. Nor from this hour
  Shall you see me again. Let those that will
  Be witness of your wickedness and folly.

          Exit

CHORUS: He is gone, my lord, in very passionate haste.
  And who shall say what a young man's wrath may do?
CREON: Let him go! Let him do! Let him rage as never man raged,
  He shall not save those women from their doom.
CHORUS: You mean, then, sire, to put them both to death?
CREON: No, not the one whose hand was innocent.
CHORUS: And to what death do you condemn the other?
CREON: I'll have her taken to a desert place
  Where no man ever walked, and there walled up
  Inside a cave, alive, with food enough
  To acquit ourselves of the blood-guiltiness
  That else would lie upon our commonwealth.
  There she may pray to Death, the god she loves,
  And ask release from death; or learn at last
  What hope there is for those who worship death.

          Exit.

CHORUS:
  Where is the equal of Love?
  Where is the battle he cannot win,
  The power he cannot outmatch?
  In the farthest corners of earth, in the midst of the sea,
  He is there; he is here
  In the bloom of a fair face

    Lying in wait;
And the grip of his madness
Spares not god or man,

    Marring the righteous man,
Driving his soul into mazes of sin
And strife, dividing a house.
For the light that burns in the eyes of a bride of desire
Is a fire that consumes.
At the side of the great gods
Aphrodite immortal
Works her will upon all.

The doors are opened and ANTIGONE *enters, guarded.*

    But here is a sight beyond all bearing,
At which my eyes cannot but weep;
Antigone forth faring
To her bridal-bower of endless sleep.

ANTIGONE: You see me, countrymen, on my last journey,
    Taking my last leave of the light of day;
    Going to my rest, where death shall take me
    Alive across the silent river.
    No wedding-day; no marriage-music;
    Death will be all my bridal dower.

CHORUS: But glory and praise go with you, lady,
    To your resting-place. You go with your beauty
    Unmarred by the hand of consuming sickness,
    Untouched by the sword, living and free,
    As none other that ever died before you.

ANTIGONE: The daughter of Tantalus, a Phrygian maid,
    Was doomed to a piteous death on the rock
    Of Sipylus, which embraced and imprisoned her,
    Merciless as the ivy; rain and snow
    Beat down upon her, mingled with her tears,
    As she wasted and died. Such was her story,
    And such is the sleep that I shall go to.

CHORUS: She was a goddess of immortal birth,
    And we are mortals; the greater the glory,
    To share the fate of a god-born maiden,
    A living death, but a name undying.

ANTIGONE: Mockery, mockery! By the gods of our fathers,
    Must you make me a laughing-stock while I yet live?
    O lordly sons of my city! O Thebes!
    Your valleys of rivers, your chariots and horses!
    No friend to weep at my banishment

    To a rock-hewn chamber of endless durance,
    In a strange cold tomb alone to linger
    Lost between life and death for ever.
CHORUS: My child, you have gone your way
    To the outermost limit of daring
    And have stumbled against Law enthroned.
    This is the expiation
    You must make for the sin of your father.
ANTIGONE: My father—the thought that sears my soul—
    The unending burden of the house of Labdacus.
    Monstrous marriage of mother and son . . .
    My father . . . my parents . . . O hideous shame!
    Whom now I follow, unwed, curse-ridden,
    Doomed to this death by the ill-starred marriage
    That marred my brother's life.
CHORUS: An act of homage is good in itself, my daughter;
    But authority cannot afford to connive at disobedience.
    You are the victim of your own self-will.
ANTIGONE: And must go the way that lies before me.
    No funeral hymn; no marriage-music;
    No sun from this day forth, no light,
    No friend to weep at my departing.

Enter CREON.

CREON: Weeping and wailing at the door of death!
    There'd be no end of it, if it had force
    To buy death off. Away with her at once,
    And close her up in her rock-vaulted tomb.
    Leave her and let her die, if die she must,
    Or live within her dungeon. Though on earth
    Her life is ended from this day, her blood
    Will not be on our hands.
ANTIGONE: So to my grave,
    My bridal-bower, my everlasting prison,
    I go, to join those many of my kinsmen
    Who dwell in the mansions of Persephone,
    Last and unhappiest, before my time.
    Yet I believe my father will be there
    To welcome me, my mother greet me gladly,
    And you, my brother, gladly see me come.
    Each one of you my hands have laid to rest,
    Pouring the due libations on your graves.
    It was by this service to your dear body, Polynices,
    I earned the punishment which now I suffer,
    Though all good people know it was for your honour.

  O but I would not have done the forbidden thing
For any husband or for any son.
For why? I could have had another husband
And by him other sons, if one were lost;
But, father and mother lost, where would I get
Another brother? For thus preferring you,
My brother, Creon condemns me and hales me away,
Never a bride, never a mother, unfriended,
Condemned alive to solitary death.
What law of heaven have I transgressed? What god
Can save me now? What help or hope have I,
In whom devotion is deemed sacrilege?
If this is God's will, I shall learn my lesson
In death; but if my enemies are wrong,
I wish them no worse punishment than mine.
CHORUS: Still the same tempest in the heart
 Torments her soul with angry gusts.
CREON: The more cause then have they that guard her
 To hasten their work; or they too suffer.
CHORUS: Alas, that word had the sound of death.
CREON: Indeed there is no more to hope for.
ANTIGONE: Gods of our fathers, my city, my home,
 Rulers of Thebes! Time stays no longer.

LIONS AT DELOS

Last daughter of your royal house
Go I, *his* prisoner, because I honoured
Those things to which honour truly belongs.

    ANTIGONE *is led away.*

CHORUS:[1]
Such was the fate, my child, of Danae
Locked in a brazen bower,
A prison secret as a tomb,
Where was no day.
Daughter of kings, her royal womb
Garnered the golden shower
Of life from Zeus. So strong is Destiny,
No wealth, no armoury, no tower,
No ship that rides the angry sea
Her mastering hand can stay.

    And Dryas' son, the proud Edonian king,
Pined in a stony cell
At Dionysus' bidding pent
To cool his fire

---

[1] *The following alternative rendering of the 'Danae' Chorus may be found more acceptable for dramatic performance. The mythological complexities of the original have here been considerably simplified in order to bring out the essential theme of the ode—precedents for the fate of Antigone.*

So, long ago, lay Danae
    Entombed within her brazen bower;
Noble and beautiful was she,
    On whom there fell the golden shower
    Of life from Zeus. There is no tower
So high, no armoury so great,
    No ship so swift, as is the power
Of man's inexorable fate.

There was the proud Edonian king,
    Lycurgus, in rock-prison pent
For arrogantly challenging
    God's laws: it was his punishment
    Of that swift passion to repent
In slow perception, for that he
    Had braved the rule omnipotent
Of Dionysus' sovereignty.

On Phineus' wife the hand of fate
    Was heavy, when her children fell
Victims to a stepmother's hate,
    And she endured a prison-cell
    Where the North Wind stood sentinel
In caverns amid mountains wild.
    Thus the grey spinners wove their spell
On her, as upon thee, my child.

Till, all his full-blown passion spent,
He came to know right well
What god his ribald tongue was challenging
When he would break the fiery spell
Of the wild Maenads' revelling
And vex the Muses' choir.

   It was upon the side
Of Bosporus, where the Black Rocks stand
By Thracian Salmydessus over the twin tide,
That Thracian Ares laughed to see
How Phineus' angry wife most bloodily
Blinded his two sons' eyes that mutely cried
For vengeance; crazed with jealousy
The woman smote them with the weaving-needle in her hand.

   Forlorn they wept away
Their sad step-childhood's misery
Predestined from their mother's ill-starred marriage-day.
She was of old Erechtheid blood,
Cave-dwelling daughter of the North-wind God;
On rocky steeps, as mountain ponies play,
The wild winds nursed her maidenhood.
On her, my child, the grey Fates laid hard hands, as upon
    thee.

Enter TEIRESIAS, *the blind prophet, led by a boy.*

TEIRESIAS:
  Gentlemen of Thebes, we greet you, my companion and I,
  Who share one pair of eyes on our journeys together—
  For the blind man goes where his leader tells him to.
CREON:
  You are welcome, father Teiresias. What's your news?
TEIRESIAS: Ay, news you shall have; and advice, if you can
    heed it.
CREON:
  There was never a time when I failed to heed it, father.
TEIRESIAS: And thereby have so far steered a steady course.
CREON: And gladly acknowledge the debt we owe to you.
TEIRESIAS:
  Then mark me now; for you stand on a razor's edge.
CREON: Indeed? Grave words from your lips, good priest.
  Say on.
TEIRESIAS: I will; and show you all that my skill reveals.
  At my seat of divination, where I sit

These many years to read the signs of heaven,
An unfamiliar sound came to my ears
Of birds in vicious combat, savage cries
In strange outlandish language, and the whirr
Of flapping wings; from which I well could picture
The gruesome warfare of their deadly talons.
Full of foreboding then I made the test
Of sacrifice upon the altar fire.
There was no answering flame; only rank juice
Oozed from the flesh and dripped among the ashes,
Smouldering and sputtering; the gall vanished in a puff,
And the fat ran down and left the haunches bare.
Thus (through the eyes of my young acolyte,
Who sees for me, that I may see for others)
I read the signs of failure in my quest.
 And why? The blight upon us is *your* doing.
The blood that stains our altars and our shrines,
The blood that dogs and vultures have licked up,
It is none other than the blood of Oedipus
Spilled from the veins of his ill-fated son.
Our fires, our sacrifices, and our prayers
The gods abominate. How should the birds
Give any other than ill-omened voices,
Gorged with the dregs of blood that man has shed?
Mark this, my son: all men fall into sin.
But sinning, he is not for ever lost
Hapless and helpless, who can make amends
And has not set his face against repentance.
Only a fool is governed by self-will.
 Pay to the dead his due. Wound not the fallen.
It is no glory to kill and kill again.
My words are for your good, as is my will,
And should be acceptable, being for your good.
CREON: You take me for your target, reverend sir,
Like all the rest. I know your art of old,
And how you make me your commodity
To trade and traffic in for your advancement.
Trade as you will; but all the silver of Sardis
And all the gold of India will not buy
A tomb for yonder traitor. No. Let the eagles
Carry his carcase up to the throne of Zeus;
Even that would not be sacrilege enough
To frighten me from my determination
Not to allow this burial. No man's act
Has power enough to pollute the goodness of God.
But great and terrible is the fall, Teiresias,

   Of mortal men who seek their own advantage
   By uttering evil in the guise of good.
TEIRESIAS: Ah, is there any wisdom in the world?
CREON: Why, what is the meaning of that wide-flung taunt?
TEIRESIAS:
   What prize outweighs the priceless worth of prudence?
CREON:
   Ay, what indeed? What mischief matches the lack of it?
TEIRESIAS: And there you speak of your own symptom, sir.
CREON: I am loth to pick a quarrel with you, priest.
TEIRESIAS: You do so, calling my divination false.
CREON: I say all prophets seek their own advantage.
TEIRESIAS: All kings, say I, seek gain unrighteously.
CREON: Do you forget to whom you say it?
TEIRESIAS: No.
   Our king and benefactor, by my guidance.
CREON: Clever you may be, but not therefore honest.
TEIRESIAS: Must I reveal my yet unspoken mind?
CREON: Reveal all; but expect no gain from it.
TEIRESIAS: Does that still seem to you my motive, then?
CREON: Nor is my will for sale, sir, in your market.
TEIRESIAS: Then hear this. Ere the chariot of the sun
   Has rounded once or twice his wheeling way,
   You shall have given a son of your own loins
   To death, in payment for death—two debts to pay:
   One for the life that you have sent to death,
   The life you have abominably entombed;
   One for the dead still lying above ground
   Unburied, unhonoured, unblest by the gods below.
   You cannot alter this. The gods themselves
   Cannot undo it. It follows of necessity
   From what you have done. Even now the avenging Furies,
   The hunters of Hell that follow and destroy,
   Are lying in wait for you, and will have their prey,
   When the evil you have worked for others falls on you.
   Do I speak this for my gain? The time shall come,
   And soon, when your house will be filled with the lamentation
   Of men and of women; and every neighbouring city
   Will be goaded to fury against you, for upon them
   Too the pollution falls when the dogs and vultures
   Bring the defilement of blood to their hearths and altars.
     I have done. You pricked me, and these shafts of wrath
   Will find their mark in your heart. You cannot escape
   The sting of their sharpness.
   Lead me home, my boy.
   Let us leave him to vent his anger on younger ears,

> Or school his mind and tongue to a milder mood
> Than that which now possesses him.
> Lead on.

Exit.

CHORUS:
> He has gone, my lord. He has prophesied terrible things.
> And for my part, I that was young and now am old
> Have never known his prophecies proved false.

CREON: It is true enough; and my heart is torn in two.
> It is hard to give way, and hard to stand and abide
> The coming of the curse. Both ways are hard.

CHORUS: If you would be advised, my good lord Creon—
CREON: What must I do? Tell me, and I will do it.
CHORUS: Release the woman from her rocky prison.
> Set up a tomb for him that lies unburied.

CREON: Is it your wish that I consent to this?
CHORUS: It is, and quickly. The gods do not delay
> The stroke of their swift vengeance on the sinner.

CREON: It is hard, but I must do it. Well I know
> There is no armour against necessity.

CHORUS: Go. Let your own hand do it, and no other.
CREON: I will go this instant.
> Slaves there! One and all.
> Bring spades and mattocks out on the hill!
> My mind is made; 'twas I imprisoned her,
> And I will set her free. Now I believe
> It is by laws of heaven that man must live.

Exit.

CHORUS:
> O Thou whose name is many,[2]
> Son of the Thunderer, dear child of his Cadmean bride,
> Whose hand is mighty
> In Italia,
> In the hospitable valley
> Of Eleusis,
> And in Thebes,
> The mother-city of thy worshippers,
> Where sweet Ismenus gently watereth
> The soil whence sprang the harvest of the dragon's teeth;
>
> Where torches on the crested mountains gleam,
> And by Castalia's stream

---

[2] *O Thou whose name is many:* believing the solution of their troubles to be now in sight, the Chorus invoke Iacchus (*alias* Bacchus, Dionysus, and other 'many names') as (1) particularly connected with Thebes, (2) giver of healing and release.

The nymph-train in thy dance rejoices,
When from the ivy-tangled glens
Of Nysa and from vine-clad plains
Thou comest to Thebes where the immortal voices
Sing thy glad strains.

   Thebes, where thou lovest most to be,
With her, thy mother, the fire-stricken one,
Sickens for need of thee.
Healer of all her ills;
Come swiftly o'er the high Parnassian hills,
Come o'er the sighing sea.

   The stars, whose breath is fire, delight
To dance for thee; the echoing night
Shall with thy praises ring.
Zeus-born, appear! With Thyiads revelling
Come, bountiful
Iacchus, King!

Enter a MESSENGER, *from the side of the stage.*

MESSENGER: Hear, men of Cadmus' city, hear and attend,
   Men of the house of Amphion, people of Thebes!
   What is the life of man? A thing not fixed
   For good or evil, fashioned for praise or blame.
   Chance raises a man to the heights, chance casts him down,
   And none can foretell what will be from what is.
   Creon was once an enviable man;
   He saved his country from her enemies,
   Assumed the sovereign power, and bore it well,
   The honoured father of a royal house.
   Now all is lost; for life without life's joys
   Is living death; and such a life is his.
   Riches and rank and show of majesty
   And state, where no joy is, are empty, vain
   And unsubstantial shadows, of no weight
   To be compared with happiness of heart.
CHORUS: What is your news? Disaster in the royal house?
MESSENGER: Death; and the guilt of it on living heads.
CHORUS: Who dead? And by what hand?
MESSENGER: Haemon is dead,
   Slain by his own—
CHORUS: His father?
MESSENGER: His own hand.
   His father's act it was that drove him to it.

CHORUS: Then all has happened as the prophet said.
MESSENGER: What's next to do, your worships will decide.

The Palace door opens.

CHORUS: Here comes the Queen, Eurydice. Poor soul,
　It may be she has heard about her son.

Enter EURYDICE, *attended by women.*

EURYDICE:
　My friends, I heard something of what you were saying
　As I came to the door. I was on my way to prayer
　At the temple of Pallas, and had barely turned the latch
　When I caught your talk of some near calamity.
　I was sick with fear and reeled in the arms of my women.
　But tell me what is the matter; what have you heard?
　I am not unacquainted with grief, and I can bear it.
MESSENGER:
　Madam, it was I that saw it, and will tell you all.
　To try to make it any lighter now
　Would be to prove myself a liar. Truth
　Is always best.
　It was thus. I attended your husband,[3]
　The King, to the edge of the field where lay the body
　Of Polynices, in pitiable state, mauled by the dogs.
　We prayed for him to the Goddess of the Roads, and to Pluto,
　That they might have mercy upon him. We washed the remains
　In holy water, and on a fire of fresh-cut branches
　We burned all that was left of him, and raised
　Over his ashes a mound of his native earth.
　That done, we turned towards the deep rock-chamber
　Of the maid that was married with death.
　Before we reached it,
　One that stood near the accursed place had heard
　Loud cries of anguish, and came to tell King Creon.
　As he approached, came strange uncertain sounds
　Of lamentation, and he cried aloud:
　'Unhappy wretch! Is my foreboding true?
　Is this the most sorrowful journey that ever I went?
　My son's voice greets me. Go, some of you, quickly

---

[3] *I attended your husband:* it is not by an oversight that the Messenger's narrative places first the attention given by Creon to the body of Polynices, and second his attempt to release Antigone. Though the king left the stage declaring his intention to save the woman's life, it is the wrong done to the dead that lies heaviest on his conscience. We misread the intention of the tragedy if we place at its centre the 'martyrdom' of Antigone; for the Athenian audience its first theme is the retribution brought upon Creon for his defiance of sacred obligations, a retribution in which Antigone and Haemon incidentally share.

Through the passage where the stones are thrown apart,
Into the mouth of the cave, and see if it be
My son, my own son Haemon that I hear.
If not, I am the sport of gods.'
We went
And looked, as bidden by our anxious master.
There in the furthest corner of the cave
We saw her hanging by the neck. The rope
Was of the woven linen of her dress.
And, with his arms about her, there stood he
Lamenting his lost bride, his luckless love,
His father's cruelty.
When Creon saw them,
Into the cave he went, moaning piteously.
'O my unhappy boy,' he cried again,
'What have you done? What madness brings you here
To your destruction? Come away, my son,
My son, I do beseech you, come away!'
His son looked at him with one angry stare,
Spat in his face, and then without a word
Drew sword and struck out. But his father fled
Unscathed. Whereon the poor demented boy
Leaned on his sword and thrust it deeply home
In his own side, and while his life ebbed out
Embraced the maid in loose-enfolding arms,
His spurting blood staining her pale cheeks red.

      EURYDICE *goes quickly back into the Palace.*

   Two bodies lie together, wedded in death,
   Their bridal sleep a witness to the world
   How great calamity can come to man
   Through man's perversity.
CHORUS: But what is this?
   The Queen has turned and gone without a word.
MESSENGER: Yes. It is strange. The best that I can hope
   Is that she would not sorrow for her son
   Before us all, but vents her grief in private
   Among her women. She is too wise, I think,
   To take a false step rashly.
CHORUS: It may be.
   Yet there is danger in unnatural silence
   No less than in excess of lamentation.
MESSENGER: I will go in and see, whether in truth
   There is some fatal purpose in her grief.
   Such silence, as you say, may well be dangerous.

He goes in. Enter Attendants preceding the King.

CHORUS: The King comes here.
   What the tongue scarce dares to tell
   Must now be known
   By the burden that proves too well
   The guilt, no other man's
   But his alone.

Enter CREON with the body of HAEMON.

CREON: The sin, the sin of the erring soul
  Drives hard unto death.
  Behold the slayer, the slain,
  The father, the son.
  O the curse of my stubborn will!
  Son, newly cut off in the newness of youth,
  Dead for my fault, not yours.
CHORUS: Alas, too late you have seen the truth.
CREON: I learn in sorrow. Upon my head
  God has delivered this heavy punishment,
  Has struck me down in the ways of wickedness,
  And trod my gladness under foot.
  Such is the bitter affliction of mortal man.

Enter the MESSENGER from the Palace.

MESSENGER: Sir, you have this and more than this to bear.
  Within there's more to know, more to your pain.
CREON: What more? What pain can overtop this pain?
MESSENGER:
  She is dead—your wife, the mother of him that is dead—
  The death-wound fresh in her heart. Alas, poor lady!
CREON: Insatiable Death, wilt thou destroy me yet?
  What say you, teller of evil?
  I am already dead,
  And is there more?
  Blood upon blood?
  More death? My wife?

The central doors open, revealing the body of EURYDICE.

CHORUS: Look then, and see; nothing is hidden now.
CREON: O second horror!
  What fate awaits me now?
  My child here in my arms . . . and there, the other . . .
  The son . . . the mother . . .

MESSENGER: There at the altar with the whetted knife
   She stood, and as the darkness dimmed her eyes
   Called on the dead, her elder son and this,
   And with her dying breath cursed you, their slayer.
CREON: O horrible ...
   Is there no sword for me,
   To end this misery?
MESSENGER: Indeed you bear the burden of two deaths.
   It was her dying word.
CREON: And her last act?
MESSENGER: Hearing her son was dead, with her own hand
   She drove the sharp sword home into her heart.
CREON: There is no man can bear this guilt but I.
   It is true, I killed him.
   Lead me away, away. I live no longer.
CHORUS: 'Twere best, if anything is best in evil times.
   What's soonest done, is best, when all is ill.
CREON: Come, my last hour and fairest,
   My only happiness ... come soon.
   Let me not see another day.
   Away ... away ...
CHORUS: The future is not to be known; our present care
   Is with the present; the rest is in other hands.
CREON: I ask no more than I have asked.
CHORUS: Ask nothing.
   What is to be, no mortal can escape.
CREON: I am nothing. I have no life.
   Lead me away ...
   That have killed unwittingly
   My son, my wife.
   I know not where I should turn,
   Where look for help.
   My hands have done amiss, my head is bowed
   With fate too heavy for me.

Exit.

CHORUS: Of happiness the crown
   And chiefest part
   Is wisdom, and to hold
   The gods in awe.
   This is the law
   That, seeing the stricken heart
   Of pride brought down,
   We learn when we are old.

EXEUNT

(Translated by E. F. Watling)

THE ACROPOLIS AT ATHENS

Euripides
(ca. 480-407 B.C.)
from *Medea*

Medea *is the tragedy of a woman whose passions are deep and spontaneous and whose love turns to hatred when she is betrayed. Her Greek audience would have kept in mind, as we should, that she was a barbarian, lacking the philosophical ideal of moderation which the Greeks admired, whether they adhered to it or not. Though they were probably horrified by the extremes to which her desire for vengeance took her, they would have recognized the basic justice—according to her standards at least—of that desire. And they would have remembered that though she was a Thracian princess, she was also endowed with gifts of magic and witchcraft which she employed in behalf of those she loved or against those she hated.*

As the Greek audience knew, Medea had given up everything she possessed because of her love for Jason, one of the most famous of Greek heroes. She helped him to steal the Golden Fleece, deceived her father, killed her brother and Jason's uncle—all in order to advance Jason—and then fled with him to Corinth, where she remained his mistress because legal marriage between Greeks and barbarians was impossible. But Jason, in this play a cold and calculating man, forgets his earlier love for Medea, and decides to put her aside so that he can marry the daughter of the king of Corinth. The king, fearing Medea's wrath and her magical powers, orders her exiled, together with the two sons whom she has borne to Jason. At this point the action of the play begins.

In the first selection that follows, Medea, who has learned that she is to be banished, bemoans the lot of women, especially of those who have come, like her, from foreign lands and have no country or friends.

MEDEA

Women of Corinth, I have come outside to you
Lest you should be indignant with me; for I know
That many people are overproud, some when alone,
And others when in company. And those who live
Quietly, as I do, get a bad reputation.
For a just judgement is not evident in the eyes
When a man at first sight hates another, before
Learning his character, being in no way injured;
And a foreigner especially must adapt himself.
I'd not approve of even a fellow-countryman
Who by pride and want of manners offends his neighbours.
But on me this thing has fallen so unexpectedly,
It has broken my heart. I am finished. I let go
All my life's joy. My friends, I only want to die.
It was everything to me to think well of one man,
And he, my own husband, has turned out wholly vile.
Of all things which are living and can form a judgement
We women are the most unfortunate creatures.
Firstly, with an excess of wealth it is required
For us to buy a husband and take for our bodies
A master; for not to take one is even worse.
And now the question is serious whether we take
A good or bad one; for there is no easy escape
For a woman, nor can she say no to her marriage.
She arrives among new modes of behaviour and manners,

And needs prophetic power, unless she has learnt at home,
How best to manage him who shares the bed with her.
And if we work out all this well and carefully,
And the husband lives with us and lightly bears his yoke,
Then life is enviable. If not, I'd rather die.
A man, when he's tired of the company of this home,
Goes out of the house and puts an end to his boredom
And turns to a friend or companion of his own age.
But we are forced to keep our eyes on one alone.
What they say of us is that we have a peaceful time
Living at home, while they do the fighting in war.
How wrong they are! I would very much rather stand
Three times in the front of battle than bear one child.
Yet what applies to me does not apply to you.
You have a country. Your family home is here.
You enjoy life and the company of your friends.
But I am deserted, a refugee, thought nothing of
By my husband,—something he won in a foreign land.
I have no mother or brother, nor any relation
With whom I can take refuge in this sea of woe.
This much then is the service I would beg from you:
If I can find the means or devise any scheme
To pay my husband back for what he has done to me,—
Him and his father-in-law and the girl who married him,—
Just to keep silent. For in other ways a woman
Is full of fear, defenceless, dreads the sight of cold
Steel; but, when once she is wronged in the manner of love,
No other soul can hold so many thoughts of blood.

After Medea persuades King Creon to give her one more day in Corinth, she is approached by Jason, whom she bitterly condemns. He tries to shrug off any responsibility.

JASON

This is not the first occasion that I have noticed
How hopeless it is to deal with stubborn temper.
For, with reasonable submission to our ruler's will,
You might have lived in this land and kept your home.
As it is you are going to be exiled for your loose speaking.
Not that I mind myself. You are free to continue
Telling everyone that Jason is a worthless man.
But as to your talk about the king, consider
Yourself most lucky that exile is your punishment.
I, for my part, have always tried to calm down
The anger of the king, and wished you to remain.
But you will not give up your folly, continually
Speaking ill of him, and so you are going to be banished.
All the same, and in spite of your conduct, I'll not desert
My friends, but have come to make some

provision for you,
So that you and the children may not be penniless
Or in need of anything in exile. Certainly
Exile brings many troubles with it. And even
If you hate me, I cannot think badly of you.

MEDEA

O coward in every way,—that is what I call you,
With bitterest reproach for your lack of manliness,
You have come, you, my worst enemy, have come to me!
It is not an example of over-confidence
Or of boldness thus to look your friends in the face,
Friends you have injured,—no, it is the worst of all
Human diseases, shamelessness. But you did well
To come, for I can speak ill of you and lighten
My heart, and you will suffer while you are listening.
And first I will begin from what happened first.
I saved your life, and every Greek knows I saved it,
Who was a ship-mate of yours aboard the Argo,
When you were sent to control the bulls that breathed fire
And yoke them, and when you would sow that deadly field.
Also that snake, who encircled with his many folds
The Golden Fleece and guarded it and never slept,
I killed, and so gave you the safety of the light.
And I myself betrayed my father and my home,
And came with you to Pelias' land of Iolcos.
And then, showing more willingness to help than wisdom,
I killed him, Pelias, with a most dreadful death
At his own daughters' hands, and took away your fear.
This is how I behaved to you, you wretched man,
And you forsook me, took another bride to bed
Though you had children; for, if that had not been,
You would have had an excuse for another wedding.
Faith in your word has gone. Indeed I cannot tell
Whether you think the gods whose names you swore by then
Have ceased to rule and that new standards are set up,
Since you must know you have broken your word to me.
O my right hand, and the knees which you often clasped
In supplication, how senselessly I am treated
By this bad man, and how my hopes have missed their mark!
Come, I will share my thoughts as though you were a friend,—
You! Can I think that you would ever treat me well?
But I will do it, and these questions will make you
Appear the baser. Where am I to go? To my father's?
Him I betrayed and his land when I came with you.
To Pelias' wretched daughters? What a fine welcome
They would prepare for me who murdered their father!
For this is my position,—hated by my friends

At home, I have, in kindness to you, made enemies
Of others whom there was no need to have injured.
And how happy among Greek women you have made me
On your side for all this! A distinguished husband
I have,—for breaking promises. When in misery
I am cast out of the land and go into exile,
Quite without friends and all alone with my children,
That will be a fine shame for the new-wedded groom,
For his children to wander as beggars and she who saved him.
O God, you have given to mortals a sure method
Of telling the gold that is pure from the counterfeit;
Why is there no mark engraved upon men's bodies,
By which we could know the true ones from the false ones?

Chorus
It is a strange form of anger, difficult to cure
When two friends turn upon each other in hatred.

Jason
As for me, it seems I must be no bad speaker.
But, like a man who has a good grip of the tiller,
Reef up his sail, and so run away from under
This mouthing tempest, woman, of your bitter tongue.
Since you insist on building up your kindness to me,
My view is that Cypris was alone responsible
Of men and gods for the preserving of my life.
You are clever enough,—but really I need not enter
Into the story of how it was love's unescapable power
Power that compelled you to keep my person safe.
On this I will not go into too much detail.
In so far as you helped me, you did well enough.
But on this question of saving me, I can prove
You have certainly got from me more than you gave.
Firstly, instead of living among barbarians,
You inhabit a Greek land and understand our ways,
How to live by law instead of the sweet will of force.
And all the Greeks considered you a clever woman.
You were honoured for it; while, if you were living at
The ends of the earth, nobody would have heard of you.
For my part, rather than stores of gold in my house
Or power to sing even sweeter songs than Orpheus,
I'd choose the fate that made me a distinguished man.
There is my reply to your story of my labours.
Remember it was you who started the argument.
Next for your attack on my wedding with the princess;
Here I will prove that, first, it was a clever move,
Secondly, a wise one, and, finally, that I made it
In your best interests and the children's. Please keep calm.

When I arrived here from the land of Iolcos,
Involved, as I was, in every kind of difficulty,
What luckier chance could I have come across than this,
An exile to marry the daughter of the king?
It was not,—the point that seems to upset you—that I
Grew tired of your bed and felt the need of a new bride,
Nor with any wish to outdo your number of children.
We have enough already. I am quite content.
But,—this was the main reason—that we might live well,
And not be short of anything. I know that all
A man's friends leave him stone-cold if he becomes poor.
Also that I might bring my children up worthily
Of my position, and, by producing more of them
To be brothers of yours, we would draw the families
Together and all be happy. You need no children.
And it pays me to do good to those I have now
By having others. Do you think this a bad plan?
You wouldn't if the love question hadn't upset you.
But you women have got into such a state of mind
That, if your life at night is good, you think you have
Everything; but, if in that quarter things go wrong,
You will consider your best and truest interests
Most hateful. It would have been better far for men
To have got their children in some other way, and women
Not to have existed. Then life would have been good.

The chorus sings of the dangers of excess—even of too much love.

Chorus

When love is in excess
It brings a man no honour
Nor any worthiness.
But if in moderation Cypris comes,
There is no other power at all so gracious.
O goddess, never on me let loose the unerring
Shaft of your bow in the poison of desire.

Let my heart be wise.
It is the gods' best gift.
On me let mighty Cypris
Inflict no wordy wars or restless anger
To urge my passion to a different love.
But with discernment may she guide women's weddings,
Honouring most what is peaceful in the bed.

O country and home,
Never, never may I be without you,
Living the hopeless life,
Hard to pass through and painful,
Most pitiable of all.
Let death first lay me low and death
Free me from this daylight.
There is no sorrow above
The loss of a native land.

I have seen it myself,
Do not tell of a secondhand story.
Neither city nor friend
Pitied you when you suffered
The worse of sufferings.

O let him die ungraced whose heart
Will not reward his friends,
Who cannot open an honest mind
No friend will he be of mine.

Medea sends her two small sons to Creusa, Jason's proposed bride, with gifts of gold that have been infused with a poison that will bring horrible deaths to Creusa and her father Creon. When the children return, she is torn between her love for them and her resolve to kill them in order to cause their father Jason the greatest possible suffering.

MEDEA

O children, O my children, you have a city,
You have a home, and you can leave me behind you,
And without your mother you may live there for ever.
But I am going in exile to another land
Before I have seen you happy and taken pleasure in you,
Before I have dressed your brides and made your marriage beds,
And held up the torch at the ceremony of wedding.
Oh, what a wretch I am in this my self-willed thought!
What was the purpose, children, for which I reared you?
For all my travail and wearing myself away?
They were sterile, those pains I had in the bearing of you.
O surely once the hopes in you I had, poor me,
Were high ones: you would look after me in old age,
And when I died would deck me well with your own hands;
A thing which all would have done. O but now it is gone,
That lovely thought. For, once I am left without you,
Sad will be the life I'll lead and sorrowful for me.
And you will never see your mother again with
Your dear eyes, gone to another mode of living.
Why, children, do you look upon me with your eyes?
Why do you smile so sweetly that last smile of all?
Oh, oh, what can I do? My spirit has gone from me,
Friends, when I saw that bright look in the children's eyes.
I cannot bear to do it. I renounce my plans
I had before. I'll take my children away from
This land. Why should I hurt their father with the pain
They feel, and suffer twice as much of pain myself?
No, no, I will not do it. I renounce my plans.
Ah, what is wrong with me? Do I want to let go
My enemies unhurt and be laughed at for it?
I must face this thing. Oh, but what a weak woman
Even to admit to my mind these soft arguments.
Children, go into the house. And he whom law forbids
To stand in attendance at my sacrifices,
Let him see to it. I shall not mar my handiwork.
Oh! Oh!
Do not, O my heart, you must not do these things!
Poor heart, let them go, have pity upon the children.
If they live with you in Athens they will cheer you.
No! By Hell's avenging furies it shall not be,—
This shall never be, that I should suffer

my children
To be the prey of my enemies insolence.
Every way is it fixed. The bride will not escape.
No, the diadem is now upon her head, and she,
The royal princess, is dying in the dress, I know it.
But,—for it is the most dreadful of roads for me
To tread, and them I shall send on a more dreadful still—
I wish to speak to the children.

She calls the children to her.

                Come, children, give
Me your hands, give your mother your hands to kiss them.
O the dear hands, and O how dear are these lips to me,
And the generous eyes and the bearing of my children!
I wish you happiness, but not here in this world.
What is here your father took. O how good to hold you!
How delicate the skin, how sweet the breath of children!
Go, go! I am no longer able, no longer
To look upon you. I am overcome by sorrow.

                (Translated by Rex Warner)

Plato
(427-347 B.C.)
The Death of Socrates
from *Phaedo*

The great philosopher Plato was not consistent in his attitude toward the arts. In his Republic, *he argues that art is too far removed from reality to be of any value. In other works he modifies this position somewhat. But in all of his writings he demonstrates his own artistic ability in his beautiful use of language. The following moving account of the death of his teacher Socrates is a good example of his literary skill.*

When he had done speaking, Crito said: And have you any commands for us, Socrates—anything to say about your children, or any matter in which we can serve you?

Nothing particular, Crito, he replied: only, as I have always told you, take care of yourselves; that is a service which you may be ever rendering to me and mine and to all of us, whether you promise to do so or not. But if you have no thought for yourselves, and care not to walk according to the rule which I have prescribed for you, not now for the first time, however much you may profess or promise at the moment, it will be of no avail.

We will do our best, said Crito: And in what way shall we bury you?

In any way that you like; but you must get hold of me, and take care that I do not run away from you. Then he turned to us, and added with a smile:—I cannot make Crito believe that I am the same Socrates who have been talking and conducting the argument; he fancies that I am the other Socrates whom he will soon see, a dead body—and he asks, How shall he bury me? And though I have spoken many words in the endeavour to show that when I have drunk the poison I shall leave you and go to the joys of the blessed,—these words of mine, with which I was comforting you and myself, have had, as I perceive, no effect upon Crito. And therefore I want you to be surety for me to him now, as at the trial he was surety to the judges for me: but let the promise be of another sort; for he was surety for me to the judges that I would remain, and you must be my surety to him that I shall not remain, but go away and depart; and then he will suffer less at my death, and not be grieved when he sees my body being burned or buried. I would not have him sorrow at my hard lot, or say at the burial, Thus we lay out Socrates, or, Thus we follow him to the grave or bury him; for false words are not only evil in themselves, but they infect the soul with evil. Be of good cheer then, my dear Crito, and say that you are burying my body only, and do with that whatever is usual, and what you think best.

When he had spoken these words, he arose and went into a chamber to bathe; Crito followed him and told us to wait. So we remained behind, talking and thinking of the subject of discourse, and also of the greatness of our sorrow; he was like a father of whom we were being bereaved, and we were about to pass the rest of our lives as orphans. When he had taken the bath his children were brought to him—(he had two young sons and an elder one); and the women of his family also came, and he talked to them and gave them a few directions in the presence of Crito; then he dismissed them and returned to us.

Now the hour of sunset was near, for a good deal of time had passed while he was within. When he came out, he sat down with us again after his bath, but not much was said. Soon the jailer, who was the servant of the Eleven, entered and stood by him, saying:—To you, Socrates, whom I know to be the noblest and gentlest and best of all who ever came to this place, I will not impute the angry feelings of other men, who rage and swear at me, when, in obedience to the authorities, I bid them drink the poison—indeed, I am sure that you will not be angry with me; for others, as you are aware, and not I, are to blame. And so fare you well, and try to bear lightly what must needs be—you know my errand. Then bursting into tears he turned away and went out.

Socrates looked at him and said: I return your good wishes, and will do as you bid. Then turning to us, he said, How charming the man is: since I have been in prison he has always been coming to see me, and at times he would talk to me, and was as good to me as could be, and now see how generously he sorrows on my account. We must do as he says, Crito; and therefore let the cup be brought, if the poison is prepared: if not, let the attendant prepare some.

Yet, said Crito, the sun is still upon the hill-tops, and I know that many a one has taken the draught late, and after the announcement has been made to him, he has eaten and drunk, and enjoyed the society of his beloved; do not hurry—there is time enough.

Socrates said: Yes, Crito, and they of whom you speak are right in so acting, for they think that they will be gainers by the delay; but I am right in not following their example, for I do not think that I should gain anything by drinking the poison a little later; I should only be ridiculous in my own eyes for sparing and saving a life which is already forfeit. Please then to do as I say, and not to refuse me.

Crito made a sign to the servant, who was standing by; and he went out, and having been absent for some time, returned with the jailer carrying the cup of poison. Socrates said: You, my good friend, who are experienced in these matters, shall give me directions how I am to proceed. The man answered: You have only to walk about until your legs are heavy, and then to lie down, and the poison will act. At the same time he handed the cup to Socrates, who in the easiest and gentlest manner, without the least fear or change of colour or feature, looking at the man with all his eyes, Echecrates, as his manner was, took the cup and said: What do you say about making a libation out of this cup to any god? May I, or not? The man answered: We only prepare, Socrates, just so much as we deem enough. I understand, he said: but I may and must ask the gods to prosper my journey from this to the other world—even so—and so be it according to my prayer. Then raising the cup to his lips, quite readily and cheerfully he drank off the poison. And hitherto most of us had been able to control our sorrow; but now when we saw him drinking, and saw too that he had finished the draught, we could no longer forbear, and in spite of myself my own tears were flowing fast; so that I covered my face and wept, not for him, but at the thought of my own calamity in having to part from such a friend. Nor was I the first; for Crito, when he found himself unable to restrain his tears, had got up, and I followed; and at that moment, Apollodorus, who had been weeping all the time, broke out in a loud and passionate cry which made cowards of us all. Socrates alone retained his calmness: What is this strange outcry? he said. I sent away the women mainly in order that they might not misbehave in this way, for I have been told that a man should die in peace. Be quiet then, and have patience. When we heard his words we were ashamed, and refrained our tears; and he walked about until, as he said, his legs began to fail, and then he lay on his back, according to the directions, and the man who gave him the poison now and then looked at his feet and legs; and after a while he pressed his foot hard, and asked him if he could feel; and he said, No; and then his leg, and so upwards and upwards, and showed us that he was cold and stiff. And he felt them himself, and said: When the poison reaches the heart, that will be the end. He was beginning to grow cold about the groin, when he uncovered his face, for he had covered himself up, and said—they were his last words—he said:

Crito, I owe a cock to Asclepius; will you remember to pay the debt? The debt shall be paid, said Crito; is there anything else? There was no answer to this question; but in a minute or two a movement was heard, and the attendants uncovered him; his eyes were set, and Crito closed his eyes and mouth.

Such was the end, Echecrates, of our friend; concerning whom I may truly say, that of all the men of his time whom I have known, he was the wisest and justest and best.

(Translated by Benjamin Jowett)

Aristotle
(384-322 B.C.)
The Nature of Tragedy
from *On Tragedy*

Unlike his teacher Plato, Aristotle is not noted for his own literary skill. In fact, most of his extant writings are probably lecture notes—either those he used or those taken by his students. Aristotle was, however, the first writer to develop important ideas about the theory of literature. The part of Aristotle's literary theory that has been preserved is concerned largely with Greek drama, specifically the tragedy. The passage given here concerns his analysis of the important parts of the drama.

Tragedy, then, is an imitation of an action that is serious, complete, and of a certain magnitude; in language embellished with each kind of artistic ornament, the several kinds being found in separate parts of the play; in the form of action, not of narrative; through pity and fear effecting the proper purgation of these emotions. By "language embellished," I mean language into which rhythm, "harmony," and song enter. By "the several kinds in separate parts," I mean, that some parts are rendered through the medium of verse alone, others again with the aid of song.

Now as tragic imitation implies persons acting, it necessarily follows, in the first place, that Spectacular equipment will be a part of Tragedy. Next, Song and Diction, for these are the medium of imitation. By "Diction" I mean the mere metrical arrangement of the words: as for "Song," it is a term whose sense every one understands.

Again, Tragedy is the imitation of an action; and an action implies personal agents, who necessarily possess certain distinctive qualities both of character and thought; for it is by these that we qualify actions themselves, and these—thought and character—are the two natural causes from which actions spring, and on actions again all success or failure depends. Hence, the Plot is the imitation of the action: for by plot I here mean the arrangement of the incidents. By Character I mean that in virtue of which we ascribe certain qualities to the agents. Thought is required wherever a statement is proved, or, it may be, a general truth is enunciated. Every Tragedy, therefore, must have six parts, which parts determine its quality—namely, Plot, Character, Diction, Thought, Spectacle, Song. Two of the parts constitute the medium of imitation, one the manner, and three the objects of imitation. And these complete the list. These elements have been employed, we may say, by the poets to a man; in fact, every play contains Spectacular elements as well as Character, Plot, Diction, Song, and Thought.

But most important of all is the structure of the incidents. For Tragedy is an imitation, not of men, but of an action and of life, and life consists in action, and its end is a mode of action, not a quality. Now character determines men's qualities, but it is by their actions that they are happy or the reverse. Dramatic action, therefore, is not with a view to the representation of character: character comes in as subsidiary to the actions. Hence the incidents and the plot are the end of a tragedy; and the end is the chief thing of all. Again, without action there cannot be a tragedy; there may be without character. The tragedies of most of our modern poets fail in the rendering of character; and of poets in general this is often true. It is the same in painting; and here lies the difference between Zeuxis and Polygnotus. Polygnotus delineates character well: the style of Zeuxis is devoid of ethical quality. Again, if you string together a set of speeches expressive of character, and well finished in point of diction and thought, you will not produce the essential tragic effect nearly so well as with a play which, however deficient in these respects, yet has a plot and artistically constructed incidents. Besides which, the most powerful elements of emotional interest in Tragedy—Peripeteia or Reversal of the Situation, and Recognition scenes—are parts of the plot. A further proof is, that novices in the art attain to finish of diction and precision of portraiture before they can construct the plot. It is the same with almost all the early poets.

The Plot, then, is the first principle, and, as it were, the soul of a tragedy: Character holds the second place. A similar fact is seen in painting. The most beautiful colors, laid on confusedly, will not give as much pleasure as the chalk outline of a portrait. Thus Tragedy is the imitation of an action, and of the agents mainly with a view to the action.

Third in order is Thought,—that is, the faculty of saying what is possible and pertinent in given circumstances. In the case of oratory, this is the function of the political art and of the art of rhetoric: and so indeed the older poets make their characters speak the language of civic life; the poets of our time, the language of the rhetoricians. Character is that which reveals moral purpose, showing what kinds of things a man chooses or avoids. Speeches, therefore, which do not make this manifest, or in which the speaker does not choose or avoid anything whatever, are not expressive of character. Thought, on the other hand, is found where something is proved to be or not to be, or a general maxim is enunciated.

Fourth among the elements enumerated comes Diction; by which I mean, as has been already said, the expression of the meaning in words; and its essence is the same both in verse and prose.

Of the remaining elements Song holds the chief place among the embellishments.

The Spectacle has, indeed, an emotional attraction of its own, but, of all the parts, it is the least artistic, and connected least with the art of poetry. For the power of Tragedy, we may be sure, is felt even apart from representation and actors. Besides, the production of spectacular effects depends more on the art of the stage machinist than on that of the poet.

These principles being established, let us now discuss the proper structure of the Plot, since this is the first and most important thing in Tragedy.

Now, according to our definition, Tragedy is an imitation of an action that is complete, and whole, and of a certain magnitude; for there may be a whole that is wanting in magnitude. A whole is that which has a beginning, a middle, and an end. A beginning is that which does not itself follow anything by causal necessity, but after which something naturally is or comes to be. An end, on the contrary, is that which itself naturally follows some other thing, either by necessity, or as a rule, but has nothing following it. A middle is that which follows something as some other thing follows it. A well constructed plot, therefore, must neither begin nor end at haphazard, but conform to these principles.

Again, a beautiful object, whether it be a living organism or any whole composed of parts, must not only have an orderly arrangement of parts, but must also be of a certain magnitude; for beauty depends on magnitude and order. Hence a very small animal organism cannot be beautiful; for the view of it is confused, the object being seen in an almost imperceptible moment of time. Nor, again, can one of vast size be beautiful; for as the eye cannot take it all in at once, the unity and sense of the whole is lost for the spectator; as for instance if there were one a thousand miles long. As, therefore, in the case of animate bodies and organisms a certain magnitude is necessary, and a magnitude which may be easily embraced in one view; so in the plot, a certain length is necessary, and a length which can be easily embraced by the memory. The limit of length in relation to dramatic competition and sensuous presentment, is no part of artistic theory. For had it been the rule for a hundred tragedies to compete together, the performance would have been regulated by the water-clock—as indeed we are told was formerly done. But the limit as fixed by the nature of the drama itself is this:—the greater the length, the more beautiful will the piece be by reason of its size, provided that the whole be perspicuous. And to define the matter roughly, we may say that the proper magnitude is comprised within such limits, that the sequence of events, according to the law of probability or necessity, will admit of a change from bad fortune to good, or from good fortune to bad.

Unity of plot does not, as some persons think, consist in the unity of the hero. For infinitely various are the incidents in one man's life which cannot be reduced to unity; and so, too, there are many actions of one man out of which we cannot make one action. Hence the error, as it appears, of all poets who have composed a Heracleid, a Theseid or other poems of the kind. They imagine that as Heracles was one man, the story of Heracles must also be a unity. But Homer, as in all else he is of surpassing merit, here too—whether from art or natural genius—seems to have happily discerned the truth. In composing the *Odyssey* he did not include all the adventures of Odysseus—such as his wound on Parnassus, or his feigned madness at the mustering of the host—incidents between which there was no necessary or probable connexion: but he made the *Odyssey*, and likewise the *Iliad*, to centre round an action that in our sense of the word is one. As therefore, in the other imitative arts, the imitation is one when the object imitated is one, so the plot, being an imitation of an action, must imitate one action and that a whole, the structural union of the parts being such that, if any one of them is displaced or removed, the whole will be disjointed and disturbed. For a thing whose presence or absence makes no visible difference, is not an organic part of the whole.

It is, moreover, evident from what has been said, that it is not the function of the poet to relate what has happened, but what may happen,—what is possible according to the law of probability or necessity. The poet and the historian differ not by writing in verse or prose. The work of Herodotus might be put into verse, and it would still be a species of history, with metre no less than without it. The true difference is that one relates what has happened, the other what may happen. Poetry, therefore, is a more philosophical and a higher thing than history: for poetry tends to express the universal, history the particular. By the universal I mean how a person of a certain type will on occasion speak or act, according to the law of probability or necessity; and it is this universality at which poetry aims in the names she attaches to the personages. The particular is—for example—what Alcibiades did or suffered. In Comedy this is already apparent: for here the poet first constructs the plots on the lines of probability, and then inserts characteristic names;—unlike the lampooners who write about particular individuals. But tragedians still keep to real names, the reason being that what is possible is credible: what has not happened we do not at once feel sure to be possible: but what has happened is manifestly possible: otherwise it would not have happened. Still there are even some tragedies in which there are only one or two well known names, the rest being fictitious. In others, none are well known,—as in Agathon's *Antheus*, where incidents and names alike are fictitious, and yet they give none the less pleasure. We must not, therefore, at all costs keep to the received legends, which are the usual subjects of Tragedy. Indeed, it would be absurd to attempt it; for even subjects that are known are known only to a few, and yet give pleasure to all. It clearly follows that the poet or "maker" should be the maker of plots rather than of verses; since he is a poet because he imitates, and what he imitates are actions. And even if he chances to take an historical subject, he is none the less a poet; for there is no reason why some events that have actually happened should not conform to the law of the probable and possible, and in virtue of that quality in them he is their poet or maker.

Of all plots and actions, the epeisodic are the worst. I call a plot "epeisodic" in which the episodes or acts succeed one another without probable or necessary sequence. Bad poets compose such pieces by their own fault, good poets, to please the players; for, as they write show pieces for competition, they stretch the plot beyond its capacity, and are often forced to break the natural continuity.

But again, Tragedy is an imitation not only of a complete action, but of events inspiring fear or pity. Such an effect is best produced when the events come on us by surprise; and the effect is heightened when, at the same time, they follow as cause and effect. The tragic wonder will then be greater than if they happened of themselves or by accident; for even coincidences are most striking when they have an air of design. We may instance the statue of Mitys at Argos, which fell upon his murderer while he was a spectator at a festival, and killed him. Such events seem not to be due to mere chance. Plots, therefore, constructed on these principles are necessarily the best.

Plots are either Simple or Complex, for the actions in real life, of which the plots are an imitation, obviously show a similar distinction. An action which is one and continuous in the sense above defined, I call Simple, when the change of fortune takes place without Reversal of the Situation and without Recognition.

A Complex action is one in which the change is accompanied by such Reversal, or by Recognition, or by both. These last should arise from the internal structure of the plot, so that what follows should be the necessary or probable result of the preceding action. It makes all the difference whether any given event is a case of *propter hoc* or *post hoc*.

Reversal of the Situation is a change by which the action veers round to its opposite, subject always to our rule of probability or necessity. Thus in the *Oedipus*, the messenger comes to cheer Oedipus and free him from his alarms about his mother, but by revealing who he is, he produces the opposite effect. Again in the *Lynceus*, Lynceus is being led away to his death, and Danaus goes with him, meaning to slay him; but the outcome of the preceding incidents is that Danaus is killed and Lynceus saved.

Recognition, as the name indicates, is a change from ignorance to knowledge, producing love or hate between the persons destined by the poet for good or bad fortune. The best form of recognition is coincident with a Reversal of the Situation, as in the *Oedipus*. There are indeed other forms. Even inanimate things of the most trivial kind may in a sense be objects of recognition. Again, we may recognise or discover whether a person has done a thing or not. But the recognition which is most intimately connected with the plot and action is, as we have said, the recognition of persons. This recognition, combined with Reversal, will produce either pity or fear; and actions producing these effects are those which, by our definition, Tragedy represents. Moreover, it is upon such situations that the issues of good or bad fortune will depend. Recognition, then, being between persons, it may happen that one person only is recognised by the other—when the latter is already known—or it may be necessary that the recognition should be on both sides. Thus Iphigenia is revealed to Orestes by the sending of the letter; but another act of recognition is required to make Orestes known to Iphigenia.

Two parts, then, of the plot—Reversal of Situation and Recognition—turn upon surprises. A third part is the Scene of Suffering. The Scene of Suffering is a destructive or painful action, such as death on the stage, bodily agony, wounds and the like.

(The parts of Tragedy which must be treated as elements of the whole have been already mentioned. We now come to the quantitative parts—the separate parts into which Tragedy is divided—namely, Prologue, Episode, Exode, Choric song; this last being divided into Parode and Stasimon. These are common to all plays: peculiar to some are the songs of actors from the stage and the Commos.

The Prologue is that entire part of a tragedy which precedes the Parode of the Chorus. The Episode is that entire part of a tragedy which is between complete choric songs. The Exode is that entire part of a tragedy which has no choric song after it. Of the Choric part the Parode is the first undivided utterance of the Chorus: the Stasimon is a Choric ode without anapests or trochaic tetrameters: the Commos is a joint lamentation of Chorus and actors. The parts of Tragedy which must be treated as elements of the whole have been already mentioned. The quantitative parts—the separate parts into which it is divided—are here enumerated.)

As the sequel to what has already been said, we must proceed to consider what the poet should aim at, and what he should avoid, in constructing his plots; and by what means the specific effect of Tragedy will be produced.

A perfect tragedy should, as we have seen, be arranged not on the simple but on the complex plan. It should, moreover, imitate actions which excite pity or fear, this being the distinctive mark of tragic imitation. It follows plainly, in the first place, that the change of fortune presented must not be the spectacle of a virtuous man brought from prosperity to adversity: for this moves neither pity nor fear; it merely shocks us. Nor, again, that of a bad man passing from adversity to prosperity: for nothing can be more alien to the spirit of Tragedy; it possesses no single tragic quality; it neither satisfies the moral sense nor calls forth pity or fear. Nor, again, should the downfall of the utter villain be exhibited. A plot of this kind would, doubtless, satisfy the moral sense, but it would inspire neither pity nor fear; for pity is aroused by unmerited misfortune, fear by the misfortune of a man like ourselves. Such an event, therefore, will be neither pitiful nor terrible. There remains, then, the character between these two extremes,—that of a man who is not eminently good and just, yet whose misfortune is brought about not by vice or depravity, but by some error or frailty. He must be one who is highly renowned and prosperous,—a personage like Oedipus, Thyestes, or other illustrious men of such families.

A well constructed plot should, therefore, be single in its issue, rather than double as some maintain. The change of fortune should be not from bad to good, but, reversely, from good to bad. It should come about as the result not of vice, but of some great error or frailty, in a character such as we have described, or better rather than worse. The practice of the stage bears out our view. At first the poets recounted any legend that came in their way. Now, the best tragedies are founded on the stories of a few houses,—on the fortunes of Alcmaeon, Oedipus, Meleager, Thyestes, Telephus, and those others who have done or suffered something terrible. A tragedy, then, to be perfect according to the rules of art should be of this construction. Hence they are in error who censure Euripides just because he follows this principle in his plays, many of which end unhappily. It is, as we have said, the right ending. The best proof is that on the stage and in dramatic competition, such plays, if well worked out, are the most tragic in effect; and Euripides, faulty though he may be in the general management of his subject, yet is felt to be the most tragic of the poets.

In the second rank comes the kind of tragedy which some place first. Like the *Odyssey,* it has a double thread of plot, and also an opposite catastrophe for the good and for the bad. It is accounted the best because of the weakness of the spectators; for the poet is guided in what he writes by the wishes of his audience. The pleasure, however, thence derived is not the true tragic pleasure. It is proper rather to Comedy, where those who, in the piece, are the deadliest enemies—like Orestes and Aegisthus—quit the stage as friends at the close, and no one slays or is slain.

Fear and pity may be aroused by spectacular means; but they may also result from the inner structure of the piece, which is the better way, and indicates a superior poet. For the plot ought to be so constructed that, even without the aid of the eye, he who hears the tale told will thrill with horror and melt to pity at what takes place. This is the impression we should receive from hearing the story of the Oedipus. But to produce this effect by the mere spectacle is a less artistic method, and dependent on extraneous aids. Those who employ spectacular means to create a sense not of the terrible but only of the monstrous, are strangers to the purpose of Tragedy; for we must not demand of Tragedy any and every kind of pleasure, but only that which is proper to it. And since the pleasure which the poet should afford is that which comes from pity and fear through imitation, it is evident that this quality must be impressed upon the incidents.

Let us then determine what are the circumstances which strike us as terrible or pitiful.

Actions capable of this effect must happen between persons who are either friends or enemies or indifferent to one another. If an enemy kills an enemy, there is nothing to excite pity either in the act or the intention,—except so far as the suffering in itself is pitiful. So again with indifferent persons. But when the tragic incident occurs between those who are near or dear to one another—if, for example, a brother kills, or intends to kill, a brother, a son his father, a mother her son, a son his mother, or any other deed of the kind is done—these are the situations to be looked for by the poet. He may not indeed destroy the framework of the received legends—the fact, for instance, that Clytemnestra was slain by Orestes and Eriphyle by Alcmaeon—but he ought to show invention of his own, and skilfully handle the traditional material. Let us explain more clearly what is meant by skilful handling.

The action may be done consciously and with knowledge of the persons, in the manner of the older poets. It is thus too that Euripides makes Medea slay her children. Or, again, the deed of horror may be done, but done in ignorance, and the tie of kinship or friendship discovered afterwards. The *Oedipus* of Sophocles is an example. Here, indeed, the incident is outside the drama proper; but cases occur where it falls within the action of the play: one may cite the *Alcmaeon* of Astydamas, or Telegonus in the *Wounded Odysseus.* Again, there is a third case,—to be about to act with knowledge of the persons and then not to act. The fourth case is when some one is about to do an irreparable deed through ignorance, and makes the discovery before it is done. These are the only possible ways. For the deed must either be done or not done,—and that wittingly or unwittingly. But of all these ways, to be about to act knowing the persons, and then not to act, is the worst. It is shocking without being tragic, for no disaster follows. It is, therefore, never, or very rarely, found in poetry. One instance, however, is in the *Antigone,* where Haemon threatens to kill Creon. The next and better way is that the deed shall be perpetrated. Still better, that it should be perpetrated in ignorance, and the discovery made afterwards. There is then nothing to shock us, while the discovery produces a startling effect. The last case is the best, as when in the *Cresphontes* Merope is about to slay her son, but recognising who he is, spares his life. So in the *Iphigenia,* the sister recognises the brother just in time. Again in the *Helle,* the son recognises the mother when on the point of giving her up. This, then, is why a few families only, as has been already observed, furnish the subjects of tragedy. It was not art, but happy chance, that led the poets in search of subjects to impress the tragic quality upon their plots. They are compelled, therefore, to have recourse to those houses whose history contains moving incidents like these.

Enough has now been said concerning the structure of the incidents, and the right kind of plot.

In respect of character there are four things to be aimed at. First, and most important, it must be good. Now any speech or action that manifests moral purpose of any kind will be expressive of character: the character will be good if the purpose is good. This rule is relative to each class. Even a woman may be good, and also a slave; though the woman may be said to be an inferior being, and the slave quite worthless. The second thing to aim at is propriety. There is a type of manly valor; but valor in a woman, or unscrupulous cleverness, is inappropriate. Thirdly, the character must be true to life: for this is a distinct thing from goodness and propriety, as here described. The fourth point is consistency: for though the subject of the imitation, who suggested the type, be inconsistent, still he must be consistently inconsistent. As an example of motiveless degradation of character, we have Menelaus in the *Orestes*: of character indecorous and inappropriate, the lament of Odysseus in the Scylla, and the speech of Melanippe: of inconsistency, the *Iphigenia at Aulis*—for Iphigenia the suppliant in no way resembles her later self.

As in the structure of the plot, so too in the portraiture of character, the poet should always aim either at the necessary or the probable. Thus a person of a given character should speak or act in a given way, by the rule either of necessity or of probability; just as this event should follow that by necessary or probable sequence. It is therefore evident that the unravelling of the plot, no less than the complication, must arise out of the plot itself, it must not be brought about by the *Deus ex Machina*—as in the *Medea,* or in the Return of the Greeks in the *Iliad.* The *Deus ex Machina* should be employed only for events external to the drama,—for antecedent or subsequent events, which lie beyond the range of human knowledge, and which require to be reported or foretold; for to the gods we ascribe the power of seeing all things. Within the action there must be nothing irrational. If the irrational cannot be excluded, it should be outside the scope of the tragedy. Such is the irrational element in the *Oedipus* of Sophocles.

Again, since Tragedy is an imitation of persons who are above the common level, the example of good portrait-painters should be followed. They, while reproducing the distinctive form of the original, make a likeness which is true to life and yet more beautiful. So to the poet, in representing men who are irascible or indolent, or have other defects of character, should preserve the type and yet ennoble it. In this way Achilles is portrayed by Agathon and Homer.

Theocritus
(ca. 270 B.C.)
The Incantation
(Idyl 2)

Though the Hellenistic period—323 to 27 B.C.,—was marked by the growth of urban centers like Alexandria and Pergamum, its finest poet wrote mostly about country life. The pastoral poetry of Theocritus is as natural and lifelike as that of most of his imitators is artificial and stilted. The idyl that follows, the second of the thirty-two that have come down to us under his name, tells how a passionate young country woman, jilted by her lover, tries by magic rites to regain his love. Gilbert Murray says that the poem is "realistic, beautiful, tragic, strangely humorous and utterly unforgettable, and has remained a unique masterpiece in literature."

Where are the bay-leaves, Thestylis, and the charms?
Fetch all; with fiery wool the caldron crown;
Let glamour win me back my false lord's heart!
Twelve days the wretch has not come nigh to me,
Nor made enquiry if I die or live,
Nor clamoured (oh, unkindness!) at my door.
Sure his swift fancy wanders otherwhere,
The slave of Aphrodite and of Love.
I'm off to Timagetus' wrestling-school
At dawn, that I may see him and denounce
His doings; but I'll charm him now with charms.
So shine out fair, O moon! To thee I sing
My soft low song: to thee and Hecate
The dweller in the shades, at whose approach
E'en the dogs quake, as on she moves through blood
And darkness and the barrows of the slain.
All hail, dread Hecate: companion me
Unto the end, and work me witcheries
Potent as Circe or Medea wrought,
Or Perimede of the golden hair!
   Turn, magic wheel, draw homeward him I love.
First we ignite the grain. Nay, pile it on:
Where are thy wits flown, timorous Thestylis?
Shall I be flouted, I, by such as you?
Pile, and still say, "This pile is of his bones."
   Turn, magic wheel, draw homeward him I love.
Delphis wracks me: I burn him in these bays.
As, flame-enkindled, they lift up their voice,
Blaze once, and not a trace is left behind:
So waste his flesh to powder in yon fire!
   Turn, magic wheel, draw homeward him I love.
E'en as I melt, not uninspired, the wax,
May Mindian Delphis melt this hour with love:
And swiftly as this brazen wheel whirls round,
May Aphrodite whirl him to my door.
   Turn, magic wheel, draw homeward him I love.
Next burn the husks. Hell's adamantine floor
And all that else stands firm can Artemis move.
Thestylis, the hounds bay up and down the town:
The goddess stands i' the crossroads: sound the gongs.
   Turn, magic wheel, draw homeward him I love.
Hushed are the voices of the winds and seas;
But O not hushed the voice of my despair.
He burns my being up, who left me here
No wife, no maiden, in my misery.
   Turn, magic wheel, draw homeward him I love.

. . .

He lost his tassel from his robe; which I
Shred thus, and cast it on the raging flames.
Ah, baleful love! why, like the marsh-born leech,
Cling to my flesh, and drain my dark veins dry?
   Turn, magic wheel, draw homeward him I love.
From a crushed eft tomorrow he shall drink
Death! But now, Thestylis, take these herbs and smear
That threshold o'er, whereto at heart I cling
Still, still—albeit he thinks scorn of me—
And spit, and say, " 'Tis Delphis' bones I smear."
   Turn, magic wheel, draw homeward him I love.
Now all alone, I'll weep a love whence sprung,
When born? Who wrought my sorrow? Anaxo came,
Her basket in her hand, to Artemis' grove.
Bound for the festival, troops of forest beasts
Stood round, and in the midst a lioness.
   Bethink thee, mistress Moon, whence came my love.
I saw, I raved, smit (weakling) to my heart.
My beauty withered, and I cared no more
For all the pomp; and how I reached my home
I know not: some strange fever wasted me.
Ten nights and days I lay upon my bed.
And wan became my flesh, as 't had been dyed,
And all my hair streamed off, and there was left
But bones and skin. Whose threshold crossed I not,
Or missed what grandam's hut who dealt in charms?
For no light thing was this, and time sped on.
   Bethink thee, mistress Moon, whence came my love.
At last I spoke the truth to that my maid:
"Seek, if you can, some cure for my sore pain.
Alas, I am all the Mindian's! But begone,
And watch by Timagetus' wrestling school:
There does he linger, there he takes his rest.
Find him alone: nod softly: say, 'she waits';
And bring him." So I spoke: she went her way,
And brought the lustrous-limbed one to my home.
And I, the instant I beheld him step
Lightfooted o'er the threshold of my door,
Became all cold like snow, and from my brow
Broke the damp dewdrops: utterance I had none,
Not e'en such utterance as a babe may make
That babbles to its mother in its dreams;
But all my fair frame stiffened into wax.
   Bethink thee, mistress Moon, whence came my love.
He bent his pitiless eyes on me; looked down,
And sat him on my couch, and sitting, said:
"You have gained on me, Simaetha (e'en as I
Gained once on young Philinus in the race),
Bidding me hither ere I came unasked.
For I had come, by Eros I had come,
This night, with comrades two or maybe more,
The fruitage of the Wine-god in my robe,
And, wound about my brow with ribbons red,
The silver leaves so dear to Heracles.

Bethink thee, mistress Moon, whence came my love.

"Had ye said 'Enter,' well; for 'mid my peers
High is my name for goodliness and speed:
I had kissed that sweet mouth once and gone my way.
But had the door been barred, and I thrust out,
With brand and axe would we have stormed you then.
Now be my thanks recorded, first to Love,
Next to thee, maiden, who did pluck me out,
A half-burned helpless creature, from the flames,
And bade me hither. It is Love that lights
A fire more fierce than his of Lipara;
Scares, mischief-mad, the maiden from her bower,
The bride from her warm couch." He spoke, and I,
A willing listener, sat, my hand in his,
Among the cushions, and his cheek touched mine,
Each hotter than its wont, and we discoursed
In soft low language. Need I speak to thee,
Sweet Moon, of all we said and all we did?
Till yesterday he found no fault with me,
Nor I with him. But lo, today there came
Philista's mother—hers who flutes with me—
With her Melampo's; just when up the sky
Gallop the mares that chariot rose-limbed Dawn:
And certain tales she brought me, with the rest
How Delphis loved, she knew not rightly whom;
But this she knew: that of the rich wine aye
He poured "to Love"; and at the last had fled
To line, she thought, the fair one's hall with flowers.
Such was my visitor's tale, and it was true:
For thrice, no, four times daily would he stroll
Hither, leave here ofttimes his Dorian flask;
Now—'tis a fortnight since I saw his face.
Does he then treasure something sweet elsewhere?
Am I forgot? I'll charm him now with charms.
But let him try me more, and by the Fates
He'll soon be knocking at the gates of hell.
Spells of such power are in this chest of mine,
Learned, lady, from mine host in Palestine.

Lady, farewell: turn oceanward thy steeds;
As I have purposed, so I shall fulfil.
Farewell, thou bright-faced Moon! Ye stars, farewell,
That wait upon the car of noiseless Night.

(Translated by C. S. Calverley)

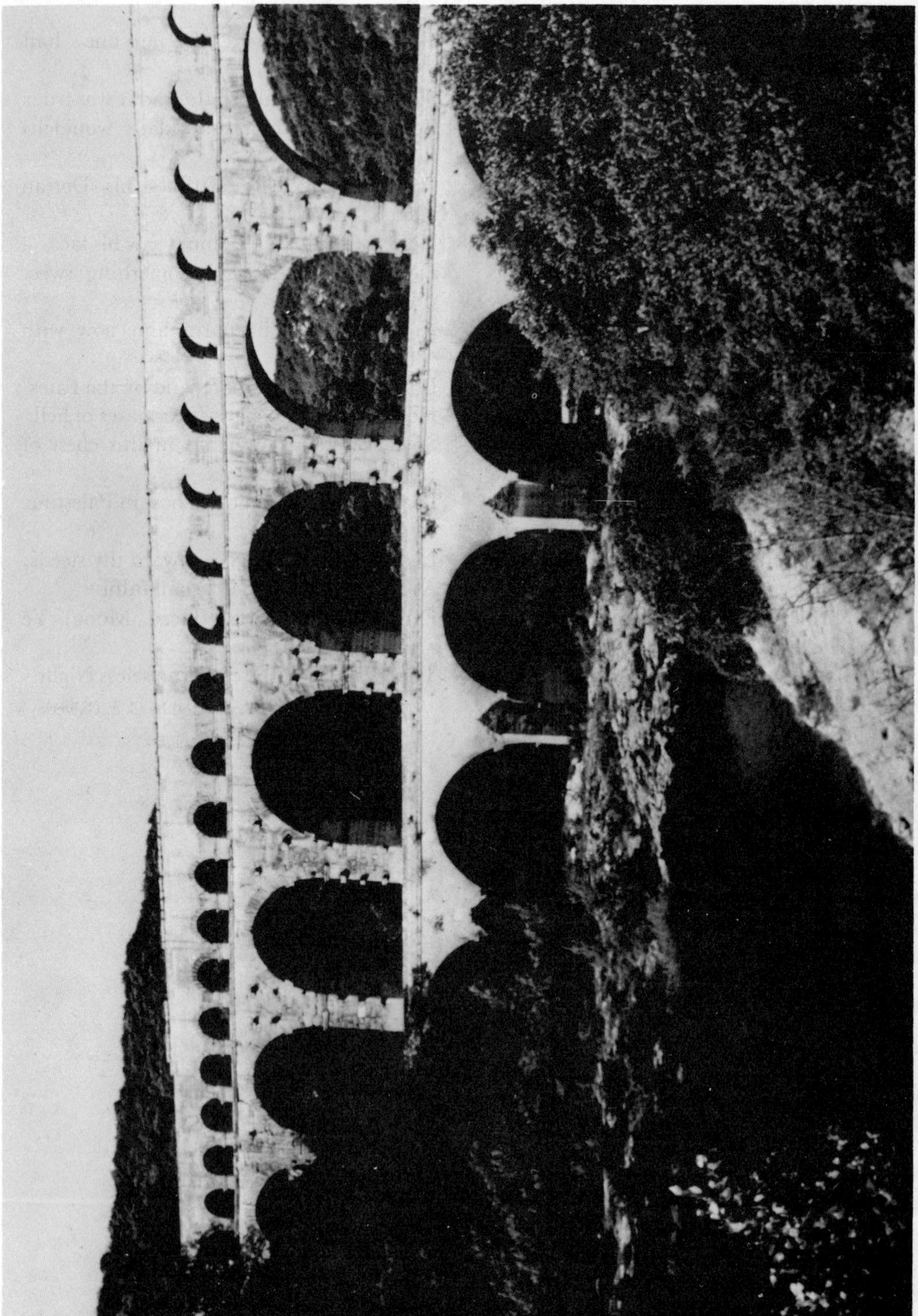

Lucretius
(ca. 99-55 B.C.)
from *Of the Nature of Things*

The greatest philosophical poem of classical antiquity, Of the Nature of Things (De Rerum Natura), *was written by Lucretius, a Roman poet about whom we know next to nothing. (There is a tradition, perpetuated by St. Jerome, that Lucretius drank a love philtre which drove him insane, that he wrote his long poem in his lucid moments, and that he committed suicide.) Lucretius was a devoted follower of Epicurus; he believed that all things, including the human soul, are made up of atoms of varying sizes that move at random throughout a boundless universe and occasionally join together to form objects of varying densities. The atoms of the spirit, when death occurs, disperse themselves, and so man is mortal. Since he ceases to exist, he has no need to fear death or the possibility of future punishment. There are gods; but they are indifferent to men, and they live in a state of untroubled contemplation to which all men should aspire. Like Epicurus, Lucretius believed men should try to gain the greatest amount of pleasure possible, partly by avoiding the pain that follows overindulgence of any kind. Hence the wise man will shun all situations that might prove disturbing. Above all, he will trust his senses, which are the infallible guides to truth.*

This philosophy, with whatever flaws it embodies, Lucretius expressed in clear and beautiful verse, imbued with a love of nature and of common things.

BOOK II
Proem

'Tis sweet, when, down the mighty main, the winds
Roll up its waste of waters, from the land
To watch another's labouring anguish far,
Not that we joyously delight that man
Should thus be smitten, but because 'tis sweet
To mark what evils we ourselves be spared;
'Tis sweet, again, to view the mighty strife
Of armies embattled yonder o'er the plains,
Ourselves no sharers in the peril; but naught
There is more goodly than to hold the high
Serene plateaus, well fortressed by the wise,
Whence thou may'st look below on other men
And see them ev'rywhere wand'ring, all dispersed
In their lone seeking for the road of life;
Rivals in genius, or emulous in rank,
Pressing through days and nights with hugest toil
For summits of power and mastery of the world.
O wretched minds of men! O blinded hearts!
In how great perils, in what darks of life
Are spent the human years, however brief!—
O not to see that nature for herself
Barks after nothing, save that pain keep off,
Disjoined from the body, and that mind enjoy
Delightsome feeling, far from care and fear!
Therefore we see that our corporeal life
Needs little, altogether, and only such
As takes the pain away, and can besides
Strew underneath some number of delights.
More grateful 'tis at times (for nature craves
No artifice nor luxury), if forsooth
There be no golden images of boys
Along the halls, with right hands holding out
The lamps ablaze, the lights for evening feasts,
And if the house doth glitter not with gold
Nor gleam with silver, and to the lyre resound
No fretted and gilded ceilings overhead,

Yet still to lounge with friends in the soft grass
Beside a river of water, underneath
A big tree's boughs, and merrily to refresh
Our frames, with no vast outlay—most of all
If the weather is laughing and the times of the year
Besprinkle the green of the grass around with flowers.
Nor yet the quicker will hot fevers go,
If on a pictured tapestry thou toss,
Or purple robe, than if 'tis thine to lie
Upon the poor man's bedding. Wherefore, since
Treasure, nor rank, nor glory of a reign
Avail us naught for this our body, thus
Reckon them likewise nothing for the mind:
Save then perchance, when thou beholdest forth
Thy legions swarming round the Field of Mars,
Rousing a mimic warfare—either side
Strengthened with large auxiliaries and horse,
Alike equipped with arms, alike inspired;
Or save when also thou beholdest forth
Thy fleets to swarm, deploying down the sea:
For then, by such bright circumstance abashed,
Religion pales and flees the mind; O then
The fears of death leave heart so free of care.
But if we note how all this pomp at last
Is but a drollery and a mocking sport,
And of a truth man's dread, with cares at heels,
Dreads not these sounds of arms, these savage swords,
But among kings and lords of all the world
Mingles undaunted, nor is overawed
By gleam of gold nor by the splendour bright
Of purple robe, canst thou then doubt that this
Is aught, but power of thinking?—when, besides
The whole of life but labours in the dark.
For just as children tremble and fear all
In the viewless dark, so even we at times
Dread in the light so many things that be
No whit more fearsome than what children feign,
Shuddering, will be upon them in the dark.
This terror then, this darkness of the mind,
Not sunrise with its flaring spokes of light,
Nor glittering arrows of morning can disperse,
But only nature's aspect and her law.

Atomic Motions

Now come: I will untangle for thy steps
Now by what motions the begetting bodies
Of the world-stuff beget the varied world,
And then forever resolve it when begot,
And by what force they are constrained to this,
And what the speed appointed unto them
Wherewith to travel down the vast inane:
Do thou remember to yield thee to my words.
For truly matter coheres not, crowds not tight,
Since we behold each thing to wane away,
And we observe how all flows on and off,
As 'twere, with age-old time, and from our eyes
How eld withdraws each object at the end,
Albeit the sum is seen to bide the same,
Unharmed, because these motes that leave each thing
Diminish what they part from, but endow
With increase those to which in turn they come,
Constraining these to wither in old age,
And those to flower at the prime (and yet
Biding not long among them).

Thus the sum
Forever is replenished, and we live
As mortals by eternal give and take.
The nations wax, the nations wane away;
In a brief space the generations pass,
And like to runners hand the lamp of life
One unto other.
          But if thou believe
That the primordial germs of things can stop,
And in their stopping give new motions birth,
Afar thou wanderest from the road of truth.
For since they wander through the void inane,
All the primordial germs of things must needs
Be borne along, either by weight their own,
Or haply by another's blow without.
For, when, in their incessancy so oft
They meet and clash, it comes to pass amain
They leap asunder, face to face: not strange—
Being most hard, and solid in their weights,
And naught opposing motion, from behind.
And that more clearly thou perceive how all
These mites of matter are darted round about,
Recall to mind how nowhere in the sum
Of All exists a bottom,—nowhere is
A realm of rest for primal bodies; since
(As amply shown and proved by reason sure)
Space has no bound nor measure, and extends
Unmetered forth in all directions round.
Since this stands certain, thus 'tis out of doubt
No rest is rendered to the primal bodies
Along the unfathomable inane; but rather,
Inveterately plied by motions mixed,
Some, at their jamming, bound aback and leave
Huge gaps between, and some from off the blow
Are hurried about with spaces small between.
And all which, brought together with slight gaps,
In more condensed union bound aback,
Linked by their own all inter-tangled shapes,—
These forms the irrefragable roots of rocks
And the brute bulks of iron, and what else
Is of their kind. . . .
The rest leap far asunder, far recoil,
Leaving huge gaps between: and these supply
For us thin air and splendour-lights of the sun.
And many besides wander the mighty void—
Cast back from unions of existing things,
Nowhere accepted in the universe,
And nowise linked in motions to the rest.
And of this fact (as I record it here)
An image, a type goes on before our eyes
Present each moment; for behold whenever
The sun's light and the rays, let in, pour down
Across dark halls of houses: thou wilt see
The many mites in many a manner mixed
Amid a void in the very light of the rays,
And battling on, as in eternal strife,
And in battalions contending without halt,
In meetings, partings, harried up and down.
From this thou mayest conjecture of what sort
The ceaseless tossing of primordial seeds
Amid the mightier void—at least so far
As small affair can for a vaster serve,
And by example put thee on the spoor
Of knowledge. For this reason too 'tis fit
Thou turn thy mind the more unto these bodies

Which here are witnessed tumbling in the light:
Namely, because such tumblings are a sign
That motions also of the primal stuff
Secret and viewless lurk beneath, behind.
For thou wilt mark here many a speck, impelled
By viewless blows, to change its little course,
And beaten backwards to return again,
Hither and thither in all directions round.
Lo, all their shifting movement is of old,
From the primeval atoms; for the same
Primordial seeds of things first move of self,
And then those bodies built of unions small
And nearest, as it were, unto the powers
Of the primeval atoms, are stirred up
By impluse of those atoms' unseen blows,
And these thereafter goad the next in size;
Thus motion ascends from the primevals on,
And stage by stage emerges to our sense,
Until those objects also move which we
Can mark in sunbeams, though it not appears
What blows do urge them.
    Herein wonder not
How 'tis that, while the seeds of things are all
Moving forever, the sum yet seems to stand
Supremely still, except in cases where
A thing shows motion of its frame as whole.
For far beneath the ken of senses lies
The nature of those ultimates of the world;
And so, since those themselves thou canst not see,
Their motion also must they veil from men—
For mark, indeed, how things we *can see*, oft
Yet hide their motions, when afar from us
Along the distant landscape. Often thus,
Upon a hillside will the woolly flocks
Be cropping their goodly food and creeping about
Whither the summons of the grass, begemmed
With the fresh dew, is calling, and the lambs
Well filled, are frisking, locking horns in sport:
Yet all for us seem blurred and blent afar—
A glint of white at rest on a green hill.
Again, when mighty legions, marching round,
Fill all the quarters of the plains below,
Rousing a mimic warfare, there the sheen
Shoots up the sky, and all the fields about
Glitter with brass, and from beneath, a sound
Goes forth from feet of stalwart soldiery,
And mountain walls, smote by the shouting, send
The voices onward to the stars of heaven,
And hither and thither darts the cavalry,
And of a sudden down the midmost fields
Charges with onset stout enough to rock
The solid earth: and yet some post there is
Up the high mountains, viewed from which they seem
To stand—a gleam at rest along the plains.

 Now what the speed to matter's atoms given
Thou mayest in few, my Memmius, learn from this:
When first the dawn is sprinkling with new light
The lands, and all the breed of birds abroad
Flit round the trackless forests, with liquid notes
Filling the regions along the mellow air,
We see 'tis forthwith manifest to man
How suddenly the risen sun is wont
At such an hour to overspread and clothe
The whole with its own splendour; but the sun's

Warm exhalations and this serene light
Travel not down an empty void; and thus
They are compelled more slowly to advance,
Whilst, as it were, they cleave the waves of air;
Nor one by one travel these particles
Of warm exhalations, but are all
Entangled and enmassed, whereby at once
Each is restrained by each, and from without
Checked, till compelled more slowly to advance.
But the primordial atoms with their old
Simple solidity, when forth they travel
Along the empty void, all undelayed
By aught outside them there, and they, each one
Being one unit from nature of its parts,
Are borne to that one place on which they strive
Still to lay hold, must then, beyond a doubt,
Outstrip in speed, and be more swiftly borne
Than light of sun, and over regions rush,
Of space much vaster, in the self-same time
The sun's effulgence widens round the sky.

(Translated by William Ellery Leonard)

Virgil
(70-19 B.C.)
from *Aeneid*

Virgil's Aeneid *is one of the greatest of epic poems and certainly one of the most important and influential books ever composed in Latin. Modeling the first half of his epic on* The Odyssey *and the second half on* The Iliad, *Virgil recounts the adventures of Aeneas, the Trojan hero who was the legendary founder of what was to become the Roman nation.*

The story begins in medias res (in the middle of things). Aeneas and his followers, after exciting adventures and severe hardships, have come to the court of the widowed queen Dido in her newly founded city of Carthage. Here Aeneas, son of the Trojan Anchises and the goddess Venus, tells the story of his experiences—of the fall of Troy; of the loss of his wife; of leading his followers toward their destined new home; of their adventures, many of them like those of Odysseus; of the death in Sicily of his father Anchises; and of the storm that has brought them to Dido's harbor.

Dido has vowed never to remarry, but as she listens to Aeneas' story, she finds herself falling desperately in love with him. What follows, one of the earliest and most celebrated of tragic romances, is related in Book IV of the Aeneid. *However one may feel about Aeneas, Virgil has made of Dido a sympathetic and truly tragic figure. Her story is the basis for Purcell's operatic masterpiece* Dido and Aeneas.

H. H. Ballard's translation, from which the following selection is taken, is written in an English approximation of the dactylic hexameter of Greek and Latin epic.

Book IV

Ah, but the queen, long since sore hurt by the arrows of Cupid,
Feeds her love with her life, and is secretly wasted by passion.
Constantly runs in her mind the man's great worth, and the noble
Honor that crowns his line; his words and his looks are still clinging
Fixed in her heart, and love disquiets the peace of her slumber.
So, when Aurora next lighted the earth with the torch of Apollo,
When she had swept from the sky cool night with its mist-laden shadows,
Thus, all distracted, she cried to the answering heart of her sister,

"Anna, dear sister, what dreams are affrighting me, sad and bewildered!
What strange guest is this who hath entered our home! How distinguished
Both in his face and mien! And his heart, how brave, how heroic!
I, for one, and with reason, believe him descended from Heaven.
Fear betrays low-born souls; but, alas, by what cruel misfortune
He hath been ever pursued! What wearisome wars he recounted!
Dwelt there not in my heart a fixed and immovable purpose
Never again to consent to be linked to another in wedlock,
Since my first love failed, since Death deceived and bereft me,
Were I not utterly weaned from the torch and the chamber of marriage,
Unto this one reproach I might, perhaps, have surrendered.
For, I will own, dear Anna, that since the sad fate of Sichaeus,
Since by my brother's crime our home was defiled and dishonored,
This man alone hath stirred my heart, and mastered my spirit.
Yielding, I feel once more the glow of long slumbering passion.
But I had rather the earth should yawn to its depths underneath me,
Rather the Father omnipotent strike me down with his thunder
Where in profoundest night pale shades of Erebus wander,
Rather, my honor, than violate thee, or break thy requirements.
He who wedded me first took with him my heart when he left me;
Still let him keep his own; in his tomb let him guard it forever."
Speaking these words, with a torrent of tears she deluged her bosom.
Anna replies, "O thou, who art dearer than life to thy sister,
Wilt thou in loneliness pine, till the days of thy youth are departed,
Knowing no children sweet, and enjoying no blessings of Venus?
Thinkest thou ashes will care; or the shades of the buried be troubled?
Grant that no lover before hath won thy heart from its grieving,
Either in Libya now, or aforetime in Tyre; bid Iarbas
Go, if thou wilt, with scorn, and the rest of the African princes,
Mighty in war; yet, why resist a love that delights thee?
Hath it not crossed thy mind whose lands these are thou hast settled?
Here are Gaetulian towns, a race unconquered in battle,—
There wild riding Numidians press, and impassable quicksands.
Here is a region made desert by drought, and ravaged by roaming
Barcans; and why do I speak of Tyre and its ominous war cloud,
Or of our brother's threats?
Guided by Heaven, I believe, and under the favor of Juno,
Hither these Ilian keels have found their way in the tempest.
What a proud city, my sister, thou yet shalt behold! What a nation
Spring from a match like this! With the arms of the Trojans to help us,
By what illustrious deeds shall we heighten the glory of Carthage!
Seek but the favor of Heaven, and when thou hast gained absolution,
Then be as kind as thou wilt; find reasons to keep him delaying
Long as the seas are rough, while stormy Orion is raging;
Urge his shattered ships, and plead the implacable heavens."
Thus by her words she fanned the flame that passion had kindled,
Thus freed a wavering heart from the

bondage of fear and of honor.
First they visit the temples, and pass from altar to altar,
Paying their vows; and sheep, selected according to custom,
Offer to law-giving Ceres, to Phoebus, and father Lyaeus,
But, before all, unto Juno, the guardian goddess of marriage.
Holding the cup in her own right hand, most beautiful Dido
Empties it fairly between the horns of a snow-white heifer;
Or, invoking the gods, draws nigh to the rich laden altars,
Hourly renewing her gifts, and still, as each sheep is laid open,
Watches with lips apart, and questions the quivering vitals.
Ah! unseeing seers! What balm can your vows and your temples
Bring to a wounded heart? For still the soft flame without ceasing
Feeds on her life; and the hidden wound still lives in her bosom.
Dido, on fire with love, goes wandering on through the city,
Frantic and sore distressed, like a deer that a shepherd pursuing,
Drawing his bow at a venture, hath pierced afar off and unwary,
Deep in the Cretan groves, and, unwitting, abandons his arrow;
But, as the wounded deer goes roaming the forests of Dicte,
Still in her side as she flies, the fatal arrow is clinging.
Now she guides Aeneas along through the midst of the city,
Shows him the wealth of Tyre, and her capital nearly completed;
Opens her lips to speak, and stops with the sentence unfinished.
Then, as the day declines, she invites him again to a banquet,
Begs, in her frenzy, to hear once more the Trojan disasters,
Hangs for the second time on his lips as he tells her the story.
Then, when her guests are gone, and the moon in turn disappearing
Puts out her light, and the stars as they set are inviting to slumber,
Lone in her empty hall she is sad, and the couch he has quitted,
Presses, and, absent, sees and listens to him who is absent;
Or to her bosom she folds Ascanius, charmed by his father's
Likeness, if thus, perhaps, she may cheat her unspeakable longing.
Towers forgot to rise; armed youth no longer are marshalled
On the parade; all work on harbor and walls is suspended;
Buildings abruptly stop; the threatening crest of the rampart
Stands unfinished and bare, and the towering derricks are idle.
Soon as the consort beloved of Jupiter sees her o'er-mastered
Thus by the fever of love, and modesty yielding to passion,
Quickly with words like these Queen Juno turns upon Venus:—
"Truly, with honor unheard of, and glorious trophies thou comest,
Thou and this boy of thine! Thy name shall be great and immortal!
If by the cunning of two of the gods one woman be vanquished,
Yet I am not so blind, for I know that thou fearest our bulwarks,
Watching the rising homes of Carthage with secret misgiving.
Where shall we make an end? What profits a quarrel so bitter?
Shall we not rather agree on perpetual peace, and a union,
Sanctioned by both? Thou has gained what thy heart hath been set on securing;

Dido is burning with love; her heart is surging with passion;
Let us with equal authority govern a nation united;
Dido shall yield her hand to the hand of a Phrygian husband,
She shall entrust to thee her dowry of Tyrian subjects."
Then, (for she clearly perceived how craftily Juno had spoken,
Hoping that Italy's power might be turned to the African seacoast,)
Thus did Venus reply: "Is there any so made as to question
Terms like these, or prefer to engage in a quarrel with Juno?
If we could only be certain that fortune would favor the project.
But I have come to distrust the fates; whether Jupiter wishes
These who have come from Troy to unite with the people of Carthage,
Whether he favors this blending of blood, and these bonds of alliance;
Thou art his wife; 't is thy right to coax him to show thee his purpose.
Lead, I will follow." Then thus quick answered imperial Juno:
"Mine shall that duty be. And now, I will briefly advise thee
How what remains to be done can be done most successfully: listen!
Into the forest together Aeneas and heart-stricken Dido
Plan to go hunting to-morrow as soon as the torch of Apollo
Flashes above the sea, unveiling the earth with its glory.
Over them then, the blackness of clouds, commingled with hailstones,
I will outpour from the sky, and shake the whole welkin with thunder
While their horsemen are spreading their toils and enclosing the jungles;
Then shall their comrades be scattered and covered by midnight darkness;
Dido and Ilium's lord shall reach the same cavern, together;
I will be there, and if thou wilt only vouchsafe us thy blessing,
I will proclaim the bans and join them by marriage forever;
This their wedding shall be." And Venus, by no means reluctant,
Nodded assent to the plan and laughed as the plot unfolded.
Meanwhile Aurora, arising, has left the waves of the ocean.
Chivalrous youth of Tyre ride out of the gates with the sunrise,
Laden with nets and toils, and hunting-spears bladed with iron.
Libya's knights rush forth with kennels of keen-scented boar-hounds.
Still, as the queen in her chamber delays, the princes of Carthage
Wait at her gates; and, proud in his trappings of gold and of purple,
Stands her own hunter, impatiently champing his foam-covered snaffle.
Lo, she appears at last, encompassed by thronging attendants;
Woven with colors the border that fringes her Tyrian mantle;
Quiver of gold she bears, with gold she hath fastened her tresses;
Golden the girdle below, that binds her vesture of purple.
Also advancing come Trojan retainers, and joyful Iulus,
While Aeneas, himself, surpassing all others in beauty,
Graces the sport with his presence, and mingles his train of attendants,
Like to Apollo, when, Lycian winter and hurrying Xanthus
Leaving behind, he visits the home of his mother in Delos.
There he renews the dance, and around bacchanalian altars,
Cretans chant, and Dryopians dance with tattooed Agathyrsi;

But on the hilltops of Cynthus he walks, intertwining his wind-tossed
Hair with a light pressing chaplet of gold and leaves of the laurel;
Arrows clang on his back. With no less grace doth Aeneas
Move than he; while beauty as godlike shines in his features.
 Soon as the mountains were reached, and the trackless haunts of the jungle,
Wild goats leap from the ledges, and scamper with pattering hoof-beats
Over the hilltops, and columns of deer, in the opposite quarter,
Thunder their way o'er the shelterless fields, until all the stampeding
Dust-covered ranks unite in flight, and abandon the mountains.
But, in the midst of the plain, Ascanius, boy-like, rejoices,
Proud of his horse; and, swiftly outrunning one after another,
Prays that instead of these spiritless herds a boar may be granted,
Or that his vows may bring from the mountains a tawny-skinned lion.
Meanwhile, the heavens are filled with an ominous rumble of thunder,
Followed at once by a storm of rain commingled with hailstones.
Hither and thither the Tyrian train and the Trojan retainers,
E'en the Dardanian grandson of Venus, have sought in their terror
Huts dispersed through the fields; wild torrents rush from the mountains.
Dido, the queen, and the Lord of Troy have reached the same cavern.
Then, first of all, Mother Earth and Juno, the goddess of wedlock,
Giving the signal, the lightnings blaze for torches of marriage,
Flames the conspiring sky, and nymphs loudly wail on the hilltop.
That day first foretokened her death and foreshadowed her anguish,
For, no longer disturbed by visions of sin or of scandal,
Dido, contented no longer with loving her lover in secret,
Cloaks her disgrace with a name, and calls Aeneas her husband.
Instantly Rumor goes flying through all the great Libyan cities,
Rumor, a curse than whom no other is swifter of motion.
Ever on swiftness she thrives, and gains new vigor by speeding.
Cringing at first with fear, she lifts herself quick to the heavens,
Treading still on the earth, but veiling her face in the storm-cloud.
Earth brought her forth, it is said, impelled by her rage against heaven.
She was the latest born of the terrible sisters of Titan.
Swift are her feet, and swifter the flight of her hurrying pinions;
Monster terrific and huge, who, under each separate feather,
Carries a watchful eye; by each eye, O marvellous story!
Babble a tongue and a mouth, and an ear pricks forward to listen.
Rustling, she flies by night, between earth and sky in the darkness,
Never closing her eyes in the sweet refreshment of slumber;
Watching by day like a spy, she perches aloft on the housetops,
Or upon lofty towers, and causes great cities to tremble;
Tale-bearer, loving the truth no better than slander and libel.
Such was the one who was filling the nation with manifold rumors,
Gloating, and equally glad whether telling a truth or a falsehood.
How that Aeneas had come, a descendant of ancestors Trojan,
How that to him fair Dido had deigned to surrender her honor,

How that in luxury now they were idling away the long winter,
Caring no more for their kingdoms, enslaved by an infamous passion.
Such were the stories the hideous goddess was scattering broadcast.

But it is Aeneas' heaven-ordained destiny to found a new Troy elsewhere, and Jove sends the messenger god Mercury to remind him of his duty.

Mercury straight attacks: "Foundations of towering Carthage,
Here for thy love thou are laying, and building a beautiful city!
Quite forgetful, alas, of thine own dominion and duty!
Now hath the king of the gods, who revolveth the sky at his pleasure,
Hastened me down unto thee from the shining Heights of Olympus,
Sent by himself, on the wings of the wind, I am come with these mandates;
What dost thou plan? With what hope dost thou loiter in Libya's borders?
Yet, if no vision of glorious victory kindle thy spirit,
Though, for thine own renown, thou covet not labor and hardship,
Think on Ascanius, growing, consider the hopes of Iulus;
He is thine heir; unto him falls Italy's throne as a birthright,
Aye, and the land of Rome." Then Mercury, thus having spoken,
Waiting for no reply, withdrew from the vision of mortals,
And afar off disappeared from their eyes in the shadowy heavens.
But, by the vision astounded, Aeneas was dumb with amazement;
Bristled his hair with fright, and his tongue became speechless with terror;
Burning to make his escape, and the land of delight to abandon,
Stunned by so great a rebuke, and Heaven's imperial mandate.
But, alas! what can he do? What speech can he risk for appeasing
Now the infuriate queen; what words adopt for his prelude?
Swiftly his wavering thoughts he despatches now hither, now thither,
Hurries them back and forth, and turns them to every quarter.
This, to his hesitant mind, appears the most hopeful solution:
Mnestheus he calls, and Sergestus, and also intrepid Serestus;
Quietly they are to order the fleet, get the men to the seashore,
See to the arms, and invent some excuse for their sudden manoeuvres.
Meanwhile, he himself, while as yet most excellent Dido
Has no suspicion, nor fears that affection so strong can be broken,
He will discover a way, the most delicate moment for speaking,
And the most feasible mode of arranging the matter. His orders
Instantly all obey, and rejoicingly follow his bidding.

Nevertheless the queen (who ever outwitted a lover?)
Fathomed their wiles, and was first to divine their approaching departure.
Fearful while all was safe. To her frenzy the same cruel Rumor
Whispered of ships equipped, and a course already determined.
Breaks her distracted heart, and wandering over the city
Madly she raves like Thyas, inspired by the frantic procession,
When the triennial orgies arouse her, and Bacchus is calling,
When she is summoned at night by the clamorous voice of Cithaeron.
Finally, breaking forth, she wildly reproaches Aeneas:—
"What perfidious man! has thou hoped

that a crime so atrocious
Thou couldst dissemble? and stealthily steal away from our borders?
Doth not our love constrain, nor the troth thou hast plighted so lately?
Nay, nor Dido doomed to a cruel death if thou leave her?
What! art thou building a fleet in the very heart of the winter?
And dost thou hasten to go on the deep while the north winds are raging?
Cruel! But what! were thy quest not an alien land and an unknown
Place of abode, nay, grant that thine ancient Troy were still standing,
Wouldst thou for Troy set sail across a tempestuous ocean?
Me dost thou flee? By these tears, by thine own right hand I implore thee,
(Since I myself have reserved to myself naught else in my sorrow,)
By our marriage bond, by the wedded life we have entered,
If I have ever well merited aught of thy love, or have ever
Found any grace in thy sight, oh, pity a house that is falling.
If there be still any place for my prayers, abandon thy purpose!
'T is for thy sake the Numidian kings and Libyan nations
Hate me, and Tyrians threat; for thee, and thee only, my honor
And the good name I bore, my only credentials to heaven,
These are no more! Unto whom dost thou leave me, while dying, my guest-friend?
Since this name alone is left to me now for my husband!
What shall I live for? for brother Pygmalion to ruin my city?
Or for Iarbas, the Moor, to carry me off as his captive?
Ah, if before thy flight, some child might have called me his mother,
One who should bear thy name; if I had any little Aeneas
Playing about my hall, who might only re-image thy features;
I should not seem to myself so wholly deceived or deserted!"
  Thus had she spoken, but he, at the bidding of Jove, remained steadfast,
Eyes unmoved, and controlled the love in his heart with a struggle.
Few were his words at last: "O queen, that thou richly deservest
All and more than all thou art able to put into language,
I will never deny; I will gladly remember you, Dido,
While I remember myself, while my body is ruled by my spirit.
There is but little to say. Think not that I hoped to elude thee,
Fleeing by stealth; not so; nor yet have I ever put forward
Claim to a husband's right, or made any compact of marriage.
Nay, if the Fates had allowed me to order my life as I wanted,
And to arrange a career in accord with mine own inclination,
I should have honored first the Trojan town and the cherished
Ashes of those I loved, and Priam's tall towers would be standing,
And I had raised with my hands a Troy new-built for the vanquished.
But, to great Italy, now, Grynaean Apollo hath called me;
Italy is the goal ordained by the Delphic responses;
There is my love and my home. If the castles of Carthage detain thee,
Thee, a Phoenician by birth, if thou lovest thy Libyan city,
Prithee, if Teurcrians settle Ausonian land, what objection
Hast thou to that? We, too, have a right to seek foreign dominions.
Often as Night enfolds the Earth in her

dews and her shadows,
Oft as the glittering stars arise, my father, Anchises,
Admonishes me in dreams, and his troubled image affrights me.
Me Ascanius warns, and the wrong I am doing my darling,
Whom I defraud of Hesperia's throne, and his destined dominions.
Nay, 't is but now that the herald of Heaven, at Jupiter's bidding,
Witness ye deities twain!—on the wings of the wind hath delivered
Heaven's command to me; I saw him myself in broad daylight
Passing within the walls; with these ears did I drink in his message.
Harrow no longer thy heart and mine by useless repining.
Not of my choice is Italy's quest."

While he is speaking thus, her gaze has long been averted,
Wandering hither and yon; but now she looks him all over,
Lifting her silent eyes, and thus indignantly answer:—
"No goddess-mother was thine, nor from Dardanus art thou descended,
Traitor! but, bristling with crags, it was Caucasus gave thee thy being,
Yea, and Hyrcanian tigers encouraged thy life with their udders.
For, what need to dissemble? What worse can I fear in the future?
Had he a groan for my tears? Did his eyes once soften with pity?
Was he constrained to weep? Did my love arouse his compassion?
What is there left to choose? Now, neither most powerful Juno
Nor the Saturnian Father looks on with aspect impartial.
Nowhere is faith secure. I welcomed thee shipwrecked and needy,
Nay, in my madness I gave thee a home and a share in my kingdom,
Rescued the fleet thou hadst lost, and from death I redeemed thy companions;
Oh, I am urged by the furies of hate! Now augur Apollo,
Now the Lycian omens, now even the herald of Heaven,
Sent by Jove himself, comes flying with terrible mandates!
This, I suppose, is the work of the gods; this care is disturbing
Heaven's tranquillity! Go! I neither detain nor dispute thee!
Italy chase with the winds; seek over the billows thy kingdom!
But, as for me, I hope, if the good gods have any power,
Thou mayest drink thy reward 'mid the rocks, till thou callest on Dido
Oft, and by name; and, from far, with terrible flames I will follow;
Ay, and when icy death shall have sundered the flesh from my spirit,
Die where thou wilt, my shade will be with thee. Thy crime shall be punished;
Wretch, I shall hear, and this tidings will reach me in nethermost Hades."
Speaking these words, she awaited no answer, but rushed from the courtyard,
Fainting, avoiding his eyes, and fleeing away from his presence;
Leaving him much that he feared to say, and much that already
Waited to spring from his lips. Her maidens sustained her, and bore her
Yielding form to a couch in her bridal chamber of marble.

Yet god-fearing Aeneas, for all that he longed to console her,
Longed to assuage her grief, and, speaking, to comfort her anguish,
Groaning aloud, and shaken in mind, by the pow'r of his passion,
None the less follows the word of the god, and returns to his galley.
Then how the Trojans toil, and down from all parts of the seacoast

Drag their lofty ships, and float the oiled keels on the billows.
Leafy the oars they bear, and the oak rough hewn in the forest,
Cut in their zeal for flight.
See! they are hurrying forth with a rush from each gate of the city,
Just like an army of ants, that, prudently mindful of winter,
Steal a great pile of grain and lay it away in their garner.
Moves a black line in the field, as they carry their spoil through the herbage,
Over the foot-worn path; part struggling hard with their shoulders
Pushing huge kernels along; part keeping the column in order,
Punishing all delay; the whole pathway is seething with labor.
What are thy feelings now, at the sight of such diligence, Dido!
How didst thou groan when, looking abroad from the top of thy castle,
Thou didst behold thy shores alive far and wide, and the ocean,
Far as thine eyes can reach, confused with so mighty an uproar?
Pitiless Love, unto what dost thou force not the spirit of mortals!
Driven again to tears, she must try him once more by entreaty;
And once more, as a suppliant, humble her pride to her passion,
Lest she should needlessly die by leaving some way unattempted.
  "Anna, thou seest them hasten all over the shore, as they gather
Rushing from every side, and the sails now call to the breezes.
See how the sailors rejoicing have covered the decks with their garlands!
If I have lived through the dread of this terrible moment of anguish,
I shall also, my sister, have strength to endure it: yet, Anna,
Grant me one boon in my grief; for only on thee hath this traitor
Looked with respect, and to thee hath confided his innermost feelings;
Thou alone knowest the time and the winning way to approach him.
Go, dear sister, and humbly entreat our imperious guest-friend.
I did not swear with the Grecians at Aulis to slaughter the Trojans;
Nor did I send out a fleet against his Pergamene city;
I have not troubled the ashes or shades of his father Anchises.
Why should his obdurate ears deny themselves to my pleading?
Wherefore this haste? Let him grant his poor queen this final concession,
Let him but wait for a prosperous flight, and for favoring breezes.
I am not asking him now to renew the old ties he hath broken,
Nor to abandon his beautiful Rome, and relinquish his kingdom;
Time, only time, do I seek, a respite and rest from my madness;
Time for my sorrow to teach me how they who are vanquished should suffer.
This do I ask as my final request: O pity thy sister!
When thou shalt grant this boon, at my death I will doubly repay thee."
  So she kept pleading, and such are the wailings her heart-broken sister
Carries and carries again; but no lamentations can move him;
There are no voices now to which he indulgently listens;
Fate stands guard, and God defends the calm ears of the hero.
And, as when Alpine winds from the north are struggling together,
Blowing now this way, now that, to tear from the earth an old oak-tree,
Strong with its centuried fibres; its foliaged boughs, 'mid the roaring,
Litter the earth from on high, as the trunk

is rocked by the tempest,
Yet the tree clings to the cliff, and as high as its crown is uplifted
Into the sky, so deep are its roots toward Tartarus reaching.
So, now this way, now that way, the hero is beaten by ceaseless
Cries, and his mighty heart is deeply stirred with compassion,
Yet is his mind unmoved, and vain are the torrents of weeping.
  Verily then, dismayed by her fate, unfortunate Dido
Prays for death; she is tired of the sight of the arches of heaven.
Further to fix her resolve the sunlight of life to relinquish,
While she was laying her gifts on the altars glowing with incense,
Shocking to tell, she beheld the milk turn black in the chalice;
While to polluted blood was changed the wine she had sprinkled.
This was a sight that she told to none, not even her sister.
Added to this, there stood in the palace a chapel of marble,
Raised to her husband of old, which she honored with wondrous devotion,
Solemnly wreathed with garlands of leaves and snow-white fillets.
Hence she seemed to hear the voice and the words of her husband
Calling her when dark night was enfolding the earth in its shadows.
Also, alone on the eaves, an owl with funereal wailing
Often complained, and prolonged her cries in long lamentation.

Concealing her real intentions, Dido induces her sister Anna to direct the building of a funeral pyre, on which are placed an effigy of Aeneas and some of his belongings. Again Mercury warns Aeneas that he and his men must leave, and so they set sail in the night.

Now they have left the shore, and the sea is hid by their vessels.
Straining, they whirl the foam, and sweep the deep blue of the ocean.
  Now the new light of dawn was Aurora beginning to sprinkle
Over the earth, as she sprang from the golden couch of Tithonus.
Soon as the queen from her windows perceives that morning is breaking,
Soon as she sees the fleet with sails wing and wing disappearing,
Sees the shore and the harbor deserted and empty of oarsmen,
Thrice and again she beats with her hand her beautiful bosom,
Tearing her golden hair, and exclaiming: "Ye Gods! shall this stranger
Thus be allowed to depart, and hold our throne in derision?
Will they not rush to arms and pursue from all parts of the city?
Are there not others to tear our boats from their moorings? What, ho, there!
Hither with torches! To arms! Row hard, my Tyrian boatmen!
What am I saying? Where am I? What madness disorders my reason?
Ah, wretched Dido, at last do deeds of disloyalty touch thee?
Then were it meet, when thou gavest thy sceptre! Oh, faith and devotion!
This is the man, they say, carries with him the gods of his fathers!
This is the man who bore on his shoulders his age-stricken parent!
I could have seized him and torn him in pieces and scattered his body
Over the waves; or his friends, Ascanius even, have slaughtered—
Why could I not?—and have served him up as a feast for his father!
But had the hazard of war been uncertain? Then let it have been so.
Whom did I fear at Death's door? I might have set fire to his galleys,

Filling his hatches with flame; and when with the son and the father
I had destroyed the race, have flung myself on the embers.
O thou Sun, who searchest all deeds of the Earth with thy glory,
Also, thou Juno, who knowest and feelest these tortures of passion,
Hecate, too, who wailest by night through the streets of the city,
Yea, ye avenging fiends, ye gods of dying Elissa,
Listen to this, and vouchsafe your presence to woes that deserve it.
Listen, and hear our prayers; and if it must certainly happen
That his accursèd head reach land and float to a harbor,
If the decrees of Jove are fixed, if this goal is determined,
Yet, undone by war and the sword of a resolute people,
Banished the realm and torn from the arms of his darling Iulus,
Let him go begging for aid, and see his best and his bravest
Slain in disgrace; and when to a treacherous peace he hath yielded.
Let him not then enjoy a throne or the day he hath longed for,
But, ere it dawn, let him fall far away on the shore, and unburied.
This is my prayer; with my blood I pour this dying petition.
Then, O ye Tyrian men! his seed to the last generation.
Follow with hate, and send these offerings down to our ashes.
Neither be love nor league between these nations forever!
Rise from my bones in the days to come, thou unknown avenger!
Follow with fire and sword the Dardanian colonists ever!
Now, and hereafter, whenever the time and the power shall be granted,
Shore against opposite shore, and sea against sea, I invoke it,—
Sword against sword, let them fight, themselves and all their descendants!"
Having thus spoken, she hurried her thoughts in ev'ry direction
Seeking the speediest way to break off the life she detested.
Then she briefly addressed old Barce, the nurse of Sychaeus,
For dark Death held her own in the ancient land of her fathers!
"Go, my dear nurse, and hither to me bring Anna, my sister.
Say she must hasten to sprinkle her body with free-flowing water,
Also to fetch, when she comes, the sheep and appointed oblations;
So shall she come; and do thou bind thy temples with consecrate fillets.
Vows unto Stygian Jove, which I have begun in due order,
It is my wish to complete, and thus put an end to my trouble,
Also to set the torch to the pyre of Dardania's chieftain."
Quickly on this the good nurse pattered off with an old woman's ardor.
But, affrighted and crazed by these gruesome beginnings, poor Dido—
Eyes with a murderous gleam, under eyelids trembling and tear-stained,
Face all white at the thought of Death so swiftly approaching—
Burst through the doors that led to the inner court, and in frenzy
Mounted the lofty pyre and unsheathed the sword of Aeneas,
Which, though not for this use, she had begged as a gift from her lover.
Here, as soon as she saw the familiar couch, and the garments
He had worn, she stood for a moment, weeping and thinking,
Then she fell on the bed, and these were the last words she uttered:

"Relics of happier days, when God and the Fates were indulgent,
Take this spirit of mine, and set me free from these troubles.
Lo, I have lived; I have finished the course that fate hath appointed;
Now my illustrious shade shall pass to the realms of the future.
I have established a glorious town; I have seen my own bulwarks;
I have avenged my husband, and punished my treacherous brother;
Happy, too happy, alas! if only the keel of the Dardan
Never had touched our shore!" Then, pressing her face to the pillow,
"Must we then die," she cried, "with no compensation of vengeance!
Yet, let us die! Thus! thus! we rejoice to enter the shadows.
Let him, afar on the sea, drink these flames with his eyes, cruel Dardan!
Yea, let him bear in his heart our death and its ominous tokens."
Dido hath spoken. The words are still on her lips when her maidens
See her sink down on the steel, see the blood foaming out round the dagger;
See her hands besprent. Then rings a loud cry through the lofty
Hall, and Rumor runs wild in the startled and terrified city;
Echoes the palace with groans, and the weeping and wailing of women;
Echoes the vaulted sky with the loud lament of the people,
Just as if Carthage or ancient Tyre were falling in ruins,
Left to the mercy of foemen, and flames were rolling in fury,
Leaping from home to home, and roaring from temple to temple.
Breathless, her sister heard, and, frantic with terror and running,
Marring her face with her nails, and frenziedly beating her bosom,
Forces her way through the throng, and calls by name on the dying:
"Was it for this, dear heart, thou didst craftily beg my assistance?
This for me were thy pyre and thy fires and thine altars preparing?
What is the first complaint of my loneliness? didst thou despise me
For a companion in death? Hadst thou called me to die with thee, sister,
Lo, one anguish had ended us both,—one hour, and one dagger!
Have I then builded this pyre, and called on the gods of our fathers
Only that thou shouldst fall like this,—I cruelly absent?
Me hast thou slain, my sister; thyself, and the princes of Sidon;
Ended thy city, thy race! Give place, good friends, that with water
I may assuage her wounds, and catch the last breath of her spirit
Should it be flickering still!" and with this, the tall pyre she ascended;
Now she is folding her dying sister close to her bosom,
Groaning aloud, and striving to staunch the dark blood with her garments.
Dido endeavored to raise her heavy eyes, but, exhausted,
Fainted again, while gurgled the wound deep fixed in her bosom.
Thrice attempting to rise, she lifted herself to her elbow,
Thrice fell back on the couch, and sought with wandering glances
Light in the lofty sky, but the light only deepened her moaning.
Then did omnipotent Juno, moved by her lingering anguish,
Touched by her struggle with death, send Iris down from Olympus,
Bidding her loose the impatient soul from the body that held it;

For, since neither by fate, nor a death
  deserved, she was dying,
But untimely and sad, and suddenly mastered by passion,
Not as yet had Proserpine stolen a lock
  of her golden
Hair, or doomed her head to the gloom
  of Stygian Orcus.
Therefore on saffron wings doth Iris fly
  down through the heavens,
Dewy, and drawing a thousand different
  hues from the sunbeams
Crossing her pathway, and hovers right
  over her head. "Under orders
This unto Pluto I bear as a sacred gift,
  and release thee
Thus, from thy body." She speaks, and
  severs the hair; the same instant
Warmth hath all vanished, and life hath
  passed to the whispering breezes.

(Translated by H. H. Ballard)

Catullus
(ca. 84-54 B.C.)
On Lesbia

Lesbia forever on me rails.
To talk of me she never fails.
Now, hang me, but for all her art,
I find that I have gained her heart.
My proof is this: I plainly see
The case is just the same with me;
I curse her every hour sincerely,
Yet, hang me, but I love her dearly.

(Translated by Jonathan Swift)

"Love Is Best"

O! Let us love and have our day,
All that bitter greybeards say
Appraising at a single mite.
My Lesbia, suns can set and rise:
For us the brief light dawns and dies
Once only, and the rest is night.
A thousand kisses, then five score,
A thousand and a hundred more,
Then one for each you gave before.
Then, as the many thousands grow,
We'll wreck the counting lest we know,
Or lest an evil eye prevail
Through knowledge of the kisses' tale.

(Translated by Hugh MacNaghton)

After a Quarrel

If that which is the heart's desire be told
Unhoped for, it is joy beyond the rest;
Therefore I count it joy more dear than gold
That, love, you turn again and make me blest;
You turn, my heart's desire so long denied,
Unasked, unhoped for. Oh! the white, bright day!
What happiness in all the world beside
Is like to mine? The rapture who shall say?

(Translated by Hugh MacNaghton)

At the Grave of His Brother

By ways remote and distant waters sped,
  Brother, to thy sad graveside am I come,
That I may give the last gifts to the dead,
  And vainly parley with thine ashes dumb;
Since She who now bestows and now denies
  Have ta'en thee, hapless brother, from mine
    eyes.
But lo! These gifts, the heirlooms of past years,
  Are made sad things to grace thy coffin-shell;
Take them, all drenchèd with a brother's tears,
  And, brother, for all time, hail and farewell.

(Translated by Aubrey Beardsley)

Horace
(65-8 B.C.)
To Postumus

Swiftly fly the rolling years, my friend!
Nor can your anxious prayers extend
    The fleeting joys of youth.
The trembling hand, the wrinkled cheek,
Too plainly life's decay bespeak,
    With sad but silent truth.

What though your daily offerings rise
In fragrant clouds of sacrifice
    To Jove's immortal seat;
You cannot fly death's cold embrace,
Where peasants—chiefs of kingly race
    An equal welcome meet.

In vain, from battlefields afar
You gently dream of waging war,
    Secure in peace and wealth:
In vain you shun the stormy wave,
The scorching breeze that others brave,
    Profuse of vigorous health.

Though zealous friends your portals throng,
They cannot still your life prolong
    By one short lingering hour;
Whate'er our plans, whate'er our state,
We mortals own one common fate,
    One stern, unbending power.

When your parched lips shall faintly press
On your fond wife their faint caress,
    And farewell murmurs breathe,
Your wandering eyes shall feebly rove
O'er each loved wood and well-trained grove,
    To seek a funeral wreath.

The purple vineyard's luscious stores,
Secured by trebly bolted doors,
    Excite, in vain, your care;
Soon shall the rich and sparkling hoard
Flow largely o'er the festive board
    Of your unsparing heir.

        (Translated by Ralph Bernal)

Ovid
(43 B.C.-A.D. 17)
Orpheus and Eurydice

In his greatest work, the Metamorphoses, *the Latin poet Ovid collected hundreds of myths and legends involving, among other things, supernatural transformations—from man to beast, bird, tree, or flower; from meteor to man, and so forth. To him, as to us, they were probably no more than fanciful tales, but he retold them with great care and often with brilliance. One of the most celebrated is the story of Orpheus and Eurydice, a tragic romance that has been retold again and again through the centuries, in mediums ranging from painting and sculpture through the operas of Monteverdi, Gluck, and Offenbach to the motion picture classic,* Black Orpheus.

    When his farewells were said at Iphis' wedding,
Hymen[1] leaped into space toward blue uncharted skies,
His golden-amber colours gliding up,
Till he sailed over Thrace where Orpheus hailed him
(But not entirely to his advantage)
To bless another wedding celebration.
Though Hymen came to help him at the feast
And waved his torch, its fires guttered out
In coiling smoke that filled the eyes with tears.
Then on the morning after, things went wrong:
While walking carelessly through sun-swept grasses,
Like Spring herself, with all her girls-in-waiting,
The bride stepped on a snake; pierced by his venom,
The girl tripped, falling, stumbled into Death.
Her bridegroom, Orpheus, poet of the hour,

[1]*Hymen:* god of marriage.

And pride of Rhadope, sang loud his loss
To everyone on earth. When this was done,
His wailing voice, his lyre, and himself
Came weaving through the tall gates of Taenarus
Down to the world of Death and flowing Darkness
To tell the story of his grief again.
He took his way through crowds of drifting shades
Who had escaped their graves to hear his music
And stood at last where Queen Persephone
Joined her unyielding lord to rule that desert
Which had been called their kingdom. Orpheus
Tuned up his lyre and cleared his throat to sing:
"O King and Queen of this vast Darkness where
All who are born of Earth at last return,
I cannot speak half flattery, half lies;
I have not come, a curious, willing guest,
To see the streets of Tartarus wind in Hell,
Nor have I come to see Medusa's children,
Three-throated beasts with wild snakes in their hair.
My mission is to find Eurydice,
A girl whose thoughts were innocent and gay,
Yet tripped upon a snake who struck his poison
Into her veins—then her short walk was done.
However much I took her loss serenely,
A god called Love had greater strength than I;
I do not know how well he's known down here,
But up on Earth his name's on every tongue,
And if I'm to believe an ancient rumour,
A dark king took a princess to his bed,
A child more beautiful than any queen;
They had been joined by Love. So at your mercy.
And by the eternal Darkness that surrounds us,
I ask you to unspin the fatal thread
Too swiftly run, too swiftly cut away,
That was my bride's brief life. Hear me, and know
Another day, after our stay on Earth,
Or swift or slow, we shall be yours forever.
Speeding at last to one eternal kingdom—
Which is our one direction and our home—
And yours the longest reign mankind has known.
When my Eurydice has spent her stay on Earth,
The child, a lovely woman in your arms,
Then she'll return and you may welcome her.
But for the present I must ask a favour:
Let her come back to me to share my love,
Yet if the Fates say 'No,' here shall I stay—
Two deaths in one—my death as well as hers."

Since these pathetic words were sung to music
Even the blood-drained ghosts of Hell fell weeping;
Tantalus[2] no longer reached toward vanished waves
And Ixion's[3] wheel stopped short, charmed by the spell;
Vultures gave up their feast on Tityus'[4] liver
And cocked their heads to stare; fifty Belides[5]
Stood gazing while their half-filled pitchers emptied,

---

[2]*Tantalus:* the king who was punished in Hades by being placed in water which receded when he tried to drink. [3]*Ixion:* king punished by Zeus for his love of Hera by being bound on an eternally revolving wheel. [4]*Tityus:* giant slain by Apollo; in Hades he was bound and two vultures continually tore at his liver. [5]*Belides:* female spirits of the Underworld, the granddaughters of Belus.

118 Classicism

And Sisyphus[6] sat down upon his stone.
Then, as the story goes, the raging Furies
Grew sobbing-wet with tears. Neither the queen
Nor her great lord of Darkness could resist
The charms of Orpheus and his matchless lyre.
They called Eurydice, and there among
The recent dead she came, still hurt and limping,
At their command. They gave him back his wife
With this proviso: that as he led her up
From where Avernus sank into a valley,
He must not turn his head to look behind him.
They climbed a hill through clouds, pitch-dark and gloomy,
And as they neared the surface of the Earth,
The poet, fearful that she'd lost her way,
Glanced backward with a look that spoke his love—
Then saw her gliding into deeper darkness,
As he reached out to hold her, she was gone;
He had embraced a world of emptiness.
This was her second death—and yet she could not blame him
(Was not his greatest fault great love for her?)
She answered him with one last faint "Good-bye,"
An echo of her voice from deep Avernus.

When Orpheus saw his wife go down to Death,
Twice dead, twice lost, he stared like someone dazed.
He seemed to be like him who saw the fighting
Three-headed Dog led out by Hercules
In chains, a six-eyed monster spitting bile;
The man was paralyzed and fear ran through him
Until his very body turned to stone.
Or rather, Orpheus was not unlike
Lethaea's husband, who took on himself
The sin of being proud of his wife's beauty,
Of which that lady bragged too much and long,
Yet since their hearts were one (in their opinion)
They changed to rocks where anyone may see them
Hold hands and kiss where Ida's fountains glitter.
Soon Orpheus went "melancholy-mad";
As often as old Charon pushed him back,
He begged, he wept to cross the Styx again.
Then for a week he sat in rags and mud,
Nor ate nor drank; he lived on tears and sorrow.
He cried against the gods of black Avernus
And said they made him suffer and go wild;
Then, suddenly, as if his mood had shifted,
He went to Thrace and climbed up windy Haemus.

Three times the year had gone through waves of Pisces,
While Orpheus refused to sleep with woman;
Whether this meant he feared bad luck in marriage,
Or proved him faithful to Eurydice,
No one can say, yet women followed him
And felt insulted when he turned them out.
One day while walking down a little hill
He sloped upon a lawn of thick green grasses,
A lovely place to rest—but needed shade.
But when the poet, great-grandson of the gods,
Sat down to sing and touched his

---

[6]*Sisyphus:* a king of Corinth, condemned to push a heavy stone uphill, only to have it always roll down again when he approached the top.

golden lyre,
There the cool grasses waved beneath green shadows,
For trees came crowding where the poet sang,
The silver poplar and the bronze-leaved oak,
The swaying lina, beech-nut, maiden-laurel,
Delicate hazel and spear-making ash,
The shining silver fir, the ilex leaning
Its flower-weighted head, sweet-smelling fir,
The shifting-coloured maple and frail willow
Whose branches trail where gliding waters flow;
Lake-haunted lotus and the evergreening boxwood,
Thin tamarisk and the myrtle of two colours,
Viburnum with its darkly shaded fruit.
And with them came the slender-footed ivy,
Grapevine and vine-grown elms and mountain ash,
The deeply wooded spruce, the pink arbutus,
The palm whose leaves are signs of victory,
And the tall pine, beloved of Cybele
Since Attis her loyal priest stripped of his manhood,
And stood sexless and naked as that tree.

    The songs that Orpheus sang brought creatures round him,
All beasts, all birds, all stones held in their spell.
But look! There on a hill that overlooked the plain,
A crowd of raging women stood, their naked breasts
Scarce covered by strips of fur. They gazed at Orpheus
Still singing, his frail lyre in one hand.
Her wild hair in the wind, one naked demon cried,
"Look at the pretty boy who will not have us!"
And shouting tossed a spear aimed at his mouth.
The leaf-grown spear scratched his white face,
Nor bruised his lips, nor was the song unbroken.
Her sister threw a stone, which as it sailed
Took on his music's charm, wavered and swayed;
As to beg free of its mistress' frenzy,
Fell at the poet's feet, At this the women
Grew more violent and madness flamed among the crowd:
A cloud of spears were thrown which flew apart
And dropped to earth, steered by the singer's voice.
The screams of women, clapping of hands on breasts and thighs,
The clattering tympanum soon won their way
Above the poet's music; spears found their aim,
And stones turned red, streaked by the singer's blood.
No longer charmed by music now unheard,
The birds, still with the echoes of Orpheus' music
Chiming through their veins, began to fly away—
Then snakes and wild things (once his pride to charm)
Turned toward their homes again and disappeared.
Now, as wild birds of prey swoop down to kill
An owl struck by a blinding light at noon,
Or as when dawn breaks over an open circus
To show a stag bleeding and put to death by dogs,

Such was the scene as Maenads[7] came at
    Orpheus,
Piercing his flesh with sharpened boughs
    of laurel,
Tearing his body with blood-streaming
    hands,
Whipping his sides with branches torn
    from trees;
He was stoned, beaten, and smeared with
    hardened clay.
Yet he was still alive; they looked for
    deadlier weapons,
And in the nearby plains, they saw the
    sweating peasants
And broad-shouldered oxen at the plough.
As they rushed toward them, peasants ran
    to shelter,
Their rakes and mattocks tossed aside
As the maddened women stormed the
    helpless oxen
To rip their sides apart, tear out their
    horns.
Armed with this gear they charged on
    Orpheus,
Who bared his breast to them to cry for
    mercy
(A prayer that never went unheard before);
They leaped on him to beat him into earth.
Then, O by Jupiter, through those same
    lips,
Lips that enchanted beasts, and dying
    rocks and trees,
His soul escaped in his last breath
To weave invisibly in waves of air.

    The saddened birds sobbed loud for Or-
        pheus;
All wept: the multitude of beasts,
Stones, and trees, all those who came to
    hear
The songs he sang, yes, even the charmed
    trees
Dropped all their leaves as if they shaved
    their hair. . . .

    The poet's shade stepped down from
        earth to Hades;
To stroll again the places that it knew,
It felt its way toward fair Elysium.
There Orpheus took his Eurydice, put arms
    around her
Folding her to rest. Today they walk to-
    gether,
Side by side—or if they wish, he follows
    her, she, him,
But as they move, however they may go,
Orpheus may not turn a backward look
    at her.

Lyaeus could not let the killing of Orpheus
Pass without revenge on his mad murder-
    ers.
Angered by loss, he captured Thracian
    women
Who saw him die, trussed them with roots,
And thrust their feet, toes downward, into
    earth.
As birds are trapped by clever fowlers in
    a net,
Then flutter to get free, drawing the net
    still tighter
Round wings and claws, so each woman
    fought,
Held by quick roots entangling feet and
    fingers,
Toenails in earth, she felt bark creeping
    up her legs,
And when she tried to slap her thighs, her
    hands struck oak;
Her neck, her shoulders, breasts were oak-
    wood carving;
You'd think her arms were bran-
    ches—you're not wrong.

        (Translated by Horace Gregory)

7*Maenads:* the bacchantes, frenzied followers of Bacchus.

Pliny the Younger
(A.D. 62-ca. 114)
The Tuscan Villa
from *The Villas of Pliny the Younger*

Pliny's letters, probably written with an eye toward publication, provide many glimpses of the life and times of this wealthy Roman, his treatment of Christians, his illustrious uncle's activities, the eruption of Vesuvius, his elegant villas. A favorite exercise of architects both professional and amateur has been to attempt to reconstruct—in drawings, at least—the Tuscan and the Laurentine villas, from Pliny's descriptions of them. Helen Tanzer's little book, The Villas of Pliny the Younger, *contains reproductions of many such drawings. The reader is invited to try his own hand.*

It is most kind of you, my dear Apollinaris, to try to dissuade me from going to my Tuscan villa because of the climate, but though you are right in thinking that the Tuscan coast is malarial, my villa is quite a distance from the shore, right at the foot of the Apennines, a very healthful situation.

Let me describe my villa to you, and when you hear how salubrious the climate is and how comfortable the house and how well situated, you will see that there is no cause for anxiety. The place is indeed so thoroughly delightful that I think you will like to hear about it as much as I shall enjoy the telling.

It is so cold in winter that we have no myrtle, olives, or other trees that require a warm climate, though the laurel flourishes and is sometimes very fine—though sometimes the frost kills it—not oftener however than it does in Rome, for that matter. But in the summer it is delightfully cool; there is always a breeze though there is seldom a high wind. You would believe that the place is healthy if you could see how many grandfathers and great-grandfathers there are among the native families. The tales the old fellows tell about their ancestors carry you back a century or two.

The country is wonderfully beautiful. It gives the impression of a huge natural amphitheatre; the arena is a wide plain surrounded by mountains which rise to a great height. At the summit is a forest of huge ancient trees providing excellent hunting of various kinds. Below the forest the slopes are covered with timber woods which grow less thick as they descend the slope. There is a great deal of underbrush, and scattered through this are hillocks of very rich soil in which you will hardly find a stone, search as you may, and these hillocks are fully as fertile as the fields in the plain and bear as rich a harvest, though somewhat later. At the foot of the hills there is a network of vines, and at the very lowest margin a vineyard forming a sort of fringe.

Then come the fields and the meadows. The soil of the fields is so heavy that it has to be ploughed nine times before it is ready for planting though they use extremely heavy plows drawn by powerful bulls. The meadows are thickly sprinkled with clover and all sorts of herbage which all grow fresh and tender. The whole basin is watered by never-failing springs, and while there is an abundance of water there are no marshes, as the ground water drains away into the river. The Tiber, which traverses these fields, carries many ships with produce of various kinds to the City, but only in the winter and spring, and again in the autumn, for in spite of its mighty name, it dries up in the summer to the size of a brook.

I know you would enjoy the view of this part of the country from the mountain: for as the land lies below you it looks more

HADRIAN'S VILLA NEAR TIVOLI, ITALY

like a beautiful landscape painting than the real thing; it is a refreshing picture both in its variety and in its regularity. The view from the house is like a mountain view though the house is really at the foot of the hills; the slope is so gradual that you never know how far you have come. Behind the house, but quite far away, are the Apennines; and so, no matter how warm the day, there is always a gentle breeze, but never a gale.

The house faces almost full south, and so the entrance porch is always sunny—in summer at noon and in winter a little earlier. Several rooms open on the porch, which is wide and comparatively deep, notably an atrium in the old style.

In front of the porch is a terrace laid out in beds of various shapes edged with box, and, sloping down from this, a bank bordered by rows of box at both sides in the form of animals facing one another, and on the level ground below, acanthus so soft that it almost seems to flow. Around it is a walk hedged in by shrubs trained and cut into various forms, and outside a driveway encircles it which is itself bordered by numerous evergreen shrubs rising in steps so as to hide it completely. Then comes a meadow the natural beauty of which is as great as the artificial beauty just described; then fields, and, stretching off into the distance, more meadows planted with trees.

At the end of the porch a dining room abuts which, from the folding doors, looks down upon the extreme end of the terrace, on the meadow and a good bit of the country beyond; and from the windows at one side looks out on the terrace and on the other at the trees and the woods around the park which lies beyond the house.

Opening from about the middle of the porch and a little behind it is a suite of rooms enclosing a small court shaded by four plane trees which are watered by the overflow from a marble basin in which stands a fountain gently spraying the surrounding verdure. One of the rooms of this suite is a little alcove for sleeping from which it is possible to exclude every ray of light and all sounds. Next door is the private dining room which we use informally; it looks out on the plane trees, the porch, and the atrium and has the same view as the porch.

Then comes another chamber, shaded by a leafy plane tree and ornamented by a marble wainscoting and, no less pleasing, a frieze above it, depicting birds perched on leafy branches. There is a fountain in a basin and the pleasant sound of running water from many jets.

At the corner of the portico a large chamber projects toward the dining room, and from the windows on one side you can look down on the terrace and from the other side on that part of the meadows which lie below, where stands a marble basin, pleasing to the eye and to the ear also as the foaming water falls back into the basin. This room is warm in winter because the sun comes streaming in all day long. Or, if the day is cloudy, the room can be heated from the hypocaust which is connected with it. Adjoining the hypocaust is a pleasant large heated dressing room for the bath and next to that a swimming pool for a cold plunge in a large shaded basin. If you wish to have a swim in warmer water, there is a pool outdoors in the court and a basin near by which you can use to refresh yourself when you want to cool off. Adjoining the swimming pool is a room warmed by the sun, warmer than a caldarium need be, since it projects. There are three pools here, two directly in the sun and the third somewhat shaded though not dark.

Above the dressing room is the gymnasium, fitted up for various kinds of exercise, with several courts marked out. Not far from the bath rooms are stairs leading first to three apartments and then to a covered gallery. One of these rooms—they have quite different exposures—overlooks the little court with the plane trees, another looks out on the terrace, and the third on the vineyard. At the upper end of the gallery and forming a part of it is a chamber which looks out on the park, the vineyard, and the mountains. Then comes a chamber which enjoys the full sun, especially in winter, and then a sitting room which extends the villa toward the park. This is the view in front.

At the side is a high two-story covered colonnade, for summer use, which seems not merely to face the vineyards but to touch them. A dining room in the center receives the freshest breezes direct from the valley of the Apennines; at the back the vineyards seem to come in through the broad windows and also through the folding doors, and almost from the colonnade. At the side of the dining room where there are no windows, stairs provide a private entrance to the banquet hall. At the end there is a chamber which has a good view of the whole colonnade as well as of the vineyards. The lower story which is underground is similar to the upper one, except that in the summer time it is quite cool; it receives no breath of outside air nor does it need it.

Behind this two-story gallery beyond the dining room is a porch which receives the sun before midday in winter and earlier in summer. The porch leads to two apartments in which there are three and four chambers respectively which are shady or sunny according to the position of the sun. This pleasantly situated group of buildings follows the course of the driveway though at some distance from it. Upon entering, the visitor at once takes in the whole view of this part of the park, with plane trees in the center, so covered with ivy that its leaves mingle with the leaves of the trees and look exactly as if they were part of them. The ivy not only covers the trunk and branches of each tree, but goes from one to another, in festoons, binding the trees together. Boxwood is planted there between the plane trees, and beyond the box is laurel, which mingles its shade with that of the plane trees. The driveway ends in a semicircle, where the view is quite different. For cypresses bound the edge of it and make a shadow that grows blacker and denser the farther it goes, but on the beds within, of which there are many, the sun shines bright, and roses grow there, making the sunlit spot a lovely contrast to the cool shadows. Then after many curves the road is straight again and branches into many paths separated by boxwood hedges. And in between there are small patches of lawn set here and there with box trees cut into numerous different shapes, even letters which spell out the name of the owner and again of the artist. There are also rows of little posts alternating with fruit trees, thus surprising one with the appearance of rustic simplicity in surroundings of studied formality. The central space has low plane trees on each side. Behind these is acanthus, some pliant and vinelike and some cut into animal forms and letters. At the head is a curved seat of white marble decked with vines and four vine clad columns of Carystian marble. From beneath the seat, water flows out from small pipes but appears to be pressed out by the weight of the bench and its occupants, and is caught in a stone basin hewn out of the rock and faced with marble, very pretty, in which the supply is so regulated that it never overflows even though it is always full. When meals are served here, the appetizers and the heavier courses are served from the bank, while the lighter ones are floated on the surface in artificial birds and little ships. There is a fountain in full view of this seat from which the water shoots up into the air and is caught in the basin as it falls back, not continuously but intermittently.

Opposite the marble bench is a chamber which adds as much to the beauty of the scene as it gains from it. It is covered with shining marble and opens into the garden by folding doors; above and below, it is embowered in greenery. A small alcove at the back of the room is almost a separate chamber. It has a bed, and though there are windows on every side, still the light is subdued, for every window is shaded most delightfully by a vine which completely covers the outside clear to the roof. It is exactly like sleeping in the woods except that you are completely protected from the rain. Another fountain plays outside. Then there are marble seats placed at intervals which offer as pleasant a rest to those wearied by walking as does the chamber with its couch. There are more fountains around the benches which all feed rivulets flowing down through the park, following a course artificially laid out and varied so as to water one or another part of the garden and sometimes all of it at once.

I should long since have stopped for fear of becoming tedious if I had not set out in my letter to take you into every corner of the house. I was not afraid that you would grow weary in reading about what it could not have tired you to visit, especially as you could rest whenever you wished and by merely laying aside the letter you could sit down, as it were, as often as you chose. Furthermore, I have indulged in the luxury of praising something that delights me, for I especially love anything that I have been responsible in beginning or successful in finishing. In short—why should I not tell you what I think, even if I am wrong—it seems to me that the chief duty of a writer is, after a careful consideration of the scope of his subject, to see that he confines himself to it and that even if his piece should turn out to be somewhat longer than he had expected, not to conclude that it is too long if it contains no extraneous matter. Just consider how many lines Homer and Virgil take to describe the armor of Achilles and of Aeneas, but they are really brief because each has done only what he set out to do. . . .

But now I am afraid that I shall transgress the laws I have myself laid down if I continue. You can readily understand, however, why I prefer my Tuscan villa to any of my others—those at Tusculum, Tibur, or Praeneste. For besides the attractions which I have mentioned, the greatest is the solid comfort of the place—nobody needs to bother to dress, the neighbors do not come to call, it is always quiet and peaceful—advantages as great as the healthful situation and good air. I always feel energetic and fit for anything at my Tuscan villa, both mentally and physically. I exercise my mind by study, my body by hunting. My household too flourishes better here than elsewhere: I have never lost a slave, none of those I brought up with me, anyway, if you will pardon my mentioning it. May the gods thus continue to bless me and my house!

Yours ever, *Secundus*

(Letter 6 Book V, translated by Helen Tanzer)

DETAIL FROM MARCUS AURELIUS COLUMN IN ROME

Marcus Aurelius
(A.D. 121-180)
from *The Meditations*

From my grandfather Verus I learned good morals and the government of my temper.

From the reputation and remembrance of my father, modesty and a manly character.

From my mother, piety and beneficence, and abstinence, not only from evil deeds, but even from evil thoughts; and further, simplicity in my way of living, far removed from the habits of the rich. . . .

From Alexander the Platonic, not frequently nor without necessity to say to any one, or to write in a letter, that I have no leisure; nor continually to excuse the neglect of duties required by our relation to those with whom we live, by alleging urgent occupations.

. . .

Begin the morning by saying to thyself, I shall meet with the busybody, the ungrateful, arrogant, deceitful, envious, unsocial. All these things happen to them by reason of their ignorance of what is good and evil. But I who have seen the nature of the good that it is beautiful, and of the bad that it is ugly, and the nature of him who does wrong, that it is akin to me, not only of the same blood or seed, but that it participates in the same intelligence and the same portion of divinity, I can neither be injured by any of them, for no one can fix on me what is ugly, nor can I be angry with my kinsman, nor hate him. For we are made for co-operation, like feet, like hands, like eyelids, like rows of upper and lower teeth. To act against one another then is contrary to nature; and it is acting against one another to be vexed and turn away.

Whatever this is that I am, it is a little flesh and breath, and the ruling part. Throw away thy books; no longer distract thyself; it is not allowed; but as if thou wast now dying, despise the flesh; it is blood and bones and a network, a contexture of nerves, veins, and arteries. See the breath also, what kind of a thing it is, air, and not always the same, but every moment sent out again and sucked in. The third then is the ruling part.

. . .

Every moment think steadily as a Roman and a man to do what thou hast in hand with perfect and simple dignity, and feeling of affection, and freedom, and justice; and to give thyself relief from all other thoughts. And thou wilt give thyself relief, if thou doest every act of thy life as if it were the last, laying aside all carelessness and passionate aversion from the commands of reason, and all hypocrisy, and self-love, and discontent with the portion which has been given to thee. Thou seest how few the things are, the which if a man lays hold of, he is able to live a life which flows in quiet, and is like the existence of the gods; for the gods on their part will require nothing more of him who observes these things.

. . .

Never value anything as profitable to thyself which shall compel thee to break thy promise, to lose thy self-respect, to hate any man, to suspect, to curse, to act the hypocrite, to desire anything which needs walls and curtains.

. . .

Throwing away then all things, hold to these only which are few; and besides bear in mind that every man lives only this present time, which is an indivisible point, and that all the rest of his life is either past or uncertain. Short then is the time which every man lives, and small the nook of the earth where he lives; and short too the longest posthumous fame, and even this only continued by a succession of poor human beings, who will very soon die, and who know not even themselves, much less him who died long ago.

. . .

Men seek retreats for themselves, houses in the country, sea-shores, and mountains; and thou too art wont to desire such things very much. But this is altogether a mark of the most common sort of men, for it is in thy power whenever thou shalt choose to retire into thyself. For nowhere either with more quiet or more freedom from trouble does a man retire than into his own soul, particularly when he has within him such thoughts that by looking into them he is immediately in perfect tranquillity; and I affirm that tranquillity is nothing else than the good ordering of the mind. Constantly then give to thyself retreat, and renew thyself; and let thy principles be brief and fundamental, which, as soon as thou shalt recur to them, will be sufficient to cleanse the soul completely, and to send thee back free from all discontent with the things to which thou returnest.

. . .

Do not act as if thou wert going to live ten thousand years. Death hangs over thee. While thou livest, while it is in thy power, be good.

. . .

Occupy thyself with few things, says the philosopher, if thou wouldst be tranquil.—But consider if it would not be better to say, Do what is necessary, and whatever the reason of the animal which is naturally social requires, and as it requires. For this brings not only the tranquillity which comes from doing well, but also that which comes from doing few things. For the greatest part of what we say and do being necessary, if a man takes this away, he will have more leisure and less uneasiness. Accordingly on every occasion a man should ask himself, Is this one of the unnecessary things? Now a man should take away not only unnecessary acts, but also unnecessary thoughts, for thus superfluous acts will not follow after.

. . .

Be like a promontory against which the waves continually break, but it stands firm and tames the fury of the water around it.

. . .

In the morning when thou risest unwilling, let this thought be present—I am rising to the work of a human being. Why then am I dissatisfied if I am going to do the things for which I exist and for which I was brought into the world? Or have I been made for this, to lie in the bedclothes and keep myself warm?—But this is more pleasant—Dost thou exist then to take thy pleasure, and not at all for action or exertion? Dost thou not see the little plants, the little birds, the ants, the spiders, the bees working together to put in order their several parts of the universe? And art thou unwilling to do the work of a human being, and doest thou not make haste to do that which is according to thy nature?—But it is necessary to take rest also—It is necessary: however nature has fixed bounds to this too: she has fixed bounds to both eating and drinking, and yet thou goest beyond these bounds, beyond what is sufficient; yet in thy acts it is not so, but thou stoppest short of what thou canst do. So thou lovest not thyself, for if thou didst, thou wouldst love thy nature and her will.

. . .

Such as are thy habitual thoughts, such also will be the character of thy mind; for the soul is dyed by the thoughts.

. . .

Reverence that which is best in the universe; and this is that which makes use of all things and directs all things. And in like manner also reverence that which is best in thyself; and this is of the same kind as that. For in thyself also, that which makes use of everything else, is this, and thy life is directed by this.

(Translated by George Long)

CHRISTIANITY AND THE MIDDLE AGES

(ROBERT CAMPIN?): Flemish Annunciation, COURTESY OF THE M. H. DE YOUNG MEMORIAL MUSEUM IN SAN FRANCISCO

CHRISTIANITY AND THE MIDDLE AGES

The term *Middle Ages* designates a long period of history that extends from the end of the Roman Empire to the beginnings of the Renaissance. However, the important point to remember is that cultural patterns do not change at any given moment in history; often, as mentioned earlier, change is merely a blending and adapting. New concepts develop and spread while older ones are still in vogue. If circumstances permit, the new may replace the old because the forces of time are ripe and permit change, or the new blends with the old. Such changes occurred during and after the fall of the Roman Empire. And of course they are reflected in the literature of this long period.

It is convenient to consider the literature of the Middle Ages in two large divisions: that of the Early Middle Ages (from the fall of the Empire to A.D. 1000); and that of the Later Middle Ages (from 1000 to the Renaissance).

Early Middle Ages

Christian Influence

The major influence of the Early Middle Ages was the rise and spread of Christianity. Paul's missionary work (and his later letters of direction) in Asia Minor, Greece, and Italy established Christian organizations in some predominantly Jewish communities in these areas. Paul and other missionaries, however, extended their efforts to the Gentiles as well. In the period of a weakening Roman Empire, with its many mystical sects and confused intellectual concepts, Christianity provided a haven of good sense. Furthermore, Christianity was able to incorporate some of the Classical religious feasts and concepts into its development, such as the establishment of holidays from long traditional feast days (gift giving at Christmas came from the Roman Saturnalia, which was celebrated in the fourth week of December) and the transference of the abstract Greek *Logos,* a divine essence or reason, to the human form of Jesus, giving this new religion the familiar embellishments of the old. By 313 Constantine had decreed official toleration for the sect. Theodosius prohibited pagan worship in 392, and Christianity became the official religion of the Roman state.

One of the most successful elements in the rise of Christianity was the ability of its leaders to organize. Scattered and remote, individual churches could not accomplish the needs of a volatile church; but leaders arose in key areas, and the development of a church hierarchy followed. The already established framework of Roman government provided excellent patterns for growth.

Though the later contentions between the churches at Rome and Constantinople ended in complete severance in 1054, the power of a centralized church carried through the centuries that were marked by Germanic invasions throughout Europe and the rise and fall of nation-states. Our surviving literature owes its life to the church—not only to the monks in the West, who served as copyists and translators, but also to the church in the East; for without the aid of the Byzantines who preserved so much of the literary art of Classical times, our knowledge of the Greek writings would be severely limited.

Early Literature

The Bible contains the primary examples of early Christian literature; furthermore, it has played an important subsidiary role in literature through the centuries. The influence of the Bible on the arts in general is immeasurable; allusions to biblical names and events are copious in Western literature from the Middle Ages to the present day. Besides the biblical writers, there were capable writers in the early church who wrote to interpret and defend doctrine; among these were men such as Jerome, Gregory, Ambrose, and Augustine, who is represented in this reader.

Augustine's *Confessions* (354-430) constitutes the first autobiography of ancient times. Writing directly to God, Augustine recounts the personal events of his life and attempts to analyze the experiences he had on the journey that led him finally to the church.

These works were written in Latin; the Bible appeared in a single Latin Vulgate (common or informal speech) version through the efforts of Jerome, a gifted scholar, in the early part of the fifth century after Christ.

Germanic Influence

The Germanic tribes that overcame the Romans and spread throughout Europe brought a new quality, a new personality, to the forms of Western culture. The Goths swept to the south (in 410 the Visigoths sacked Rome); the Angles, Saxons, and Jutes, to the north and west; the Franks (Charlemagne came from this people) settled along the Rhineland. These were only a few of the influential Germanic tribes. There were centuries of pillaging, upheaval, and wars.

The Germanic tribes had few observable art forms, but their personalities marked later developments in art. Vigorous and imaginative, they explained the workings of nature with equally bizarre supernatural phenomena: ghosts, creatures that taunted men, animals that changed to human form. Fiercely loyal to leaders who had won their places by their deeds of strength and daring, the Germanic peoples were also active and independent. They had a strong respect for women. Their gods, not as human as the Classical gods nor as loving as the Hebraic God, rewarded valor attained even at the cost of life.

As these people gradually settled the lands once under the influence of the Roman Empire and began to accept Christianity, an imaginative, romantic mixture of Christian religious purpose and pagan excitement colored the literature. The Old English epic *Beowulf* serves as a perfect example of this blending. Written somewhere between the late seventh and early ninth centuries, *Beowulf* resembles in purpose, and to an extent in style, the *Aeneid* of Virgil. The cleric who wrote *Beowulf* combines the Christ-like character of Beowulf with the pagan mystery of sea monsters and dragons. Adventure-filled and colorful, this epic presents well the life and tribal experiences of the sixth-century sea-nomad.

Later Middle Ages

Feudalism and the Crusades

The Early Middle Ages were chaotic in one sense, stagnant in another; cultural and educational development was minimal. The church and tribal polities operated separately. The earliest important move toward order in the church and state was successfully accomplished in the ninth century. With the naming of Charlemagne as Emperor of the Romans in 800 by Pope Leo III, a tie was again established between church and state. Under Charlemagne's promptings a new impetus to learning was revived; in a sense this was an early "Renaissance." Following his death in 814, however, there was a return to the political disorganization that had stifled the preceding centuries.

During the years of the Carolingians (Carolus or Charlemagne and his successors), a new political concept, feudalism, was introduced into Western Europe. Its development and dissemination encouraged the qualities of order and loyalty on a localized scale. Feudalism survived the chaos after Charlemagne. Though wars and land conflicts were common in a feudal society, order was slowly coming back to Europe.

The church recognized the need for order too. Even though it suffered with weak popes through the ninth and tenth centuries, the church saw its role as that of unifier and leader. Monastic orders that had developed earlier went through the same reforms that the general church body attempted. One of the more important changes in the church was its effort to become more human-oriented. The introduction of the worship of Mary found a welcome place in the minds of people who needed to identify more with "this world," and it helped enhance the role of women generally.

The feudal knights accepted with enthusiasm the function of protecting their lords' lands and womankind; chivalry was born. Chivalry directed toward freeing the Holy Land from the clutches of "infidels" was a natural cause for feudal lords, who recognized the worth of religion and the power the church had to offer. The church, on the other hand, saw the importance of encouraging the involvement of these lords in a good, energy-consuming cause. The Crusades did both.

Though disastrous to many feudal fortunes, the Crusades had some happy consequences. They prompted the exchange of cultural ideas and helped to strengthen the towns that were developing as centers of trade and services. Religious orders grew powerful and wealthy.

The world was again changing. The early kings who had been largely replaced by the feudal hierarchy were once again finding a place in society as lords and lands banded together around strong and wealthy leaders. Commerce developed and nations came into being. The world was aware of knowledge and a *past*. The scholasticism that took form in the eleventh and twelfth centuries represented the attempt of scholars in the church to reconcile church dogma with newly identified Aristotelian thought. The past made the present conscious of itself. National awareness was one result.

Later Literature

The *Song of Roland* is an example of the *chanson de geste* or song of deeds. Medieval French narrative poems, the *chansons* are short epics. Based at least remotely on historical fact, they are usually stories already long associated with oral tradition. The author of the *Song of Roland* is unknown, but tradition holds that it was probably composed somewhere in the eleventh century. Written in the feudal and heroic tradition, it deals with the days of Charlemagne.

Another type of literature, flourishing during the twelfth and thirteenth centuries, is the Arthurian romance. Originally the term *romance* connoted adventure and mystery, but love was included too. Subject matter revolved around the exciting days of the past: heroes of the classical world, the France of Charlemagne, and the stories of Arthur and his Round Table. Celtic in origin, these tales are familiar because they have appeared in so many modern versions. *Sir Gawain and the Green Knight* is one of the finest Arthurian romances.

Literature of the Late Middle Ages is representative of the brilliant and alert minds of its writers. These men are supremely interested in the blossoming world of ideas and people around them. Writers in the church often extol the beauties of the world and praise the God that created it. Their hymns and prose writings hold a new awareness and delicacy of expression coupled with intense feeling.

Then the strong trend toward nationalism was reflected in the fourteenth and fifteenth-century literature that appeared in the vernacular (the native language or dialect). Dante and Chaucer both composed masterpieces in their native tongues, opening doors to literary expression that have never since closed. Life and experience gained a momentum that led overwhelmingly to that period we call the *Renaissance*.

GERARD DAVID: *The Rest on the Flight into Egypt*, ANDREW MELLON COLLECTION, NATIONAL GALLERY OF ART, WASHINGTON, D. C.

from the *Bible*

The passages from the Bible that have been selected for inclusion in this book of readings are only a few of the many that have provided inspiration for countless thousands of artists—sculptors, painters, composers, poets, playwrights, novelists. It will be valuable for the student to identify with particular works of art the selections that follow—the story of the Creation, three Psalms, the Messianic passages from Isaiah, Luke's account of the Annunciation and the birth of the Savior, and John's account of the Last Supper.

The Creation

(Genesis 1; 2:1-3)

In the beginning God created the heaven and the earth. And the earth was without form, and void; and darkness was upon the face of the deep. And the Spirit of God moved upon the face of the waters. And God said, "Let there be light": and there was light. And God saw the light, that it was good: and God divided the light from the darkness. And God called the light Day, and the darkness he called Night. And the evening and the morning were the first day.

And God said, "Let there be a firmament in the midst of the waters, and let it divide the waters from the waters." And God made the firmament, and divided the waters which were under the firmament from the waters which were above the firmament: and it was so. And God called the firmament Heaven. And the evening and the morning were the second day.

And God said, "Let the waters under the heaven be gathered together unto one place, and let the dry land appear": and it was so. And God called the dry land Earth; and the gathering together of the waters called he Seas; and God saw that it was good. And God said, "Let the earth bring forth grass, the herb yielding seed, and the fruit tree yielding fruit after his kind, whose seed is in itself, upon the earth": and it was so. And the earth brought forth grass, and herb yielding seed after his kind, and the tree yielding fruit, whose seed was in itself, after his kind: and God saw that it was good. And the evening and the morning were the third day.

And God said, "Let there be lights in the firmament of the heaven to divide the day from the night; and let them be for signs, and for seasons, and for days, and years; and let them be for lights in the firmament of the heaven to give light upon the earth."

And it was so. And God made two great lights; the greater light to rule the day, and the lesser light to rule the night: he made the stars also. And God set them in the firmament of the heaven to give light upon the earth. And to rule over the day and over the night, and to divide the light from the darkness: and God saw that it was good. And the evening and the morning were the fourth day.

And God said, "Let the waters bring forth abundantly the moving creature that hath life, and fowl that may fly above the earth in the open firmament of heaven." And God created great whales, and every living creature that moveth, which the waters brought forth abundantly, after their kind, and every winged fowl after his kind: and God saw that it was good. And God blessed them, saying, "Be fruitful, and multiply, and fill the waters in the seas, and let fowl multiply in the earth." And the evening and the morning were the fifth day.

And God said, "Let the earth bring forth the living creature after his kind, cattle, and creeping thing, and beast of the earth after his kind": and it was so. And God made the beast of the earth after his kind, and cattle after their kind, and every thing that creepeth upon the earth after his kind: and God saw that it was good.

And God said, "Let us make man in our image, after our likeness: and let them have dominion over the fish of the sea, and over the fowl of the air, and over the cattle, and over all the earth, and over every creeping thing that creepeth upon the earth." So God created man in his own image, in the image of God created he him; male and female created he them. And God blessed them, and God said unto them, "Be fruitful, and multiply, and replenish the earth, and subdue it: and have dominion over the fish of the sea, and over the fowl of the air, and over every living thing that moveth upon the earth." And God said, "Behold, I have given you every herb bearing seed, which is upon the face of all the earth, and every tree, in the which is the fruit of a tree yielding seed; to you it shall be for meat. And to every beast of the earth, and to every fowl of the air, and to every thing that creepeth upon the earth, wherein there is life, I have given every green herb for meat." And it was so. And God saw every thing that he had made, and behold, it was very good. And the evening and the morning were the sixth day.

Thus the heavens and the earth were finished, and all the host of them. And on the seventh day God ended his work which he had made; and he rested on the seventh day from all his work which he had made. And God blessed the seventh day, and sanctified it: because that in it he had rested from all his work which God had created and made.

The Messiah

(Isaiah 9:2-6)

The people that walked in darkness have seen a great light: they that dwell in the land of the shadow of death, upon them hath the light shined.

Thou has multiplied the nation, and not increased the joy: they joy before thee according to the joy in harvest, and as men rejoice when they divide the spoil.

For thou has broken the yoke of his burden, and the staff of his shoulder, the rod of his oppressor, as in the day of Midian.

For every battle of the warrior is with confused noise, and garments rolled in blood; but this shall be with burning and fuel of fire.

For unto us a child is born, unto us a son is given: and the government shall be upon his shoulder: and his name shall be called Wonderful, Counsellor, The mighty God, the everlasting Father, the Prince of Peace.

(Isaiah 35:1-6)

The wilderness and the solitary place shall be glad for them; and the desert shall rejoice, and blossom as the rose.

It shall blossom abundantly, and rejoice even with joy and singing: the glory of Lebanon shall be given unto it, the excellency of Carmel and Sharon, they shall see the glory of the Lord, and the excellency of our God.

Strengthen then ye the weak hands, and confirm the feeble knees.

Say to them that are of a fearful heart, Be strong, fear not: behold, your God will come with vengeance, even God with a recompence; he will come and save you.

Then the eyes of the blind shall be opened, and the ears of the deaf shall be unstopped.

Then shall the lame man leap as an

hart, and the tongue of the dumb shall sing: for in the wilderness shall waters break out, and streams in the desert.

(Isaiah 40:1-11)

Comfort ye, comfort ye my people, saith your God.

Speak ye comfortably to Jerusalem, and cry unto her, that her warfare is accomplished, that her iniquity is pardoned: for she hath received of the Lord's hand double for all her sins.

The voice of him that crieth in the wilderness, Prepare ye the way of the Lord, make straight in the desert a highway for our God.

Every valley shall be exalted, and every mountain and hill shall be made low: and the crooked shall be made straight, and the rough places plain:

And the glory of the Lord shall be revealed, and all flesh shall see it together: for the mouth of the Lord hath spoken it.

The voice said, Cry, And he said, What shall I cry? All flesh is grass, and all the goodliness thereof is as the flower of the field:

The grass withereth, the flower fadeth: but the word of our God shall stand for ever.

O Zion, that bringest good tidings, get thee up into the high mountain; O Jerusalem, that bringest good tidings, lift up thy voice with strength; lift it up, be not afraid; say unto the cities of Judah, Behold your God!

Behold, the Lord God will come with strong hand, and his arm shall rule for him: behold, his reward is with him, and his work before him.

He shall feed his flock like a shepherd: he shall gather the lambs with his arm, and carry them in his bosom, and shall gently lead those that are with young.

(Isaiah 53:1-6)

Who hath believed our report? and to whom is the arm of the Lord revealed?

For he shall grow up before him as a tender plant, and as a root out of a dry ground: he hath no form nor comeliness; and when we shall see him, there is no beauty that we should desire him.

He is despised and rejected of men; a man of sorrows, and acquainted with grief: and we hid as it were our faces from him; he was despised, and we esteemed him not.

Surely he hath borne our griefs, and carried our sorrows: yet we did esteem him stricken, smitten of God, and afflicted.

But he was wounded for our transgressions, he was bruised for our iniquities: the chastisement of our peace was upon him; and with his stripes we are healed.

All we like sheep have gone astray; we have turned everyone to his own way; and the Lord hath laid on him the iniquity of us all.

Psalm 8

O Lord our Lord, How excellent is thy name in all the earth! who hast set thy glory above the heavens.

Out of the mouths of babes and sucklings hast thou ordained strength because of thine enemies, that thou mightest still the enemy and the avenger.

When I consider thy heavens, the work of thy fingers, the moon and the stars, which thou hast ordained;

What is man, that thou art mindful of him? and the son of man, that thou visitest him?

For thou hast made him a little lower than the angels, and hast crowned him with glory and honour.

Thou madest him to have dominion over the works of thy hands; thou hast put all things under his feet:

All sheep and oxen, yea, and the beasts of the field;

The fowl of the air, and the fish of the sea, and whatsoever passeth through the paths of the seas.

O Lord our Lord, how excellent is thy name in all the earth!

Psalm 23

The Lord is my shepherd; I shall not want.

He maketh me to lie down in green pastures: he leadeth me beside the still waters.

He restoreth my soul: he leadeth me in the paths of righteousness for his name's sake.

Yea, though I walk through the valley of the shadow of death, I will fear no evil: for thou art with me; thy rod and thy staff they comfort me.

Thou preparest a table before me in the presence of mine enemies: thou anointest my head with oil; my cup runneth over.

Surely goodness and mercy shall follow me all the days of my life: and I will dwell in the house of the Lord for ever.

Psalm 24

The earth is the Lord's, and the fulness thereof; the world, and they that dwell therein.

For he hath founded it upon the seas, and established it upon the floods.

Who shall ascend into the hill of the

THE GOOD SHEPHERD MOSAIC, TOMB OF GALLA PLACIDIA, RAVENNA

Lord? or who shall stand in his holy place?

He that hath clean hands and a pure heart; who hath not lifted up his soul unto vanity, nor sworn deceitfully.

He shall receive the blessing from the Lord, and righteousness from the God of his salvation.

This is the generation of them that seek him, that seek thy face, O Jacob, Selah.

Lift up your heads, O ye gates; and be ye lifted up, ye everlasting doors; and the King of glory shall come in.

Who is this King of glory? The Lord strong and mighty, the Lord mighty in battle.

Lift up your heads, O ye gates; even lift them up, ye everlasting doors; and the King of glory shall come in.

Who is this King of glory? The Lord of hosts, he is the King of glory. Selah.

The Annunciation

(Luke 1:26-38)

And in the sixth month the angel Gabriel was sent from God unto a city of Galilee, named Nazareth,

To a virgin espoused to a man whose name was Joseph, of the house of David; and the virgin's name was Mary.

And the angel came in unto her, and said, Hail, thou that art highly favoured, the Lord is with thee: blessed art thou among women.

And when she saw him, she was troubled at his saying, and cast in her mind what manner of salutation this should be.

And the angel said unto her, Fear not, Mary: for thou hast found favour with God.

And, behold, thou shalt conceive in thy womb, and bring forth a son, and shall call his name JESUS.

He shall be great, and shall be called the Son of the Highest: and the Lord God shall give unto him the throne of his father David:

And he shall reign over the house of Jacob for ever; and of his kingdom there shall be no end.

Then said Mary unto the angel, How shall this be, seeing I know not a man?

And the angel answered and said unto her, The Holy Ghost shall come upon thee, and the power of the Highest shall overshadow thee: therefore also that holy thing which shall be born of thee shall be called the Son of God.

And behold, thy cousin Elisabeth, she hath also conceived a son in her old age: and this is the sixth month with her, who was called barren.

For with God nothing shall be impossible.

And Mary said, Behold the handmaid of the Lord; be it unto me according to thy word. And the angel departed from her.

The Birth of Christ

(Luke 2:1-20)

And it came to pass in those days, that there went out a decree from Caesar Augustus, that all the world should be taxed....

And all went to be taxed, every one into his own city.

And Joseph also went up from Galilee, out of the city of Nazareth, into Judaea, unto the city of David, which is called Bethlehem; (because he was of the house and lineage of David:)

To be taxed with Mary his espoused wife, being great with child.

And so it was, that, while they were there, the days were accomplished that she should be delivered.

And she brought forth her first-born son, and wrapped him in swaddling clothes, and laid him in a manger; because there was no room for them in the inn.

And there were in the same country shepherds abiding in the field, keeping watch over their flock by night.

And, lo, the angel of the Lord came upon them, and the glory of the Lord shone round about them: and they were sore afraid.

And the angel said unto them, Fear not: for, behold, I bring you good tidings of great joy, which shall be to all people.

For unto you is born this day in the city of David, a Saviour, which is Christ the Lord.

And this shall be a sign unto you; Ye shall find the babe wrapped in swaddling clothes, lying in a manger.

And suddenly there was with the angel a multitude of the heavenly host praising God, and saying,

Glory to God in the highest, and on earth peace, good will toward men.

And it came to pass, as the angels were gone away from them into heaven, the shepherds said one to another, Let us now go even unto Bethlehem, and see this thing which is come to pass, which the Lord hath made known unto us.

And they came with haste, and found Mary, and Joseph, and the babe lying in a manger.

And when they had seen it, they made known abroad the saying which was told them concerning this child.

And all they that heard it wondered at those things which were told them by the shepherds.

But Mary kept all these things, and pondered them in her heart.

And the shepherds returned, glorifying and praising God for all the things that they had heard and seen, as it was told unto them.

The Last Supper

(*John 13:1-34*)

Now before the feast of the passover, when Jesus knew that his hour was come that he should depart out of this world unto the Father, having loved his own which were in the world, he loved them unto the end.

And supper being ended, the devil having now put into the heart of Judas Iscariot, Simon's son, to betray him;

Jesus knowing that the Father had given all things into his hands, and that he was come from God, and went to God;

He riseth from supper, and laid aside his garments; and took a towel, and girded himself.

After that he poureth water into a bason, and began to wash the disciples' feet, and to wipe them with the towel wherewith he was girded.

Then cometh he to Simon Peter: and Peter saith unto him, Lord, dost thou wash my feet?

Jesus answered and said unto him, What I do thou knowest not now; but thou shalt know hereafter.

Peter said unto him, Thou shalt never wash my feet. Jesus answered him, If I wash thee not, thou hast no part with me.

Simon Peter saith unto him, Lord, not my feet only, but also my hands and my head.

Jesus saith to him, He that is washed needeth not save to wash his feet, but is clean every whit: and ye are clean, but not all.

For he knew who should betray him; therefore said he, Ye are not all clean.

So after he had washed their feet, and had taken his garments, and was set down again, he said unto them, Know ye what I have done to you?

Ye call me Master and Lord: and ye

say well; for so I am.

If I then, your Lord and Master, have washed your feet; ye also ought to wash one another's feet.

For I have given you an example, that ye should do as I have done to you.

Verily, verily, I say unto you, The servant is not greater than his lord; neither he that is sent greater than he that sent him.

If ye know these things, happy are ye if ye do them.

I speak not of you all: I know whom I have chosen: but that the scripture may be fulfilled, He that eateth bread with me hath lifted up his heel against me.

Now I tell you before it come, that, when it is come to pass, ye may believe that I am he.

Verily, verily, I say unto you, He that receiveth whomsoever I send receiveth me; and he that receiveth me receiveth him that sent me.

When Jesus had thus said, he was troubled in spirit, and testified, and said, Verily, verily, I say unto you, that one of you shall betray me.

Then the disciples looked one to another, doubting of whom he spake.

Now there was leaning on Jesus' bosom one of his disciples, whom Jesus loved.

Simon Peter therefore beckoned to him, that he should ask who it should be of whom he spake.

He then lying on Jesus' breast said unto him, Lord, who is it?

Jesus answered, He it is, to whom I shall give a sop, when I have dipped it. And when he had dipped the sop, he gave it to Judas Iscariot, the son of Simon.

And after the sop Satan entered into him. Then said Jesus unto him, That thou doest, do quickly.

Now no man at the table knew for what intent he spake this unto him.

For some of them thought, because Judas had the bag, that Jesus had said unto him, Buy those things that we have need of against the feast; or, that he should give something to the poor.

He then having received the sop went immediately out: and it was night.

Therefore, when he was gone out, Jesus said, Now is the Son of man glorified, and God is glorified in him.

If God be glorified in him, God shall also glorify him in himself, and shall straightway glorify him.

Little children, yet a little while I am with you. Ye shall seek me; and as I said unto the Jews, Whither I go, ye cannot come; so now I say to you.

A new commandment I give unto you. That ye love one another; as I have loved you, that ye also love one another.

Saint Augustine
(A.D. 354-430)
from *Confessions*
from BOOK I

In boyhood itself (so much less dreaded for me than youth), I loved not study, and hated to be forced to it. Yet I was forced; and this was well done towards me, but I did not well; for, unless forced, I had not learnt. But no one doth well against his will, even though what he doth, be well. Yet neither did they well who forced me, but what was well came to me from Thee, my God. For they were regardless how I should employ what they forced me to learn, except to satiate the insatiate desires of a wealthy beggary, and a shameful glory. But Thou, by whom the very hairs of our head are numbered, didst use for my good the error of all who urged me

CHRIST THE WAY MOSAIC IN MONASTERY OF ST. LUKE

to learn; and my own, who would not learn, Thou didst use for my punishment—a fit penalty for one, so small a boy and so great a sinner. So by those who did not well, Thou didst well for me; and by my own sin Thou didst justly punish me. For Thou hast commanded, and so it is, that every inordinate affection should be its own punishment.

But why did I so much hate the Greek, which I studied as a boy? I do not yet fully know. For the Latin I loved; not what my first masters, but what the so-called grammarians taught me. For those first lessons, reading, writing, and arithmetic, I thought as great a burden and penalty as any Greek. And yet whence was this too, but from the sin and vanity of this life, because I was flesh, and a breath that passeth away and cometh not again? For those first lessons were better certainly, because more certain; by them I obtained, and still retain, the power of reading what I find written, and myself writing what I will; whereas in the others, I was forced to learn the wanderings of one Aeneas, forgetful of my own, and to weep for dead Dido, because she killed herself for love; the while, with dry eyes, I endured my miserable self dying among these things, far from thee, O God my life.

For what more miserable than a miserable being who commiserates not himself; weeping the death of Dido for love to Aeneas, but weeping not his own death for want of love to Thee, O God. Thou light of my heart, Thou bread of my inmost soul, Thou power who givest vigour to my mind, who quickenest my thoughts, I love Thee not. I committed fornication against Thee, and all around me thus fornicating there echoed "Well done! well done!" for the friendship of this world is fornication against Thee; and "Well done! well done!" echoes on till one is ashamed not to be thus a man. And for all this I wept not, I who wept for Dido slain, and "seeking by the sword a stroke and wound extreme," myself seeking the while a worse extreme, the extremest and lowest of Thy creatures, having forsaken Thee, earth passing into the earth. And if forbid to read all this, I was grieved that I might not read what grieved me. Madness like this is thought a higher and a richer learning, than that by which I learned to read and write.

But now, my God, cry Thou aloud in my soul; and let Thy truth tell me, "Not so, not so. Far better was that first study." For, lo, I would readily forget the wanderings of Aeneas and all the rest, rather than how to read and write. But over the entrance of the Grammar School is a veil drawn! true; yet is this not so much an emblem of aught recondite, as a cloak of error. Let not those, whom I no longer fear, cry out against me, while I confess to Thee, my God, whatever my soul will, and acquiesce in the condemnation of my evil ways, that I may love Thy good ways. Let not either buyers or sellers of grammar-learning cry out against me. For if I question them whether it be true that Aeneas came on a time to Carthage, as the poet tells, the less learned will reply that they know not, the more learned that he never did. But should I ask with what letters the name "Aeneas" is written, every one who has learnt this will answer me aright, as to the signs which men have conventionally settled. If, again, I should ask which might be forgotten with least detriment to the concerns of life, reading and writing or these poetic fictions? who does not foresee what all must answer who have not wholly forgotten themselves? I sinned, then, when as a boy I preferred those empty to those more profitable studies, or rather loved the one and hated the other. "One and one, two"; "two and two, four"; this was to me a hateful singsong: "the wooden horse lined with armed men," and "the burning of Troy," and "Creusa's shade and sad similitude," were the choice spectacle of my vanity.

Why then did I hate the Greek classics, which have the like tales? For Homer also curiously wove the like fictions, and is most sweetly-vain, yet was he bitter to my boyish taste. And so I suppose would Virgil be to Grecian children, when forced to learn him as I was Homer. Difficulty, in truth, the difficulty of a foreign tongue, dashed, as it were, with gall all the sweetness of Grecian fable. For not one word of it did I understand, and to make me understand I was urged vehemently with cruel threats and punishments. Time was also (as an infant) I knew no Latin; but this I learned without fear or suffering, by mere observation, amid the caresses of my nursery and jests of friends, smiling and sportively encouraging me. This I learned without any pressure of punishment to urge me on, for my heart urged me to give birth to its conceptions, which I could only do by learning words not of those who taught, but of those who talked with me; in whose ears also I gave birth to the thoughts, whatever I conceived. No doubt, then, that a free curiosity has more force in our learning these things, than a frightful enforcement. Only this enforcement restrains the rovings of that freedom, through Thy laws, O my God, Thy laws, from the master's came to the martyr's trials, being able to temper for us a wholesome bitter, recalling us to Thyself from that deadly pleasure which lures us from Thee.

Hear, Lord, my prayer; let not my soul faint under Thy discipline, nor let me faint in confessing unto Thee all Thy mercies, whereby Thou hast drawn me out of all my most evil ways, that Thou mightest become a delight to me above all the allurements which I once pursued; that I may most entirely love Thee, and clasp Thy hand with all my affections, and Thou mayest yet rescue me from every temptation, even unto the end. For lo, O Lord, my King and my God, for Thy service be whatever useful thing my childhood learned; for Thy service, that I speak, write, read, reckon. For Thou didst grant me Thy discipline, while I was learning vanities; and my sin of delighting in those vanities Thou hast forgiven. In them, indeed, I learnt many a useful word, but these may as well be learned in things not vain; and that is the safe path for the steps of youth.

from BOOK II

Behold with what companions I walked the streets of Babylon, and wallowed in the mire thereof, as if in a bed of spices and precious ointments. And that I might cleave the faster to its very centre, the invisible enemy trod me down, and seduced me, for that I was easy to be seduced. Neither did the mother of my flesh (who had now fled out of the centre of Babylon, yet went more slowly in the skirts thereof), as she advised me to chastity, so heed what she had heard of me from her husband, as to restrain within the bounds of conjugal affection (if it could not be pared away to the quick) what she felt to be pestilent at present and for the future dangerous. She heeded not this, for she feared lest a wife should prove a clog and hindrance to my hopes. Not those hopes of the world to come, which my mother reposed in Thee; but the hope of learning, which both my parents were too desirous I should attain; my father, because he had next to no thought of Thee, and of me but vain conceits; my mother, because she accounted that those usual courses of learning would not only be no hindrance, but even some furtherance towards attaining Thee. For thus I conjecture, recalling, as well as I may, the disposition of my parents. The reins, meantime, were slackened to me, beyond all temper of due severity, to spend my time in sport, yea, even unto dissoluteness in whatsoever I affected. And in all was a mist, intercepting from me, O my God, the brightness of Thy truth; and mine iniquity burst out as from very fatness.

Theft is punished by Thy law, O Lord, and the law written in the hearts of men, which iniquity itself effaces not. For what thief will abide a thief? not even a rich thief, one stealing through want. Yet I lusted to thieve, and did it, compelled by no hunger, nor poverty, but through a cloyedness of well-doing, and a pamperedness of iniquity. For I stole that, of which I had enough, and much better. Nor cared I to enjoy what I stole, but joyed in the theft and sin itself. A pear tree there was near our vineyard, laden with fruit, tempting neither for colour nor taste. To shake and rob this, some lewd young fellows of us went, late one night (having according to our pestilent custom prolonged our sports in the streets till then), and took huge loads, not for our eating, but to fling to the very hogs, having only tasted them. And this, but to do what we liked only, because it was misliked. Behold my heart, O God, behold my heart, which Thou hadst pity upon in the bottom of the bottomless pit. Now, behold let my heart tell Thee what it sought there, that I should be gratuitously evil, having no temptation to ill, but the ill itself. It was foul, and I loved it; I loved to perish, I loved mine own fault, not that for which I was faulty, but my fault itself. Foul soul, falling from Thy firmament to utter destruction; not seeking aught through the shame, but the shame itself! . . .

from BOOK III

To Carthage I came, where there sang all around me in my ears a cauldron of unholy loves. I loved not yet, yet I loved to love, and out of a deep-seated want, I hated myself for wanting not. I sought what I might love, in love with loving, and safety I hated, and a way without snares. For within me was a famine of that inward food, Thyself, my God; yet, through that famine I was not hungered; but was without all longing for incorruptible sustenance, not because filled therewith, but the more empty, the more I loathed it. For this cause my soul was sickly and full of sores, it miserably cast itself forth, desiring to be scraped by the touch of objects of sense. Yet if these had not a soul, they would not be objects of love. To love then, and to be beloved, was sweet to me; but more, when I obtained to enjoy the person I loved I defiled, therefore, the spring of friendship with the filth of concupiscence, and I beclouded its brightness with the hell of lustfulness; and thus foul and unseemly, I would fain, through exceeding vanity, be fine and courtly. I fell headlong then into the love wherein I longed to be ensnared. My God, my Mercy, with how much fall didst Thou out of Thy great goodness besprinkle for me that sweetness? For I was both beloved, and secretly arrived at the bond of enjoying; and was with joy fettered with sorrow-bringing bonds, that I might be scourged with the iron burning rods of jealousy, and suspicions, and fears, and angers, and quarrels.

Stage-plays also carried me away, full of images of my miseries, and of fuel to my fire. Why is it, that man desires to be made sad, beholding doleful and tragical things, which yet himself would by no means suffer? yet he desires as a spectator to feel sorrow at them, and this very sorrow is his pleasure. What is this but miserable madness? for a man is the more affected with these actions, the less free he is from such affections. Howsoever, when he suffers in his own person, it uses to be styled misery: when he compassionates others, then it is mercy. But what sort of compassion is this for feigned and scenical passions? for the auditor is not called on to relieve, but only to grieve: and he applauds the actor of these fictions the more, the more he grieves. And if the calamities of those persons (whether of old times, or mere fiction) be so acted, that the spectator is not moved to tears, he goes away disgusted and criticising; but if he be moved to passion, he stays intent, and weeps for joy.

(Translated by Edward B. Pusey)

from *Beowulf*
(ca. 8th Century)

Beowulf is one of the best-known poems written in Old English. Scholars conjecture that it was written sometime during the eighth century, although it deals with a much earlier period in Germanic history. Weaving a curious mixture of Christianity and paganism, Beowulf was probably either transcribed by a monk who inserted the Christian elements, or else it was written by a Christian who occasionally neglected his assumed pagan point of view.

Beowulf gives an exciting picture of sixth-century Scandinavian warriors and the bravery of the Anglo-Saxon lord and his comitatus (warrior band). There are two parts to the story: the first deals with Beowulf's valor as a young man, and the second tells of his old age and death.

The hero of the poem, Beowulf, is a Geat, who is living in South Sweden when he hears of the crimes of Grendel. Grendel is a sea-monster who is ravaging Heorot, the hall of the Danish king, Hrothgar. Beowulf sets out with a small band of men and has two battles: first he fights with Grendel in the hall; then he encounters Grendel's mother in her sea lair. The following excerpts tell about the first encounter Beowulf has with the monster Grendel. Beowulf emerges from the battles victorious and returns home. Eventually he becomes king of the Geats. Some fifty years later, he fights a fire-breathing dragon that is threatening his kingdom. Beowulf is mortally wounded as he destroys the dragon. The story of his funeral ends the poem.

Grendel invades Heorot and kills a Geat. Beowulf attacks the monster.

From the stretching moors, from the misty hollows,
Grendel came creeping, accursed of God,
A murderous ravager minded to snare
Spoil of heroes in high-built hall.
Under clouded heavens he held his way
Till there rose before him the high-roofed house,
Wine-hall of warriors gleaming with gold.
Nor was it the first of his fierce assaults
On the home of Hrothgar; but never before
Had he found worse fate or hardier hall-thanes!
Storming the building he burst the portal,
Though fastened of iron, with fiendish strength;
Forced open the entrance in savage fury
And rushed in rage o'er the shining floor.
A baleful glare from his eyes was gleaming
Most like to a flame. He found in the hall
Many a warrior sealed in slumber,
A host of kinsmen. His heart rejoiced;
The savage monster was minded to sever
Lives from bodies ere break of day,
To feast his fill of the flesh of men.
But he was not fated to glut his greed
With more of mankind when the night was ended!
The hardy kinsman of Hygelac waited

To see how the monster would make his attack.
The demon delayed not, but quickly clutched
A sleeping thane in his swift assault,
Tore him in pieces, bit through the bones,
Gulped the blood, and gobbled the flesh,
Greedily gorged on the lifeless corpse,
The hands and the feet. Then the fiend stepped nearer,
Sprang on the Sea-Geat lying outstretched,
Clasping him close with his monstrous claw.
But Beowulf grappled and gripped him hard,
Struggled up on his elbow; the shepherd of sins
Soon found that never before had he felt
In any man other in all the earth
A mightier hand-grip; his mood was humbled,
His courage fled; but he found no escape!
He was fain to be gone; he would flee into the darkness,
The fellowship of devils. Far different his fate
From that which befell him in former days!
The hardy hero, Hygelac's kinsman,
Remembered the boast he had made at the banquet;
He sprang to his feet, clutched Grendel fast,
Though fingers were cracking, the fiend pulling free.
The earl pressed after; the monster was minded
To win his freedom and flee to the fens.
He knew that his fingers were fast in the grip
Of a savage foe. Sorry the venture,
The raid that the ravager made on the hall.
> There was din in Heorot. For all the Danes,
The city-dwellers, the stalwart Scyldings,
That was a bitter spilling of beer!
The walls resounded, the fight was fierce,
Savage the strife as the warriors struggled.
The wonder was that the lofty wine-hall
Withstood the struggle, nor crashed to earth,
The house so fair; it was firmly fastened
Within and without with iron bands
Cunningly smithied; though men have said
That many a mead-bench gleaming with gold
Sprang from its sill as the warriors strove.
The Scylding wise men had never weened
That any ravage could wreck the building,
Firmly fashioned and finished with bone,
Or any cunning compass its fall,
Till the time when the swelter and surge of fire
Should swallow it up in a swirl of flame.
> Continuous tumult filled the hall;
A terror fell on the Danish folk
As they heard through the wall the horrible wailing.
The groans of Grendel, the foe of God
Howling his hideous hymn of pain,
The hell-thane shrieking in sore defeat.
He was fast in the grip of the man who was greatest
Of mortal men in the strength of his might,
Who would never rest while the wretch was living,
Counting his life-days a menace to man.

Beowulf rips out Grendel's arm and wins the fight. The monster, mortally wounded, escapes to the fen.

> Many an earl of Beowulf brandished
His ancient iron to guard his lord,
To shelter safely the peerless prince.
They had no knowledge, those daring thanes,
When they drew their weapons to hack and hew,
To thrust to the heart, that the

sharpest sword,
The choicest iron in all the world,
Could work no harm to the hideous foe.
On every sword he had laid a spell,
On every blade; but a bitter death
Was to be his fate; far was the journey
The monster made to the home of fiends.
 Then he who had wrought such wrong to men,
With grim delight as he warred with God,
Soon found that his strength was feeble and failing
In the crushing hold of Hygelac's thane.
Each loathed the other while life should last!
There Grendel suffered a grievous hurt,
A wound in the shoulder, gaping and wide;
Sinews snapped and bone-joints broke,
And Beowulf gained the glory of battle.
Grendel, fated, fled to the fens,
To his joyless dwelling, sick unto death.
He knew in his heart that his hours were numbered,
His days at an end. For all the Danes
Their wish was fulfilled in the fall of Grendel.
The stranger from far, the stalwart and strong,
Had purged of evil the hall of Hrothgar,
And cleansed of crime; the heart of the hero
Joyed in the deed his daring had done.
The lord of the Geats made good to the East-Danes
The boast he had uttered; he ended their ill,
And all the sorrow they suffered long
And needs must suffer—a foul offense.
The token was clear when the bold in battle
Laid down the shoulder and dripping claw—
Grendel's arm—in the gabled hall!

Rejoicing of the Danes. They go to follow the track of the fleeing Grendel. On their return to the Hall of the Hart, they listen to the tales of the bard.

When the morning came, as they tell the tale,
Many a warrior hastened to hall,
Folk-leaders faring from far and near
Over wide-running ways, to gaze and wonder,
The trail of the demon. Nor seemed his death
A matter of sorrow to any man
Who viewed the tracks of the vanquished monster
As he slunk weary-hearted away from the hall,
Doomed and defeated and marking his flight
With bloody prints to the nicors' pool.
The crimson currents bubbled and heaved
In eddying reaches reddened with gore;
The surges boiled with the fiery blood.
But the monster had sunk from sight of men.
In that fenny covert the cursed fiend
Not long thereafter laid down his life,
His heathen spirit; and hell received him.
 Then all the comrades, the old and young,
The brave of heart, in a blithesome band
Came riding their horses home from the mere.
Beowulf's prowess was praised in song;
And many men stated that south or north,
Over all the world, or between the seas,
Or under the heaven, no hero was greater,
More worthy of rule. But no whit they slighted
The gracious Hrothgar, their good old king.
Time and again they galloped their horses,
Racing their roans where the roads seemed fairest;
Time and again a gleeman chanted,
A ministrel mindful of saga and lay.
He wove his words in a winsome pattern,
Hymning the burden of Beowulf's feat,
Clothing the story in skilful verse.

(Translated by Charles W. Kennedy)

from *The Song of Roland*

The most important Old French epic poem, The Song of Roland, is based on a song in celebration of an engagement between Charlemagne and the Basques in 778. By the eleventh century the story has assumed epic proportions. The hero, Roland, has come to be typical for his bravery, his friend Olivier for his wisdom, and Ganelon for his treachery. In the epic, Roland is attacked by the Saracen king on the advice of Ganelon. Roland refuses to summon aid until too late to save himself and his army. Then he blows his horn and Charlemagne comes to the rescue and punishes Ganelon and the Moors. The passage below is the conclusion of the first half of the poem.

When Roland saw that life had fled
And with face to earth his comrade dead,
He thus bewept him, soft and still:
"Ah, friend, thy prowess wrought thee ill!
So many days and years gone by
We lived together, thou and I:
And thou hast never done me wrong,
Nor I to thee, our lifetime long.
Since thou art dead, to live is pain."
He swooned on Veillantif again,
Yet may not unto earth be cast,
His golden stirrups held him fast.

When passed away had Roland's swoon,
With sense restored, he saw full soon
What ruin lay beneath his view.
His Franks have perished all save two—
The archbishop and Walter of Hum alone.
From the mountain-side hath Walter flown,
Where he met in battle the bands of Spain,
And the heathen won and his men were slain.
In his own despite to the vale he came;
Called unto Roland, his aid to claim.
"Ah, count! brave gentleman, gallant peer!
Where art thou? With thee I know not fear.
I am Walter, who vanquished Maelgut of yore,
Nephew to Drouin, the old and hoar.
For knightly deeds I was once thy friend.
I fought the Saracen to the end;
My lance is shivered, my shield is cleft,
Of my broken mail are but fragments left.
I bear in my body eight thrusts of spear;
I die, but I sold my life right dear."
Count Roland heard as he spake the word,
Pricked his steed, and anear him spurred.

"Walter," said Roland, "thou hadst affray
With the Saracen foe on the heights today.
Thou wert wont a valorous knight to be:
A thousand horsemen gave I to thee;
Render them back, for my need is sore."
"Alas, thou seest them never more!
Stretched they lie on the dolorous ground,
Where myriad Saracen swarms we found,—
Armenians, Turks, and the giant brood
Of Balisa, famous for hardihood,
Bestriding their Arab coursers fleet,
Such host in battle 'twas ours to meet;
Not vaunting thence shall the heathen go,—
Full sixty thousand on earth lie low.
With our brands of steel we avenged us well,
But every Frank by the foeman fell.
My hauberk plates are riven wide,
And I bear such wounds in flank and side,
That from every part the bright blood flows,
And feebler ever my body grows.
I am dying fast, I am well aware:
Thy liegeman I, and claim thy care.
If I fled perforce, thou wilt forgive
And yield me succor while thou dost live."
Roland sweated with wrath and pain,
Tore the skirts of his vest in twain,
Bound Walter's every bleeding vein.

In Roland's sorrow his wrath arose,
Hotly he stuck at the heathen foes,

TOWERS OF CARCASSONNE, IN SOUTHERN FRANCE

Nor left he one of a score alive;
Walter slew six, the archbishop five.
The heathens cry, "What a felon three!
Look to it, lords, that they shall not flee.
Dastard is he who confronts them not;
Craven, who lets them depart this spot."
Their cries and shoutings begin once more,
And from every side on the Franks they pour.
Count Roland in sooth is a noble peer;
Count Walter, a valorous cavalier;
The archbishop, in battle proved and tried,
Each struck as if knight there were none beside.
From their steeds a thousand Saracens leap,
Yet forty thousand their saddles keep;
I trow they dare not approach them near,
But they hurl against them lance and spear,
Pike and javelin, shaft and dart.
Walter is slain as the missiles part;
The archbishop's shield in pieces shred,
Riven his helm, and pierced his head;
His corselet of steel they rent and tore;
Wounded his body with lances four;
His steed beneath him dropped withal:
What woe to see the archbishop fall!

When Turpin felt him flung to ground,
And four lance wounds within him found,
He swiftly rose, the dauntless man,
To Roland looked, and nigh him ran.
Spake but, "I am not overthrown—
Brave warrior yields with life alone."
He drew Almace's burnished steel,
A thousand ruthless blows to deal.
In after time, the Emperor said
He found four hundred around him spread,—
Some wounded, others cleft in twain;
Some lying headless on the plain.
So Giles the saint, who saw it, tells,
From whom High God wrought miracles.
In Laon cell the scroll he wrote;
He little weets who knows it not.

Count Roland combateth nobly yet,
His body burning and bathed in sweat;
In his brow a mighty pain, since first,
When his horn he sounded, his temple burst;
But he yearns of Karl's approach to know,
And lifts his horn once more—but oh!
How faint and feeble a note to blow!
The Emperor listened, and stood full still.
"My lords," he said, "we are faring ill.
This day is Roland my nephew's last;
Like dying man he winds that blast.
On! Who would aid, for life must press.
Sound every trump our ranks possess."
Peal sixty thousand clarions high,
The hills re-echo, the vales reply.
It is now no jest for the heathen band.
"Karl!" they cry, "it is Karl at hand!"

They said, " 'Tis the Emperor's advance,
We hear the trumpets resound of France.
If he assail us, hope in vain;
If Roland live, 'tis war again,
And we lose for aye the land of Spain."
Four hundred in arms together they drew,
The bravest of the heathen crew;
With serried power they on him press,
And dire in sooth is the count's distress.

When Roland saw his coming foes,
All proud and stern his spirit rose;
Alive he shall never be brought to yield:
Veillantif spurred he across the field,
With golden spurs he pricked him well,
To break the ranks of the infidel;
Archbishop Turpin by his side.
"Let us flee, and save us," the heathen cried;
"These are the trumpets of France we hear—
It is Karl, the mighty Emperor, near."

Count Roland never hath loved the base,
Nor the proud of heart, nor the dastard race,—
Nor knight, but if he were vassal good,—

And he spake to Turpin, as there he stood;
"On foot are you, on horseback I;
For your love I halt, and stand you by.
Together for good and ill we hold;
I will not leave you for man of mold.
We will pay the heathen their onset back,
Nor shall Durindana of blows be slack."
"Base," said Turpin, "Who spares to smite;
When the Emperor comes, he will all requite."

The heathens said, "We were born to shame.
This day for our disaster came:
Our lords and leaders in battle lost,
And Karl at hand with his marshaled host;
We hear the trumpets of France ring out,
And the cry 'Montjoie!' their rallying shout.
Roland's pride is of such a height,
Not to be vanquished by mortal wight;
Hurl we our missiles, and hold aloof."
And the word they spake, they put in proof,—
They flung, with all their strength and craft,
Javelin, barb, and plumed shaft.
Roland's buckler was torn and frayed,
His cuirass broken and disarrayed,
Yet entrance none to his flesh they made.
From thirty wounds Veillantif bled,
Beneath his rider they cast him, dead;
Then from the field have the heathen flown:
Roland remaineth, on foot, alone.

The heathens fly in rage and dread;
To the land of Spain have their footsteps sped;
Nor can Count Roland make pursuit—
Slain is his steed, and he rests afoot;
To succor Turpin he turned in haste,
The golden helm from his head unlaced,
Ungirt the corselet from his breast,
In stripes divided his silken vest;
The archbishop's wounds hath he staunched and bound,
His arms around him softly wound;
On the green sward gently his body laid,
And, with tender greeting, thus him prayed:
"For a little space, let me take farewell;
Our dear companions, who round us fell,
I go to seek; if I haply find,
I will place them at thy feet reclined."
"Go," said Turpin; "the field is thine—
To God the glory, 'tis thine and mine."

Alone seeks Roland the field of fight,
He searcheth vale, he searcheth height.
Ivon and Ivor he found, laid low,
And the Gascon Engelier of Bordeaux,
Gerein and his fellow in arms, Gerier;
Otho he found, and Berengier;
Samson the duke, and Anseis bold,
Gerard of Roussillon, the old.
Their bodies, one after one, he bore,
And laid them Turpin's feet before.
The archbishop saw them stretched arow,
Nor can he hinder the tears that flow;
In benediction his hands he spread:
"Alas! for your doom, my lords," he said,
"That God in mercy your souls may give,
On the flowers of Paradise to live;
Mine own death comes, with anguish sore
That I see mine Emperor never more."

Once more to the field doth Roland wend,
Till he findeth Olivier, his friend;
The lifeless form to his heart he strained,
Bore him back with what strength remained,
On a buckler laid him beside the rest,
The archbishop assoiled them all, and blessed.
Their dole and pity anew find vent,
And Roland maketh his fond lament:
"My Olivier, my chosen one,
Thou wert the noble Duke Renier's son,
Lord of the March unto River vale.
To shiver lance and shatter mail,
The brave in council to guide and cheer,

To smite the miscreant foe with fear,—
Was never on earth such cavalier."

Dead around him his peers to see,
And the man he loved so tenderly,
Fast the tears of Count Roland ran,
His visage discolored became, and wan,
He swooned for sorrow beyond control.
"Alas," said Turpin, "how great thy dole!"

To look on Roland swooning there,
Surpassed all sorrow he ever bare;
He stretched his hand, the horn he took,—
Through Roncesvalles there flowed a brook,—
A draught to Roland he thought to bring;
But his steps were feeble and tottering,
Spent his strength, from waste of blood,—
He struggled on for scarce a rood,
When sank his heart, and dropped his frame,
And his mortal anguish on him came.

Roland revived from his swoon again;
On his feet he rose, but in deadly pain;
He looked on high, and he looked below,
Till, a space his other companions fro,
He beheld the baron, stretched on sward,
The archbishop, vicar of God our Lord.
Mea Culpa was Turpin's cry,
While he raised his hands to heaven on high,
Imploring Paradise to gain.
So died the soldier of Carlemaine,—
With word or weapon, to preach or fight,
A champion ever of Christian right,
And a deadly foe to the infidel.
God's benediction within him dwell!

When Roland saw him stark on earth
(His very vitals were bursting forth,
And his brain was oozing from out his head),
He took the fair white hands outspread,
Crossed and clasped them upon his breast,
And thus plaint to the dead addressed,—

So did his country's law ordain:—
"Ah, gentleman of noble strain,
I trust thee unto God the True,
Whose service never man shall do
With more devoted heart and mind:
To guard the faith, to win mankind,
From the apostles' day till now,
Such prophet never rose as thou.
Nor pain or torment thy soul await,
But of Paradise the open gate."

Roland feeleth his death is near,
His brain is oozing by either ear.
For his peers he prayed—God keep them well;
Invoked the angel Gabriel.
That none reproach him, his horn he clasped;
His other hand Durindana grasped;
Then, far as quarrel from crossbow sent,
Across the march of Spain he went,
Where, on a mound, two trees between,
Four flights of marble steps were seen;
Backward he fell, on the field to lie;
And he swooned anon, for the end was nigh.

High were the mountains and high the trees,
Bright shone the marble terraces;
On the green grass Roland hath swooned away.
A Saracen spied him where he lay:
Stretched with the rest he had feigned him dead,
His face and body with blood bespread.
To his feet he sprang, and in haste he hied,—
In pride and wrath he was overbold,—
And on Roland, body and arms, laid hold.
"The nephew of Karl is overthrown!
To Araby bear I this sword, mine own."
He stooped to grasp it, but as he drew,
Roland returned to his sense anew.

He saw the Saracen seize his sword;

His eyes he oped, and he spake one word—
"Thou are not one of our band, I trow,"
And he clutched the horn he would ne'er forego;
On the golden crest he smote him full,
Shattering steel and bone and skull,
Forth from his head his eyes he beat,
And cast him lifeless before his feet.
"Miscreant, makest thou then so free,
As, right or wrong, to lay hold on me?
Who hears it will deem thee a madman born;
Behold the mouth of mine ivory horn
Broken for thee, and the gems and gold
Around its rim to earth are rolled."

Roland feeleth his eyesight reft,
Yet he stands erect with what strength is left;
From his bloodless cheek is the hue dispelled,
But his Durindana all bare he held.
In front a dark brown rock arose—
He smote upon it ten grievous blows.
Grated the steel as it struck the flint,
Yet it brake not, nor bore its edge one dint.
"Mary, Mother, be thou mine aid!
Ah, Durindana, my ill-starred blade,
I may no longer thy guardian be!
What fields of battle I won with thee!
What realms and regions 'twas ours to gain,
Now the lordship of Carlemaine!
Never shalt thou possessor know
Who would turn from face of mortal foe;
A gallant vassal so long thee bore,
Such as France the free shall know no more."

He smote anew on the marble stair,
It grated, but breach nor notch was there.
When Roland found that it would not break,
Thus began he his plaint to make.
"Ah, Durindana, how fair and bright
Thou sparklest, flaming against the light!

When Karl in Maurienne valley lay,
God sent his angel from heaven to say—
'This sword shall a valorous captain's be,'
And he girt it, the gentle king, on me.
With it I vanquished Poitou and Maine,
Provence I conquered and Aquitaine;
I conquered Normandy the free,
Anjou, and the marches of Brittany;
Romagna I won, and Lombardy,
Bavaris, Flanders from side to side,
And Burgundy, and Poland wide;
Constantinople affiance vowed,
And the Saxon soil to his bidding bowed;
Scotia, and Wales, and Ireland's plain,
Of England made he his own domain.
What mighty regions I won of old,
For the hoary-headed Karl to hold!
But there presses on me a grievous pain,
Lest thou in heathen hands remain.
O God our Father, keep France from stain!"

His strokes once more on the brown rock fell,
And the steel was bent past words to tell;
Yet it brake not, nor was notched the grain,
Erect it leaped to the sky again.
When he failed at the last to break his blade,
His lamentation he inly made.
"Oh, fair and holy, my peerless sword,
What relics lie in the pommel stored!
Tooth of Saint Peter, Saint Basil's blood,
Hair of Saint Denis beside them strewed,
Fragment of holy Mary's vest.
'Twere shame that thou with the heathen rest;
Thee should the hand of a Christian serve,
One who would never in battle swerve.
What regions won I with thee of yore,
The empire now of Karl the hoar!
Rich and mighty is he therefore."

That death was on him he knew full well;
Down from his head to his heart it fell.
On the grass beneath a pine-tree's shade,

With face to earth, his form he laid,
Beneath him placed he his horn and sword,
And turned his face to the heathen horde.
Thus hath he done the sooth to show,
That Karl and his warriors all may know,
That the gentle count a conqueror died,
Mea Culpa full oft he cried;
And, for all his sins, unto God above,
In sign of penance, he raised his glove.

Roland feeleth his hour at hand;
On a knoll he lies towards the Spanish land.
With one hand beats he upon his breast:
"In thy sight, O God, be my sins confessed.
From my hour of birth, both the great and small,
Down to this day, I repent of all."
As his glove he raised to God on high,
Angels of heaven descend him nigh.

Beneath a pine was his resting-place,
To the land of Spain hath he turned his face,
On his memory rose full many a thought—
Of the lands he won and the fields he fought;
Of his gentle France, of his kin and line;
Of his nursing father, King Karl benign;—
He may not the tear and sob control,
Nor yet forgets he his parting soul.
To God's compassion he makes his cry:
"O Father true, who canst not lie,
Who didst Lazarus raise unto life again,
And Daniel shield in the lions' den;
Shield my soul from its peril, due
For the sins I sinned my lifetime through."
He did his right-hand glove uplift—
Saint Gabriel took from his hand the gift;
Then drooped his head upon his breast,
And with clasped hands he went to rest.
God from on high sent down to him
One of his angel Cherubim—
Saint Michael of Peril of the sea,
Saint Gabriel in company—
From heaven they came for that soul of price,
And they bore it with them to Paradise.

(Translated by John O'Hagan)

Te Deum

The Te Deum—from the Latin Te Deum Laudamus, *"We Praise Thee, O God," originally an Ambrosian chant or plain song, goes back at least to the fifth century. Since that time it has been used in the Western church in morning services and as a festival hymn. The text was probably written by Nicetas of Remesiana. It has been set to music by many composers, including Palestrina, Purcell, De Lalande, Handel, Berlioz, Bruckner, Verdi, and Sullivan. Bach used the plain song melody in one of his choral preludes.*

Thee, Sovereign God, our grateful accents praise;
We own thee Lord, and bless thy wondrous ways;
To thee, Eternal Father, earth's whole frame,
With loudest trumpets, sounds immortal fame.

Lord God of Hosts! for thee the heavenly powers
With sounding anthems fill the vaulted towers.
Thy Cherubims thrice, Holy, Holy, Holy, cry:
Thrice, Holy, all the Seraphims reply,
And thrice returning echoes endless songs supply.
Both heaven and earth thy majesty display;
They owe their beauty to thy glorious ray.
Thy praises fill the loud apostles' choir;
The train of prophets in the song conspire.
Legions of martyrs in the chorus shine,
And vocal blood with vocal music join.
By these thy church, inspir'd by heavenly art,
Around the world maintains a second part;
And tunes her sweetest notes, O God, to thee,
The Father of unbounded majesty;
The Son, ador'd copartner of thy seat,
And equal everlasting Paraclete.
Thou King of Glory, Christ, of the most high,
Thou coeternal filial Deity;
Thou who, to save the world's impending doom,
Vouchsaf'dst to dwell within a Virgin's womb;
Old tyrant Death disarm'd, before thee flew
The bolts of heaven, and back the foldings drew,
To give access, and make thy faithful way;
From God's right hand thy filial beams display.
Thou art to judge the living and the dead;
Then spare those souls for whom thy veins have
    bled.
O take us up among thy blest above,
To share with them thy everlasting love.
Preserve, O Lord, thy people, and enhance
Thy blessing on thine own inheritance.
For ever raise their hearts, and rule their ways;
Each day we bless thee, and proclaim thy praise:
No age shall fail to celebrate thy name,
No hour neglect thy everlasting fame.
Preserve our souls, O Lord, this day from ill;
Have mercy on us, Lord, have mercy still:
As we have hop'd, do thou reward our pain;
We've hoped in thee—let not our hope be vain.
        (Translated by John Dryden)

Saint Francis of Assisi
(ca. 1182-1226)
from *Little Flowers*
CHAPTER XXI

Of the most holy miracle which St. Francis wrought when he converted the very fierce wolf of Agobio.

During the time that St. Francis dwelt in the city of Agobio, there appeared in the territory of Agobio a very great wolf, terrible and fierce, the which not only devoured animals but also men and women, so that all the citizens stood in great fear, because ofttimes he came nigh unto the city; and all men went armed when they went forth from the city, as if they were going to battle; and therewithal they were not able to defend themselves from him, when haply any man encountered him alone; and for dread of this wolf things came to such a pass that no one dared to leave the city. Wherefore, St. Francis, having compassion on the men of the city, was minded to go forth to meet this wolf, albeit the citizens altogether counselled him not to do so; and, making the sign of the cross, he went forth from the city with his companions, putting all his trust in God. And because the others feared to go farther, St. Francis alone took the road toward the place where the wolf was. And lo! while many citizens who had come out to behold this miracle were looking on, the said wolf made at St. Francis with open mouth. Whereupon St. Francis advanced toward him, and making over him the sign of the most holy Cross, called him unto him and spake to him after this manner. "Come hither, friar wolf, I command thee in Christ's name that thou do no harm to me nor to any other." O marvelous thing! Scarcely had St. Francis made the sign of the cross than the terrible wolf instantly closed his mouth and stayed his running; and, in obedience to that command, came gentle as a lamb, and laid himself down at the feet of St. Francis. Then St. Francis spake unto him thus: "Friar wolf, thou dost much damage in these parts, and thou hast committed great crimes, destroying and slaying the creatures of God without His license; and not only hast thou slain and devoured beasts, but thou hast also had the hardihood to slay men, made in the image of God; for the which cause thou dost merit the gallows as a thief and most iniquitous murderer; and all men cry out against thee and complain, and all this city is thine enemy. But I desire, friar wolf, to make peace between thee and them; to the end that thou mayest no more offend them and that they may forgive thee all thy past offences and neither men nor dogs may pursue thee any more." At these words, the wolf, by movements of his body and tail and eyes, and by bowing his head, showed that he accepted that which St. Francis said and was minded to observe the same. Thereupon St. Francis spake unto him again, saying: "Friar wolf, inasmuch as it seemeth good unto thee to make and keep this peace, I promise thee that, so long as thou shalt live, I will cause thy food to be given thee continually by the men of the city, so that thou shalt no more suffer hunger; for I know full well that whatever of evil thou hast done, thou hast done it through hunger. But seeing that I beg for thee this grace, I desire, friar wolf, that thou shouldst promise me that never from henceforward wilt thou injure any human being or any animal. Dost thou promise me this?" And the wolf, by bowing its head, gave evident token that he promised it. And St. Francis said: "Friar wolf, I desire that thou swear me fealty touching this promise, to the end that I may trust thee utterly." Then St. Francis held forth his hand to receive his fealty, and the wolf

GIOTTO: *Saint Francis' Sermon to the Birds*, IN THE BASILICA DI SAN FRANCESCO IN ASSISI

lifted up his right fore-foot and put it with friendly confidence in the hand of St. Francis, giving thereby such token of fealty as he was able. Thereupon St. Francis said: "Friar wolf, I command thee in the name of Jesus Christ to come now with me, nothing doubting, and let us go and stablish this peace in the name of God." And the wolf went with him obediently, like a gentle lamb; wherefore the citizens beholding the same marveled greatly. And anon, the fame thereof was noised abroad through all the city, and all the people, men and women, great and small, young and old, thronged to the piazza to see the wolf with St. Francis. And when all the folk were gathered together, St. Francis rose up to preach unto them, saying, among other things, how, by reason of sin, God permits such pestilences; and far more perilous is the fire of Hell, the which must forever torment the damned, than is the fury of a wolf which can only kill the body; how much then are the jaws of Hell to be feared when the jaws of a little beast can hold so great a multitude in fear? "Turn ye then, most dear ones, turn ye to God, and do befitting penance for your sins, and God will save you from the wolf in this present world and from the fire of Hell in that which is to come." And when he had done preaching, St. Francis said: "Hear ye, my brethren. Friar wolf, who is here before you, hath promised and sworn fealty to me, that he will make peace with you and never more offend you in anything; do ye now promise him to give him every day that whereof he hath need; and I become surety unto you for him that he will faithfully observe this covenant of peace." Then all the people with one voice promised to provide him food continually, and St. Francis spake unto the wolf before them all, saying: "And thou, friar wolf, dost promise to observe the covenant of peace which thou hast made with this folk, that thou wilt offend neither men nor beasts nor any creature?" And the wolf kneeled him down and bowed his head, and, with gentle movements of his body and tail and ears, showed as far as he was able his determination to keep that covenant wholly. Said St. Francis: "Friar wolf, as thou didst me fealty touching this promise, without the gate, so now I desire that thou do me fealty, before all the people, touching thy promise, and that thou wilt not deceive me concerning my promise and surety which I have given for thee." Then the wolf, lifting up its right foot, put it in the hand of St. Francis. By which act, and by the other acts aforesaid, all the people were fulfilled with so great joy and wonder, alike for devotion toward the saint, and for the strangeness of the miracle, and for the peace with the wolf, that they all began to shout to Heaven, praising and blessing God who had sent them St. Francis, who, by his merits, had freed them from the jaws of the cruel beast. And thereafter, the said wolf lived two years in Agobio, and entered familiarly into the houses, going from door to door, neither doing injury to any one nor receiving any; and he was courteously nourished by the people; and, as he thus went through the town and through the houses, never did any dog bark after him. Finally, after two years, friar wolf died of old age, whereat the citizens lamented much, because as long as they saw him going so gently through their city, they recalled the better the virtue and sanctity of St. Francis.

Thomas of Celano
(ca. 1200-1255)
Dies Irae

Hear'st thou, my soul, what serious things
Both the Psalm and Sibyl sings

Of a sure Judge, from whose sharp ray
The world in flames shall fly away!

O that fire! before whose face
Heaven and earth shall find no place:
O those Eyes! whose angry light
Must be the day of that dread night.

O that trump! whose blast shall run
An even round with th' circling sun,
And urge the murmuring graves to bring
Pale mankind forth to meet his King.

Horror of Nature, Hell, and Death!
When a deep groan from beneath
Shall cry, "We come, we come!" and all
The caves of night answer one call.

O that book! whose leaves so bright
Will set the world in severe light.
O that judge! whose hand, whose eye
None can endure, yet none can fly.

Ah then, poor soul! what wilt thou say?
And to what patron choose to pray,
When stars themselves shall stagger, and
The most firm foot no more shall stand?

But Thou giv'st leave, dread Lord, that we
Take shelter from Thyself in Thee;
And with the wings of Thine own dove
Fly to Thy scepter of soft love!

Dear Lord, remember in that day
Who was the cause Thou cam'st this way;
Thy sheep was strayed, and Thou wouldst be
Even lost Thyself in seeking me!

Shall all that labor, all that cost
Of love, and even that loss, be lost?
And this loved soul judged worth no less
Than all that way and weariness?

Just mercy, then, Thy reck'ning be
With my price, and not with me;
'Twas paid at first with too much pain
To be paid twice, or once in vain.

Mercy, my Judge, mercy I cry,
With blushing cheek and bleeding eye;
The conscious colors of my sin
Are red without, and pale within.

O let Thine own soft bowels pay
Thyself, and so discharge that day!
If Sin can sigh, Love can forgive,
O, say the word, my soul shall live!

Those mercies which Thy Mary found,
Or who Thy cross confess'd and crowned,
Hope tells my heart the same loves be
Still alive, and still for me.

Though both my prayers and tears combine,
Both worthless are, for they are mine;
But Thou Thy bounteous self still be,
And show Thou art by saving me.

O when Thy last frown shall proclaim
The flocks of goats to folds of flame,
And all Thy lost sheep found shall be,
Let "Come ye blessed!" then call me!

When the dread "ITE" shall divide
Those limbs of death from Thy left side,
Let those life-speaking lips command
That I inherit Thy right hand!

O, hear a suppliant heart all crush'd,
And crumbled into contrite dust!
My hope, my fear—my Judge, my Friend!
Take charge of me, and of my end!

(Translated by Richard Crashaw)

Dante Alighieri
(1265-1321)
Five Cantos from
the *Inferno*
from the *Divine Comedy*

In a recent article commemorating the seven hundredth anniversary of the birth of the Italian poet Dante, Time *says, "For seven centuries* La Commedia, *which in 14,233 lines of lordly language describes the poet's descent into hell and ascent into heaven through the refining fires of purgatory, has been widely considered the greatest poem ever composed; and its author has been virtually deified by the critics. T.S. Eliot pronounced him 'the most universal of poets in the modern languages,' and added: 'Shakespeare gives the greatest width of human passion; Dante the greatest depth. They divide the modern world between them; there is no third.'"*

Dante's great poem, an epic in size and scope if not in certain technical respects, is divided into three large sections or canticles—Hell or the Inferno, Purgatory, *and* Paradise. *Each contains thirty-three cantos or short poetic chapters, and there is an extra one in the* Inferno *by way of introduction; thus the total comes to one hundred cantos. These numbers, plus many others that appear in one way or another in the poem—usually based on three, seven, nine, or ten—have symbolic significance. But surprisingly, in spite of numerology and the mathematical logic of the poem's structure, it does not seem mechanical or burdened with symbolism. In fact, it contains numerous episodes that are more concrete in their imagery and intense in their emotional impact—even when dealing with angels, devils, and monsters—than are most contemporary novels.*

On its simplest level, the Divine Comedy *is a straightforward account of a journey which the poet takes through Hell, where are found the unrepentant sinners; then through Purgatory, where the penitent gladly accept their penance; and finally into Paradise, where Dante has a beatific vision of redeemed souls dwelling with God and the angels. This is on the simplest level; on others, the poem is rich in theological, political, moral, and other implications, which will yield themselves to the reader who uses insight and a good set of notes. Two points are most important: first, the* Comedy *is a poem, not a theological atlas; Dante did not believe for a moment that Hell is literally a cone-shaped pit under the surface of the earth, or that Purgatory is a terraced mountain situated at the South Pole. Second, the poem is among other things an allegory of this life—of what happens to people who are incapable of penitence, or who have begun the process of spiritual cleansing through repentance, or who have attained a measure of godliness here on earth.*

In the Inferno *or Hell, five cantos of which are included in this anthology, Dante is guided by the spirit of the Roman poet Virgil—here symbolizing human reason—through the abodes of the self-damned. Dante imagines Hell as a vast cone-shaped region with the tip at the center of the globe. Circular terraces line the inside of the cone, each smaller in circumference but more terrible in the symbolic torments that it metes out than the one above. At the center, waist-deep in a lake of ice, is Satan, the ultimate figure of ignorance, impotence, and hatred.*

The Inferno *is available in many translations, including several fine ones by such modern poets as John Ciardi, Lawrence Binyon, Dorothy Sayers, and Lawrence Grant White.*

Canto I

THE STORY. *Dante finds that he has strayed from the right road and is lost in a Dark Wood. He tries to escape by climbing a beautiful Mountain, but is turned aside, first by a gambolling Leopard, then by a fierce Lion, and finally by a ravenous She-Wolf. As he is fleeing back into the Wood, he is stopped by the shade of Virgil, who tells him that he cannot hope to pass the*

AUGUSTE RODIN: *The Gates of Hell*, PHILADELPHIA MUSEUM OF ART: GIVEN BY THE ESTATE OF JULES MASTBAUM

Wolf and ascend the Mountain by that road. One day a Greyhound will come and drive the Wolf back to Hell; but the only course at present left open to Dante is to trust himself to Virgil, who will guide him by a longer way, leading through Hell and Purgatory. From there, a worthier spirit than Virgil (Beatrice) will lead him on to see the blessed souls in Paradise. Dante accepts Virgil as his "master, leader, and lord," and they set out together.

Midway this way of life we're bound upon,
   I woke to find myself in a dark wood,
   Where the right road was wholly lost and gone.

Ay me! how hard to speak of it—that rude
   And rough and stubborn forest! the mere breath
   Of memory stirs the old fear in the blood;

It is so bitter, it goes nigh to death;
   Yet there I gained such good, that, to convey
   The tale, I'll write what else I found therewith.

How I got into it I cannot say,
   Because I was so heavy and full of sleep
   When first I stumbled from the narrow way;

But when at last I stood beneath a steep
   Hill's side, which closed that valley's wandering maze
   Whose dread had pierced me to the heart-root deep,

Then I looked up, and saw the morning rays
   Mantle its shoulder from that planet bright
   Which guides men's feet aright on all their ways;

And this a little quieted the affright
   That lurking in my bosom's lake had lain
   Through the long horror of that piteous night.

And as a swimmer, panting, from the main
   Heaves safe to shore, then turns to face the drive
   Of perilous seas, and looks, and looks again,

So, while my soul yet fled, did I contrive
   To turn and gaze on that dread pass once more
   Whence no man yet came ever out alive.

Weary of limb I rested a brief hour,
   Then rose and onward through the desert hied,
   So that the fixed foot always was the lower;

And see! not far from where the mountain-side
   First rose, a Leopard, nimble and light and fleet,
   Clothed in a fine furred pelt all dapple-dyed,

Came gambolling out, and skipped before my feet,
   Hindering me so, that from the forthright line
   Time and again I turned to beat retreat.

The morn was young, and in his native sign
   The Sun climbed with the stars whose glitterings
   Attended on him when the Love Divine

First moved those happy, prime-created things:
   So the sweet reason and the new-born day
   Filled me with hope and cheerful augurings

Of the bright beast so speckled and so gay;
   Yet not so much but that I fell to quaking
   At a fresh sight—a Lion in the way.

I saw him coming, swift and savage, making
   For me, head high, with ravenous hunger raving
   So that for dread the very air seemed shaking.

And next, a Wolf, gaunt with the famished craving
   Lodged ever in her horrible lean flank,
   The ancient cause of many men's enslaving;—

She was the worst—at that dread sight a blank
   Despair and whelming terror pinned me fast,
   Until all hope to scale the mountain sank.

Like one who loves the gains he has amassed,
   And meets the hour when he must lose his loot,
   Distracted in his mind and all aghast,

Even so was I, faced with that restless brute
   Which little by little edged and thrust me back,
   Back, to that place wherein the sun is mute.

Then, as I stumbled headlong down the track,
   Sudden a form was there, which dumbly crossed
   My path, as though grown voiceless from long lack

Of speech; and seeing it in that desert lost,
   "Have pity on me!" I hailed it as I ran,
   "Whate'er thou art—or very man, or ghost!"

It spoke: "No man, although I once was man;
   My parents' native land was Lombardy
   And both by citizenship were Mantuan.

Sub Julio born, though late in time, was I,
   And lived at Rome in good Augustus' days,
   When the false gods were worshipped ignorantly.

Poet was I, and tuned my verse to praise
   Anchises' righteous son, who sailed from Troy
   When Ilium's pride fell ruined down ablaze

But thou—oh, why run back where fears destroy
   Peace? Why not climb the blissful mountain yonder,
   The cause and first beginning of all joy?"

"Canst thou be Virgil? thou that fount of splendour
   Whence poured so wide a stream of lordly speech?"
   Said I, and bowed my awe-struck head in wonder;

"Oh honour and light of poets all and each,
   Now let my great love stead me—the bent brow
   And long hours pondering all thy book can teach!

Thou art my master, and my author thou,
   From thee alone I learned the singing strain,
   The noble style, that does me honour now.

See there the beast that turned me back again—
   Save me from her, great sage—I fear her so,
   She shakes my blood through every pulse and vein."

"Nay, by another path thou needs must go
   If thou wilt ever leave this waste," he said,
   Looking upon me as I wept, "for lo!

The savage brute that makes thee cry for dread
   Lets no man pass this road of hers, but still
   Trammels him, till at last she lays him dead.

Vicious her nature is, and framed for ill;
   When crammed she craves more fiercely than before;
   Her raging greed can never gorge its fill.

With many a beast she mates, and shall with more,
   Until the Greyhound come, the Master-hound,
   And he shall slay her with a stroke right sore.

He'll not eat gold nor yet devour the ground;
   Wisdom and love and power his food shall be,
   His birthplace between Feltro and Feltro found;

Saviour he'll be to that low Italy
   For which Euryalus and Nisus died,
   Turnus and chaste Camilla, bloodily.

He'll hunt the Wolf through cities far and wide,
   Till in the end he hunt her back to Hell,
   Whence Envy first of all her leash untied.

But, as for thee, I think and deem it well
   Thou take me for thy guide, and pass with me
   Through an eternal place and terrible

Where thou shalt hear despairing cries, and see
   Long-parted souls that in their torments dire
   Howl for the second death perpetually.

Next, thou shalt gaze on those who in the fire
   Are happy, for they look to mount on high,
   In God's good time, up to the blissful quire;

To which glad place, a worthier spirit than I
   Must lead thy steps, if thou desire to come,
   With whom I'll leave thee then, and say good-bye;

For the Emperor of that high Imperium
   Wills not that I, once rebel to His crown,
   Into that city of His should lead men home.

Everywhere is His realm, but there His throne,
   There is His city and exalted seat:
   Thrice-blest whom there He chooses for His own!"

Then I to him: "Poet, I thee entreat,
   By that great God whom thou didst never know,
   Lead on, that I may free my wandering feet

From these snares and from worse; and I will go
   Along with thee, St Peter's Gate to find,
   And those whom thou portray'st as suffering so."

So he moved on; and I moved on behind.

In Canto II, as the two poets begin their journey, Virgil tells how Beatrice had descended into Limbo to entreat him to go to Dante's rescue. In Canto III the poets arrive at the gates of Hell, where they read on the lintel, "Abandon hope, all you who enter here." Inside the gates, on the vestibule of Hell, the futile and indecisive spirits run perpetually, following a wavering banner. Then, in Canto IV, the poets enter Limbo, a place where there is no torment but likewise no hope, and where are found the spirits of virtuous pagans —poets, philosophers, and so forth.

Canto V

THE STORY. *Dante and Virgil descend from the First Circle to the Second (the first of the Circles of Incontinence). On the threshold sits Minos, the judge of Hell, assigning the souls to their appropriate places of torment. His opposition is overcome by Virgil's word of power, and the Poets enter the Circle, where the souls of the Lustful are tossed for ever upon a howling wind. After Virgil has pointed out a number of famous lovers, Dante speaks to the shade of Francesca da Rimini, who tells him her story.*

From the first circle thus I came descending
   To the second, which, in narrower compass turning,
   Holds greater woe, with outcry loud and rending.

There in the threshold, horrible and girning,
   Grim Minos sits, holding his ghastly session,
   And, as he girds him, sentencing and spurning;

For when the ill soul faces him, confession
   Pours out of it till nothing's left to tell;
   Whereon that connoisseur of all transgression

Assigns it to its proper place in hell,
   As many grades as he would have it fall,
   So oft he belts him round with his own tail.

Before him stands a throng continual;
    Each comes in turn to abye the fell arraign;
    They speak—they hear—they're whirled down one and all.

"Ho! thou that comest to the house of pain,"
    Cried Minos when he saw me, the appliance
    Of his dread powers suspending, "think again

How thou dost go, in whom is thy reliance;
    Be not deceived by the wide open door!"
    Then said my guide: "Wherefore this loud defiance?

Hinder not thou his fated way; be sure
    Hindrance is vain; thus it is willed where will
    And power are one; enough; ask now no more."

And now the sounds of grief begin to fill
    My ear; I'm come where cries of anguish smite
    My shrinking sense, and lamentation shrill—

A place made dumb of every glimmer of light,
    Which bellows like tempestuous ocean birling
    In the batter of a two-way wind's buffet and fight.

The blast of hell that never rests from whirling
    Harries the spirits along in the sweep of its swath,
    And vexes them, for ever beating and hurling.

When they are borne to the rim of the ruinous path
    With cry and wail and shriek they are caught by the gust,
    Railing and cursing the power of the Lord's wrath.

Into this torment carnal sinners are thrust,
    So I was told—the sinners who make their reason
    Bond thrall under the yoke of their lust.

Like as the starlings wheel in the wintry season
    In wide and clustering flocks wing-borne, wind-borne,
    Even so they go, the souls who did this treason,

Hither and thither, and up and down, outworn,
    Hopeless of any rest—rest, did I say?
    Of the least minishing of their pangs forlorn.

And as the cranes go chanting their harsh lay,
    Across the sky in long procession trailing,
    So I beheld some shadows borne my way,

Driven on the blast and uttering wail on wailing;
   Wherefore I said: "O Master, art thou able
   To name these spirits thrashed by the black wind's flailing?"

"Among this band," said he, "whose name and fable
   Thou seek'st to know, the first who yonder flies
   Was empress of many tongues, mistress of Babel.

She was so broken to lascivious vice
   She licensed lust by law, in hopes to cover
   Her scandal of unnumbered harlotries.

This was Semiramis; 'tis written of her
   That she was wife to Ninus and heiress, too,
   Who reigned in the land the Soldan now rules over.

Lo! she that slew herself for love, untrue
   To Sychaeus' ashes. Lo! tost on the blast,
   Voluptuous Cleopatra, whom love slew.

Look, look on Helen, for whose sake rolled past
   Long evil years. See great Achilles yonder,
   Who warred with love, and that war was his last.

See Paris, Tristram see!" And many—oh, wonder
   Many—a thousand more, he showed by name
   And pointing hand, whose life love rent asunder.

And when I had heard my Doctor tell the fame
   Of all those knights and ladies of long ago,
   I was pierced through with pity, and my head swam.

"Poet," said I, "fain would I speak those two
   That seem to ride as light as any foam,
   And hand in hand on the dark wind drifting go."

And he replied: "Wait till they nearer roam,
   And thou shalt see; summon them to thy side
   By the power of the love that leads them, and they will come."

So, as they eddied past on the whirling tide,
   I raised my voice: "O souls that wearily rove,
   Come to us, speak to us—if it be not denied."

And as desire wafts homeward dove with dove
   To their sweet nest, on raised and steady wing
   Down-dropping through the air, impelled by love,

So these from Dido's flock came fluttering
    And dropping toward us down the cruel wind,
    Such power was in my affectionate summoning.

"O living creature, gracious and so kind,
    Coming through this black air to visit us,
    Us, who in death the globe incarnadined,

Were the world's King our friend and might we thus
    Entreat, we would entreat Him for thy peace,
    That pitiest so our pangs dispiteous!

Hear all thou wilt, and speak as thou shalt please,
    And we will gladly speak with thee and hear,
    While the winds cease to howl, as they now cease.

There is a town upon the sea-coast, near
    Where Po with all his streams comes down to rest
    In ocean; I was born and nurtured there.

Love, that so soon takes hold in the gentle breast,
    Took this lad with the lovely body they tore
    From me; the way of it leaves me still distrest.

Love, that to no loved heart remits love's score,
    Took me with such great joy of him, that see!
    It holds me yet and never shall leave me more.

Love to a single death brought him and me;
    Cain's place lies waiting for our murderer now."
    These words came wafted to us plaintively.

Hearing those wounded souls, I bent my brow
    Downward, and thus bemused I let time pass,
    Till the poet said at length: "What thinkest thou?"

When I could answer, I began: "Alas!
    Sweet thoughts how many, and desire how great,
    Brought down these twain unto the dolorous pass!"

And then I turned to them: "Thy dreadful fate,
    Francesca, makes me weep, it so inspires
    Pity," said I, "and grief compassionate.

Tell me—in that time of sighing-sweet desires,
    How, and by what, did love his power disclose
    And grant you knowledge of your hidden fires?"

Then she to me: "The bitterest woe of woes
   Is to remember in our wretchedness
   Old happy times; and this thy Doctor knows;

Yet, if so dear desire thy heart possess
   To know that root of love which wrought our fall,
   I'll be as those who weep and who confess.

One day we read for pastime how in thrall
   Lord Lancelot lay to love, who loved the Queen;
   We were alone—we thought no harm at all.

As we read on, our eyes met now and then,
   And to our cheeks the changing colour started,
   But just one moment overcame us—when

We read of the smile, desired of lips long-thwarted,
   Such smile, by such a lover kissed away,
   He that may never more from me be parted

Trembling all over, kissed my mouth. I say
   The book was Galleot, Galleot the complying
   Ribald who wrote; we read no more that day."

While the one spirit thus spoke, the other's crying
   Wailed on me with a sound so lamentable,
   I swooned for pity like as I were dying,

And, as a dead man falling, down I fell.

> *In Cantos VI through XII, the poets descend through a series of circles in which they encounter the shades of the gluttonous, the hoarders and spendthrifts, the wrathful and sullen, the heretics in their burning tombs, and the violent against their neighbors.*

Canto XIII

The Story. The Poets enter a pathless Wood. Here Harpies sit shrieking among the withered trees, which enclose the souls of Suicides. Pier delle Vigne tells Dante his story, and also explains how these shades come to be changed into trees and what will happen to their bodies at the Last Day. The shades of two Profligates rush through the wood, pursued and torn by black hounds. Dante speaks to a bush containing the soul of a Florentine.

Ere Nessus had regained the bank beyond
    We'd pushed into a forest, where no mark
    Of any beaten path was to be found.

No green here, but discoloured leaves and dark,
    No tender shoots, but writhen and gnarled and tough,
    No fruit, but poison-galls on the withered bark.

Wild beasts, from tilth and pasture slinking off
    'Twixt Cecina and Corveto, never come
    To lurk in scrub so tangled or so rough.

There the foul Harpies nest and are at home,
    Who chased the Trojans from the Strophades
    With dismal outcry ominous of doom.

Wide-winged like birds and lady-faced are these,
    With feathered belly broad and claws of steel;
    And there they sit and shriek on the strange trees.

And the good master thus began: "'Twere well,
    Ere going further, thou shouldst understand,
    Thou'rt now in the second ring, and shalt be, till

Thou comest to the abominable sand.
    But now, look well, and see a thing whose telling
    Might kill my credit with thee out of hand."

Already all round I heard a mournful wailing,
    But, seeing none to wail, I stopped short, blinking
    Bewilderedly, as though my wits were failing.

I think he must have thought that I was thinking
    That all these voices through the boles resounding
    Were those of folk who from our gaze hid shrinking,

Because he said: "If from these boughs abounding
    Thou wilt pluck off one small and single spray,
    Thy thoughts will stagger at their own dumbfounding."

So I put forth my hand a little way,
    And broke a branchlet from a thorn-tree tall;
    And the trunk cried out: "Why tear my limbs away?"

Then it grew dark with blood, and therewithal
    Cried out again: "Why dost thou rend my bones?
    Breathes there no pity in thy breast at all?

We that are turned to trees were human once;
    Nay, thou shouldst tender a more pious hand
    Though we had been the souls of scorpions."

As, when you burn one end of a green brand,
    Sap at the other oozes from the wood,
    Sizzling as the imprisoned airs expand,

So from that broken splint came words and blood
    At once: I dropped the twig, and like to one
    Rooted to the ground with terror, there I stood.

"O wounded soul," my sage replied anon,
    "Might I have brought him straightway to believe
    The thing he'd read of in my verse alone,

Never had he lifted finger to mischieve
    Thee thus; but 'twas incredible; so I
    Prompted his deed, for which myself must grieve.

But tell him who thou wast, that he may try
    For some amends, to right thee with mankind
    When, by permission, he returns on high."

To this the trunk made answer: "Words so kind
    Tempt me to speech; nor take it in ill part
    If at some length I'm lured to speak my mind.

I am he that held both keys of Frederick's heart,
    To lock and to unlock; and well I knew
    To turn them with so exquisite an art,

I kept his counsel and let few men through;
    Loyal to my glorious charge did I remain,
    And sacrificed my sleep and my strength too.

But that great harlot which can ne'er refrain
    From Caesar's household her adulterous eyes,
    The vice of kings' courts and their common bane,

Inflamed all hearts against me, and these likewise,
    Flaming, inflamed Augustus to distrust,
    Till my glad honours turned to obloquies.

So, in a scornful spirit of disgust,
   And thinking to escape from scorn by death,
   To my just self I made myself unjust;

But by these strange new roots my trunk beneath,
   Never to my most honourworthy lord,
   I swear to you, was I found false of faith;

And if to that bright world indeed restored
   One of you goes, oh, heal my memory,
   Which lies and bleeds from envy's venomed sword."

He paused there; and the poet said to me:
   "While he is mute, let not this moment go,
   But speak, and ask what more seems good to thee."

And I: "Ask thou, whate'er thou think'st will do
   My hunger good and satisfy me well;
   I cannot ask, pity unhearts me so."

Wherefore: "So may this man prove liberal,"
   Thus he resumed, "thine errand to perform,
   Imprisoned spirit, do thou be pleased to tell

How souls get cramped into this knotty form,
   And, if thou canst, if any shall do off
   These limbs one day and find release therefrom."

At this the trunk blew hard, and the windy puff
   After this wise soon whistled into speech:
   "You shall be answered with brief words enough.

When the wild soul leaps from the body, which
   Its own mad violence forces it to quit,
   Minos dispatches it down to the seventh ditch.

It falls in the wood; no place is picked for it,
   But as chance carries it, there it falls to be,
   And where it falls, it sprouts like a corn of wheat,

And grows to a sapling, and thence to a wild tree;
   Then the Harpies feed on its leaves, and the sharp bite
   Gives agony, and a vent to agony.

We shall take our flight, when all souls take their flight,
   To seek our spoils, but not to be rearrayed,
   For the spoils of the spoiler cannot be his by right;

Here shall we drag them, to this gloomy glade;
   Here shall they hang, each body evermore
   Borne on the thorn of its own self-slaughtering shade."

Thinking the trunk might wish to tell us more,
   We stood intent, when suddenly there came crashing
   On our astonished ears a wild uproar,

As the huntsman hears the boar and the chase dashing
   Down on his post like the noise of a hurricane,
   With trampling of beasts and all the branches smashing.

And lo! on the left of us came two that ran
   Naked and torn, with such a furious burst
   As snapped to flinders every forest fan.

"O death, come now, come quickly!" thus the first;
   And the second, finding himself outstripped in the rush,
   Cried: "Lano, thy legs were not so nimble erst

At the jousts of Toppo." So in the last push,
   His breath failing perhaps, he shot sidelong
   And made one group of himself and a thick bush.

And filling the woods behind them came a throng
   Of great black braches, fleet of foot and grim,
   And keen as greyhounds fresh-slipped from the thong;

They seized the skulker, and set their teeth in him,
   And rent him piecemeal, and away they went
   Carrying the wretched fragments limb by limb.

Then my guide drew me by the hand, and bent
   His steps to the poor bush, left mangled there,
   Gasping vain protests through each bleeding rent.

"O Jacomo," it cried, "of Sant' Andrea,
   Why make a screen of me? What was the good?
   Am I to blame for thy misspent career?"

Then said my gentle master when he stood
   Beside it: "Who wast thou, that through such tattered
   Wounds sighest out thy grief mingled with blood?"

"O spirits, who come in time to see me battered
   Thus shamefully, and all my foliage torn,"
   It said, "bring back the leaves that lie there scattered,

Gather them close beneath the shrub forlorn.
  My city was she that for the Baptist changed
  Her ancient patron, wherefore on her scorn

Still by his art he makes himself avenged;
  Yea, did not Arno's bridge even now retain
  Some image of the guardian she estranged,

Those citizens who built her walls again
  On the ashes left by Attila, had been baffled
  Wholly, and all their labour spent in vain;

I am one that made my own roof-tree my scaffold."

> *In Cantos XIV through XXV, the poets continue their descent through circles in which are found the violent against God and Nature, the seducers, the sellers of holy things, the grafters, the hypocrites in their gilded leaden cloaks, the thieves in their snake pit, and so forth—more often than not represented by spirits well known to Dante and his contemporaries.*

Canto XXVI

The Story. Dante, with bitter irony, reproaches Florence. The Poets climb up and along the rugged spur to the arch of the next bridge, from which they see the Counsellors of Fraud moving along the floor of the Eighth Bowge, each wrapped in a tall flame. Virgil stops the twin-flame which contains the souls of Ulysses and Diomede, and compels Ulysses to tell the story of his last voyage.

Florence, rejoice, because thy soaring fame
  Beats its broad wings across both land and sea,
  And all the deep of Hell rings with thy name!

Five of thy noble townsmen did I see
  Among the thieves; which makes me blush anew,
  And mighty little honour it does to thee.

But if toward the morning men dream true,
  Thou must ere long abide the bitter boon
  That Prato craves for thee, and others too;

Nay, were't already here, 'twere none too soon;
    Let come what must come, quickly—I shall find
    The burden heavier as the years roll on.

We left that place; and by the stones that bind
    The brink, which made the stair for our descent,
    My guide climbed back, and drew me up behind.

So on our solitary way we went,
    Up crags, up boulders, where the foot in vain
    Might seek to speed, unless the hand were lent.

I sorrowed then; I sorrow now again,
    Pondering the things I saw, and curb my hot
    Spirit with an unwontedly strong rein

For fear it run where virtue guide it not,
    Lest, if kind star or greater grace have blest
    Me with good gifts, I mar my own fair lot.

Now, thickly clustered,—as the peasant at rest
    On some hill-side, when he whose rays illume
    The world conceals his burning countenance least,

What time the flies go and mosquitoes come,
    Looks down the vale and sees the fire-flies sprinkling
    Fields where he tills or brings the vintage home—

So thick and bright I saw the eighth moat twinkling
    With wandering fires, soon as the arching road
    Laid bare the bottom of the deep rock-wrinkling.

Such as the chariot of Elijah showed
    When he the bears avenged beheld it rise,
    And straight to Heaven the rearing steeds upstrode,

For he could not so follow it with his eyes
    But that at last it seemed a bodiless fire
    Like a little shining cloud high in the skies,

So through that gulf moved every flaming spire;
    For though none shows the theft, each, like a thief,
    Conceals a pilfered sinner. To admire,

I craned so tip-toe from the bridge, that if
    I had not clutched a rock I'd have gone over,
    Needing no push to send me down the cliff.

Seeing me thus intently lean and hover,
    My guide said: "In those flames the spirits go
    Shrouded, with their own torment for their cover."

"Now thou hast told me, sir," said I, "I know
    The truth for sure; but I'd already guessed,
    And meant to ask—thinking it must be so—

Who walks in that tall fire cleft at the crest
    As though it crowned the pyre where those great foes,
    His brother and Eteocles, were placed?"

"Tormented there," said he, "Ulysses goes
    With Diomede, for as they ran one course,
    Sharing their wrath, they share the avenging throes.

In fire they mourn the trickery of the horse,
    That opened up the gates through which the high
    Seed of the Romans issued forth perforce;

There mourn the cheat by which betrayed to die
    Deïdamia wails Achilles still;
    And the Palladium is avenged thereby."

Then I: "O Master! if these sparks have skill
    To speak, I pray, and re-pray that each prayer
    May count with thee for prayers innumerable,

Deny me not to tarry a moment here
    Until the horned flame come; how much I long
    And lean to it I think thee well aware."

And he to me: "That wish is nowise wrong,
    But worthy of high praise; gladly indeed
    I grant it; but do thou refrain thy tongue

And let me speak to them; for I can read
    The question in thy mind; and they, being Greek,
    Haply might scorn thy speech and pay no heed."

So, when by time and place the twin-fire peak,
    As to my guide seemed fitting, had come on,
    In this form conjuring it, I heard him speak:

"You that within one flame go two as one,
    By whatsoever I merited once of you,
    By whatsoever I merited under the sun

When I sang the high songs, whether little or great my due,
   Stand; and let one of you say what distant bourne,
   When he voyaged to loss and death, he voyaged unto."

Then of that age-old fire the loftier horn
   Began to mutter and move, as a wavering flame
   Wrestles against the wind and is over-worn;

And, like a speaking tongue vibrant to frame
   Language, the tip of it flickering to and fro
   Threw out a voice and answered: "When I came

From Circe at last, who would not let me go,
   But twelve months near Caieta hindered me
   Before Aeneas ever named it so,

No tenderness for my son, nor piety
   To my old father, nor the wedded love
   That should have comforted Penelope

Could conquer in me the restless itch to rove
   And rummage through the world exploring it,
   All human worth and wickedness to prove.

So on the deep and open sea I set
   Forth, with a single ship and that small band
   Of comrades that had never left me yet.

Far as Morocco, far as Spain I scanned
   Both shores; I saw the island of the Sardi,
   And all that sea, and every wave-girt land.

I and my fellows were grown old and tardy
   Or ere we made the straits where Hercules
   Set up his marks, that none should prove so hardy

To venture the uncharted distances;
   Ceuta I'd left to larboard, sailing by,
   Seville I now left in the starboard seas.

'Brothers,' said I, 'that have come valiantly
   Through hundred thousand jeopardies undergone
   To reach the West, you will not now deny

To this last little vigil left to run
   Of feeling life, the new experience
   Of the uninhabited world behind the sun.

Think of your breed; for brutish ignorance
   Your mettle was not made; you were made men,
   To follow after knowledge and excellence.'

My little speech made every one so keen
   To forge ahead, that even if I'd tried
   I hardly think I could have held them in.

So, with our poop shouldering the dawn, we plied,
   Making our oars wings to the witless flight,
   And steadily gaining on the larboard side.

Already the other pole was up by night
   With all it stars, and ours had sunk so low,
   It rose no more from the ocean-floor to sight;

Five times we had seen the light kindle and grow
   Beneath the moon, and five times wane away,
   Since to the deep we had set course to go,

When at long last hove up a mountain, grey
   With distance, and so lofty and so steep,
   I never had seen the like on any day.

In Cantos XXVII through XXXIII we pass through a circle in which the sowers of discord within the church, including Mahomet, are continually cut and ripped asunder by a demon with a sword; then through a disease-ridden pit in which are falsifiers of various kinds; and finally to the bottom circle of Hell, a vast lake of ice in which are encased the shades of traitors to kindred, to country, to guests, or to their lords. Canto XXXIII tells the terrible story of Count Ugolino, a traitor who was himself betrayed, imprisoned, and allowed to starve to death by Count Roger. Now they are frozen together in the ice, and Ugolino gnaws continually at the nape of Roger's neck.

Canto XXXIV

The Story. *After passing over the region of Judecca, where the Traitors to their Lords are wholly immersed in the ice, the Poets see Dis (Satan) devouring the shades of Judas, Brutus, and Cassius. They clamber along his body until, passing through the centre of the Earth, they emerge into a rocky cavern. From here they follow the stream of Lethe upwards until it brings them out on the island of Mount Purgatory in the Antipodes.*

"Vexilla regis prodeunt inferni
   Encountering us; canst thou distinguish him,
   Look forward," said the master, "as we journey."

As, when a thick mist breathes, or when the rim
   Of night creeps up across our hemisphere,
   A turning windmill looms in the distance dim,

I thought I saw a shadowy mass appear;
   Then shrank behind my leader from the blast,
   Because there was no other cabin here.

I stood (with fear I write it) where at last
   The shades, quite covered by the frozen sheet,
   Gleamed through the ice like straws in crystal glassed;

Some lie at length and others stand in it,
   This one upon his head, and that upright,
   Another like a bow bent face to feet.

And when we had come so far that it seemed right
   To my dear master, he should let me see
   That creature fairest once of the sons of light,

He moved him from before me and halted me,
   And said: "Behold now Dis! behold the place
   Where thou must steel thy soul with constancy."

How cold I grew, how faint with fearfulness,
   Ask me not, Reader; I shall not waste breath
   Telling what words are powerless to express;

This was not life, and yet it was not death;
   If thou hast wit to think how I might fare
   Bereft of both, let fancy aid thy faith.

The Emperor of the sorrowful realm was there,
   Out of the girding ice he stood breast-high,
   And to his arm alone the giants were

Less comparable than to a giant I;
   Judge then how huge the stature of the whole
   That to so huge a part bears symmetry.

If he was once as fair as now he's foul,
   And dared outface his Maker in rebellion,
   Well may he be the fount of all our dole.

And marvel 'twas, out-marvelling a million,
   When I beheld three faces in his head;
   The one in front was scarlet like vermilion;

And two, mid-centred on the shoulders, made
   Union with this, and each with either fellow
   Knit at the crest, in triune junction wed.

The right was of a hue 'twixt white and yellow;
   The left was coloured like the men who dwell
   Where Nile runs down from source to sandy shallow.

From under each sprang two great wings that well
   Befitted such a monstrous bird as that;
   I ne'er saw ship with such a spread of sail.

Plumeless and like the pinions of a bat
   Their fashion was; and as they flapped and whipped
   Three winds went rushing over the icy flat

And froze up all Cocytus; and he wept
   From his six eyes, and down his triple chin
   Runnels of tears and bloody slaver dripped.

Each mouth devoured a sinner clenched within,
   Frayed by the fangs like flax beneath a brake;
   Three at a time he tortured them for sin.

But all the bites the one in front might take
   Were nothing to the claws that flayed his hide
   And sometimes stripped his back to the last flake.

"That wretch up there whom keenest pangs divide
   Is Judas called Iscariot," said my lord,
   "His head within, his jerking legs outside;

As for the pair whose heads hang hitherward:
   From the black mouth the limbs of Brutus sprawl—
   See how he writhes and utters never a word;

And strong-thewed Cassius is his fellow-thrall.
   But come; for night is rising on the world
   Once more; we must depart; we have seen all."

Then, as he bade, about his neck I curled
   My arms and clasped him. And he spied the time
   And place; and when the wings were wide unfurled

Set him upon the shaggy flanks to climb,
   And thus from shag to shag descended down
   'Twixt matted hair and crusts of frozen rime.

And when we had come to where the huge thigh-bone
   Rides in its socket at the haunch's swell,
   My guide, with labour and great exertion,

Turned head to where his feet had been, and fell
   To hoisting himself up upon the hair,
   So that I thought us mounting back to Hell.

"Hold fast to me, for by so steep a stair,"
   My master said, panting like one forspent,
   "Needs must we quit this realm of all despair."

At length, emerging through a rocky vent,
   He perched me sitting on the rim of the cup
   And crawled out after, heedful how he went.

I raised my eyes, thinking to see the top
   Of Lucifer, as I had left him last;
   But only saw his great legs sticking up.

And if I stood dumbfounded and aghast,
   Let those thick-witted gentry judge and say,
   Who do not see what point it was I'd passed.

"Up on thy legs!" the master said; "the way
   Is long, the road rough going for the feet,
   And at mid-terce already stands the day."

The place we stood in was by no means fit
   For a king's palace, but a natural prison,
   With a vile floor, and very badly lit.

"One moment, sir," said I, when I had risen;
   "Before I pluck myself from the Abyss,
   Lighten my darkness with a word in season.

Kindly explain; what's happened to the ice?
   What's turned him upside-down? or in an hour
   Thus whirled the sun from dusk to dawning skies?"

"Thou think'st," he said, "thou standest as before
   Yon side the centre, where I grasped the hair
   Of the ill Worm that pierces the world's core.

So long as I descended, thou wast there;
   But when I turned, then was the point passed by
   Toward which all weight bears down from everywhere.

The other hemisphere doth o'er thee lie—
   Antipodal to that which land roofs in,
   And under whose meridian came to die

The Man born sinless and who did no sin;
   Thou hast thy feet upon a little sphere
   Of whose far side Judecca forms the skin.

When it is evening there, it's morning here;
   And he whose pelt our ladder was, stands still
   Fixt in the self-same place, and does not stir.

This side the world from out high Heaven he fell;
   The land which here stood forth fled back dismayed,
   Pulling the sea upon her like a veil,

And sought our hemisphere; with equal dread,
   Belike, that peak of earth which still is found
   This side, rushed up, and so this void was made."

There is a place low down there underground,
   As far from Belzebub as his tomb's deep,
   Not known to sight, but only by the sound

Of a small stream which trickles down the steep,
   Hollowing its channel, where with gentle fall
   And devious course its wandering waters creep.

By that hid way my guide and I withal,
   Back to the lit world from the darkened dens
   Toiled upward, caring for no rest at all,

He first, I following; till my straining sense
   Glimpsed the bright burden of the heavenly cars
   Through a round hole; by this we climbed, and thence

Came forth, to look once more upon the stars.

from *Sir Gawain and the Green Knight*
(ca. Fourteenth Century)

Sir Gawain and the Green Knight is a masterpiece of Middle English alliterative poetry. Though the author is unknown, the work is obviously the creation of a superb artist. It has beautiful descriptive passages that show the poet's deep love for nature. The work is balanced; the dialogue is rich and controlled; and the dramatic progress is tight. The moral purpose of the poem is integrated so skillfully into the story that modern readers still enjoy it.

Gawain is a familiar figure in Arthurian lore. The story, in this instance, begins on New Year's Day at the court of King Arthur. In the middle of the festivities the company is startled by the interruption of the Green Knight. His clothes, hair, horse, and all are green. He challenges each knight to meet him in hand-axe combat. Gawain cuts off the knight's head; then the Green Knight picks it up, arranges to meet Gawain a year from then in a rematch, and gallops away.

A year later on Christmas Day, Gawain reaches a castle near the Green Chapel where he is to meet the knight. For three days the master of the castle goes hunting and Gawain rests. Daily, while the lord hunts, Gawain is tempted by the lord's wife. The involvement of each day's hunt equals the involvement of each day's temptation for Gawain. The lord and Gawain exchange gifts in the evenings, but Gawain holds back the girdle or belt that the lady has given him on the third day.

On New Year's Day Gawain meets the Green Knight and receives two blows. The third blow cuts him slightly. Then he discovers that the Green Knight is lord of the castle, and that he and his wife have been sent to tempt Gawain. Gawain would have received no harm if he had not concealed the magic belt. When Gawain returns home and tells his story, the court decides to wear green belts in his honor.

The excerpts following are from the early scenes, in which the Green Knight interrupts the festivities, and from later scenes of the hunt and the lady's temptings.

7

Now will I of their merry-making no more describe,
For each of you may guess no guest went hungry.
A new blast of music was boldly blown forth,
Signal to the banqueteers the banquet was begun,
But merely had the music melted into echoes
And the opening course had been commanded and carved,
When suddenly came crashing in a frightening great creature,
Terrible to look upon, tall as a forest tree;
From his throat to his thigh so sturdy and so thick,
And his loins and limbs so powerful and long,
Half legendary giant I jest not to name him,
But nonetheless a man I must believe him to be,
And that the likeliest and mightiest ever lanced or galloped,
For, back and breast, full-muscled was his body,
But his sides and waist were worthily slim,
And all his facial features likewise were fair,
   Cheery and clean.
  But wonder of his color!
  The like I've never seen.
  This strange and ominous fellow
  Was a vivid green.

8

And everything was green, all this creature with his weeds:
A close, clipped jacket that clung to his sides,
Over that mantle made and masked within
With featly trimmed fur fair for to see,
A white ermine hem handsome on the hood,
That loosely from his locks lay upon his shoulders;
Neat, tight hose, green like hood and habit,

That clung to his calves, and golden, clanking spurs,
Joined to silken straps and richly gemmed and jeweled,
And long pointed slippers both proper and neat:
Forth this rider fares clad all in forest green,
Even the bars of his belt and the other bright stones
Richly arrayed about his verdant robe,
About his suit and saddle and all his silk belongings;
Too tedious it were to tell half the bonny trifles
That were embroidered there, birds and butterflies,
In gay gaudy green studded round with gold.
His beast's breast-trappings, the studs of its bit,
All his gear and rigging, were greenly enameled;
The stirrups that he stood in, they were stained the same,
And all his sparkling tackle from saddle-bows to spurs
Gleamed and glittered grandly with green, glinting stones;
The steed that he straddled, stoutest of stallions,
   Green was beside him,
  A steed strong and thick,
  Straining at the bridle,
  Mettlesome and quick,
  Well-suited to his rider.

9

And this giant was full gay, geared all in green,
The hair of his head matching his horse,
Fair fanning flax falling round his shoulders;
A brave bushy beard hung before his breast,
Which, like the hair hanging from his head,
Was clipped all about just above his elbows,
So half his arms thereunder were hidden as it were
Beneath a king's cape enclosing his neck;
That mane of his mount in much the same fashion,
Well crisped and combed in many curious knots
And plaited with gold throughout the goodly green:
Here a strand of green, there a gleam of gold;
His tail and his forelock likewise framed and fitted
And bound with a band of bright glittering green
And studded to the tip with the starriest of stones,
Then twisted with a thong and tied into a knot,
Where many bright bells of burnished gold rang.
Such a rare horse, such a rarer rider
Had never before been seen at one of Arthur's banquets.
   His gaze
  Was blinding, bold and bright,

Dazzling to his foes.
It seemed no mortal wight
Might stand beneath his blows.

10

However, he wore no helmet, neither any halberd,
No gorgeret nor greaves, grim plates of battle,
No shaft nor shield wherewith to shear and smite,
But he held in one hand a giant branch of holly
That waxes and grows great when the green groves are bare,
And in his other an ax, horrible and huge,
A deadly weapon to describe or deal with in words.
The ax head measured long as an ell in length,
The spike of green steel beat with goodly gold,
The bit burnished bright with a biting edge,
As shaped to split or shear as the sharpest razor.
And this grim knight gripped and grasped it tight
By a stout shaft spun and wound with iron,
All engraved in green in grave and curious fashion;
A thong tied around that was twisted at the head
And along the handle's length was looped round about,
With tassels tied thereto and tightly attached
On bosses of bright green, rich with splendid braid.
Boldly then this burly fellow bursts into the hall,
Fares forward to the very dais, fearless and free;
Never once he spoke, but coolly looked about.
The first sound that he uttered: "Show me," he said,
"The governor of this gathering. Gladly I would
See and speak with him, whosoe'er he be."
  Silent and strong,
  He rode before the dais
  And seemed to study long,
  Searching that still place
  For the leader of the throng.

11

Great was the goggling and gaping at that creature,
And each man in his heart thought what it might mean,
This stranger and his steed stained so rich and strangely,
As green as growing grass and seeming even greener
Than enamel on a golden ground, glowing even brighter.
All stood still about him, staring curiously,
Full of fear and wonder, what work he planned there.
For many marvels had they seen, but never such a monster,

Wherefore they deemed him a phantom, troll or fay,
And full of goodly fear all this folk were then;
And all, astonished at his voice, sat stone-still;
And a breathing silence settled on the scene;
All, as though enchanted, ceased their cheery chatter.
       (See,
    Some are hushed with fear,
    Some out of courtesy,
    But every person there
    Leans forward, tensed to see.)

56

And after by the chimney they sat in the chamber;
Servants brought the choice wine cheerfully unto them.
And soon in their jollity, their jesting and joking,
They planned to repeat their pact upon the morrow:
Each to give the other whatever goods he gained
Swiftly and nimbly at night when next they met.
They agreed to the covenant before the gathered group;
The beverage was brought forth blithely and with laughter,
Then lightly they took their leave in merriment and love;
Each lord and lady hurried to his lodging.
By the time the cock had crowed and cackled but thrice,
The lord had leaped up from his bed, and all his merry lads;
The meat and the mass were meetly delivered,
And all the court clad for the chase before the dawn came,
       And ho!
    With holloing and horns
    To the deep woods they go;
    Through thickets, through thorns,
    A brave and noisy show.

57

Soon they called for a search beneath a bankside;
The huntsman hailed those hounds who had first howled;
Wild words he shouted there, with a warlike sound;
All the hounds who heard him hastened thither swiftly
And forty sprang upon the spoor like growling despoilers.
Then such a baying and bellowing, such howling and barking
Rose, that the rocks rang all about,
And the hunters heartened them with horn and with voice.
Then all rushed together in a thrashing throng

Between a still pool and a steep, stark cliff,
In a rocky copse beneath a knobby crag
Where the rough rocks ruggedly had fallen
They fell upon the scent, with all those fellows following;
They broke down the bushes, rushed through the underbrush,
And those wights well knew that within there was
A bold goodly beast; and the bloodhounds richly bayed.
So they beat upon the bushes and bade him uprise
And suddenly he rushed out, roaring and rampaging,
The hugest of boars, a bold and a burly one;
Long from the herd had he wandered alone,
And now he was tough and old, with strong teeth and tusks,
Full grim when he grunted, and many there grieved,
For three at the first thrust he thrashed to the earth
And snorting sped him forth to spy out more sport.
Then they holloed: "Heigh!" and "Hay! Hay!" they cried,
Sounded on the horns the high hunting cry;
And many were the mingled sounds of men and of hounds
Pursuing this boar with bellowing and blaring
        To the kill.
    Full oft he turns and stands
    And drives them back at will;
    He gores the baying hounds
    And loud they yowl and yell.

58

Bowmen to shoot the boar were bidden forth then,
Showered their sharp arrows on him, struck him full often;
But the trenchant points were turned by the toughness of his thews
And no barb could bite his hard, bristled brow;
All the spearing shafts splintered into pieces,
And the barbs rebounded as though from off a boulder.
But, as the dints are dealt him of their dire strokes,
Thus, frenzied in the fight, he rushes at his foe,
Goring those who goaded him; grievously he hurt them,
And many then felt fear and fell back before him.
But the lord upon a light horse launched in full pursuit;
Like a boldened warrior he blew upon his bugle.
Blaringly he blew, rushing through the deep brush,
Pursuing this wild swine until the sun set.
Thus the hours flew within the fierce forest,
While our hardy hero harbored him in bed,
Gawain, the good, in raiment and gear
        Full bright.
    The lady was not late

In coming to his side,
Nor had he long to wait
Her lovely face to greet.

59

She came to the curtain and peeped coyly in,
And Gawain, he greeted her with most goodly gallantry
And she replied to him prettily and pertly,
Set her softly by his side, and sweetly she laughed
And with a lovely look she delivered these words:
"Sir, if you are Gawain, strange it seems to me
That one so well disposed always to do good
Cannot in lady's company comprehend the code,
And if one craves to know you you coolly discard her;
You have forgotten utterly what yesterday I taught you
By the truest of tokens in the talk that I know best."
"What is that?" said Gawain. "By God, I cannot guess.
Though if what you say is true, then truly I'm to blame."
"I instructed you in kissing," cried that gay lady,
"That which a Christian knight is always quick to claim,
As beauteously becomes his manners and behavior."
"No more," he said, "my dear, of such sweet merriment,
For I dare not do, lest I be denied;
Were I refused, I were wrong to have proffered."
"My faith," cried the merry wife, "how may one refuse you?
You are strong enough stoutly to constrain me
If I were so foolish as to refuse or flout you."
Said Gawain, "Before God, goodly is your speaking,
But force is not thought fitting in the land where I fare from
And worthless that gift not given with goodwill.
I am at your commandment to kiss at your content,
You may start as you will and cease when you think seemly,
    In peace."
The lady drops down
And kisses his face,
And long then they expound
Upon love's subtle grace.

60

"I would know of you, knight," that lady said neatly,
"If you would not resent it rudely, what is the riddle
Of one so young and yearning as you seem at this season,
So free and so fair as your fame declares you?
For of all princely chivalry the principle most praised

Is the lore of love, the liberty of arms;
When the deeds of noble knights are loudly sung and named,
It is the truest title and text of their works,
How heroes for their ladies' love have ventured their lives,
Endured for their dear ones dire, doleful trails,
Avenged them with valor, verily, in contest,
And brought bliss to the bower with bounty and virtue—
And you are the comeliest of the king's courtiers,
Your grace and your fairness are famed wide and far,
And I have sat beside you two separate times,
Yet never have I heard the slightest hint of love,
The smallest hint of gallantry, greatly or lightly:
Oh, you who are so quaint and careful in your conduct
Ought to yield and yearn to show unto a young thing
Some traits and some tokens of true love's craft.
What! are you a fool, who possesses this false fame?
Or do you deem me too dull to hark unto your dalliance?
   For shame!
  I come here and sit,
  To learn from you some game.
  Come, teach me of your wit,
  While my lord is far from home."

61

"In good faith," said Gawain, "may God reward you!
Great is my gladness and goodly my pleasure;
That so worthy as you would wend her way hither
And play with so poor a man as plainly I am
With any dint of pleasure, it drowns me in delight;
But to take the task upon myself true love to expound
And touch upon romantic themes and tell tales of arms
To you who, well I know, are wiser by far
In that awesome art a hundred times again
Than I am, or ever shall aspire to attain to,
That would be a foolish folly, by my goodly faith.
I will do your desires, as dearly as I may,
For thus I am beholden and bound to obey—
To serve you and succor you, as God is my savior."
Thus that lovely lady, lovingly she tempted him
To win him to sin and to serve her desire,
But he defended him so fair no fault there seemed,
Nothing on either side, nor naught did they know
   But bliss.
  They laughed and lingered long;
  She took a second kiss;

    He smiled, but held strong,
    And she went her way with this.

62

Then the man rises and goes to morning mass
And after, food was fixed and fetched unto the tables.
This knight with the ladies thus lingered long that day,
But the lord over the land launched his furious chase,
Pursuing his ferocious pig, which turned upon the pack
And bit the backs in sunder of the best dogs
And he stood at bay, till the bowmen broke upon him
And forced him to fight or flee to the open plain,
Where the flying arrows fell fiercely about him.
Still he made the stoutest-hearted stop and step back,
Till at last he was so weak he could walk or run no more,
But hastily as he might he hied him to a hole
In a bank beneath a rock where a brook bubbled.
He got the bank at his back and began to snort and blow;
The froth foamed at his mouth foul around his whiskers,
And he whetted his white tusks; oh, loth were those warriors,
Heavy with their hurts, to draw nearer to him;
They dallied at a distance, avoiding the danger
    Like fire.
    He had hurt them so much
    That none had desire
    To feel again his tearing tusks
    Or face his savage ire.

63

Till the lord sprang among them, spurring on his steed,
Saw the boar at bay, bloody but unchastened;
He leaped lightly down, leaving the reins a-dangle,
Snatched from the scabbard his long, shining sword,
Fared swashing through the ford to where the fell brute lurked.
The wild beast was wary of the man with the weapon;
All his bristles stiffened, and he stamped and blew and snorted,
So all the fellows in the field feared for their lord.
Then the boar charged savagely straight for the waiting knight,
And down they crashed together, thrashing and struggling,
In the deepest part of the water. But woe for the wild beast!
For the man caught him keenly as they clashed head-on,
Set the sharp sword-blade in the slot beneath the throat,
Drove it direly in to the hilt, and the heart burst,
And, snarling bloody bubbles, the boar grimly yielded

And died.
A hundred hounds then leapt
To tear at him and bite,
For now no keepers kept
Their dogs from his side.

64

Then they blew triumphantly their brave silver bugles,
And there was hallooing on the heights by all those hearty hunters;
And the bloodhounds bayed while their masters cheered beside them,
They who were the chiefest in that charging chase;
Then an ancient woodsman, wise in the ways of woodcraft,
Began in careful fashion to butcher this great boar.
First he hewed off the head and set it on high,
Then roughly he ripped down the ridged backbone,
Carved out the bowels and cast them on the coals,
And the brachs he rewarded with the baked bowels and bread.
Then he slices up the flesh in fat sleek slabs
And portions out the pieces as is fitting and proper;
And then he loops and harnesses the halves of the boar together
And stoutly he hangs them upon a strong stick.
So then with this swine they swing toward the castle;
The boar's head, it was borne aloft before the lord,
He who in the swirling ford had felled the fierce beast
In man's view.
And when the lord saw Gawain
He called him forward, too,
To trade once more their day's gain,
As they had sworn to do.

65

The lord with merry jest then laughed loud and long
When he saw Sir Gawain and joyously he spoke;
The good ladies were gotten, and the company gathered;
He showed for them the sheared meat and shaped for them the tale
Of the largeness and length, the litheness and savagery
Of that wild snarling swine in woodlands where he fled.
Gawain in full comeliness courteously commended him
And praised the wondous prize that he had proved and won.
For such a brawny beast, the bold Gawain said,
Or such a splendid boar he had never seen.
Then they handled the horrible head and praised the high prowess
Of that noble warrior who worthily had won it.

"Now, Gawain," said the good man, "this gain is your own,
According to our covenant, on which we clasped hands."
"It is true," said the knight, "and as surely true,
All my gains I give to you, as goodly we compacted."
He hasped the lord about the neck and heartily he kissed him,
And likewise once again he served him in that fashion.
"Now we're even," said the knight, "upon this sweet evening,
Of all the covenants we claimed since I came hither."
  Then
  The lord cried, "By Saint Giles,
  You are the best of men!
  Sure, in a little while
  You'll be as rich as ten!"

66

Then the tables were set atop the neat trestles,
Cloths were cast upon them; clear light then
From the waxen torches whispered on the walls.
Servants came and went, serving in the hall;
Much din and merriment mingled gaily there
About the friendly fire, and many fair times,
At the supper and after, many artful songs,
Old Christmas carols and carefree roundelays,
With all the mannerly mirth men may devise,
And ever our lovely knight beside the fair lady.
Such sweetness she showed to that stalwart knight
With sly secret looks and with silent smiling,
That all bewildered was that man and angry with himself,
But it proved against his nature for him to deny her,
So daintily he dealt with her, dearly he dallied there,
  Come what may.
  As long as she pleased
  He agreed to play.
  Then the tables were upraised
  And they moved away.

(Translated by James L. Rosenberg)

Geoffrey Chaucer
(ca. 1340-1400)
The Prioress's Tale
from *The Canterbury Tales*

For examples of Chaucer's realism, insight into character, broad range of humor, or good-natured tolerance, one would probably turn to other of his writings than "The Prioress's Tale"—to Troilus and Criseyde *or the celebrated prologue to the* Canterbury Tales *or to some of the other tales themselves. But for pure artistry—the faultless beauty of the verse, the economy and simplicity of the telling, the sustained tone of reverence and tenderness —there is nothing better in Chaucer or elsewhere in the literature of the Middle Ages. There is nothing more characteristically medieval in theme and subject matter. And there is no Canterbury tale more completely appropriate to its teller, whom Chaucer has described in the prologue as a gentle nun who has cultivated courteous manners and who is "al conscience and tendre herte."*

The seven-line stanza form employed in "The Prioress's Tale" was a favorite with Chaucer; later it came to be known as rime royal. *The poem is given in Frank Ernest Hill's translation.*

There was in Asia, in a city great,
Mid Christian folk, a Jewish colony,
Protected by a lord who ruled that state,
For wicked gain and foulest usury,
Hateful to Christ and to His company;
And through the street all men could walk or ride;
For it was free, with both ends open wide.

A little school of Christian people stood
Down at the farther end, in which there were
Children full many come of Christian blood
That studied in that school from year to year
The kind of lessons taught to students there—
Singing, that is to say, and reading too,
Such things as children in their childhood do.

Among these children was a widow's son—
A little chorister but seven years old;
Who day by day to school had always gone;
And any time he might the form behold
Of Jesu's mother, then, as he was schooled,
It was his custom down to kneel and say
His *Ave Maria* as he went his way.

The widow thus her little son had taught
Always to worship Christ's own mother dear,
Lady of bliss; and nowise he forgot,
For a good child is quick of eye and ear,
But when I call to mind this story here,
St. Nicholas himself appears to me,
For he when young served Christ so reverently.

This little child, while studying among
The others in the school was soon aware
Of *Alma Redemptoris* being sung
By children that were learning anthems there;
And ever he edged as close as he might dare,
And listened to the singing, word and note,
Until he had the whole first verse by rote.

Nothing he knew of what this Latin said,
Being too tender in his years, and young,
But with a comrade on a day he plead
To explain this song to him in his own tongue,
Or tell him wherefore it was being sung;
To know the words and what was meant by these
Eager and oft he prayed him on bare knees.

His comrade was an older boy than he,
And answered thus: "This song, I hear folk say,
Was made about our blissful Lady free,
To hail and give her greeting, and to pray
Her help and grace when we shall pass away.
No more about the matter can I tell;
Singing I learn, but grammar not so well."

"And is this song made then in reverence
Of Christ's dear mother?" cried this innocent;
"Now truly, I will make great diligence
To know it all, ere Christmastide be spent,
Though in my work I suffer punishment
And thrice an hour be beaten for it," said he,
"Yet will I learn it, honoring our Lady."

Each day his fellow taught him privately
While going home, until he knew by rote
The whole, and sang it well and lustily
From word to word, according to the note,
And twice a day the song would pass his throat,
Once when to school and once when home he went;
On Christ's dear mother was his whole intent.

This child passed through the Jewish colony,
As I have said, in going to and fro,
And there full merry would he sing, and cry
"O Alma Redemptoris;" for the glow
And sweetness pierced his little spirit so
Of Christ's dear mother, that he could not stay
His song to pray to her along the way.

Satan, that serpent and our ancient foe,
That hath in Jewish heart his hornet's nest,
Swelled up and cried, "Woe, Hebrew people, woe!
In such dishonor do ye dwell at rest?
Must ye endure these accents ye detest,
Hearing this boy that goes with evil cause
To desecrate by song your faith and laws?"

And from that day the wicked Jews conspired
How they could bring this innocent to die,
And to this end a homicide they hired
That had his dwelling in an alley nigh,
And as the little child was going by,
This Jew leapt forth and seized him fast, and slit
His throat, and cast his body in a pit.

Into a privy they his body threw,
Where all these Jews had purged them commonly,
O cursed folk, O Herods born anew,
What shall avail you all your infamy?
Murder will out; yea, this is certainty;
And where God's honor lifteth voice to plead,
Loud cries the blood against your cursèd deed!

O martyr wedded to virginity
Now mayst thou sing indeed, and follow on
After the white celestial Lamb (cried she);
Of thee the great evangelist, St. John
In Patmos wrote, saying of martyrs gone
Before the Lamb, and singing songs all new,
That never women in the flesh they knew!

This widow sat awaiting all the night
Her little child, and yet he cometh not;
So when the day drew once again to light,
Her face all pale with fear and heavy thought
At school and every place about she sought,
Until thus much she learned at

length—that he
Was seen last in the Jewish colony.

With mother's pity burning in her breast,
She goes as if she had but half her mind,
To every place where there could be the least
Of likelihood her little child to find;
And ever on Christ's mother meek and mild
She called, and so at length, and long distraught,
Among the cursèd Jews her child she sought.

She asketh and she prayeth piteously
Of all the Jews that dwelt within that place,
To tell her if they saw her child go by,
And they said "No." But Jesu, of His grace,
This impulse gave her in a little space:
That for her little son she stood and cried
Where he within the pit lay close beside.

O mighty God, who let'st Thy praise be called
By mouths of innocents, lo, here Thy might!
This gem of chastity, this emerald
Of martyrdom, this blessèd ruby bright,
There where he lay with throat all gashed and white,
"*O Alma Redemptoris*" clearly sang—
So loud that all the place about him rang.

The Christians on the street, that came and went,
Rushed up with wonder as they heard him sing,
And for the provost hastily they sent;
And he came thither without tarrying,
And Christ he praised that is of heaven the King,
And His dear mother, glory of mankind;
And after that, the Jews he bade them bind.

This little child with piteous lamentation
Was lifted up the while he sang his song,
And, honored by a mighty congregation,
Unto the nearest abbey borne along;
There by the bier his mother swooning hung,
And scarcely could the people that were there
This second Rachel from his body tear.

This provost bade at once that every Jew
With torture and by shameful death should die
That anything about this murder knew;
He would not tolerate such iniquity;
Evil to them where evil ought to lie!
So first he had them dragged behind wild horses,
Then hanged: the judgment which the law enforces.

Upon his bier still lay this innocent
By the chief altar while the mass was said
And after that, the priests and abbot went
With all dispatch to burial of the dead;
But sprinkling holy water on his head,
They heard him speak, at sprinkling of the water.
And sing—"*O Alma Redemptoris Mater!*"

Now this good abbot was a holy man,
As all monks are (or leastwise ought to be!)
And so to conjure his young child began,
And said, "Beloved child, I ask of thee,
By virtue of the Holy Trinity,
Tell me the reason why, though it appear
Thy throat is cut, thou singest still so clear."

"My throat is cut, yea, to the very bone,"
Answered this child, "and following nature's way,
Long time ago I should have died and gone,
But Jesu Christ, as find ye books to say,
Will that His glory be in mind, and stay,

And so for honor of His mother dear,
Still may I sing *O Alma* loud and clear.

"Always I loved Christ's Mother, well of grace,
My wit and knowledge wholly thus applying,
And when they threw my body in that place,
She came to me and spoke as I was lying,
And bade me sing this song when I was dying,
As ye have heard, and, after I had sung,
I thought she laid a grain upon my tongue.

"Therefore I sing, and sing I must indeed,
In honor of that sainted maiden free,
Till from my tongue ye take away the seed;
And afterwards these words she said to me:
'My little child, I will come back for thee
When from thy tongue the grain at last is taken;
Be not dismayed, thou shalt not be forsaken.'"

This holy monk, this abbot, instantly
Drew out the tongue and took away the grain,
And he gave up his spirit quietly;
And when the abbot saw this wonder plain,
His salt tears trickled down his cheeks like rain,
Face down he fell all flat upon the ground,
And lay there still as he with cords were bound.

And all the convent on the pavement lay
Weeping and praising Christ's own mother dear,
And after that they rose and went away
Taking this blessed martyr from his bier
And made for him a tomb of marble clear,
And in it closed his little body sweet;
Where he is now, pray God we all shall meet!

O Hugh of Lincoln, slain in youth also
By cursèd Jews, as all the world knows well,
For it was but a little time ago,
Pray too for us, sinful and changeable,
That God, in whom abounding mercies dwell,
May multiply His grace on us, and thence
Do to His mother Mary reverence!

(Translated by Frank Ernest Hill)

John Ruskin
(1819-1900)
St. Mark's
from *The Stones of Venice*

... Between those pillars there opens a great light, and, in the midst of it, as we advance slowly, the vast tower of St. Mark seems to lift itself visibly forth from the level field of chequered stones; and, on each side, the countless arches prolong themselves into ranged symmetry, as if the rugged and irregular houses that pressed together above us in the dark alley had been struck back into sudden obedience and lovely order, and all their rude casements and broken walls had been transformed into arches charged with goodly sculpture, and fluted shafts of delicate stone.

And well may they fall back, for beyond those troops of ordered arches there rises a vision out of the earth, and all the great square seems to have opened from it in a kind of awe, that we may see it far away;—a multitude of pillars and white domes, clustered into a long low pyramid of coloured light; a treasure-heap, it seems, partly of gold, and partly of opal and mother-of-pearl, hollowed beneath into five great vaulted porches, ceiled with fair mosaic, and beset with sculpture of alabaster, clear as amber and delicate as ivory,—sculpture fantastic and involved, of palm leaves and lilies, and grapes and pomegranates, and birds clinging and fluttering among the branches all twined together into an endless network of buds and plumes; and in the midst of it, the solemn forms of angels, sceptred, and robed to the feet, and leaning to each other across the gates, their figures indistinct among the gleaming of the golden ground through the leaves beside them interrupted and dim, like the morning light as it faded back among the branches of Eden, when first its gates were angel-guarded long ago. And round the walls of the porches there are set pillars of variegated stones, jasper and porphyry, and deep-green serpentine spotted with flakes of snow, and marbles, that half refuse and half yield to the sunshine, Cleopatra-like, "their bluest veins to kiss"—the shadow, as it steals back from them, revealing line after line of azure undulation, as a receding tide leaves the waved sand; their capitals rich with interwoven tracery, rooted knots of herbage, and drifting leaves of acanthus and vine, and mystical signs, all beginning and ending in the Cross; and above them, in the broad archivolts, a continuous chain of language and of life—angels, and the signs of heaven, and the labours of men, each in its appointed season upon the earth; and above these, another range of glittering pinnacles, mixed with white arches edged with scarlet flowers,—a confusion of delight, amidst which the breasts of the Greek horses are seen blazing in their breadth of golden strength, and the St. Mark's lion, lifted on a blue field covered with stars, until at last, as if in ecstasy, the crests of the arches break into a marble foam, and toss themselves far into the blue sky in flashes and wreaths of sculptured spray, as if the breakers on the Lido shore had been frost-bound before they fell, and the sea-nymphs had inlaid them with coral and amethyst....

Let us enter the church itself. It is lost in still deeper twilight, to which the eye must be accustomed for some moments before the form of the building can be traced; and then there opens before us a vast cave, hewn out into the form of a Cross, and divided into shadowy aisles by many pillars. Round the domes of its roof the light enters only through narrow apertures like large stars; and here and there a ray or two from some far-away casement wanders into the darkness, and casts a narrow phosphoric stream upon the waves of marble that heave and fall in a thousand colours along the floor. What else there is of light is from torches, or silver lamps, burning ceaselessly in the recesses of the chapels; the roof sheeted with gold, and the polished walls covered with alabaster, give back at every curve and angle some feeble gleaming to the flames; and the glories round the heads of the sculptured saints flash out upon us as we pass them, and sink again into the gloom. Under foot and over head, a continual succession of crowded imagery, one picture passing into another, as in a dream; forms beautiful and terrible mixed together; dragons and serpents, and ravening beasts of prey, and graceful birds that in the midst of them drink from running fountains and feed from vases of crystal; the passions and the pleasures of human life symbolized together, and the mystery of its redemption; for the mazes of interwoven lines and changeful pictures lead always at last to the Cross, lifted and carved in every place and upon every stone; sometimes with the serpent of eternity wrapt round it, sometimes with doves beneath its arms, and sweet herbage growing forth from its feet; but conspicuous most of all on the great rood that crosses the church before the altar, raised in bright blazonry against the shadow of the apse. And although in the recesses of the aisles and chapels, when the mist of the incense hangs heavily, we may see continually a figure traced in faint lines upon their marble, a woman standing with her eyes raised to heaven, and the inscription above her, "Mother of God," she is not here the presiding deity. It is the Cross that is first seen, and always, burning in the centre of the temple; and every dome and hollow of its roof has the figure of Christ in the utmost height of it, raised in power, or returning in judgment.

Henry Adams
(1838-1918)
The Virgin of Chartres
from *Mont-Saint-Michel and Chartres*

The American historian Henry Adams conceived of his Mont-Saint-Michel and Chartres, *"a study in 13th Century unity," as a contrast to his autobiography,* The Education of Henry Adams, *"a study of 20th Century multiplicity." Both have become classics. In prose that is clear and often beautiful, the former book describes two of the greatest of medieval architectural monuments, relates them to the artistic and religious thought of the time, and demonstrates why he, like so many others, "felt irresistibly attracted to an age in which he saw spiritual unity and peace."*

We must take ten minutes to accustom our eyes to the light, and we had better use them to seek the reason why we came to Chartres rather than to Rheims or Amiens or Bourges, for the cathedral that fills our ideal. The truth is, there are several reasons; there generally are, for doing the things we like; and after you have studied Chartres to the ground, and got your reasons settled, you will never find an antiquarian to agree with you; the architects will probably listen to you with contempt; and even these excellent priests, whose kindness is great, whose patience is heavenly, and whose good opinion you would so gladly gain, will turn from you with pain, if not with horror. The Gothic is singular in this; one seems easily at home in the Renaissance; one is not too strange in the Byzantine; as for the Roman, it is ourselves; and we could walk blindfolded through every chink and cranny of the Greek mind; all these styles seem modern, when we come close to them; but the Gothic gets away. No two men think alike about it, and no woman agrees with either man. The Church itself never agreed about it, and the architects agree even less than the priests. To most minds it casts too many shadows; it wraps itself in mystery; and when people talk of mystery, they commonly mean fear. To others, the Gothic seems hoary with age and decrepitude, and its shadows mean death. What is curious to watch is the fanatical conviction of the Gothic enthusiast, to whom the twelfth century means exuberant youth, the eternal child of Wordsworth, over whom its immortality broods like the day; it is so simple and yet so complicated; it seems so much and so little; it loves so many toys and cares for so few necessities; its youth is so young, its age so old, and its youthful yearning for old thought is so disconcerting, like the mysterious senility of the baby that

Deaf and silent, reads the eternal deep
Haunted forever by the eternal mind.

One need not take it more seriously than one takes the baby itself. Our amusement is to play with it, and to catch its meaning in its smile; and whatever Chartres may be now, when young it was a smile. To the Church, no doubt, its cathedral here has a fixed and administrative meaning, which is the same as that of every bishop's seat and with which we have nothing whatever to do. To us, it is a child's fancy; a toyhouse to please the Queen of Heaven—to please her so much that she would be happy in it—to charm her till she smiled.

CHARTRES CATHEDRAL, FRANCE

MONT-SAINT-MICHEL, IN FRANCE

The Queen Mother was as majestic as you like; she was absolute; she could be stern; she was not above being angry; but she was still a woman, who loved grace, beauty, ornament—her toilette, robes, jewels;—who considered the arrangements of her palace with attention, and liked both light and colour; who kept a keen eye on her Court, and exacted prompt and willing obedience from king and archbishops as well as from beggars and drunken priests. She protected her friends and punished her enemies. She required space, beyond what was known in the Courts of kings, because she was liable at all times to have ten thousand people begging her for favours—most inconsistent with law—and deaf to refusal. She was extremely sensitive to neglect, to disagreeable impressions, to want of intelligence in her surroundings. She was the greatest artist, as she was the greatest philosopher and musician and theologist, that ever lived on earth, except her Son, Who, at Chartres, is still an infant under her guardianship. This church was built for her in this spirit of simple-minded, practical, utilitarian faith—in this singleness of thought, exactly as a little girl sets up a dollhouse for her favourite blonde doll. Unless you can go back to your dolls, you are out of place here. If you can go back to them, and get rid for one small hour of the weight of custom, you shall see Chartres in glory. . . .

If you are to get the full enjoyment of Chartres, you must, for the time, believe in Mary as Bernard and Adam did, and feel her presence as the architects did in every stone they placed, and every touch they chiselled. You must try first to rid your mind of the traditional idea that the Gothic is an intentional expression of religious gloom. The necessity for light was the motive of the Gothic architects. They needed light and always more light, until they sacrificed safety and common sense in trying to get it. They converted their walls into windows, raised their vaults, diminished their piers, until their churches could no longer stand. You will see the limits at Beauvais; at Chartres we have not got so far, but even here, in places where the Virgin wanted it—as above the high altar—the architect has taken all the light there was to take. For the same reason, fenestration became the most important part of the Gothic architect's work, and at Chartres was uncommonly interesting because the architect was obliged to design a new system, which should at the same time satisfy the laws of construction and the taste and imagination of Mary. No doubt the first command of the Queen of Heaven was for light, but the second, at least equally imperative, was for colour. Any earthly queen, even though she were not Byzantine in taste, loved colour; and the truest of queens—the only true Queen of Queens—had richer and finer taste in colour than the queens of fifty earthly kingdoms, as you will see when we come to the immense effort to gratify her in the glass of her windows. Illusion for illusion—granting for the moment that Mary was an illusion—the Virgin Mother in this instance repaid to her worshippers a larger return for their money than the capitalist has ever been able to get, at least in this world, from any other illusion of wealth which he has tried to make a source of pleasure and profit.

The next point on which Mary evidently insisted was the arrangement for her private apartments, the apse, as distinguished from her throne-room, the choir; both being quite distinct from the hall, or reception-room of the public, which was the nave with its enlargement in the transepts. This arrangement marks the distinction between churches built as shrines for the deity and churches built as halls of worship for the public. The difference is chiefly in the apse, and the apse of Chartres is the most interesting of all apses from this point of view.

The Virgin required chiefly these three things, or, if you like, these four: space, light, convenience; and colour decoration to unite and harmonize the whole. This concerns the interior; on the exterior she required statuary, and the only complete system of decorative sculpture that existed seems to belong to her churches: Paris, Rheims, Amiens, and Chartres. Mary required all this magnificence at Chartres for herself alone, not for the public. As far as one can see into the spirit of the builders, Chartres was exclusively intended for the Virgin, as the Temple of Abydos was intended for Osiris. The wants of man, beyond a mere roof-cover, and perhaps space to some degree, enter to no very great extent into the problems of Chartres. Man came to render homage or to ask favours. The Queen received him in her palace, where she alone was at home, and alone gave commands. . . .

Among all the thirteenth-century windows the western rose alone seems to affect a rivalry in brilliancy with the lancets, and carries it so far that the separate medallions and pictures are quite lost—especially in the direct sunshine—blending in a confused effect of opals, in a delirium of colour and light, with a result like a cluster of stones in jewelry. Assuming as one must, in want of the artist's instruction, that he knew what he wanted to do, and did it, one must take for granted that he treated the rose as a whole, and aimed at giving it harmony with the three precious windows beneath. The effect is that of a single large ornament; a round breastpin, or what is now called a sunburst, of jewels, with pendants beneath.

We are ignorant tourists, liable to much error in trying to seek motives in artists who worked seven hundred years ago for a society which thought and felt in forms quite unlike ours, but the mediaeval pilgrim was more ignorant than we, and much simpler in mind; if the idea of an ornament occurs to us, it certainly occurred to him, and still more the glassworker whose business was to excite his illusions. An artist, if good for anything, foresees what his public will see; and what his public will see is what he ought to have intended—the measure of his genius. If the public sees more than he himself did, this is his credit; if less, this is his fault. No matter how simple or ignorant we are, we ought to feel a discord or a harmony where the artist meant us to feel it, and when we see a motive, we conclude that other people have seen it before us, and that it must, therefore, have been intended. Neither of the transept roses is treated like this one; neither has the effect of a personal ornament; neither is treated as a jewel. No one knew so well as the artist that such treatment must give the effect of a jewel. . . .

No artist would have ventured to put up, before the eyes of Mary in Majesty, above the windows so dear to her, any object that she had not herself commanded. Whether a miracle was necessary, or whether genius was enough, is a point of casuistry which you can settle with Albertus Magnus or Saint Bernard, and which you will understand as little when settled as before; but for us, beyond the futilities of unnecessary doubt, the Virgin designed this rose; not perhaps in quite the same perfect spirit in which she designed the lancets, but still wholly for her own pleasure and as her own idea. She placed upon the breast of her Church—which symbolized herself—a jewel so gorgeous that no earthly majesty could bear comparison with it, and which no other heavenly majesty has rivalled. As one watches the light play on it, one is still overcome by the glories of the jewelled rose and its three gemmed pendants; one feels a little of the effect she meant it to produce even on infidels, Moors, and heretics, but infinitely more on the men who feared and the women who adored her;—not to dwell too long upon it, one admits that hers is the only Church. One would admit anything that she should require. If you had only the soul of a shrimp, you would crawl, like the Abbé Suger, to kiss her feet. . . .

In the chapter entitled "The Court of the Queen of Heaven," Adams describes the seven windows of the apse, with the image of the Virgin in the center window. He concludes the chapter in this way.

There she actually is—not in symbol or in fancy, but in person, descending on her errands of mercy and listening to each one of us, as her miracles prove, or satisfying our prayers merely by her presence which calms our excitement as that of a mother calms her child. She is there as Queen, not merely as intercessor, and her power is such that to her the difference between us earthly beings is nothing. Her quiet, masculine strength enchants us most. Pierre Mauclerc and Philippe Hurepel and their men-at-arms are afraid of her, and the Bishop himself is never quite at his ease in her presence; but to peasants, and beggars, and people in trouble, this sense of her power and calm is better than active sympathy. People who suffer beyond the formulas of expression—who are crushed into silence, and beyond pain—want no display of emotion—no bleeding heart—no weeping at the foot of the Cross—no hysterics—no phrases! They want to see God, and to know that He is watching over His own. How many women are there, in this mass of thirteenth-century suppliants, who have lost children? Probably nearly all, for the death rate is very high in the conditions of mediaeval life. There are thousands of such women here, for it is precisely this class who come most; and probably every one of them has looked up to Mary in her great window, and has felt actual certainty, as though she saw with her own eyes—there, in heaven, while she looked—her own lost baby playing with the Christ-Child at the Virgin's knee, as much at home as the saints, and much more at home than the kings. Before rising from her knees, every one of these women will have bent down and kissed the stone pavement in gratitude for Mary's mercy. The earth, she says, is a sorry place, and the best of it is bad enough, no doubt, even for Queen Blanche and the Duchess Alix who has had to leave her children here alone; but there above is Mary in heaven who sees and hears me as I see her, and who keeps my little boy till I come; so I can wait with patience, more or less! Saints and prophets and martyrs are all very well, and Christ is very sublime and just, but Mary *knows*!

It was very childlike, very foolish, very beautiful, and very true—as art, at least: so true that everything else shades off into vulgarity, as you see the Persephone of a Syracusan coin shade off into the vulgarity of a Roman emperor; as though the heaven that lies about us in our infancy too quickly takes colours that are not so much sober as sordid, and would be welcome if no worse than that. Vulgarity, too, has feeling, and its expression in art has truth and even pathos, but we shall have time enough in our lives for that, and all the more because, when we rise from our knees now, we have finished our pilgrimage. We have done with Chartres. For seven hundred years Chartres has seen pilgrims, coming and going more or less like us, and will perhaps see them for another seven hundred years; but we shall see it no more, and can safely leave the Virgin in her majesty, with her three great prophets on either hand, as calm and confident in their own strength and in God's providence as they were when Saint Louis was born, but looking down from a deserted heaven, into an empty church, on a dead faith.

RENAISSANCE

RENAISSANCE

The term *renaissance* could aptly be applied to many periods in the history of the world's development. Earlier we spoke of the interest Charlemagne had in the arts and learning (the Carolingian Renaissance); and the term is also applied to the nineteenth-century American literary surge (the American Renaissance). Renaissance means *rebirth*. Historically, rebirth has often been demonstrated in the arts through a renewed interest, a cultivation. However, the renaissance that occurred from as early as the twelfth and thirteenth centuries and extended in many respects to the eighteenth is *the* Renaissance; more specifically, scholars mean the fourteenth, fifteenth, sixteenth, and early seventeenth centuries in speaking of it. The Renaissance is that period that marked the change from the medieval to the modern world. Intellectual and creative emphasis shifted from the religious aspects of life to the secular.

Secular Trends and the Church

This shifting from religious to secular emphasis owed its impetus to several circumstances. One of the primary ones was the weakening of the church. The papacy grew increasingly worldly through the fourteenth and fifteenth centuries. And, of course, the confusion that resulted when Urban VI in Rome and Clement VII in Avignon both claimed to be the "sole representatives of God on earth" did not help. The consequences of these and other worldly acts encouraged the reforming attempts that spread throughout the church and in many instances prompted men such as Wycliffe and Luther to challenge them.

Couple this weakening of the church with the impact of Classicism, and the result is a trend to secularism. From the earlier investigations of scholasticism and its attempt to find a compromise between the knowledge and attainments of the classical world and the dogma of Christianity came many new concepts. The medieval man saw himself as part of a large hierarchy, assigned a place and a function and no more. This idea would have been anathema to the Greeks. To them man's potential was what he would make of it; the only limits were those he imposed on himself.

In the search to find a means for combining the two, Classicism and Christianity, several important developments took place. Scholars gathered at the universities and gradually the keys of education were handed to the layman. Before, educated men were churchmen. But specialization and professionalism grew as knowledge increased. *Humanism* (the movement that formed the highest expression of human values in the Greek and Roman writings) took root and was even supported by the popes, who were happy to find an outlet for possible detractors.

The Renaissance humanists sought to exalt man, to endow him with power and reason, to make him higher than the medieval near-animal image and elevate him to a sphere nearer the angels. Whereas the philosophers of the Middle Ages set their hopes and minds on the next world, the humanists wanted to demonstrate that man's interests and resources were of importance in this world. The humanist found his basis or touchstone in the Greek and Roman writers, the ancients, who considered man a reasonable, intelligent entity and therefore provided him with a graceful, expressive, and effective culture. In the classical writings and discourses the humanists found the qualities of thought, reason, form, and control which they felt would best serve as models for the progressive intellectual future man. Not only on the intellectual basis would man improve himself with the proper study and guidance, but also on the physical level. The classical Greeks of course emphasized physical grace and strength as well as intellectual.

Besides this, as the development of independent philosophies and intense interest in the sciences took place (thanks to Arabic influences as well as Greek), theology no longer held all the answers for questing minds. The church did not influence the arts as strongly as before. Religious artistic conventions, particularly evidenced in literature by symbolism and allegory, were employed less often as writers turned more and more to the world around them, the world of reality and facts.

Travel, too, was a strong influence for change. Travel, of course, promotes the interchange of ideas and widens man's view of the world. Travel also encourages commercialism. And what is more natural than the dissemination of knowledge that came as a result of the development of printing about 1450? No longer laboriously copied by hand, works became readily available to those who could afford them and who showed an interest in them.

As we mentioned earlier, the strong move toward nationalism helped shape the spirit of the Renaissance. Nations vied for supremacy, on land and sea. Horizons broadened, and the world was opened for exploration and conquest. There is no time nor place for stagnation when the tides of change are sweeping the land.

There was much to be learned and much to be regained.

Literature

The rediscovery of classical writing with its many literary forms—lyric poetry, drama, and philosophy—strongly influenced the literature of the Renaissance. There were writers who tried to compose in the style and form of these ancient literary models. And though many of the Greek writings were translated into Latin, the vernacular was not neglected, especially in Italy. Two early Italian Renaissance humanists who successfully wrote in the vernacular were Petrarch (1304-1374) and Boccaccio (1313-1375).

Petrarch wrote numerous works, some in Latin imitating Virgil. He is best remembered, however, for his collections of love poems, sonnets, addressed to Laura. Though she was happily married and at times found him a bit of a nuisance, he continued to address poems to her for over twenty-five years. Initially the poems expressed a love that was human and real. But over the years the love was transformed. Laura's beauty and Petrarch's love became symbolic of the way to attain God, a neo-Platonic concept that continued to be significant in most of the humanistic Renaissance poetry that followed. Intense and personal, the poems express real feelings, typifying the concerns and struggles of a "modern man."

Petrarch reacted against the ideals of the Middle Ages; Boccaccio, even more so. Boccaccio was a part of the "new society" that was founded on wit and pleasure. His early writing reflected the life he had led in Florence and Naples; the *Decameron* belongs to this period. After meeting Petrarch, the poet laureate of Italy, in 1350, his writing changed. His later years were spent in writing long works in Latin, all designed to teach and elevate.

A great deal of the study of Classicism often missed the point. Some court writers failed to see below the surface knowledge and application: they became more concerned with form than content, cleverness than wisdom. But a new spirit did grow from this study, the spirit of individual inquiry. Rather than accept long-established tradition and dogma, the Renaissance man began to look at the facts. This idea is applied to statesmanship in Machiavelli's (1469-1527) *The Prince,* greatly influential during the Renaissance.

The church also had an impact on the humanistic movement. Erasmus (1466-1536) in *The Praise of Folly* helped the course of the Reformation with that satire and other writings directed at the weakness of the church and national leaders. Northern humanists attempted to reform the church from within or break entirely.

Renaissance literature abounded in lyrics. The sonnet was a particularly popular form that prompted the writing of many sonnet cycles. Wyatt and Surrey picked up the sonnet from Petrarch, giving it a peculiarly English "sound." The conventions of unrequited love and elaborate conceits to illustrate them were carried on. Despite the fact that the sonnet form was characterized by artifice and concern with form, it nevertheless had great popularity.

The writers of the Renaissance wrote under circumstances much different from today's. The court supported many writers; the courtier, however, did not publish his work. It was disseminated privately among court members. Many writers were supported by the universities. Other writers had patrons who subsidized them in their literary endeavors. A few publishers began to appear in the sixteenth century, but the pay was minimal. The state maintained too tight a rein over publications yet for them to have much freedom.

Edmund Spenser
(1552-1599)
from *An Hymn in Honour of Beauty*

The influence of Plato can clearly be seen in much Renaissance art, including the following selection from Spenser's Four Hymns.

Ah! whither, Love! wilt thou now carry me?
What wontless fury dost thou now inspire
Into my feeble breast, too full of thee?
Whilst seeking to aslake thy raging fire,
Thou in me kindlest much more great desire,
And up aloft above my strength dost raise
The wondrous matter of my fire to praise.

That as I erst, in praise of thine own name,
So now in honour of thy mother dear,
An honourable hymn I eke should frame,
And, with the brightness of her beauty clear,
The ravisht hearts of gazeful men might rear
To admiration of that heavenly light,
From whence proceeds such soul-enchanting might.

Thereto do thou, great goddess! Queen of Beauty,
Mother of love, and of all world's delight,
Without whose sovereign grace and kindly duty
Nothing on earth seems fair to fleshly sight,
Do thou vouchsafe with thy love-kindling light
T' illuminate my dim and dullèd eyne,
And beautify this sacred hymn of thine:

That both to thee, to whom I mean it most,
And eke to her, whose fair immortal beam
Hath darted fire into my feeble ghost,
That now it wasted is with woes extreme,
It may so please, that she at length will stream
Some dew of grace into my withered heart,
After long sorrow and consuming smart.

What time this world's great Workmaster did cast
To make all things such as we now behold,
It seems that he before his eyes had placed
A goodly pattern, to whose perfect mould
He fashioned them as comely as he could;
That now so fair and seemly they appear,
As nought may be amended anywhere.

That wondrous pattern, wheresoe'er it be,
Whether in earth laid up in secret store,
Or else in heaven, that no man may it see
With sinful eyes, for fear it to deflore,
Is perfect Beauty, which all men adore;
Whose face and feature doth so much excel
All mortal sense, that none the same may tell.

Thereof as every earthly thing partakes
Or more or less, by influence divine,
So it more fair accordingly it makes,
And the gross matter of this earthly mine
Which clotheth it, thereafter doth refine,
Doing away the dross which dims the light
Of that fair beam which therein is empight.

For, through infusion of celestial power,
The duller earth it quick'neth with delight,
And lifeful spirits privily doth pour
Through all the parts, that to the looker's sight
They seem to please. That is thy sovereign might,
O Cyprian queen! which flowing from the beam
Of thy bright star, thou into them dost stream.

That is the thing which giveth pleasant grace
To all things fair, that kindleth lively fire,

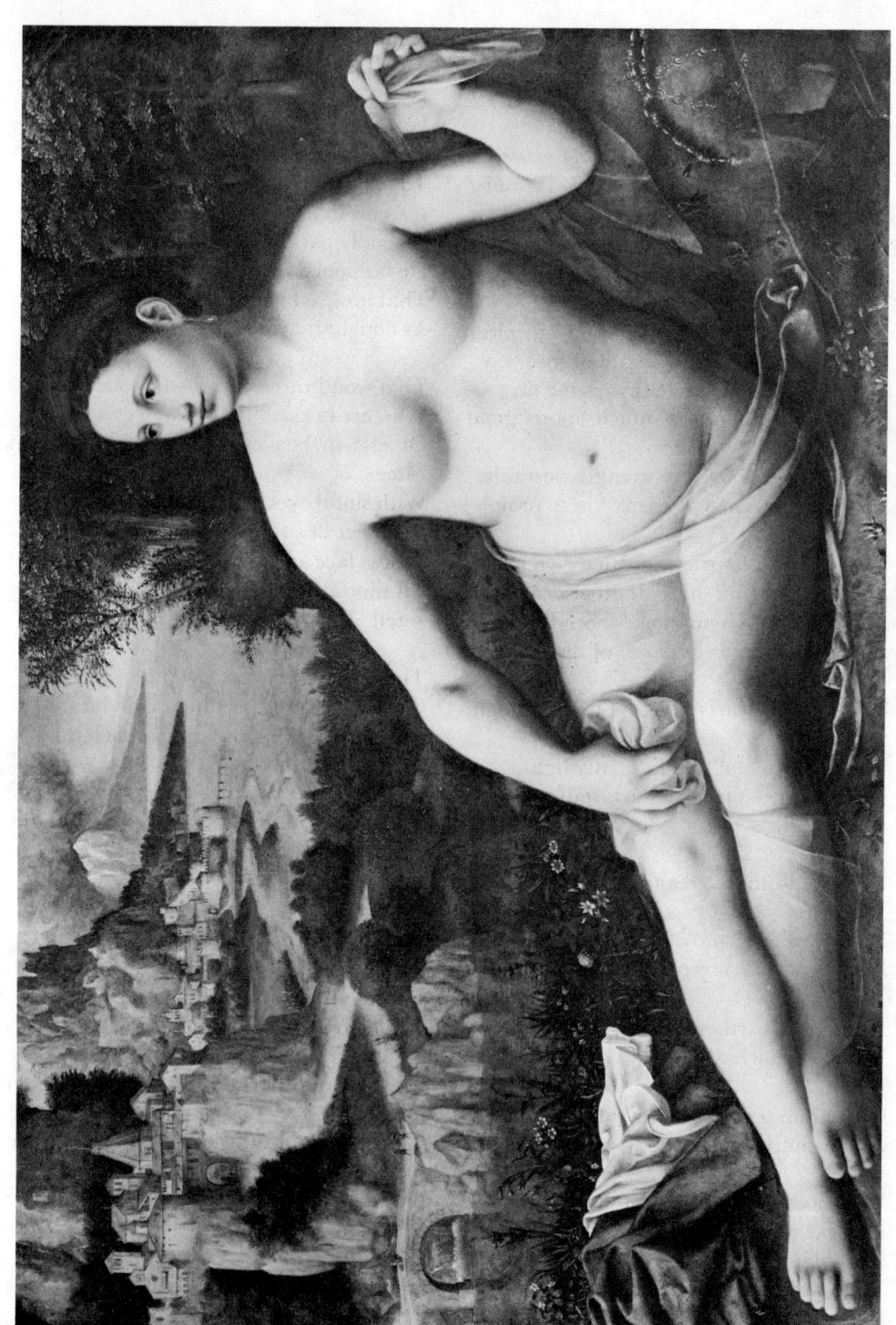

BERNARDINO LUINI: *Venus*, SAMUEL H. KRESS COLLECTION, NATIONAL GALLERY OF ART, WASHINGTON, D. C.

Light of thy lamp, which, shining in the face,
Thence to the soul darts amorous desire,
And robs the hearts of those which it admire;
Therewith thou pointest thy son's pois'ned arrow,
That wounds the life, and wastes the inmost marrow.

How vainly then do idle wits invent,
That beauty is nought else but mixture made
Of colours fair, and goodly temp'rament
Of pure complexions, that shall quickly fade
And pass away, like to a summer's shade;
Or that it is but comely composition
Of parts well measured, with meet disposition!

Hath white and red in it such wondrous power,
That it can pierce through th' eyes unto the heart,
And therein stir such rage and restless stour,
As nought but death can stint his dolour's smart?
Or can proportion of the outward part
Move such affection in the inward mind,
That it can rob both sense and reason blind?

Why do not then the blossoms of the field,
Which are arrayed with much more orient hue,
And to the sense most dainty odours yield,
Work like impression in the looker's view?
Or why do not fair pictures like power shew,
In which of-times we nature see of art
Excelled, in perfect limning every part?

But ah! believe me there is more than so,
That works such wonders in the minds of men;
I, that have often proved, too well it know,
And whoso list the like assays to ken,
Shall find by trial, and confess it then,
That Beauty is not, as fond men misdeem,
An outward shew of things that only seem.

For that same goodly hue of white and red,
With which the cheeks are sprinkled, shall decay,
And those sweet rosy leaves, so fairly spread
Upon the lips, shall fade and fall away
To that they were, even to corrupted clay;
That golden wire, those sparkling stars so bright,
Shall turn to dust, and lose their goodly light.

But that fair lamp, from whose celestial ray
That light proceeds, which kindleth lovers' fire,
Shall never be extinguished nor decay;
But, when the vital spirits do expire,
Unto her native planet shall retire;
For it is heavenly born and cannot die,
Being a parcel of the purest sky.

For when the soul, the which derived was,
At first, out of that great immortal Sprite,
By whom all life to lofe, whilom did pass
Down from the top of purest heaven's height
To be embodied here, it then took light
And lively spirits from that fairest star,
Which lights the world forth from his fiery car.

Which power retaining still or more or less,
When she in fleshly seed is eft enraced,
Through every part she doth the same impress,

According as the heavens have her graced,
And frames her house, in which she will be placed,
Fit for herself, adorning it with spoil
Of th' heavenly riches which she robbed erewhile.

Thereof it comes that these fair souls, which have
The most resemblance of that heavenly light,
Frame to themselves most beautiful and brave
Their fleshly bower, most fit for their delight,
And the gross matter by a sovereign might
Tempers so trim, that it may well be seen
A palace fit for such a Virgin Queen.

So every spirit, as it is more pure,
And hath in it the more of heavenly light,
So it the fairer body doth procure
To habit in, and it more fairly dight
With cheerful grace and amiable sight.
For of the soul the body form doth take:
For soul is form, and doth the body make.

Therefore wherever that thou dost behold
A comely corpse, with beauty fair endued,
Know this for certain, that the same doth hold
A beauteous soul, with fair conditions thewed,
Fit to receive the seed by virtue strewed.
For all that fair is, is by nature good;
That is a sign to know the gentle blood.

Yet oft it falls that many a gentle mind
Dwells in deformèd tabernacle drowned,
Either by chance, against the course of kind,
Or through unaptness in the substance found,
Which it assumèd of some stubborn ground,
That will not yield unto her form's direction,
But is deformed with some foul imperfection.

And oft it falls, (ay me, the more to rue!)
That goodly beauty, albe heaven born,
Is foul abused, and that celestial hue,
Which doth the world with her delight adorn,
Made but the bait of sin, and sinners' scorn,
Whilst every one doth seek and sue to have it,
But every one doth seek but to deprave it.

Yet nathemore is that fair beauty's blame,
But theirs that do abuse it unto ill:
Nothing so good, but that through guilty shame
May be corrupt, and wrested unto will:
Natheless the soul is fair and beauteous still,
However flesh's fault it filthy make;
For things immortal no corruption take.

(Lines 1-161; spelling and capitalization modernized by McGinn and Howerton)

Desiderius Erasmus
(1466-1536)
The Powers and Pleasures of Folly
from *The Praise of Folly*
from PART II

I must not pass over those nobodies who take enormous pride in empty titles of nobility. One will trace his family back to Aeneas, another to Brutus, and a third to King Arthur. They are surrounded by busts and portraits of their ancestors. They name over their grandfathers and great-grandfathers, and have the old titles by heart. At the same time, they are not far from being senseless statues themselves, and are probably worth less than the ones they show off. My follower, Self-love, enables them to live happily, however; and there are always other fools who regard monsters like these as gods.

Of course Self-love brings joy to others too. This ape-like fellow here seems handsome enough to himself. That one drawing circles over there thinks he is another Euclid. The man with the rooster's voice considers himself a great musician. The happiest fool, however, is the dolt who glories in some talent which is really made possible by his followers. Seneca tells of that doubly-happy rich man, for example, who had servants on hand to refresh his memory whenever he told stories. He was so weak he could hardly stand, but he was a great fighter—with the support of hired thugs.

Artists are notoriously conceited. They would rather lose the family homestead than any part of their talent. This is especially true of actors, singers, orators, and poets. The worse they are, the more insolent, pushing, and conceited they become. And the more applause they receive. The worst always please the most, because the majority of people, as I have remarked, are fools. If the poorer artist is most pleased with himself and is admired by the largest number, why should he wish to have true skill? It will cost him more; it will make him self-conscious and critical; and it will please far fewer of his audience.

I observe that races and cities are also attended by self-love. The English pride themselves on their good looks, their music, and their fine food, among other things. Noble or royal lineage is the claim of all Scots, together with argumentative skill. The French are the masters of courtesy; and the Parisians, in addition, are the only ones who understand theology. The Italians have a monopoly on literature and eloquence, and they are pleased to admit that they alone are not barbarians. Happiest in this delusion are the Romans, who dream pleasantly of their ancient glories. The Venetians are content with their own nobility. The Greeks, of course, discovered the arts and possess the heroes of antiquity. Christian superstitions entertain the Turks and the other actual barbarians, who boast of their own religions. Better yet, the Jews steadfastly await the Messiah, and still hold grimly to Moses. The Spaniards scorn all other soldiers; and the Germans pride themselves on their great size and their knowledge of magic. I believe this is sufficient to convince you that the happiness of men, individually and collectively, springs from self-love.

Another source of pleasure is flattery, an extension of self-love. Instead of admiring yourself, you simply admire someone else. Nowadays flattery is condemned, but only among those who confuse the names of things with the things themselves. They think that flattery is necessarily insincere. The example of dumb animals should show them how wrong they are. What is more fawning than a dog? And yet, what is more faithful and a better friend to man? Or perhaps you prefer fierce lions, tigers, and leopards? Of course there is a harmful kind of flattery, the kind with which traitors and mockers destroy their victims; but my kind springs from kindliness and candor. It is much closer to virtue than is its opposite, surliness—or what Horace calls a heavy and awkward rudeness. It raises the spirits and dispels grief; it stimulates the faint, enlivens the dull, and eases the suffering; it brings lovers together and keeps them together. It entices boys to study literature; it inspires the old. Disguised as praise, it warns and instructs princes without offense. In short, it makes everyone more pleased with himself—which is the chief part of happiness. What is more courteous than the way two mules scratch each other? There is no need to point out that flattery is important in the admired art of oratory, that it is a great part of medicine, and that it is a still greater part of poetry. It is nothing less than the sugar and spice of all human intercourse.

Still, it is a sad thing, they say, to be deceived: No; the saddest thing is not to be deceived. The notion that happiness comes from a knowledge of things as they really are is wrong. Happiness resides in opinion. Human affairs are so obscure and various that nothing can be clearly known. This was the sound conclusion of the Academics, who were the least surly of the philosophers. At least if something can be truly known, it is rarely anything that adds to the pleasure of life. Anyway, man's mind is much more taken with appearances than with reality. This can be easily and surely tested by going to church. When anything serious is being said, the congregation dozes or squirms. But if the ranter—I mean the reverend—begins some old wives' tale, as often happens, everyone wakes up and strains to hear. You will also see more devotion being paid to such fabulous and poetic saints as George, Christopher, or Barbara than to Peter or Paul or even to Christ Himself. But these examples belong elsewhere.

The price of this kind of happiness is very low. Much more must be paid for substantial things, even for the least of them—grammar, for instance. It is easy enough to acquire mere opinions; nevertheless they bring greater happiness than knowledge does. The satisfaction of a man who thinks rotten kippers taste and smell like ambrosia is not affected by the fact that his neighbor cannot abide their odor. On the other hand, if the finest fish turn your stomach, their quality has no bearing on your happiness. A man who thinks his extremely ugly wife is another Venus is as well off as if she really were beautiful. Here's a person who gazes admiringly at a picture made of red lead and mud which he believes is by Apelles or Zeuxis. Isn't he happier than someone who has paid a high price for an authentic masterpiece, but who gets little pleasure from it? I know a man by my name, a practical joker, who gave his new wife some imitation jewels and persuaded her that they were genuine and very valuable. Now what difference did it make to the girl? She was delighted with the glass trinkets and kept them locked in a secret place. In the meantime, the husband had saved money, had enjoyed fooling his wife, and had won her devotion as well as he would have by a more expensive present.

What difference do you see between the self-satisfied inhabitants of Plato's cave who contentedly admire the shadows of things, and the wise man who emerges from the cave and sees reality? If Lucian's Micyllus could have dreamed forever his rich and golden dream, there would have been no reason for him to desire any other kind of happiness. Evidently, then, there is either no difference between a fool and a wise man, or if there is a difference, a fool has the better of it. A fool's happiness costs least—no more than a bit of illusion. In addition, it is enjoyed in the company of a great many others. The good things of life must be shared to be delightful; and who has not heard of the scarcity of wise men, if indeed any exist at all. The Greeks listed seven all told; a more accurate census would do well to turn up one-half or one-third of a wise man.

Of course drink will drown your sorrows, but only for a time. The next morning they come galloping back, riding four white horses, as the saying is. Folly, on the other hand, is a spree that never ends. Its effect is complete and immediate. Without requiring any bothersome preparations, it fills the heart with joy. It is available to all, rather than to a chosen few, as with other gifts of the gods. Vintage wine is not made everywhere; beauty comes to few, and eloquence to fewer still. Not many are rich, and not many can be kings. Mars often favors neither side; Neptune drowns more than he saves. The majority are turned away from wisdom. Jove himself thunders, and the anti-Joves—Pluto, Ate, Poena, Febris, and the others—are executioners rather than gods. Only I, great-hearted Folly, embrace all men equally. Nor do I come only when prayed for. If some devotion is neglected, I don't grow testy and demand expiation. I don't upset heaven and earth if I have been left at home and not invited along with the other gods to smell the sacrifices. In fact, the other gods are so hard to please that it is safer and wiser not to try to worship them, but rather to avoid them altogether. Men are sometimes like that; so thin-skinned and irritable that hands off is the best policy.

Even though all this is so, I understand that no one sacrifices to Folly or builds a temple for her. Such ingratitude, I repeat, is amazing. At the same time, I good-naturedly persuade myself that respect is not really lacking. What need have I for incense, meal, a he-goat, or a she-hog, so long as men everywhere wholeheartedly worship me in the way that preachers tell us is best? Let Diana have her human sacrifices! I am not envious when I consider that all men honor me in the truest way, that is, by taking me to their hearts and manifesting me in their lives and actions. This kind of worship of the saints is not exactly customary among Christians. Plenty of them burn little candles to the Virgin, and in the middle of the day, when it does no good; but how few of them burn with zeal to imitate her in chastity, temperance, and love of heavenly things! That, after all, is the true worship, and it is by far the most pleasing to those above.

(Translated by Leonard F. Dean)

Giovanni Boccaccio
(1313-1375)
The Plague of 1348
from the Introduction to the *Decameron*

Art historians have drawn attention to the impact on the arts of the terrible plague of 1348. A remarkable firsthand description of the immediate effects of the plague on the city of Florence is found in Boccaccio's introduction to his Decameron; *here he uses the ravaging of the stricken city to provide a framework for the telling of his tales. Some of the more famous of those stories are included here following the selection from the introduction.*

In the year of our Lord 1348, there happened at Florence, the finest city in all Italy, a most terrible plague; which, whether owing to the influence of the planets, or that it was sent from God as a just punishment for our sins, had broken out some years before in the Levant, and after passing from place to place, and making incredible havoc all the way, had now reached the west. There, in spite of all the means that art and human foresight could suggest, such as keeping the city clear from filth, the exclusion of all suspected persons, and the publication of copious instructions for the preservation of health; and notwithstanding manifold humble supplications offered to God in processions and otherwise, it began to show itself in the spring of the year mentioned, in a sad and wonderful manner. Unlike what had been seen in the east, where bleeding from

ROGIER VAN DER WEYDEN: *Portrait of a Lady*, ANDREW MELLON COLLECTION, NATIONAL GALLERY OF ART, WASHINGTON, D. C.

the nose is the fatal sign of a swift death to follow, here there appeared certain tumors in the groin or under the armpits, some as big as a small apple, others the size of an egg; and afterwards purple spots in most parts of the body, in some cases large but few in number, in other smaller and more numerous—both sorts the usual messengers of death. To the cure of this disease, neither medical knowledge nor the power of drugs was of any effect. Whether because the disease was in its own nature mortal, or that the physicians (the number of whom, taking quacks and women pretenders into account, was grown very great) could form no just idea of the cause, nor consequently devise a true method of cure—whichever was the reason, few escaped. Nearly all died the third day after the first appearance of the symptoms, some sooner, some later, without any fever or other accessory symptoms. What gave the more virulence to this plague was that, by being communicated from the sick to the well, it spread daily, like fire that catches everything combustible near it. Nor was it caught only by conversing with or coming near the sick, but even by touching their clothes, or anything that they had touched before. It is wonderful, what I am going to mention; and had I not seen it with my own eyes, and were there not many witnesses to attest it besides myself, I should never venture to relate it. Such, I say, was the malignancy of this plague as to pass not only from man to man but from the infected garments of a man to another creature, and even to kill that creature in a short space of time. One instance of this kind I took particular notice of: the rags of a poor man just dead had been thrown into the street; two hogs came up, and after rooting among the rags and shaking them about in their mouths, in less than an hour they both turned round and died on the spot.

These facts and others of the same sort prompted various fears and practices among those who survived, all tending to the same cruel and uncharitable end, which was to avoid the sick and everything that had been near them. They expected by that means to save themselves.

Some, considering it best to live temperately and to avoid excesses of all kinds, formed small communities and shut themselves up from the rest of the world, eating and drinking moderately of the best, and diverting themselves with music and such other entertainments as they might have within doors. They never listened to anything from without which might make them uneasy. Others maintained free living to be a better preservative, and they would restrain no passion or appetite that they wished to gratify, drinking and reveling incessantly from tavern to tavern or in private houses (which were frequently found to be deserted by their owners and therefore open to everyone); and, in all this brutal indulgence, strenuously avoiding contact with the infected. And such, at this time, was the public distress, that the laws, human and divine, were no longer regarded; since the officers who were to enforce them were either dead, sick, or in want of persons to assist them, everyone did just as he pleased.

Many others chose a course of life between these two, not confining themselves to rules of diet like the former and yet avoiding the intemperance of the latter. They ate and drank what their appetites required and walked everywhere with flowers or perfumes in their hands, thinking it best to comfort the brain in this way; for the whole atmosphere seemed to them tainted with the stench of the dead bodies, of the sick persons, and of the medicines they were using.

Others, with less humanity but with a greater desire to be secure from danger, decided that the only remedy for the pestilence was to avoid it. Convinced of this and taking care for themselves only, men and women in great numbers left the city, their houses, relations, and effects, and fled into the country, as if the wrath of God had been restrained to visit only those within the walls of the city; or else concluding that none ought to stay in a place thus doomed to destruction.

Thus divided as they were in their views, neither did all die nor all escape. Those who first set the example of forsaking others now often languished themselves unpitied. I pass over the little regard that citizens and relatives showed to each other. Their terror was such that a brother even fled from his brother, a wife from her husband, and, what is more uncommon, a parent from his own child.

Hence many that fell sick could have no help but what the charity of friends (who were few) or the greed of servants supplied; for servants were scarce and hardly available even at extravagant wages, and they were so little used to the business that they were only fit to hand the sick what they asked for and watch them as they died. And this desire of the servants to get money often cost them their own lives. As a result of this desertion of friends and scarcity of servants, a custom unheard of before now prevailed: no lady, however young or beautiful, would hesitate to be attended by a man-servant, whether young or old it mattered not, and to expose herself naked to him because of the necessity of her disease, as though it were to a woman. This practice might make those who survived less modest thereafter.

Many lost their lives who might have escaped if they had been looked after at all. Between the scarcity of servants and the violence of the disease, such numbers were continually dying as made it terrible to hear about as well as to behold. Hence, from mere necessity, many customs were introduced that were different from what had been before known in the city.

It had been customary, as it now is, for the women who were friends and neighbors of the deceased to meet together at his house, and to lament with his relatives. At the same time the men would get together at the door, with a number of the clergy, according to the person's circumstances. Then the corpse was carried by people of his own rank, with the solemnity of tapers and singing, to the church where the deceased had desired to be buried. This custom was now laid aside, and, far from having a crowd of women to lament over them, great numbers of persons passed out of the world without a witness. Few were they who had the tears of their friends at their departure; on the contrary, their friends were laughing and making themselves merry—even the women had learned to ignore every other concern except their own lives. Few were the bodies that were attended by more than ten or a dozen; nor were these honorable citizens, but men of low rank hired for the purpose. They would put themselves under the bier and carry it with all possible haste to the nearest church; and the corpse was interred, without any great ceremony, wherever they could find room.

As for the lower and many of the middle classes, the scene was still more affecting. For they stayed at home either through poverty or hope of relief in distress, fell sick daily by thousands, and, having nobody to attend them, generally died. Some breathed their last in the streets, and others were shut up in their own houses, where the stench that came from them made their deaths known to their neighbors. And indeed, every place was filled with the dead. Hence it became a general practice—more from regard for the living than from pity for the dead—for the neighbors, with the aid of porters if they could get them, to clear all the houses and lay the bodies at the doors. Every morning great numbers of bodies might be seen brought out in this manner, to be carried away on biers or on tables, two or three at a time. Sometimes it happened that a wife and her husband, two or three brothers, or a father and son were carried off on the same bier.

It frequently happened that while two or three priests walked before a corpse with their crucifixes, several sets of porters fell in behind them; and where the priests thought they had but one body to bury, there would be six or eight or more. Nor were there any to follow and shed a few tears over them, for things had reached such a pass that men's lives were no more regarded than the lives of so many beasts. . . .

Since the consecrated ground could no longer contain the numbers which were continually brought there, especially as they were desirous of laying everyone in the parts allotted to their families, they were forced to dig trenches and put them in by hundreds, piling them up in rows, as goods are stored in a ship, and throwing in a little earth till they were filled to the top.

Not to dwell upon every particular of our misery, I shall observe that it fared no better with the adjacent country. The villages on a smaller scale were like the city; you might see the poor, distressed laborers, with their families, without either the aid of physicians or help of servants, languishing on the highways, in the fields, and in their own houses, and dying rather like cattle than human creatures. The result was that, growing dissolute and indifferent in their ways like the townspeople, and careless of everything, thinking every day to be their last, their thoughts were not employed with how to improve their substance but rather with how to use it for their present satisfaction. The cows, asses, sheep, goats, swine, and even the dogs, those faithful companions, were left to roam at will about the fields and among the standing corn, which no one cared to gather or reap; and many times, after they had filled themselves in the day, the animals would return to the farms at night of their own free will.

What more can I say, if I return to the city? I can only add that such was the cruelty of heaven, and perhaps of men, that between March and July, according to authentic reckonings, upwards of a hundred thousand souls perished in the city alone; before the calamity, it was not thought to have contained that many inhabitants. What magnificent dwellings, what noble palaces were then emptied to the last inhabitant! What families became extinct! What riches and vast possessions were left, and no known heir to inherit them! What numbers of both sexes, in the prime and vigor of youth, whom in the morning Galen, Hippocrates, or Aesculapius himself would have considered in perfect health, at noon dined with their relatives and friends, and supped at night with their departed friends in the other world!

(This is a modified version of a translation which first appeared anonymously in 1741.)

The Falcon of Federigo

In Florence dwelt a young gentleman named Federigo, son of Filippo Alberighi, who, in feats of arms and gentility, surpassed all the youth in Tuscany. This gentleman was in love with a lady called Monna Giovanna, one of the most agreeable women in Florence, and to gain her affection, he was continually making tilts, balls, and such diversions, lavishing away his money in rich presents and everything that was extravagant. But she, pure in conduct as she was fair, made no account either of what he did for her sake, or of himself.

As Federigo continued to live in this manner, spending profusely and acquiring nothing, his wealth failed, till at last he had nothing left but a small farm, the income of which was most slender, and a single falcon, one of the best in the world. Yet loving still more than ever, and finding he could subsist no longer in the city in the manner he would choose to live, he retired to his farm, where he went out hawking as often as the weather would permit, and bore his poverty patiently.

Now it happened, after he was thus brought low, that the lady's husband fell sick. Being very rich, he made a will by which he left all his substance to an only son, who was almost grown up; and if the son should die without issue, the substance should then revert to his lady, whom he was extremely fond of. When he had thus disposed of his fortune, he died. Monna Giovanna, being left a widow, retired to a house of hers in the country, near to that of Federigo. Thus it happened that her son became acquainted with him, and they used to divert themselves together with dogs and falcons; and the boy, having often seen Federigo's falcon and taking great delight in it, wanted to have it, but he dared not ask for it because he knew how Federigo valued it.

This being so, the boy soon fell sick. His mother felt great concern, for he was her only child, and she loved him extremely. She attended him and comforted him constantly, often requesting, if there was any particular thing that he wanted, to let her know it, and promising to get it for him if it was possible. After many offers of this kind, the boy at last said:

"Mother, if you could get Federigo's falcon for me, I should soon be well."

She was in some perplexity at this, and began to consider how best to act. She knew that Federigo had long had a liking for her, without the least encouragement on her part, and so she said to herself:

"How can I send or go to ask for this falcon, which I understand is the very best of its kind, and which is all he has in the world to support him? Or how can I ask to take away from a gentleman all the pleasure that he has in life?"

Though she was sure of having the falcon for the asking, she stood without making a reply, till her love for her son so far prevailed that she resolved, at all events, to put him at ease, and not to send for the falcon but to go herself. She then replied:

"Be comforted, my boy, and think only of your recovery. For I promise you that I will go for it tomorrow the first thing I do."

This gave him such joy that he immediately showed signs of improvement.

The next morning she went, as if walking for exercise with another lady in company, to Federigo's little cottage. At that time, since it was too early for him to go out hawking, he was at work in his garden. Hearing that his mistress inquired for him at the door, he ran there surprised and full of joy; while she, with womanly charm, went to meet him, and after the usual greetings, she said:

"Sir, I am come to make you some amends for the losses you have suffered on my account. What I mean is that I have brought a companion to take a neighborly dinner with you today."

He replied, with a good deal of humility, "Madam, I do not remember that I have suffered any losses because of you; but rather, I have received so much good that if I was worth anything at any time it was due to your worth and the love I had for you. This courteous visit is more welcome to me than if I had all that I have wasted returned to me to spend over again. But you have come to a very poor host."

With these words he modestly showed her into his house, and thence they went into the garden. Since he had no one else to leave in her company, he said:

"Madam, as I have no one else, please allow this honest woman, a laborer's wife, to remain with you, while I go to set the table."

Although his poverty was extreme, never till now had he been so aware of his past extravagance. Finding nothing to entertain the lady with, he was in the utmost perplexity, cursing his evil fortune and running up and down like a man out of his wits. At length, having neither money nor anything he could pawn, longing to give her something, and not being willing to ask help even from his own workman, he spied his falcon upon the perch, seized it, and finding it very fat, decided it might make a dish not unworthy of such a lady. Without further thought, then, he wrung its head off and gave it to a girl to dress and roast carefully, while he laid the cloth, having a small quantity of linen left. And then he returned, with a smile on his face, to the garden, to tell Monna Giovanna that what little dinner he was able to provide was now ready. She and her friend, therefore, entered and sat down with Federigo, who served them all the time with great devotion while they ate the good falcon, not knowing what it was.

After dinner was over and they had sat chatting a little while together, the lady thought it was a good time to tell him what she had come for, and she addressed him courteously in this manner:

"Sir, if you remember your past life and my resistance, which perhaps you may call cruelty, you may wonder at my presumption when you hear what I have come for. But if you had children of your own and could know how strong our natural affection is towards them, I am very sure you would excuse me. Now, my having a son forces me, against my own desire, to request a thing of you which I know you value extremely—especially so, because you have no other comfort or diversion left to you. I mean your falcon, which my son has taken such a fancy to that unless I bring it back with me, I very much fear his illness will grow so much worse that I will lose him. Therefore I beg you, not for any regard you may have for me, but for that generosity which you have so often shown, that you will let me have the falcon, so that I may be able to say that my child's life has been restored to me through your gift, and that he and I are forever under obligation to you."

Federigo, hearing the lady's request and knowing it was out of his power to fulfill it, began to weep before he was able to make a word of reply. The lady thought at first that his grief was due to his reluctance to part with his favorite bird, and she expected that he was going to give her a flat denial. But after she had waited a little for his answer, he said:

"Madam, ever since I have fixed my love upon you, fortune has been contrary to me in many things, and I have grieved for it. But all the rest is nothing compared to what has now come to pass. You are here to visit me in this my poor dwelling, which you never deigned to visit when I was prosperous. You also ask a small present from me, which it is wholly out of my power to give. Why this is so, I will briefly tell you. As soon as I knew of the great favor you had granted me in desiring to dine with me, I thought it proper to treat you with something more choice than is usually given to other persons. Remembering the falcon you now ask for and its value, I judged him a fit repast for you, and you have had him, roasted. Nor could I have thought him better used, had you not now desired him in a different manner, which is such a grief to me that I shall never be at peace as long as I live."

Saying this, he produced the falcon's feathers, feet, and talons. The lady now began to blame him for killing such a bird to entertain any woman with, in her heart all the while commending his greatness of soul, which poverty had no power to abate.

Having now no further hope of obtaining the falcon, she took leave of Federigo and returned sadly to her son. Either from grief for the disappointment or through the violence of his disorder, the boy died in a few days, to the mother's extreme grief.

She continued sorrowful for some time, but being left rich and young, she was pressed by her brothers to marry again. This went against her desires, but finding them still insistent, and remembering Federigo's great worth and his last act of generosity in killing such a bird for her entertainment, she said:

"I should rather choose to continue as I am; but since it is your desire that I take a husband, I will have none but Federigo de gli Alberighi."

They smiled contemptuously at this and said:

"You simple woman, what are you talking about? He hasn't a penny in the world!"

She replied, "I believe it, brothers, to be as you say. But know that I would sooner have a man that stands in need of money than money that needs a man."

Hearing her resolution and well knowing his generous disposition, her brothers gave her to him with all her wealth. And he, seeing himself possessed of a lady whom he dearly loved, and of such a vast fortune, lived in all true happiness with her, and was a better manager of his affairs than he had been before.

(Anonymous 1741 translation, revised)

Chichibio and the Crane

Chichibio, cook to Currado Gianfigliazzi, by a sudden reply which he made to his master, turns his wrath into laughter, and so escapes the punishment with which he had threatened him.

Though ready wit and invention furnish people with words proper to their different occasions, yet sometimes does Fortune, an assistant to the timorous, tip the tongue with a sudden and yet more pertinent reply than the most mature deliberation could ever have suggested, as I shall now briefly relate to you.

Currado Gianfigliazzi, as most of you have both known and seen, was always esteemed a gallant and worthy citizen, delighting much in hounds and hawks, to omit his other excellencies, as no way relating to our present purpose. Now he having taken a crane one day with his hawk, near the village of Peretola, and finding it to be young and fat, sent it home to his cook, who was a Venetian, and called Chichibio, with orders to prepare it delicately for supper. The cook, a poor simple fellow, trussed and spitted it, and when it was nearly roasted, and began to smell pretty well, it chanced that a woman in the neighbourhood called Brunetta, of whom he was much enamoured, came into the kitchen, and, being taken with the high savour, earnestly begged of him to give her a leg. He replied very merrily, singing all the time, "Donna Brunetta, you shall have no leg from me." Upon this she was a good deal nettled, and said, "As I hope to live, if you do not give it me, you need never expect any favour more from me." The dispute, at length, was carried to a great height between them; when, to make her easy, he was forced to give her one of the legs. Accordingly the crane was served up at supper, with only one leg, whereat a friend whom Currado had invited to sup with him expressed surprise. He therefore sent for the fellow, and demanded what was become of the other leg. The Venetian (a liar by nature) answered directly, "Sir, cranes have only one leg." Currado, in great wrath, said, "What the devil does the man talk of? Only one leg! Thou rascal, dost thou think I never saw a crane before?" Chichibio still persisted in his denial, saying, "Believe me, sir, it is as I say, and I will convince you of it whenever you please, by such fowls as are living." Currado was willing to have no more words, out of regard to his friend; only he added, "As thou undertakest to show me a thing which I never saw or heard of before, I am content to make proof thereof to-morrow morning; but I vow and protest, if I find it otherwise, I will make thee remember it the longest day thou hast to live."

Thus there was an end for that night, and the next morning Currado, whose passion would scarcely suffer him to get any rest, arose betimes, and ordered his horses to be brought out, taking Chichibio along with him towards a river where he used early in the morning to see plenty of cranes; and he said, "We shall soon see which of us spoke truth last night." Chichibio, finding his master's wrath not at all abated, and that he was now to make good what he had asserted, nor yet knowing how to do it, rode on first with all the fear imaginable; gladly would he have made his escape, but he saw no possible means, whilst he was continually looking about him, expecting everything that appeared to be a crane with two feet. But being come near to the river, he chanced to see, before anybody else, a dozen or so of cranes, each standing upon one leg, as they use to do when they are sleeping; whereupon, showing them quickly to his master, he said, "Now, sir, you yourself may see that I spoke nothing but truth, when I said that cranes have only one leg: look at those there, if you please." Currado, beholding the cranes, replied. "Yes, sirrah! but stay a while, and I will show thee that they have two." Then riding something nearer to them, he cried out, "Shough! shough!" which made them set down the other foot, and after taking a step or two they all flew away. Then Currado, turning to him, said, "Well, thou lying knave, art thou now convinced that they have two legs?" Chichibio, quite at his wits' end, and knowing scarcely what he said himself, suddenly made answer, "Yes, sir, but you did not shout out to that crane last night, as you have done to these; had you called to it in the same manner, it would have put down the other leg, as these have now done." This pleased Currado so much that, turning all wrath into mirth and laughter, he said, "Chichibio, thou sayest right; I should have done so indeed."

By this sudden and comical answer, Chichibio escaped a sound drubbing, and made peace with his master.

The Patient Griselda

The Marquis of Saluzzo, having been prevailed upon by his subjects to marry, in order to please himself in the affair, made choice of a countryman's daughter, by whom he had two children, which he pretended to put to death. Afterwards, feigning that he was weary of her, and had taken another, he had his own daughter brought home, as if he had espoused her, whilst his wife was sent away destitute. At length, being convinced of her patience, he brought her home again, presenting her children, now grown up, and ever afterwards loved and honoured her as his lady.

Gracious ladies, it appears to me that this day has been wholly given up to kings, soldans, and such-like people; therefore, that I may not be left too far behind, I intend to speak of a marquis—not with regard to anything noble and great, but rather monstrously vile and brutish, although it ended well at last—whose conduct being highly reprehensible, I counsel none to imitate, however it may have resulted in his case.

It is a long time ago, that, amongst the Marquises of Saluzzo, the principal or head of the family was a youth called Gualtieri, who, as he was a bachelor, spent his whole time in hawking and hunting, without any thought of ever being encumbered with a wife and children, in which respect, no doubt, he was very wise. But, this being disagreeable to his subjects, they often pressed him to marry, to the end he might neither die without an heir, nor they be left without a lord, offering themselves to provide such a lady for him, and of such a family, that they should have great hopes from her, and he reason enough to be satisfied. "Worthy friends," he replied, "you urge me to do a thing which I was fully resolved against, considering what a difficult matter it is to find a person of a suitable temper, with the great abundance everywhere of such as are otherwise, and how miserable also that man's life must be who is tied to a disagreeable woman. As to your getting at a woman's temper from her family, and so choosing one to please me, that seems quite a ridiculous fancy; for I cannot see how you can tell who are their true fathers, still less know their mothers' secret doings; and even were it otherwise, how many daughters do we see resembling neither father nor mother! Nevertheless, as you are so fond of having me noosed, I will agree to be so. Therefore, that I may have nobody to blame but myself should it happen amiss, I will make my own choice; and I protest, let me marry whom I will, that, unless you show her the respect that is due to her as my lady, you shall know to your cost how grievous it is to me to have taken a wife at your request, contrary to my own inclination." The honest men replied that they were well satisfied, provided he would but make the trial.

Now he had taken a fancy, some time before, to the behaviour of a poor country girl, who lived in a village not far from his palace; and being pleased with her beauty, thinking too that he might live comfortably enough with her, he determined, without seeking any farther, to espouse her. Accordingly he sent for her father, who was a very poor man, and told him that he would marry her. Afterwards he summoned all his subjects together, and said to them, "Gentlemen, it was and is your desire that I take a wife; I do it rather to please you than out of any liking I have to matrimony. You know that you promised me to be satisfied, and to pay her due honour whoever she be that I shall make choice of. The time is now come when I shall fulfil my promise to you, and I expect you to do the like to me. I have found a young woman in the neighbourhood after my own heart, whom I intend to espouse, and bring home in a very few days. Let it be your care, then, to do honour to my nuptials, and to respect her as your sovereign lady; so that I may be satisfied with the performance of your promise, even as you are with that of mine."

The people all declared themselves pleased, and promised to regard her in all things as their mistress. Afterwards they made preparations for a most noble feast, and the like did the prince, inviting all his relations, and the great lords in all parts and provinces about him; he had also most rich and costly robes made, shaped by a person that seemed to be of the same figure as his intended spouse; and provided girdles, rings, and a fine coronet, with everything requisite for a bride. When the day appointed was come, about nine in the morning he mounted his horse, attended by all his friends and vassals; and, having everything in readiness, he said, "My lords and gentlemen, it is now time to go for my new spouse." So on they rode to the village, and when they were come near the father's house, they saw her carrying some water from the well, in great haste, intending to go afterwards with some of her acquaintance to see the new marchioness, when the marquis called her by name, which was Griselda, and inquired where her father was. She modestly replied, "My lord, he is in the house." He then alighted from his horse, commanding them all to wait for him, and went alone into the cottage, where he found the father, who was called Giannucolo, and said to him, "Honest man, I am come to espouse thy daughter Griselda, but would first ask her some questions before thee." He then inquired whether she would make it her study to please him, and not be uneasy at any time, whatever he should do or say, and whether she would always be obedient, with more to that purpose. To all which she answered, "Yes." He then led her out by the hand, and made her unclothe herself before them all; and ordering the rich apparel which he had provided to be brought, he had her attired completely, and a coronet set upon her head, all disordered as her hair was; after which, every one being in amaze, he said, "Behold, this is the person whom I intend for my wife, provided she will accept of me for her husband." Then, turning towards her, who stood quite abashed, "Will you," said he, "have me for your husband?" She replied, "Yes, if so please your lordship." "Well," he replied, "and I take you for my wife."

So he espoused her in that public manner, and mounting her on a palfrey, conducted her honourably to his palace, celebrating the nuptials with as much pomp and grandeur as though he had been married to the daughter of the King of France; and the young bride showed apparently that with her garments she had changed both her mind and behaviour. She was, as we have said, beautiful both in face and person, and was so amiable, so good-natured withal, that she seemed rather a lord's daughter than a poor shepherdess, whereat every one who knew her before was greatly surprised. She was besides so obedient to her husband, and so obliging in all respects, that he thought himself the happiest man in the world, and to his subjects likewise so gracious and condescending that they all honoured and loved her as their own lives, praying for her health and prosperity, and declaring, contrary to their former assertion, that Gualtieri was the most prudent and sharp-sighted prince in the whole world; for that no one else could have discerned such virtues under a mean habit, and country garb, but himself. In a very short time, her discreet behaviour and good works were the common subject of discourse, not in that country only, but everywhere else; and what had been objected to the prince, with regard to his marrying her, now took a contrary turn.

They had not lived long together before she proved with child, and in due time brought forth a daughter, for which he made great rejoicings. But soon afterwards a new fancy came into his head; and that was to make a trial of her patience by long and intolerable sufferings: so he began with harsh words, and an appearance of great uneasiness, telling her that his subjects were greatly displeased with her mean parentage, especially as they saw she bore children, and did nothing but murmur at the daughter already born. She hearing this, without changing countenance or her resolution in any respect, replied, "My lord, pray dispose of me as you think most for your honour and happiness; I shall entirely acquiesce, knowing myself to be less than the least, and that I was altogether unworthy of that dignity to which your favour was pleased to advance me." This was very agreeable to the prince, seeing that she was no way exalted in mind with the honour he had conferred upon her.

Afterwards, having often told her, in general terms, that his subjects could not bear with the daughter that was born of her, he sent to her one of his servants, whom he had instructed what to do, who, with a very sorrowful countenance, said, "Madam, I must either lose my own life or obey my lord's commands. Now he has ordered me to take your daughter, and—" whereupon he was silent. She, hearing these words, and noting the fellow's looks, remembering also what she had heard before from her lord, concluded that he had orders to destroy the child. So she took it out of the cradle, kissed it, and gave it her blessing, when, without changing countenance, though her heart throbbed with maternal affection, she tenderly laid it in the servant's arms, and said, "Take it, and do what thy lord and mine has commanded; but prithee leave it not to be devoured by the fowls or wild beasts, unless that be his will." Taking the child, he acquainted the prince with what she had said; he was greatly surprised at her constancy, and sent the same person with it to a relation at Bologna, desiring him, without revealing whose child it was, to see it carefully brought up and educated.

Afterwards the lady became with child the second time, and was delivered of a son, at which the marquis was extremely pleased; but, not satisfied with what he had already done, he began to grieve and persecute her still more, saying one day to her, seemingly much out of temper, "Since thou has brought me this son, I am able to live no longer with my people; for they resent so strongly the succession of a poor shepherd's grandson, that unless I would run the risk of being driven out of my dominions I must be obliged to dispose of this child as I did the other, and then to send thee away, in order to take a more suitable wife." She heard this with a great deal of resignation, making only this reply: "My lord, study only your own ease and happiness, without the least care for me; for nothing is agreeable to me but what is pleasing to yourself." Not many days after, he sent for the son in the same manner as he had sent for the daughter; and, seeming also as if he had procured him to be slain, had him conveyed to Bologna, to be taken care of with the girl. This the lady bore with the same silence and resolution as she had shown at the taking away of her daughter, whereat the prince wondered greatly, declaring to himself that no other woman was capable of doing the like; and, were it not that he had observed her extremely fond of her children whilst that was agreeable to him, he would have thought it want of affection in her; but he saw it was only her entire wisdom and obedience. The people, imagining that the children were both put to death, blamed him to the last degree, thinking him the most cruel of men, and showing great compassion for the lady, who, whenever she was in company with ladies of her acquaintance who expressed pity for her lost children, would only say, "It was not my will, but his who begot them."

But more years being now passed, and the marquis resolving to make the last trial of her patience, he declared before many people that he could no longer bear to keep Griselda as his wife, owning that he had done very foolishly, and like a young man, in marrying her, and that he meant to solicit the Pope for a dispensation to take another, and send her away. For this he was much blamed by many worthy persons; but he said nothing in return, only that it should be so. She, hearing this, and expecting to go home to her father's, and possibly tend the sheep as she had done before, whilst she saw some other lady possessed of him whom she dearly loved and honoured, was secretly grieved; but, as she had withstood other strokes of fortune, so she determined resolutely to do now. Soon afterwards, Gualtieri caused counterfeit letters to be brought to him, as from Rome, acquainting all his people that his holiness enabled him by dispensation to take another wife and put away Griselda. Accordingly he had her brought before him in presence of his lords, when he said, "Woman, by the Pope's leave I may dispose of thee, and take another wife. As my ancestors, then, have been all of gentle birth and sovereign princes of this country, and thine only peasants, I intend to keep thee no longer, but to send thee back to thy father's cottage, with the same portion which thou broughtest me, and afterwards I shall take one whom I find to be suitable in quality to myself." It was with much difficulty that she could now refrain from tears, and she replied, "My lord, I was always sensible that my servile condition would no way accord with your high rank and descent. For what I have been, I own myself indebted to Providence and to you; nor ever have looked on it as mine, but as a thing lent, not given; since now you require it again, it should please me, and does please me, to restore it. Behold the ring with which you espoused me; I deliver it to you. You bid me take back the dowry which I brought you; you will have no need for a teller to count it, nor I for a purse wherein to put it, much less a sumpter-horse to carry it away; for I have not forgotten that you took me naked, and, if you think it decent to expose that body which has borne you two children in that manner, I am contented; but I would entreat you, as a recompense for my virginity, which I brought you, and do not carry away, that you would please to let me have one smock over and above my dowry." He, though ready to weep, yet put on a stern countenance, and said, "Thou shalt have one only then." And, notwithstanding the people all desired that she might have an old gown to keep her body from shame, having been his wife for thirteen years and upwards, yet it was all in vain. So she left his palace in a single garment, barefooted and bareheaded, and returned to her father, accompanied by the tears of the people.

The poor man, who, indeed, had never supposed that the prince would keep her long as his wife, and expected this thing to happen every day, had safely laid up the garments of which she had been despoiled on the day the marquis espoused her, wherefore he now brought them to her, and she put them on, and went as usual about her father's little household affairs, bearing this fierce trial of adverse fortune with the greatest courage imaginable. The prince then gave it out that he was to espouse a daughter of one of the Counts of Panago; and, seeming as if he made great preparations for his nuptials, he sent for Griselda to come to him, and said to her, "I am going to bring home this lady whom I have just married, and intend to show her all possible respect at her first coming: thou knowest that I have no women with me able to set out the rooms, and do many other things which are requisite on so solemn an occasion. As, therefore, thou art best acquainted with the state of the house, I would have thee make such provision as thou shalt judge proper, invite what ladies thou wilt, and receive them as though thou wert mistress of the house; and when the marriage is ended, thou mayst return home to thy father's again."

Though these words pierced like daggers to the heart of Griselda, who was unable to part with her love for the prince so easily as she had parted with her great fortune, she yet replied, "My lord, I am ready to fulfil all your commands." She then went in her coarse attire into the palace, from whence she had but just before departed in her smock, and with her own hands did she begin to sweep, and set all the rooms in order, cleaning the stools and benches in the hall like the meanest servant, and directing what was to be done in the kitchen, never giving over till everything was as it ought to be. After this was done, she invited, in the prince's name, all the ladies in the country to come to the feast; and on the day appointed for the marriage, meanly clad as she was, she received them in the most polished and cheerful manner imaginable.

Now Gualtieri, who had had his children carefully brought up at Bologna by one of his family who was related to the Counts of Panago (the girl being about twelve years old, and one of the prettiest creatures that ever was seen, and the boy about six), had sent to his kinsman to desire he would bring them, with an honourable retinue, to Saluzzo, giving it out all the way he came that he was bringing the young lady to be married to the marquis, without letting any one know to the contrary. Accordingly, they all set forward, attended by a goodly train of gentry, and, after travelling some days, reached Saluzzo about dinner-time, when they found the whole country assembled, waiting to see their new lady. The young lady was most graciously received by all the women present; and Griselda, meanly dressed as she was, being come into the hall where the tables were all covered, went cheerfully to meet her, saying, "Your ladyship is most welcome." The ladies, who had greatly importuned the prince, though to no purpose, to let Griselda be in a room by herself, or else that she might have some of her own clothes, and not appear before strangers in that manner, were now seated, and going to be served; whilst the young lady was universally admired, and every one said that the prince had made a good change, but Griselda in particular highly commended both her and her brother.

The marquis now thinking that he had seen enough with regard to his wife's patience, and perceiving that in all her trials she was still unchanged, being persuaded likewise that this proceeded from no want of understanding in her, because he knew her to be singularly prudent, he thought it time to take her from that anguish which he supposed she might conceal under her firm and constant deportment. So, making her come before all the company, he said, with a smile, "What thinkest thou, Griselda, of my bride?" "My lord," she replied, "I like her extremely well; and, if she be as prudent as she is fair, I doubt not you will be the happiest man in the world with her; but I must humbly beg you would not sting her with those sharp sayings that you addressed to her who was formerly yours; because this one is young, and has been tenderly educated, whereas the other was inured to hardships from a child."

Gualtieri perceiving that, though Griselda thought that person was to be his wife, she nevertheless answered him with great frankness and sweetness of temper, made her sit down by him, and said, "Griselda, it is now time for you to reap the fruit of your long patience, and that they who have reputed me to be cruel, unjust, and a monster in nature may know that what I have done has been all along with a view to teach you how to behave as a wife; to show them how to choose and keep a wife; and, lastly, to secure my own ease and quiet as long as we live together, which I was apprehensive might have been endangered by my marrying. Therefore I had a mind to prove you by harsh and injurious treatment; and, not being sensible that you have ever transgressed my will, either in word or deed, I now seem to have met with that happiness I desired. I intend, then, to restore in one hour what I had taken away from you in many, and to make you the sweetest recompense for the many bitter pangs I have caused you to suffer. Joyfully accept, therefore, this young lady, whom you thought my spouse, and her brother, as your children and mine. They are the same which you and many others believed that I had been the means of cruelly murdering; and I am your husband, who love and value you above all things, assuring myself that no person in the world can be happier in a wife than I am."

With this he embraced her most affectionately, when, rising up together (she weeping for joy), they went where their daughter was sitting, quite astonished with these things, and tenderly saluted both her and her brother, undeceiving them and the whole company. At this the women all arose, overjoyed, from the tables, and taking Griselda into the chamber, they pulled off her coarse garments, and clothed her with her own noble apparel, like a marchioness, she resembling such an one even in rags, and brought her into the hall. And being extremely rejoiced with her son and daughter, and every one expressing the utmost satisfaction at what had come to pass, the feasting was prolonged many days.

The marquis was judged a very wise man, though abundantly too severe, and the trial of his lady most intolerable; but as for Griselda, all esteemed her as a most wise and virtuous lady. In a few days the Count of Panago returned to Bologna, and the marquis took Giannucolo from his drudgery, and maintained him as his father-in-law, and so he lived very comfortably to a good old age. Gualtieri afterwards married his daughter to one of equal nobility, continuing the rest of his life with Griselda, and showing her all the respect and honour that was possible.

What can we say, then, but that divine spirits may descend from heaven into the meanest cottages; whilst royal palaces shall produce such as seem rather adapted to have the care of hogs than the government of men? Who but Griselda could, not only without a tear; but even with seeming satisfaction, undergo the most rigid and unheard-of trials of her husband? Many women there are who, if turned out of doors almost naked in that manner, would have revenged themselves in another fashion, and so procured abundance of fine clothes.

Petrarch
(1304-1374)
If It Be Destined

If it be destined that my Life, from thine
Divided, yet with thine shall linger on
Till, in the later twilight of Decline,
I may behold those Eyes, their lustre gone;
When the gold tresses that enrich thy brow
Shall all be faded into silver-gray,
From which the wreaths that well bedeck
   them now
For many a Summer shall have fallen
   away:
Then should I dare to whisper in your ears
The pent-up Passion of so long ago,
That Love which hath survived the wreck
   of years
Hath little else to pray for, or bestow,
Thou wilt not to the broken heart deny
The boon of one too-late relenting sigh.

(Translated by Edward FitzGerald)

When I Reflect

When I reflect and turn me to that part
Whence my sweet lady beamed in purest
   light,
And in my inmost thought remains that
   light

Which burns me and consumes in every part,
I, who yet dread lest from my heart it part
And see at hand the end of this my light,
Go lonely, like a man deprived of light,
Ignorant where to go; whence to depart.
Thus flee I from the stroke which lays me dead,
Yet flee not with such speed but that desire
Follows, companion of my flight alone.
Silent I go:—but these my words, though dead,
Others would cause to weep—this I desire,
That I may weep and waste myself alone.

(Translated by Lofft)

In Gratitude to Love

Blest be the day, and blest the month, the year,
The spring, the hour, the very moment blest,
The lovely scene, the spot, where first oppressed
I sunk, of two bright eyes the prisoner:
And blest the first soft pang, to me most dear,
Which thrilled my heart, when Love became its guest;
And blest the bow, the shafts which pierced my breast.
And even the wounds, which bosomed thence I bear.
Blest too the strains which, poured through glade and grove,
Have made the woodlands echo with her name;
The sighs, the tears, the languishment, the love:
And blest those sonnets, sources of my fame;
And blest that thought—Oh! never to remove!
Which turns to her alone, from her alone which came.

(Translated by Wrangham)

Her Golden Hair

She used to let her golden hair fly free
For the wind to toy and tangle and molest;
Her eyes were brighter than the radiant west.
(Seldom they shine so now.) I used to see
Pity look out of those deep eyes on me.
('It was false pity,' you would now protest.)
I had love's tinder heaped within my breast;
What wonder that the flame burned furiously?
She did not walk in any mortal way,
But with angelic progress; when she spoke,
Unearthly voices sang in unison,
She seemed divine among the dreary folk
Of earth. You say she is not so today?
Well, though the bow's unbent, the wound bleeds on.

(Translated by Morris Bishop)

On Hearing of Laura's Death

Alas, that gentle look, and that fair face!
Alas, for the body's beauty when you wended
Your gracious way! Alas, your words that mended
The wicked, and taught honor to the base!
Alas, that smile of yours, whose wounding grace
Has come to death, and all my hope is ended!
You'd have been queen of earth, had you descended
To a younger world, to a less evil race.
Still I must burn in you, in you respire!
I was yours utterly; my stricken heart
Can feel no other hurt, after today.
You showered hope upon me and desire
In our last moment, ere we came to part;
And then the wind blew all your words away.

(Translated by Morris Bishop)

He Sees Her Everywhere

If I do hear regretful birds complain
—Or the leaves ruffling in the summer light,
Or water whispering huskily toward the plain—
From my resort, where streamside flowers are bright,
And where I sit, and dream of love, and write;
Then do I see and hear her once again
Whom heaven vouchsafed a moment to our sight;
Her far voice comes in answer to my pain:
"Why do you waste away in such advance
Of time? and why—" so, gently does she chide,
"Do you walk always in a tearful trance?
Weep not for me; out of the death I died
I rose immortal; and in radiance
My eyes, that seemed to shut, have opened wide."

(Translated by Morris Bishop)

Final Sonnet

Valley, my sorrow's refuge and retreat;
River, whereto my tears are tributary;
Wild birds and beasts; and fishes, shy and wary,
Within the green walls of your narrow street;
Air, that receives and soothes my passion's heat;
Pathway of grief, where once I was so merry;
Hill, joyful once, and now pain's sanctuary,
Whither Love still compels my docile feet;
Your dear familiar forms I recognize,
But not myself; I am no longer gay,
I am an inn for everlasting dole.
Here where we walked, I see her spirit rise,
Naked and pure, to take the heavenly way,
Leaving on earth the garments of her soul.

(Translated by Morris Bishop)

Niccolo Machiavelli
(1469-1527)
from *The Prince*
In What Way Faith Should Be Kept by Princes

Everybody knows how laudable it is in a prince to keep this faith and to be an honest man and not a trickster. Nevertheless, the experience of our times shows that the princes who have done great things are the ones who have taken little account of their promises and who have known how to addle the brains of men with craft. In the end they have conquered those who have put their reliance on good faith.

You must realize, then, that there are two ways to fight. In one kind the laws are used, in the other, force. The first is suitable to man, the second to animals. But because the first often falls short, one has to turn to the second. Hence a prince must know perfectly how to act like a beast and like a man. This truth was covertly taught to princes by ancient authors, who write that Achilles and many other ancient princes were turned over for their upbringing to Chiron the centaur,[1] that he might keep them under his tuition. To have as teacher one who is half beast and half man means nothing else than that a prince needs to know how to use the qualities of both creatures. The one without the other will not last long.

Since, then, it is necessary for a prince to understand how to make good use of the conduct of the animals, he should select among them the fox and the lion, because the lion cannot protect himself from traps,

---

[1]Reputed in myth to be the educator of many heroes, among them Achilles, Theseus, Jason, and Hercules.

and the fox cannot protect himself from the wolves. So the prince needs to be a fox that he may know how to deal with traps, and a lion that he may frighten the wolves. Those who act like the lion alone do not understand their business. A prudent ruler, therefore, cannot and should not observe faith when such observance is to his disadvantage and the causes that made him give his promise have vanished. If men were all good, this advice would not be good, but since men are wicked and do not keep their promises to you, you likewise do not have to keep yours to them. Lawful reasons to excuse his failure to keep them will never be lacking to a prince. It would be possible to give innumerable modern examples of this and to show many treaties and promises that have been made null and void by the faithlessness of princes. And the prince who has best known how to act as a fox has come out best. But one who has this capacity must understand how to keep it covered, and be a skilful pretender and dissembler. Men are so simple and so subject to present needs that he who deceives in this way will always find those who will let themselves be deceived.

I do not wish to keep still about one of the recent instances. Alexander VI[2] did nothing else than deceive men, and had no other intention; yet he always found a subject to work on. There never was a man more effective in swearing that things were true, and the greater the oaths with which he made a promise, the less he observed it. Nonetheless his deceptions always succeeded to his wish, because he thoroughly understood this aspect of the world.

It is not necessary, then, for a prince really to have all the virtues mentioned above, but it is very necessary to seem to have them. I will even venture to say that they damage a prince who possesses them and always observes them, but if he seems to have them they are useful. I mean that he should seem compassionate, trustworthy, humane, honest, and religious, and actually be so; but yet he should have his mind so trained that, when it is necessary not to practice these virtues, he can change to the opposite, and do it skilfully. It is to be understood that a prince, especially a new prince, cannot observe all the things because of which men are considered good, because he is often obliged, if he wishes to maintain his government, to act contrary to faith, contrary to charity, contrary to humanity, contrary to religion. It is therefore necessary that he have a mind capable of turning in whatever direction the winds of Fortune and the variations of affairs require, and, as I said above, that he should not depart from what is morally right, if he can observe it, but should know how to adopt what is bad, when he is obliged to.

A prince, then, should be very careful that there does not issue from his mouth anything that is not full of the above-mentioned five qualities. To those who see and hear him he should seem all compassion, all faith, all honesty, all humanity, all religion. There is nothing more necessary to make a show of possessing than this last quality. For men in general judge more by their eyes than by their hands; everybody is fitted to see, few to understand. Everybody sees what you appear to be; few make out what you really are. And these few do not dare to oppose the opinion of the many, who have the majesty of the state to confirm their view. In the actions of all men, and especially those of princes, where there is no court to which to appeal, people think of the outcome. A prince

---

[2] Rodrigo Borgia, father of Cesare Borgia; he was pope from 1492 to 1503.

needs only to conquer and to maintain his position. The means he has used will always be judged honorable and will be praised by everybody, because the crowd is always caught by appearance and by the outcome of events, and the crowd is all there is in the world; there is no place for the few when the many have room enough. A certain prince of the present day,[3] whom it is not good to name, preaches nothing else than peace and faith, and is wholly opposed to both of them, and both of them, if he observed them, would many times have taken from him either his reputation or his throne.

The Power of Fortune in Human Affairs, and to What Extent She Should Be Relied On

"Fortune Is a Woman"

It is not unknown to me that many have been and still are of the opinion that the affairs of this world are so under the direction of Fortune and of God that man's prudence cannot control them; in fact, that man has no resource against them. For this reason many think there is no use in sweating much over such matters, but that one might as well let Chance take control. This opinion has been the more accepted in our times, because of the great changes in the state of the world that have been and now are seen every day, beyond all human surmise. And I myself, when thinking on these things, have now and then in some measure inclined to their view. Nevertheless, because the freedom of the will should not be wholly annulled, I think it may be true that Fortune is arbiter of half of our actions, but that she still leaves the control of the other half, or about that, to us.

I liken her to one of those raging streams that, when they go mad, flood the plains, ruin the trees and the buildings, and take away the fields from one bank and put them down on the other. Everybody flees before them; everybody yields to their onrush without being able to resist anywhere. And though this is their nature, it does not cease to be true that, in calm weather, men can make some provisions against them with walls and dykes, so that, when the streams swell, their waters will go off through a canal, or their currents will not be so wild and do so much damage. The same is true of Fortune. She shows her power where there is no wise preparation for resisting her, and turns her fury where she knows that no walls and dykes have been made to hold her in. And if you consider Italy—the place where these variations occur and the cause that has set them in motion—you will see that she is a country without dykes and without any wall of defence. If, like Germany, Spain, and France, she had had a sufficient bulwark of military vigor, this flood would not have made the great changes it has, or would not have come at all.

And this, I think, is all I need to say on opposing oneself to Fortune, in general. But limiting myself more to particulars, I say that a prince may be seen prospering today and falling in ruin tomorrow, though it does not appear that he has changed in his nature or any of his qualities. I believe this comes, in the first place, from the causes that have been discussed at length in preceding chapters. That is, if a prince bases himself entirely on Fortune, he will fall when she varies. I also believe that a ruler will be successful who adapts his mode of procedure to the quality of the times, and likewise that he will be unsuccessful if the times are out of

---

[3]Ferdinand II, "the Catholic," king of Spain. In refraining from mentioning him, Machiavelli apparently had in mind the good relations existing between Spain and the house of Medici.

accord with his procedure. Because it may be seen that in things leading to the end each has before him, namely glory and riches, men proceed differently. One acts with caution, another rashly; one with violence, another with skill; one with patience, another with its opposite; yet with these different methods each one attains his end. Still further, two cautious men will be seen, of whom one comes to his goal, the other does not. Likewise you will see two who succeed with two different methods, one of them being cautious and the other rash. These results are caused by nothing else than the nature of the times, which is or is not in harmony with the procedure of men. It also accounts for what I have mentioned, namely, that two persons, working differently, chance to arrive at the same result; and that of two who work in the same way, one attains his end, but the other does not.

On the nature of the times also depends the variability of the best method. If a man conducts himself with caution and patience, times and affairs may come around in such a way that his procedure is good, and he goes on successfully. But if times and circumstances change, he is ruined, because he does not change his method of action. There is no man so prudent as to understand how to fit himself to this condition, either because he is unable to deviate from the course to which nature inclines him, or because, having always prospered by walking in one path, he cannot persuade himself to leave it. So the cautious man, when the time comes to go at a reckless pace, does not know how to do it. Hence he comes to ruin. Yet if he could change his nature with the times and with circumstances, his fortune would not be altered.

Pope Julius II proceeded rashly in all his actions, and found the times and circumstances so harmonious with his mode of procedure that he was always so lucky as to succeed. Consider the first enterprise he engaged in, that of Bologna, while Messer Giovanni Bentivogli[4] was still alive. The Venetians were not pleased with it; the King of Spain felt the same way; the Pope was debating such an enterprise with the King of France. Nevertheless, in his courage and rashness Julius personally undertook that expedition. This movement made the King of Spain and the Venetians stand irresolute and motionless, the latter for fear, and the King because of his wish to recover the entire kingdom of Naples. On the other side, the King of France was dragged behind Julius, because the King, seeing that the Pope had moved and wishing to make him a friend in order to put down the Venetians, judged he could not refuse him soldiers without doing him open injury. Julius, then, with his rash movement, attained what no other pontiff, with the utmost human prudence, would have attained. If he had waited to leave Rome until the agreements were fixed and everything arranged, as any other pontiff would have done, he would never have succeeded, for the King of France would have had a thousand excuses, and the others would have raised a thousand fears. I wish to omit his other acts, which are all of the same sort, and all succeeded perfectly. The brevity of his life did not allow him to know anything different. Yet if times had come in which it was necessary to act with caution, they would have ruined him, for he would never have deviated from the methods to which nature inclined him.

I conclude, then, that since Fortune is variable and men are set in their ways,

---

[4]Of the ruling family Bentivogli (the prefix *Messer* means "my lord"); the Pope untertook to dislodge him from Bologna, in 1506.

they are successful when they are in harmony with Fortune and unsuccessful when they disagree with her. Yet I am of the opinion that it is better to be rash than over-cautious, because Fortune is a woman and, if you wish to keep her down, you must beat her and pound her. It is evident that she allows herself to be overcome by men who treat her in that way rather than by those who proceed coldly. For that reason, like a woman, she is always the friend of young men, because they are less cautious, and more courageous, and command her with more boldness.

Benvenuto Cellini
(1500-1571)
The Casting of the Perseus

The autobiography of Cellini, the celebrated Florentine goldsmith and sculptor, has been called "the nearest approach there is to a great Italian novel of life and character." And Goethe said that Cellini's Life, *which he translated into German, gave a better view of the sixteenth century than could be found in the clearest historical account. After allowance has been made for exaggeration and for some inaccurate reminiscences, much remains that is informative and even exciting. One of the most dramatic passages is the artist's story of his difficulties in casting the bronze statue of Perseus which he made on the order of Duke Cosimo and which still stands in the Loggia dei Lanzi in Florence. This account remains our best guide to the Renaissance techniques of casting bronze.*

Having succeeded so well with the cast of the Medusa, I had great hope of bringing my Perseus through; for I had laid the wax on, and felt confident that it would come out in bronze as perfectly as the Medusa. The waxen model produced so fine an effect, that when the Duke saw it and was struck with its beauty—whether somebody had persuaded him it could not be carried out with the same finish in metal, or whether he thought so for himself—he came to visit me more frequently than usual, and on one occasion said: "Benvenuto, this figure cannot succeed in bronze; the laws of art do not permit of it." These words of his Excellency stung me so sharply that I answered: "My lord, I know how very little confidence you have in me; and I believe the reason of this is that your most illustrious Excellency lends too ready an ear to my calumniators, or else indeed that you do not understand my art." He hardly let me close the sentence when he broke in: "I profess myself a connoisseur, and understand it very well indeed." I replied: "Yes, like a prince, not like an artist; for if your Excellency understood my trade as well as you imagine, you would trust me on the proofs I have already given. These are, first, the colossal bust of your Excellency, which is now in Elba; secondly, the restoration of the Ganymede in marble, which offered so many difficulties and cost me so much trouble, that I would rather have made the whole statue new from the beginning; thirdly, the Medusa, cast by me in bronze, here now before your Excellency's eyes, the execution of which was a greater triumph of strength and skill than any of my predecessors in this fiendish art have yet achieved. Look you, my lord! I constructed that furnace anew on principles quite different from those of other founders; in addition to many technical improvements and ingenious devices, I supplied it with two issues for the metal, because this difficult and twisted figure could not otherwise have come out perfect. It is only owing to my intelligent insight into means and appliances that the statue turned out as it did; a triumph judged impossible by all the practitioners of this art. I should like you furthermore to be aware, my lord, for cer-

BENVENUTO CELLINI: *Perseus.* MUSEO DEL BARGELLO, FLORENCE

tain, that the sole reason why I succeeded with all those great and arduous works in France under his most admirable Majesty King Francis, was the high courage which that good monarch put into my heart by the liberal allowances he made me, and the multitude of work-people he left at my disposal. I could have as many as I asked for, and employed at times above forty, all chosen by myself. These were the causes of my having there produced so many masterpieces in so short a space of time. Now then, my lord, put trust in me; supply me with the aid I need. I am confident of being able to complete a work which will delight your soul. But if your Excellency goes on disheartening me, and does not advance me the assistance which is absolutely required, neither I nor any man alive upon this earth can hope to achieve the slightest thing of value."

It was as much as the Duke could do to stand by and listen to my pleadings. He kept turning first this way and then that; while I, in despair, poor wretched I, was calling up remembrance of the noble state I held in France, to the great sorrow of my soul. All at once he cried: "Come, tell me, Benvenuto, how is it possible that yonder splendid head of Medusa, so high up there in the grasp of Perseus, should ever come out perfect?" I replied upon the instant: "Look you now, my lord! If your Excellency possessed that knowledge of the craft which you affirm you have, you would not fear one moment for the splendid head you speak of. There is good reason, on the other hand, to feel uneasy about this right foot, so far below and at a distance from the rest." When he heard these words, the Duke turned, half in anger, to some gentlemen in waiting, and exclaimed: "I verily believe that this Benvenuto prides himself on contradicting everything one says." Then he faced round to me with a touch of mockery, upon which his attendants did the like, and began to speak as follows: "I will listen patiently to any argument you can possibly produce in explanation of your statement, which may convince me of its probability." I said in answer: "I will adduce so sound an argument that your Excellency shall perceive the full force of it." So I began: "You must know, my lord, that the nature of fire is to ascend, and therefore I promise you that Medusa's head will come out famously; but since it is not in the nature of fire to descend, and I must force it downwards six cubits by artificial means, I assure your Excellency upon this most convincing ground of proof that the foot cannot possibly come out. It will, however, be quite easy for me to restore it." "Why, then," said the Duke, "did you not devise it so that the foot should come out as well as you affirm the head will?" I answered: "I must have made a much larger furnace, with a conduit as thick as my leg; and so I might have forced the molten metal by its own weight to descend so far. Now, my pipe, which runs six cubits to the statue's foot, as I have said, is not thicker than two fingers. However, it was not worth the trouble and expense to make a larger; for I shall easily be able to mend what is lacking. But when my mould is more than half full, as I expect, from this middle point upwards, the fire ascending by its natural property, then the heads of Perseus and Medusa will come out admirably; you may be quite sure of it." After I had thus expounded these convincing arguments, together with many more of the same kind, which it would be tedious to set down here, the Duke shook his head and departed without further ceremony.

Abandoned thus to my own resources, I took new courage, and banished the sad thoughts which kept recurring to my mind, making me often weep bitter tears of repentance for having left France; for though

I did so only to revisit Florence, my sweet birthplace, in order that I might charitably succour my six nieces, this good action, as I well perceived, had been the beginning of my great misfortune. Nevertheless, I felt convinced that when my Perseus was accomplished, all these trials would be turned to high felicity and glorious well-being.

Accordingly I strengthened my heart, and with all the forces of my body and my purse, employing what little money still remained to me, I set to work. First I provided myself with several loads of pinewood from the forests of Serristori, in the neighborhood of Montelupo. While these were on their way, I clothed my Perseus with the clay which I had prepared many months beforehand, in order that it might be duly seasoned. After making its clay tunic (for that is the term used in this art) and properly arming it and fencing it with iron girders, I began to draw the wax out by means of a slow fire. This melted and issued through numerous air-vents I had made; for the more there are of these, the better will the mould fill. When I had finished drawing off the wax, I constructed a funnel-shaped furnace all round the model of my Perseus. It was built of bricks, so interlaced, the one above the other, that numerous apertures were left for the fire to exhale at. Then I began to lay on wood by degrees, and kept it burning two whole days and nights. At length, when all the wax was gone, and the mould was well baked, I set to work at digging the pit in which to sink it. This I performed with scrupulous regard to all the rules of art. When I had finished that part of my work, I raised the mould by windlasses and stout ropes to a perpendicular position, and suspending it with the greatest care one cubit above the level of the furnace, so that it hung exactly above the middle of the pit, I next lowered it gently down into the very bottom of the furnace, and had it firmly placed with every possible precaution for its safety. When this delicate operation was accomplished, I began to bank it up with the earth I had excavated; and, ever as the earth grew higher, I introduced its proper air-vents, which were little tubes of earthenware, such as folk use for drains and such-like purposes. At length, I felt sure that it was admirably fixed, and that the filling-in of the pit and the placing of the air-vents had been properly performed. I also could see that my work-people understood my method, which differed very considerably from that of all the other masters in the trade. Feeling confident, then, that I could rely upon them, I next turned to my furnace, which I had filled with numerous pigs of copper and other bronze stuff. The pieces were piled according to the laws of art, that is to say, so resting one upon the other that the flames could play freely through them, in order that the metal might heat and liquify the sooner. At last I called out heartily to set the furnace going. The logs of pine were heaped in, and, what with the unctuous resin of the wood and the good draught I had given, my furnace worked so well that I was obliged to rush from side to side to keep it going. The labour was more than I could stand; yet I forced myself to strain every nerve and muscle. To increase my anxieties, the workshop took fire, and we were afraid lest the roof should fall upon our heads; while, from the garden, such a storm of wind and rain kept blowing in, that it perceptibly cooled the furnace.

Battling thus with all these untoward circumstances for several hours, and exerting myself beyond even the measure of my powerful constitution, I could at last bear up no longer, and a sudden fever, of the utmost possible intensity, attacked me. I felt absolutely obliged to go and fling myself upon my bed. Sorely against my will having to drag myself away from the spot, I turned to my assistants, about ten or more in all, what with master-founders, hand-workers, country-fellows, and my own special journeymen, among whom was Bernardino Mannellini of Mugello, my apprentice through several years. To him in particular I spoke: "Look, my dear Bernardino, that you observe the rules which I have taught you; do your best with all despatch, for the metal will soon be fused. You cannot go wrong; these honest men will get the channels ready; you will easily be able to drive back the two plugs with this pair of iron crooks; and I am sure that my mould will fill miraculously. I feel more ill than I ever did in all my life, and verily believe that it will kill me before a few hours are over." Thus, with despair at heart, I left them, and betook myself to bed.

No sooner had I got to bed, than I ordered my serving-maids to carry food and wine for all the men into the workshop; at the same time I cried: "I shall not be alive tomorrow." They tried to encourage me, arguing that my illness would pass over, since it came from excessive fatigue. In this way I spent two hours battling with the fever, which steadily increased, and calling out continually: "I feel that I am dying." My housekeeper, who was named Mona Fiore da Castel del Rio, a very notable manager and no less warmhearted, kept chiding me for my discouragement; but, on the other hand, she paid me every kind attention which was possible. However, the sight of my physical pain and moral dejection so affected her, that, in spite of that brave heart of hers, she could not refrain from shedding tears; and yet, so far as she was able, she took good care that I should not see them. While I was thus terribly afflicted, I beheld the figure of a man enter my chamber, twisted in his body into the form of a capital S. He raised a lamentable, doleful voice, like one who announces their last hour to men condemned to die upon the scaffold, and spoke these words: "O Benvenuto! your statue is spoiled, and there is no hope whatever of saving it." No sooner had I heard the shriek of that wretch than I gave a howl which might have been heard from the sphere of flame. Jumping from my bed, I seized my clothes and began to dress. The maids, and my lad, and every one who came round to help me, got kicks or blows of the fist, while I kept crying out in lamentation: "Ah! traitors! enviers! This is an act of treason, done by malice prepense! But I swear by God that I will sift it to the bottom, and before I die will leave such witnesses to the world of what I can do as shall make a score of mortals marvel."

When I had got my clothes on, I strode with soul bent on mischief toward the worship; there I beheld the men, whom I had left erewhile in such high spirits, standing stupefied and downcast. I began at once and spoke: "Up with you! Attend to me! Since you have not been able or willing to obey the directions I gave you, obey me now that I am with you to conduct my work in person. Let no one contradict me, for in cases like this we need the aid of hand and hearing, not of advice." When I had uttered these words, a certain Maestro Alessandro Lastricati broke silence and said: "Look you, Benvenuto, you are going to attempt an enterprise which the laws of art do not sanction, and which cannot succeed." I turned upon him with such fury and so full of mischief, that he and all the rest of them exclaimed with one voice: "On then! Give orders! We will obey your least commands, so long as life is left in us." I believe they spoke thus feelingly because they thought I must fall shortly dead upon the ground. I went immediately to inspect the furnace, and found that the metal was all curdled; an accident which we express by "being caked." I told two of the hands to cross the road, and fetch from the house of the butcher Capretta, a load of young oakwood, which had lain dry for above a year; this wood had been previously offered me by Madame Ginevra, wife of the said Capretta. So soon as the first armfuls arrived, I began to fill the grate beneath the furnace. Now oak-wood of that kind heats more powerfully than any other sort of tree; and for this reason, where a slow fire is wanted, as in the case of gun-foundry, alder or pine is preferred. Accordingly, when the logs took fire, oh! how the cake began to stir beneath that awful heat, to glow and sparkle in a blaze! At the same time I kept stirring up the channels, and sent men upon the roof to stop the conflagration, which had gathered force from the increased combustion in the furnace; also I caused boards, carpets, and other hangings to be set up against the garden, in order to protect us from the violence of the rain.

When I had thus provided against these several disasters, I roared out first to one man and then to another: "Bring this thing here! Take that thing there!" At this crisis, when the whole gang saw the cake was on the point of melting, they did my bidding, each fellow working with the strength of three. I then ordered half a pig of pewter to be brought, which weighed about sixty pounds, and flung it into the middle of the cake inside the furnace. By this means, and by piling on wood and stirring now with pokers and now with iron rods, the curdled mass rapidly began to liquify. Then, knowing I had brought the dead to life again, against the firm opinion of those ignoramuses, I felt such vigour fill my veins, that all those pains of fever, all those fears of death, were quite forgotten.

All of a sudden an explosion took place, attended by a tremendous flash of flame, as though a thunder-bolt had formed and been discharged amongst us. Unwonted and appalling terror astonished every one, and me more even than the rest. When the din was over and the dazzling light extinguished, we began to look each other in the face. Then I discovered that the cap of the furnace had blown up, and the bronze was bubbling over from its source beneath. So I had the mouths of my mould immediately opened, and at the same time drove in the two plugs which kept back the molten metal. But I noticed that it did not flow as rapidly as usual, the reason being probably that the fierce heat of the fire we kindled had consumed its base alloy. Accordingly I sent for all my pewter platters, porringers, and dishes, to the number of some two hundred pieces, and had a portion of them cast, one by one, into the channels, and the rest into the furnace. This expedient succeeded, and every one could now perceive that my bronze was in most perfect liquefaction, and my mould was filling; whereupon they all with heartiness and happy cheer assisted and obeyed my bidding, while I, now here, now there, gave orders, helped with my own hands, and cried aloud: "O God! Thou that by Thy immeasurable power didst rise from the dead, and in Thy glory didst ascend to heaven!"...even thus in a moment my mould was filled; and seeing my work finished, I fell upon my knees, and with all my heart gave thanks to God.

After all was over, I turned to a plate of salad on a bench there, and ate with hearty appetite, and drank together with the whole crew. Afterwards I retired to bed, healthy and happy, for it was now two hours before morning, and slept as sweetly as though I had never felt a touch of illness. My good housekeeper, without my giving any orders, had prepared a fat capon for my repast. So that, when I rose, about the hour for breaking fast, she presented herself with a smiling countenance, and said: "Oh! is that the man who felt that he was dying? Upon my word, I think the blows and kicks you dealt us last night, when you were so enraged, and had that demon in your body as it seemed, must have frightened away your mortal fever! The fever feared that it might catch it too, as we did!" All my poor household, relieved in like measure from anxiety and overwhelming labour, went at once to buy earthen vessels in order to replace the pewter I had cast away. Then we dined together joyfully; nay, I cannot remember a day in my whole life when I dined with greater gladness or a better appetite.

After our meal I received visits from the several men who had assisted me. They exchanged congratulations, and thanked God for our success, saying they had learned and seen things done which other masters judged impossible. I too grew somewhat glorious; and deeming I had shown myself a man of talent, indulged in a boastful humour. So I thrust my hand into my purse, and paid them all to their full satisfaction.

That evil fellow, my mortal foe, Messer Pier Francesco Ricci, majordomo of the Duke, took great pains to find out how the affair had gone. In answer to his questions, the two men whom I suspected of having caked my metal for me, said I was no man, but of a certainty some powerful devil, since I had accomplished what no craft of the art could do; indeed they did not believe a mere ordinary fiend could work such miracles as I in other ways had shown. They exaggerated the whole affair so much, possibly in order to excuse their own part in it, that the majordomo wrote an account to the Duke, who was then in Pisa, far more marvellous and full of thrilling incidents than what they had narrated.

After I had let my statue cool for two whole days, I began to uncover it by slow degrees. The first thing I found was that the head of Medusa had come out most admirably, thanks to the air-vents; for, as I had told the Duke, it is the nature of fire to ascend. Upon advancing farther, I discovered that the other head, that, namely, of Perseus, had succeeded no less admirably; and this astonished me far more, because it is at a considerably lower level than that of the Medusa. Now the mouths of the mould were placed above the head of Perseus and behind his shoulders; and I found that all the bronze my furnace contained had been exhausted in the head of this figure. It was a miracle to observe that not one fragment remained in the orifice of the channel, and that nothing was wanting to the statue. In my great astonishment I seemed to see in this the hand of God arranging and controlling all.

I went on uncovering the statue with success, and ascertained that everything had come out in perfect order, until I reached the foot of the right leg on which the statue rests. There the heel itself was formed, and going farther, I found the foot apparently complete. This gave me great joy on the one side, but was half unwelcome to me on the other, merely because I had told the Duke that it could not come out. However, when I reached the end, it appeared that the toes and a little piece above them were unfinished, so that about half the foot was wanting. Although I knew that this would add a trifle to my labour, I was very well pleased, because I could now prove to the Duke how well I understood my business. It is true that far more of the foot than I had expected had been

BOTTICELLI: *The Adoration of the Magi*, ANDREW MELLON COLLECTION, NATIONAL GALLERY OF ART, WASHINGTON, D. C.

perfectly formed; the reason of this was that, from causes I have already described, the bronze was hotter than our rules of art prescribe; also that I had been obliged to supplement the alloy with my pewter cups and platters, which no one else, I think, had ever done before.

Having now ascertained how successfully my work had been accomplished, I lost no time in hurrying to Pisa, where I found the Duke. He gave me a most gracious reception, as did also the Duchess; and although the majordomo had informed them of the whole proceedings, their Excellencies deemed my performance far more stupendous and astonishing when they heard the tale from my own mouth. When I arrived at the foot of the Perseus, and said it had not come out perfect, just as I had previously warned his Excellency, I saw an expression of wonder pass over his face, while he related to the Duchess how I had predicted this beforehand. Observing the princes to be so well disposed towards me, I begged leave from the Duke to go to Rome. He granted it in most obliging terms, and bade me return as soon as possible to complete his Perseus....

(Translated by John Addington Symonds)

Sir Thomas Wyatt
(1503-1542)
Description of the Contrarious Passions in a Lover

I find no peace, and all my war is done;
I fear and hope, I burn, and freeze like ice;
I fly above the wind, yet can I not arise;
And nought I have, and all the world I seize on,
That loseth nor locketh, holdeth me in prison,
And holdeth me not, yet can I scape no wise;
Nor letteth me live, nor die, at my devise,
And yet of death it giveth me occasion.
Without eye I see; and without tongue I plain.
I desire to perish, and yet I ask health;
I love another, and thus I hate myself;
I feed me in sorrow, and laugh in all my pain.
Likewise displeaseth me both death and life,
And my delight is causer of this strife.

Henry Howard, Earl of Surrey
(1517?-1547)
Complaint of a Lover Rebuked

Love, that doth reign and live within my thought,
And build his seat within my captive breast,
Clad in the arms wherein with me he fought,
Oft in my face he doth his banner rest.
But she that taught me love and suffer pain,
My doubtful hope and eke my hot desire
With shamefast look to shadow and refrain,
Her smiling grace converteth straight to ire.
And coward Love then to the heart apace
Taketh his flight, where he doth lurk and plain
His purpose lost, and dare not show his face.
For my lord's guilt thus faultless bide I pain.
Yet from my lord shall not my foot remove;
Sweet is the death that taketh end by love.

Pierre de Ronsard
(1525-1585)
To Marie

Two flowers I love, the March-flower and
the rose,
The lovely rose that is to Venus dear,
The March-flower that of her the name
doth bear,
Who will not leave my spirit in repose:
Three birds I love; one, moist with May-
dew, goes
To dry his feathers in the sunshine clear;
One for his mate laments throughout the
year,
And for his child the other wails his woes:
And Bourgueil's pine I love, where Venus
hung,
  For a proud trophy on the darksome
bough,
Ne'er since released my youthful liberty:
And Phoebus' tree love I, the laurel tree,
Of whose fair leaves, my mistress, when
I sung,
Bound with her locks a garland for my
brow.

            (Translated by H. F. Cary)

Edmund Spenser
(1552-1599)
Sonnet 15
Ye Tradeful Merchants

Ye tradeful merchants, that with weary toil
Do seek most precious things to make your
gain;
And both the Indias of their treasures spoil;
What needeth you to seek so far in vain?
For lo, my love doth in herself contain
All this world's riches that may far be
found;
If sapphires, lo, her eyes be sapphires plain;
If rubies, lo, her lips be rubies sound;
If pearls, her teeth be pearls, both pure
and round;
If ivory, her forehead ivory ween;
If gold, her locks are finest gold on ground;
If silver, her fair hands are silver sheen:
  But that which fairest is, but few be-
hold,
  Her mind adorned with virtues mani-
fold.

Sir Philip Sidney
(1554-1586)
With How Sad Steps

With how sad steps, O Moon, thou climb'st
the skies!
How silently, and with how wan a face!
What, may it be that even in heavenly
place
That busy archer his sharp arrows tries?
Sure, if that long-with-love-acquainted
eyes
Can judge of love, thou feel'st a lover's
case.
I read it in thy looks; thy languished grace,
To me that feel the like, thy state descries.
Then, even of fellowship, O Moon, tell me,
Is constant love deemed there but want
of wit?
Are beauties there as proud as here they
be?
Do they above love to be loved, and yet
  Those lovers scorn whom that love doth
possess?
  Do they call virtue there ungrateful-
ness?

Leave Me, O Love

Leave me, O love which reachest but to
dust;
And thou, my mind, aspire to higher
things;

Grow rich in that which never taketh rust,
Whatever fades but fading pleasure brings.
Draws in thy beams, and humble all thy might
To that sweet yoke where lasting freedoms be;
Which breaks the clouds and opens forth the light,
That doth both shine and give us sight to see.
O take fast hold; let that light be thy guide
In this small course which birth draws out to death,
And think how evil becometh him to slide,
Who seeketh heav'n, and comes of heav'nly breath.
Then farewell, world; thy uttermost I see;
Eternal Love, maintain thy life in me.

Michael Drayton
(1563-1631)
Since There's No Help

Since there's no help, come let us kiss and part;
Nay, I have done, you get no more of me,
And I am glad, yea glad with all my heart
That thus so cleanly I myself can free;
Shake hands forever, cancel all our vows,
And when we meet at any time again,
Be it not seen in either of our brows
That we one jot of former love retain.
Now at the last gasp of love's latest breath,
When, his pulse failing, passion speechless lies,
When faith is kneeling by his bed of death,
And innocence is closing up his eyes,
Now if thou wouldst, when all have given him over,
From death to life thou mightst him yet recover.

William Shakespeare
(1564-1616)
Sonnet 8
Music to Hear

Music to hear, why hear'st thou music sadly?
Sweets with sweets war not, joy delights in joy;
Why lov'st thou that which thou receiv'st not gladly,
Or else receiv'st with pleasure thine annoy?
If the true concord of well-tuned sounds,
By union married, do offend thine ear,
They do but sweetly chide thee, who confounds
In singleness the parts that thou shouldst bear:
Mark how one string, sweet husband to another,
Strikes each in each by mutual ordering;
Resembling sire and child and happy mother,
Who all in one, one pleasing note do sing:
   Whose speechless song, being many, seeming one,
   Sings this to thee: "Thou single wilt prove none."

There was an Elizabethan mathematical notion that the number one is no number. The instrument in this sonnet is the lute, the strings of which, except for the highest, are double. Stravinsky has set the sonnet to music for mezzo-soprano, flute, clarinet, and viola.

Sonnet 18
Shall I Compare Thee

Shall I compare thee to a summer's day?
Thou art more lovely and more temperate:
Rough winds do shake the darling buds of May,

And summer's lease hath all too short a date:
Sometime too hot the eye of heaven shines,
And often is his gold complexion dimm'd;
And every fair from fair sometime declines,
By chance, or nature's changing course, untrimmed;
But thy eternal summer shall not fade
Nor lose possession of that fair thou ow'st,
Nor shall Death brag thou wand'rest in his shade
When in eternal lines to time thou grow'st:
   So long as men can breathe or eyes can see,
   So long lives this, and this gives life to thee.

Sonnet 30
When to the Sessions

When to the sessions of sweet silent thought
I summon up remembrance of things past,
I sign the lack of many a thing I sought
And with old woes new wail my dear time's waste;
Then can I drown an eye unused to flow,
For precious friends hid in death's dateless night,
And weep afresh love's long since cancell'd woe,
And moan th' expense of many a vanish'd sight;
Then can I grieve at grievances foregone,
And heavily from woe to woe tell o'er
The sad account of fore-bemoaned moan,
Which I new pay as if not paid before:
   But if the while I think on thee, dear friend,
   All losses are restor'd and sorrows end.

Sonnet 55
Not Marble Nor the Guilded Monuments

Not marble nor the gilded monuments
Of princes shall outlive this pow'rful rhyme,
But you shall shine more bright in these contents,
Than unswept stone, besmear'd with sluttish time.
When wasteful war shall statues overturn,
And broils root out the work of masonry,
Not Mars this sword nor war's quick fire shall burn
The living record of your memory.
'Gainst death and all oblivious enmity
Shall you pace forth, your praise shall still find room
Even in the eyes of all posterity
That wear this world out to the ending doom.
   So, till the judgment that yourself arise,
   You live in this, and dwell in lovers' eyes.

Sonnet 73
That Time of Year

That time of year thou mayst in me behold
When yellow leaves, or none, or few, do hang
Upon those boughs which shake against the cold,
Bare ruin'd choirs, where late the sweet birds sang:
In me thou see'st the twilight of such day
As after sunset fadeth in the west;
Which by and by black night doth take away,
Death's second self, that seals up all in rest:
In me thou see'st the glowing of such fire,
That on the ashes of his youth doth lie,

As the death-bed whereon it must expire,
Consum'd with that which it was nourish'd by.
    This thou perceiv'st, which makes thy love more strong,
    To love that well which thou must leave ere long.

Who Is Sylvia?

Of the many musical settings of this charming song from one of Shakespeare's earliest plays, Franz Schubert's is probably the best.

Who is Sylvia? what is she,
    That all our swains commend her?
Holy, fair, and wise is she;
    The heaven such grace did lend her,
That she might admired be.

Is she kind as she is fair?
    For beauty lives with kindness:
Love doth to her eyes repair
    To help him of his blindness;
And being help'd, inhabits there.

Then to Sylvia let us sing
    That Sylvia is excelling;
She excels each mortal thing
    Upon the dull earth dwelling.
To her garlands let us bring.

Orlando Gibbons
(1583-1625)
The Silver Swan

The silver swan, who living had no note,
When death approached unlocked her silent throat;

Leaning her breast against the reedy shore,
Thus sung her first and last, and sung no more:

"Farewell, all joys, O death, come close mine eyes;
More geese than swans now live, more fools than wise."

Walter Pater
(1839-1894)
La Gioconda
from *The Renaissance*

Walter Pater, probably the most important critical writer of the late Victorian period, devoted the same painstaking care to the writing of his prose that he would have done to the composing of poetry. He is at his best in the following famous passage from his chapter on Leonardo da Vinci in The Renaissance.

"La Gioconda" is, in the truest sense, Leonardo's masterpiece, the revealing instance of his mode of thought and work. In suggestiveness, only the "Melancholia" of Dürer is comparable to it; and no crude symbolism disturbs the effect of its subdued and graceful mystery. We all know the face and hands of the figure, set in its marble chair, in that circle of fantastic rocks, as in some faint light under sea. Perhaps of all ancient pictures time has chilled it least. As often happens with works in which invention seems to reach its limit, there is an element in it given to, not invented by, the master. In that inestimable folio of drawings, once the possession of Vasari, were certain designs by Verrocchio, faces of such impressive beauty that Leonardo in his boyhood copied them many times. It is hard not to connect with these designs of the elder, by-past master, as with its germinal principle, the unfathomable smile, always with a touch of something sinister in it, which plays over all Leonardo's work. Besides, the picture is a portrait. From childhood we see this image defining itself on the fabric of his dreams, and but for express historical testimony, we might fancy that this was but his ideal lady, embodied and beheld at last. What was the relationship of a living Florentine to this creature of his thought? By what strange affinities had the dream and the person grown up thus apart, and yet so closely together? Present from the first incorporeally in Leonardo's brain, dimly traced in the designs of Verrocchio, she is found present at last in Il Giocondo's house. That there is much of mere portraiture in the picture is attested by the legend that by artificial means, the presence of mimes and flute-players, that subtle expression was protracted on the face. Again, was it in four years and by renewed labor never really completed, or in four months and as by stroke of magic, that the image was projected?

The presence that rose thus so strangely beside the waters, is expressive of what in the ways of a thousand years men had come to desire. Hers is the head upon which all "the ends of the world are come," and the eyelids are a little weary. It is a beauty wrought out from within upon the flesh, the deposit, little cell by cell, of strange thoughts and fantastic reveries and exquisite passions. Set it for a moment beside one of those white Greek goddesses or beautiful women of antiquity, and how would they be troubled by this beauty, into which the soul with all its maladies has passed! All the thoughts and experiences of the world have etched and molded there, in that which they have of power to refine and make expressive the outward form, the animalism of Greece, the lust of Rome, the mysticism of the Middle Ages with its spiritual ambition and imaginative loves, the return of the Pagan world, the sins of the Borgias. She is older than the rocks among which she sits; like the vampire, she has been dead many times, and learned the secrets of the grave; and has been a diver in deep seas, and keeps their fallen day about her; and trafficked for strange webs with Eastern merchants, and, as Leda, was the mother of Helen of Troy, and, as Saint Anne, the mother of Mary; and all this has been to her but as the sound of lyres and flutes, and lives only in the delicacy with which it has molded the changing lineaments, and tinged the eyelids and the hands. The fancy of a perpetual life, sweeping together ten thousand experiences, is an old one; and modern philosophy has conceived the idea of humanity as wrought upon by, and summing itself up in itself, all modes of thought and life. Certainly Lady Lisa might stand as the embodiment of the old fancy, the symbol of the modern idea.

Dmitri Merezhkovsky
(1865-1941)
Monna Lisa Gioconda
from *The Romance of Leonardo da Vinci*

One of the most influential of Russian novelists and philosophers at the turn of the century, Merezhkovsky reflected his mysticism and his neo-Christian beliefs in a trilogy of novels published under the general title Christ and the Antichrist. *The second novel of the three has as its hero Leonardo da Vinci, who was to the novelist a forerunner of the ideal man of the future. "Alien alike to the moribund Christianity of the Renaissance Church, the sterile revival of pagan antiquity, the expiring medievalism of Savonarola and—Merezhkovsky is careful to make the point—the positivism and narrow specialization of modern science, Leonardo was the man who thought for himself, the universal consciousness, 'the poet of the hypothesis, the organizer of the materials of analysis,' as Paul Valéry characterizes him."*

Leonardo used to say:—

"For portraits, have a special studio; a

court, oblong and rectangular, ten *braccia* in width, twenty in length, the walls painted black, with a projecting roof and canvas curtains for the sun. Or, if you haven't the canvas curtains, paint only in the twilight, or when it is clouded and dull. That is the perfect light."

Just such a court for the painting of portraits he had made for himself in the house of the Florentine citizen who lodged him; a notable personage, commissary of the Signoria, a mathematician, a man of intellect and amiability, his name Ser Piero di Braccio Martelli. His house was the second in the Via Martelli, on the left as one goes from San Giovanni to the Palazzo Medici.

It was a warm misty afternoon, towards the close of spring, in the year 1505. The sun shone through clouds; there was a dull light, which seemed as if shining under water, throwing delicate liquid shadows—Leonardo's favorite condition of the atmosphere; which, he thought, gave special charm to the face of a woman.

"Will she come?" he asked himself, thinking of her whose portrait he had been painting for nearly three years, with a tenacity and a zeal unwonted.

He arranged the studio for her reception. Boltraffio, watching him, marvelled at his unusual solicitude.

He prepared palette, brushes, and skins of paint, each one coated with a transparent film of gum arabic. He removed the cover from the portrait, which was disposed on a movable three-legged stand called a *leggio*. He set the fountain playing in the middle of the court. It had been constructed for her delight—falling streams striking against glass spheres put them in motion and produced a strange low music. Her favorite flowers had been planted round the fountain—pale irises—the lilies of Florence. Then he crumbled bread in a basket for the tame doe which lived in the court, and which she used to feed with her own hands; lastly, he arranged her chair, of smooth dark oak with carved back and arms; before it placed a soft rug, upon which was soon curled and purring a white cat of a rare breed, procured for her pleasure, a dainty foreign beast with vari-coloured eyes, the right yellow as a topaz, the left sapphire blue.

Meantime, Andrea Salaino had begun to tune the viol; another musician, one Atalante, whom Leonardo had known at the Milanese court, brought the silver lyre, shaped like a horse's head, which the artist had invented.

The best musicians, singers, story-tellers, and poets, the most witty talkers, were invited by Leonardo to his studio to amuse *her*, and avert the tedium of her sittings. He studied the changeful beauty of her expression as reflects of thought and feeling were awakened by talk, music, poetry, in turn.

Now all was ready, but still she delayed her coming.

"Where is she?" he thought; "the light and shadow today are just her own. Shall I send to seek her? Nay, but she knows how ardently I await her! She will come." And Giovanni noticed that his impatience grew.

Suddenly a light waft of the breeze swayed the jet of the fountain, the delicate irises shook as the spray fell on them. The keen-eared doe was on the alert, with outstretched neck. Leonardo listened. And Giovanni, though he heard nothing, knew it was she.

First, with a humble reverence, came Sister Camilla, a lay-companion who lived with her, and always attended her to the studio, sitting quietly apart studying a prayer-book, and effacing herself, so that in three years Leonardo had hardly heard her voice. The sister was followed by the woman all expected; a woman of thirty,

LEONARDO DA VINCI: *Mona Lisa*, PHOTO DES MUSÉES NATIONAUX, LOUVRE

in a plain dark dress, and a dark transparent veil which reached to the center of her forehead—Monna Lisa Gioconda.

She was a Neapolitan of noble birth; her father, Antonio Gherardini, had lost his wealth in the French invasion of 1495, and had married his daughter to the Florentine, Francesco del Giocondo, who had seen the death of two wives already. Messer Francesco was five years younger than Leonardo; was one of the twelve *Bonuomini*, and was likely later to be made Prior. He was a mediocre personage, of a type to be found in every country and in every age; neither good nor bad; busy in a commonplace way, absorbed in his affairs, content with daily routine. He regarded his young wife as nothing more than an ornament for his house. Her essential charm he understood less than the points of his Sicilian cattle, or the impost upon raw sheepskins. She was said to have married this man solely to please her father, and by her marriage to have driven an earlier lover to a voluntary death. It was also said that she still had a crowd of passionate adorers—persevering, but hopeless. The scandalmongers could find nothing worse than this to insinuate. Calm, gentle, retiring, pious, charitable to the poor, she was a faithful wife, a good housekeeper, a most tender mother to Dianora, her twelve-year-old stepdaughter.

Giovanni knew all this of Monna Lisa. Yet she never visited Leonardo's studio without seeming to the pupil a wholly different person from Messer Francesco's wife. She had been coming now for three years, and Giovanni's first impressions had only been confirmed by subsequent observations. He found something mysterious, illusory, phantasmal about her which filled him with awe. Leonardo's portrait seemed more real than she was herself. She and the painter—whom she never saw except when sitting to him, and then never alone—appeared to share some secret; not a love-secret, at least not in the ordinary sense of the term.

Leonardo had once spoken of the tendency felt by every artist to reproduce his own likeness in his pictures of others, the reason of this tendency being that both his own material semblance and his work are the creation and manifestation of his soul. In this case Giovanni found that not merely the portrait, but the woman herself, was growing daily more like the painter. The likeness was less in the features than in the expression of eyes and in the smile. But he had already seen this smile on the lips of Verrocchio's Unbelieving Thomas; of Eve before the Tree of Science, Leonardo's first picture; in the Leda, in the Angel of the Madonna of the Rocks; and in a hundred other drawings, executed before ever he had met Monna Lisa: as though, throughout life, he had sought his own reflection, and had found it completely at last.

When Giovanni looked at that smile, he felt perturbed, alarmed, as if in presence of the supernatural: reality seemed a dream, and the dream-world reality; Monna Lisa, not the wife of Giocondo, the very ordinary Florentine citizen, but a phantom evoked by the will of the Master, a female semblance of Leonardo himself.

Lisa took her seat, and the white cat jumped on her lap; she stroked it with delicate fingers, and faint cracklings and sparks came from the silky fur. Leonardo began his work; but presently he laid it aside and sat silent, looking into her face with an intentness that no faintest shadow of change in her expression could have escaped.

"Madonna," he said at last, "you are preoccupied—troubled about something today."

Giovanni had observed that today she did not resemble the portrait.

"I am a little troubled," she replied; "Dianora is ill, and I have been up with her the whole night."

"Then you are wearied, and the pose will try you. We will defer the sitting to another time."

"Nay, we cannot lose this delightful day! See the misty sunlight and the delicate shadows! It is *my* day!"

There was a short silence. Then she went on: "I knew you expected me. I was ready to come earlier; but I was kept. Madonna Sophonisba—"

"Who? Ah, I know. She with the voice of a fishwife and the scent of a perfumer's shop!"

Monna Lisa smiled quietly. "She had to tell me about the fete at the Palazzo Vecchio, given by Argentina, wife of the *Gonfaloniere;* of the supper, the dresses, the lovers—"

"Ay, 'tis not Dianora's illness that has disturbed you, but this woman's senseless gossip. Strange case! Have you never noticed, madonna, how sometimes a single absurdity on an indifferent subject from an uninteresting person will throw a gloom over the mind, and afflict us more than our real cares?"

She bent her head silently; it was clear they understood each other too well for words to be always necessary.

Leonardo again addressed himself to his work.

"Tell me something!" she cried.

"What shall I tell you?"

She smiled. "Tell me about *The Realm of Venus.*"

The artist had certain favorite stories for La Gioconda; tales of travel, of natural phenomena, of plans for pictures. He knew them by heart, and would recite always in the same simple half-childlike words, accompanied by soft music, in his feminine voice, the old fable, or cradle-tale. Andrea and Atalante took their instruments, and when they had executed the *motif* which invariably preluded *The Realm of Venus,* he began:—

"The seafarers who live on the coasts of Cilicia tell of him who is destined to drown, that for a moment, during the most tremendous storms, he is permitted to behold the island of Cyprus, realm of the Goddess of Love. Around boil whirlwinds and whirlpools, and the voices of the waters; and great in number are the navigators who, attracted by the splendour of that island, have lost ships upon its rocks. Many a gallant bark has there been dashed to pieces, many sunk for ever in the deep! Yonder on the coast lie piteous hulks, overgrown with seaweed, half buried by sand. Of one the prow juts exposed; of another the stern; of another the gaping beams of its side, like the blackened ribs of a corpse. So many are they, that there it looks like the Resurrection Day, when the Sea shall give up its dead! But over the isle itself is a curtain of eternal azure, and the sun shines on flowery hills. And the stillness of the air is such, that when the priest swings the censer on the temple steps, the flame ascends to heaven straight, unwavering as the white columns and the giant cypresses mirrored in an untroubled lake lying inland, far from the shore. Only the streams that flow from that lake, and cascades leaping from one porphyry basin to another, trouble the solitude with their pleasant sound. Those drowning far at sea hear for a moment that soft murmur, and see the still lake of sweet waters, and the wind carries to them the perfume of myrtle and rose. Ever the more terrible the outer tempest, the profounder that calm in the island realm of the Cyprian."

He ceased; the strains of lute and viol died away, and that silence followed which is sweeter than any music. As if lulled by the words just spoken, as caught away from actual life by the long hush, a stranger to all things except the will of the artist, Monna Lisa, like calm and pure and fathomless water, looked into Leonardo's eyes with that mystic smile which was the very counterpart of his own. Giovanni Boltraffio, watching now one, now the other, thought of two mirrors, each reflecting, absorbing the other into infinity. . . .

On leaving the Palazzo Vecchio Leonardo paused in the piazza before Michelangelo's "David." It stood as if on guard, a giant of white marble, relieved against the background of dark stone. Young, thin, naked, the veins swollen in his right hand which held the sling, his left arm was raised in front of his breast, the stone within the hand. His brows were knit, his gaze far away, like one taking aim. The curls upon his low forehead seemed already the garland of victory. . . . Seeing him stand there where Savonarola had been burned, he thought of the prophet Fra Girolamo had desired in vain, the hero for whom Machiavelli was still waiting.

In this work of his rival's Leonardo recognised the expression of a soul as great as his own, but eternally opposed to it; opposed as action is to contemplation, passion to apathy, storm to tranquility. This alien force attracted him; he felt the inevitable fascination of something new, the desire to come close to it, to study it, to understand it.

Two years earlier, among the building stones of Santa Maria del Fiore, lay a huge block of white marble, spoilt by an unskilled sculptor. The best masters had refused it, thinking it no longer good for anything. It had been offered to Leonardo himself, and with his usual slowness he had meditated, measured, calculated, hesitated. Then came another, twenty-three years younger than he, who had undertaken the task without misgiving; with incredible rapidity, working by night as well as by day, he had made this giant in two years and one month. Leonardo had worked six years at the clay of his Colossus; he dared not think how long he would have required for a marble statue like this David.

The Florentines had proclaimed Michelangelo Leonardo's rival in the art of sculpture, and the young man had not hesitated to accept his challenge. Now it seemed he was about to place himself in competition with the older Master as a painter also. He had yet hardly taken a brush in his hand, but with a daring which might seem presumption, he was about to paint the second war-picture in the council chamber.

Leonardo had met his youthful rival with goodwill and every consideration; but Michelangelo hated him with all the fire of his impetuous nature. Leonardo's calm he fancied contempt; he listened to calumnies, he sought pretexts for quarrels, he seized every occasion to damage his rival. When the "David" was finished the best painters and sculptors were invited by the Signoria to discuss where it should be placed. Leonardo agreed with Giuliano da San Gallo, the architect, that the most suitable position would be under the Loggia de' Priori, and not, as others suggested, in front of the Palazzo della Signoria. Michelangelo swore that Leonardo, prompted by envy, wished his rival's work hidden in a corner where no one could properly see it.

Discussions on abstract questions were at this time much the vogue, and on one occasion a company, including the brothers Pollaiuoli, the aged Botticelli, Filippino Lippi, and Lorenzo di Credi, assembled in Leonardo's studio to debate whether sculpture or painting held the higher place among the arts. Leonardo quickly, with a whimsical expression, gave his opinion thus:—

"The further art is removed from a

handicraft the nearer it approaches perfection. The major distinction between the two arts lies in the fact that painting demands greater effort of mind, sculpture greater effort of body. The shape, contained like a kernel in the block of marble, is slowly set free by the sculptor's blows of chisel and mallet, needing the exertion of all his bodily powers. Great fatigue ensues, the labourer is drenched with sweat, which mingling with dust becomes a miry crust upon his garments; his face is smeared and covered with white like a baker's, his studio is filled with chips. Whereas the painter, perfectly calm, in elegant habiliments, seated at ease in his chair, plies a light brush and manipulates pleasant paints. His house is clean, and quiet, so that his toil can be sweetened by converse, or music, or reading, undisturbed by hammerings or scrapings."

These words came to the ears of Michelangelo, who imagined them aimed at himself. He took occasion to make venomous reply:—

"Let this Messer da Vinci, a kitchen-wench's bastard, be ashamed of dirty work; I, the heir of an old and honourable house, despise neither sweat nor mire. The dispute is foolish, for all the arts are equal, proceeding from one source, aiming at one goal. He who maintains that painting is nobler than sculpture knows no more of either than my serving-maid."

He set to work with feverish energy on his picture for the council chamber, wishing to overtake his rival—a feat by no means difficult. His subject was an incident in the Pisan campaign: a sudden attack by the enemy while the soldiers were bathing. The men hurry to the bank, scramble out of the pleasant waves, draw on their sweated and dusty clothes, don their cuirasses and helmets, which are burning hot under the fiery sunshine. Michelangelo thus showed war as a contrast to Leonardo's representation: not as "the most bestial of madnesses," but as the performance of hard and manful duty to the denial of ease and pleasure; as the struggle of heroes for the greatness and glory of their country.

The Florentines watched the growth of the two pictures and the rivalry between the artists with all the keenness of spectators at a street show; and as strife unconnected with politics seemed to them tasteless as broth without salt, they affirmed that Michelangelo was for the republic against the Medici, Leonardo for the Medici against the republic. The artistic duel now became intelligible to everybody; the town was divided into two parties; and men, to whom art was a sealed book, declared themselves the adherents of one or other of the two artists whose works had become the ensigns of hostile camps. Stones were thrown secretly at the "David"; the rich accused the poor of this outrage, the demagogues accused the substantial burghers; the artists, the pupils; and Buonarroti, in the presence of the *Gonfaloniere,* asserted that ruffians had been hired by Leonardo to damage his statue.

One day Leonardo, working at his portrait in the presence of Boltraffio and Salaino, said to Monna Lisa:—

"Could I but come to speech with Messer Michelangelo, face to face, as I speak with you, madonna, all would be explained, and no trace would remain of this stupid quarrel. He would learn that I am not his enemy, and that there is no man living could love him better than I."

Madonna Lisa shook her head.

"Nay, Messer Leonardo, he would not understand you."

"Such a man could not fail to understand. The mischief is that he is diffident and has too little self-confidence. He fears and tortures himself and is jealous, because he does not yet know his own strength. It is folly in him. I would reassure him. What has he to fear in me? I have seen his sketch for the 'Soldiers Bathing' and, believe me, madonna, I was astounded, and could scarce believe my own eyes. No one can conceive the value of this young man, nor what he will rise to. Even now he is not only my equal, but stronger than I. Deny it not, madonna, for I speak what I know to be true: he is my superior."

She smiled, reflecting his expression like an image in a mirror.

"Messer," she said, "do you remember the words the Lord spoke to the prophet Elijah when he fled from the wicked King Ahab into the desert on the Mountain Horeb:—

" 'Go forth, and stand upon the mountain before the Lord. And behold, the Lord passed by; and a great and strong wind rent the mountains, and brake in pieces the rocks before the Lord; but the Lord was not in the wind: and after the wind an earthquake; but the Lord was not in the earthquake: and after the earthquake a fire; but the Lord was not in the fire: and after the fire a still small voice—and the Lord was in it. . . .'

"Perhaps Messer Buonarroti has the strength of the wind, which rends mountains and dashes rocks to pieces before the Lord; but the still small voice is not in him, which is the stillness of God. This he knows and hates you, for you are mightier than he, as stillness is mightier than the tempest. . . ."

The next day, at her habitual hour, Monna Lisa came to the studio for the first time unaccompanied. She knew it was their last interview. It was a brilliant morning, and Leonardo lowered the canvas curtain to produce that dim and tender light, transparent as submarine shadows, which gave her face its greatest charm.

They were alone.

He kept working on in silence, calm and absorbed, forgetting his thoughts of the previous night, forgetting the parting, the inevitable choice. Past and Future had alike vanished from his memory; time had come to a standstill; it seemed as if she had always sat, and would ever thus sit before him with that calm strange smile. What he could not do in life he did by imagination: he blended the two images in one—mingled the reality and its reflection—the living woman and the immortal. He had now the sense of a great deliverance. He no longer either pitied her or feared her. He knew her submissiveness, that she would accept all, endure all; die, perhaps, but never revolt. And momently he looked at her with that curiosity which had taken him to the execution of the condemned, that he might watch the last shudders of fear on the dying faces.

Suddenly he fancied that a strange shadow, as of an unbidden thought, which he had not evoked, which he wished away, appeared upon her countenance, like the cloud of human breath upon the surface of a mirror. To preserve her, to recall her anew to the Type, to banish from her this human shadow, he related gravely, like a magician pronouncing an incantation, one of his mystic tales.

"Unable to resist the desire of beholding new forms, the secret creations of nature, I at length reached the cavern, and there at the entrance stood still in terror. I stooped, the left hand on the right knee, and shading my eyes with my hand to accustom myself to the darkness, I presently took heart and entered, and moved forward for several steps. Then, frowning, straining my sight to the utmost, I unwittingly changed my course and wandered hither and thither in the darkness, feeling my way and groping after the definite. But the obscurity was overpowering, and when I had passed some time in it, Fear and Curiosity contended most mightily within me: fear of searching that dark cavern, and curiosity after its secret."

He was silent. The unwonted shadow still lay upon her face.

"Which of the two feelings gained the day?" La Gioconda murmured.

"Curiosity."

"And you learned the stupendous secret?"

"I learned...what could be learned."

"And will reveal it to men?"

"I would not, nor could not, reveal all. But I would inspire them also with curiosity strong enough to vanquish fear."

"And if curiosity be not enough, Messer Leonardo?" she said slowly, an unwonted fire in her eyes; "if something further, a profounder feeling were needed to lay bare the cavern's last and greatest treasure?"

And she turned toward him a smile he had never seen before.

"What more is needed?" he asked.

She was silent. Just then a slender, blinding ray shone through a rent in the curtain; the dimness vanished; the mystery, the clear shadows, tender as distant music, fled.

"You leave tomorrow?" she said suddenly.

"No. Tonight."

"I, too, am soon departing."

The artist looked at her steadily, attempted speech, and said nothing. He divined her meaning; that she would not stay in Florence without him.

"Messer Francesco," she continued, "goes presently for three months to Calabria. I have asked him to take me with him."

He frowned. This sunshine was not to his mind; the fountain had been ghostly white; now it had taken the rainbow hues of life. Leonardo felt that he was returning to life, timid, weak, pitiable.

"No matter," said Monna Lisa, "draw closer the curtain. It is early yet. I am not tired."

"I have painted enough," he said, throwing down his brush.

"You will not finish my portrait?"

"Why not?" he cried hastily, as if alarmed. "Will you not come to me when you return?"

"I will come. But shall I be the same? You have told me that faces, especially the faces of women, quickly change."

"I long to finish it. But sometimes to me it seems impossible."

"Impossible?" wondered La Gioconda. "Ay, they tell me you finish nothing because you are always seeking the impossible."

In these words he fancied a tender reproach.

She rose and said with her usual calm:—

"Farewell, Messer Leonardo. I wish you a good journey."

He also had risen, and looking at her he saw again helpless entreaty and reproach on her face. He knew that this moment was irrevocable for both—final and solemn as death. He felt he must break this pregnant silence, yet no words came to him. The more he forced his will to find a solution, the more he was conscious of his own powerlessness and the profundity of the abyss which must divide them. Monna Lisa still smiled her quiet smile; that calmness, that brightness, seemed to him now the smile of the dead. Intolerable pity filled his heart and weakened him still more.

She stretched out her hand; he took it and kissed it for the first time since he had known her. As he did so she bent quickly, and he felt that La Gioconda touched his hair with her lips.

"May God have you in His keeping," she said simply.

When he recovered from his wonder—she was gone. Around him was the dead silence of a summer afternoon, more menacing than midnight. Again he heard the heavy measured clanging of the clock, telling of the irremediable flight of time, of the darkness and loneliness of age, of the past, which can return no more. And as the last vibrations died away the words of the plaintive love song echoed in his ears:—

"Di doman non v'è certezza."
"And count not on the day to come."

(Translated by Herbert Trench)

Irving Stone
(1903-   )
The Sculpturing of the David
from *The Agony and the Ecstasy*

Irving Stone, successful contemporary American novelist and historian, has written both biographies—of Jack London, Clarence Darrow, and others—and biographical novels. Among the latter are Love is Eternal, *on the life of Mary Todd Lincoln;* The President's Lady, *on Rachel Jackson; and two based on the lives of artists:* Lust for Life, *on Vincent Van Gogh, and* The Agony and the Ecstasy, *on Michelangelo. In preparation for writing the last-named novel, Irving Stone lived for several years in Italy, where he did extensive research and even learned firsthand the techniques of carving marble. His publishers, Doubleday and Company, have graciously granted the editors of this anthology permission to include here one of Stone's many excellent accounts of the artist at work on a masterpiece.*

from BOOK VI

He (Michelangelo) sat in his shed before the column, drawing David's head, face, and eyes, asking himself:

"What is David feeling at this moment of conquest? Glory? Gratification? Would he feel himself to be the biggest and strongest man in the world? Would there be a touch of contempt for Goliath, of arrogance as he watched the fleeing Philistines, and then turned to accept the plaudits of the Israelites?"

All unworthy emotions, none of which he could bring himself to draw. What could he find in David triumphant, he asked himself, worthy of sculpturing? Tradition portrayed him after the fact. Yet David after the battle was certainly an anticlimax, his great moment already gone.

Which then was the important David? When did David become a giant? After killing Goliath? Or at the moment he decided that he must try? David as he was releasing, with brilliant and deadly accuracy, the shot from the sling? Or David before he entered the battle, when he decided that the Israelites must be freed from their vassalage to the Philistines? Was not the decision more important than the act itself, since character was more critical than action? For him, then, it was David's decision that made him a giant, not his killing of Goliath. He had been floundering because he had imprisoned himself and David at the wrong moment in time.

How could he have been so stupid, so blind? David pictured after Goliath could be no one but the Biblical David, a special individual. He was not content to portray one man; he was seeking universal man, Everyman, all of whom, from the beginning of time, had faced a decision to strike for freedom.

This was the David he had been seeking, caught at the exultant height of resolution, still reflecting the emotions of fear, hesitation, repugnance, doubt; the man who wished to follow his own ways among the hills of Jerusalem, who cared little for the clash of arms and material reward. The man who killed Goliath would be committed all his life to warfare and its consequence, power. The reluctance would still be fading from his face, this giving up of

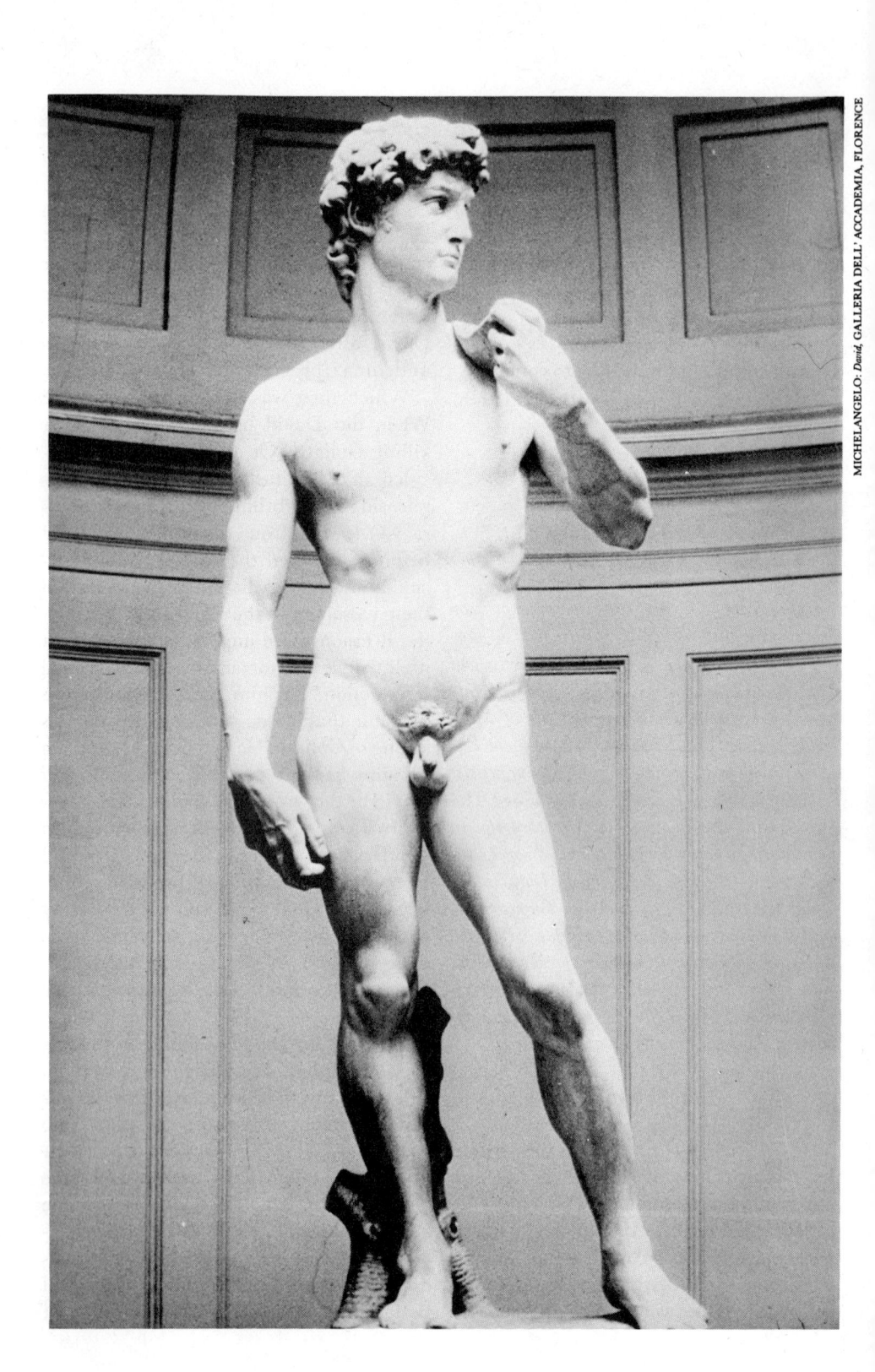

MICHELANGELO: *David*, GALLERIA DELL' ACCADEMIA, FLORENCE.

the pastoral life in which he had been happy for a life of courts and kings, of jealousy and intrigue, of control and disposition of other men's destinies. This was the dichotomy in all men: the reflective life and the active. David would know that the man who gave himself to action would have sold himself to an inexorable master who would command him all the days and years of his life; he would know intuitively that nothing gained as reward for action, no kingdom or power or wealth, could compensate a man for the loss of his privacy.

To act was to join. David would not be sure he wanted to join. He had been a man alone. Once he tackled Goliath there would be no turning back, far more true if he vanquished Goliath than if he were vanquished. It was what he sensed that he would do to himself, as well as what the world would do to him, that made him doubtful and averse to changing the pattern of his days. His had been a hard choice, indeed. This concept opened wide vistas to Michelangelo. He soared, he drew with authority and power; he modeled in clay, eighteen inches high, his fingers unable to keep pace with his thoughts and emotions; and with astonishing facility he knew where the David lay. The limitations of the block began to appear as assets, forcing his mind into a simplicity of design that might never have occurred to him had it been whole and perfect. The marble came alive now.

When he tired of drawing or modeling he would join his fellow members of the Cauldron for an evening of talk. Sansovino moved into the Duomo workyard to begin carving a marble St. John Baptizing Christ for over the east door of the Baptistery, setting up his workshed between Michelangelo and Beppe's stonemasons. When Rustici became bored with working alone on his drawings for a Boccaccio head and an Annunciation in marble, he would come to the yard and sketch with Michelangelo or Sansovino. Next Baccio joined them in the Duomo workyard, to design a crucifix which he hoped the church of San Lorenzo was going to commission. Bugiardini would bring in a hot dinner in pots from a nearby *osteria,* and the former apprentices would spend a companionable hour, Argiento serving the food on Michelangelo's plank worktable against the rear wall. Soggi, proud of his former associates, visited once in a while, wheeling in a cart of cooked sausages for the communal dinner. . . .

Argiento swept out the shop each evening when he returned from the Duomo. He too was content in Florence, working in the Duomo workshed all day, at night having the company of the other young apprentices of the piazza who also slept in their shops, each providing food for a common cookpot.

Best of all, Giuliano da Sangallo returned from Savona where he had completed a palace for Cardinal Rovere at the family estate. Leaving Savona, Sangallo had been intercepted and kept a prisoner for six months by the Pisans and had had to be ransomed for three hundred ducats. Michelangelo visited with him at the family home in the Quarter of the Sun, near Santa Maria Novella. He still insisted that Cardinal Rovere would be the next Pope.

"Tell me about your design for the Giant," he demanded. "And what have you heard of interesting architectural jobs in Florence?"

"There are several of great urgency," said Michelangelo. "A revolving table strong enough to turn a two-thousand-pound column of marble, so I can control the light and sun. A fifteen-foot scaffold, one in which I can change the height and work all around the block."

Sangallo was amused. "You are my best

client. Let's get pen and paper. What you need is a series of four towers, with open shelves that take planks from either direction, like this. . . . As for your turntable, that's an engineering task. . . ."

There were heavy rain clouds overhead. Beppe and his crew built a wooden roof that arched upward at a sharp angle from the back wall, leaving space for the seventeen-foot column, then tiled it securely to keep out the rain.

His marble was still lying flat on the ground. He made a wooden lid to fit its length, with lead-weighted strings hanging over the sides to show at what level in the block he would be seeking for the back of David's head, the arm raised to take the slingshot, the hips swiveled away from the gouge, the rock inside the huge right hand, the tree trunk supporting the right calf. He marked these depths with charcoal and then, helped by Beppe's augmented crew of fifteen, roped the column, attached a block and tackle, slowly raised it to stand upright on Sangallo's turntable. He and Argiento then built the scaffold towers that had open shelves to take wide planks at any height he needed to work.

Now the column cried out to him, giving itself wholly. His tools tore into its flesh with a terrifying penetration, searching for elbows and thighs and chest and groin and kneecap. The white crystals that had lain dormant for half a century yielded lovingly to every touch, from the subtlest nuance to the driving "Go!" in which his hammer and chisel swept upward from the ankle through the knee and thigh without stopping, the routine count of seven for work, followed by four for rest, abandoned as he felt within himself the strength of a hundred men.

This was his most glorious experience in working marble; never had he had such an expanse of figure, such a simplicity of design; never before had he been so possessed by a sense of precision, force, penetration or depth of passion. He could think of nothing else now, could not bring himself to stop for food or change of clothes. He fed his marble hunger twenty hours a day, the acrid dust coagulating in his nostrils, his hair covered as white as old Ficino's, the vibrations of the marble consistency running from the chisels and hammer up his shoulders, then down his chest into his loins and thighs and knees, throbbing and vibrating through his body and brain long after he had thrown himself across his bed in exultant exhaustion. When his right hand tired of driving the hammer he shifted it to the left, the chisel in his right moving with the same precision and probing sensitivity. He carved at night by candlelight, in absolute quiet, for Argiento retired at sundown to the other shop. To Sangallo, who sometimes walked over after supper to check the turntable and scaffold, he commented:

"I'd like to carve for a year of days and nights, with no break at all."

"It's midnight, and freezing in this shed. Aren't you cold?"

Michelangelo flashed his friend a mischievous grin, the amber eyes shining as a cat's do at night.

"Cold? I'm burning with fever. Look how the tension of the torso is beginning to emerge. Another few days and life will break through."

He had met the challenge of the deeply gouged area by tilting the figure twenty degrees inside the column, designing it diagonally, on the bias, down the thickness of the marble, so that David's left side could be fitted into the remaining marble. Now it was as an engineer that he buried in his design a strong vertical structure beginning at the right foot, continuing up through the right leg supported by the short tree trunk, through the thigh and torso and the width of the giant neck, face and head. With this shaft of solid marble his David would stand erect; there could never be an inner collapse.

The key to the beauty and balance of the composition was David's right hand enclosing the stone. This was the form from which the rest of David's anatomy and feeling grew; as the key to the Bacchus had been the arm raised high to hold the wine cup, the Virgin's face the key to the Pieta. This hand with its bulging veins created a width and a bulk to compensate for the leanness with which he had to carve the straight left hip opposite, even as the right arm and elbow would be the most delicate form in the composition.

As he became increasingly absorbed, Granacci could no longer persuade him to come to the villa for supper; he went rarely to the meetings at Rustici's, and then only if the night were too wet and raw to continue work. He could hardly concentrate on what was being said, let alone contribute anything to his friends. Leonardo da Vinci was the only one who complained, claiming that Michelangelo had no right to come to them in his filthy clothes and dust-matted hair. From the pained expression on Leonardo's face, the slight sniffing of the patrician nostrils, he saw that Leonardo thought he smelled bad. He imagined that he probably did, for he did not take his clothes off for a week at a time, even to sleep; but he was too involved to care. Easier to stop going to the Company of the Cauldron.

Christmas came, he accompanied his family to high mass at Santa Croce. The New Year he ignored, not even going to the celebration at Rustici's to help the Company usher in 1502. He stormed through the dark days of January, Argiento feeding coal to four braziers so that he would be warm enough to work, turning the table to catch the most light, moving the plank-platform up and down the David, forward and back as he worked the four sides simultaneously, keeping a heavy webbing between the legs and between the arms and the bulk of the body. The neck was so tremendous he could work it without fear of the head breaking off. He left considerable marble about the heroic head so that later he could carve a shock of short wavy hair....

To mark the frontal projections, David's left foot, left knee, right wrist, the left elbow and hand at the shoulder, he affixed nailheads in the marble. With these fixed points established he was able to carve the upsurging line from the knee through the thigh and chest, delineating David's hard physical stamina; the flesh of the belly in which David was feeling quiverings of anxiety; the left hand holding the slingshot, the great right hand standing cocked, rock at the ready. To protect himself he had left half again as much marble at the rear as he would ultimately need, keeping in mind the fact that there were forty views of a statue as one walked around it.

He had designed David as an independent man, standing clear of all space around him. The statue must never be fitted into a niche, stood against a wall, used to decorate a facade or soften the harsh corner of a building. David must always be free. The world was a battlefield, man forever under strain, precarious on his perch. David was a fighter; not a brutal, senseless ravager, but capable of achieving freedom.

Now the figure became aggressive, began to push out of its mass, striving to define itself in space. His own pace matched the drive of the material, so that Sangallo and Sansovino, visiting with him of a Sunday afternoon, were staggered by his passion.

"I've never seen anything like it," cried Sangallo. "He's knocked off more chips from this hard marble in the last quarter of an hour than any three of his stonecutter friends in the quarry could cut in four."

"It's not the quantity that frightens me," added Sansovino, "It's the impetuosity. I've been watching fragments get hurled four feet in the air, until I thought the whole marble would fly to pieces."

Michelangelo stopped work, turned and faced his friends.

"Once marble is out of its quarry, it is no longer a mountain, it is a river. It can flow, change its course. That's what I'm doing, helping this marble river change its bed."

When the others had returned to their homes, Michelangelo sat at the David's feet and gazed up at him. He thought, "It takes as long for a marble column to bear, as it does a fruit tree." Yet each separate form within the sculpture was beginning to mirror the time and love he had lavished on it. Nor was he frightened by Sansovino's warning, for he identified himself with the center of gravity of the block, fitting himself into the core, feeling the balancing weight of the arms, legs, torso, head, as though they were his own. When he sliced off marble he did so with the precise knowledge of how much flesh he could safely spare.

The one thorn in this flesh, his own and the David's, was Leonardo da Vinci's belittling of the sculptor's art. To Michelangelo it appeared a serious threat. Leonardo's influence in Florence was spreading; if it should convince enough people that marble carving was a second-rate craft, when his David was completed it would be received with indifference. Growing within him was a need to counterattack.

The following Sunday, when the Company of the Cauldron was meeting at Rustici's and Leonardo made light of stone carving, Michelangelo said:

"True, sculpture shares nothing with painting. It exists on its own premises. But primitive man carved in stone for thousands of years before he began to paint on cave walls. Sculpture is the first and original art."

"By that very claim it is condemned," answered Leonardo in his high-pitched voice. "It satisfied only until the fine art of painting was developed. It is now becoming extinct."

Infuriated, Michelangelo struck back with a personal attack.

"Isn't it true, Leonardo," he demanded, "that your equestrian statue in Milan is so colossal that it can never be cast? And hence will never come into existence as bronze sculpture? And that your huge clay model is disintegrating so fast that it's becoming the joke of Milan? No wonder you talk against sculpture, you're not capable of bringing a piece to completion!"

There was an uncomfortable silence in the room.

MANNERISM TO NEO CLASSICISM

GIOVANNI BATTISTA TIEPOLO: *Apollo Pursuing Daphne*, SAMUEL H. KRESS COLLECTION, NATIONAL GALLERY OF ART, WASHINGTON, D. C.

MANNERISM TO NEOCLASSICISM

The artistic trends covered by the designation *Mannerism to Neoclassicism* are excellent examples of adaptation to changing attitudes and ideals. In reality, three distinct styles of art will be under consideration: mannerism, baroque, and neoclassicism. International, civil, and religious unrest had a direct effect on the art of the late sixteenth, seventeenth, and eighteenth centuries.

Mannerism and Baroque

National and Religious Trends

The late sixteenth century was marked by international conflict. England and Spain were vying for supremacy on the seas. France was expanding her holdings. The Germanic countries were struggling to hold their own. Furthermore, the Catholic Counter Reformation was moving to reestablish the position of the church.

The Counter Reformation started first with words and then moved to wars. It had two primary purposes: to resist the spread of Protestantism and to revitalize the church from within, through both religious reform and cultural expression. The Council of Trent encouraged the cultivation of the arts but determined to guide them toward proper representation of the church.

The seventeenth century saw a continuation of unrest and instability. The period of the Thirty Years' War (1618-1648) was devastating to Western Europe, but it also saw the emerging of the great age of France, the *Grand Siecle*. Nationalism and absolutism were at their peak in the France of Louis XIV and strongly influenced the thinking of the rest of Western Europe. England suffered severe internal conflicts during the seventeenth century, and her Elizabethan-Age power weakened accordingly.

Southern Europe, trying to support a Holy Roman Empire that had long been only a name, was caught in the force of the Counter Reformation and the harassment of the Moslems. Northern Europe felt the rising force of Protestantism.

Even though the political and religious atmosphere seemed unprogressive, gains in the intellectual sphere were enormous. Science and the arts were highly productive; men such as Descartes, Hobbes, Galileo, Locke, and Newton furnished their world with new discoveries about itself and its organization. Music, painting, and sculpture—all knew the impact of sharpened awareness. Literature became the means by which many tried either to react to the upheaval of their world or instruct their peers in the way things ought to be.

Literature

Mannerism in literature has only as recently as the last thirty or forty years been acknowledged a legitimate style. Distinguished by such elements as unresolved tensions, word play, highly figurative language, and paradoxes of tone, mannerism is at once sophisticated and self-conscious. The trend first appeared in Spain during that period called the *Golden Age* of Spain. Works such as Cervante's *Don Quixote* and "The Obscure

Night of the Soul" by St. John of the Cross represent the Spanish mannerists. It was not long before the style influenced English writers.

English mannerism had a highly emotional content; reality and illusion shifted place continuously. Paradox became an important device of expression, and the elaborate conceits of the metaphysical writers communicated this groping for both emotional and intellectual expression. They were severely criticized for it by later writers such as Johnson. One of America's first poets, Edward Taylor a Puritan minister, employed the mannerist style. From Spain's Golden Age to England, mannerism was the forerunner to the baroque style that followed.

The baroque influence in literature was rather short-lived, but elements of baroque are found in the modern period as well. Baroque flourished from around 1600 to the middle of the century, leading into the rise of neoclassicism. Developing slowly after the Council of Trent, baroque arts constituted one attempt of the church to counteract the distrust and uncertainty that some mannerist writers expressed regarding the faith and dogma of the church. As in the High Renaissance, baroque was a patronized art form, supported by the wealthy and the church. Largely inspired by the antique world, baroque employed order and logic but not restraint. Baroque literature has texture, color, and embellishment. Substance, however, still predominates over form, to a greater degree than in the neoclassic style that ruled the arts from the last of the seventeenth century to the French Revolution of the eighteenth. Milton's *Paradise Lost* is an expansive, rich, baroque work.

Neoclassicism

Order and Reason

The Neoclassic Period was exactly what its name implies, an attempt to restore the atmosphere of the classical world. From the Renaissance on, scholars were comparing, copying, and challenging the classical heritage. Now, their search into classicism was even more intense; it was a highly self-conscious and determined effort to return society and art to what the neoclassicists felt was the ideal—the Golden Age of Greece. In an age of unrest, Athenian Greece represented the epitome of order, balance, and restraint. The neoclassicist was a strong advocate of order. He needed reason and laws. Correctness became his guiding principle.

Neoclassicists were determined to find order in the world around them. When they did not, they attempted to point out this failing to society. To them, society was all-important; the individual had importance only insofar as he fitted into his allotted place in society.

Deism was particularly prevalent during the eighteenth century. For the deist, God became the prime creator, but a remote one. He had prepared the perfect organization for man, the world; now society's task was to keep it running smoothly.

Literature

This desire to control society and give it form accounts for the major role that satire played in the literature of the day. Humor directed at the foibles of mankind provides the perfect vehicle for writers who are concerned about improving society. Molière in France and Swift in England were brilliant satirists.

There are other characteristics that typify the neoclassic style of literature. The neoclassicist paid strict attention to form, basing many of his arguments for this practice on Aristotle's emphasis on structure and the Greek adherence to form. Furthermore, neoclassicism is concerned with wit, controlled and educated intelligence. Since the writers of this period wanted to improve society and were concerned with society's faults, they looked for the universals in literature. Reason was all-important; the heart was to be directed by the mind. The French *salons* were primarily instrumental in forming many of the standards for wit and style that were transferred to English writing.

A writer such as Pope was eager to analyze and dictate the form and style of writing. In a world that needed order, it was gratifying to attempt to provide it by setting up rules. Neoclassicism missed much of the spirituality and wisdom of classicism because of this concern with rules; it also missed one of the basic focuses of the Greek people, the promise of the individual.

Now that the common man was able to share in the ideas around him, this emphasis on order and rules took care of almost every problem except the strength and needs of the individual. Too many were unhappy with their "assigned" place in society and the outmoded political structures that surrounded them. This discontent began to evidence itself early in the eighteenth century, gathering momentum in political and intellectual areas as well as around the dinner table. The currents of thought were changing, and these changes were, of course, reflected in the arts.

Saint Teresa of Avila
(1515-1582)
from *The Flaming Heart or the Life of the Glorious Saint Teresa*

Saint Teresa, a Spanish mystic, was an important force in the Counter Reformation. Her autobiography records her trances, visions, fear of Hell, and spiritual marriage to the Lord. Mystic though she was, she was also a skillful administrator and organizer; she founded an order of Carmelite nuns and assisted Saint John of the Cross in establishing groups of friars. Gertrude Stein in Four Saints in Three Acts,"has tried to capture St. Teresa's paradoxical combination of practicality and mysticism." The following selection from her autobiography has inspired several works of art, particularly Bernini's famous sculptural group, "The Ecstasy of St. Teresa," in the Roman church of Santa Maria della Vittoria.

And now his Divine Majesty hath begun very lately to perform what he had been pleased to promise me before, as, namely, to assure me yet better that it was he, for there grew in me so great a love of Almighty God that I knew not how it could get into my heart. And it was of a very supernatural kind, nor was it I who procured it. I then found myself even as it were to die through a desire wherein I was to see Almighty God, nor could I come to know how I might be able to seek out this kind of life but by the way of death. There came upon me so great impetuosities, or impulses, of this love that howsoever they were not insupportable not yet altogether of so high value as those others were which I have related before. Yet knew I not what to do with myself, for nothing could now give me satisfaction, nor was I able even to contain my very self, but really it was with me as if my soul had been directly torn out of my body....

Whosoever hath never tried and felt these so great impetuosities of divine love, it is impossible that he should be able to understand them, for this is not a kind of restlessness of the breast or heart not any of that kind of devotions which are wont sometimes, as it were, to stop the breath in such sort as that the soul is not able to contain herself. But this is an inferior kind of prayer to that, and herein we are to procure to remove such kind of promptitudes and vehemences as those and to endeavor to retire them sweetly into themselves so as to appease and calm the soul....

It is not in our power to express, and much less to relate with advantage, the manner how God approaches and arrives to such a soul as this or the excessive pain that he gives which makes her not to know even what to do with herself. For the soul ... would always be very glad if she might be ever dying of this disease. This pain and glory together did carry my understanding into such distraction and disorder that I knew not how they both could possibly consist together. O what a thing it is to see a soul so wounded! For it is just in such sort as that one may very well affirm it to be wounded and that for a most excellent cause; for now she sees very clearly that she herself did contribute no part of the reason why this Love should grow, but only it seems that some little spark fell down upon her from that immense love of our Lord, which set her so totally on fire....

It pleased our Blessed Lord that I should have sometimes this following vision. I saw an angel very near me towards my left side, and he appeared to me in a corporeal form, though yet I am not wont to see anything of that kind but very rarely. For though angels be represented often to me, it is yet without my seeing them but only according to that other kind of vision whereof

BERNINI: *St. Teresa in Ecstasy*, SANTA MARIA DELLA VITTORIA, ROME

I spake before [intellectual apprehension]. But in this vision our Lord was pleased that I should see this angel after this other manner. He was not great but rather little, yet withal he was of very much beauty. His face was so inflamed that he appeared to be of those most superior angels who seem to be all in a fire, and he well might be of them whom we call Seraphims. But as for me, they never tell me their names or ranks, yet howsoever I see thereby that there is of so great a difference in Heaven between one angel and another as I am no way able to express. I saw that he had a long dart of gold in his hand, and at the end of the iron below methought there was a little fire. And I conceived that he thrust it some several times through my very heart after such a manner as that it passed the very inwards of my bowels, and when he drew it back methought it carried away as much as it had touched within me and left all that which remained wholly inflamed with a great love of Almighty God. The pain of it was so excessive that it forced me to utter those groans, and the suavity which that extremity of pain gave was also very excessive that there was no desiring at all to be rid of it. Nor can the soul then receive any contentment at all in less than God Almighty himself.

This is no corporeal but a spiritual pain, though yet the body do not fail to participate some part thereof, yea, and that not a little ... During the time when I was in this state I went up and down that world like an odd kind of transported fool. Neither cared I either to see anything or to speak but contented myself to consume with burning up in my pain which was to be the greatest glory for me that this whole world could afford.

(Translated in 1642 by "M.T."; modernized by McGinn and Howerton)

Miguel de Cervantes
(1547-1616)
from *Don Quixote*

Cervantes had little literary training, and his novel was not well received by the Spanish intellectuals of his day. But to the common man in seventeenth-century Spain and to critic and average reader alike since that time, Don Quixote *is one of the supreme literary masterpieces. The story concerns a poor retired gentleman who has read so many romances of chivalry that he decides to revive the tradition of knight-errantry. He sets forth on a series of hilarious adventures, often aided by his "squire," Sancho Panza. Though he is beaten and ridiculed, Quixote maintains a dignity that in the end makes him a worthy follower of the chivalric custom. The experience with the lions is a typical adventure.*

V. The happily terminated adventure of the lions, and the story of Camacho's wedding feast

Don Quixote continued his journey full of the joy, satisfaction and high spirits we have described, fancying himself the most valiant knight-errant in the world owing to his late victory. All the adventures that might happen to him from that day onwards he reckoned as already successfully accomplished; he despised enchanters and enchantments, and he gave no thought to the innumerable beatings he had received in the course of his knight-errantry, nor to the stoning which had knocked out half his teeth, nor to the ingratitude of the galley-slaves, nor to the bold insolence of the Yanguesans who had belaboured him with their staves. Finally he said to himself that if he could only discover a method of disenchanting his Lady Dulcinea, he would not envy the highest good fortune which the most fortunate knight-errant of past ages ever achieved or could achieve. He was riding along entirely absorbed in these fancies, when Sancho said to him:

"Isn't it strange, master, that I've still before my eyes that monstrous and hugeous nose of my gossip Tom Cecial?"

"Can it be, Sancho, that you really believe that the Knight of the Mirrors was the bachelor Samson Carrasco, and his squire Tom Cecial, your gossip?"

"I don't know what I'm to say to that," answered Sancho. "I only know that the details he gave me about my house, my wife and my children, no one but himself could have given me; and as for his face, once he had removed the nose, 'twas the very face of Tom Cecial, for I've often seen him in my village, and there was but a wall between my house and his; and the tone of his voice was just the same."

"Let us be reasonable, Sancho," replied Don Quixote. "Now tell me how it can be argued that the bachelor Samson Carrasco would come as a knight-errant armed with arms offensive and defensive to do battle with me? Have I, perchance, ever been his enemy? Have I ever given him cause to have a grudge against me? Am I his rival, or does he make profession of arms that he should envy the fame I have earned in them?"

"Yes, but what shall we say then," replied Sancho, "about that knight, whosoe'er he was, being the very image of the bachelor Carrasco, and his squire the dead spit of my gossip, Tom Cecial? And if that is enchantment, as your worship says, was there no other form in the world for them to take the likeness of?"

"It is all," said Don Quixote, "an artifice and trick of the malignant magicians who persecute me, and who, guessing that I was to be victorious in the conflict, settled that the vanquished knight should display the face of my friend the bachelor in order that my affection for him might intervene to halt my sharp blade and restrain my mighty arm and moderate the righteous indignation of my heart, so that he who sought to rob me of my life by trickery should save his own. And in proof, you know already, Sancho, through experience, which cannot lie or deceive, how easy it is for enchanters to change some countenances into others, making the beautiful ugly and the ugly beautiful, for not two days ago you saw with your own eyes the beauty and elegance of the peerless Dulcinea in all its perfection and natural grace, while I saw her in the ugly and mean form of a coarse country wench, with cataracts in her eyes and a stinking breath from her mouth. Seeing that the perverse enchanter caused such a wicked transformation, it is no wonder that he effected that of Samson Carrasco and of your gossip, in order to snatch away my victory. Nevertheless, I console myself, because, when all is said and done, I have been victorious over my enemy, no matter what shape he took."

"God knows the truth of all," answered Sancho. Knowing as he did that the transformation of Dulcinea had been a device and trick of his own, he was not at all pleased by his master's wild fancies; but he did not like to reply, for fear of saying anything that would reveal his trickery.

As the discourse was not much to his taste, he turned aside from the road to beg a little milk from some shepherds who were milking their ewes near by.

Just then Don Quixote, happening to raise his head, perceived a waggon covered with royal flags, coming along the road they were travelling, and, convinced that this must be some new adventure, he shouted to Sancho to bring him his helmet. At that moment Sancho was buying some curds from the shepherds, and, being flustered by his master's hurried call, he did not know what to do with them or how to carry them, so, not to lose them, for he had already paid for them, he thought it best to pour them into his master's helmet, and, using this clever shift, he turned back to see what his master needed. Don Quixote cried out to him: "Give me that helmet, my friend, for either I know precious little of adventures, or what I see yonder is one which should require me to arm myself."

The squire, as he had no time to take out the curds, had to give it him just as it was. Don Quixote took it, and, without noticing what was in it, clapped it on his head hastily, and as the curds were pressed and squeezed, the whey began to pour down over Don Quixote's face and beard, which gave him such a start that he exclaimed to Sancho: "What's this, Sancho? I think my head is softening, or my brains are melting, or else I am sweating from head to foot. And if I am sweating 'tis certainly not from fear. Now I am truly sure that the adventure is a terrible one which I must face. Give me something to wipe myself with, for this copious sweat is blinding my eyes." Sancho held his tongue and handed him a cloth, thanking God that his master had not found out the truth.

Don Quixote wiped himself and took off the helmet to see what it was that made his head feel cool, and seeing the white mess inside the helmet he put it up to his nose, and sniffing he said: "By my Lady Dulcinea del Toboso, these are curds you have put here, you treacherous, impudent, ill-favoured squire."

To which with calm composure Sancho replied: "If they are curds, master, give them to me, and I'll eat them; but let the Devil eat them, for it must be he who put them there. But how could you ever imagine that I would have the impudence to soil your worship's helmet? Indeed you must already know the culprit. In faith, master, from the understanding which God has given me, I am convinced that I too must have enchanters who persecute me as a creature and limb of your worship, and they must have put that nasty mess there in order to drive your patience into anger and make you drub my ribs as you are wont to do; but this time they have missed their mark, for I put my trust in my master's good sense; he must have considered that I have no curds or milk, or anything of the kind, and if I had, 'tis in my belly I would put it and not in the helmet."

"That may be," said Don Quixote. When he had wiped clean his head, face, beard and helmet, he put it on, and sitting himself firmly in his stirrups, feeling for his sword and grasping his lance, he cried: "Now come what may: here I stand ready to face Satan himself in battle."

The waggon with the flags now approached. In it was nobody, but the carter rode one of the mules and a man was seated in front. Don Quixote stood in front of it, and said: "Whither are you going, brothers? What cart is this? What have you got in it? What flags are those?"

To this the carter replied: "The cart is mine, but in it is a fine pair of caged lions which the Governor of Oran is sending as a present to His Majesty, and the flags are the King, our master, and signify that what is inside the cart is his property."

"Are the lions large?" asked Don Quixote.

"So large," said the man at the door of the waggon, "that none larger, or even as large, have ever crossed from Africa into Spain. I am the keeper and I've carried many, but never a pair like these. They are male and female; the male is in the front cage, and the female in the one behind. They are now very hungry, for they've eaten nought today, so 'twere best for your worship to stand aside, for we must make haste to reach the place where we may give them their feed."

To this Don Quixote answered, smiling slightly: "Lion-whelps to me? To me lion-

EL GRECO: *Laocoön*, SAMUEL H. KRESS COLLECTION, NATIONAL GALLERY OF ART, WASHINGTON, D. C.

whelps? At such a time too? Then, by God, those gentlemen who send them here will soon see whether I am the man to be frightened by lions. Dismount, my good man, and since you are the keeper, open the cages and drive out those beasts. In the midst of this open field I will let them know who Don Quixote of La Mancha is, in spite of the enchanters who have sent them to me."

The carter tried to remonstrate with Don Quixote, but the latter then said sharply: "I swear, Sir Rogue, that if you don't open the cages at once I'll stitch you to the cart with this lance."

The carter then, seeing the grim determination of the armed phantom, said to him: "Please, sir, for charity's sake, let me unyoke the mules and place myself in safety along with them before the lions are unleashed, for if they kill them on me I'm ruined for life, seeing that all I possess is this cart and the mules."

"O man of little faith," replied Don Quixote, "get down and unyoke, and do what you will: soon you will see that your toils were in vain, and you might have spared yourself the trouble."

The carter got down and in haste unyoked, and the keeper called out in a loud voice: "Bear witness all who are here, how against my will and under compulsion I open the cages and let loose the lions. And I protest to this gentleman that all the harm and mischief these beasts shall do will be put to his account, together with my wages and dues as well. You, sir, take cover before I open: as for myself, I am sure they will do me no harm."

Hearing this, Sancho besought his master with tears in his eyes to give up such an enterprise, compared with which that of the windmills, and the fearsome one of the fulling-mills, and, in fact, all the deeds his master had attempted in the whole course of his life, were nought but cakes and fancy bread. "Look, sir," quoth he, "here there is no enchantment nor anything of the kind, for between the bars of the cage I have seen the paw of a real lion, and I infer that a lion with such a paw must be bigger than a mountain."

"Fear, at any rate," answered Don Quixote, "will make it seem bigger to you than half the earth. Retire, Sancho, and leave me. If I die here, you know our old compact. You will go straight to Dulcinea; I say no more."

Sancho now began to weep over his master's death, for this time he firmly believed that it would come for him from the claws of the lions. He cursed his fate and called it an unlucky hour when he took it into his head to take service with him again. Nevertheless, despite all his tears and groans he took good care to flog up Dapple so as to drive him a good distance away from the cart.

While the keeper was engaged in opening the first cage, Don Quixote was wondering whether it would not be best to do battle on foot, instead of on horseback, and in the end he decided to fight on foot, for he was afraid lest Rozinante might take fright at the lions. He therefore sprang off his horse, flung his lance aside, braced his buckler on his arm, drew his sword and advanced at leisurely speed to take up his position in front of the cart, commending himself to God and then to his Lady Dulcinea.

The keeper, seeing that Don Quixote had taken up his position, and that it was impossible for him to avoid letting loose the male lion without falling under the rage of the wrathful and undaunted knight, opened wide the doors of the first cage, containing, as we have said, the male lion. The beast was now seen to be of extraordinary size and of grim and awful aspect. The first thing he did was to turn round in the cage in which he lay, and extend his claws and stretch himself out at his full length. Then he opened his mouth and yawned very leisurely, and with about two palms-length of tongue, which he put out, he licked the dust from his eyes and washed his face. When this was done, he put his head out of the cage and gazed all around with eyes like blazing coals, a sight that would have struck terror into rash bravery itself. Don Quixote alone stood looking at him intently, longing for him to leap out of the cart and come to close grips with him, when he hoped to hack him to pieces.

Up to this point did his unheard-of madness raise him. The noble lion, however, more courteous than arrogant, took scant notice of such childish bravado, but after looking around about him, as we have said, turned his back and showed Don Quixote his hinder parts, after which coolly and calmly he flung himself down in the cage. Seeing this, Don Quixote ordered the keeper to prod him and tease him to make him come out.

"I will not so," replied the keeper, "for if I excite him, the first he will tear to pieces will be myself. Be content, sir, with what you've done, which leaves no more to be said on the score of courage, and don't try to tempt fortune a second time. The lion has the door open; he's free to come out or not; since he hasn't come out up to this, he won't come out all day. Your worship's sturdy heart has been already shown to the world; no gallant champion, to my way of thinking, is bound to do more nor challenge his enemy and wait for him on the field. If his rival don't come, to him sticks the disgrace, and the man who waits his ground carries off the crown of victory."

"That is true," said Don Quixote; "close the door, my friend, and now give me, in the best form you are able, a voucher to prove what you have seen me do; to wit, how you did open for the lion, that I waited for him, that he did not come, that still I waited for him, that still he did not come out, but lay down again. I am not bound to do more. Away with enchantments, and God protect right, truth and true chivalry! Close the door, as I have said, while I make signs to the fugitives to return and hear this exploit from your lips."

The keeper did so, and Don Quixote, sticking on the point of his lance the cloth with which he had wiped the shower of curds off his face, began to signal to those who were still continuing to flee, though looking round at every step. Sancho, happening to notice the signal of the white cloth, exclaimed: "May I be blowed, if my master has not conquered the wild beasts, for he's calling us!"

They stopped, and saw that it was Don Quixote who was making signals, and, losing some of their fear, they approached little by little, until they clearly heard the voice of Don Quixote calling to them. At length they reached the cart, and as they came up Don Quixote said to the carter: "Yoke your mules once more, my friend, and continue your journey, and you, Sancho, give him two gold crowns for himself and for the keeper, as a compensation for the delay they have had through me."

"I'll give them with a heart and a half," said Sancho, "but what has happened to the lions? Are they alive or dead?"

Then the keeper gave a detailed account of the encounter, praising to the skies the power and valour of Don Quixote, at whose sight the cowed lion dared not to come out of his cage, though he had held the door open a good while, and that it was only because he had told the knight that it was tempting Providence to excite the lion and force him to come out, as he wanted him to do, that the knight had, against his will, allowed him to close the door.

"What do you think of this, Sancho," said Don Quixote: "are any enchantments able to prevail against true valour? The enchanters may be able to rob me of fortune, but of courage they cannot."

Sancho gave the gold crowns, the carter yoked up, the keeper kissed Don Quixote's hands for the guerdon received and promised to give an account of the brave exploit to the King himself as soon as he saw him at court.

"Then," said Don Quixote, "if His Majesty should happen to ask who performed it, you must say the Knight of the Lions, for it is my wish that from this day onwards there may be changed, altered and transformed the name which till now I have borne of the Knight of the Rueful Figure. In this I follow the ancient custom of knights-errant, who changed their names when they pleased or when it suited them."

The cart of the lions then went on its way and Don Quixote and Sancho went theirs.

(Translated by Walter Starkie)

Saint John of the Cross
(1549-1591)
The Obscure Night of the Soul

Upon an obscure night
Fevered with love in love's anxiety
(O hapless-happy plight!)
I went, none seeing me,
Forth from my house where all things be.

By night, secure from sight,
And by the secret stair, disguisedly,
(O hapless-happy plight)
By night, and privily,
Forth from my house where all things quiet be.

Blest night of wandering,
In secret, where by none might I be spied,
Nor I see anything;
Without a light or guide,
Save that which in my heart burnt in my side.

That light did lead me on,
More surely than the shining of noontide,
Where well I knew that one
Did for my coming bide;
Where He abode, might none but He abide.

O night that didst lead thus,
O night more lovely than the dawn of light,
O night that broughtest us,
Lover to lover's sight,
Lover with loved in marriage of delight!

Upon my flowery breast
Wholly for Him, and save Himself for none,
There did I give sweet rest
To my belovèd one;
The fanning of the cedars breathed thereon.

When the first moving air
Blew from the tower and waved His locks aside,
His hand, with gentle care,
Did wound me in the side,
And in my body all my senses died.

All things I then forgot,
My cheek on Him who for my coming came;
All ceased, and I was not,
Leaving my cares and shame
Among the lilies, and forgetting them.

(Translated by Arthur Symons)

John Donne
(1571-1631)
Meditation 17

Perchance he for whom this bell tolls may be so ill as that he knows not it tolls for him; and perchance I may think myself so much better than I am, as that they who are about me and see my state, may have caused it to toll for me, and I know not that. The church is catholic, universal; so are all her actions; all that she does, belongs to all. When she baptizes a child, that action concerns me, for that child is thereby connected to that Head which is my Head too, and engraffed into that body, whereof I am a member. And when she buries a man, that action concerns me. All mankind is of one author, and is one volume; when one man dies, one chapter is not torn out of the book, but translated into a better language, and every chapter must be so translated. God employs several translators; some pieces are translated by age, some by sickness, some by war, some by justice; but God's hand is in every translation; and his hand shall bind up all our scattered leaves again for that library where every book shall lie open to one another. As therefore the bell that rings to a sermon calls not upon the preacher only, but upon the congregation to come, so this bell calls us all; but how much more he, who am brought so near the door by this sickness. There was a contention as far as a suit, (in which both piety and dignity, religion and estimation, were mingled) which of the religious orders should ring to prayers first in the morning; and it was determined, that they should ring first that rose earliest. If we understand aright the dignity of this bell that tolls for our evening prayer, we would be glad to make it ours by rising early, in that application, that it might be ours as well as his whose indeed it is. The bell doth toll for him that thinks it doth; and though it intermit again, yet from that minute that that occasion wrought upon him, he is united to God. Who casts not up his eye to the sun when it rises? But who takes off his eye from a comet when that breaks out? Who bends not his ear to any bell which upon any occasion rings? But who can remove it from that bell which is passing a piece of himself out of this world? No man is an island, entire of itself; every man is a piece of the continent, a part of the main; if a clod be washed away by the sea, Europe is the less, as well as if a promontory were, as well as if a manor of thy friend's or of thine own were. Any man's death diminishes me, because I am involved in mankind; and therefore never send to know for whom the bell tolls; it tolls for thee. Neither can we call this a begging of misery or a borrowing of misery, as though we were not miserable enough of ourselves, but must fetch in more from the next house, in taking upon us the misery of our neighbors. Truly it were an excusable covetousness if we did; for affliction is a treasure, and scarce any man hath enough of it. No man hath affliction enough that is not matured and ripened by it, and made fit for God by that affliction. If a man carry treasure in bullion, or in a wedge of gold, and have none coined into current monies, his treasure will not defray him as he travels. Tribulation is treasure in the nature of it, but it is not current money in the use of it, except we get nearer and nearer our home, heaven, by it. Another man may be sick too, and sick to death, and this affliction may lie in his bowels, as gold in a mine, and be of no use to him; but this bell, that tells me of his affliction, digs out and applies that gold to me, if by this consideration of another's danger, I take mine own into contemplation, and so secure myself by making my recourse to my God, who is our only security.

Song

Go and catch a falling star,
   Get with child a mandrake root,[1]
Tell me where all past years are,
   Or who cleft the Devil's foot,
Teach me to hear mermaids singing,
   Or to keep off envy's stinging,
        And find
        What wind
Serves to advance an honest mind.

If thou beest born to strange sights,
   Things invisible to see,
Ride ten thousand days and nights,
   Till age snow white hairs on thee,
Thou, when thou return'st, wilt tell me
All strange wonders that befell thee,
        And swear
        Nowhere
Lives a woman true, and fair.

If thou findst one, let me know,
   Such a pilgrimage were sweet;
Yet do not, I would not go,
   Though at next door we might meet;
Though she were true when you met her,
And last till you write your letter,
        Yet she
        Will be
False, ere I come, to two, or three.

Song

Sweetest love, I do not go,
   For weariness of thee,
Nor in hope the world can show
   A fitter love for me;
       But since that I
Must die at last, 'tis best,
To use my self in jest
   Thus by fained deaths to die;

Yesternight the sun went hence,
   And yet is here today,
He hath no desire nor sense,
   Nor half so short a way:
       Then fear not me
But believe that I shall make
Speedier journeys, since I take
   More wings and spurs than he.

O how feeble is man's power,
   That if good fortune fall,
Cannot add another hour,
   Nor a lost hour recall!
       But come bad chance,
And we join to it our strength
And we teach it art and length,
   It self o'er us t' advance.

When thou sigh'st, thou sigh'st not wind,
   But sigh'st my soul away,
When thou weep'st, unkindly kind,
   My life's blood doth decay.
       It cannot be
That thou lov'st me, as thou say'st,
If in thine my life thou waste,
   That art the best of me.

Let not thy divining heart
   Forethink me any ill,
Destiny may take thy part,
   And may thy fears fulfill;
       But think that we
Are but turn'd aside to sleep;
They who one another keep
   Alive, ne'er parted be.

---

[1] The forked root of the mandrake was often thought to resemble a human body; there were many legends and superstitions about it.

from *Holy Sonnets*

1

Thou hast made me, and shall Thy work decay?
Repair me now, for now mine end doth haste;
I run to death, and death meets me as fast,
And all my pleasures are like yesterday.
I dare not move my dim eyes any way,
Despair behind, and death before doth cast
Such terror, and my feeble flesh doth waste
By sin in it, which it towards hell doth weigh.
Only Thou art above, and when towards Thee
By Thy leave I can look, I rise again;
But our old subtle foe so tempteth me
That not one hour myself I can sustain.
Thy grace may wing me to prevent his art,
And Thou like adamant draw mine iron heart.

10

Death, be not proud, though some have callèd thee
Mighty and dreadful, for thou art not so;
For those whom thou think'st thou dost overthrow
Die not, poor Death, nor yet canst thou kill me.
From rest and sleep, which but thy pictures be,
Much pleasure; then from thee much more must flow,
And soonest our best men with thee do go,
Rest of their bones, and soul's delivery.
Thou art slave to fate, chance, kings, and desperate men,
And dost with poison, war, and sickness dwell,
And poppy or charms can make us sleep as well
And better than thy stroke; why swell'st thou then?
One short sleep past, we wake eternally
And death shall be no more; Death, thou shalt die.

A Hymn to God the Father

Wilt thou forgive that sin where I begun,
   Which was my sin, though it were done before?
Wilt thou forgive that sin through which I run,
   And do run still, though still I do deplore?
     When thou hast done, thou hast not done,
       For I have more.

Wilt thou forgive that sin which I have won
   Others to sin, and made my sin their door?
Wilt thou forgive that sin which I did shun
   A year or two, but wallowed in a score?
      When thou hast done, thou hast not done,
         For I have more.

I have a sin of fear, that when I have spun
   My last thread I shall perish on the shore;
But swear by thyself, that at my death thy son
   Shall shine as he shines now, and heretofore;
      And, having done that, thou hast done;
         I fear no more.

George Herbert
(1593-1633)
The Altar

A broken ALTAR, Lord, thy servant rears,
Made of a heart, and cemented with tears;
  Whose parts are as thy hand did frame
  No workman's tool hath touched the same.
        A   HEART   alone
        Is   such   a   stone
        As   nothing   but
        Thy power doth cut.
        Wherefore each part
        Of my hard heart
        Meets in this frame
        To praise thy name;
  That, if I chance to hold my peace
  These stones to praise thee may not cease.
Oh let thy blessed SACRIFICE be mine
And sanctify this ALTAR to be thine.

Easter Wings

Lord, who createdst man in wealth and store,
Though foolishly he lost the same,
Decaying more and more
Till he became
Most poor:
With thee
O let me rise
As larks, harmoniously,
And sing this day thy victories:
Then shall the fall further the flight in me.

My tender age in sorrow did begin:
And still with sicknesses and shame
Thou didst so punish sin,
That I became
Most thin.
With thee
Let me combine,
And feel this day thy victory;
For, if I imp my wing on thine,
Affliction shall advance the flight in me.

Calderón
(1600-1681)
The Dream Called Life
from *Life Is a Dream*

A dream it was in which I found myself.
And you that hail me now, then hailed me king,
In a brave palace that was all my own,
Within, and all without it, mine; until,
Drunk with excess of majesty and pride,
Methought I towered so big and swelled so wide
That of myself I burst the glittering bubble
Which my ambition had about me blown
And all again was darkness. Such a dream
As this, in which I may be walking now,
Dispensing solemn justice to yon shadows,
Who make believe to listen; but anon
Kings, princes, captains, warriors, plume and steel,
Ay, even with all your airy theater,
May flit into the air you seem to rend
With acclamations, leaving me to wake
In the dark tower; or dreaming that I wake
From this that waking is; or this and that,
Both waking and both dreaming; such a doubt
Confounds and clouds our mortal life about.
But whether wake or dreaming, this I know
How dreamwise human glories come and go;
Whose momentary tenure not to break,
Walking as one who knows he soon may wake,
So fairly carry the full cup, so well

Disordered insolence and passion quell,
That there be nothing after to upbraid
Dreamer or doer in the part he played;
Whether tomorrow's dawn shall break the spell,
Or the last trumpet of the Eternal Day,
When dreaming, with the night, shall pass away.

              (Translated by Edward FitzGerald)

John Milton
(1608-1674)
Lycidas

In this monody the author bewails a learned friend, unfortunately drowned in his passage from Chester on the Irish Seas, 1637. And by occasion foretells the ruin of our corrupted clergy, then in their height.

Yet once more, O ye laurels, and once more,
Ye myrtles brown, with ivy never sere,
I come to pluck your berries harsh and crude,
And with forced fingers rude
Shatter your leaves before the mellowing year.
Bitter constraint, and sad occasion dear,
Compels me to disturb your season due;
For Lycidas is dead, dead ere his prime,
Young Lycidas, and hath not left his peer.
Who would not sing for Lycidas? he knew
Himself to sing, and build the lofty rhyme.
He must not float upon his watery bier
Unwept, and welter to the parching wind,
Without the meed of some melodious tear.
   Begin then, Sisters of the sacred well
That from beneath the seat of Jove doth spring,
Begin, and somewhat loudly sweep the string.
Hence with denial vain, and coy excuse;
So may some gentle Muse
With lucky words favor my destined urn,
And as he passes turn,
And bid fair peace be to my sable shroud.
For we were nursed upon the self-same hill,
Fed the same flock, by fountain, shade, and rill.
   Together both, ere the high lawns appeared
Under the opening eyelids of the morn,
We drove afield, and both together heard
What time the gray-fly winds her sultry horn,
Battening our flocks with the fresh dews of night,
Oft till the star that rose, at evening, bright
Toward Heaven's descent had sloped his westering wheel.
Meanwhile the rural ditties were not mute,
Tempered to the oaten flute;
Rough Satyrs danced, and Fauns with cloven heel
From the glad sound would not be absent long,
And old Damoetas loved to hear our song.
   But O the heavy change, now thou art gone,
Now thou art gone, and never must return!
Thee, Shepherd, thee the woods and desert caves,
With wild thyme and the gadding vine o'ergrown,
And all their echoes mourn.
The willows and the hazel copses green
Shall now no more be seen
Fanning their joyous leaves to thy soft lays.
As killing as the canker to the rose,
Or taint-worm to the weanling herds that graze,
Or frost to flowers, that their gay wardrobe wear,
When first the white-thorn blows;
Such, Lycidas, thy loss to shepherd's ear.
   Where were ye, Nymphs, when the remorseless deep
Closed o'er the head of your loved Lycidas?
For neither were ye playing on the steep

Where your old bards, the famous Druids, lie,
Nor on the shaggy top of Mona high,
Nor yet where Deva spreads her wizard stream.
Ay me, I fondly dream,
Had ye been there!—for what could that have done?
What could the Muse herself that Orpheus bore,
The Muse herself, for her enchanting son,
Whom universal Nature did lament,
When by the rout that made the hideous roar
His gory visage down the stream was sent,
Down the swift Hebrus to the Lesbian shore?
    Alas! what boots it with uncessant care
To tend the homely slighted shepherd's trade,
And strictly meditate the thankless Muse?
Were it not better done as others use,
To sport with Amaryllis in the shade,
Or with the tangles of Neaera's hair?
Fame is the spur that the clear spirit doth raise
(That last infirmity of noble mind)
To scorn delights, and live laborious days;
But the fair guerdon when we hope to find,
And think to burst out into sudden blaze,
Comes the blind Fury with the abhorrèd shears,
And slits the thin-spun life. "But not the praise,"
Phoebus replied, and touched my trembling ears:
"Fame is no plant that grows on mortal soil,
Nor in the glistering foil
Set off to the world, nor in broad rumor lies,
But lives and spreads aloft by those pure eyes
And perfect witness of all-judging Jove;
As he pronounces lastly on each deed,
Of so much fame in Heaven expect thy meed."
    O fountain Arethuse, and thou honored flood,
Smooth-sliding Mincius, crowned with vocal reeds,
That strain I heard was of a higher mood.
But now my oat proceeds,
And listens to the Herald of the Sea,
That came in Neptune's plea.
He asked the waves, and asked the felon winds,
What hard mishap hath doomed this gentle swain?
And questioned every gust of rugged wings
That blows from off each beakèd promontory;
They knew not of his story,
And sage Hippotades their answer brings,
That not a blast was from his dungeon strayed;
The air was calm, and on the level brine
Sleek Panope with all her sisters played.
It was that fatal and perfidious bark,
Built in the eclipse, and rigged with curses dark,
That sunk so low that sacred head of thine.
    Next Camus, reverend sire, went footing slow,
His mantle hairy, and his bonnet sedge,
Inwrought with figures dim, and on the edge
Like to that sanguine flower inscribed with woe.
"Ah, who hath reft," quoth he, "my dearest pledge?"
Last came, and last did go,
The Pilot of the Galilean Lake;
Two massy keys he bore of metals twain
(The golden opes, the iron shuts amain).
He shook his mitered locks, and stern bespake:
"How well could I have spared for thee, young swain,
Enow of such as for their bellies' sake

Creep and intrude and climb into the fold!
Of other care they little reckoning make
Than how to scramble at the shearers' feast,
And shove away the worthy bidden guest.
Blind mouths! that scarce themselves know how to hold
A sheep-hook, or have learned aught else the least
That to the faithful herdman's art belongs!
What recks it them? What need they? They are sped;
And when they list, their lean and flashy songs
Grate on their scrannel pipes of wretched straw;
The hungry sheep look up, and are not fed,
But swoln with wind and the rank mist they draw,
Rot inwardly, and foul contagion spread;
Besides what the grim wolf with privy paw
Daily devours apace, and nothing said;
But that two-handed engine at the door
Stands ready to smite once, and smite no more."
   Return, Alpheus, the dread voice is past
That shrunk thy streams; return, Sicilian Muse,
And call the vales, and bid them hither cast
Their bells and flowerets of a thousand hues.
Ye valleys low where the mild whispers use
Of shades and wanton winds and gushing brooks,
On whose fresh lap the swart star sparely looks,
Throw hither all your quaint enameled eyes,
That on the green turf suck the honied showers,
And purple all the ground with vernal flowers.
Bring the rathe primrose that forsaken dies,
The tufted crow-toe, and pale jessamine.
The white pink, and the pansy freaked with jet,
The glowing violet,
The musk-rose, and the well-attired woodbine,
With cowslips wan that hang the pensive head,
And every flower that sad embroidery wears.
Bid amaranthus all his beauty shed,
And daffadillies fill their cups with tears,
To strew the laureate hearse where Lycid lies.
For so to interpose a little ease,
Let our frail thoughts dally with false surmise;
Ay me! whilst thee the shores and sounding seas
Wash far away, where'er thy bones are hurled,
Whether beyond the stormy Hebrides,
Where thou perhaps under the whelming tide
Visit'st the bottom of the monstrous world;
Or whether thou, to our moist vows denied,
Sleep'st by the fable of Bellerus old,
Where the great Vision of the guarded mount
Looks toward Namancos and Bayona's hold;
Look homeward, Angel, now, and melt with ruth;
And, O ye dolphins, waft the hapless youth.
   Weep no more, woeful shepherds, weep no more,
For Lycidas, your sorrow, is not dead,
Sunk though he be beneath the watery floor;
So sinks the day-star in the ocean bed,
And yet anon repairs his drooping head,
And tricks his beams, and with new-spangled ore
Flames in the forehead of the morning sky:

So Lycidas sunk low, but mounted high,
Through the dear might of him that walked the waves,
Where, other groves and other streams along,
With nectar pure his oozy locks he laves,
And hears the unexpressive nuptial song,
In the blest kingdoms meek of joy and love.
There entertain him all the saints above,
In solemn troops and sweet societies
That sing, and singing in their glory move,
And wipe the tears for ever from his eyes.
Now, Lycidas, the shepherds weep no more;
Henceforth thou art the Genius of the shore,
In thy large recompense, and shalt be good
To all that wander in that perilous flood.
   Thus sang the uncouth swain to the oaks and rills,
While the still morn went out with sandals gray;
He touched the tender stops of various quills,
With eager thought warbling his Doric lay.
And now the sun had stretched out all the hills,
And now was dropped into the western bay;
At last he rose, and twitched his mantle blue:
To-morrow to fresh woods, and pastures new.

from *Paradise Lost*

At the time Milton began composing Paradise Lost, *he was fifty years old, blind for over six years, and a man of stature in letters and government. Milton began working on his epic poem around 1658, and it was 1663 before it was completed. He rose early in the morning, mentally writing a section until the later arrival of his secretary, who would then transcribe the morning's work.*

Well versed in Greek literary traditions, Milton had long considered writing an epic; at first he intended to write about King Arthur's court. Instead he chose the rich biblical account of Adam and Eve and their loss of Paradise. The work begins in medias res *after the expulsion of Satan from heaven. The theme centers around the war between good and evil, both in the individual and public world. Milton begins his poem with the epic invocation to the Muse, but his muses are Moses and the prophets. Then he gives a brief survey of the action of the entire poem. Satan meets with his legions on the lake fires of Hell and calls a council. They build Satan's palace, Pandemonium. The balance of the work tells of Christ's offer of intercession when He learns of Satan's proposed tempting of Adam and Eve and, in the final book, Adam and Eve learn of Christ's future coming before they are quietly expelled from Paradise.*

Milton's portrayal of Satan is masterful; in fact, he has often been accused of making Satan the hero of the work. But, there is no way to appreciate Satan's strength and loss without understanding his magnificent abilities and his misguided potentialities.

The poem has a vast canvas for its setting, the universe. Its language is allusive, descriptive, and consciously controlled. The reader is aware that the work constitutes an organic whole, for each episode relates to the previous one and extends smoothly into the next. The selection here presents only a sampling of one of the finest works from the last truly great Christian humanist of the Renaissance.

Book I

THE ARGUMENT

This first book proposes, first in brief, the whole subject, man's disobedience, and the loss thereupon of Paradise wherein he was placed: then touches the prime cause of his fall, the Serpent, or rather Satan in the Serpent; who, revolting from God, and drawing to his side many legions of angels, was by the command of God driven out of Heaven with all his crew into the great Deep. Which action passed over, the poem hastes into the midst of things, presenting Satan with his angels now fallen into Hell—described here, not in the center (for Heaven and Earth may be supposed as yet not made, certainly not yet accursed), but in a place of utter darkness, fitliest called Chaos. Here Satan with his angels lying on the burning lake, thunder-struck and astonished, after a certain space recovers, as from confusion; calls up him who, next in order and dignity, lay by him; they confer of their miserable fall. Satan awakens all his legions, who lay till then in the same manner confounded. They rise: their numbers, array of battle, their chief leaders named, according to the idols known afterwards in Canaan and the countries adjoining. To these Satan directs his speech, comforts them with hope yet of regaining Heaven, but tells them lastly of a new world and new kind of creature to be created, according to an ancient prophecy or report in Heaven; for that angels were long before this visible creation was the opinion of many ancient Fathers. To find out the truth of this prophecy, and what to determine thereon, he refers to a full council. What his associates thence attempt. Pandemonium, the palace of Satan, rises, suddenly built out of the Deep; the infernal peers there sit in council.

Of man's first disobedience, and the fruit
Of that forbidden tree, whose mortal taste
Brought death into the world, and all our
    woe,
With loss of Eden, till one greater Man
Restore us, and regain the blissful seat,
Sing, Heavenly Muse that on the secret
    top
Of Oreb, or of Sinai, didst inspire
That shepherd, who first taught the chosen
    seed
In the beginning how the Heavens and
    Earth
Rose out of Chaos; or if Sion hill
Delight thee more, and Siloa's brook that
    flowed
Fast by the oracle of God, I thence
Invoke thy aid to my adventurous song,
That with no middle flight intends to soar
Above the Aonian mount, while it pursues
Things unattempted yet in prose or rhyme.
And chiefly thou, O Spirit, that dost prefer
Before all temples the upright heart and
    pure,
Instruct me, for thou know'st; thou from
    the first
Wast present, and with mighty wings outspread
Dove-like sat'st brooding on the vast abyss
And mad'st it pregnant: what in me is dark
Illumine, what is low raise and support;
That to the highth of this great argument
I may assert Eternal Providence,
And justify the ways of God to men.
   Say first, for Heaven hides nothing from
    thy view,
Nor the deep tract of Hell, say first what
    cause
Moved our grand parents in that happy
    state,
Favored of Heaven so highly, to fall off
From their Creator, and transgress his will
For one restraint, lords of the world besides?
Who first seduced them to that foul revolt?
The infernal Serpent; he it was, whose
    guile,
Stirred up with envy and revenge, deceived
The mother of mankind, what time his
    pride
Had cast him out from Heaven, with all
    his host
Of rebel angels, by whose aid aspiring
To set himself in glory above his peers,
He trusted to have equaled the Most High,
If he opposed; and with ambitious aim
Against the throne and monarchy of God,

Raised impious war in Heaven and battle proud
With vain attempt. Him the Almighty Power
Hurled headlong flaming from the ethereal sky
With hideous ruin and combustion down
To bottomless perdition, there to dwell
In adamantine chains and penal fire,
Who durst defy the Omnipotent to arms.
Nine times the space that measures day and night
To mortal men, he with his horrid crew
Lay vanquished, rolling in the fiery gulf,
Confounded though immortal. But his doom
Reserved him to more wrath; for now the thought
Both of lost happiness and lasting pain
Torments him; round he throws his baleful eyes,
That witnessed huge affliction and dismay
Mixed with obdúrate pride and steadfast hate.
At once as far as angels ken he views
The dismal situation waste and wild:
A dungeon horrible on all sides round
As one great furnace flamed, yet from those flames
No light; but rather darkness visible
Served only to discover sights of woe,
Regions of sorrow, doleful shades, where peace
And rest can never dwell, hope never comes
That comes to all; but torture without end
Still urges, and a fiery deluge, fed
With ever-burning sulphur unconsumed:
Such place Eternal Justice had prepared
For those rebellious, here their prison ordained
In utter darkness, and their portion set
As far removed from God and light of Heaven
As from the center thrice to the utmost pole.
O how unlike the place from whence they fell!
There the companions of his fall, o'erwhelmed
With floods and whirlwinds of tempestuous fire,
He soon discerns, and weltering by his side
One next himself in power, and next in crime,
Long after known in Palestine, and named
Beëlzebub. To whom the Arch-Enemy,
And thence in Heaven called Satan, with bold words
Breaking the horrid silence thus began:
    "If thou beest he—but O how fallen! how changed
From him, who in the happy realms of light
Clothed with transcendent brightness didst outshine
Myriads though bright—if he whom mutual league,
United thoughts and counsels, equal hope
And hazard in the glorious enterprise,
Joined with me once, now misery hath joined
In equal ruin: into what pit thou seest
From what highth fallen! so much the stronger proved
He with his thunder; and till then who knew
The force of those dire arms? Yet not for those,
Nor what the potent Victor in his rage
Can else inflict, do I repent or change,
Though changed in outward luster, that fixed mind
And high disdain, from sense of injured merit,
That with the Mightiest raised me to contend,
And to the fierce contention brought along
Innumerable force of spirits armed
That durst dislike his reign, and, me preferring,
His utmost power with adverse power opposed
In dubious battle on the plains of Heaven,
And shook his throne. What though

the field be lost?
All is not lost; the unconquerable will,
And study of revenge, immortal hate,
And courage never to submit or yield:
And what is else not to be overcome?
That glory never shall his wrath or might
Extort from me. To bow and sue for grace
With suppliant knee, and deify his power
Who from the terror of this arm so late
Doubted his empire, that were low indeed,
That were an ignominy and shame beneath
This downfall; since by fate the strength of gods
And this empyreal substance cannot fail,
Since through experience of this great event,
In arms not worse, in foresight much advanced,
We may with more successful hope resolve
To wage by force or guile eternal war
Irreconcilable to our grand Foe,
Who now triumphs, and in the excess of joy
Sole reigning holds the tyranny of Heaven."
   So spake the apostate Angel, though in pain,
Vaunting aloud, but racked with deep despair;
And him thus answered soon his bold compeer:
   "O Prince, O Chief of many thronèd Powers,
That led the embattled Seraphim to war
Under thy conduct, and in dreadful deeds
Fearless, endangered Heaven's perpetual King,
And put to proof his high supremacy,
Whether upheld by strength, or chance, or fate;
Too well I see and rue the dire event,
That with sad overthrow and foul defeat
Hath lost us Heaven, and all this mighty host
In horrible destruction laid thus low,
As far as gods and heavenly essences
Can perish: for the mind and spirit remains
Invincible, and vigor soon returns,
Though all our glory extinct, and happy state
Here swallowed up in endless misery.
But what if he our Conqueror (whom I now
Of force believe almighty, since no less
Than such could have o'erpowered such force as ours)
Have left us this our spirit and strength entire
Strongly to suffer and support our pains,
That we may so suffice his vengeful ire,
Or do him mightier service as his thralls
By right of war, whate'er his business be,
Here in the heart of Hell to work in fire,
Or do his errands in the gloomy deep?
What can it then avail, though yet we feel
Strength undiminished, or eternal being
To undergo eternal punishment?"
   Whereto with speedy words the Arch-Fiend replied:
"Fallen Cherub, to be weak is miserable,
Doing or suffering: but of this be sure,
To do aught good never will be our task,
But ever to do ill our sole delight,
As being the contrary to his high will
Whom we resist. If then his providence
Out of our evil seek to bring forth good,
Our labor must be to pervert that end,
And out of good still to find means of evil;
Which ofttimes may succeed, so as perhaps
Shall grieve him, if I fail not, and disturb
His inmost counsels from their destined aim.
But see the angry Victor hath recalled
His ministers of vengeance and pursuit
Back to the gates of Heaven; the sulphurous hail
Shot after us in storm, o'erblown hath laid
The fiery surge, that from the precipice
Of Heaven received us falling, and the thunder,
Winged with red lightning and impetuous rage,
Perhaps hath spent his shafts, and ceases now

To bellow through the vast and boundless deep.
Let us not slip the occasion, whether scorn
Or satiate fury yield it from our Foe.
Seest thou yon dreary plain, forlorn and wild,
The seat of desolation, void of light,
Save what the glimmering of these livid flames
Casts pale and dreadful? Thither let us tend
From off the tossing of these fiery waves,
There rest, if any rest can harbor there,
And reassembling our afflicted powers,
Consult how we may henceforth most offend
Our Enemy, our own loss how repair,
How overcome this dire calamity,
What reinforcement we may gain from hope,
If not, what resolution from despair."
   Thus Satan talking to his nearest mate
With head uplift above the wave, and eyes
That sparkling blazed; his other parts besides,
Prone on the flood, extended long and large,
Lay floating many a rood, in bulk as huge
As whom the fables name of monstrous size,
Titanian or Earth-born, that warred on Jove,
Briareos or Typhon, whom the den
By ancient Tarsus held, or that sea-beast
Leviathan, which God of all his works
Created hugest that swim the ocean stream:
Him haply slumbering on the Norway foam,
The pilot of some small night-foundered skiff,
Deeming some island, oft, as seamen tell,
With fixèd anchor in his scaly rind
Moors by his side under the lee, while night
Invests the sea, and wishèd morn delays:
So stretched out huge in length the Arch-Fiend lay
Chained on the burning lake; nor ever thence
Had risen or heaved his head, but that the will
And high permission of all-ruling Heaven
Left him at large to his own dark designs,
That with reiterated crimes he might
Heap on himself damnation, while he sought
Evil to others, and enraged might see
How all his malice served but to bring forth
Infinite goodness, grace and mercy shown
On man by him seduced, but on himself
Treble confusion, wrath and vengeance poured.
   Forthwith upright he rears from off the pool
His mighty stature; on each hand the flames
Driven backward slope their pointing spires, and rolled
In billows, leave in the midst a horrid vale.
Then with expanded wings he steers his flight
Aloft, incumbent on the dusky air
That felt unusual weight, till on dry land
He lights, if it were land that ever burned
With solid, as the lake with liquid fire;
And such appeared in hue, as when the force
Of subterranean wind transports a hill
Torn from Pelorus, or the shattered side
Of thundering Etna, whose combustible
And fueled entrails thence conceiving fire,
Sublimed with mineral fury, aid the winds,
And leave a singèd bottom all involved
With stench and smoke: such resting found the sole
Of unblest feet. Him followed his next mate,
Both glorying to have scaped the Stygian flood
As gods, and by their own recovered strength,

Not by the sufferance of supernal power.
  "Is this the region, this the soil, the clime,"
Said then the lost Archangel, "this the seat
That we must change for Heaven, this mournful gloom
For that celestial light? Be it so, since he
Who now is sovran can dispose and bid
What shall be right: farthest from him is best,
Whom reason hath equaled, force hath made supreme
Above his equals. Farewell, happy fields,
Where joy for ever dwells! Hail, horrors! hail,
Infernal world! and thou, profoundest Hell,
Receive thy new possessor; one who brings
A mind not to be changed by place or time.
The mind is its own place, and in itself
Can make a Heaven of Hell, a Hell of Heaven.
What matter where, if I be still the same,
And what I should be, all but less than he
Whom thunder hath made greater? Here at least
We shall be free; the Almighty hath not built
Here for his envy, will not drive us hence:
Here we may reign secure, and in my choice
To reign is worth ambition, though in Hell:
Better to reign in Hell than serve in Heaven.
But wherefore let we then our faithful friends,
The associates and copartners of our loss,
Lie thus astonished on the oblivious pool,
And call them not to share with us their part
In this unhappy mansion, or once more
With rallied arms to try what may be yet
Regained in Heaven, or what more lost in Hell?"
  So Satan spake, and him Beëlzebub
Thus answered: "Leader of those armies bright,
Which but the Omnipotent none could have foiled,
If once they hear that voice, their liveliest pledge
Of hope in fears and dangers, heard so oft
In worst extremes, and on the perilous edge
Of battle when it raged, in all assaults
Their surest signal, they will soon resume
New courage and revive, though now they lie
Groveling and prostrate on yon lake of fire,
As we erewhile, astounded and amazed;
No wonder, fallen such a pernicious highth!"
  He scarce had ceased when the superior Fiend
Was moving toward the shore; his ponderous shield,
Ethereal temper, massy, large, and round,
Behind him cast; the broad circumference
Hung on his shoulders like the moon, whose orb
Through optic glass the Tuscan artist views
At evening from the top of Fesole,
Or in Valdarno, to descry new lands,
Rivers or mountains in her spotty globe.
His spear, to equal which the tallest pine
Hewn on Norwegian hills, to be the mast
Of some great ammiral, were but a wand,
He walked with, to support uneasy steps
Over the burning marl, not like those steps
On Heaven's azure; and the torrid clime
Smote on him sore besides, vaulted with fire.
Nathless he so endured, till on the beach
Of that inflamèd sea he stood and called
His legions, angel forms, who lay entranced,
Thick as autumnal leaves that strow the brooks
In Vallombrosa, where the Etrurian shades
High over-arched embower; or scattered sedge
Afloat, when with fierce winds Orion armed

Hath vexed the Red Sea coast, whose waves o'erthrew
Busiris and his Memphian chivalry,
While with perfidious hatred they pursued
The sojourners of Goshen, who beheld
From the safe shore their floating carcasses
And broken chariot wheels; so thick bestrown,
Abject and lost lay these, covering the flood,
Under amazement of their hideous change.
He called so loud, that all the hollow deep
Of Hell resounded: "Princes, Potentates,
Warriors, the flower of Heaven, once yours, now lost,
If such astonishment as this can seize
Eternal spirits! or have ye chosen this place
After the toil of battle to repose
Your wearied virtue, for the ease you find
To slumber here, as in the vales of Heaven?
Or in this abject posture have ye sworn
To adore the Conqueror, who now beholds
Cherub and Seraph rolling in the flood
With scattered arms and ensigns, till anon
His swift pursuers from Heaven gates discern
The advantage, and descending tread us down
Thus drooping, or with linkèd thunderbolts
Transfix us to the bottom of this gulf?
Awake, arise, or be forever fallen!"
   They heard, and were abashed, and up they sprung
Upon the wing, as when men wont to watch
On duty, sleeping found by whom they dread,
Rouse and bestir themselves ere well awake.
Nor did they not perceive the evil plight
In which they were, or the fierce pains not feel;
Yet to their general's voice they soon obeyed
Innumerable. As when the potent rod
Of Amram's son in Egypt's evil day
Waved round the coast, up called a pitchy cloud
Of locusts, warping on the eastern wind,
That o'er the realm of impious Pharaoh hung
Like night, and darkened all the land of Nile:
So numberless were those bad angels seen
Hovering on wing under the cope of Hell
'Twixt upper, nether, and surrounding fires;
Till, as a signal given, the uplifted spear
Of their great Sultan waving to direct
Their course, in even balance down they light
On the firm brimstone, and fill all the plain;
A multitude like which the populous North
Poured never from her frozen loins, to pass
Rhene or the Danaw, when her barbarous sons
Came like a deluge on the South, and spread
Beneath Gibraltar to the Libyan sands.
Forthwith from every squadron and each band
The heads and leaders thither haste where stood
Their great commander; godlike shapes and forms
Excelling human, princely dignities,
And powers that erst in Heaven sat on thrones;
Though of their names in heavenly records now
Be no memorial, blotted out and rased
By their rebellion from the Books of Life.
Nor had they yet among the sons of Eve
Got them new names, till wandering o'er the Earth,
Through God's high sufferance for the trial of man,
By falsities and lies the greatest part
Of mankind they corrupted to forsake
God their Creator, and the invisible

Glory of him that made them to transform
Oft to the image of a brute, adorned
With gay religions full of pomp and gold,
And devils to adore for deities:
Then were they known to men by various names,
And various idols through the heathen world.
  Say, Muse, their names then known, who first, who last,
Roused from the slumber on that fiery couch,
At their great emperor's call, as next in worth
Came singly where he stood on the bare strand,
While the promiscuous crowd stood yet aloof.
  The chief were those who from the pit of Hell,
Roaming to seek their prey on Earth, durst fix
Their seats long after next the seat of God,
Their altars by his altar, gods adored
Among the nations round, and durst abide
Jehovah thundering out of Sion, throned
Between the Cherubim; yea, often placed
Within his sanctuary itself their shrines,
Abominations; and with cursèd things
His holy rites and solemn feasts profaned,
And with their darkness durst affront his light.
First Moloch, horrid king besmeared with blood
Of human sacrifice, and parents' tears,
Though for the noise of drums and timbrels loud
Their children's cries unheard, that passed through fire
To his grim idol. Him the Ammonite
Worshiped in Rabba and her watery plain,
In Argob and in Basan, to the stream
Of utmost Arnon. Nor content with such
Audacious neighborhood, the wisest heart
Of Solomon he led by fraud to build
His temple right against the temple of God
On that opprobrious hill, and made his grove
The pleasant valley of Hinnom, Tophet thence
And black Gehenna called, the type of Hell.
Next Chemos, the obscene dread of Moab's sons,
From Aroer to Nebo, and the wild
Of southmost Abarim, in Hesebon
And Horonaim, Seon's realm, beyond
The flowery dale of Sibma clad with vines,
And Elealè to the Asphaltic pool:
Peor his other name, when he enticed
Israel in Sittim on their march from Nile
To do him wanton rites, which cost them woe.
Yet thence his lustful orgies he enlarged
Even to that hill of scandal, by the grove
Of Moloch homicide, lust hard by hate;
Till good Josiah drove them thence to Hell.
With these came they, who from the bordering flood
Of old Euphrates to the brook that parts
Egypt from Syrian ground, had general names
Of Baalim and Ashtaroth, those male,
These feminine. For spirits when they please
Can either sex assume, or both; so soft
And uncompounded is their essence pure,
Not tied or manacled with joint or limb,
Nor founded on the brittle strength of bones,
Like cumbrous flesh; but in what shape they choose,
Dilated or condensed, bright or obscure,
Can execute their aery purposes,
And works of love or enmity fulfil.
For those the race of Israel oft forsook
Their Living Strength, and unfrequented left
His righteous altar, bowing lowly down
To bestial gods; for which their heads as low
Bowed down in battle, sunk before the spear

Of despicable foes. With these in troop
Came Astoreth, whom the Phoenicians called
Astarte, queen of heaven, with crescent horns;
To whose bright image nightly by the moon
Sidonian virgins paid their vows and songs;
In Sion also not unsung, where stood
Her temple on the offensive mountain, built
By that uxorious king whose heart though large,
Beguiled by fair idolatresses, fell
To idols foul. Thammuz came next behind,
Whose annual wound in Lebanon allured
The Syrian damsels to lament his fate
In amorous ditties all a summer's day,
While smooth Adonis from his native rock
Ran purple to the sea, supposed with blood
Of Thammuz yearly wounded: the love-tale
Infected Sion's daughters with like heat,
Whose wanton passions in the sacred porch
Ezekiel saw, when by the vision led
His eye surveyed the dark idolatries
Of alienated Judah. Next came one
Who mourned in earnest, when the captive ark
Maimed his brute image, head and hands lopped off
In his own temple, on the grunsel edge,
Where he fell flat, and shamed his worshipers:
Dagon his name, sea monster, upward man
And downward fish; yet had his temple high
Reared in Azotus, dreaded through the coast
Of Palestine, in Gath and Ascalon,
And Accaron and Gaza's frontier bounds.
Him followed Rimmon, whose delightful seat
Was fair Damascus, on the fertile banks
Of Abbana and Pharphar, lucid streams.
He also against the house of God was bold:
A leper once he lost and gained a king,
Ahaz his sottish conqueror, whom he drew
God's altar to disparage and displace
For one of Syrian mode, whereon to burn
His odious offerings, and adore the gods
Whom he had vanquished. After these appeared
A crew who under names of old renown,
Osiris, Isis, Orus, and their train,
With monstrous shapes and sorceries abused
Fanatic Egypt and her priests, to seek
Their wandering gods disguised in brutish forms
Rather than human. Nor did Israel scape
The infection when their borrowed gold composed
The calf in Oreb; and the rebel king
Doubled that sin in Bethel and in Dan,
Likening his Maker to the grazèd ox—
Jehovah, who in one night when he passed
From Egypt marching, equaled with one stroke
Both her first-born and all her bleating gods.
Belial came last, than whom a spirit more lewd
Fell not from Heaven, or more gross to love
Vice for itself. To him no temple stood
Or altar smoked; yet who more oft than he
In temples and at altars, when the priest
Turns atheist, as did Eli's sons, who filled
With lust and violence the house of God?
In courts and palaces he also reigns
And in luxurious cities, where the noise
Of riot ascends above their loftiest towers,
And injury and outrage; and when night
Darkens the streets, then wander forth the sons
Of Belial, flown with insolence and wine.
Witness the streets of Sodom, and that night
In Gibeah, when the hospitable door
Exposed a matron to avoid worse rape.

These were the prime in order and in
    might;
The rest were long to tell, though far re-
    nowned,
The Ionian gods, of Javan's issue held
Gods, yet confessed later than Heaven and
    Earth,
Their boasted parents; Titan, Heaven's
    first-born,
With his enormous brood, and birthright
    seized
By younger Saturn; he from mightier Jove,
His own and Rhea's son, like measure
    found;
So Jove usurping reigned. These, first in
    Crete
And Ida known, thence on the snowy top
Of cold Olympus ruled the middle air,
Their highest Heaven; or on the Delphian
    cliff,
Or in Dodona, and through all the bounds
Of Doric land; or who with Saturn old
Fled over Adria to the Hesperian fields,
And o'er the Celtic roamed the utmost
    isles.
   All these and more came flocking; but
    with looks
Downcast and damp, yet such wherein
    appeared
Obscure some glimpse of joy, to have
    found their Chief
Not in despair, to have found themselves
    not lost
In loss itself; which on his countenance cast
Like doubtful hue. But he, his wonted
    pride
Soon recollecting, with high words, that
    bore
Semblance of worth, not substance, gently
    raised
Their fainting courage, and dispelled their
    fears.
Then straight commands that, at the war-
    like sound
Of trumpets loud and clarions, be upreared
His mighty standard; that proud honor claimed
Azazel as his right, a Cherub tall;
Who forthwith from the glittering staff
    unfurled
The imperial ensign, which full high ad-
    vanced
Shone like a meteor streaming to the wind,
With gems and golden luster rich em-
    blazed,
Seraphic arms and trophies; all the while
Sonorous metal blowing martial sounds;
At which the universal host upsent
A shout that tore Hell's concave, and
    beyond
Frighted the reign of Chaos and old Night.
All in a moment through the gloom were
    seen
Ten thousand banners rise into the air
With orient colors waving; with them rose
A forest huge of spears; and thronging
    helms
Appeared, and serried shields in thick
    array
Of depth immeasurable. Anon they move
In perfect phalanx to the Dorian mood
Of flutes and soft recorders; such as raised
To highth of noblest temper heroes old
Arming to battle, and instead of rage
Deliberate valor breathed, firm and un-
    moved
With dread of death to flight or foul re-
    treat,
Nor wanting power to mitigate and swage
With solemn touches troubled thoughts,
    and chase
Anguish and doubt and fear and sorrow
    and pain
From mortal or immortal minds. Thus
    they,
Breathing united force with fixèd thought,
Moved on in silence to soft pipes that
    charmed
Their painful steps o'er the burnt soil; and
    now
Advanced in view they stand, a horrid
    front

Of dreadful length and dazzling arms, in guise
Of warriors old with ordered spear and shield,
Awaiting what command their mighty Chief
Had to impose. He through the armèd files
Darts his experienced eye, and soon traverse
The whole battalion views, their order due,
Their visages and stature as of gods;
Their number last he sums. And now his heart
Distends with pride, and hardening in his strength
Glories; for never, since created man,
Met such embodied force as named with these
Could merit more than that small infantry
Warred on by cranes: though all the giant brood
Of Phlegra with the heroic race were joined
That fought at Thebes and Ilium, on each side
Mixed with auxiliar gods; and what resounds
In fable or romance of Uther's son
Begirt with British and Armoric knights;
And all who since, baptized or infidel,
Jousted in Aspramont or Montalban,
Damasco, or Marocco, or Trebisond,
Or whom Biserta sent from Afric shore
When Charlemain with all his peerage fell
By Fontarabbia. Thus far these beyond
Compare of mortal prowess, yet observed
Their dread commander. He above the rest
In shape and gesture proudly eminent
Stood like a tower; his form had yet not lost
All her original brightness, nor appeared
Less than Archangel ruined, and the excess
Of glory obscured: as when the sun new risen
Looks through the horizontal misty air
Shorn of his beams, or from behind the moon
In dim eclipse disastrous twilight sheds
On half the nations, and with fear of change
Perplexes monarchs. Darkened so, yet shone
Above them all the Archangel; but his face
Deep scars of thunder had intrenched, and care
Sat on his faded cheek, but under brows
Of dauntless courage, and considerate pride
Waiting revenge. Cruel his eye, but cast
Signs of remorse and passion to behold
The fellows of his crime, the followers rather
(Far other once beheld in bliss), condemned
For ever now to have their lot in pain,
Millions of spirits for his fault amerced
Of Heaven, and from eternal splendors flung
For his revolt, yet faithful how they stood,
Their glory withered: as when Heaven's fire
Hath scathed the forest oaks or mountain pines,
With singèd top their stately growth though bare
Stands on the blasted heath. He now prepared
To speak; whereat their doubled ranks they bend
From wing to wing, and half enclose him round
With all his peers: attention held them mute.
Thrice he assayed, and thrice in spite of scorn,
Tears such as angels weep burst forth; at last
Words interwove with sighs found out their way:
   "O myriads of immortal spirits, O Powers
Matchless, but with the Almighty, and that strife

Was not inglorious, though the event was dire,
As this place testifies, and this dire change
Hateful to utter. But what power of mind
Foreseeing or presaging, from the depth
Of knowledge past or present, could have feared
How such united force of gods, how such
As stood like these, could ever know repulse?
For who can yet believe, though after loss,
That all these puissant legions, whose exile
Hath emptied Heaven, shall fail to reascend
Self-raised, and repossess their native seat?
For me, be witness all the host of Heaven,
If counsels different, or danger shunned
By me, have lost our hopes. But he who reigns
Monarch in Heaven, till then as one secure
Sat on his throne, upheld by old repute,
Consent or custom, and his regal state
Put forth at full, but still his strength concealed,
Which tempted our attempt, and wrought our fall.
Henceforth his might we know, and know our own,
So as not either to provoke, or dread
New war, provoked; our better part remains
To work in close design, by fraud or guile,
What force effected not; that he no less
At length from us may find, who overcomes
By force hath overcome but half his foe.
Space may produce new worlds; whereof so rife
There went a fame in Heaven that he ere long
Intended to create, and therein plant
A generation, whom his choice regard
Should favor equal to the sons of Heaven.
Thither, if but to pry, shall be perhaps
Our first eruption, thither or elsewhere;
For this infernal pit shall never hold
Celestial spirits in bondage, nor the abyss
Long under darkness cover. But these thoughts
Full counsel must mature. Peace is despaired,
For who can think submission? War then, war
Open or understood, must be resolved."
   He spake; and to confirm his words, out flew
Millions of flaming swords, drawn from the thighs
Of mighty Cherubim; the sudden blaze
Far round illumined Hell. Highly they raged
Against the Highest, and fierce with graspèd arms
Clashed on their sounding shields the din of war,
Hurling defiance toward the vault of Heaven.
   There stood a hill not far, whose grisly top
Belched fire and rolling smoke; the rest entire
Shone with a glossy scurf, undoubted sign
That in his womb was hid metallic ore,
The work of sulphur. Thither winged with speed
A numerous brígade hastened: as when bands
Of pioneers with spade and pickaxe armed
Forerun the royal camp, to trench a field,
Or cast a rampart. Mammon led them on,
Mammon, the least erected spirit that fell
From Heaven, for even in Heaven his looks and thoughts
Were always downward bent, admiring more
The riches of Heaven's pavement, trodden gold,
Than aught divine or holy else enjoyed
In vision beatific. By him first
Men also, and by his suggestion taught,
Ransacked the center, and with impious hands

Rifled the bowels of their mother Earth
For treasures better hid. Soon had his crew
Opened into the hill a spacious wound
And digged out ribs of gold. Let none admire
That riches grow in Hell; that soil may best
Deserve the precious bane. And here let those
Who boast in mortal things, and wondering tell
Of Babel, and the works of Memphian kings,
Learn how their greatest monuments of fame,
And strength and art, are easily outdone
By spirits reprobate, and in an hour
What in an age they with incessant toil
And hands innumerable scarce perform.
Nigh on the plain in many cells prepared,
That underneath had veins of liquid fire
Sluiced from the lake, a second multitude
With wondrous art founded the massy ore,
Severing each kind, and scummed the bullion dross.
A third as soon had formed within the ground
A various mold, and from the boiling cells
By strange conveyance filled each hollow nook,
As in an organ from one blast of wind
To many a row of pipes the sound-board breathes.
Anon out of the earth a fabric huge
Rose like an exhalation, with the sound
Of dulcet symphonies and voices sweet,
Built like a temple, where pilasters round
Were set, and Doric pillars overlaid
With golden architrave; nor did there want
Cornice or frieze, with bossy sculptures graven;
The roof was fretted gold. Not Babylon,
Nor great Alcairo such magnificence
Equaled in all their glories, to enshrine
Belus or Serapis their gods, or seat
Their kings, when Egypt with Assyria strove
In wealth and luxury. The ascending pile
Stood fixed her stately highth, and straight the doors
Opening their brazen folds discover, wide
Within, her ample spaces, o'er the smooth
And level pavement; from the archèd roof,
Pendent by subtle magic, many a row
Of starry lamps and blazing cressets, fed
With naphtha and asphaltus, yielded light
As from a sky. The hasty multitude
Admiring entered, and the work some praise,
And some the architect: his hand was known
In Heaven by many a towered structure high,
Where sceptered angels held their residence,
And sat as princes, whom the supreme King
Exalted to such power, and gave to rule,
Each in his hierarchy, the orders bright.
Nor was his name unheard or unadored
In ancient Greece, and in Ausonian land
Men called him Mulciber; and how he fell
From Heaven, they fabled, thrown by angry Jove
Sheer o'er the crystal battlements: from morn
To noon he fell, from noon to dewy eve,
A summer's day; and with the setting sun
Dropped from the zenith like a falling star,
On Lemnos the Aegean isle. Thus they relate,
Erring; for he with this rebellious rout
Fell long before; nor aught availed him now
To have built in Heaven high towers; nor did he scape
By all his engines, but was headlong sent
With his industrious crew to build in Hell.
    Meanwhile the winged heralds by command

Of sovran power, with awful ceremony
And trumpet's sound, throughout the host
     proclaim
A solemn council forthwith to be held
At Pandemonium, the high capitol
Of Satan and his peers; their summons
     called
From every band and squarèd regiment
By place or choice the worthiest; they anon
With hundreds and with thousands troop-
     ing came
Attended. All access was thronged, the
     gates
And porches wide, but chief the spacious
     hall
(Though like a covered field, where cham-
     pions bold
Wont ride in armed, and at the Soldan's
     chair
Defied the best of paynim chivalry
To mortal combat or career with lance)
Thick swarmed, both on the ground and
     in the air,
Brushed with the hiss of rustling wings. As
     bees
In springtime, when the sun with Taurus
     rides,
Pour forth their populous youth about the
     hive
In clusters; they among fresh dews and
     flowers
Fly to and fro, or on the smoothèd plank,
The suburb of their straw-built citadel,
New rubbed with balm, expatiate and
     confer
Their state affairs. So thick the aery crowd
Swarmed and were straitened; till the sig-
     nal given,
Behold a wonder! they but now who seemed
In bigness to surpass Earth's giant sons,
Now less than smallest dwarfs, in narrow
     room
Throng numberless, like that Pygmean
     race
Beyond the Indian mount, or fairy elves,
Whose midnight revels, by a forest side
Or fountain, some belated peasant sees,
Or dreams he sees, while overhead the
     moon
Sits arbitress, and nearer to the Earth
Wheels her pale course; they on their mirth
     and dance
Intent, with jocund music charm his ear;
At once with joy and fear his heart re-
     bounds.
Thus incorporeal spirits to smallest forms
Reduced their shapes immense, and were
     at large,
Though without number still, amidst the
     hall
Of that infernal court. But far within,
And in their own dimensions like them-
     selves,
The great Seraphic Lords and Cherubim
In close recess and secret conclave sat,
A thousand demi-gods on golden seats,
Frequent and full. After short silence then
And summons read, the great consult
     began.

Andrew Marvell
(1621-1678)
To His Coy Mistress

Had we but world enough, and time,
This coyness, lady, were no crime.
We would sit down, and think which way
To walk, and pass our long love's day.
Thou by the Indian Ganges' side
Shouldst rubies find: I by the tide
Of Humber would complain. I would
Love you ten years before the flood,
And you should, if you please, refuse
Till the conversion of the Jews;
My vegetable love should grow
Vaster than empires and more slow;
An hundred years should go to praise
Thine eyes, and on thy forehead gaze;

PETER PAUL RUBENS: *Marchesa Brigida Spinola Doria*, SAMUEL H. KRESS COLLECTION, NATIONAL GALLERY OF ART, WASHINGTON, D.C.

Two hundred to adore each breast,
But thirty thousand to the rest;
An age at least to every part,
And the last age should show your heart.
For, lady, you deserve this state,
Nor would I love at lower rate.
   But at my back I always hear
Time's wingèd chariot hurrying near,
And yonder all before us lie
Deserts of vast eternity.
Thy beauty shall no more be found,
Nor, in thy marble vault, shall sound
My echoing song; then worms shall try
That long-preserved virginity,
And your quaint honour turn to dust,
And into ashes all my lust:
The grave's a fine and private place,
But none, I think, do there embrace.
   Now therefore, while the youthful hue
Sits on thy skin like morning dew,
And while thy willing soul transpires
At every pore with instant fires,
Now let us sport us while we may,
And now, like amorous birds of prey,
Rather at once our time devour,
Than languish in his slow-chapt power.
Let us roll all our strength and all
Our sweetness up into one ball,
And tear our pleasures with rough strife,
Thorough the iron gates of life;
Thus, though we cannot make our sun
Stand still, yet we will make him run.

Molière
(1622-1673)
from *The Bourgeois Gentleman*
(First performed for Louis XIV at Chambord Castle, October 1670)

French classical drama, in the main, deals with timeless situations—hence their continuing appeal. Unlike the Romantic authors of the nineteenth century who prize those differences which make each man an individual, classical writers focus on the common denominator, those attributes shared by many of us. Molière zeroes in on Monsieur Jourdain, a rather uncultivated, middle-class person who aspires to be a gentleman. He has no difficulty hiring tutors willing to polish and refine him as long as his money holds out. Unfortunately, he is one of those whose aesthetic sensitivity appears to lie too deep for anyone to uncover, which poses the question as to his powers of discernment in selecting the proper people to educate him. As the second act opens, he is observing four young fellows dance under the direction of two somewhat effeminate individuals, his music teacher and his dancing teacher.

LIST OF CHARACTERS:
    MONSIEUR JOURDAIN—
       The would-be gentleman
    DANCING TEACHER
    MUSIC TEACHER
    FENCING MASTER
    PHILOSOPHY TEACHER
    TAILOR
    SERVANTS AND APPRENTICES

ACT TWO
SCENE 1.
   JOURDAIN
That's pretty sharp! Those fellows really know how to bob around.
   MUSIC TEACHER
When the dance is blended with the music, it will be even more effective, and in the little ballet that we have written up for you you're going to see something quite elegant.
   JOURDAIN
I hope it's about ready to go. The person I'm getting this all up for is supposed to do me the honor of coming to dine here.
   DANCING TEACHER
Everything's ready.
   MUSIC TEACHER
May I say, sir, that you may well need more than this. A person such as your-

self—and by that I mean a princely person, one who is inclined to appreciate beautiful things—should be offering a musical concert at his home each Wednesday and Thursday.

JOURDAIN

Is that what people with rank do?

MUSIC TEACHER

Yes sir.

JOURDAIN

Well, that's for me. I guess it'll be something pretty nice, eh?

MUSIC TEACHER

Of course. You will obviously need three voices: a tenor, alto, and baritone, accompanied by a bass-viol, a theorbo, and by a harpsichord for the figured basses with two first violins for the ritornellos.[1]

JOURDAIN

Could you work a marine trumpet in there, too? That's one instrument I really like, the marine trumpet. It's . . . well, it's musical.[2]

MUSIC TEACHER

You may have the utmost confidence in us that we will attend to all these matters for you in the best of taste.

JOURDAIN

Don't forget at least to send me a few musicians pretty soon to sing at the table.

MUSIC TEACHER

You'll have everything you need.

JOURDAIN

But especially, I want the ballet to be good.

MUSIC TEACHER

You will be pleased with it and also with certain minuets that you will see performed.

JOURDAIN

Ah! now minuets are my type of dance, and I'd like you to see how I'm coming along with them. [*To the dancing teacher*] Let's show him, teacher.

DANCING TEACHER

Your hat on, sir, if you please.[3] La, la, la; La, la, la, la, la, la; La, la, la, once more; La, la, la; la, la. Keep the time up, please. La, la, la, la. Your leg should be straight. La, la, la. Nor free play with the shoulders. La, la, la, la, la; La, la, la, la, la. More graceful with the arms. Don't just let them dangle. La, la, la, la, la. Head up. Point the foot out. La, la, la. Keep the body straight.

JOURDAIN

[*To the music teacher*] There, what do you think of that?

MUSIC TEACHER

Positively superb.

JOURDAIN

By the way, I'd like you to teach me how to bow when I greet a marquise. I'll need to be doing that pretty soon.

DANCING TEACHER

A bow to greet a marquise? a marchioness?

JOURDAIN

Yes, a marchioness whose name is Dorimène.

---

[1] *Theorbo:* One of numerous types of lute. Tremendously popular at the end of the sixteenth century, and during the seventeenth century (especially during the reign of Louis XIV), this instrument was widely used in early chamber music concerts and also for accompanying voices. It differed from the regular lute in that it had two necks, to the longest of which the bass strings—usually eight of them—were attached. On the shorter neck it was not uncommon to find eleven or more strings. A few years after the first performance of this play the theorbo fell into disfavor and was generally replaced by the guitar. *Figured basses:* Continual accompaniment behind the singers by the bass-viol, the theorbo, and the harpsichord. *Ritornello:* A short passage serving as an introduction to a piece of music and repeated when the singers pause at the end of a verse. [2] *Marine trumpet:* A one-stringed instrument sometimes six feet in length. The sound it produced has been compared to a harsh, noisy snoring or buzzing. Although there were apparently three marine trumpets in the orchestra of Louis XIV, this was an instrument commonly used in street music. Even M. Jourdain, then, might feel qualified to talk about the marine trumpet. [3] It was proper at that time for men to wear a three-cornered hat when dancing.

DANCING TEACHER
Give me your hand.
JOURDAIN
No, just show me. I'll remember.
DANCING TEACHER
If you wish to greet her with a great deal of respect, you should first of all step back and bow, then walk toward her bowing three times,—lowering yourself on the last one to her knees.
JOURDAIN
Show me how that goes. [*He watches as the dancing master demonstrates.*]⁴ Good.
FIRST SERVANT
Sir, your fencing master is here.
JOURDAIN
Tell him to come in here for my lesson. [*To the other two teachers:*] I want you to see how I'm getting along.

SCENE 2.
FENCING MASTER
[*Handing Jourdain a foil*] Very well sir, the salute. Your body straight. Lean slightly on the left thigh. The legs need not be separated quite so much. Keep your heels in line. The wrist is opposite the hip. The point of your sword is on the same level as your shoulder. The arm is not so extended. The left hand is at the same height as the eye. The left shoulder needs to be pulled back a little. Keep the head straight. Look confident.⁵ Advance. Keep the body steady, shoulders level. Touch my blade in position four, and finish that attack. One, two. Recover. When you make your lunge, sir, your sword must lead up, and the body must present the smallest target possible. One, two. Now, touch my blade in position six, and finish that attack. Advance. The body straight. Advance. Now attack, sir. One, two. Recover. Lunge. Relax. En garde, sir, en garde. [*The fencing master lunges at him two or three times saying "En garde."*]
JOURDAIN
[*To the other teachers*] How am I doing?⁶
MUSIC TEACHER
Wonderfully.
FENCING MASTER
As I have told you, the whole secret of weapons consists simply of two things, of giving, and not receiving; and as I showed you the other day by demonstrative reasoning, it is impossible for you to receive if you know how to turn your enemy's blade away from the line of your body: all of which requires only a slight movement of the wrist either in, or out.⁷
JOURDAIN
So in that way a man ... who isn't necessarily too brave ... is sure of killing his man and of not being killed?
FENCING MASTER
Of course. Didn't you watch the demonstration?
JOURDAIN
Yes.
FENCING MASTER
And it's precisely because of that that you can understand just how much we men of the sword count in a nation such as ours,⁸ and just how much the science of

---

⁴It would be proper for a man to remove his hat when bowing to a lady. ⁵Jourdain's facial expressions, of course, add greatly to the humor. Here he probably squints and tries his best to "look confident." As he proceeds through this ridiculous demonstration with his fencing master one can even imagine Jourdain, as he is instructed to advance to the attack, instinctively closing his eyes like a small boy first learning to catch a ball. ⁶Jourdain could hand his foil back to the fencing master at this point. However, it is just as logical for him to keep it in his hand, making it possible to use it again in a little action later on. ⁷If you are right-handed, try extending your right arm somewhat as though holding a foil. Turning the wrist slightly in a counter-clockwise direction would be turning it in, while turning it slightly in a clockwise direction would be turning it out. ⁸Student editions of this play in France indicate that, in 1656, Louis XIV granted permanent noble rank to six former fencing masters in Paris. This meant that not only they but also their descendants belonged to the nobility.

weaponry surpasses all other useless sciences such as dancing, music, ...
DANCING TEACHER
Just a minute, master swordsman: When you speak of dancing try to show the proper respect.
MUSIC TEACHER
You have a few things to learn about the true worth of music.
FENCING MASTER
Are you fellows serious about comparing your professions to mine?
MUSIC TEACHER
Well now, doesn't he think he's someone!
DANCING TEACHER
You couldn't expect proper manners from him. Look at the ridiculous cut of that fencing jacket!
FENCING MASTER
My little dancing master, I'll teach you a few steps in a moment. And you, my little musician, I'll have you singing in a way that will not, shall we say, lack "appeal."
DANCING TEACHER
You big swashbuckler, I'll teach you something about your profession.
JOURDAIN
[*To the dancing master*] Are you crazy to pick a quarrel with him? He understands positions four and six, and can kill a man by demonstrative reasoning!
DANCING TEACHER
His demonstrative reasoning leaves me cold, and so do his positions four and six.
[*The following lines are said quickly, not one after the other—no one pays any attention to Jourdain, and they all end up talking at once.*]
JOURDAIN
Take it easy, I'm telling you.
FENCING MASTER
[*To the dancing master*] What? You impertinent little. . .
JOURDAIN
Hold on now, fencing master.

DANCING TEACHER
Listen, as big a horse as you are ought to be pulling a beer wagon!
JOURDAIN
Oh no! Dancing master. . .
FENCING MASTER
Suppose I just jump on you instead.
JOURDAIN
Will you take it easy!
DANCING TEACHER
All I need to do is to lay just one hand on you. . .
JOURDAIN
Calm down.
FENCING MASTER
Try it, you scruffy little pipsqueak.
JOURDAIN
Please, not that!
DANCING TEACHER
So help me, I'm going to rough you up like a. . .
JOURDAIN
Please, I'm asking you. . .
MUSIC TEACHER
[*To Jourdain*] All we want to do is teach him a little about public speaking.
JOURDAIN
For heaven's sake! Stop!

SCENE 3.

JOURDAIN
Aha, Mr. Philosopher, have you ever arrived in the nick of time. Philosophy is just what we need! Come on over here and make peace between these people.
PHILOSOPHY TEACHER
What's the matter, gentlemen? What's going on?
JOURDAIN
They began to lose their tempers arguing about their professions to the point that they have been insulting each other, and they were just about to come to blows.
PHILOSOPHY TEACHER
What's that? Gentlemen, is it necessary to

get so carried away? Haven't you read the learned treatise that Seneca wrote on anger?[9] Is there anything more base and shameful than that passion which degrades a man to the level of a beast? Are we not to be governed in everything we do by reason?

DANCING TEACHER

Reason? When he comes in here insulting both of us, scorning the dance in which I am trained, and music which is his profession?

PHILOSOPHY TEACHER

A wise man rises above all the insults that can be heaped on him; and the one great answer which must be made to all insults is one of moderation and patience.

FENCING TEACHER

They have both dared, right to my face, to compare their professions with mine.

PHILOSOPHY TEACHER

Why should that upset you? It's not because of idle boasting or because of circumstances that men should begin quarreling among themselves; you see, what makes any of us stand out from all the rest is clear thinking and self discipline.

DANCING TEACHER

I have simply been pointing out to him that dancing is a science, the importance of which would be difficult to overemphasize.

MUSIC TEACHER

And I, that knowledge of music has commanded respect throughout the ages.

FENCING MASTER

And all I have been doing is to defend the position that fencing is the noblest and most indispensable of all sciences.

PHILOSOPHY TEACHER

And where does that leave philosophy? All three of you, as far as I can see, are downright insolent to stand there in front of me so arrogantly, applying the word *science*—without cowering in shame—to things that you couldn't even call art, and which don't deserve to be identified except as the petty trades of a gladiator, a vocalist, and a buffoon.

FENCING MASTER

Listen, you crummy philosopher!

MUSIC TEACHER

What a conceited ass!

DANCING TEACHER

You're a bare-faced liar!

PHILOSOPHY TEACHER

What? I don't have to take that! [*The philosopher leaps on them, and all three pound him. They go out slowly during the following, fighting all the way.*]

JOURDAIN

[*To the philosopher*] Sir. [*Perhaps tapping him on the arm with the handle of the foil.*]

FENCING MASTER

String him up!

JOURDAIN

Look, fellows. . . .

PHILOSOPHY TEACHER

You contemptible show-offs!

DANCING TEACHER

Let's give it to him!

JOURDAIN

Gentlemen. . . .

PHILOSOPHY TEACHER

You dirty rats!

JOURDAIN

[*To the philosophy master*] Sir.

MUSIC TEACHER

Paste him!

JOURDAIN

Gentlemen. . . .

PHILOSOPHY TEACHER

Crooks! Bums! Traitors! Imposters! [*They finally go out.*]

JOURDAIN

[*Standing at the exit looking after them, crying*

---

[9]Seneca's *De Ira* is a three-volume work.

now to one, now to the other:] Please sir, gentlemen, please sir, gentlemen, Please sir ... Oh! Fight it out. It's none of my business. I'm not going to get my clothes all ripped up trying to separate you. A man would be crazy to get in the middle of that. I could really get hurt.

PHILOSOPHY TEACHER
[*Comes back in adjusting his collar*] Let's get down to our lesson.

JOURDAIN
I'm really sorry about how they beat you up.

PHILOSOPHY TEACHER
It's nothing at all. A philosopher, you understand, is not exactly thin-skinned, and I am going to compose against them a satire in the style of Juvenal,[10] which will rip them up one side and down the other, I promise you. Well, let's leave that. What would you like to learn?

JOURDAIN
Everything I can, because I really want to be well-informed; nothing makes me angrier than to think of how my mother and father didn't have me study all the sciences when I was young.

PHILOSOPHY TEACHER
That's quite a reasonable feeling: *Nam sine doctrina vita est quasi mortis imago.* You understand what I mean; that is, I assume you know Latin.

JOURDAIN
Yes, but go on just as if I didn't understand it: Explain to me what that means.

PHILOSOPHY TEACHER
That means that without science life is almost an image of death.

JOURDAIN
Hmm. That's right.

PHILOSOPHY TEACHER
Don't you have any basic principles, or point from which we may begin?

JOURDAIN
Oh yes, I know how to read and write.

PHILOSOPHY TEACHER
Where would you like to start? Do you want me to teach you logic?

JOURDAIN
What's logic?

PHILOSOPHY TEACHER
That's the science which teaches the three operations of the intellect.

JOURDAIN
And what are they, the three operations of the intellect?

PHILOSOPHY TEACHER
The first, second, and third. The first is to think properly by means of the universals. The second is to form good judgments by the means of using categories correctly; and the third to draw a valid conclusion by means of the figures, *Barbara, Celarent, Darii, Ferio, Baralipton,* etc.[11]

JOURDAIN
Hmm, I'm afraid I don't follow much of that. None of that type of logic comes back to me at all. Let's learn something else which has a little nicer ring to it.

PHILOSOPHY TEACHER
Would you like to learn about ethics?

JOURDAIN
Ethics?

PHILOSOPHY TEACHER
Yes.

JOURDAIN
What does that have to say, ethics?

PHILOSOPHY TEACHER
It deals with happiness, teaches men to moderate their passions, and...

---

[10]*Juvenal:* A Roman satirist whose birth and death dates are uncertain, but who apparently lived sometime between A. D. 60 and 140. [11]The *universals:* A term used in logic and referring to something which is common to many things. The *categories:* The order or class to which several things having the same general nature belong. The *figures:* Refers to different arrangements possible for the three propositions of a syllogism. The syllogistic type of reasoning with the categories, the universals, and the figures is derived from Aristotle's book on the subject, *The Organon.*

JOURDAIN
No, let's not do that. I'm as crotchety as the devil; and ethics or not, I want to get as angry as I feel like it, whenever the desire strikes me.

PHILOSOPHY TEACHER
How would you like to try physics?

JOURDAIN
What's the story on physics?

PHILOSOPHY TEACHER
Physics is that science which explains the principles of natural things, and the characteristics of matter; it discourses on the nature of the elements, metals, minerals, rocks, plants and animals, and teaches us the causes of all the phenomena produced in the atmosphere, the rainbow, Saint-Elmo's Fire, comets, lightning, thunder, thunderbolts, rain, snow, hail, wind, and whirlwinds.

JOURDAIN
There's too much racket in all that, too much confusion.

PHILOSOPHY TEACHER
What would you like me to teach you then?

JOURDAIN
How about spelling?

PHILOSOPHY TEACHER
Spelling it is.

JOURDAIN
Afterwards you'll teach me about the almanac so that I'll know when there's a moon and when there isn't any.

PHILOSOPHY TEACHER
So be it. Now then, to follow along with your thought and to treat this subject as a philosopher, I must of course begin according to the proper order of things, by a precise knowledge of the nature of the letters, and of the differences involved in pronouncing each of them. And on that particular item let me say that the letters are divided into vowels, called vowels because they express the different voices or tones of the voice; and into consonants, called consonants because they sound with—*con* in Latin, you see—the vowels, and do nothing other than mark the different articulations of the voices.[12] There are five vowels or voices: *A, E, I, O, U*.[13]

JOURDAIN
I understand all that.

PHILOSOPHY TEACHER
The voice *A* [*pronounced like the open A in the English word "dance"*] is formed by opening wide the mouth: A.

JOURDAIN
[*Probably fumbling it the first time*] A, A. That's right.

PHILOSOPHY TEACHER
The vowel or voice *E* [*pronounced in French something like the E in the English "Bert"*] is formed by bringing the lower jaw in closer proximity to the upper one: A, E.

JOURDAIN
A, E, A, E. For heaven's sakes! Yes. Oh! That's beautiful!

PHILOSOPHY TEACHER
And the voice *I* [*pronounced like a double E in the English word "feet"*] by closing still more the jaws, and by separating the two corners of the mouth in the direction of the ears: A, E, I.

JOURDAIN
A, E, I, I, I, I. That's true! Three cheers for science!

PHILOSOPHY TEACHER
The voice *O* is formed by opening the jaws again and by bringing the corners of the lips toward each other: O.

JOURDAIN
O, O. That's exactly right. A, E, I, O, I, O. That's just great! I, O, I, O.[14]

---

[12]The following scene was apparently inspired by a book on pronunciation published in 1668 and dedicated to Louis XIV. [13]It will be necessary, as you will see, to retain the French pronunciation for these vowels.
[14]In French, this is very close to the sound made by a donkey.

PHILOSOPHY TEACHER
The opening of the mouth is exactly like a little circle which represents an O.

JOURDAIN
[*No doubt feeling with his finger*] O, O, O. You're right. O. You know, it's really a wonderful thing to know something!

PHILOSOPHY TEACHER
[*To produce this sound an English reader should pretend he is drinking iced tea through a straw. His lips are tight around the straw when someone asks him what he is drinking. He looks up, his lips tight around the straw, and attempts to say "tea." The sound will come out like the French "tu." The vowel here is the French U.*] The voice *U* is formed by bringing the teeth together without touching them completely and by extending the two lips forward, bringing them together also one toward the other but without letting them touch each other: U.

JOURDAIN
U, U. That's the pure truth: U.

PHILOSPHY TEACHER
Your two lips are extended as if you were pouting, which leads me to say that if you wanted to pout at someone, and make fun of him, there is nothing else you could say but U.

JOURDAIN
[*Pouting*] U, U. That's true. [*He sighs.*] Why didn't I study sooner to learn all that?

PHILOSOPHY TEACHER
Tomorrow we will look at the other letters, the consonants.

JOURDAIN
Will there be as many interesting things to talk about as with these things we've been discussing today?

PHILOSOPHY TEACHER
Of course. The consonant *D*, for example, is pronounced by touching the tip of the tongue above the upper teeth: DA.

JOURDAIN
[*Probably sounding like a small child talking to its father*] DA, DA. DA, DA. Yes. It's beautiful! Just beautiful!

PHILOSOPHY TEACHER
The F is pronounced by resting the upper teeth on the lower lip: FA.

JOURDAIN
FA, FA. That's the truth! Oh! My mother and father, when I think....!

PHILOSOPHY TEACHER
And the R by bringing the tip of the tongue up to the palate, in such a way that being brushed over by the air which surrounds it on all sides and which is being expelled with some force, it yields to that air, but continually returns to the same spot, producing a sort of trembling: Rra.[15]

JOURDAIN
R, r, ra; R, r, r, r, r, r, ra. That's true! You really know your business. I've just been wasting my time: R, r, r, ra.

PHILOSOPHY TEACHER
I will explain all these things to you in depth.

JOURDAIN
Please do. Besides, I'll have to let you in on a little secret. See, I'm in love with a person of noble rank, and I'd like you to help me write something to her in a little note that I want to drop at her feet.

PHILOSOPHY TEACHER
Very well.

JOURDAIN
A gentleman could well do that, couldn't he?

PHILOSOPHY TEACHER
Of course. Is it verse that you wish to write to her?

JOURDAIN
No, no, no verse.

PHILOSOPHY TEACHER
You want only prose?

---

[15] The tongue trill.

JOURDAIN
No, I don't want either prose or verse.
PHILOSOPHY TEACHER
It has to be one or the other.
JOURDAIN
Why?
PHILOSOPHY TEACHER
By reason of the fact, sir, that in order to express oneself there is only prose or verse.
JOURDAIN
There is only prose, or verse.
PHILOSOPHY TEACHER
You see, everything which is not prose is verse; and everything which is not verse is prose.
JOURDAIN
And the way we talk, what's that?
PHILOSOPHY TEACHER
Prose.
JOURDAIN
What? When I say: "Nicole, bring me my slippers and my nightcap," that's prose?
PHILOSOPHY TEACHER
Yes sir.
JOURDAIN
Well I'll be! I've been speaking prose for more than forty years and I didn't know it. I can't thank you enough for having taught me that. Well, here's what I'd like to put in this little note:[16] *Beautiful Marquise, your beautiful eyes are causing me to die of love;* but I'd like that put in a polite, mannerly way, a neatly turned phrase, you know what I mean?
PHILOSOPHY TEACHER
Why not write that the fire of her eyes is reducing your heart to ashes and that for her, day and night, you have actually been writhing in the frenzied throes of...[17]
JOURDAIN
No, no, no, I don't want all that; I only want what I told you: *Beautiful Marquise, your beautiful eyes are causing me to die of love.*
PHILOSOPHY TEACHER
I think it would be better to extend your thought a little.
JOURDAIN
No, I tell you, I don't want to change the words; I just want to say them and arrange them in the proper way. Couldn't you just show me the different ways to put them, so that I can see for myself?
PHILOSOPHY TEACHER
They could be arranged first of all as you have said: *Beautiful Marquise, your beautiful eyes are causing me to die of love.* Or else: *Of love are causing me to die, Beautiful Marquise, your beautiful eyes.* Or else: *Your beautiful eyes of love are causing me, Beautiful Marquise, to die.* Or else: *To die, your beautiful eyes, Beautiful Marquise, of love are causing me.* Or else: *Your beautiful eyes are causing me to die, Beautiful Marquise, of love.*
JOURDAIN
I see...Now, of all those ways, which is the best?
PHILOSOPHY TEACHER
The one you said: *Beautiful Marquise, your beautiful eyes are causing me to die of love.*
JOURDAIN
And I've never studied these things at all! I did that first crack! I don't know how I can ever thank you. Please come early tomorrow, will you?

---

[16]At this point he perhaps gets out a piece of paper on which he has written the words. The paper can provide an amusing bit of stage business if both Jourdain and the philosopher have to refer to the paper every time they want to recall the particular words Jourdain wants in the note. [17]If Jourdain has kept the foil dangling in one hand all this time, it is precisely for this moment. As the philosopher begins to get carried away by his own creativity, he perhaps turns slowly away from Jourdain, begins to rise to his toes and spread his arms apart while closing his eyes and lifting his face upwards in a very paroxysm of emotion. At the very height, and before he is allowed to finish, Jourdain jabs him—gently, of course—from behind with the foil.

PHILOSOPHY TEACHER
I shall be here.
JOURDAIN
[*Calling to his servant after the philosophy master leaves*] What in the world! My new clothes still haven't come?
SECOND SERVANT
No sir.
JOURDAIN
That blasted tailor![18] Making me wait on a day when I've already got so blasted much to do! I could kill him! I hope he comes down with something that really grabs him where it hurts, dang him! The devil with him! A guy like that ought to be strangled by the plague! If I had my hands on him right now! How I hate him, that dirty so and so! Talk about treacherous, I . . .

SCENE 5.
[*Enter the tailor and an apprentice who is carrying Jourdain's new clothes.*]
JOURDAIN
[*His face brightens*] So there you are! I was just about to say some naughty things about you!
TAILOR
I couldn't get here any sooner. I had twenty people working on your clothes.
JOURDAIN
The stockings you sent me were so blinking tight that it was all I could do to get them on, and so I've already got two runs in them.
TAILOR
You'll find that they'll soon be slipping on easily.
JOURDAIN
Yes, if I keep getting runs in them. And those shoes you sent me pinch like mad.
TAILOR
Not at all, sir.

JOURDAIN
What do you mean, not at all?
TAILOR
No, they don't pinch you.
JOURDAIN
I'm telling you that they pinch me.
TAILOR
It's all in your head.
JOURDAIN
I tell you it's in my feet. That's where I feel it. I ought to know the difference.
TAILOR
[*Pointing to the new clothes*] Here you go, sir. There are no finer clothes at the palace, and none better matched. It's simply a master creation to have invented formal attire which isn't black; I defy the best tailors to come up with anything like it.
JOURDAIN
What's this? You put the flowers growing downward?
TAILOR
You didn't say that you wanted them growing up.
JOURDAIN
Did I have to say that?
TAILOR
You should have, yes. But all the noblemen are wearing them that way.
JOURDAIN
The nobility are wearing the flowers growing down?
TAILOR
Yes sir.
JOURDAIN
Well, that's okay then.
TAILOR
If you want, I'll put them the other way.
JOURDAIN
No. No.
TAILOR
You have only to say the word . . .
JOURDAIN
No, I tell you, that's all right. What do

---

[18]If Jourdain is still holding the foil, he can begin using it as he sees fit to better make his point during the following lines.

you think? Do you think they'll fit?[19]

TAILOR
What a question! I challenge any painter, with his brush, to produce anything that would suit you better. I have a fellow in my establishment who, so far as getting up a Rhinegrave[20] is concerned is the greatest in the world; and another whose ability to put together a jacket makes him the hero of our time.

JOURDAIN
How about the wig and the feathers? Have you been careful with them?

TAILOR
Everything's perfect.

JOURDAIN
[Looking at the tailor's clothes] Am I seeing right? That cloth comes from the last outfit you made for me! I recognize it.

TAILOR
No, it's just that the material seemed so beautiful that I wanted to make clothes for myself out of it.

JOURDAIN
Yes, but you shouldn't have cut it out of the same bolt as mine.

TAILOR
Do you want to try on your new clothes?

JOURDAIN
Yes, let's have them.

TAILOR
Just a moment. That doesn't go like that. I have brought a few of my people with me who will clothe you rhythmically. You appreciate that this type of outfit is to be put on ceremoniously. Hey there! Come in, the rest of you. Dress this gentleman in the same way you do for noblemen. [Four apprentice tailors come in, two of whom pull off his breeches, and two others his jacket; then they put on his new clothes, and Mr. Jourdain promenades around among them, showing them his new outfit, to see if he will make the proper impression. The whole scene is choreographed carefully so that all movements are performed in rhythm.]

FIRST APPRENTICE
May I ask the gentleman if he would care to give the apprentices something with which they can drink to his health.

JOURDAIN
What are you calling me?

FIRST APPRENTICE
A gentleman.

JOURDAIN
A gentleman! That's what dolling up like a nobleman does for you! Just keep dressing like a bourgeois and no one will say to you "gentleman." There, that's for "gentleman."

FIRST APPRENTICE
Milord, we're grateful.

JOURDAIN
"Milord," Oh, Oh! Milord! Just a minute there, my friend. "Milord" merits something, and "Milord" is not just a tiny little word. There you go, there's what "Milord" gives you.

FIRST APPRENTICE
Milord, we shall all be delighted to drink to the health of your Highness.

JOURDAIN
"Your Highness!" Aha ha! Hold on there, don't go yet. "Your Highness" to me! By gosh, if he goes as far as your Imperial Highness he'll get all the money I've got on me. There you go, that's for "My Highness."

FIRST APPRENTICE
Milord, we are most appreciative of your generosity.

JOURDAIN
Whew! I'm lucky there! He quit while I was still ahead.

(Translated by John Green)

---

[19]If the tailor were to answer this question truthfully, he should probably say: "Fit? They'll be nothing short of a convulsion." That's what others think, later in the play. His servant Nicole, for example, upon seeing him, bursts spontaneously into an uncontrollable fit of laughter. His wife, too, tells him he looks like a complete ninny. [20]*Rhinegrave:* A particular type of knee-breeches fitted with ribbons at the knee. They were very popular at that time, the style having been imported to Paris.

John Dryden
(1631-1700)
A Song for St. Cecilia's Day

1

From harmony, from heavenly harmony
  This universal frame began:
    When Nature underneath a heap
      Of jarring atoms lay,
And could not heave her head,
The tuneful voice was heard from high:
  "Arise, ye more than dead."
Then cold, and hot, and moist, and dry,
In order to their stations leap,
    And Music's power obey.
From harmony, from heavenly harmony
  This universal frame began:
  From harmony to harmony
Through all the compass of the notes it ran,
The diapason closing full in man.

2

What passion cannot Music raise and quell!
    When Jubal struck the corded shell,
    His listening brethren stood around,
    And, wondering, on their faces fell
    To worship that celestial sound.
Less than a god they thought there could not dwell
    Within the hollow of that shell
    That spoke so sweetly and so well.
What passion cannot Music raise and quell!

Edward Taylor
(ca. 1642-1729)
Housewifery

Make me, O Lord, Thy spinning-wheel complete.
  Thy holy Word my distaff make for me;
Make mine affections Thy swift flyers neat;
  And make my soul Thy holy spool to be;
  My conversation make to be Thy reel,
And reel the yarn thereon spun of Thy wheel.

Make me Thy loom then; knit therein this twine;
  And make Thy Holy Spirit, Lord, wind quills;
Then weave the web Thyself. The yarn in fine.
  Thine ordinances make my fulling mills.
  Then dye the same in heavenly colors choice,
All pinked with varnished flowers of paradise.

Then clothe therewith mine understanding, will,
  Affections, judgment, conscience, memory,
My words and actions, that their shine may fill
  My ways with glory and Thee glorify.
  Then mine apparel shall display before Ye
That I am clothed in holy robes for glory.

Jonathan Swift
(1667-1745)
Part II
A Voyage to Brobdingnag[1]
from *Gulliver's Travels*

Gulliver's Travels *was written by Jonathan Swift over a period of years, probably beginning as early as 1720. It was published, however, in 1726. Swift possessed a critical eye and a sharp wit. He spent his life pointing out human inconsistencies. Widely read by the people of his day,* Gulliver's Travels *can be equally appreciated by young and old. The work is a satire in the form of a travel narrative: travel and adventure were the themes of the day. Satirizing both men and institutions,* Gulliver's Travels *is fascinating reading.*

The excerpt here comes from the second part, the voyage to Brobdingnag, where the inhabitants are as tall as church steeples.

Chapter I

A great storm described. The longboat sent to fetch water, the Author goes with it to discover the country. He is left on shore, is seized by one of the natives, and carried to a farmer's house. His reception there, with several accidents that happened there. A description of the inhabitants.

Having been condemned by nature and fortune to an active and restless life, in two months after my return, I again left my native country, and took shipping in the Downs on the 20th day of June, 1702, in the *Adventure,* Captain John Nicholas, a Cornish man, Commander, bound for Surat. We had a very prosperous gale till we arrived at the Cape of Good Hope, where we landed for fresh water, but discovering a leak we unshipped our goods and wintered there; for the Captain falling sick of an ague, we could not leave the Cape till the end of March. We then set sail, and had a good voyage till we passed the Straits of Madagascar; but having got northward of that island, and to about five degrees south latitude, the winds, which in those seas are observed to blow a constant equal gale between the north and west from the beginning of December to the beginning of May, on the 19th of April began to blow with much greater violence, and more westerly than usual, continuing so for twenty days together, during which time we were driven a little to the east of the Molucca Islands, and about three degrees northward of the Line, as our Captain found by an observation he took the 2nd of May, at which time the wind ceased, and it was a perfect calm, whereat I was not a little rejoiced. But he, being a man well experienced in the navigation of those seas, bid us all prepare against a storm, which accordingly happened the day following: for a southern wind, called the southern monsoon, began to set in.

Finding it was likely to overblow, we took in our spritsail, and stood by to hand the foresail; but making foul weather we looked the guns were all fast, and handed the mizzen. The ship lay very broad off, so we thought it better spooning before the sea, than trying or hulling. We reefed the foresail and set him, we hauled aft the foresheet; the helm was hard aweather. The ship wore bravely. We belayed the fore-down-haul; but the sail was split, and we hauled down the yard, and got the sail into the ship, and unbound all the things clear of it. It was a very fierce storm; the sea broke strange and dangerous. We hauled off upon the lanyard of the whipstaff, and helped the man at helm. We would not get down our topmast, but

---
[1] Brobdingnag is a great island or continent, jutting out into the Pacific from the northwest coast of North America.

JEAN-HONORÉ FRAGONARD: *A Young Girl Reading*, GIFT OF MRS. MELLON BRUCE IN MEMORY OF HER FATHER ANDREW MELLON, NATIONAL GALLERY OF ART, WASHINGTON, D. C.

let all stand, because she scudded before the sea very well, and we knew that the topmast being aloft, the ship was the wholesomer, and made better way through the sea, seeing we had sea room. When the storm was over, we set foresail and mainsail, and brought the ship to. Then we set the mizzen, main topsail, and the fore topsail. Our course was east northeast, the wind was at southwest. We got the starboard tack aboard, we cast off our weather braces and lifts; we set in the lee braces, and hauled forward by the weather bowlines, and hauled them tight, and belayed them, and hauled over the mizzen tack to windward, and kept her full and by as near as she would lie.

During this storm, which was followed by a strong wind west southwest, we were carried by my computation about five hundred leagues to the east, so that the oldest sailor on board could not tell in what part of the world we were. Our provisions held out well, our ship was staunch, and our crew all in good health; but we lay in the utmost distress for water. We thought it best to hold on the same course, rather than turn more northerly, which might have brought us to the northwest parts of Great Tartary, and into the frozen sea.

On the 16th day of June, 1703, a boy on the topmast discovered land. On the 17th we came in full view of a great island or continent (for we knew not whether) on the south side whereof was a small neck of land jutting out into the sea, and a creek too shallow to hold a ship of above one hundred tons. We cast anchor within a league of this creek, and our Captain sent a dozen of his men well armed in the longboat, with vessels for water if any could be found. I desired his leave to go with them, that I might see the country, and make what discoveries I could. When we came to land we saw no river or spring, nor any sign of inhabitants. Our men therefore wandered on the shore to find out some fresh water near the sea, and I walked alone about a mile on the other side, where I observed the country all barren and rocky. I now began to be weary, and seeing nothing to entertain my curiosity, I returned gently down towards the creek; and the sea being full in my view, I saw our men already got into the boat, and rowing for life to the ship. I was going to hollow after them, although it had been to little purpose, when I observed a huge creature walking after them in the sea, as fast as he could: he waded not much deeper than his knees, and took prodigious strides: but our men had the start of him half a league, and the sea thereabouts being full of sharp-pointed rocks, the monster was not able to overtake the boat. This I was afterwards told, for I durst not stay to see the issue of that adventure; but ran as fast as I could the way I first went, and then climbed up a steep hill, which gave me some prospect of the country. I found it fully cultivated; but that which first surprised me was the length of the grass, which in those grounds that seemed to be kept for hay, was above twenty foot high.

I fell into a highroad, for so I took it to be, though it served to the inhabitants only as a footpath through a field of barley. Here I walked on for some time, but could see little on either side, it being now near harvest, and the corn rising at least forty foot. I was an hour walking to the end of this field, which was fenced in with a hedge of at least one hundred and twenty foot high, and the trees so lofty that I could make no computation of their altitude. There was a stile to pass from this field into the next. It had four steps, and a stone to cross over when you came to the uppermost. It was impossible for me to climb this stile, because every step was six foot high, and the upper stone above twenty.

I was endeavoring to find some gap in the hedge, when I discovered one of the inhabitants in the next field, advancing towards the stile, of the same size with him whom I saw in the sea pursuing our boat. He appeared as tall as an an ordinary spire steeple, and took about ten yards at every stride, as near as I could guess. I was struck with the utmost fear and astonishment, and ran to hide myself in the corn, from whence I saw him at the top of the stile, looking back into the next field on the right hand, and heard him call in a voice many degrees louder than a speaking trumpet: but the noise was so high in the air, that at first I certainly thought it was thunder. Whereupon seven monsters like himself came towards him with reaping hooks in their hands, each hook about the largeness of six scythes. These people were not so well clad as the first, whose servants or laborers they seemed to be: for, upon some words he spoke, they went to reap the corn in the field where I lay. I kept from them at as great a distance as I could, but was forced to move with extreme difficulty, for the stalks of the corn were sometimes not above a foot distant, so that I could hardly squeeze my body betwixt them. However, I made a shift to go forward till I came to a part of the field where the corn had been laid by the rain and wind. Here it was impossible for me to advance a step; for the stalks were so interwoven that I could not creep through, and the beards of the fallen ears so strong and pointed that they pierced through my clothes into my flesh. At the same time I heard the reapers not above an hundred yards behind me. Being quite dispirited with toil, and wholly overcome by grief and despair, I lay down between two ridges, and heartily wished I might there end my days. I bemoaned my desolate widow, and fatherless children. I lamented my own folly and willfulness in attempting a second voyage against the advice of all my friends and relations. In this terrible agitation of mind I could not forbear thinking of Lilliput, whose inhabitants looked upon me as the greatest prodigy that ever appeared in the world; where I was able to draw an Imperial Fleet in my hand, and perform those other actions which will be recorded forever in the chronicles of that empire, while posterity shall hardly believe them, although attested by millions. I reflected what a mortification it must prove to me to appear as inconsiderable in this nation as one single Lilliputian would be among us. But this I conceived was to be the least of my misfortunes: for, as human creatures are observed to be more savage and cruel in proportion to their bulk, what could I expect but to be a morsel in the mouth of the first among these enormous barbarians who should happen to seize me? Undoubtedly philosophers are in the right when they tell us, that nothing is great or little otherwise than by comparison. It might have pleased fortune to let the Lilliputians find some nation, where the people were as diminutive with respect to them, as they were to me. And who knows but that even this prodigious race of mortals might be equally overmatched in some distant part of the world, whereof we have yet no discovery?

Scared and confounded as I was, I could not forbear going on with these reflections, when one of the reapers approaching within ten yards of the ridge where I lay, made me apprehend that with the next step I should be squashed to death under his foot, or cut in two with his reaping hook. And therefore when he was again about to move, I screamed as loud as fear could make me. Whereupon the huge creature trod short, and looking round about under him for sometime, at last espied me as I lay on the ground. He considered a while with the caution of one who endeavors to lay hold on a small dangerous animal in such a manner that it shall not be able either to scratch or bite him, as I myself have sometimes done with a weasel in England. At length he ventured to take me up behind by the middle between his forefinger and thumb, and brought me within three yards of his eyes, that he might behold my shape more perfectly. I guessed his meaning, and my good fortune gave me so much presence of mind, that I resolved not to struggle in the least as he held me in the air about sixty foot from the ground, although he grievously pinched my sides, for fear I should slip through his fingers. All I ventured was to raise my eyes towards the sun, and place my hands together in a supplicating posture, and to speak some words in an humble melancholy tone, suitable to the condition I then was in. For I apprehended every moment that he would dash me against the ground, as we usually do any little hateful animal which we have a mind to destroy. But my good star would have it, that he appeared pleased with my voice and gestures, and began to look upon me as a curiosity, much wondering to hear me pronounce articulate words, although he could not understand them. In the meantime I was not able to forbear groaning and shedding tears, and turning my head towards my sides; letting him know, as well as I could, how cruelly I was hurt by the pressure of his thumb and finger. He seemed to apprehend my meaning; for, lifting up the lappet of his coat, he put me gently into it, and immediately ran along with me to his master, who was a substantial farmer, and the same person I had first seen in the field.

The farmer having (as I supposed by their talk) received such an account of me as his servant could give him, took a piece of a small straw, about the size of a walking staff, and therewith lifted up the lappets of my coat; which it seems he thought to be some kind of covering that nature had given me. He blew my hairs aside to take a better view of my face. He called his hinds about him, and asked them (as I afterwards learned) whether they had ever seen in the fields any little creature that resembled me. He then placed me softly on the ground upon all fours, but I got immediately up, and walked slowly backwards and forwards, to let those people see I had no intent to run away. They all sat down in a circle about me, the better to observe my motions. I pulled off my hat, and made a low bow towards the farmer. I fell on my knees, and lifted up my hands and eyes, and spoke several words as loud as I could: I took a purse of gold out of my pocket, and humbly presented it to him. He received it on the palm of his hand, then applied it close to his eye, to see what it was, and afterwards turned it several times with the point of a pin (which he took out of his sleeve), but could make nothing of it. Whereupon I made a sign that he should place his hand on the ground. I then took the purse, and opening it, poured all the gold into his palm. There were six Spanish pieces of four pistoles each, beside twenty or thirty smaller coins. I saw him wet the tip of his little finger upon his tongue, and take up one of my largest pieces, and then another, but he seemed to be wholly ignorant what they were. He made me a sign to put them again into my purse, and the purse again into my pocket, which after offering to him several times, I thought it best to do.

The farmer by this time was convinced I must be a rational creature. He spoke often to me, but the sound of his voice pierced my ears like that of a water mill, yet his words were articulate enough. I answered as loud as I could, in several languages, and he often laid his ear within two yards of me, but all in vain, for we were wholly unintelligible to each other. He then sent his servants to their work, and taking his handkerchief out of his pocket, he doubled and spread it on his hand, which he placed flat on the ground, with the palm upwards, making me a sign to step into it, as I could easily do, for it was not above a foot in thickness. I thought it my part to obey, and for fear of falling, laid myself at full length upon the handkerchief, with the remainder of which he lapped me up to the head for further security, and in this manner carried me home to his house. There he called his wife, and showed me to her; but she screamed and ran back, as women in England do at the sight of a toad or a spider. However, when she had a while seen my behavior, and how well I observed the signs her husband made, she was soon reconciled, and by degrees grew extremely tender of me.

It was about twelve at noon, and a servant brought in dinner. It was only one substantial dish of meat (fit for the plain condition of an husbandman) in a dish of about four-and-twenty foot diameter. The company were the farmer and his wife, three children, and an old grandmother. When they were sat down, the farmer placed me at some distance from him on the table, which was thirty foot high from the floor. I was in a terrible fright, and kept as far as I could from the edge for fear of falling. The wife minced a bit of meat, then crumbled some bread on a trencher, and placed it before me. I made her a low bow, took out my knife and fork, and fell to eat, which gave them exceeding delight. The mistress sent her maid for a small dram cup, which held about two gallons, and filled it with drink; I took up the vessel with much difficulty in both hands, and in a most respectful manner drank to her ladyship's health, expressing the words as loud as I could in English, which made the company laugh so heartily that I was almost deafened with the noise. This liquor tasted like a small cider, and was not unpleasant. Then the master made me a sign to come to his trencher side; but as I walked on the table, being in great surprise all the time, as the indulgent reader will easily conceive and excuse, I happened to stumble against a crust, and fell flat on my face, but received no hurt. I got up immediately, and observing the good people to be in much concern, I took my hat (which I held under my arm out of good manners) and waving it over my head, made three huzzas, to show I had got no mischief by the fall. But advancing forwards toward my master (as I shall henceforth call him), his youngest son who sat next him, an arch boy of about ten years old, took me up by the legs, and held me so high in the air, that I trembled every limb; but his father snatched me from him, and at the same time gave him such a box on the left ear, as would have felled an European troop of horse to the earth, ordering him to be taken from the table. But being afraid the boy might owe me a spite, and well remembering how mischievous all children among us naturally are to sparrows, rabbits, young kittens, and puppy dogs, I fell on my knees, and pointing to the boy, made my master understand, as well as I could, that I desired his son might be pardoned. The father complied, and the lad took his seat again; whereupon I went to him and kissed his hand, which my master took, and made him stroke me gently with it.

In the midst of dinner, my mistress's favorite cat leapt into her lap. I heard a noise behind me like that of a dozen stocking weavers at work; and turning my head, I found it proceeded from the purring of this animal, who seemed to be three times larger than an ox, as I computed by the view of her head, and one of her paws, while her mistress was feeding and stroking her. The fierceness of this creature's countenance altogether discomposed me; though I stood at the farther end of the table, above fifty foot off; and although my mistress held her fast for fear she might give a spring, and seize me in her talons. But it happened there was no danger; for the cat took not the least notice of me when my master placed me within three yards of her. And as I have been always told, and found true by experience in my travels, that flying, or discovering fear before a fierce animal, is a certain way to make it pursue or attack you, so I resolved in this dangerous juncture to show no manner of concern. I walked with intrepidity five or six times before the very head of the cat, and came within half a yard of her; whereupon she drew herself back, as if she were more afraid of me: I had less apprehension concerning the dogs, whereof three or four came into the room, as it is usual in farmers' houses; one of which was a mastiff, equal in bulk to four elephants, and a greyhound, somewhat taller than the mastiff, but not so large.

When dinner was almost done, the nurse came in with a child of a year old in her arms, who immediately spied me, and began a squall that you might have heard from London Bridge to Chelsea, after the usual oratory of infants, to get me for a plaything. The mother out of pure indulgence took me up, and put me towards the child, who presently seized me by the middle, and got my head in his mouth, where I roared so loud that the urchin was frighted, and let me drop; and I should infallibly have broke my neck if the mother had not held her apron under me. The nurse to quiet her babe made use of a rattle, which was a kind of hollow vessel filled with great stones, and fastened by a cable to the child's waist: but all in vain, so that she was forced to apply the last remedy by giving it suck. I must confess no object ever disgusted me so much as the sight of her monstrous breast, which I cannot tell what to compare with, so as to give the curious reader an idea of its bulk, shape and color. It stood prominent six foot, and could not be less than sixteen in circumference. The nipple was about half the bigness of my head, and the hue both of that and the dug so varified with spots, pimples, and freckles, that nothing could appear more nauseous: for I had a near sight of her, she sitting down the more conveniently to give suck, and I standing on the table. This made me reflect upon the fair skins of our English ladies, who appear so beautiful to us, only because they are of our own size, and their defects not to be seen but through a magnifying glass, where we find by experiment that the smoothest and whitest skins look rough and coarse, and ill colored.

I remember when I was at Lilliput, the complexion of those diminutive people appeared to me the fairest in the world; and talking upon this subject with a person of learning there, who was an intimate friend of mine, he said that my face appeared much fairer and smoother when he looked on me from the ground, than it did upon a nearer view when I took him up in my hand and brought him close, which he confessed was at first a very shocking sight. He said he could discover great holes in my skin; that the stumps of my beard were ten times stronger than the bristles of a boar, and my complexion made up of several colors altogether disagreeable: although I must beg leave to say for myself, that I am as fair as most of my sex and country, and very little sunburnt by all my travels. On the other side, discoursing of the ladies in that Emperor's court, he used to tell me, one had freckles, another too wide a mouth, a third too large a nose, nothing of which I was able to distinguish. I confess this reflection was obvious enough; which, however, I could not forbear, lest the reader might think those vast creatures were actually deformed: for I must do them justice to say they are a comely race of people; and particularly the features of my master's countenance, although he were but a farmer, when I beheld him from the height of sixty foot, appeared very well proportioned.

When dinner was done, my master went out to his laborers, and as I could discover by his voice and gesture, gave his wife a strict charge to take care of me. I was very much tired, and disposed to sleep, which my mistress perceiving, she put me on her own bed, and covered me with a clean white handkerchief, but larger and coarser than the mainsail of a man-of-war.

I slept about two hours, and dreamed I was at home with my wife and children, which aggravated my sorrows when I awaked and found myself alone in a vast room, between two and three hundred foot wide, and above two hundred high, lying in a bed twenty yards wide. My mistress was gone about her household affairs, and had locked me in. The bed was eight yards from the floor. Some natural necessities required me to get down; I durst not presume to call, and if I had, it would have been in vain, with such a voice as mine, at so great a distance from the room where I lay to the kitchen where the family kept. While I was under these circumstances, two rats crept up the curtains, and ran smelling backwards and forwards on the bed. One of them came up almost to my face, whereupon I rose in a fright, and drew out my hanger to defend myself. These horrible animals had the boldness to attack me on both sides, and one of them held his forefeet at my collar; but I had the good fortune to rip up his belly before he could do me any mischief. He fell down at my feet, and the other seeing the fate of his comrade, made his escape, but not without one good wound on the back, which I gave him as he fled, and made the blood run trickling from him. After this exploit, I walked gently to and fro on the bed, to recover my breath and loss of spirits. These creatures were of the size of a large mastiff, but infinitely more nimble and fierce, so that if I had taken off my belt before I went to sleep, I must have infallibly been torn to pieces and devoured. I measured the tail of the dead rat, and found it to be two yards long, wanting an inch; but it went against my stomach to drag the carcass off the bed, where it lay still bleeding; I observed it had yet some life, but with a strong slash across the neck, I thoroughly dispatched it.

Soon after my mistress came into the room, who seeing me all bloody, ran and took me up in her hand. I pointed to the dead rat, smiling and making other signs to show I was not hurt, whereat she was extremely rejoiced, calling the maid to take up the dead rat with a pair of tongs, and throw it out of the window. Then she set me on a table, where I showed her my hanger all bloody, and wiping it on the lappet of my coat, returned it to the scabbard. I was pressed to do more than one thing, which another could not do for me, and therefore endeavored to make my mistress understand that I desired to be set down on the floor; which after she had done, my bashfulness would not suffer me to express myself farther than by pointing to the door, and bowing several times. The good woman with much difficulty at last perceived what I would be at, and taking me up again in her hand, walked into the garden, where she set me down. I went on one side about two hundred yards, and beckoning to her not to look or to follow me, I hid myself between two leaves of sorrel, and there discharged the necessities of nature.

I hope the gentle reader will excuse me for dwelling on these and the like particulars, which however insignificant they may appear to groveling vulgar minds, yet will certainly help a philosopher to enlarge his thoughts and imagination, and apply them to the benefit of public as well as private life, which was my sole design in presenting this and other accounts of my travels to the world; wherein I have been chiefly studious of truth, without affecting any ornaments of learning or of style. But the whole scene of this voyage made so strong an impression on my mind, and is so deeply fixed in my memory, that in committing it to paper I did not omit one material circumstance: however, upon a strict review, I blotted out several passages of less moment which were in my first copy, for fear of being censured as tedious and trifling, whereof travelers are often, perhaps not without justice, accused.

Chapter 2

A description of the farmer's daughter. The Author carried to a market town, and then to the metropolis. The particulars of his journey.

My mistress had a daughter of nine years old, a child of towardly parts for her age, very dexterous at her needle, and skillful in dressing her baby. Her mother and she contrived to fit up the baby's cradle for me against night: the cradle was put into a small drawer of a cabinet, and the drawer placed upon a hanging shelf for fear of the rats. This was my bed all the time I stayed with those people, although made more convenient by degrees, as I began to learn their language, and make my wants known. This young girl was so handy, that after I had once or twice pulled off my clothes before her, she was able to dress and undress me, although I never gave her that trouble when she would let me do either myself. She made me seven shirts, and some other linen, of as fine cloth as could be got, which indeed was coarser than sackcloth; and these she constantly washed for me with her own hands. She was likewise my schoolmistress to teach me the language: when I pointed to anything she told me the name of it in her own tongue, so that in a few days I was able to call for whatever I had a mind to. She was very good-natured, and not above forty foot high, being little for her age. She gave me the name of *Grildrig,* which the family took up, and afterwards the whole kingdom. The word imports what the Latins call *nanunculus,* the Italians *homunceletino,* and the English *mannikin.* To her I chiefly owe my preservation in that country: we never parted while I was there; I called her my *Glumdalclitch,* or little nurse: and I should be guilty of great ingratitude, if I omitted this honorable mention of her care and affection towards me, which I heartily wish it lay in my power to requite as she deserves, instead of being the innocent but unhappy instrument of her disgrace, as I have too much reason to fear.

It now began to be known and talked of in the neighborhood, that my master had found a strange animal in the field, about the bigness of a *splacknuck,* but exactly shaped in every part like a human creature; which it likewise imitated in all its actions; seemed to speak in a little language of its own, had already learned several words of theirs, went erect upon two legs, was tame and gentle, would come when it was called, do whatever it was bid, had the finest limbs in the world, and a complexion fairer than a nobleman's daughter of three years old. Another farmer who lived hard by, and was a particular friend of my master, came on a visit on purpose to inquire into the truth of this story. I was immediately produced, and placed upon a table, where I walked as I was commanded, drew my hanger, put it up again, made my reverence to my master's guest, asked him in his own language how he did, and told him he was welcome, just as my little nurse had instructed me. This man who was old and dimsighted, put on his spectacles to behold me better, at which I could not forbear laughing very heartily, for his eyes appeared like the full moon shining into a chamber at two windows. Our people, who discovered the cause of my mirth, bore me company in laughing, at which the old fellow was fool enough to be angry and out of countenance. He had the character of a great miser, and to my misfortune he well deserved it, by the cursed advice he gave my master to show me as a sight upon a market day in the next town, which was half an hour's riding, about two and twenty miles from our house. I guessed there was some mischief contriving, when I observed my master and his friend whispering long together, sometimes pointing at me; and my fears made me fancy that I overheard and understood some of their words. But the next morning Glumdalclitch, my little nurse, told me the whole matter, which she had cunningly picked out from her mother. The poor girl laid me on her bosom, and fell a weeping with shame and grief. She apprehended some mischief would happen to me from rude vulgar folks, who might squeeze me to death, or break one of my limbs by taking me in their hands. She had also observed how modest I was in my nature, how nicely I regarded my honor, and what an indignity I should conceive it to be exposed for money as a public spectacle to the meanest of the people. She said, her papa and mamma had promised that Grildrig should be hers, but now she found they meant to serve her as they did last year, when they pretended to give her a lamb, and yet, as soon as it was fat, sold it to a butcher. For my own part, I may truly affirm that I was less concerned than my nurse. I had a strong hope, which never left me, that I should one day recover my liberty; and as to the ignominy of being carried about for a monster, I considered myself to be a perfect stranger in the country, and that such a misfortune could never be charged upon me as a reproach, if ever I should return to England; since the King of Great Britain himself, in my condition, must have undergone the same distress.

My master, pursuant to the advice of his friend, carried me in a box the next market day to the neighboring town, and took along with him his little daughter, my nurse, upon a pillion behind him. The box was close on every side, with a little door for me to go in and out, and a few gimlet holes to let in air. The girl had been so careful to put the quilt of her baby's bed into it, for me to lie down on. However, I was terribly shaken and discomposed in this journey, though it were but of half an hour. For the horse went about forty foot at every step, and trotted so high, that the agitation was equal to the rising and falling of a ship in a great storm, but much more frequent. Our journey was somewhat further than from London to St. Albans. My master alighted at an inn which he used to frequent; and after consulting a while with the innkeeper, and making some necessary preparations, he hired the *Grultrud,* or crier, to give notice through the town of a strange creature to be seen at the Sign of the Green Eagle, not so big as a *splacknuck* (an animal in that country very finely shaped, about six foot long), and in every part of the body resembling an human creature, could speak several words, and perform an hundred diverting tricks.

I was placed upon a table in the largest room of the inn, which might be near three hundred foot square. My little nurse stood on a low stool close to the table, to take care of me, and direct what I should do. My master, to avoid a crowd, would suffer only thirty people at a time to see me. I walked about on the table as the girl commanded: she asked me questions as far as she knew my understanding of the language reached, and I answered them as loud as I could. I turned about several times to the company, paid my humble respects, said they were welcome, and used some other speeches I had been taught. I took up a thimble filled with liquor, which Glumdalclitch had given me for a cup, and drank their health. I drew out my hanger, and flourished with it after the manner of fencers in England. My nurse gave me part of a straw, which I exercised as a pike, having learned the art in my youth. I was that day shown to twelve sets of company, and as often forced to go over again with the same fopperies, till I was half dead with weariness and vexation. For those who had seen me made such wonderful reports, that the people were ready to break down the doors to come in. My master for his own interest would not suffer anyone to touch me except my nurse; and, to prevent danger, benches were set around the table at such a distance as put me out of everybody's reach. However, an unlucky schoolboy aimed a hazelnut directly at my head, which very narrowly missed me; otherwise, it came with so much violence, that it would have infallibly knocked out my brains, for it was almost as large as a small pumpion: but I had the satisfaction to see the young rogue well beaten, and turned out of the room.

My master gave public notice, that he would show me again the next market day, and in the meantime he prepared a more convenient vehicle for me, which he had reason enough to do; for I was so tired with my first journey, and with entertaining company eight hours together, that I could hardly stand upon my legs, or speak a word. It was at least three days before I recovered my strength; and that I might have no rest at home, all the neighboring gentlemen from an hundred miles round, hearing of my fame, came to see me at my master's own house. There could not be fewer than thirty persons with their wives and children (for the country is very populous); and my master demanded the rate of a full room whenever he showed me at home, although it were only to a single family; so that for some time I had but little ease every day of the week (except Wednesday, which is their Sabbath) although I were not carried to the town.

My master finding how profitable I was like to be, resolved to carry me to the most considerable cities of the kingdom. Having therefore provided himself with all things necessary for a long journey, and settled his affairs at home, he took leave of his wife, and upon the 17th of August, 1703, about two months after my arrival, we set out for the metropolis, situated near the middle of that empire, and about three thousand miles distance from our house. My master made his daughter Glumdalclitch ride behind him. She carried me on her lap in a box tied about her waist. The girl had lined it on all sides with the softest cloth she could get, well quilted underneath, furnished it with her baby's bed, provided me with linen and other necessaries, and made everything as convenient as she could. We had no other company but a boy of the house, who rode after us with the luggage.

My master's design was to show me in all the towns by the way, and to step out of the road for fifty or an hundred miles, to any village or person of quality's house where he might expect custom. We made easy journeys of not above seven or eight score miles a day: for Glumdalclitch, on purpose to spare me, complained she was tired with the trotting of the horse. She often took me out of my box, at my own desire, to give me air, and show me the country, but always held me fast by leading strings. We passed over five or six rivers many degrees broader and deeper than the Nile or the Ganges; and there was hardly a rivulet so small as the Thames at London Bridge. We were ten weeks in our journey, and I was shown in eighteen large towns beside many villages and private families.

On the 26th day of October, we arrived at the metropolis, called in their language *Lorbrulgrud,* or Pride of the Universe. My master took a lodging in the principal street of the city, not far from the royal palace, and put out bills in the usual form, containing an exact description of my person and parts. He hired a large room between three and four hundred foot wide. He provided a table sixty foot in diameter, upon which I was to act my part, and pallisadoed it round three foot from the edge, and as many high, to prevent my falling over. I was shown ten times a day to the wonder and satisfaction of all people. I could now speak the language tolerably well, and perfectly understood every word that was spoken to me. Besides, I had learnt their alphabet, and could make a shift to explain a sentence here and there; for Glumdalclitch had been my instructor while we were at home, and at leisure hours during our journey. She carried a little book in her pocket, not much larger than a Sanson's Atlas; it was a common treatise for the use of young girls, giving a short account of their religion: out of this she taught me my letters, and interpreted the words.

Chapter 3

The Author sent for to court. The Queen buys him of his master the farmer, and presents him to the King. He disputes with his Majesty's great scholars. An apartment at court provided for the Author. He is in high favor with the Queen. He stands up for the honor of his own country. His quarrels with the Queen's dwarf.

The frequent labors I underwent every day made in a few weeks a very considerable change in my health: the more my master got by me, the more insatiable he grew. I had quite lost my stomach, and was almost reduced to a skeleton. The farmer observed it, and concluding I soon must die, resolved to make as good a hand of me as he could. While he was thus reasoning and resolving with himself, a *Slardral,* or Gentleman Usher, came from court, commanding my master to bring me immediately thither for the diversion of the Queen and her ladies. Some of the latter had already been to see me, and reported strange things of my beauty, behavior, and good sense. Her Majesty and those who attended her were beyond measure delighted with my demeanor. I fell on my knees, and begged the honor of kissing her Imperial foot; but this gracious princess held out her little finger towards me (after I was set on a table), which I embraced in both my arms, and put the tip of it, with the utmost respect, to my lip. She made me some general questions about my country and my travels, which I answered as distinctly and in as few words as I could. She asked whether I would be content to live at court. I bowed down to the board of the table, and humbly answered, that I was my master's slave, but if I were at my own disposal, I should be proud to devote my life to her Majesty's service. She then asked my master whether he were willing to sell me at a good price. He, who apprehended I could not live a month, was ready enough to part with me, and demanded a thousand pieces of gold, which were ordered him on the spot, each piece being about the bigness of eight hundred moidores; but, allowing for the proportion of all things between that country and Europe, and the high price of gold among them, was hardly so great a sum as a thousand guineas would be in England. I then said to the Queen, since I was now her Majesty's most humble creature and vassal, I must beg the favor, that Glumdalclitch, who had always tended me with so much care and kindness, and understood to do it so well, might be admitted into her service, and continue to be my nurse and instructor. Her Majesty agreed to my petition, and easily got the farmer's consent, who was glad enough to have his daughter preferred at court: and the poor girl herself was not able to hide her joy. My late master withdrew, bidding me farewell, and saying he had left me in a good service; to which I replied not a word, only making him a slight bow.

The Queen observed my coldness, and when the farmer was gone out of the apartment, asked me the reason. I made bold to tell her Majesty that I owed no other obligation to my late master, than his not dashing out the brains of a poor harmless creature found by chance in his field; which obligation was amply recompensed by the gain he had made in showing me through half the kingdom, and the price he had now sold me for. That the life I had since led, was laborious enough to kill an animal of ten times my strength. That my health was much impaired by the continual drudgery of entertaining the rabble every hour of the day, and that if my master had not thought my life in danger, her Majesty perhaps would not have got so cheap a bargain. But as I was out of all fear of being ill treated under the protection of so great and good an Empress, the Ornament of Nature, the Darling of the World, the Delight of her Subjects, the Phoenix of the Creation; so I hoped my late master's apprehensions would appear to be groundless, for I already found my spirits to revive by the influence of her most august presence.

This was the sum of my speech, delivered with great improprieties and hesitation; the latter part was altogether framed in the style peculiar to that people, whereof I learned some phrases from Glumdalclitch, while she was carrying me to court.

The Queen giving great allowance for my defectiveness in speaking, was however surprised at so much wit and good sense in so diminutive an animal. She took me in her own hand, and carried me to the King, who was then retired to his cabinet. His Majesty, a prince of much gravity, and austere countenance, not well observing my shape at first view, asked the Queen after a cold manner, how long it was since she grew fond of a *splacknuck;* for such it seems he took me to be, as I lay upon my breast in her Majesty's right hand. But this princess, who hath an infinite deal of wit and humor, set me gently on my feet upon the scrutore, and commanded me to give his Majesty an account of myself, which I did in a very few words; and Glumdalclitch, who attended at the cabinet door, and could not endure I should be out of her sight, being admitted, confirmed all that had passed from my arrival at her father's house.

The King, although he be as learned a person as any in his dominions, and had been educated in the study of philosophy, and particularly mathematics; yet when he observed my shape exactly, and saw me walk erect, before I began to speak, conceived I might be a piece of clockwork (which is in that country arrived to a very great perfection), contrived by some ingenious artist. But when he heard my voice, and found what I delivered to be regular and rational, he could not conceal his astonishment. He was by no means satisfied with the relation I gave him of the manner I came into his kingdom, but thought it a story concerted between Glumdalclitch and her father, who had taught me a set of words to make me sell at a higher price. Upon this imagination he put several other questions to me, and still received rational answers, no otherwise defective than by a foreign accent, and an imperfect knowledge in the language, with some rustic phrases which I had learned at the farmer's house, and did not suit the polite style of a court.

His Majesty sent for three great scholars who were then in their weekly waiting, according to the custom in that country. These gentlemen, after they had a while examined my shape with much nicety, were of different opinions concerning me. They all agreed that I could not be produced according to the regular laws of nature, because I was not framed with a capacity of preserving my life, either by swiftness, or climbing of trees, or digging holes in the earth. They observed by my teeth, which they viewed with great exactness, that I was a carnivorous animal; yet most quadrupeds being an overmatch for me, and field mice, with some others, too nimble, they could not imagine how I should be able to support myself, unless I fed upon snails and other insects, which they offered, by many learned arguments, to evince that I could not possibly do. One of them seemed to think that I might be an embryo, or abortive birth. But this opinion was rejected by the other two, who observed my limbs to the perfect and finished, and that I had lived several years, as it was manifested from my beard, the stumps whereof they plainly discovered through a magnifying glass. They would not allow me to be a dwarf, because my littleness was beyond all degrees of comparison; for the Queen's favorite dwarf, the smallest ever known in that kingdom, was near thirty foot high. After much debate, they concluded unanimously that I was on only *relplum scalcath,* which is interpreted literally, *lusus naturae;* a determination exactly agreeable to the modern philosophy of Europe, whose professors, disdaining the old evasion of *occult causes,* whereby the followers of Aristotle endeavor in vain to disguise their ignorance, have invented this wonderful solution of all difficulties, to the unspeakable advancement of human knowledge.

After this decisive conclusion, I entreated to be heard a word or two. I applied myself to the King, and assured his Majesty, that I came from a country which abounded with several millions of both sexes, and of my own stature; where the animals, trees, and houses were all in proportion, and where by consequence I might be as able to defend myself, and to find sustenance, as any of his Majesty's subjects could do here; which I took for a full answer to those gentlemen's arguments. To this they only replied with a smile of contempt, saying, that the farmer had instructed me very well in my lesson. The King, who had a much better understanding, dismissing his learned men, sent for the farmer, who by good fortune was not yet gone out of town. Having therefore first examined him privately, and then confronted him with me and the young girl, his Majesty began to think that what we told might possibly be true. He desired the Queen to order that a particular care should be taken of me, and was of opinion that Glumdalclitch should still continue in her office of tending me, because he observed we had a great affection for each other. A convenient apartment was provided for her at court:

she had a sort of governess appointed to take care of her education, a maid to dress her, and two other servants for menial offices; but the care of me was wholly appropriated to herself. The Queen commanded her own cabinetmaker to contrive a box that might serve me for a bedchamber, after the model that Glumdalclitch and I should agree upon. This man was a most ingenious artist, and according to my directions, in three weeks finished for me a wooden chamber of sixteen foot square, and twelve high, with sash windows, a door, and two closets, like a London bedchamber. The board that made the ceiling was to be lifted up and down by two hinges, to put a bed ready furnished by her Majesty's upholsterer, which Glumdalclitch took out every day to air, made it with her own hands, and letting it down at night, locked up the roof over me. A nice workman, who was famous for little curiosities, undertook to make me two chairs, with backs and frames, of a substance not unlike ivory, and two tables, with a cabinet to put my things in. The room was quilted on all sides, as well as the floor and the ceiling, to prevent any accident from the carelessness of those who carried me, and to break the force of a jolt when I went in a coach. I desired a lock for my door, to prevent rats and mice from coming in: the smith, after several attempts, made the smallest that was ever seen among them, for I have known a larger at the gate of a gentleman's house in England. I made a shift to keep the key in a pocket of my own, fearing Glumdalclitch might lose it. The Queen likewise ordered the thinnest silks that could be gotten, to make me clothes, not much thicker than an English blanket, very cumbersome till I was accustomed to them. They were after the fashion of the kingdom, partly resembling the Persian, and partly the Chinese, and are a very grave, decent habit.

The Queen became so fond of my company, that she could not dine without me. I had a table placed upon the same at which her Majesty eat, just at her left elbow, and a chair to sit on. Glumdalclitch stood upon a stool on the floor, near my table, to assist and take care of me. I had an entire set of silver dishes and plates, and other necessaries, which, in proportion to those of the Queen, were not much bigger than what I have seen in a London toyshop, for the furniture of a baby-house: these my little nurse kept in her pocket, in a silver box, and gave me at meals as I wanted them, always cleaning them herself. No person dined with the Queen but the two Princesses Royal, the elder sixteen years old, and the younger at that time thirteen and a month. Her Majesty used to put a bit of meat upon one of my dishes, out of which I carved for myself, and her diversion was to see me eat in miniature. For the Queen (who had indeed but a weak stomach) took up at one mouthful, as much as a dozen English farmers could eat at a meal, which to me was for some time a very nauseous sight. She would craunch the wing of a lark, bones and all, between her teeth, although it were nine times as large as that of a full-grown turkey; and put a bit of bread into her mouth, as big as two twelve-penny loaves. She drank out of a golden cup, above a hogshead at a draught. Her knives were twice as long as a scythe set straight upon the handle. The spoons, forks, and other instruments were all in the same proportion. I remember when Glumdalclitch carried me out of curisoity to see some of the tables at court, where ten or a dozen of these enormous knives and forks were lifted up together, I thought I had never till then beheld so terrible a sight.

It is the custom that every Wednesday (which, as I have before observed, was their

Sabbath) the King and Queen, with the royal issue of both sexes, dine together in the apartment of his Majesty, to whom I was now become a favorite; and at these times my little chair and table were placed at his left hand, before one of the saltcellars. This prince took a pleasure in conversing with me, inquiring into the manners, religion, laws, government, and learning of Europe; wherein I gave him the best account I was able. His apprehension was so clear, and his judgment so exact, that he made very wise reflections and observations upon all I said. But, I confess, that after I had been a little too copious in talking of my own beloved country, of our trade, and wars by sea and land, of our schisms in religion, and parties in the state; the prejudices of his education prevailed so far, that he could not forbear taking me up in his right hand, and stroking me gently with the other, after an hearty fit of laughing, asked me, whether I were a Whig or a Tory. Then turning to his first minister, who waited behind him with a white staff, near as tall as the mainmast of the *Royal Sovereign,* he observed how contemptible a thing was human grandeur, which could be mimicked by such diminutive insects as I. "And yet," said he, "I dare engage, those creatures have their titles and distinctions of honor, they contrive little nests and burrows, that they call houses and cities; they make a figure in dress and equipage; they love, they fight, they dispute, they cheat, they betray." And thus he continued on, while my color came and went several times, with indignation to hear our noble country, the mistress of arts and arms, the scourge of France, the arbitress of Europe, the seat of virtue, piety, honor, and truth, the pride and envy of the world, so contemptuously treated.

But as I was not in a condition to resent injuries, so, upon mature thoughts, I began to doubt whether I were injured or no. For, after having been accustomed several months to the sight and converse of this people, and observed every object upon which I cast my eyes, to be of proportionable magnitude, the horror I had first conceived from their bulk and aspect was so far worn off, that if I had then beheld a company of English lords and ladies in their finery and birthday clothes, acting their several parts in the most courtly manner, of strutting, and bowing, and prating; to say the truth, I should have been strongly tempted to laugh as much at them as this King and his grandees did at me. Neither indeed could I forbear smiling at myself, when the Queen used to place me upon her hand towards a looking glass, by which both our persons appeared before me in full view together; and there could be nothing more ridiculous than the comparison; so that I really began to imagine myself dwindled many degrees below my usual size.

Nothing angered and mortified me so much as the Queen's dwarf, who being of the lowest stature that was ever in that country (for I verily think he was not full thirty foot high) became so insolent at seeing a creature so much beneath him, that he would always affect to swagger and look big as he passed by me in the Queen's antechamber, while I was standing on some table talking with the lords or ladies of the court, and he seldom failed of a smart word or two upon my littleness; against which I could only revenge myself by calling him brother, challenging him to wrestle, and such repartees as are usual in the mouths of court pages. One day at dinner this malicious little cub was so nettled with something I had said to him, that raising himself upon the frame of her Majesty's chair, he took me up by the middle, as I was sitting down, not thinking any harm, and let me drop into a large silver bowl of cream, and then ran away as fast as he could. I fell over head and ears, and if I had not been a good swimmer, it might have gone very hard with me; for Glumdalclitch in that instant happened to be at the other end of the room, and the Queen was in such a fright that she wanted presence of mind to assist me. But my little nurse ran to my relief, and took me out, after I had swallowed above a quart of cream. I was put to bed; however, I received no other damage than the loss of a suit of clothes, which was utterly spoiled. The dwarf was soundly whipped, and as a farther punishment, forced to drink up the bowl of cream, into which he had thrown me: neither was he ever restored to favor: for, soon after the Queen bestowed him on a lady of high quality, so that I saw him no more, to my very great satisfaction; for I could not tell to what extremity such a malicious urchin might have carried his resentment.

He had before served me a scurvy trick, which set the Queen a laughing, although at the same time she was heartily vexed, and would have immediately cashiered him, if I had not been so generous as to intercede. Her Majesty had taken a marrow bone upon her plate, and after knocking out the marrow, placed the bone again in the dish erect as it stood before; the dwarf watching his opportunity, while Glumdalclitch was gone to the sideboard, mounted the stool that she stood on to take care of me at meals, took me up in both hands, and squeezing my legs together, wedged them into the marrow bone above my waist, where I stuck for some time, and made a very ridiculous figure. I believe it was near a minute before anyone knew what was become of me, for I thought it below me to cry out. But, as princes seldom get their meat hot, my legs were not scalded, only my stockings and breeches in a sad condition. The dwarf, at my entreaty, had no other punishment than a sound whipping.

I was frequently rallied by the Queen upon account of my fearfulness, and she used to ask me whether the people of my country were as great cowards as myself. The occasion was this: the kingdom is much pestered with flies in summer; and these odious insects, each of them as big as a Dunstable lark, hardly gave me any rest while I sat at dinner. with their continual humming and buzzing about my ears. They would sometimes alight upon my victuals, and leave their loathsome excrement or spawn behind, which to me was very visible, though not to the natives of that country, whose large optics were not so acute as mine in viewing smaller objects. Sometimes they would fix upon my nose or forehead, where they stung me to the quick, smelling very offensively, and I could easily trace that viscous matter, which our naturalists tell us enables those creatures to walk with their feet upwards upon a ceiling. I had much ado to defend myself against these detestable animals, and could not forbear starting when they came on my face. It was the common practice of the dwarf to catch a number of these insects in his hand, as schoolboys do among us, and let them out suddenly under my nose, on purpose to frighten me, and divert the Queen. My remedy was to cut them in pieces with my knife as they flew in the air, wherein my dexterity was much admired.

I remember one morning when Glumdalclitch had set me in my box upon a window, as she usually did in fair days to give me air (for I durst not venture to let the box be hung on a nail out of the window, as we do with cages in England), after I had lifted up one of my sashes, and sat down at my table to eat a piece of sweet cake for my breakfast, above twenty wasps, allured by the smell, came flying into the room, humming louder than the drones of as many bagpipes. Some of them seized my cake, and carried it piecemeal away, others flew about my head and face, confounding me with the noise, and putting me in the utmost terror of their stings. However I had the courage to rise and draw my hanger, and attack them in the air. I dispatched four of them, but the rest got away, and I presently shut my window. These insects were as large as partridges: I took out their stings, found them an inch and a half long, and as sharp as needles. I carefully preserved them all, and having since shown them with some other curiosities in several parts of Europe; upon my return to England I gave three of them to Gresham College, and kept the fourth for myself.

Alexander Pope
(1688-1744)
from *An Essay on Man*

Pope was one of England's great literary craftsmen; he is seldom equalled in clarity and precision. His major works are generally written in heroic couplets, a type of rhymed iambic pentameter. His ideas are not particularly original, but his poems can be described in his own words: "What oft was thought, but ne'er so well expressed." His Essay on Man *shows his confidence in a world in which reason is the answer to all problems.*

TO HENRY ST. JOHN, LORD BOLINGBROKE

Epistle I. Of the Nature and State of Man, With Respect to the Universe

Awake, my St. John! leave all meaner things
To low ambition, and the pride of kings.
Let us (since life can little more supply
Than just to look about us and to die)
Expatiate free o'er all this scene of man;
A mighty maze! but not without a plan;
A wild, where weeds and flowers promiscuous shoot,
Or garden, tempting with forbidden fruit.
Together let us beat this ample field,
Try what the open, what the covert yield;
The latent tracts, the giddy heights, explore
Of all who blindly creep, or sightless soar;
Eye Nature's walks, shoot folly as it flies,
And catch the manners living as they rise;
Laugh where we must, be candid where we can;
But vindicate the ways of God to man.

1. Say first, of God above, or man below,
What can we reason, but from what we know?
Of man, what see we but his station here,
From which to reason, or to which refer?
Through worlds unnumbered though the God be known,
'Tis ours to trace him only in our own.
He, who through vast immensity can pierce,
See worlds on worlds compose one universe,
Observe how system into system runs,
What other planets circle other suns,
What varied Being peoples every star,
May tell why Heaven has made us as we are.
But of this frame the bearings, and the ties,
The strong connections, nice dependencies,
Gradations just, has thy pervading soul
Looked through? or can a part contain the whole?
Is the great chain, that draws all to agree,
And drawn supports, upheld by God, or thee?

2. Presumptuous man! the reason wouldst thou find,

Why formed so weak, so little, and so blind?
First, if thou canst, the harder reason guess,
Why formed no weaker, blinder, and no less!
Ask of thy mother earth, why oaks are made
Taller or stronger than the weeds they shade?
Or ask of yonder argent fields above,
Why Jove's satellites are less than Jove?
   Of systems possible, if 'tis confessed
That Wisdom Infinite must form the best,
Where all must full or not coherent be,
And all that rises, rise in due degree;
Then, in the scale of reasoning life, 'tis plain,
There must be, somewhere, such a rank as man:
And all the question (wrangle e'er so long)
Is only this, if God has placed him wrong?
   Respecting man, whatever wrong we call,
May, must be right, as relative to all.
In human works, though labored on with pain,
A thousand movements scarce one purpose gain;
In God's, one single can its end produce;
Yet serves to second too some other use.
So man, who here seems principal alone,
Perhaps acts second to some sphere unknown,
Touches some wheel, or verges to some goal;
'Tis but a part we see, and not a whole.
   When the proud steed shall know why man restrains
His fiery course, or drives him o'er the plains;
When the dull ox, why now he breaks the clod,
Is now a victim, and now Egypt's god:
Then shall man's pride and dullness comprehend
His actions', passions', being's use and end;
Why doing, suffering, checked, impelled; and why
This hour a slave, the next a deity.
   Then say not man's imperfect, Heaven in fault;
Say rather, man's as perfect as he ought:
His knowledge measured to his state and place
His time a moment, and a point his space.
If to be perfect in a certain sphere,
What matter, soon or late, or here or there?
The blest today is as completely so,
As who began a thousand years ago.

   3. Heaven from all creatures hides the book of Fate,
All but the page prescribed, their present state:
From brutes what men, from men what spirits know:
Or who could suffer Being here below?
The lamb thy riot dooms to bleed today,
Had he thy reason, would he skip and play?
Pleased to the last, he crops the flowery food,
And licks the hand just raised to shed his blood.
O blindness to the future! kindly given,
That each may fill the circle marked by Heaven:
Who sees with equal eye, as God of all,
A hero perish, or a sparrow fall,
Atoms or systems into ruin hurled,
And now a bubble burst, and now a world.
   Hope humbly then; with trembling pinions soar;
Wait the great teacher Death, and God adore!
What future bliss, he gives not thee to know,
But gives that hope to be thy blessing now.
Hope springs eternal in the human breast:
Man never is, but always to be blest:

The soul, uneasy and confined from home,
Rests and expatiates in a life to come.
   Lo! the poor Indian, whose untutored mind
Sees God in clouds, or hears him in the wind;
His soul proud Science never taught to stray
Far as the solar walk, or milky way;
Yet simple Nature to his hope has given,
Behind the cloud-topped hill, an humbler heaven;
Some safer world in depth of woods embraced,
Some happier island in the watery waste,
Where slaves once more their native land behold,
No fiends torment, no Christians thirst for gold!
To be, contents his natural desire,
He asks no angel's wing, no seraph's fire;
But thinks, admitted to that equal sky,
His faithful dog shall bear him company.

   4. Go, wiser thou! and, in thy scale of sense,
Weigh thy opinion against Providence;
Call imperfection what thou fancy'st such,
Say, here he gives too little, there too much;
Destroy all creatures for thy sport or gust,
Yet cry, if man's unhappy, God's unjust;
If man alone engross not Heaven's high care,
Alone made perfect here, immortal there:
Snatch from his hand the balance and the rod,
Rejudge his justice, be the God of God!
In pride, in reasoning pride, our error lies;
All quit their sphere, and rush into the skies.
Pride still is aiming at the blest abodes,
Men would be angels, angels would be gods.
Aspiring to be gods, if angels fell,
Aspiring to be angels, men rebel:
And who but wishes to invert the laws
Of order, sins against the Eternal Cause.

   5. Ask for what end the heavenly bodies shine,
Earth for whose use? Pride answers, " 'Tis for mine:
For me kind Nature wakes her genial power,
Suckles each herb, and spreads out every flower;
Annual for me, the grape, the rose renew
The juice nectareous, and the balmy dew;
For me, the mine a thousand treasures brings;
For me, health gushes from a thousand springs;
Seas roll to waft me, suns to light me rise;
My footstool earth, my canopy the skies."
   But errs not Nature from this gracious end,
From burning suns when livid deaths descend,
When earthquakes swallow, or when tempests sweep
Towns to one grave, whole nations to the deep?
"No," 'tis replied, "the first Almighty Cause
Acts not by partial, but by general laws;
The exceptions few; some change since all began,
And what created perfect?"—Why then man?
If the great end be human happiness,
Then Nature deviates; and can man do less?
As much that end a constant course requires
Of showers and sunshine, as of man's desires;
As much eternal springs and cloudless skies,
As men forever temperate, calm, and wise.
If plagues or earthquakes break not Heaven's design,

Why then a Borgia, or a Catiline?
Who knows but he whose hand the lightning forms,
Who heaves old ocean, and who wings the storms,
Pours fierce ambition in a Caesar's mind,
Or turns young Ammon loose to scourge mankind?
From pride, from pride, our very reasoning springs;
Account for moral, as for natural things:
Why charge we Heaven in those, in these acquit?
In both, to reason right is to submit.
   Better for us, perhaps, it might appear,
Were there all harmony, all virtue here;
That never air or ocean felt the wind;
That never passion discomposed the mind:
But ALL subsists by elemental strife;
And passions are the elements of life.
The general ORDER, since the whole began,
Is kept in Nature, and is kept in man.

   6. What would this man? Now upward will he soar,
And little less than angel, would be more;
Now looking downwards, just as grieved appears
To want the strength of bulls, the fur of bears.
Made for his use all creatures if he call,
Say what their use, had he the powers of all?
Nature to these, without profusion, kind,
The proper organs, proper powers assigned;
Each seeming want compénsated of course,
Here with degrees of swiftness, there of force;
All in exact proportion to the state;
Nothing to add, and nothing to abate.
Each beast, each insect, happy in its own;
Is Heaven unkind to man, and man alone?
Shall he alone, whom rational we call,
Be pleased with nothing, if not blessed with all?
The bliss of man (could pride that blessing find)
Is not to act or think beyond mankind;
No powers of body or of soul to share,
But what his nature and his state can bear.
Why has not man a microscopic eye?
For this plain reason, man is not a fly.
Say what the use, were finer optics given,
To inspect a mite, not comprehend the heaven?
Or touch, if tremblingly alive all o'er,
To smart and agonize at every pore?
Or quick effluvia darting through the brain,
Die of a rose in aromatic pain?
If nature thundered in his opening ears,
And stunned him with the music of the spheres,
How would he wish that Heaven had left him still
The whispering zephyr, and the purling rill?
Who finds not Providence all good and wise,
Alike in what it gives, and what denies?

   7. Far as creation's ample range extends,
The scale of sensual, mental powers ascends:
Mark how it mounts, to man's imperial race,
From the green myriads in the peopled grass:
What modes of sight betwixt each wide extreme,
The mole's dim curtain, and the lynx's beam:
Of smell, the headlong lioness between,
And hound sagacious on the tainted green:
Of hearing, from the life that fills the flood,
To that which warbles through the vernal wood:
The spider's touch, how exquisitely fine!

Feels at each thread, and lives along the line:
In the nice bee, what sense so subtly true
From poisonous herbs extracts the healing dew:
How instinct varies in the groveling swine,
Compared, half-reasoning elephant, with thine!
'Twixt that, and reason, what a nice barrier;
Forever separate, yet forever near!
Remembrance and reflection how allied;
What thin partitions sense from thought divide:
And middle natures, how they long to join,
Yet never pass the insuperable line!
Without this just gradation, could they be
Subjected, these to those, or all to thee?
The powers of all subdued by thee alone,
Is not thy reason all these powers in one?

8. See, through this air, this ocean, and this earth,
All matter quick, and bursting into birth.
Above, how high progressive life may go!
Around, how wide! how deep extend below!
Vast Chain of Being! which from God began,
Natures ethereal, human, angel, man,
Beast, bird, fish, insect, what no eye can see,
No glass can reach! from Infinite to thee,
From thee to nothing.—On superior powers
Were we to press, inferior might on ours:
Or in the full creation leave a void,
Where, one step broken, the great scale's destroyed:
From Nature's chain whatever link you strike,
Tenth or ten thousandth, breaks the chain alike.
And, if each system in gradation roll
Alike essential to the amazing Whole,
The least confusion but in one, not all
That system only, but the Whole must fall.
Let earth unbalanced from her orbit fly,
Planets and suns run lawless through the sky,
Let ruling angels from their spheres be hurled,
Being on being wrecked, and world on world,
Heaven's whole foundations to their center nod,
And Nature tremble to the throne of God:
All this dread ORDER break—for whom? for thee?
Vile worm!—oh, madness, pride, impiety!

9. What if the foot, ordained the dust to tread,
Or hand, to toil, aspired to be the head?
What if the head, the eye, or ear repined
To serve mere engines to the ruling Mind?
Just as absurd for any part to claim
To be another, in this general frame:
Just as absurd, to mourn the tasks or pains,
The great directing MIND of ALL ordains.
  All are but parts of one stupendous whole,
Whose body Nature is, and God the soul;
That, changed through all, and yet in all the same,
Great in the earth, as in the ethereal frame,
Warms in the sun, refreshes in the breeze,
Glows in the stars, and blossoms in the trees,
Lives through all life, extends through all extent,
Spreads undivided, operates unspent,
Breathes in our soul, informs our mortal part,
As full, as perfect, in a hair as heart;
As full, as perfect, in vile man that mourns,
As the rapt seraph that adores and burns;
To him no high, no low, no great, no small;
He fills, he bounds, connects, and equals all.

10. Cease then, nor ORDER imperfection name:
Our proper bliss depends on what we blame.
Know thy own point: this kind, this due degree
Of blindness, weakness, Heaven bestows on thee.
Submit—In this, or any other sphere,
Secure to be as blest as thou canst bear:
Safe in the hand of one disposing Power,
Or in the natal, or the mortal hour.
All Nature is but art, unknown to thee;
All chance, direction, which thou canst not see;
All discord, harmony not understood;
All partial evil, universal good:
And, spite of pride, in erring reason's spite,
One truth is clear: Whatever IS, is RIGHT.

from *Epistle II. Of the Nature and State of Man With Respect to Himself, as an Individual*

1. Know then thyself, presume not God to scan;
The proper study of mankind is Man.
Placed on this isthmus of a middle state,
A being darkly wise, and rudely great:
With too much knowledge for the skeptic side,
With too much weakness for the Stoic's pride,
He hangs between; in doubt to act, or rest,
In doubt to deem himself a god, or beast;
In doubt his mind or body to prefer,
Born but to die, and reasoning but to err;
Alike in ignorance, his reason such,
Whether he thinks too little, or too much:
Chaos of thought and passion, all confused;
Still by himself abused, or disabused;
Created half to rise, and half to fall;
Great lord of all things, yet a prey to all;
Sole judge of truth, in endless error hurled:
The glory, jest, and riddle of the world!

Voltaire
(1694-1778)
from *Candide*

Voltaire (real name, Francois-Marie Arouet) was the foremost figure of the French intellectual-literary world during much of the eighteenth century. He was a successful novelist, essayist, playwright, poet, and writer of epics. As a philosopher, he tended to agree with the principal thinkers of his age that reason could solve most of man's problems, but he refused to succumb to the uncritical and naive optimism of some of his contemporaries.

In Candide, *or* Optimism, *Voltaire satirizes those who feel that "everything is for the best." The title character is a young man who has been reared in the castle of a German Baron. There he has fallen in love with the Baron's daughter, Cunegonde, and has studied philosophy with Pangloss, who "proved admirably that there is no effect without a cause and that in this best of all possible worlds, My Lord the Baron's castle was the best of castles and his wife the best of all possible Baronesses." Candide is expelled from the castle because he is too familiar with Cunegonde. Later, he is forced into the army of the King of Bulgaria, where he suffers greatly; after fleeing the army, he is saved from starvation by Jacques, an Anabaptist. Jacques also saves Pangloss, who has himself suffered greatly. The three then set out by ship on a voyage to Lisbon.*

V

Storm, Shipwreck, Earthquake, and What Happened to Dr. Pangloss, to Candide and the Anabaptist Jacques

Half the enfeebled passengers, suffering from that inconceivable anguish which the rolling of a ship causes in the nerves and in all the humours of bodies shaken in contrary directions, did not retain strength enough even to trouble about the danger. The other half screamed and prayed; the sails were torn, the masts broken, the vessel leaking. Those worked who could, no one cooperated, no one commanded. The Anabaptist tried to help the crew a little; he was on the main-deck; a furious sailor struck him violently and stretched him on the deck; but the blow he delivered gave the sailor so violent a shock that he fell head-first out of the ship. He remained hanging and clinging to part of the broken mast. The good Jacques ran to his aid, helped him to climb back, and from the effort he made was flung into the sea in full view of the sailor, who allowed him to drown without condescending even to look at him. Candide came up, saw his benefactor reappear for a moment and then be engulfed for ever. He tried to throw himself after him into the sea; he was prevented by the philosopher Pangloss, who proved to him that the Lisbon roads had been expressly created for the Anabaptist to be drowned in them. While he was proving this *a priori*, the vessel sank, and every one perished except Pangloss, Candide and the brutal sailor who had drowned the virtuous Anabaptist; the blackguard swam successfully to the shore and Pangloss and Candide were carried there on a plank. When they had recovered a little, they walked toward Lisbon; they had a little money by the help of which they hoped to be saved from hunger after having escaped the storm. Weeping the death of their benefactor, they had scarcely set foot in the town when they felt the earth tremble under their feet; the sea rose in foaming masses in the port and smashed the ships which rode at anchor. Whirlwinds of flame and ashes covered the streets and squares; the houses collapsed, the roofs were thrown upon the foundations, and the foundations were scattered; thirty thousand inhabitants of every age and both sexes were crushed under the ruins. Whistling and swearing, the sailor said: "There'll be something to pick up here." "What can be the sufficient reason for this phenomenon?" said Pangloss. "It is the last day!" cried Candide. The sailor immediately ran among the debris, dared death to find money, found it, seized it, got drunk, and having slept off his wine, purchased the favors of the first woman of good-will he met on the ruins of the houses and among the dead and dying. Pangloss, however, pulled him by the sleeve. "My friend," said he, "this is not well, you are disregarding universal reason, you choose the wrong time." "Blood and 'ounds!" he retorted, "I am a sailor and I was born in Batavia; four times have I stamped on the crucifix during four voyages to Japan; you have found the right man for your universal reason!" Candide had been hurt by some falling stones; he lay in the street covered with debris. He said to Pangloss: "Alas! Get me a little wine and oil; I am dying." "This earthquake is not a new thing," replied Pangloss. "The town of Lima felt the same shocks in America last year; similar causes produce similar effects; there must certainly be a train of sulphur underground from Lima to Lisbon." "Nothing is more probable," replied Candide; "But, for God's sake, a little oil and wine." "What do you mean, probable?" replied the philosopher; "I maintain that it is proved." Candide lost consciousness, and Pangloss brought him a little water from a neighboring fountain. Next day they found a little food as they wandered among the ruins and regained a little strength. Afterwards they worked like others to help the inhabitants who had escaped death. Some citizens they had assisted gave them as good a dinner as could be expected in such a disaster; true, it was a dreary meal; the hosts watered their bread with their tears, but Pangloss consoled them by assuring them that things could not be otherwise. "For," said he, "all this is for the best; for, if there is a volcano at Lisbon, it cannot be anywhere else; for it is impossible that things should not be where they are; for all is well." A little, dark man, a familiar of the Inquisition, who sat beside him, politely took up the conversation, and said: "Apparently, you do not believe in original sin; for, if everything is for the best, there was neither fall nor punishment." "I most humbly beg your excellency's pardon," replied Pangloss still more politely, "for the fall of man and the curse necessarily entered into the best of all possible worlds." "Then you do not believe in free-will?" said the familiar. "Your excellency will pardon me," said Pangloss; "free-will can exist with absolute necessity; for it was necessary that we should be free; for in short, limited will. . ." Pangloss was in the middle of his phrase when the familiar nodded to his armed attendant who was pouring out port or Oporto wine for him.

VI

How a Splendid Auto-da-fé Was Held to Prevent Earthquakes and How Candide Was Flogged

After the earthquake which destroyed three-quarters of Lisbon, the wise men of that country could discover no more efficacious way of preventing a total ruin than by giving the people a splendid *auto-da-fé*. It was decided by the university of Coimbre that the sight of several persons being slowly burned in great ceremony is an infallible secret for preventing earthquakes. Consequently they had arrested a Biscayan convicted of having married his fellow-godmother, and two Portuguese who, when eating a chicken, had thrown away the fat; after dinner they came and bound Dr. Pangloss and his disciple Candide, one because he had spoken and the other because he had listened with an air of approbation; they were both carried separately to extremely cool apartments, where there was never any discomfort from the sun; a week afterwards each was dressed in a sanbenito and their heads were ornamented with paper mitres; Candide's mitre and sanbenito were painted with flames upside down and with devils who had neither tails nor claws; but Pangloss's devils had claws and tails, and his flames were upright. Dressed in this manner they marched in procession and listened to a most pathetic sermon, followed by lovely plain-song music. Candide was flogged in time to the music, while the singing went on; the Biscayan and the two men who had not wanted to eat fat were burned, and Pangloss was hanged, although this is not the custom. The very same day, the earth shook again with a terrible clamor. Candide, terrified, dumbfounded, bewildered, covered with blood, quivering from head to foot, said to himself: "If this is the best of all possible worlds, what are the others? Let it pass that I was flogged, for I was flogged by the Bulgarians, but, O my dear Pangloss! The greatest of philosophers! Must I see you hanged without knowing why! O my dear Anabaptist! The best of men! Was it necessary that you should be drowned in port! O Mademoiselle Cunegonde! The pearl of women! Was it necessary that your belly should be slit!" He was returning, scarcely able to support himself, preached at, flogged, absolved and blessed, when an old woman accosted him and said: "Courage, my son, follow me."

VII

How an Old Woman Took Care of Candide and How He Regained That Which He Loved

Candide did not take courage, but he followed the old woman to a hovel; she gave him a pot of ointment to rub on, and left him food and drink; she pointed out a fairly clean bed; near the bed there was a suit of clothes. "Eat, drink, sleep," said she, "and may our Lady of Atocha, my Lord Saint Anthony of Padua and my Lord Saint James of Compostella take care of you; I shall come back tomorrow." Candide, still amazed by all he had seen, by all he had suffered, and still more by the old woman's charity, tried to kiss her hand. "'Tis not my hand you should kiss," said the old woman, "I shall come back tomorrow. Rub on the ointment, eat and sleep." In spite of all his misfortune, Candide ate and went to sleep. Next day the old woman brought him breakfast, examined his back and smeared him with another ointment; later she brought him dinner, and returned in the evening with supper. The next day she went through the same ceremony. "Who are you?" Candide kept asking her. "Who has inspired you with so much kindness? How can I thank you?" The good woman never made any reply; she returned in the evening but without any supper. "Come with me," said she, "and do not speak a word." She took him by the arm and walked into the country with him for about a quarter of a mile; they came to an isolated house, surrounded with gardens and canals. The old woman knocked at a little door. It was opened; she led Candide up a back stairway into a gilded apartment, left him on a brocaded sofa, shut the door and went away. Candide thought he was dreaming, and felt that his whole life was a bad dream and the present moment an agreeable dream. The old woman soon reappeared; she was supporting with some difficulty a trembling woman of majestic stature, glittering with precious stones and covered with a veil. "Remove the veil," said the old woman to Candide. The young man advanced and lifted the veil with a timid hand. What a moment! What a surprise! He thought he saw Mademoiselle Cunegonde, in fact he was looking at her, it was she herself. His strength failed him, he could not utter a word and fell at her feet. Cunegonde fell on the sofa. The old woman dosed them with distilled waters; they recovered their senses and began to speak: at first they uttered only broken words, questions and answers at cross purposes, sighs, tears, exclamations. The old woman advised them to make less noise and left them alone. "What! Is it you?" said Candide. "You are alive, and I find you here in Portugal! Then you were not raped? Your belly was not slit, as the philosopher Pangloss assured me?" "Yes, indeed," said the fair Cunegonde; "but those two accidents are not always fatal." "But your father and mother were killed?" "'Tis only too true," said Cunegonde, weeping. "And your brother?" "My brother was killed too." "And why are you in Portugal? And how did you know I was here? And by what strange adventure have you brought me to this house?" "I will tell you everything," replied the lady, "but first of all you must tell me everything that has happened to you since the innocent kiss you gave me and the kicks you received." Candide obeyed with profound respect; and, although he was bewildered, although his voice was weak and trembling, although his back was still a little painful, he related in the most natural manner all he had endured since the moment of their separation. Cunegonde raised her eyes to heaven; she shed tears at the death of the good Anabaptist and Pangloss, after which she spoke as follows to Candide, who did not miss a word and devoured her with his eyes.

Candide continues through a series of incredible adventures. He is at times separated from both Cunegonde and Pangloss, who are both presumed dead. Finally he again is reunited with both of his friends. Cunegonde has become old and ugly, but her brother, the Baron, still forbids Candide to marry her.

XXX
Conclusion

At the bottom of his heart Candide had not the least wish to marry Cunegonde. But the Baron's extreme impertinence determined him to complete the marriage, and Cunegonde urged it so warmly that he could not retract. He consulted Pangloss, Martin and the faithful Cacambo. Pangloss wrote an excellent memorandum by which he proved that the Baron had no rights over his sister and that by all the laws of the empire she could make a left-handed marriage with Candide. Martin advised that the Baron should be thrown into the sea; Cacambo decided that he should be returned to the Levantine captain and sent back to the galleys, after which he would be returned by the first ship to the Vicar-General at Rome. This was thought to be very good advice; the old woman approved it; they said nothing to the sister; the plan was carried out with the aid of a little money and they had the pleasure of duping a Jesuit and punishing the pride of a German Baron.

It would be natural to suppose that when, after so many disasters, Candide was married to his mistress, and living with the philosopher Pangloss, the philosopher Martin, the prudent Cacambo and the old woman, having brought back so many diamonds from the country of the ancient Incas, he would lead the most pleasant life imaginable. But he was so cheated by the Jews that he had nothing left but his little farm; his wife, growing uglier every day, became shrewish and unendurable; the old woman was ailing and even more bad-tempered than Cunegonde. Cacambo, who worked in the garden and then went to Constantinople to sell vegetables, was overworked and cursed his fate. Pangloss was in despair because he did not shine in some German university. As for Martin, he was firmly convinced that people are equally uncomfortable everywhere; he accepted things patiently. Candide, Martin and Pangloss sometimes argued about metaphysics and morals. From the windows of the farm they often watched the ships going by, filled with effendis, pashas, and cadis, who were being exiled to Lemnos, to Mitylene and Erzerum. They saw other cadis, other pashas and other effendis coming back to take the place of the exiles and to be exiled in their turn. They saw the neatly impaled heads which were taken to the Sublime Porte. These sights redoubled their discussions; and when they were not arguing, the boredom was so excessive that one day the old woman dared to say to them: "I should like to know which is worse, to be raped a hundred times by Negro pirates, to have a buttock cut off, to run the gauntlet among the Bulgarians, to be whipped and flogged in an *auto-da-fé*, to be dissected, to row in a galley, in short, to endure all the miseries through which we have passed, or to remain here doing nothing?" " 'Tis a great question," said Candide.

These remarks led to new reflections, and Martin especially concluded that man was born to live in the convulsions of distress or in the lethargy of boredom. Candide did not agree, but he asserted nothing. Pangloss confessed that he had always suffered horribly; but, having once maintained that everything was for the best, he had continued to maintain it without believing it.

One thing confirmed Martin in his detestable principles, made Candide hesitate more than ever, and embarrassed Pangloss. And it was this. One day there came to their farm Paquette and Friar Giroflée, who were in the most extreme misery; they had soon wasted their three thousand piastres, had left each other, made up, quarrelled again, been put in prison, escaped, and finally Friar Giroflée had turned Turk. Paquette continued her occupation everywhere and now earned nothing by it. "I foresaw," said Martin to Candide, "that your gifts would soon be wasted and would only make them the more miserable. You and Cacambo were once bloated with millions of piastres and you are no happier than Friar Giroflée and Paquette." "Ah! Ha!" said Pangloss to Paquette, "so Heaven brings you back to us, my dear child? Do you know that you cost me the end of my nose, an eye and an ear! What a plight you are in! Ah! What a world this is!" This new occurrence caused them to philosophize more than ever.

In the neighborhood there lived a very famous Dervish, who was supposed to be the best philosopher in Turkey; they went to consult him; Pangloss was the spokesman and said: "Master, we have come to beg you to tell us why so strange an animal as man was ever created." "What has it to do with you?" said the Dervish. "Is it your business?" "But, reverend father," said Candide, "there is a horrible amount of evil in the world." "What does it matter," said the Dervish, "whether there is evil or good? When his highness sends a ship to Egypt, does he worry about the comfort or discomfort of the rats in the ship?" "Then what should we do?" said Pangloss. "Hold your tongue," said the Dervish. "I flattered myself," said Pangloss, "that I should discuss with you effects and causes, this best of all possible worlds, the origin of evil, the nature of the soul and pre-established harmony." At these words the Dervish slammed the door in their faces.

During this conversation the news went round that at Constantinople two viziers and the mufti had been strangled and several of their friends impaled. This catastrophe made a prodigious noise everywhere for several hours. As Pangloss, Candide and Martin were returning to their little farm, they came upon an old man who was taking the air under a bower of orange-trees at his door. Pangloss, who was as curious as he was argumentative, asked him what was the name of the mufti who had just been strangled. "I do not know," replied the old man. "I have never known the name of any mufti or of any vizier. I am entirely ignorant of the occurrence you mention; I presume that in general those who meddle with public affairs sometimes perish miserably and that they deserve it; but I never inquire what is going on in Constantinople; I content myself with sending there for sale the produce of the garden I cultivate." Having spoken thus, he took the strangers into his house. His two daughters and his two sons presented them with several kinds of sherbet which they made themselves, caymac flavored with candied citron peel, oranges, lemons, limes, pineapples, dates, pistachios and Mocha coffee which had not been mixed with the bad coffee of Batavia and the Isles. After which this good Mussulman's two daughters perfumed the beards of Candide, Pangloss and Martin. "You must have a vast and magnificent estate?" said Candide to the Turk. "I have only twenty acres," replied the Turk. "I cultivate them with my children; and work keeps at bay three great evils: boredom, vice and need."

As Candide returned to his farm he reflected deeply on the Turk's remarks. He said to Pangloss and Martin: "That good old man seems to me to have chosen an existence preferable by far to that of the six kings with whom we had the honor to sup." "Exalted rank," said Pangloss, "is very dangerous, according to the testimony of all philosophers; for Eglon, King of the Moabites, was murdered by Ehud; Absalom was hanged by the hair and pierced by three darts; King Nadab, son of Jeroboam, was killed by Baasha; King Elah by Zimri; Ahaziah by Jehu; Athaliah by Jehoiada; the Kings Jehoiakim, Jeconiah and Zedekiah were made slaves. You know in what manner died Croesus, Astyages, Darius, Denys of Syracuse, Pyrrhus, Perseus, Hannibal, Jugurtha, Ariovistus, Caesar, Pompey, Nero, Otho, Vitellius, Domitian, Richard II of England, Edward II, Henry VI, Richard III, Mary Stuart, Charles I, the three Henrys of France, the Emperor Henry IV. You know . . ." "I also know," said Candide, "that we should cultivate our garden." "You are right," said Pangloss, "for, when man was placed in the Garden of Eden, he was placed there *ut operaretur eum*, to dress it and to keep it; which proves that man was not born for idleness." "Let us work without theorizing," said Martin; "'tis the only way to make life endurable."

The whole small fraternity entered into this praiseworthy plan, and each started to make use of his talents. The little farm yielded well. Cunegonde was indeed very ugly, but she became an excellent pastry-cook; Paquette embroidered; the old woman took care of the linen. Even Friar Giroflée performed some service; he was a very good carpenter and even became a man of honor; and Pangloss sometimes said to Candide: "All events are linked up in this best of all possible worlds; for, if you had not been expelled from the noble castle, by hard kicks in your backside for love of Mademoiselle Cunegonde, if you had not been clapped into the Inquisition, if you had not wandered about America on foot, if you had not stuck your sword in the Baron, if you had not lost all your sheep from the land of Eldorado, you would not be eating candied citrons and pistachios here." "That's well said," replied Candide, "but we must cultivate our garden."

Robert Herrick
(1591-1678)
To Daffodils

Fair daffodils, we weep to see
    You haste away so soon;
As yet the early-rising sun
    Has not attained his noon.
      Stay, stay,
    Until the hasting day
      Has run
    But to the even-song;
And, having prayed together, we
    Will go with you along.

We have short time to stay, as you;
    We have as short a spring;
As quick a growth to meet decay,
    As you, or any thing.
      We die,
    As your hours do, and dry
      Away
    Like to the summer's rain;
Or as the pearls of morning's dew,
    Ne'er to be found again.

Corinna's Going A-Maying

Get up, get up, for shame, the blooming
    morn
Upon her wings presents the god unshorn.
    See how Aurora throws her fair
    Fresh-quilted colors through the air!
    Get up, sweet slug-a-bed, and see
    The dew bespangling herb and tree.
Each flower has wept, and bowed toward
    the East,
Above an hour since; yet you not dressed,
    Nay! not so much as out of bed?
    When all the birds have matins said,
    And sung their thankful hymns, 'tis sin,
    Nay, profanation to keep in;
Whenas a thousand virgins on this day
Spring, sooner than the lark, to fetch in
    May.

Rise, and put on your foilage, and be seen
To come forth, like the spring-time, fresh
    and green
    And sweet as Flora. Take no care
    For jewels for your gown, or hair;
    Fear not, the leaves will strew
    Gems in abundance upon you;
Besides, the childhood of the day has kept,
Against you come, some orient pearls un-
    wept;
    Come, and receive them while the light
    Hangs on the dew-locks of the night:
    And Titan on the eastern hill
    Retires himself, or else stands still
Till you come forth. Wash, dress, be brief
    in praying:
Few beads are best, when once we go a-
    maying.

Come, my Corinna, come; and, coming,
    mark
How each field turns a street, each street
    a park
    Made green, and trimmed with trees;
    see how
    Devotion gives each house a bough,
    Or branch; each porch, each door, ere
    this,
    An ark, a tabernacle is,
Made up of white-thorn neatly interwove;
As if here were those cooler shades of love.
    Can such delights be in the street,
    And open fields, and we not see't?
    Come, we'll abroad; and let's obey
    The proclamation made for May:
And sin no more, as we have done, by
    staying;
But, my Corinna, come, let's go a-maying.

There's not a budding boy or girl this day
But is got up, and gone to bring in May.
    A deal of youth, ere this, is come
    Back, and with white-thorn laden home.
    Some have dispatched their cakes and
    cream,
    Before that we have left to dream;
And some have wept, and wooed, and
    plighted troth,
And chose their priest, ere we can cast off
    sloth.
    Many a green-gown has been given;
    Many a kiss, both odd and even:
    Many a glance too has been sent
    From out the eye, love's firmament;
Many a jest told of the keys betraying
This night, and locks picked, yet we're not
    a-maying.

Come, let us go, while we are in our prime,
And take the harmless folly of the time.
    We shall grow old apace and die
    Before we know our liberty.
    Our life is short, and our days run
    As fast away as does the sun;
And as a vapor, or a drop of rain,
Once lost, can ne'er be found again:
    So when or you or I are made
    A fable, song, or fleeting shade,
    All love, all liking, all delight
    Lies drowned with us in endless night.
Then while time serves, and we are but
    decaying,
Come, my Corinna, come, let's go a-maying.

Gladys Schmitt
(1909-   )
The Syndics
from *Rembrandt*

Gladys Schmitt's long and excellent biographical novel Rembrandt *traces the career of the master painter from his boyhood in Leyden to his peaceful death, after years of triumph and of personal and professional tragedy, in Amsterdam. The novel recounts the circumstances in which many of the painter's astonishing number of masterpieces were created—among them* The Anatomy Lesson, Aristotle Contemplating a Bust of Homer, *and—in a period of relative serenity in his later years—the group picture called* The Syndics.

The door moved slowly inwards, and the presence on the threshold was such that he wondered whether it was really there, whether he had not called it up out of some forgotten corridor of his past. The intruder was a small man, dressed as impeccably as Master van Swanenburgh used to dress to pay a formal visit: black beaver, black velvet jacket and breeches, black shoes with silver buckles, black gloves, and a large white linen collar so stiffly starched and impressive that it looked for an instant like the outmoded ruff. And—pink, fresh, almost infantine against all this blackness and whiteness—the Dutch face showed between the dip of the beaver and the rise of the collar, a singularly guileless and puzzled face made softer by reddish curls threaded with white and flecked with melting snow. "Excuse me," said the stranger in a gentle tenor voice, "but is this the warehouse of Vrouw Anna Weijmar Six?"

"Yes, it is." Since the small and inoffensive apparition apparently wanted no dealings with him, had obviously only come from Jan's mother on some errand in connection with the property, he did not bother to put down the scrubbing brush or get up off his knees.

"Good. They told me over on the Rozengracht that this is the place where I can find Master Rembrandt van Rijn as if he were in some cupboard or in the antechamber with the water barrel, and would come out now, washed and brushed and in the clothing of a gentleman."

"I'm van Rijn," he said, letting the brush slide into the bucket and shaking the grey and soapy drippings from his fingers.

For an instant the pink face puckered in childlike surprise: little dents appeared where another man would have had wrinkles, in the fresh cheeks and between the sandy eyebrows. Then he subsided into immediate self-possession, as if he had seen stranger things in his fifty-odd years. The corners of his mouth moved in a cordial smile, and he stripped off his glove and held out his small well-fleshed hand to shake hands formally and—most informally—to help the man who was squatting before him to his feet. "I don't mind the wetness, it's only a little soapy water after all," he said, insisting on the contact with a kind of warm authority. "It's a great honor to make your acquaintance, Master. I'm Duart Simonszoon van Hudde, the treasurer of the Syndics of the Drapers' Guild. I hope you'll excuse me for coming over here at this hour—your good wife seemed disturbed about it and did everything she could to put me off—but there's a meeting of the Syndics tomorrow, and I *did* want to settle my business with you tonight."

But what business could the man have with him—this impeccable little burgher who held the purse strings of the oldest and most respected merchants' guild in Holland? He stared at him and said nothing, the eyes of the newcomer—of an indefinite color, neither blue nor brown nor grey—gazed back at him shyly but without embarrassment. "Don't you want to dry your hands, Heer van Rijn?" he said after a long but unstressful silence. "They'll chap and crack, and that's unpleasant for anybody, and especially so for a painter, I would think."

He bowed and went into the antechamber and plunged his arms into the icy water in the storage barrel and dried himself carefully. Peculiar as the whole incident was, he would have been scarcely more surprised to find the caller vanished when he came back than he was to see him sitting at his ease on one of the high paint-spattered stools, with his heels on the topmost rung and his hands curled around his knees. "It's a long way from the Rozengracht, and I sat down without begging your leave," he said, "Won't you sit down too? I'm here on behalf of the other four Syndics of the Cloth Hall, to talk over the possibility of your doing something for us—a commission, you know, a Regents' piece."

He stopped in the act of pulling up another stool—stopped and straightened to his full height, his cheeks turning hot and the old wild pulse of rage and shame hammering in his chest. Then the fellow *had* come from the house of Six: they had been up to their old scheming in his favor, and this Duart Simonszoon van Hudde had stepped out of the snowy night to bring him the sop that was to soothe him in his disgrace. He wheeled around and glared at the visitor. "Who sent you?" he said.

"Who sent me? Why, I suppose you could say the Syndics of the Cloth Hall sent me, though, to tell you the truth, I made the choice by myself—"

"Not Jan Six? Not Anna Weijmar Six?"

"The young Burgomaster? His mother?" The whole rosy face was broken up with little depressions of confusion. "Unfortunately, I can't claim the honor of counting either of them among my acquaintances. That's the trouble with being a member of the Board of Syndics. We work so hard at it, Heer van Rijn, that there's not much time left for meeting the people we'd like to meet."

"Am I to understand you came to offer me a commission?"

"Yes, with certain reservations. But then, by the time a man comes to our age, he takes it for granted that everything comes with certain reservations—isn't that so?"

He looked up so eagerly, he smiled with such a strange mingling of resignation and cheerfulness that it was impossible not to nod back at him. "So the Six family didn't send you? You don't know them?" he said.

"Why, no, nobody sent me—nobody but the Syndics of the Cloth Hall, and as I said a moment ago, they left the matter pretty much to me. I suppose it's because I own a few things—a Hals, a Seghers, a Brouwer—that they do me the honor of considering me an expert. And though it's nothing to boast of, I do know a little more about it than the other four. Look, my friend"—his tenor voice took on a sudden reedy tone of concern—"won't you please sit down? You've been doing manual labor here, your wife says you've been ill, and I'm sure you must be very tired."

Tired he was, so tired that his heart, once he was settled face to face with his visitor, left off pounding and moved as weakly as a dying fish. Over its irregular movements he heard the visitor talking; through the mist that the paroxysm and its aftermath had put before his eyes he saw the candid face. Nobody had sent the treasurer of the Syndics of the Cloth Hall. The said treasurer, charged by his fellow Board members to find the proper painter for their Regents' piece, had gone about the business with the same uncompromising thoroughness and inviolable honesty that had made the woolens of Amsterdam the most faultless item on the European market for the last hundred years. He had made a list of all the notable painters in the city and had gone from one Guild Hall and charitable institution and private house to another, examining and evaluating their productions. It had been an education, Heer van Rijn, a real education. Some whom he had thought of as minor painters had risen markedly in his esteem, and some whom he had approached with the highest hopes had turned out to be downright trivial. And now that *that* part of the business was over—to tell the truth, he had come to his decision some time ago and had gone on only to satisfy his conscience—he knew that the one painter who could handle the commission properly was Rembrandt van Rijn. If it had been possible for the Syndics to call back the great Dürer from the dead, they could not hope to get a better product than they would get right here—he bent forward, too earnest to smile, and laid his hand briefly on the stained and icy hand.

"Thank you, Heer van Hudde," he said; and realizing that his unbelief had made the thanks sound cold, he added, "Those are kind words, and I stand in need of a few kind words these days."

"We hope, then, Master, that you'll consider the commission—"

"*You're* the one to do the considering, Heer van Hudde. I couldn't say I've given much satisfaction with such commissions in the past. Plenty of bad blood came out of what I did for Banning Coq, God rest his soul, and the *Anatomy Lesson of Doctor Deijman* pleased nobody very much, and this last one they'll not be hanging up again—that lunette I did for the City Hall."

"No?" said the visitor, shaking his head and pursing his mild pink mouth and making a clucking sound. "But aren't they *dreadful?*—the pictures that are up there for good, I mean. So blown-up, so false, if you'll excuse my saying so. My, my, if poor Seghers could see what they've got up there he'd turn over in his grave."

That speech, delivered without malice in the quiet tenor, had an unmanning effect upon him. It was as if some hidden spring of life within him, long sealed over with ice, had suddenly been released to well up and infused his weary body with some freshening essence, to fill his aching eyes with tears. "I don't paint like that. I paint what I see, not something that people believe they ought to see," he said.

"I know it, my dear friend, I know it." The small and rosy hand, as undeliberate as a child's, reached out again and patted him on the wrist. "That's why the other four agreed with me that you're the one we should get. And now"—he took a piece of paper out of his pocket, unfolded it, and spread it on his knee—"now shall we go through this list of what I referred to earlier as the reservations?"

There was a change in him then: it was as if he had assumed the tasseled mortarboard of the professor. He took a stub of crayon out of his pocket and held it poised between thumb and finger; and it was plain that he was a man about to speak in his official capacity, but his authority was so old and well worn and sat so comfortably upon him that it could not give offense. "First of all, let's consider the kind of painting that our members want," he said. "We're an ancient guild, Heer van Rijn, and all five of us feel that any painting for the Guild Hall should be—well, why mince words?—a little old-fashioned. Innovations such as you introduced, and perfectly properly I'm sure, in the lunette for the City Hall are very interesting, but in our particular case they won't do. Close up or far away—wherever the viewer stands—a table must look like a table, an account book like an account book, a moneybag like a moneybag. I've not the slightest doubt that you can do what's required; any number of your paintings prove it. But the question is: Would you *want* to do it that way? That's something we'd better settle from the start."

He should have bridled, he should have said that the painter's concept of his subject was inalienably his own affair; and why he continued to sit courteously listening he did not know. Was it because he was too weary, body and soul, to assert his rights? Was it because the little treasurer saw nothing preposterous in his request and would have been amazed to learn that he had overstepped himself? Or was it that the fresh and blameless face before him, precluding visionary fantasy, could be painted only with directness and truth? "I would give you recognizable objects and good likenesses, worked up to the smallest detail," he said at last.

"Good!" He uttered it with real satisfaction, checked off the first item on his list with his stub of crayon, and smiled an open and gratified smile. "Now, as to what we would like to have brought out—if such things ever *can* be brought out—it's not so much our dignity as our honesty. The one thing you can say of the five of us is that our honesty has never been called into question. We examine and classify and stamp every bolt of cloth that comes off the looms in this city, and we have never—it may seem a small matter to you, but it's everything to us—let one flawed yard of goods go through our hands. We don't expect you to make us handsome or intelligent or aristocratic. Honest and conscientious—that's what we've been in our duties, and that's what we mean to be until we die, and that's what we want to look like when we're hung up in the Cloth Hall."

He did not speak, he only nodded, trying to envision the group—five men who could say of themselves that the creeping corruption of the times had not tainted them, that in their calling they had never lied to themselves or among themselves or to the buyers on the market—it was an assembly he wanted to see.

The visitor nodded too and made another check mark on his list. Then he lifted his face, which had grown even more schoolmasterly, and fixed the painter with his steady, earnest eyes. "And now, third and last—except, of course, for the monetary terms—there's this business of giving every one of the sitters his just due. That's very important. I wouldn't want to make a final commitment until we had come to an understanding about that," he said. "Far be it from me to criticize the very important canvas you did for the late lamented Captain Banning Coq—as a pure piece of painting, it's as fine as any in Holland, I have no doubt. But if certain members of that Company had their complaints, I must say I can't really blame them. A few of the faces are cut up by intervening objects and others are lost in shadows. They'd naturally feel cheated and a little ridiculous, though I'm certain that wasn't your intention. No doubt you were carried away by the enthusiasm of youth—a tendency we won't have to reckon with here, the more's the pity: you and I are both beyond such transports now. There are to be six sitters in our Regents' piece: five Syndics and our loyal servant who has been with us over twenty years and deserves to be memorialized as much as we do. And every one of the six must be a finished portrait, each man getting what he deserves and no man profiting by the suppression of any of the rest."

It must have been taxing for him to deliver himself of all that: he had wrinkled his paper by pressing his elbow nervously down on it. It was hard, too, to answer him, to ask without implications of scorn or anger—for which there was really no cause—"What do you want, then, Heer van Hudde? Five Syndics and a servant all sitting in one long row?"

"Oh, no, certainly not, Heer van Rijn. You only say that because you're worn out with your sickness and aren't drawing on your remarkable imagination. Arrange us any way you like—some sitting, some standing—anything you want. One could be speaking and one could be thinking and another could be listening—but why should I say such things to *you*? Come down to the Cloth Hall—we'd like you to paint us in the room we meet in—come down and have a look at us and move us around as you please. I'm sure you'll find an arrangement that will be completely satisfactory to all parties concerned; there must be dozens of possibilities."

He had never been inside the Cloth Hall, though the fame of its integrity had brought many to visit it from England and Denmark and Poland and Germany and France. He would go tomorrow or the day after—with trimmed hair and a shaven face and in decent clothes, so that Heer Duart Simonszoon van Hudde would not think he was always as slovenly as he was tonight. "I won't do it like the one of the Military Guild," he said. "You're quite right—some of the men *did* have reason to complain about what I did to them." And though he had uttered it with difficulty, it was as if some long illness passed miraculously from him as he spoke.

"You'll consider it, then, in spite of the reservations?" He checked the last item off, folded up the paper, and returned it to his pocket.

"Yes, definitely." He sighed and straightened on his stool and became aware of the room again: the half-scrubbed floor, the steady flame of the lamp, the snow piled up outside so that a thin, uneven band of it showed at the bottom of the black windowpane.

"It's an honorable commission, Heer van Rijn, even if I say so myself, and I'm happy to be able to offer you a solid and equitable price. Each of the Syndics is prepared to put down two hundred florins, and an additional two hundred for the portrait of our good servingman will be provided by the president and the secretary and myself. That's twelve hundred in all—will that be satisfactory?"

"Entirely satisfactory, Heer van Hudde."

"Well, good, then; very good!" said the little visitor, sliding down from his stool, his broad face dimpled all over with the dents of his gratification. "We'll be expecting you to call on us at the Cloth Hall one of these days. Not that there's any hurry. Eager as we are, I'd rather see you stay at home until you're quite yourself again. And, if I may say so, I wouldn't stay here much longer without a fire if I were you. You've got a long walk ahead of you, and the sooner you're to bed the better. There's no use trying to tell you how delighted I am that we've come to an agreement—I only hope you know."

The small figure was over the threshold, moving off in a swirl of big flakes, before Rembrandt realized that there was a way to exchange kindness for kindness, to make some return for the faith that had survived the twists and turns of fashion, to let some of the clean waters that had welled up in him at the touch of this stranger flow out of his closed spirit into the world. "Heer van Hudde, Heer van Hudde," he shouted, running out after him into the soft, agitated whiteness. "Wait a moment—there was something I wanted to say—" The treasurer of the Syndics of the Cloth Hall stopped short while the flakes gathered on his beaver and the fine velvet in which he had dressed himself to pay a formal call on the Master Rembrandt van Rijn. "You said it would be twelve hundred florins—let it be a thousand," the master said.

"A thousand? Why a thousand?"

"Because the portrait of your servingman—*I* would like to make a gift of that to him and to the Drapers' Guild and to you."

For an instant he was afraid that the purity of their exchange would be shattered by some protest, but no protest came. The small mouth opened, closed, and shaped itself into a smile. "Well, now, that's very generous of you, very generous indeed," he said; and the light touch that he laid upon the bare chapped arm before he went his way was as giving and as satisfying as an embrace.

The board had been spread in the meeting chamber of the Syndics of the Cloth Hall, and the candles had been lighted,

REMBRANDT: *Young Girl at an Open Half Door*, THE ART INSTITUTE OF CHICAGO, CHICAGO even though the golden midsummer sunlight still lay in squares on the good china plates and the crystal goblets, on the beautiful wainscoting and the pale wall above it, and on the finished picture which hung on that wall, itself a source of light. Summer—ripe, peaceful summer—would bloom in it forever: so he thought as he saw it from the threshold, saw the white and black and cream and scarlet of it across the festal table. He stood there, decent in the grey jacket and breeches that Hendrikje had insisted he buy for the occasion, unnoticed by the loyal servant of twenty years' service who was laying pears and peaches on the boxwood garland in the middle of the board; he stood there and thanked God—listening or unlistening—that such a blasted tree, beaten by so many storms and rooted in such inhospitable soil, should have borne such fruit. Nothing as radiant and whole and true had ever before issued from him. He hoped that they also would know it, the five who were to sit with him at this little supper which, in their courteous fashion, they had arranged to celebrate the consummation of his eight months of labor. But whether they knew it or not was a secondary consideration: God and the great dead against whom he had measured himself all his days would know if He or they knew anything; and, furthermore, he knew it himself.

The frame of the picture—they had ordered it without thought of cost from the best framemaker in the city—put a gilded but simple boundary around the best of his works and the best that a man could hope to find on earth. The light of the liberal sun fell on the six faces and merged there with the inner light of the human spirit unclouded by compromise, glowing in ripe serenity. The black velvet, the black beaver hats, the fine scarlet and gold of the Oriental carpet that covered the table at which they sat, the ancient wood of the wainscoting behind them, the account book and the moneybag they touched with their seasoned and eloquent hands—all these, carefully as he had wrought them, were mere accessories to the faces; and the faces, varied as they were and perfect likenesses, were subordinate to the ultimate intention: the light of Man shining in the light of the world. He looked his fill and then cleared his throat to make his presence known to the servant, who had laid the last yellow pear in the waxy green of the boxwood. "Oh, your honor, I hadn't seen you," he said, straightening and smiling and glancing at the picture. "It does look fine, doesn't it? It's almost as if there were two of me. And now, before the others come, may I thank your honor for the portrait? Wonderful as it is in itself—and I've never seen anything like it—it's still more wonderful because of your honor's generosity."

The best he could do in return for that was to bring himself to look cordially at the well-known face: the merry mouth, the lineless cheeks, the gentle eyes, the balding brow. "The table looks very festive—very elegant," he said.

"Thank you. I'm glad your honor thinks so. The extra place is for a friend of your honor's, the Burgomaster Tulp. Heer van Hudde thought you might find it pleasant to have him here, since he was the subject of your first Regents' piece and has known your honor for so many years."

"That was very kind of Heer van Hudde," he said, feeling the easy tears filming his eyes and doing his best to keep them out of his voice. The celebratory supper, the elaborate garland on the table, the beautiful frame, even the fact that the other pictures had been removed for this one evening so that nothing would draw attention from his masterpiece—all these, gracious as they were, were formal courtesies. But that the treasurer of the Syndics should have thought of inviting his old friend to share the occasion—this surpassed graciousness, this came from the heart.

"Your honor will sit here at the head," said the servant. "Heer van Hudde, because it was he who arranged this happy business, will sit at your left; and Burgomaster Tulp, as the guest of the Syndics, will sit at your right. Wait—I think I hear them coming. I believe the gentlemen would like your honor to stand over there, a little to one side of the picture. They'll want to shake your hand and thank you separately before you all sit down to supper, you know."

He had not known it, nor was he prepared for the grave procedure that followed. Each one of the Syndics, dressed in the formal clothes in which he had been painted, stepped in by himself, paused just this side of the threshold, and looked up at the painting solemnly and with complete attention, as if he had never laid eyes on it before. The second waited outside the room until the first had come at an unhurried pace across the broad carpet, to take the master's hand and express his gratification and move on to his appointed place at the board in the mingled sun and candlelight. It was a ritual so perfectly planned that his own awkwardness could not mar it: it overrode whatever rigid and insufficient things he said in response to their varied compliments; and it reached its consummation with the last of the line, when the good doctor came in and kissed his cheek and held him in his arms as he had done in Hendrik Uylenburgh's shop thirty years ago.

Once they were seated and grace had been said, the atmosphere was lightened by a fine flurry of unfolding napkins; and while the servant poured out the excellent white wine, everybody began to jest about what they should toast. Their beavers, said the secretary; plainly their beavers were the most significant part of the picture for the master, since he had repainted them nine or ten times. The president proposed his own eyebrows because they, too, had given no end of trouble, but then withdrew his suggestion in favor of Heer van Hudde's hand, which had grown stiff with holding the moneybag a dozen unsatisfactory ways. There was a warmth in all that jesting which told him they looked back on the long sessions of sitting—the puttings on and the scrapings off, the tag-ends of time when they had hurried away from a completed piece of Guild business to slip into the chairs he had set for them the days when the sun had stubbornly refused to shine for him—as the stuff of happy memory. And lest he should be taking their harmless levity ill—he had not been able to call up one feeble sally to add to theirs—the president rapped his plate with his knife, rose and lifted his goblet, and said in a voice quavering partly with age and partly with feeling: "To the brush of Rembrandt van Rijn, which he does not dip into paint like other masters, but into the light of God's pure sun."

As the brightness at the windows faded and the quiet shining of the candles intensified, the servant brought in the great tureen of soup and ladled it out and set it still steaming before them—a rich and creamy whiteness dappled with bits of melted butter and broken here and there by the tender green of summer leeks. They ate with seemly slowness, talking of this and that: of the boy Prince Willem and his mother and the great Pensionary de Witte, who was gathering more power into his hands than any citizen since Oldenbarneveldt, of French Belligerence and Flemish complacency, of the fate of the settlers who might be left to their own devices if the great land was lost in the West, and of the hazards of the merchant vessels moving across the northern and the eastern seas. But whatever they talked of, they returned unfailingly to the business of the evening, to the canvas that shone scarcely less now that the light of day was withdrawn and it was left to shine with its own light. "The pages of the account book are so real that you can hear them crack and rustle," said the vice-president. "The scarlet in the carpet burns like a fire," said the secretary. "I pity poor Heer van Hudde," said the president. "Here we are, saying it all beforehand, and poor Heer van Hudde is the one who has to make a speech."

Little was expected of the guest of honor. They were so at ease with him and each other that he had to furnish nothing but a "Thank you" and a nod and a smile. Now that the windows were darkened, he was more aware of the city than he had been when he was only able to see the roofs and canals and sycamores and poplars which had become so familiar to him over the eight months he had sketched and painted: out there lay Amsterdam, where the names of Lievens and von Sandrart and Juriaen Ovens meant more than his—it was only in this one small chamber that he was the painter of painters, the peer of Dürer and Titian and Michelangelo. But it was a serenely melancholy thought rather than a bitter one; the worst it could do to him was to make way for the remembrance of another celebratory evening, when Hendrik Uylenburgh had made a foolish speech and the dead beloved had come to stand beside him and watch the sun go down, her face and hair on fire with molten gold. What had he hoped for then? More than he had gotten? No, it was only that what he had gotten was more exalted and more terrible, different only as that which was wrought by destiny or the hand of God was different from what men, poor artificers that they were, fashioned vainly and shallowly in their waking dreams. For one generation gave way to another, and the nations coalesced and drifted apart like bits of light on a wind-troubled pool, and only one who was blind in his vanity would presume to say what tomorrow would bring. But tonight was tonight, and the picture hung on the wall gloriously completed, and Heer van Hudde was tapping on his goblet and getting up to make a speech, partly from carefully written notes, but mostly from the heart.

"Great and beloved Master, dear and respected Burgomaster and Physician, good friends who have had an equal share with me in this happy enterprise, I promise to speak briefly, but I pray God I may speak sufficiently," he said. "They say that the time of miracles is past, and yet it seems to me that what we celebrate here tonight is a kind of secular miracle, a blessing given to us in spite of so many possibilities to the contrary that we ought to bow our heads and offer thanks with all our hearts. We have our Regents' piece, our incomparable Regents' piece, but we must not take such a rare thing for granted. Think for a minute how much might have stood in the way of it, and it may seem to some of you as it seems to me: that there is a Providence that concerns itself with such things. Heer van Rijn might not have lived to be called to our service—I know that he was one of the numerous family and that all the other issue of his mother and father are now with God. Any one of us might have had his reasons for turning me away when I came to offer him the commission. Good friends, when you come to think of it, what might *not* have happened? The full brightness of the sun might never have shone on that gold and scarlet carpet on our table; we might, like many other guilds, have ripped out our fine old wainscoting and replaced it with plaster ten years ago; our good and loyal servant might have been so burdened with private cares that he would have been unable to smile; those troublesome beavers of ours might never have been arranged to the master's satisfaction—and any one of these possibilities would have been enough to diminish the unique treasure which hangs, to our honor and for the preservation of our memory, finished and safe on that wall. Vision itself is vulnerable, and Heer van Rijn has eyes to paint and we have eyes to see. For all these reasons, and many more, I offer thanks to that Providence which works its miracles quietly in spite of a thousand possibilities that stand against them, but in thanking Providence I do not in the least stint my thanks to our honored master here. I say to him now what I said to him on our first meeting: we could not have been better served if the great Dürer himself had risen from the dead to paint us. And to our thanks will be added those of our children who will see us living here when we live no more, and the gratefulness of generations who will look at us when we are long since forgotten, and think that man is good and life is worthy, even if there is much of it that lies in the dark. Dr. Tulp, old friends and fellow Syndics—yes, and you, too, Mathias, put down the tureen and join us in this: I give you, by the grace of Providence, Heer Rembrandt van Rijn."

ROMANTICISM

JOHN CONSTABLE: *Wivenhoe Park, Essex*, WIDENER COLLECTION, NATIONAL GALLERY OF ART, WASHINGTON, D. C.

ROMANTICISM

The designation *Romantic Period* applies to the particular spirit that developed in the later eighteenth and nineteenth centuries as a result of an intellectual and artistic revolt against the formal rigidity of neoclassicism. As mentioned earlier, romanticism appears in classical and medieval literature. But the romanticism that evidenced itself in Europe and America was a full-blown counterattack against neoclassicism.

Revolution

With more and more land coming under cultivation and the population growing, society was changing. The Industrial Revolution was making inroads on ways of life that had long been accepted. Quiet villages were being replaced by towns that were strategically located around factories. Machines began to put many men out of work. The wealthy were not too affected, but the poor were suffering. It was only natural that the oppressed as well as the thinking man became concerned with the "rights of man" in general. The focus had changed.

Early romanticism reflected this change. It was characterized by a strong belief in the value of the individual, an intense interest in and communion with nature, and a concern for the organic forms of art. The early period is usually thought of as extending from sporadic writings of the 1720s and on to the great flowering of romanticism from 1789 through 1832.

The influence of the Victorian Era tempered the later romanticism. Men were feeling the impact of the Industrial Revolution. Romanticism conflicted with the reality in the world around it; this conflict showed in the arts. Most intelligent men were aware of the suffering of the masses and were disturbed by it. Steam power, long hours of labor, starving workers, the growth of democracy, franchise, education—all led to extremes in the literary temperament.

Much of this unrest and dissatisfaction had spurred the American and French revolutions, promoted democratic movements in Greece and Italy, and prompted the establishment of constitutional government in Russia and nationalism in Germany.

The Romantic Spirit

Since there are many qualities that comprise romanticism, there is no easy way to label or define it. Romanticism is a mood, a spirit. As with other cultural influences, romanticism reflects the milieu from which it arises. There are, however, certain qualities that help to classify it. A brief description follows.

The romantic spirit is first of all a reaction against the formalism and impersonality of classicism. It values spontaneity, intuition, and emotion more than reason. Love serves a primary role in romantic literature, as do the concepts of individual liberty, democracy, and nationalism. The common man is extolled, the man of nature with his simplicity and virtues. The romanticist enjoys the remote and exotic; he particularly finds expression and escape in the "good old days," be they medieval times or a period some fifty years ago. The fanciful and supernatural also provide inspiration. Romantic writers lean toward a use of natural diction; style is diversified and suited to the mood.

Nature plays another primary role in romanticism. Inspiration lies in her streams and woods; her moods reflect the moods of man. God is found in nature. And, finally, romanticism believes in the potential divinity that lies in one's self. Man has the capability to accomplish anything. Ideals and imagination are important; from them the rest will follow.

Literature

The literature of romanticism is varied and represents many of the qualities previously discussed. For example, an early essay by Rousseau (*Confessions 1749*) says that man is by nature good and innocent and that he is only corrupted by the social institutions around him. Heine's interest centers on the revival of medievalism. Hugo exalts the artist who is free from restraint. Goethe's *Faust*, a tragic drama, shows the world and the universe to be a dynamic force, not a static entity. And from Russia, Pushkin's verse novel *Eugene Onegin* demonstrates well the move to romanticism which extended from the Continent outward.

In England early writers such as Gray and Thomson regret the passing of village life and exult in nature. Burns and Wordsworth reflect the use of common diction and the inspiration of nature, among other romantic elements. Coleridge's "Kubla Khan" and Keats' "La Belle Dame Sans Mercy" represent the exotic and medieval. And Browning's "The Bishop Orders His Tomb" exemplifies the movement toward reality. He viewed people as they were, yet expressed an optimistic hope for them. Many later English romantics move from romanticism to a form of realism as they attempt to cope with their changing world.

Romanticism flowered in American literature too, especially between 1830 and 1865. Writers such as Bryant, Poe, Hawthorne, and Whitman, to list just a few, wrote in the strong romantic spirit. And Emerson's belief in the individual and his highly quotable writing have long made him a favorite. Writers now had something they had never had before, an ever expanding reading public. Works were read and discussed; and besides this, there were many different kinds of reading material. Periodicals, novels, and the short story broadened the audience appeal of literature. The romantic age was a prolific writing period.

The problem of coping with the "ideal" and the "real" occupied more and more attention as men recognized the disparity between the present and what they hoped it would be. Darwin's *Origin of the Species* broke many long-held patterns of thought. The perceptive writer's eye was forced to closer and more realistic representation of the here and now. This reaction took several interesting forms which will be considered in the next section "Realism and Impressionism."

JEAN LOUIS ANDRÉ THÉODORE GÉRICAULT: *Officer of the Imperial Guard*, PHOTO DES MUSÉES NATIONAUX, LOUVRE

CONTINENTAL

Heinrich Heine
(1799-1856)
Du Bist wie eine Blume

E'en as a lovely flower,
   So fair, so pure thou art;
I gaze on thee, and sadness
   Comes stealing o'er my heart.

My hands I fain had folded
   Upon thy soft brown hair,
Praying that God may keep thee
   So lovely, pure and fair.

(Translated by Kate Freiligrath Kroeker)

The Two Grenadiers

Toward France there traveled two grenadiers,
   Their Russian captivity leaving;
As through the German camp slowly they drew,
   Their heads were bowed down with grieving.

For there first they heard of a sorrowful tale;
   Disaster their country had shaken.
The army so brave had borne rout and defeat,
   And the Emperor, the Emperor was taken.

Then sorrowed together the Grenadiers,
   Such doleful news to be learning;
And one spoke out amidst his tears:
   "My wounds once again are burning."

The other spoke: "The song is done;
   Would that I too were dying.
Yet I have wife and child at home,
   On me for bread relying."

"Nor wife nor child give care to me.
   What matter if they are forsaken?
Let them beg their food, if they hungry be;
   My Emperor, my Emperor is taken!

"Oh, grant a last request to me,
    If here my life be over:
Then take thou my body to France with thee,
    No soil but of France my cover.

"The cross of honor, with its band,
    Leave on my bosom lying;
My musket place within my hand,
    My dagger round me tying.

"Then there I shall lie within the tomb,
    A sentry still and unstirring,
Till the war of cannon resounds through the gloom,
    And tramp of the horsemen spurring.

"Then rideth my Emperor swift over my grave,
    While swords with clash are descending;
Then will I arise fully armed from my grave,
    My Emperor, my Emperor defending."

                        (Translator unknown)

Victor Hugo
(1802-1885)
The Djinns

    Town, tower,
    Shore, deep,
    Where lower
    Cliffs steep;
    Waves gray,
    Where play
    Winds gay,—
    All sleep.

    Hark! a sound,
    Far and slight,
    Breathes around
    On the night:
    High and higher,
    Nigh and nigher,
    Like a fire
    Roaring bright.

Now on 't is sweeping
With rattling beat,
Like dwarf imp leaping
In gallop fleet:
He flies, he prances,
In frolic fancies,
On wave-crest dances
With pattering feet.

Hark, the rising swell,
With each nearer burst!
Like the toll of bell
Of a convent cursed;
Like the billowy roar
On a storm-lashed shore,—
Now hushed, now once more
Maddening to its worst.

O God! the deadly sound
Of the Djinns' fearful cry!
Quick, 'neath the spiral round
Of the deep staircase fly!
See, see our lamplight fade!
And of the balustrade
Mounts, mounts the circling shade
Up to the ceiling high!

'T is the Djinns' wild streaming swarm
Whistling in their tempest-flight;
Snap the tall yews 'neath the storm,
Like a pine-flame crackling bright.
Swift and heavy, lo, their crowd
Through the heavens rushing loud,
Live a livid thunder-cloud
With its bolt of fiery night!

Ha! they are on us, close without!
Shut tight the shelter where we lie!
With hideous din the monster rout,
Dragon and vampire, fill the sky!
The loosened rafter overhead
Trembles and bends like quivering reed;
Shakes the old door with shuddering dread,
As from its rusty hinge 't would fly!

Wild cries of hell! voices that howl and shriek!
The horrid swarm before the tempest tossed—
O Heaven!—descends my lowly roof to seek:
Bends the strong wall beneath the furious host.
Totters the house, as though, like dry leaf shorn
From autumn bough and on the mad blast borne,
Up from its deep foundations it were torn
To join the stormy whirl. Ah! all is lost!

   O Prophet! if thy hand but now
   Save from these foul and hellish things,
   A pilgrim at thy shrine I'll bow,
   Laden with pious offerings.
   Bid their hot breath its fiery rain
   Stream on my faithful door in vain,
   Vainly upon my blackened pane
   Grate the fierce claws of their dark wings!

   They have passed!—and their wild legions
   Cease to thunder at my door;
   Fleeting through night's rayless region,
   Hither they return no more.
   Clanking chains and sounds of woe
   Fill the forests as they go;
   And the tall oaks cower low,
   Bent their flaming flight before.

   On! on! the storm of wings
   Bears far the fiery fear,
   Till scarce the breeze now brings
   Dim murmurings to the ear;
   Like locusts' humming hail,
   Or thrash of tiny flail
   Plied by the old pattering hail
   On some old roof-tree near.

     Fainter now are borne
     Fitful mutterings still;
     As, when Arab horn
     Swells its magic peal,
     Shoreward o'er the deep
     Fairy voices sweep,
     And the infant's sleep
     Golden visions fill.

Each deadly Djinn,
Dark child of fright,
Of death and sin,
Speeds the wild flight
Hark, the dull moan,
Like the deep tone
Of ocean's groan,
Afar, by night!

More and More
Fades it now,
As on the shore
Ripple's flow,—
As the plaint
Far and faint
Of a saint
Murmured low.

Hark! hist!
Around,
I list!
The bounds
Of space
All trace
Efface
Of sound.

(Anonymous translation, revised)

Théophile Gautier
(1811-1872)
Art

All things are doubly fair
If patience fashion them
   And care—
Verse, enamel, marble, gem

No idle chains endure:
Yet, Muse, to walk aright
   Lace tight
Thy buskin proud and sure.

Fie on facile measure,
A shoe where every lout

    At pleasure
Slips his foot in and out!

Sculptor, lay by the clay
On which thy nerveless finger
    May linger,
Thy thoughts flown far away.

Keep to Carrara rare,
Struggle with Paros cold,
    That hold
The subtle line and fair.

Lest haply nature lose
That proud, that perfect line,
    Make thine
The bronze of Syracuse.

And with a tender dread
Upon an agate's face
    Retrace
Apollo's golden head.

Despise a watery hue
And tints that soon expire.
    With fire
Burn thine enamel true.

Twine, twine in artful wise
The blue-green mermaid's arms,
    Mid charms
Of thousand heraldries.

Show in their triple lobe
Virgin and Child, that hold
    Their globe,
Cross crowned and aureoled.

—All things return to dust
Save beauties fashioned well;
    The bust
Outlasts the citadel.

Oft doth the plowman's heel,
Breaking an ancient clod,
    Reveal
A Cæsar or a god.

The gods too die, alas!
But deathless and more strong
   Than brass
Remains the sovereign song.

Chisel and carve and file
Till thy vague dream imprint
   Its smile
On the unyielding flint.

    (Translated by George Santayana)

Charles Baudelaire
(1821-1867)
Sois Sage O Ma Douleur

Peace, be at peace, O thou my heaviness,
Thou calledst for the evening, lo! 'tis here,
The City wears a somber atmosphere
That brings repose to some, to some distress.
Now while the heedless throng make haste to press
Where pleasure drives them, ruthless charioteer,
To pluck the fruits of sick remorse and fear,
Come thou with me, and leave their fretfulness.

See how they hang from heaven's high balconies,
The old lost years in faded garments dressed,
And see Regret with faintly smiling mouth;
And while the dying sun sinks in the west,
Hear how, far off, Night walks with velvet tread,
And her long robe trails all about the south.

    (Translated by Lord Alfred Douglas)

Correspondences

Nature stands as a temple in which living columns
Will release now and then words' confused interplay,
As through forests of symbols mankind makes his way
That observe him with glances familiar and solemn.

Thin-drawn echoes from far interblendings will reach
And through shadowy depths into oneness unite
As immense as pure brightness, as vast as the night
Colors, perfumes and sounds now respond each to each.

Some sweet odors there be cool as flesh of a babe,
Gentle as plaining oboes, with bright meadow green,
And still others corrupted, triumphant and brave,

Possessed of expansion of objects unseen,
Benjamin, amber light and musk and incense,
That sing ecstasies of the spirit and sense.

(Translated by Irene Osmond Spears)

Jean-Jacques Rousseau
(1712-1778)
from *The Confessions*
PART THE FIRST

Book One
[*1712-1719*]

I am commencing an undertaking, hitherto without precedent, and which will never find an imitator. I desire to set before my fellows the likeness of a man in all the truth of nature, and that man myself.

I alone. I know my heart, and I know men. I am not made like any of those I have seen; I dare to believe that I am not made like any of those who are in existence. If I am not better, at least I am different. Whether Nature has acted rightly or wrongly in destroying the mould in which she cast me, can only be decided after I have been read.

Let the trumpet of the Day of Judgment sound when it will, I will present myself before the Sovereign Judge with this book in my hand. I will say boldly: "This is what I have done, what I have thought, what I was. I have told the good and the bad with equal frankness. I have neither omitted anything bad, nor interpolated anything good. If I have occasionally made use of some immaterial embellishments, this has only been in order to fill a gap caused by lack of memory. I may have assumed the truth of that which I knew might have been true, never of that which I knew to be false. I have shown myself as I was: mean and contemptible, good, high-minded and sublime, according as I was one or the other. I have unveiled my inmost self even as Thou hast seen it, O Eternal Being. Gather round me the countless host of my fellow-men; let them hear my confessions, lament for my unworthiness, and blush for my imperfections. Then let each of them in turn reveal, with the same frankness, the secrets of his heart at the foot of the Throne, and say, if he dare, '*I was better than that man!*' "

I was born at Geneva, in the year 1712, and was the son of Isaac Rousseau and Susanne Bernard, citizens. The distribution of a very moderate inheritance amongst fifteen children had reduced my father's portion almost to nothing; and his only means of livelihood was his trade of watchmaker, at which he was really very clever. My mother, a daughter of the Protestant minister Bernard, was better off. She was clever and beautiful, and my father had found difficulty in obtaining her hand. Their affection for each other had begun almost as soon as they were born. When only eight years old, they walked every evening upon the Treille; at ten, they were inseparable. Sympathy and union of soul strengthened in them the feeling produced by intimacy. Both, naturally full of tender sensibility, only waited for the moment when they should find the same disposition in another—or, rather, this moment waited for them, and each abandoned his heart to the first which opened to receive it. Destiny, which appeared to oppose their passion, only encouraged it. The young lover, unable to obtain possession of his mistress, was consumed by grief. She advised him to travel, and endeavour to forget her. He travelled, but without result, and returned more in love than ever. He found her whom he loved still faithful and true. After this trial of affection, nothing was left for them but to love each other all their lives. This they swore to do, and Heaven blessed their oath.

Gabriel Bernard, my mother's brother, fell in love with one of my father's sisters, who only consented to accept the hand of the brother, on condition that her own brother married the sister. Love arranged everything, and the two marriages took place on the same day. Thus my uncle became the husband of my aunt, and their children were doubly my first cousins. At the end of a year, a child was born to both, after which they were again obliged to separate.

My uncle Bernard was an engineer. He took service in the Empire and in Hungary; under Prince Eugène. He distinguished himself at the siege and battle of Belgrade. My father, after the birth of my only brother, set out for Constantinople, whither he was summoned to undertake the post of watchmaker to the Sultan. During his absence, my mother's beauty, intellect and talents gained for her the devotion of numerous admirers. M. de la Closure, the French Resident, was one of the most eager to offer his. His passion must have been great, for, thirty years later, I saw him greatly affected when speaking to me of her. To enable her to resist such advances, my mother had more than her virtue: she loved her husband tenderly. She pressed him to return; he left all, and returned. I was the unhappy fruit of this return. Ten months later I was born, a weak and ailing child; I cost my mother her life, and my birth was the first of my misfortunes.

I have never heard how my father bore this loss, but I know that he was inconsolable. He believed that he saw his wife again in me, without being able to forget that it was I who had robbed him of her; he never embraced me without my perceiving, by his sighs and the convulsive manner in which he clasped me to his breast, that a bitter regret was mingled with his caresses, which were on that account only the more tender. When he said to me, "Jean-Jacques, let us talk of your mother," I used to answer, "Well, then, my father, we will weep!"—and this word alone was sufficient to move him to tears. "Ah!" said he, with a sigh, "give her back to me, console me for her loss, fill the void which she has left in my soul. Should I love you as I do, if you were only my son?" Forty years after he had lost her, he died in the arms of a second wife, but the name of the first was on his lips and her image at the bottom of his heart.

Such were the authors of my existence. Of all the gifts which Heaven had bestowed upon them, a sensitive heart is the only one they bequeathed to me; it had been the source of their happiness, but for me it proved the source of all the misfortunes of my life.

I was brought into the world in an almost dying condition; little hope was entertained of saving my life. I carried within me the germs of a complaint which the course of time has strengthened, and which at times allows me a respite only to make me suffer more cruelly in another manner. One of my father's sisters, an amiable and virtuous young woman, took such care of me that she saved my life. At this moment, while I am writing, she is still alive, at the age of eighty, nursing a husband younger than herself, but exhausted by excessive drinking. Dear aunt, I forgive you for having preserved my life; and I deeply regret that, at the end of your days, I am unable to repay the tender care which you lavished upon me at the beginning of my own. My dear old nurse Jacqueline is also still alive, healthy and robust. The hands which opened my eyes at my birth will be able to close them for me at my death.

I felt before I thought: this is the common lot of humanity. I experienced it more than others. I do not know what I did until I was five or six years old. I do not know how I learned to read; I only remember my earliest reading; and the effect it had upon me; from that time I date my uninterrupted self-consciousness. My mother had left some romances behind her, which my father and I began to read after supper. At first it was only a question of practising me in reading by the aid of amusing books; but soon the interest became so lively, that we used to read in turn without stopping, and spent whole nights in this occupation. We were unable to leave off until the volume was finished. Sometimes, my father, hearing the swallows begin to twitter in the early morning, would say, quite ashamed, "Let us go to bed; I am more of a child than yourself."

In a short time I acquired, by this dangerous method, not only extreme facility in reading and understanding what I read, but a knowledge of the passions that was unique in a child of my age. I had no idea of things in themselves, although all the feelings of actual life were already known to me. I had conceived nothing, but felt everything. These confused emotions which I felt one after the other, certainly did not warp the reasoning powers which I did not as yet possess; but they shaped them in me of a peculiar stamp, and gave me odd and romantic notions of human life, of which experience and reflection have never been able wholly to cure me.

Johann Wolfgang von Goethe
(1749-1832)
from *Faust I*

One of the genuinely universal geniuses in history, Goethe was not only a writer but also an anatomist, physicist, lawyer, and theater producer. His literary output was extensive: he was a great lyricist, a fine novelist, and the supreme playwright of his age.

Goethe's major literary project, upon which he worked intermittently throughout most of his mature life, was the writing of two plays based on the old story of Faust, the man who sells his soul to the devil in return for increased knowledge and power. The second of these plays, Faust II, *is a complex philosophical and often lyrical drama. In it, Faust eventually earns salvation through his constantly striving spirit. It is* Faust I, *however, that has touched the imagination of readers throughout the world. Gounod, Berlioz, and Boito all set parts of it to music, and Delacroix made a fine set of drawings based on the play.*

Faust I *opens with a "Prelude on the Stage," in which Goethe expounds some of his ideas on drama and acting. Next comes a "Prologue in Heaven," a scene based upon the Book of Job. In this prologue, God agrees to allow Mephistopheles to tempt His "servant Faust." The actual drama begins at night in Faust's study.*

FIRST PART OF THE TRAGEDY.
I.
NIGHT.

(*A lofty-arched, narrow, Gothic chamber.* FAUST, *in a chair at his desk, restless.*)

FAUST.

I've studied now Philosophy
And jurisprudence, Medicine,—
And even, alas! Theology,—
From end to end, with labor keen;
And here, poor fool! with all my lore
I stand, no wiser than before:
I'm Magister—yea, Doctor—hight,
And straight or cross-wise, wrong or right,
These ten years long, with many woes,
I've led my scholars by the nose,—
And see, that nothing can be known!
That knowledge cuts me to the bone.
I'm cleverer, true, than those fops of teachers,
Doctors and Magisters, Scribes and Preachers;
Neither scruples nor doubts come now to smite me,
Nor Hell nor Devil can longer affright me.
For this, all pleasure am I foregoing;
I do not pretend to aught worth knowing,
I do not pretend I could be a teacher
To help or convert a fellow-creature.
Then, too, I've neither lands nor gold,
Nor the world's least pomp or honor hold—
No dog would endure such a curst existence!
Wherefore, from Magic I seek assistance,
That many a secret perchance I reach
Through spirit-power and spirit-speech,
And thus the bitter task forego
Of saying the things I do not know,—
That I may detect the inmost force
Which binds the world, and guides its course;
Its germs, productive powers explore,
And rummage in empty words no more!

O full and splendid Moon, whom I
Have, from this desk, seen climb the sky
So many a midnight,—would thy glow
For the last time beheld my woe!
Ever thine eye, most mournful friend,
O'er books and papers saw me bend;

But would that I, on mountains grand,
Amid thy blessed light could stand,
With spirits through mountain-caverns hover,
Float in thy twilight the meadows over,
And, freed from the fumes of lore that swathe me,
To health in thy dewy fountains bathe me!

Ah, me! this dungeon still I see,
This drear, accursed masonry,
Where even the welcome daylight strains
But duskly through the painted panes.
Hemmed in by many a toppling heap
Of books worm-eaten, gray with dust,
Which to the vaulted ceiling creep,
Against the smoky papers thrust,—
With glasses, boxes, round me stacked,
And instruments together hurled,
Ancestral lumber, stuffed and packed—
Such is my world: and what a world!

And do I ask, wherefore my heart
Falters, oppressed with unknown needs?
Why some inexplicable smart
All movement of my life impedes?
Alas! in living Nature's stead,
Where God His human creature set,
In smoke and mould the fleshless dead
And bones of beasts surround me yet!

Fly! Up, and seek the broad, free land!
And this one Book of Mystery
From Nostradamus' very hand,
Is 't not sufficient company?
When I the starry courses know,
And Nature's wise instruction seek,
With light of power my soul shall glow,
As when to spirits spirits speak.
'T is vain, this empty brooding here,
Though guessed the holy symbols be:
Ye, Spirits, come—ye hover near—
Oh, if you hear me, answer me!

(*He opens the Book, and perceives the sign of the Macrocosm.*)

Ha! what a sudden rapture leaps from this
I view, through all my senses swiftly flowing!

I feel a youthful, holy, vital bliss
In every vein and fibre newly glowing.
Was it a God, who traced this sign,
With calm across my tumult stealing,
My troubled heart to joy unsealing,
With impulse, mystic and divine,
The powers of Nature here, around my path,
    revealing?
Am I a God?—so clear mine eyes!
In these pure features I behold
Creative Nature to my soul unfold.
What says the sage, now first I recognize:
"The spirit-world no closures fasten;
Thy sense is shut, thy heart is dead:
Disciple, up! untiring, hasten
To bathe thy breast in morning-red!"

    (He contemplates the sign.)

How each the Whole its substance gives,
Each in the other works and lives!
Like heavenly forces rising and descending,
Their golden urns reciprocally lending,
With wings that winnow blessing
From Heaven through Earth I see them pressing,
Filling the All with harmony unceasing!
How grand a show! but, ah! a show alone.
Thee, boundless Nature, how make thee my own?
Where you, ye breasts? Founts of all Being, shining,
Whereon hang Heaven's and Earth's desire,
Whereto our withered hearts aspire,—
Ye flow, ye feed: and am I vainly pining?

    *(He turns the leaves impatiently, and perceives the
        sign of the Earth-Spirit.)*

How otherwise upon me works this sign!
Thou, Spirit of the Earth, art nearer:
Even now my powers are loftier, clearer;
I glow, as drunk with new-made wine:
New strength and heart to meet the world incite me,
The woe of earth, the bliss of earth, invite me,
And though the shock of storms may smite me,
No crash of shipwreck shall have power to fright me!
Clouds gather over me—
The moon conceals her light—

The lamp's extinguished!—
Mists rise,—red, angry rays are darting
Around my head!—There falls
A horror from the vaulted roof,
And seizes me!
I feel thy presence, Spirit I invoke!
Reveal thyself!
Ha! in my heart what rending stroke!
With new impulsion
My senses heave in this convulsion!
I feel thee draw my heart, absorb, exhaust me:
Thou must! thou must! and though my life it cost me!

(*He seizes the book, and mysteriously pronounces the sign of the Spirit. A ruddy flame flashes: the Spirit appears in the flame.*)

SPIRIT.

Who calls me?

FAUST (*with averted head*).
Terrible to see!

SPIRIT.

Me hast thou long with might attracted,
Long from my sphere thy food exacted,
And now—

FAUST.

Woe! I endure not thee!

SPIRIT.

To view me is thine aspiration,
My voice to hear, my countenance to see;
Thy powerful yearning moveth me,
Here am I!—what mean perturbation
Thee, superhuman, shakes? Thy soul's high calling,
    where?
Where is the breast, which from itself a world did
    bear,
And shaped and cherished—which with joy expanded,
To be our peer, with us, the Spirits, banded?
Where art thou, Faust, whose voice has pierced to me,
Who towards me pressed with all thine energy?
He art thou, who, my presence breathing, seeing,
Trembles through all the depths of being,
A writhing worm, a terror-stricken form?

FAUST.
Thee, form of flame, shall I then fear?
Yes, I am Faust: I am thy peer!

SPIRIT.
In the tides of Life, in Action's storm,
A fluctuant wave,
A shuttle free,
Birth and the Grave,
An eternal sea,
A weaving, flowing
Life, all-glowing,
Thus at Time's humming loom 't is my hand prepares
The garment of Life which the Deity wears!

FAUST.
Thou, who around the wide world wendest,
Thou busy Spirit, how near I feel to thee!

SPIRIT.
Thou 'rt like the Spirit which thou comprehendest,
Not me!

(*Disappears.*)

FAUST (*overwhelmed*).
Not thee!
Whom then?
I, image of the Godhead!
Not even like thee!

(*A knock.*)

O Death!—I know it—'t is my Famulus!
My fairest luck finds no fruition:
In all the fulness of my vision
The soulless sneak disturbs me thus!

Faust is interrupted by his student Wagner. After a conversation about learning and art, Faust is again alone.

FAUST (*solus*).
That brain, alone, not loses hope, whose choice is
To stick in shallow trash forevermore,—
Which digs with eager hand for buried ore,
And, when it finds an angle-worm, rejoices!

Dare such a human voice disturb the flow,
Around me here, of spirit-presence fullest?
And yet, this once my thanks I owe
To thee, of all earth's sons the poorest, dullest!
For thou hast torn me from that desperate state
Which threatened soon to overwhelm my senses:
The apparition was so giant-great,
It dwarfed and withered all my soul's pretences!

I, image of the Godhead, who began—
Deeming Eternal Truth secure in nearness—
To sun myself in heavenly light and clearness,
And laid aside the earthly man;—
I, more than Cherub, whose free force had planned
To flow through Nature's veins in glad pulsation,
To reach beyond, enjoying in creation
The life of Gods, behold my expiation!
A thunder-word hath swept me from my stand.

With thee I dare not venture to compare me.
Though I possessed the power to draw thee near me,
The power to keep thee was denied my hand.
When that ecstatic moment held me,
I felt myself so small, so great;
But thou hast ruthessly repelled me
Back upon Man's uncertain fate.
What shall I shun? Whose guidance borrow?
Shall I accept that stress and strife?
Ah! every deed of ours, no less than every sorrow,
Impedes the onward march of life.
Some alien substance more and more is cleaving
To all the mind conceives of grand and fair;
When this world's Good is won by our achieving,
The Better, then, is named a cheat and snare.
The fine emotions, whence our lives we mould,
Lie in the earthly tumult dumb and cold.
If hopeful Fancy once, in daring flight,
Her longings to the Infinite expanded,
Yet now a narrow space contents her quite,
Since Time's wild wave so many a fortune stranded.
Care at the bottom of the heart is lurking:
Her secret pangs in silence working,
She, restless, rocks herself, disturbing joy and rest:
In newer masks her face is ever drest,
By turns as house and land, as wife and child,
    presented,—

As water, fire, as poison, steel:
We dread the blows we never feel,
And what we never lose is yet by us lamented!
I am not like the Gods! That truth is felt too deep;
The worm am I, that in the dust doth creep,—
That, while in dust it lives and seeks its bread,
Is crushed and buried by the wanderer's tread.
Is not this dust, these walls within them hold,
The hundred shelves, which cramp and chain me,
The frippery, the trinkets thousand-fold,
That in this mothy den restrain me?
Here shall I find the help I need?
Shall here a thousand volumes teach me only
That men, self-tortured, everywhere must bleed,—
And here and there one happy man sits lonely?
What mean'st thou by that grin, thou hollow skull,
Save that thy brain, like mine, a cloudy mirror,
Sought once the shining day, and then, in twilight
    dull,
Thirsting for Truth, went wretchedly to Error?
Ye instruments, forsooth, but jeer at me
With wheel and cog, and shapes uncouth of wonder;
I found the portal, you the keys should be;
Your wards are deftly wrought, but drive no bolts
    asunder!
Mysterious even in open day,
Nature retains her veil, despite our clamors:
That which she doth not willingly display
Cannot be wrenched from her with levers, screws, and
    hammers.
Ye ancient tools, whose use I never knew,
Here, since my father used ye, still ye moulder:
Thou, ancient scroll, hast worn thy smoky hue
Since at this desk the dim lamp wont to smoulder.
'T were better far, had I my little idly spent,
Than now to sweat beneath its burden, I confess it!
What from your fathers' heritage is lent,
Earn it anew, to really possess it!
What serves not, is a sore impediment:
The Moment's need creates the thing to serve and bless
    it!
Yet, wherefore turns my gaze to yonder point so
    lightly?
Is yonder flask a magnet for mine eyes?
Whence, all around me, glows the air so brightly,
As when in woods at night the mellow moonbeam lies?

I hail thee, wondrous, rarest vial!
I take thee down devoutly, for the trial:
Man's art and wit I venerate in thee.
Thou summary of gentle slumber-juices,
Essence of deadly finest powers and uses,
Unto thy master show thy favor free!
I see thee, and the stings of pain diminish;
I grasp thee, and my struggles slowly finish:
My spirit's flood-tide ebbeth more and more.
Out on the open ocean speeds my dreaming;
The glassy flood before my feet is gleaming,
A new day beckons to a newer shore!

A fiery chariot, borne on buoyant pinions,
Sweeps near me now! I soon shall ready be
To pierce the ether's high, unknown dominions,
To reach new spheres of pure activity!
This godlike rapture, this supreme existence,
Do I, but now a worm, deserve to track?
Yes, resolute to reach some brighter distance,
On Earth's fair sun I turn my back!
Yes, let me dare those gates to fling asunder,
Which every man would fain go slinking by!
'T is time, through deeds this word of truth to
    thunder:
That with the height of Gods Man's dignity may vie!
Nor from that gloomy gulf to shrink affrighted,
Where Fancy doth herself to self-born pangs
    compel,—
To struggle toward that pass benighted,
Around whose narrow mouth flame all the fires of
    Hell,—
To take this step with cheerful resolution,
Though Nothingness should be the certain, swift
    conclusion!

And now come down, thou cup of crystal clearest!
Fresh from thine ancient cover thou appearest,
So many years forgotten to my thought!
Thou shon'st at old ancestral banquets cheery,
The solemn guests thou madest merry,
When one thy wassail to the other brought.
The rich and skilful figures o'er thee wrought,
The drinker's duty, rhyme-wise to explain them,
Or in one breath below the mark to drain them,

From many a night of youth my memory caught.
Now to a neighbor shall I pass thee never,
Nor on thy curious art to test my wit endeavor:
Here is a juice whence sleep is swiftly born.
It fills with browner flood thy crystal hollow;
I chose, prepared it: thus I follow,—
With all my soul the final drink I swallow,
A solemn festal cup, a greeting to the morn!
     [*He sets the goblet to his mouth.*]

 (*Chime of bells and choral song.*)

   CHORUS OF ANGELS.
  Christ is arisen!
  Joy to the Mortal One,
  Whom the unmerited,
  Clinging, inherited
  Needs did imprison.

    FAUST.
What hollow humming, what a sharp, clear stroke,
Drives from my lip the goblet's, at their meeting?
Announce the booming bells already woke
The first glad hour of Easter's festal greeting?
Ye choirs, have ye begun the sweet, consoling chant,
Which, through the night of Death, the angels
  ministrant
Sang, God's new Covenant repeating?

   CHORUS OF WOMEN.
  With spices and precious
  Balm, we arrayed him;
  Faithful and gracious,
  We tenderly laid him:
  Linen to bind him
  Cleanlily wound we:
  Ah! when we would find him,
  Christ no more found we!

   CHORUS OF ANGELS.
  Christ is ascended
  Bliss hath invested him,
  Woes that molested him,
  Trials that tested him,
  Gloriously ended!

FAUST.

Why, here in dust, entice me with your spell,
Ye gentle, powerful sounds of Heaven?
Peal rather there, where tender natures dwell.
Your messages I hear, but faith has not been given;
The dearest child of Faith is Miracle.
I venture not to soar to yonder regions
Whence the glad tidings hither float;
And yet, from childhood up familiar with the note,
To Life it now renews the old allegiance.
Once Heavenly Love sent down a burning kiss
Upon my brow, in Sabbath silence holy;
And, filled with mystic presage, chimed the church-
    bell slowly,
And prayer dissolved me in a fervent bliss.
A sweet, uncomprehended yearning
Drove forth my feet through woods and meadows free,
And while a thousand tears were burning,
I felt a world arise for me.
These chants, to youth and all its sports appealing,
Proclaimed the Spring's rejoicing holiday;
And Memory holds me now, with childish feeling,
Back from the last, the solemn way.
Sound on, ye hymns of Heaven, so sweet and mild!
My tears gush forth: the Earth takes back her child!

CHORUS OF DISCIPLES.

Has He, victoriously,
Burst from the vaulted
Grave, and all-gloriously
Now sits exalted?
Is He, in glow of birth,
Rapture creative near?
Ah! to the woe of earth
Still are we native here.
We, his aspiring
Followers, Him we miss;
Weeping, desiring,
Master, Thy bliss!

CHORUS OF ANGELS.

Christ is arisen,
Out of Corruption's womb:
Burst ye the prison,
Break from your gloom!
Praising and pleading him,

Lovingly needing him,
Brotherly feeding him,
Preaching and speeding him.
Blessing, succeeding Him,
Thus is the Master near,—
Thus is He here!

Faust and Wagner walk together through the crowds of villagers and receive the acknowledgment of their friends. After more talk, Faust returns to his study, followed by a poodle.

III.

THE STUDY.

FAUST.

(*Entering, with the poodle.*)
Behind me, field and meadow sleeping,
I leave in deep, prophetic night,
Within whose dread and holy keeping
The better soul awakes to light.
    The wild desires no longer win us,
    The deeds of passion cease to chain;
    The love of Man revives within us,
    The love of God revives again.

Be still, thou poodle! make not such racket and riot!
Why at the threshold wilt snuffing be?
Behind the stove repose thee in quiet!
My softest cushion I give to thee.
As thou, up yonder, with running and leaping
Amused us hast, on the mountain's crest,
So now I take thee into my keeping,
A welcome, but also a silent, guest.

    Ah, when, within our narrow chamber
    The lamp with friendly lustre glows,
    Flames in the breast each faded ember,
    And in the heart, itself that knows.
    Then Hope again lends sweet assistance,
    And Reason then resumes her speech:
    One yearns, the rivers of existence,
    The very founts of Life, to reach.

Snarl not, poodle! To the sound that rises,
The sacred tones that my soul embrace,
This bestial noise is out of place.
We are used to see, that Man despises
What he never comprehends,
And the Good and the Beautiful vilipends,
Finding them often hard to measure:
Will the dog, like man, snarl *his* displeasure?

But ah! I feel, though will thereto be stronger,
Contentment flows from out my breast no longer.
Why must the stream so soon run dry and fail us,
And burning thirst again assail us?
Therein I've borne so much probation!
And yet, this want may be supplied us;
We call the Supernatural to guide us;
We pine and thirst for Revelation,
Which nowhere worthier is, more nobly sent,
Than here, in our New Testament.
I feel impelled, its meaning to determine,—
With honest purpose, once for all,
The hallowed Original
To change to my beloved German.

(*He opens a volume, and commences.*)

'T is written: "In the Beginning was the *Word*."
Here am I balked: who, now, can help afford?
The *Word*?—impossible so high to rate it;
And otherwise must I translate it,
If by the Spirit I am truly taught.
Then thus: "In the Beginning was the *Thought*."
This first line let me weigh completely,
Lest my impatient pen proceed too fleetly.
Is it the *Thought* which works, creates, indeed?
"In the Beginning was the *Power*," I read.
Yet, as I write, a warning is suggested,
That I the sense may not have fairly tested.
The Spirit aids me: now I see the light!
"In the Beginning was the *Act*," I write.

If I must share my chamber with thee,
Poodle, stop that howling, prithee!
Cease to bark and bellow!
Such a noisy, disturbing fellow
I'll no longer suffer near me.

One of us, dost hear me!
Must leave, I fear me.
No longer guest-right I bestow:
The door is open, art free to go.
But what do I see in the creature?
Is that in the course of nature?
Is't actual fact? or Fancy's shows?
How long and broad my poodle grows!
He rises mightily:
A canine form that cannot be!
What a spectre I've harbored thus!
He resembles a hippopotamus,
With fiery eyes, teeth terrible to see:
O, now am I sure of thee!
For all of thy half-hellish brood
The Key of Solomon is good.

   SPIRITS (*in the corridor*).
 Some one, within, is caught!
 Stay without, follow him not!
 Like the fox in a snare,
 Quakes the old hell-lynx there.
 Take heed—look about!
 Back and forth hover,
 Under and over,
 And he'll work himself out.
 If your aid can avail him,
 Let it not fail him;
 For he, without measure,
 Has wrought for our pleasure.

    FAUST.
First, to encounter the beast,
The Words of the Four be addressed:
 Salamander, shine glorious!
 Wave, Undine, as bidden!
 Sylph, be thou hidden!
 Gnome, be laborious!

Who knows not their sense
(These elements),—
Their properties
And power not sees,—
No mastery he inherits
Over the Spirits.

Vanish in flaming ether,
Salamander!
Flow foamingly together,
Undine!
Shine in meteor-sheen,
Sylph!
Bring help to hearth and shelf,
Incubus! Incubus!
Step forward, and finish thus!
Of the Four, no feature
Lurks in the creature.
Quiet he lies, and grins disdain:
Not yet, it seems, have I given him pain.
Now, to undisguise thee,
Hear me exorcise thee!
Art thou, my gay one,
Hell's fugitive stray-one?
The sign witness now,
Before which they bow,
The cohorts of Hell!

With hair all bristling, it begins to swell.

    Base Being, hearest thou?
    Knowest and fearest thou
    The One, unoriginate,
    Named inexpressibly,
    Through all Heaven impermeate,
    Pierced irredressibly!

Behind the stove still banned,
See it, an elephant, expand!
It fills the space entire,
Mist-like melting, ever faster.
'T is enough: ascend no higher,—
Lay thyself at the feet of the Master!
Thou seest, not vain the threats I bring thee:
With holy fire I'll scorch and sting thee!
Wait not to know
The threefold dazzling glow!
Wait not to know
The strongest art within my hands!

        MEPHISTOPHELES

(while the vapor is dissipating, steps forth from behind the stove in the costume of a Travelling Scholar).

Why such a noise? What are my lord's commands?

MEPHISTOPHELES.

FAUST.
This was the poodle's real core,
A traveling scholar, then? The *casus* is diverting.

MEPHISTOPHELES.
The learned gentleman I bow before:
You've made me roundly sweat, that's certain!

FAUST.
What is thy name?

MEPHISTOPHELES.
        A question small, it seems,
For one whose mind the Word so much despises;
Who, scorning all external gleams,
The depths of being only prizes.

FAUST.
With all you gentlemen, the name's a test,
Whereby the nature usually is expressed.
Clearly the latter implies
In names like Beelzebub, Destroyer, Father of Lies.
What art thou, then?

MEPHISTOPHELES.
        Part of that Power, not understood,
Which always wills the Bad, and always works the
    Good.

FAUST.
What hidden sense in this enigma lies?

MEPHISTOPHELES.
I am the Spirit that Denies!
And justly so: for all things, from the Void
Called forth, deserve to be destroyed:
'T were better, then, were naught created.
Thus, all which you as Sin have rated,—
Destruction,—aught with Evil blent,—
That is my proper element.

FAUST.
Thou nam'st thyself a part, yet show'st complete to
    me?

MEPHISTOPHELES.
The modest truth I speak to thee.
If Man, that microcosmic fool, can see
Himself a whole so frequently,
Part of the Part am I, once All, primal Night,—
Part of the Darkness which brought forth the Light,
The haughty Light, which now disputes the space.
And claims of Mother Night her ancient place.
And yet, the struggle fails; since Light, howe'er it
    weaves,
Still, fettered, unto bodies cleaves:
It flows from bodies, bodies beautifies;
By bodies is its course impeded;
And so, but little time is needed,
I hope, ere, as the bodies die, it dies!

FAUST.
I see the plan thou art pursuing:
Thou canst not compass general ruin,
And hast on smaller scale begun.

MEPHISTOPHELES.
And truly 'tis not much, when all is done.
That which to Naught is in resistance set,—
The Something of this clumsy world,—has yet,
With all that I have undertaken,
Not been by me disturbed or shaken:
From earthquake, tempest, wave, volcano's brand,
Back into quiet settle sea and land!
And that damned stuff, the bestial, human brood,—
What use, in having that to play with?
How many have I made away with!
And ever circulates a newer, fresher blood.
It makes me furious, such things beholding:
From Water, Earth, and Air unfolding,
A thousand germs break forth and grow,
In dry, and wet, and warm, and chilly;
And had I not the Flame reserved, why, really,
There's nothing special of my own to show!

FAUST.
So, to the actively eternal
Creative force, in cold disdain
You now oppose the fist infernal,
Whose wicked clench is all in vain!

Some other labor seek thou rather,
Queer Son of Chaos, to begin!

MEPHISTOPHELES.
Well, we'll consider: thou canst gather
My views, when next I venture in.
Might I, perhaps, depart at present?

FAUST.
Why thou shouldst ask, I don't perceive.
Though our acquaintance is so recent,
For further visits thou hast leave.
The window's here, the door is yonder;
A chimney, also, you behold.

MEPHISTOPHELES.
I must confess that forth I may not wander,
My steps by one slight obstacle controlled,—
The wizard's-foot, that on your threshold made is.

FAUST.
The pentagram prohibits thee?
Why, tell me now, thou Son of Hades,
If that prevents, how cam'st thou in to me?
Could such a spirit be so cheated?

MEPHISTOPHELES.
Inspect the thing: the drawing's not completed.
The outer angle, you may see,
Is open left—the lines don't fit it.

FAUST.
Well,—Chance, this time, has fairly hit it!
And thus, thou'rt prisoner to me?
It seems the business has succeeded.

MEPHISTOPHELES.
The poodle naught remarked, as after thee he speeded;
But other aspects now obtain:
The Devil can't get out again.

FAUST.
Try, then, the open window-pane!

MEPHISTOPHELES.
For Devils and for spectres this is law:

Where they have entered in, there also they withdraw.
The first is free to us; we're governed by the second.

MEPHISTOPHELES.

FAUST.

In Hell itself, then, laws are reckoned?
That's well! So might a compact be
Made with you gentleman—and binding,—surely?

MEPHISTOPHELES.

All that is promised shall delight thee purely;
No skinflint bargain shalt thou see.
But this is not of swift conclusion;
We'll talk about the matter soon.
And now, I do entreat this boon—
Leave to withdraw from my intrusion.

FAUST.

One moment more I ask thee to remain,
Some pleasant news, at least, to tell me.

MEPHISTOPHELES.

Release me, now! I soon shall come again;
Then thou, at will, mayst question and compel me.

FAUST.

I have not snares around thee cast;
Thyself hast led thyself into the meshes.
Who traps the Devil, hold him fast!
Not soon a second time he'll catch a prey so precious.

MEPHISTOPHELES.

An't please thee, also I'm content to stay,
And serve thee in a social station;
But stipulating, that I may
With arts of mine afford thee recreation.

FAUST.

Thereto I willingly agree,
If the diversion pleasant be.

MEPHISTOPHELES.

My friend, thou 'lt win, past all pretences,
More in this hour to soothe thy senses,
Than in the year's monotony.
That which the dainty spirits sing thee,
The lovely pictures they shall bring thee.

Are more than magic's empty show.
Thy scent will be to bliss invited;
Thy palate then with taste delighted,
Thy nerves of touch ecstatic glow!
All unprepared, the charm I spin:
We're here together, so begin!

   SPIRITS.
  Vanish, ye darkling
  Arches above him!
  Loveliest weather,
  Born of blue ether,
  Break from the sky!
  O that the darkling
  Clouds had departed!
  Starlight is sparkling,
  Tranquiller-hearted
  Suns are on high.
  Heaven's own children
  In beauty bewildering,
  Waveringly bending,
  Pass as they hover;
  Longing unending
  Follows them over.
  They, with their glowing
  Garments, out-flowing,
  Cover, in going,
  Landscape and bower,
  Where, in seclusion,
  Lovers are plighted,
  Lost in illusion.
  Bower on bower!
  Tendrils unblighted!
  Lo! in a shower
  Grapes that o'ercluster
  Gush into must, or
  Flow into rivers
  Of foaming and flashing
  Wine, that is dashing
  Gems, as it boundeth
  Down the high places,
  And spreading, surroundeth
  With crystalline spaces,
  In happy embraces,
  Blossoming forelands,
  Emerald shore-lands!

And the winged races
Drink, and fly onward—
Fly ever sunward
To the enticing
Islands, that flatter,
Dipping and rising
Light on the water!
Hark, the inspiring
Sound of their quiring!
See, the entrancing
Whirl of their dancing!
All in the air are
Freer and fairer.
Some of them scaling
Boldly the highlands,
Circling the islands;
Others are flying;
Life-ward all hieing,—
All for the distant
Star of existent
Rapture and Love!

MEPHISTOPHELES.
He sleeps! Enough, ye fays! your airy number
Have sung him truly into slumber:
For this performance I your debtor prove.—
Not yet art thou the man, to catch the Fiend and hold
    him!—
With fairest images of dreams infold him,
Plunge him in seas of sweet untruth!
Yet, for the threshold's magic which controlled him,
The Devil needs a rat's quick tooth.
I use no lengthened invocation:
Here rustles one that soon will work my liberation.

The lord of rats and eke of mice,
Of flies and bed-bugs, frogs and lice,
Summons thee hither to the door-sill,
To gnaw it where, with just a morsel
Of oil, he paints the spot for thee:—
There com'st thou, hopping on to me!
To work, at once! The point which made me craven
Is forward, on the ledge, engraven.
Another bit makes free the door:
So, dream thy dreams, O Faust, until we meet once
    more!

FAUST (*awakening*).
Am I again so foully cheated?
Remains there naught of lofty spirit-sway,
But that a dream the Devil counterfeited,
And that a poodle ran away?

IV.

THE STUDY.

FAUST. MEPHISTOPHELES.

FAUST.
A Knock? Come in! Again my quiet broken?

MEPHISTOPHELES.
'T is I!

FAUST.
Come in!

MEPHISTOPHELES.
Thrice must the words be spoken,

FAUST.
Come in, then!

MEPHISTOPHELES.
Thus thou pleasest me.
I hope we'll suit each other well;
For now, thy vapors to dispel,
I come, a squire of high degree,
In scarlet coat, with golden trimming,
A cloak in silken lustre swimming,
A tall cock's-feather in my hat,
A long, sharp sword for show or quarrel,—
And I advise thee, brief and flat,
To don the self-same gay apparel,
That, from this den released, and free,
Life be at last revealed to thee!

FAUST.
This life of earth, whatever my attire,
Would pain me in its wonted fashion.
Too old am I to play with passion;
Too young, to be without desire.

What from the world have I to gain?
Thou shalt abstain—renounce—refrain!
Such is the everlasting song
That in the ears of all men rings,—
That unrelieved, our whole life long,
Each hour, in passing, hoarsely sings.
In very terror I at morn awake,
Upon the verge of bitter weeping,
To see the day of disappointment break,
To no one hope of mine—not one—its promise
    keeping:—
That even each joy's presentiment
With wilful cavil would diminish,
With grinning masks of life prevent
My mind its fairest work to finish!
Then, too, when night descends, how anxiously
Upon my couch of sleep I lay me:
There, also, comes no rest to me,
But some wild dream is sent to fray me.
The God that in my breast is owned
Can deeply stir the inner sources;
The God, above my powers enthroned,
He cannot change external forces.
So, by the burden of my days oppressed,
Death is desired, and Life a thing unblest!

    MEPHISTOPHELES.
And yet is never Death a wholly welcome guest.

    FAUST.
O fortunate, for whom, when victory glances,
The bloody laurels on the brow he bindeth!
Whom, after rapid, maddening dances,
In clasping maiden-arms he findeth!
O would that I, before that spirit-power,
Ravished and rapt from life, had sunken!

    MEPHISTOPHELES.
And yet, by some one, in that nightly hour,
A certain liquid was not drunken.

    FAUST.
Eavesdropping, ha! thy pleasure seems to be.

    MEPHISTOPHELES.
Omniscient am I not; yet much is known to me.

FAUST.
Though some familiar tone, retrieving
My thoughts from torment, led me on,
And sweet, clear echoes came, deceiving
A faith bequeathed from Childhood's dawn,
Yet now I curse whate'er entices
And snares the soul with visions vain;
With dazzling cheats and dear devices
Confines it in this cave of pain!
Cursed be, at once, the high ambition
Wherewith the mind itself deludes!
Cursed be the glare of apparition
That on the finer sense intrudes!
Cursed be the lying dream's impression
Of name, and fame, and laurelled brow!
Cursed, all that flatters as possession,
As wife and child, as knave and plow!
Cursed Mammon be, when he with treasures
To restless action spurs our fate!
Cursed when, for soft, indulgent leisures,
He lays for us the pillows straight!
Cursed be the vine's transcendent nectar,—
The highest favor Love lets fall!
Cursed, also, Hope!—cursed Faith, the spectre!
And cursed be Patience most of all!

CHORUS OF SPIRITS (*invisible*).
Woe! woe!
Thou hast it destroyed,
The beautiful world,
With powerful fist:
In ruin 't is hurled,
By the blow of a demigod shattered!
The scattered
Fragments into the Void we carry,
Deploring
The beauty perished beyond restoring,
Mightier
For the children of men,
Brightlier
Build it again,
In thine own bosom build it anew!
Bid the new career
Commence,
With clearer sense,
And the new songs of cheer
Be sung thereto!

MEPHISTOPHELES.
These are the small dependants
Who give me attendance.
Hear them, to deeds and passion
Counsel in shrewd old-fashion!
Into the world of strife,
Out of this lonely life
That of senses and sap has betrayed thee,
They would persuade thee.
This nursing of the pain forego thee,
That, like a vulture, feeds upon thy breast!
The worst society thou find'st will show thee
Thou art a man among the rest.
But 'tis not meant to thrust
Thee into the mob thou hatest!
I am not one of the greatest,
Yet, wilt thou to me entrust
Thy steps through life, I'll guide thee,—
Will willingly walk beside thee,—
Will serve thee at once and forever
With best endeavor,
And, if thou art satisfied,
Will as servant, slave, with thee abide.

FAUST.
And what shall be my counter-service therefor?

MEPHISTOPHELES.
The time is long: thou need'st not now insist.

FAUST.
No—no! The Devil is an egotist,
And is not apt, without a why or wherefore,
"For God's sake," others to assist.
Speak thy conditions plain and clear!
With such a servant danger comes, I fear.

MEPHISTOPHELES.
Here, an unwearied slave, I'll wear thy tether,
And to thine every nod obedient be:
When *There* again we come together,
Then shalt thou do the same for me.

FAUST.
The *There* my scruples naught increases.
When thou hast dashed this world to pieces,

The other, then, its place may fill.
Here, on this earth, my pleasures have their sources;
Yon sun beholds my sorrows in his courses;
And when from these my life itself divorces,
Let happen all that can or will!
I'll hear no more: 't is vain to ponder
If there we cherish love or hate,
Or, in the spheres we dream of yonder,
A High and Low our souls await.

        MEPHISTOPHELES.
In this sense, even, canst thou venture.
Come, bind thyself by prompt indenture,
And thou mine arts with joy shalt see:
What no man ever saw, I'll give to thee.

        FAUST.
Canst thou, poor Devil, give me whatsoever?
When was a human soul, in its supreme endeavor,
E'er understood by such as thou?
Yet, hast thou food which never satiates, now,—
The restless, ruddy gold hast thou,
That runs, quicksilver-like, one's fingers through,—
A game whose winnings no man ever knew,—
A maid, that, even from my breast,
Beckons my neighbor with her wanton glances,
And Honor's godlike zest,
The meteor that a moment dances,—
Show me the fruits that, ere they're gathered, rot,
And trees that daily with new leafage clothe them!

        MEPHISTOPHELES.
Such a demand alarms me not:
Such treasures have I, and can show them.
But still the time may reach us, good my friend,
When peace we crave and more luxurious diet.

        FAUST.
When on an idler's bed I stretch myself in quiet,
There let, at once, my record end!
Canst thou with lying flattery rule me,
Until, self-pleased, myself I see,—
Canst thou with rich enjoyment fool me,
Let that day be the last for me!
The bet I offer.

MEPHISTOPHELES.
>Done!

FAUST.
>And heartily!
When thus I hail the Moment flying:
"Ah, still delay—thou art so fair!"
Then bind me in thy bonds undying,
My final ruin then declare!
Then let the death-bell chime the token,
Then art thou from thy service free!
The clock may stop, the hand be broken,
Then Time be finished unto me!

MEPHISTOPHELES.
Consider well: my memory good is rated.

FAUST.
Thou hast a perfect right thereto.
My powers I have not rashly estimated:
A slave am I, whate'er I do—
If thine, or whose? 't is needless to debate it.

MEPHISTOPHELES.
Then at the Doctor's-banquet I, to-day,
Will as a servant wait behind thee.
But one thing more! Beyond all risk to bind thee,
Give me a line or two, I pray.

FAUST.
Demand'st thou, Pedant, too, a document?
Hast never known a man, nor proved his word's
>intent?
Is't not enough, that what I speak to-day
Shall stand, with all my future days agreeing?
In all its tides sweeps not the world away,
And shall a promise bind my being?
Yet this delusion in our hearts we bear:
Who would himself therefrom deliver?
Blest he, whose bosom Truth makes pure and fair!
No sacrifice shall he repent of ever.
Nathless a parchment, writ and stamped with care,
A spectre is, which all to shun endeavor.
The word, alas! dies even in the pen,
And wax and leather keep the lordship then.

What wilt from me, Base Spirit, say?—
Brass, marble, parchment, paper, clay?
The terms with graver, quill, or chisel, stated?
I freely leave the choice to thee.

       MEPHISTOPHELES.
Why heat thyself, thus instantly,
With eloquence exaggerated?
Each leaf for such a pact is good;
And to subscribe thy name thou 'lt take a drop of
    blood.

       FAUST.
If thou therewith art fully satisfied,
So let us by the farce abide.

       MEPHISTOPHELES.
Blood is a juice of rarest quality.

       FAUST.
Fear not that I this pact shall seek to sever!
The promise that I make to thee
Is just the sum of my endeavor.
I have myself inflated all too high;
My proper place is thy estate:
The Mighty Spirit deigns me no reply,
And Nature shuts on me her gate.
The threat of Thought at last is broken,
And knowledge brings disgust unspoken.
Let us the sensual deeps explore,
To quench the fervors of glowing passion!
Let every marvel take form and fashion
Through the impervious veil it wore!
Plunge we in Time's tumultuous dance,
In the rush and roll of Circumstance!
Then may delight and distress,
And worry and success,
Alternately follow, as best they can:
Restless activity proves the man!

       MEPHISTOPHELES.
For you no bound, no term is set.
Whether you everywhere be trying,
Or snatch a rapid bliss in flying,
May it agree with you, what you get!
Only fall to, and show no timid balking.

FAUST.

But thou hast heard, 't is not of joy we're talking.
I take the wildering whirl, enjoyment's keenest pain,
Enamored hate, exhilarant disdain.
My bosom, of its thirst for knowledge sated,
Shall not, henceforth, from any pang be wrested,
And all of life for all mankind created
Shall be within mine inmost being tested:
The highest, lowest forms my soul shall borrow,
Shall heap upon itself their bliss and sorrow,
And thus, my own sole self to all their selves expanded
I too, at last, shall with them all be stranded!

MEPHISTOPHELES.

Believe me, who for many a thousand year
The same tough meat have chewed and tested.
That from the cradle to the bier
No man the ancient leaven has digested!
Trust one of us, this Whole supernal
Is made but for a God's delight!
He dwells in splendor single and eternal,
But *us* he thrusts in darkness, out of sight,
And *you* he dowers with Day and Night.

FAUST.

Nay, but I will!

MEPHISTOPHELES.

A good reply!
One only fear still needs repeating:
The art is long, the time is fleeting.
Then let thyself be taught, say I!
Go, league thyself with a poet,
Give the rein to his imagination,
Then wear the crown, and show it,
Of the qualities of his creation,—
The courage of the lion's breed.
The wild stag's speed,
The Italian's fiery blood,
The North's firm fortitude!
Let him find for thee the secret tether
That binds the Noble and Mean together,
And teach thy pulses of youth and pleasure
To love by rule, and hate by measure!
I'd like, myself, such a one to see:
Sir Microcosm his name should be.

FAUST.
What am I, then, if 't is denied my part
The crown of all humanity to win me,
Whereto yearns every sense within me?

MEPHISTOPHELES.
Why, on the whole, thou 'rt—what thou art.
Set wigs of million curls upon thy head, to raise thee
Wear shoes on ell in height,—the truth betrays thee.
And thou remainest—what thou art.

FAUST.
I feel, indeed, that I have made the treasure
Of human thought and knowledge mine, in vain;
And if I now sit down in restful leisure,
No fount of newer strength is in my brain:
I am no hair's-breadth more in height,
Nor nearer to the Infinite.

MEPHISTOPHELES.
Good Sir, you see the facts precisely
As they are seen by each and all.
We must arrange them now, more wisely,
Before the joys of life shall pall.
Why, Zounds! Both hands and feet are, truly—
And head and virile forces—thine:
Yet all that I indulge in newly,
Is't thence less wholly mine?
If I've six stallions in my stall,
Are not their forces also lent me?
I speed along, completest man of all,
As though my legs were four-and-twenty.
Take hold, then! let reflection rest,
And plunge into the world with zest!
I say to thee, a speculative wight
Is like a beast on moorlands lean,
That round and round some fiend misleads to evil
    plight,
While all about lie pastures fresh and green.

FAUST.
Then how shall we begin?

MEPHISTOPHELES.
           We'll try a wider sphere.
What place of martyrdom is here!

Is 't life, I ask, is 't even prudence,
To bore thyself and bore the students?
Let Neighbor Paunch to that attend!
Why plague thyself with threshing straw forever?
The best thou learnest, in the end
Thou dar'st not tell the youngsters—never!
I hear one's footsteps, hither steering.

         FAUST.
To see him now I have no heart.

        MEPHISTOPHELES.
So long the poor boy waits a hearing,
He must not unconsoled depart.
Thy cap and mantle straightway lend me!
I'll play the comedy with art.

      (*He disguises himself.*)

My wits, be certain, will befriend me.
But fifteen minutes' time is all I need;
For our fine trip, meanwhile, prepare thyself with
    speed!

                     [*Exit* FAUST.]

   Mephistopheles meets with the student and thoroughly confuses him. Then, he and Faust, now a younger man, leave to seek adventure. Among their adventures, Faust and Mephistopheles visit a cellar-tavern in Leipzig, where Mephistopheles causes wine to pour from a table. Then they visit a Witches' Kitchen and learn of various types of magic and alchemy. Finally, Faust is led to Margaret, a young and innocent girl whom he immediately desires.

                VII.

           A STREET.

     FAUST. MARGARET (*passing by*).

         FAUST.
Fair lady, let it not offend you,
That arm and escort I would lend you!

MARGARET.
I'm neither lady, neither fair,
And home I can go without your care.
[*She releases herself, and exits.*]

FAUST.
By Heaven, the girl is wondrous fair!
Of all I 've seen, beyond compare;
So sweetly virtuous and pure,
And yet a little pert, be sure!
The lip so red, the cheek's clear dawn,
I'll not forget while the world rolls on!
How she cast down her timid eyes,
Deep in my heart imprinted lies:
How short and sharp of speech was she,
Why, 't was a real ecstasy!

(MEPHISTOPHELES *enters.*)

FAUST.
Hear, of that girl I'd have possession!

MEPHISTOPHELES.
Which, then?

FAUST.
The one who just went by.

MEPHISTOPHELES.
She, there? She's coming from confession,
Of every sin absolved; for I,
Behind her chair, was listening nigh.
So innocent is she, indeed,
That to confess she had no need.
I have no power o'er souls so green.

FAUST.
And yet, she's older than fourteen.

MEPHISTOPHELES.
How now! You're talking like Jack Rake,
Who every flower for himself would take,
And fancies there are no favors more,
Nor honors, save for him in store;
Yet always doesn't the thing succeed.

FAUST.
Most Worthy Pedagogue, take heed!
Let not a word of moral law be spoken!
I claim, I tell thee, all my right;
And if that image of delight
Rest not within mine arms to-night,
At midnight is our compact broken.

MEPHISTOPHELES.
But think, the chances of the case!
I need, at least, a fortnight's space,
To find an opportune occasion.

FAUST.
Had I but seven hours for all,
I should not on the Devil call,
But win her by my own persuasion.

MEPHISTOPHELES.
You almost like a Frenchman prate;
Yet, pray, don't take it as annoyance!
Why, all at once, exhaust the joyance?
Your bliss is by no means so great
As if you'd use, to get control,
All sorts of tender rigmarole,
And knead and shape her to your thought,
As in Italian tales 't is taught.

FAUST.
Without that, I have appetite.

MEPHISTOPHELES.
But now, leave jesting out of sight!
I tell you, once for all, that speed
With this fair girl will not succeed;
By storm she cannot captured be;
We must make use of strategy.

FAUST.
Get me something the angel keeps!
Lead me thither where she sleeps!
Get me a kerchief from her breast,—
A garter that her knee has pressed!

MEPHISTOPHELES.
That you may see how much I'd fain

Further and satisfy your pain,
We will no longer lose a minute;
I'll find her room to-day, and take you in it.

FAUST.
And shall I see—possess her?

MEPHISTOPHELES.
                No!
Unto a neighbor she must go,
And meanwhile thou, alone, mayst glow
With every hope of future pleasure,
Breathing her atmosphere in fullest measure.

FAUST.
Can we go thither?

MEPHISTOPHELES.
                'T is too early yet.

FAUST.
A gift for her I bid thee get!   [*Exit.*]

MEPHISTOPHELES.
Presents at once? That's good: he's certain to get at her!
Full many a pleasant place I know,
And treasures, buried long ago:
I must, perforce, look up the matter.
                            [*Exit.*]

VIII.

EVENING.

A SMALL, NEATLY KEPT CHAMBER.

MARGARET.
(*plaiting and binding up the braids of her hair*).
I'd something give, could I but say
Who was that gentleman, to-day.
Surely a gallant man was he,
And of a noble family;
So much could I in his face behold,—
And he wouldn't, else, have been so bold!
                            [*Exit.*]

MEPHISTOPHELES. FAUST.

MEPHISTOPHELES.
Come in, but gently: follow me!

FAUST (*after a moment's silence*).
Leave me alone, I beg of thee!

MEPHISTOPHELES (*prying about*).
Not every girl keeps things so neat.

FAUST (*looking around*).
O welcome, twilight soft and sweet,
That breathes throughout this hallowed shrine!
Sweet pain of love, bind thou with fetters fleet
The heart that on the dew of hope must pine!
How all around a sense impresses
Of quiet, order, and content
This poverty what bounty blesses!
What bliss within this narrow den is pent!

(*He throws himself into a leather arm-chair near the bed.*)

Receive me, thou, that in thine open arms
Departed joy and pain wert wont to gather!
How oft the children, with their ruddy charms,
Hung here, around this throne, where sat the father!
Perchance my love, amid the childish band,
Grateful for gifts the Holy Christmas gave her,
Here meekly kissed the grandsire's withered hand.
I feel, O maid! thy very soul
Of order and content around me whisper,—
Which leads thee with its motherly control,
The cloth upon thy board bids smoothly thee unroll,
The sand beneath thy feet makes whiter, crisper.
O dearest hand, to thee 't is given
To change this hut into a lower heaven!
And here!

(*He lifts one of the bed-curtains.*)

What sweetest thrill is in my blood!
Here could I spend whole hours, delaying:
Here Nature shaped, as if in sportive playing,
The angel blossom from the bud.

Here lay the child, with Life's warm essence
The tender bosom filled and fair,
And here was wrought, through holier, purer
    presence.
The form diviner beings wear!

And I? What drew me here with power?
How deeply am I moved, this hour!
What seek I? Why so full my heart, and sore?
Miserable Faust! I know thee now no more.

Is there a magic vapor here?
I came, with lust of instant pleasure,
And lie dissolved in dreams of love's sweet leisure!
Are we the sport of every changeful atmosphere?

And if, this moment, came she in to me,
How would I for the fault atonement render!
How small the giant lout would be,
Prone at her feet, relaxed and tender!

        MEPHISTOPHELES.
Be quick! I see her there, returning.

        FAUST.
Go! go! I never will retreat.

        MEPHISTOPHELES.
Here is a casket, not unmeet,
Which elsewhere I have just been earning.
Here, set it in the press, with haste!
I swear, 't will turn her head, to spy it:
Some baubles I therein had placed,
That you might win another by it.
True, child is child, and play is play.

        FAUST.
I know not, should I do it?

        MEPHISTOPHELES.
                Ask you, pray?
Yourself, perhaps, would keep the bubble?
Then I suggest, 't were fair and just
To spare the lovely day your lust,
And spare to me the further trouble.

You are not miserly, I trust?
I rub my hands, in expectation tender—

(*He places the casket in the press, and locks it
again.*)
Now quick, away!
The sweet young maiden to betray,
So that by wish and will you bend her;
And you look as though
To the lecture-hall you were forced to go,—
As if stood before you, gray and loath,
Physics and Metaphysics both!
But away!
[*Exeunt.*]

MARGARET (*with a lamp*).
It is so close, so sultry, here!

(*She opens the window.*)

And yet 't is not so warm outside.
I feel, I know not why, such fear!—
Would mother came!—where can she bide?
My body's chill and shuddering,—
I'm but a silly, fearsome thing!

(*She begins to sing, while undressing.*)

There was a King in Thule,
Was faithful till the grave,—
To whom his mistress, dying,
A golden goblet gave.

Naught was to him more precious:
He drained it at every bout:
His eyes with tears ran over.
As oft as he drank thereout.

When came his time of dying,
The towns in his land he told,
Naught else to his heir denying
Except the goblet of gold.

He sat at the royal banquet
With his knights of high degree,

In the lofty hall of his fathers
In the Castle by the Sea.

There stood the old carouser,
And drank the last life-glow;
And hurled the hallowed goblet
Into the tide below.

He saw it plunging and filling,
And sinking deep in the sea:
Then fell his eyelids forever,
And never more drank he!

(*She opens the press in order to arrange her clothes, and perceives the casket of jewels.*)

How comes that lovely casket here to me?
I locked the press, most certainly.
'T is truly wonderful! What can within it be?
Perhaps 't was brought by some one as a pawn,
And mother gave a loan thereon?
And here there hangs a key to fit:
I have a mind to open it.
What is that? God in Heaven! Whence came
Such things? Never beheld I aught so fair!
Rich ornaments, such as a noble dame
On highest holidays might wear!
How would the pearl-chain suit my hair?
Ah, who may all this splendor own?

(*She adorns herself with the jewelry, and steps before the mirror.*)

Were but the ear-rings mine, alone!
One has at once another air.
What helps one's beauty, youthful blood?
One may possess them, well and good;
But none the more do others care.
They praise us half in pity, sure:
To gold still tends,
On gold depends
All, all! Alas, we poor!

Mephistopheles arranges for Faust and Margaret to be alone, and their love develops. Margaret becomes unsure of herself and her passion.

XV.

MARGARET'S ROOM.

MARGARET
(*at the spinning-wheel, alone*).

My peace is gone,
My heart is sore:
I never shall find it
Ah, nevermore!

Save I have him near,
The grave is here;
The world is gall
And bitterness all.

My poor weak head
Is racked and crazed;
My thought is lost,
My senses mazed.

My peace is gone,
My heart is sore:
I never shall find it,
Ah, nevermore!

To see him, him only,
At the pane I sit;
To meet him, him only,
The house I quit.

His lofty gait,
His noble size,
The smile of his mouth,
The power of his eyes,

And the magic flow
Of his talk, the bliss
In the clasp of his hand,
And, ah! his kiss!

My peace is gone,
My heart is sore:
I never shall find it,
Ah, nevermore!

My bosom yearns
For him alone;
Ah, dared I clasp him,
And hold, and own!

And kiss his mouth,
To heart's desire,
And on his kisses
At last expire!

XVI.

MARTHA'S GARDEN.

Margaret. Faust.

MARGARET.
Promise me, Henry!—

FAUST.
What I can!

MARGARET.
How is 't with thy religion, pray?
Thou art a dear, good-hearted man,
And yet, I think, dost not incline that way.

FAUST.
Leave that, my child! Thou know'st my love is tender;
For love, my blood and life would I surrender,
And as for Faith and Church, I grant to each his own.

MARGARET.
That's not enough: we must believe thereon.

FAUST.
Must we?

MARGARET.
Would that I had some influence!
Then, too, thou honorest not the Holy Sacraments.

FAUST.
I honor them.

MARGARET.
            Desiring no possession.
'T is long since thou hast been to mass or to confession.
Believest thou in God?

FAUST.
                 My darling, who shall dare
"I believe in God!" to say?
Ask priest or sage the answer to declare,
And it will seem a mocking play,
A sarcasm on the asker.

MARGARET.
            Then thou believest not!

FAUST.
Hear me not falsely, sweetest countenance!
Who dare express Him?
And who profess Him,
Saying: I believe in Him!
Who, feeling, seeing,
Deny His being,
Saying: I believe Him not!
The All-enfolding,
The All-upholding,
Folds and upholds he not
Thee, me, Himself?
Arches not there the sky above us?
Lies not beneath us, firm, the earth?
And rise not, on us shining,
Friendly, the everlasting stars?
Look I not, eye to eye, on thee,
And feel'st not, thronging
To head and heart, the force,
Still weaving its eternal secret,
Invisible, visible, round thy life?
Vast as it is, fill with that force thy heart,
And when thou in the feeling wholly blessed art,
Call it, then, what thou wilt,—
Call it Bliss! Heart! Love! God!
I have no name to give it!
Feeling is all in all:
The Name is sound and smoke,
Obscuring Heaven's clear glow.

MARGARET.
All that is is fine and good, to hear it so:
Much the same way the preacher spoke,
Only with slightly different phrases.

FAUST.
The same thing, in all places,
All hearts that beat beneath the heavenly day—
Each in its language—say;
Then why not I, in mine, as well?

MARGARET.
To hear it thus, it may seem passable;
And yet, some hitch in 't there must be
For thou hast no Christianity.

FAUST.
Dear love!

MARGARET.
    I've long been grieved to see
That thou art in such company.

FAUST.
How so?

MARGARET.
    The man who with thee goes, thy mate,
Within my deepest, inmost soul I hate.
In all my life there's nothing
Has given my heart so keen a pang of loathing,
As his repulsive face has done.

FAUST.
Nay, fear him not, my sweetest one!

MARGARET.
I feel his presence like something ill.
I've else, for all, a kindly will,
But, much as my heart to see thee yearneth,
The secret horror of him returneth;
And I think the man a knave, as I live!
If I do him wrong, may God forgive!

FAUST.
There must be such queer birds, however.

MARGARET.
Live with the like of him, may I never!
When once inside the door comes he,
He looks around so sneeringly,
And half in wrath:
One sees that in nothing no interest he hath:
'T is written on his very forehead
That love, to him, is a thing abhorréd.
I am so happy on thine arm,
So free, so yielding, and so warm,
And in his presence stifled seems my heart.

FAUST.
Foreboding angel that thou art!

MARGARET.
It overcomes me in such degree,
That wheresoe'er he meets us, even,
I feel as though I'd lost my love for thee.
When he is by, I could not pray to Heaven.
That burns within me like a flame,
And surely, Henry, 't is with thee the same.

FAUST.
There, now, is thine antipathy!

MARGARET.
But I must go.

FAUST.
Ah, shall there never be
A quiet hour, to see us fondly plighted,
With breast to breast, and soul to soul united?

MARGARET.
Ah, if I only slept alone!
I'd draw the bolts to-night, for thy desire;
But mother's sleep so light has grown,
And if we were discovered by her,
'T would be my death upon the spot!

FAUST.
Thou angel, fear it not!
Here is a phial: in her drink
But three drops of it measure,
And deepest sleep will on her senses sink.

MARGARET.
What would I not, to give thee pleasure?
It will not harm her, when one tries it?

FAUST.
If 't would, my love, would I advise it?

MARGARET.
Ah, dearest man, if but thy face I see,
I know not what compels me to thy will:
So much have I already done for thee,
That scarcely more is left me to fulfil.
                    [*Exit.*]

(*Enter* MEPHISTOPHELES.)

MEPHISTOPHELES.
The monkey! Is she gone?

FAUST.
                Hast played the spy again?

MEPHISTOPHELES.
I've heard, most fully, how she drew thee.
The doctor has been catechised, 't is plain;
Great good, I hope, the thing will do thee.
The girls have much desire to ascertain
If one is prim and good, as ancient rules compel:
If there he's led, they think, he'll follow them as well.

FAUST.
Thou, monster, wilt nor see nor own
How this pure soul, of faith so lowly,
So loving and ineffable,—
The faith alone
That her salvation is,—with scruples holy
Pines, lest she hold as lost the man she loves so well!

MEPHISTOPHELES.
Thou, full of sensual, super-sensual desire,
A girl by the nose is leading thee.

FAUST.
Abortion, thou, of filth and fire!

MEPHISTOPHELES.
And then, how masterly she reads physiognomy!

When I am present she's impressed, she knows not
    how;
She in my mask a hidden sense would read:
She feels that surely I'm a genius now,—
Perhaps the very Devil, indeed!
Well, well,—to-night—?

    FAUST.
      What's that to thee?

   MEPHISTOPHELES.
Yet my delight 't will also be!

Margaret, tormented in soul because she has sinned with Faust, is soon in double sorrow when her brother Valentine, returning from war, is slain by Faust and Mephistopheles. As he dies, Valentine curses her for the shame she has brought upon herself and her family. Faust abandons her and travels with Mephistopheles to the Hartz Mountains, where he attends a gathering of unearthly and satanic creatures—the Walpurgis-Night. During Faust's absence, Margaret, in mad despair, has killed the child that she has borne him. She is condemned to death and is in prison as Faust comes again to her.

XXV.

DUNGEON.

    FAUST.
(*with a bunch of keys and a lamp, before an iron door*)
A shudder, long unfelt, comes o'er me;
Mankind's collected woe o'erwhelms me, here.
She dwells within the dark, damp walls before me,
And all her crime was a delusion dear!
What! I delay to free her?
I dread, once again to see her?
On! my shrinking but lingers Death more near.
 (*He grasps the lock: the sound of singing is heard inside.*)
  My mother, the harlot,

Who put me to death;
My father, the varlet,
Who eaten me hath!
Little sister, so good,
Laid my bones in the wood,
In the damp moss and clay:
Then was I a beautiful bird o' the wood;
Fly away! Fly away!

    FAUST (*unlocking*).
She does not dream her lover listens near;
That he the rattling chain, the rustling straw, can hear.
    (*He enters.*)

   MARGARET (*hiding herself on the pallet*).
Woe! woe!
They come. O death of bitterness!

    FAUST (*whispering*).
Hush! hush! The hour is come that frees thee.

   MARGARET (*throwing herself before him*).
Art thou a man, then pity my distress!

    FAUST.
Thy cries will wake the guards, and they will seize
 thee!
  (*He takes hold of the fetters to unlock them.*)

   MARGARET (*on her knees*).
Who, headsman! unto thee such power
Over me could give?
Thou 'rt come for me at midnight-hour:
Have mercy on me, let me live!
Is 't not soon enough when morning chime has rung?
    (*She rises.*)
And I am yet so young, so young!
And now Death comes, and ruin!
I, too, was fair, and that was my undoing.
My love was near, but now he's far;
Torn lies the wreath, scattered the blossoms are.
Seize me not thus so violently!
Spare me! What have I done to thee?
Let me not vainly entreat thee!
I never chanced, in all my days, to meet thee!

FAUST.
Shall I outlive this misery?

MARGARET.
Now am I wholly in thy might.
But let me suckle, first, my baby!
I blissed it all this livelong night;
They took 't away, to vex me, maybe,
And now they say I killed the child outright.
And never shall I be glad again.
They sing songs about me! 't is bad of the folk to do it!
There's an old story has the same refrain;
Who bade them so construe it?

FAUST (*falling upon his knees*).
Here lieth one who loves thee ever,
The thraldom of thy woe to sever.

MARGARET (*flinging herself beside him*).
O let us kneel, and call the Saints to hide us!
Under the steps beside us,
The threshold under,
Hell heaves in thunder!
The Evil One
With terrible wrath
Seeketh a path
His prey to discover!

FAUST (*aloud*).
Margaret! Margaret!

MARGARET (*attentively listening*).
That was the voice of my lover!
    (*She springs to her feet: the fetters fall off.*)
Where is he? I heard him call me.
I am free! No one shall enthrall me.
To his neck will I fly,
On his bosom lie!
On the threshold he stood, and *Margaret!* calling,
Midst of Hell's howling and noises appalling,
Midst of the wrathful, infernal derision,
I knew the sweet sound of the voice of the vision!

FAUST.
'T is I!

MARGARET.
        'T is thou! O, say it once again!
           (*Clasping him.*)
'T is he! 't is he! Where now is all my pain?
The anguish of the dungeon, and the chain?
'T is thou! Thou comest to save me,
And I am saved!—
Again the street I see
Where first I looked on thee;
And the garden, brightly blooming,
Where I and Martha wait thy coming.

      FAUST (*Struggling to leave*).
Come! Come with me!

      MARGARET.
           Delay, now!
So fain I stay, when thou delayest!
    (*Caressing him.*)

      FAUST.
Away, now!
If longer here thou stayest,
We shall be made to dearly rue it.

      MARGARET.
Kiss me!—canst no longer do it?
My friend, so short a time thou 'rt missing,
And hast unlearned thy kissing?
Why is my heart so anxious, on thy breast?
Where once a heaven thy glances did create me,
A heaven thy loving words expressed,
And thou didst kiss, as thou wouldst suffocate me—
Kiss me!
Or I'll kiss thee!
      (*She embraces him.*)
Ah, woe! thy lips are chill,
And still.
How changed in fashion
Thy passion!
Who has done me this ill?
      (*She turns away from him.*)

      FAUST.
Come, follow me! My darling, be more bold:

I'll clasp thee, soon, with warmth a thousand-fold;
But follow now! 'T is all I beg of thee.

   MARGARET (*turning to him*).
And is it thou? Thou, surely, certainly?

   FAUST.
 'T is I! Come on!

   MARGARET.
   Thou wilt unloose my chain,
And in thy lap wilt take me once again.
How comes it that thou dost not shrink from me?—
Say, dost thou know, my friend, whom thou mak'st
 free?

   FAUST.
Come! come! The night already vanisheth.

   MARGARET.
My mother have I put to death;
I've drowned the baby born to thee.
Was it not given to thee and me?
Thee, too!—'T is thou! It scarcely true doth seem—
Give me thy hand! 'T is not a dream!
Thy dear, dear hand!—But, ah, 't is wet!
Why, wipe it off! Methinks that yet
There's blood thereon.
Ah, God! what hast thou done?
Nay, sheathe thy sword at last!
Do not affray me!

   FAUST.
O, let the past be past!
Thy words will slay me!

   MARGARET.
No, no! Thou must outlive us.
Now I'll tell thee the graves to give us:
Thou must begin to-morrow
The work of sorrow!
The best place give to my mother,
Then close at her side my brother,
And me a little away.
But not too very far, I pray!

And here, on my right breast, my baby lay!
Nobody else will lie beside me!—
Ah, within thine arms to hide me,
That was a sweet and a gracious bliss,
But no more, no more can I attain it!
I would force myself on thee and constrain it,
And it seems thou repellest my kiss:
And yet 't is thou, so good, so kind to see!

          FAUST.

If thou feel'st it is I, then come with me!

          MARGARET.

Out yonder?

          FAUST.

To freedom.

          MARGARET.

      If the grave is there,
Death lying in wait, then come!
From here to eternal rest:
No further step—no, no!
Thou goest away! O Henry, if I could go!

          FAUST.

Thou canst! Just will it! Open stands the door.

          MARGARET.

I dare not go: there's no hope any more.
Why should I fly? They'll still my steps waylay!
It is so wretched, forced to beg my living,
And a bad conscience sharper misery giving!
It is so wretched, to be strange, forsaken,
And I'd still be followed and taken!

          FAUST.

I'll stay with thee.

          MARGARET.

Be quick! Be quick!
Save thy perishing child!
Away! Follow the ridge
Up by the brook,
Over the bridge,
Into the wood,
To the left, where the plank is placed

In the pool!
Seize it in haste!
'T is trying to rise,
'T is struggling still!
Save it! Save it!

        FAUST.

Recall thy wandering will!
One step, and thou art free at last!

        MARGARET.

If the mountain we had only passed!
There sits my mother upon a stone,—
I feel an icy shiver!
There sits my mother upon a stone,
And her head is wagging ever.
She beckons, she nods not, her heavy head falls o'er;
She slept so long that she wakes no more.
She slept, while we were caressing:
Ah, those were the days of blessing!

        FAUST.

Here words and prayers are nothing worth;
I'll venture, then, to bear thee forth.

        MARGARET.

No—let me go! I'll suffer no force!
Grasp me not so murderously!
I've done, else, all things for the love of thee.

        FAUST.

The day dawns: Dearest! Dearest!

        MARGARET.

Day? Yes, the day comes,—the last day breaks for me!
My wedding-day it was to be!
Tell no one thou hast been with Margaret!
Woe for my garland! The chances
Are over—'t is all in vain!
We shall meet once again,
But not at the dances!
The crowd is thronging, no word is spoken:
The square below
And the streets overflow:
The death-bell tolls, the wand is broken.
I am seized, and bound, and delivered—
Shoved to the block—they give the sign!

Now over each neck has quivered
The blade that is quivering over mine.
Dumb lies the world like the grave!

FAUST.

O had I ne'er been born!

MEPHISTOPHELES (*appears outside*).

Off! or you're lost ere morn.
Useless talking, delaying and praying!
My horses are neighing:
The morning twilight is near.

MARGARET.

What rises up from the threshold here?
He! he! suffer him not!
What does he want in this holy spot?
He seeks me!

FAUST.

Thou shalt live.

MARGARET.

Judgement of God! myself to thee I give.

MEPHISTOPHELES (*to* FAUST).

Come! or I'll leave her in the lurch, and thee!

MARGARET.

Thine am I, Father! rescue me!
Ye angels, holy cohorts, guard me,
Camp around, and from evil ward me!
Henry! I shudder to think of thee.

MEPHISTOPHELES.

She is judged!

VOICE (*from above*).

She is saved!

MEPHISTOPHELES (*to* FAUST).

Hither to me!

(*He disappears with* FAUST.)

VOICE (*from within, dying away*).

Henry! Henry!

(Translated by Bayard Taylor)

The Erl-King

Who rides there so late through the night dark and drear?
A father it is, with his infant so dear;
He holdeth the boy tightly clasp'd in his arm,
He holdeth him safely, he keepeth him warm.

"My son, wherefore seek'st thou thy face thus to hide?"
"Look, father, the Erl-King is close by our side!
Dost see not the Erl-King, with crown and with train?"
"My son, 'tis the mist rising over the plain."

"Oh come, thou dear infant! oh, come thou with me!
Full many a game I will play there with thee;
On my strand, lovely flowers their blossoms unfold,
My mother shall grace thee with garments of gold."

"My father, my father, and dost thou not hear
The words that the Erl-King now breathes in my ear?"
"Be calm, dearest child, 'tis thy fancy deceives;
'Tis the sad wind that sighs through the withering leaves."

"Wilt go, then, dear infant, wilt go with me there?
My daughters shall tend thee with sisterly care;
My daughters by night their glad festival keep,
They'll dance thee, and rock thee, and sing thee to sleep."

"My father, my father, and dost thou not see
How the Erl-King his daughters has brought here for me?"
"My darling, my darling, I see it aright,
'Tis the aged gray willows deceiving thy sight."

"I love thee, I'm charmed by thy beauty, dear boy!
And if thou'rt unwilling, then force I'll employ."
"My father, my father, he seizes me fast,
Full sorely the Erl-King has hurt me at last."

The father now gallops, with terror half wild,
He grasps in his arms the poor shuddering child;
He reaches his courtyard with toil and with dread,—
The child in his arms is motionless, dead.

(Translated by E. A. Bowring)

Alexander Pushkin
(1799-1837)
from *Eugene Onegin*

Pushkin was the first Russian writer to gain international fame, and he remains one of his country's most loved poets and dramatists. Byronesque in both his literary attitudes and his way of living, he wrote in praise of freedom, advocated the overthrow of oppressive governments, got himself exiled for his political activities, and was killed at thirty-eight, in a duel that grew out of his wife's unfaithfulness.

A prolific writer, Pushkin produced many poems, narratives in verse and prose, and dramas. Russian composers found his writings invaluable; his stories provided plots for a number of important operas—for Glinka's Russlan and Ludmilla; *for Moussorgsky's great* Boris Godunov; *for Rimski-Korsakov's* Le Coq d'Or (The Golden Cockerel); *and for Tchaikovsky's* Pique-Dame (The Queen of Spades) *and* Eugene Onegin.

Eugene Onegin, a novel in verse, is modeled on Byron's long narrative poems, particularly on Don Juan. *Though its story is often serious and even tragic, it is told in light, vigorous verse, with numerous passages of realistic description and an abundance of satire.*

Eugene Onegin, a handsome, bored young breaker of hearts, inherits his uncle's large estate and moves to the country. Here he becomes friendly with a neighbor, the young poet Vladimir Lensky. He also meets Lensky's fiancée, a dimpled blonde named Olga Larina, and Olga's sister Tatyana (Tanya), a quiet girl who reads romantic novels and dreams of love. Though Eugene pays little attention to Tatyana, she writes him the letter that follows.

Tatyana's Letter to Onegin

I write you; is my act not serving
As an avowal? Well I know
The punishment I am deserving:
That you despise me. Even so,
Perhaps for my sad fate preserving
A drop of pity, you'll forbear
To leave me here to my despair.
I first resolved upon refraining
From speech: you never would have learned
The secret shame with which I burned,
If there had been a hope remaining
That I should see you once a week
Or less, that I should hear you speak,
And answer with the barest greeting,
But have one thing when you were gone,
One thing alone to think upon
For days, until another meeting.
But you're unsociable, they say,
The country, and its dulness, bore you;
We . . . we don't shine in any way,
But have a hearty welcome for you.

Why did you come to visit us?
Here in this village unfrequented,
Not knowing you, I would not thus
Have learned how hearts can be tormented.
I might (who knows?) have grown contented,
My girlish dreams forever stilled,
And found a partner in another,
And been a faithful wife and mother,
And loved the duties well fulfilled.

Another? . . . No, my heart is given
To one forever, one alone!
It was decreed . . . the will of Heaven
Ordained it so: I am your own.
All my past life has had one meaning—
That I should meet you. God on High
Has sent you, and I shall be leaning
On your protection till I die.
I saw you in my dreams; I'd waken
To know I loved you; long ago
I languished in your glance, and oh!
My soul, hearing your voice, was shaken.
Only a dream? It could not be!
The moment that I saw you coming,
I thrilled, my pulses started drumming,
And my heart whispered: it is he!
Yes, deep within I had the feeling,

When at my tasks of charity,
Or when, the world about me reeling,
I looked for peace in prayer, kneeling,
That silently you spoke to me.
Just now, did I not see you flitting
Through the dim room where I am sitting,
To stand, dear vision, by my bed?
Was it not you who gently gave me
A word to solace and to save me:
The hope on which my heart is fed?
Are you a guardian angel to me
Or but a tempter to undo me?
Dispel my doubts! My mind's awhirl;
Perhaps mere folly has created
These fancies of a simple girl
And quite another end is fated . . .
So be it! Now my destiny
Lies in your hands, for you to fashion;
Forgive the tears you wring from me,
I throw myself on your compassion . . .
Imagine: here I am alone,
With none to understand or cherish
My restless thoughts, and I must perish,
Stifled, in solitude, unknown.
I wait: when once your look has spoken,
My heart once more with hope will glow,
Or a deserved reproach will show
The painful dream forever broken!

Reread I cannot . . . I must end . . .
The fear, the shame, are past endurance . . .
Upon your honor I depend,
And lean upon it with assurance . . .

. . .

Tatyana's letter moves Eugene a little, but he gives her no encouragement—nothing but a self-satisfied lecture about learning to control her emotions. She is heartbroken, but she hides her sorrow as the months pass. At a name-day party in honor of Tatyana, Eugene flirts with her sister Olga. In a jealous fury, the poet Lensky challenges Eugene to a duel, which takes place the next morning.

The gleaming pistols are held steady
As hammers on the ramrods knock,
And bullets are crammed down; already
One hears the clicking of a cock.
Powder into the pan is sifted,
The jagged flint, still harmless, lifted.
Behind a stump among the trees
Guillot is standing, ill at ease.
Their gestures arguing decision,
The enemies their mantles doff.
And now Zaretzky measures off
Thirty-two paces with precision;
At either end the two friends stand
Each with a pistol in his hand.

"Approach!" How calm and cold their faces,
As the two foes, with even tread,
Not aiming yet, advance four paces,
Four steps toward a narrow bed.
First Eugene, still advancing duly,
Begins to raise his pistol coolly.
Now five steps more the pair have made,
And Lensky, firm and unafraid,
Screws up his eye and is preparing
To take aim also—but just then
Onegin fires . . . Once again
Fate shows herself to be unsparing.
The hour is fled beyond recall;
The poet lets his pistol fall,

His hand upon his breast lays lightly,
And drops. His clouded eyes betray
Not pain, but death. Thus, sparkling whitely
Where the quick sunbeams on it play,
A snowball down the hill goes tumbling
And sinks from sight, soon to be crumbling.
Eugene, with ice in all his veins,
Runs to the youth, whose life-blood stains
The ground, looks, calls him . . . But no power
Avails to rouse him: he is gone.
The poet in the very dawn
Of life has perished like a flower
That from its stem a gale has wrenched;
Alas! the altar-fire is quenched.

He did not stir, but like one dreaming
He lay most strangely there at rest.
The blood from the fresh wound was steaming:
The ball had pierced clean through the breast.
A moment since, this heart was quickened
By poetry and love, or sickened
By hate and dread, and strongly beat
With dancing blood, with living heat.
But now it is a house forsaken,
Where all is silent, dark and drear,
The shutters closed, chalked windows blear.
The lady of the house has taken
Her leave. She's gone. Where to, God knows,
She left no trace behind that shows.

. . .

In a digression, the poet wonders what might have happened had Lensky lived, and he bids an ironical farewell to his own youth.

. . . I love my hero truly,
Return to him I will, I vow,
And shall complete his story duly,
But that is not my pleasure now.
The years to rugged prose constrain me,
No more can hoyden rhymes detain me,
And I admit, in penitence,
I court the Muse with indolence.
No more I find it quite so pressing
To soil the sheets with flying quill;
But other fancies bleak and chill,
And other cares, austere, distressing,
In festive crowds, in solitude,
Upon my dreaming soul intrude.

By new desires I am enchanted,
New sorrows come, my heart to fret;
The hopes of old will not be granted,
The olden sorrows I regret.
Ah, dreams! where has your sweetness vanished?
Where's youth(the rhyme comes glibly)banished?
And is the vernal crown of youth
Quite withered now in very truth?
Can the sad thought with which I flirted
In elegiac mood at last
Be fact, and can my spring be past
(As I in jest so oft asserted)?
Will it no more return to me?
Shall I be thirty presently?

The afternoon of life is starting,
I must admit the sorry truth.
Amen: but friendly be our parting,
My frivolous and merry youth!
My thanks for all the hours of gladness,
The tender torments, and the sadness,
The storm and strife, the frequent feast;
For all your great gifts and your least,
My thanks. Alike in peace and riot
I found you good, and I attest
I tasted all your joys with zest;
Enough! My soul is calm and quiet
As a new road I choose at last,
To rest from cares and labors past.

Let me look back. Farewell, sweet bowers
Where days would drift by lazily,
Where first I yielded to the powers
Of passion and of reverie.
And you, oh, youthful inspiration,
Come, rouse anew imagination—
Upon the dull mind's slumbers break,
My little nook do not forsake;
Let not the poet's heart know capture
By sullen time, and soon grow dry
And hard and cold, and petrify
Here in the world's benumbing rapture,
This pool we bathe in, friends, this muck
In which, God help us, we are stuck.

. . .

Olga soon ends her mourning for Lensky and marries a military man. Tatyana's mother takes her to Moscow, where the once-shy girl acquires the social graces, becomes a great lady, and marries a prince. Still bored with life, Eugene comes to Moscow, sees Tatyana, and promptly falls in love with her; in fact, he writes a pathetic letter that is much like her earlier one to him. She ignores him; but some weeks later he visits her and finds her tearfully reading his letter.

Her voiceless grief was past disguising;
In that swift moment one could see
The former Tanya, recognizing
Her in the princess readily.
Eugene in a blind gust of feeling
Dropped at her feet and stayed there, kneeling.
She shuddered, wordless, yet her eyes
Betrayed no anger, no surprise,
As she surveyed him. . . . His dejected
And healthless look, his dumb remorse—
These spoke to her with silent force.
And in her soul was resurrected
The simple girl whose dreams, whose ways,
Whose heart belonged to other days.

She does not raise him, does not falter:
Nor from his greedy lips withdraws
Her passive hand; naught seems to alter
Her look throughout that endless pause. . . .
What are her reveries unspoken?
The silence is at long last broken
As she says gently: "Rise, have done.
I must say candid words, or none.
Onegin, need I ask you whether
You still retain the memory
Of that lost hour beneath the tree
When destiny brought us together?
You preached at me, I listened, meek;
Today it is my turn to speak.

"Then I was younger, maybe better,
Onegin, and I loved you; well?
How did you take my girlish letter?
Your heart responded how? Pray, tell!
Most harshly: there was no disguising
Your scorn. You did not find surprising
The plain girl's love? Why, even now,
I freeze—good God!—recalling how
You came and lectured me so brightly—
Your look that made my spirit sink!
But for that sermon do not think

I blame you. . . .For you acted rightly;
Indeed, you played a noble role:
I thank you from my inmost soul. . . .

"Then, far from urban noise and glitter,
Off in the wilds—is it not true?—
You did not like me. . . . That was bitter,
But worse, what now you choose to do!
Why do you pay me these attentions?
Because society's conventions,
Deferring to my wealth and rank,
Have given me prestige? Be frank!
Because my husband's decoration,
A soldier's, wins us friends at court,
And all would blazon the report
That I had stained my reputation—
'Twould give you in society
A tempting notoriety?

"I cannot help it: I am weeping. . . .
If you recall your Tanya still,
There is one thought you should be keeping
In mind: if I but had my will,
You'd treat me in the old harsh fashion,
Not offer this insulting passion,
These endless letters and these tears.
My childish dreams, my tender years
Aroused your pity then. . . . You're kneeling
Here at my feet. But dare you say
In truth what brought you here today?
What petty thought, what trivial feeling?
Can you, so generous, so keen,
Be ruled by what is small and mean?

"To me, Onegin, all these splendors,
The tinsel of unwelcome days,
The homage that the great world tenders,
My modish house and my soirées—
To me all this is naught. This minute
I'd give my house and all that's in it,
This dizzy whirl in fancy dress,
For a few books, a wilderness
Of flowers, for our modest dwelling,
The scene where first I saw your face,
Onegin, that familiar place,

And for the simple churchyard, telling
Its tale of humble lives, where now
My poor nurse sleeps beneath the bough. . . .

"And happiness, before it glided
Away forever, was so near! . . .
But now my fate is quite decided.
I was in too much haste, I fear;
My mother coaxed and wept; the sequel
You know; besides, all lots were equal
To hapless Tanya. . . . Well, and so
I married. Now, I beg you, go.
I know your heart; I need not tremble,
Because your honor and your pride
Will in this matter be your guide.
I love you (why should I dissemble?)
But I became another's wife;
I shall be true to him through life."

She left him. There Eugene, forsaken,
Stood thunderstruck. He could not stir.
By what a storm his heart was shaken,
What pride, what grief, what thoughts of her!
But are those stirrups he is hearing?
Tatyana's husband is appearing.
At this unhappy moment, we
Must leave my hero; it will be
For a long time. . .indeed, forever.
Together we have traveled far.
Congratulations! Now we are
Ashore at last, and our endeavor
Is at an end. Hurrah, three cheers!
You'll grant it's time to part, my dears.

(Translated by Babette Deutsch)

Ivan Turgenev
(1818-1883)
The Singers

The small village of Kolotovka, which once belonged to a lady known in the neighborhood as Filly because of her mettlesome, lively disposition, and which is now the property of some German from St. Petersburg, lies on the slope of a bare hill split from top to bottom by a terrible ravine. A yawning chasm, gullied by the action of water, it winds its way along the very middle of the village street and divides the wretched hamlet more completely than a river would, for a river can at least be spanned by a bridge. A few gaunt willows straggle timidly down its sandy sides; at the very bottom, which is dry and yellow as brass, lie enormous slabs of limestone. A cheerless sight, certainly—yet the people of the neighborhood know the road to Kolotovka well: they go there often and gladly.

At the very head of the ravine, a few steps from the point where it starts as a narrow cleft in the ground, there is a small square cottage. It stands alone, apart from the others, and has a thatched roof and a chimney. One window faces the ravine, like a vigilant eye, and on winter evenings when it is lighted from within, it is visible from afar in the foggy, frosty air and twinkles like a guiding star to many a wayfaring peasant. A blue signboard is nailed above the door: the cottage is a tavern, called The Cheerful Nook. Liquor is sold there probably not cheaper than the set price, but the tavern is frequented far more than all the other establishments of the kind in the vicinity. The reason for this is the tavernkeeper, Nikolay Ivanych.

Once a slender, curly-headed and applecheeked lad, now an extraordinarily stout man, already grizzled, his features buried in fat, with sly, good-natured little eyes, and a fleshy forehead creased with threadlike wrinkles, Nikolay Ivanych has lived in Kolotovka for more than twenty years. He is a shrewd, wide-awake fellow, like most tavernkeepers. Although he is not particularly amiable or talkative, he has the gift of attracting and keeping customers. For some reason they find it extremely pleasant to sit in front of his bar under the placid and cordial though watchful gaze of the phlegmatic host. He has a great deal of common sense; he is thoroughly familiar with the life of the landed gentry, the peasants, the townspeople; in a crisis he can give sensible advice, but being selfish and cautious, prefers to keep aloof and at most by distant hints, dropped as if unintentionally, to lead his customers—and at that only his favorite customers—into the right path. He is a good judge of everything that is of importance or interest to a Russian: horses and cattle, timber, bricks, crockery, dry goods and leather goods, songs and dances. When he has no customers, he generally sits like a sack on the ground in front of his cottage, his thin little legs tucked under him, exchanging friendly remarks with all the passers-by.

Nikolay Ivanych has seen a great deal in his time; he has survived scores of petty landowners who used to come to him for liquor; he knows everything that goes on within a radius of sixty miles and he never blabs, never gives the slightest sign of knowing what is unsuspected even by the most astute rural police officer. He holds his tongue, chuckles to himself and shifts his tumblers about. His neighbors respect him; General Shcherspetenko, the ranking landowner of the district, nods to him condescendingly whenever he drives past his cottage. Nikolay Ivanych is a man of influence: he made a well-known horse thief return a horse he had stolen from one of his friends; he brought to their senses the peasants of a neighboring village who had refused to accept a new steward, and so on. It should not be thought, however, that he does such things out of love of justice, or concern for his neighbors. No, he simply tries to prevent anything from happening that might in any way disturb his peace of mind. Nikolay Ivanych is married and has children. His wife, a pert, sharp-nosed and keen-eyed woman of the burgher class, has, like her husband, of late years grown rather stout. He relies on her in all things, and she keeps the key to the cashbox. Boisterous drunks are afraid of her; she doesn't like them: they bring little profit and make much noise; the sullen, taciturn ones are more to her taste. The children are still small; their older brothers and sisters died young; those who survived favor their parents: it is a pleasure to look at the intelligent faces of these robust youngsters.

It was an intolerably hot day in July when, slowly dragging my feet, I was climbing up the Kolotovka ravine together with my dog on the way to The Cheerful Nook. The sun was blazing furiously in the sky; the sticky heat was relentless, and the air was thick with stifling dust. Glossy cocks and crows with gaping beaks stared piteously at passers-by, as though begging for sympathy; alone the sparrows were undaunted. Ruffling their feathers, they chirped and fought in the hedges more ferociously than ever, flew up from the dusty road in a flock, or soared in gray clouds over the green patches of hemp. Thirst tormented me. There was no water near by: in Kolotovka, as in many villages of the steppes, the peasants, in the absence of springs and wells, drink a kind of liquid mud—for no one could call such vile slops water—out of a pond.... I wanted to get a glass of beer or kvass at Nikolay Ivanych's.

It must be admitted that at no season does Kolotovka present a cheerful spectacle; it has a particularly depressing effect when the pitiless rays of the dazzling July sun beat down upon the brown, tattered roofs of the cottages, on the deep ravine, on the parched, dusty pasture over which lean, long-legged hens are wandering hopelessly, on the gray aspenwood frame with holes for windows, the remains of a former manor house, overgrown with nettles, wormwood and rank weeds. The sun beats down on the pond too, black and scorched, as it were, strewn with goose down and rimmed with half-dried mud; it beats down on the ramshackle dam, near which, on the ashen earth trodden fine, sheep, breathless and sneezing with the dust, huddle sadly together, dejectedly and patiently bowing their heads as low as possible, apparently waiting for the intolerable heat to give over.

With weary steps I approached Nikolay Ivanych's dwelling, as usual arousing in the village children an astonishment which expressed itself in an intense and meaningless stare, and in the dogs an indignation that manifested itself in a barking so hoarse and furious that it seemed to tear at their very entrails and left them coughing and choking. Suddenly on the threshold of the tavern there appeared a tall, bare-headed man in a frieze coat with a low blue belt. He looked like a house-serf; thick gray hair rose in disorder above his withered and wrinkled face. He was calling someone all the while, rapidly sawing the air, and his arms were making wider circles than he desired. It could be seen that he had been drinking. "Come, do come!" he jabbered, raising his thick eyebrows with difficulty. "Come, Blinkard, come! How you crawl along, brother, upon my word! That isn't right, brother. People are waiting for you, and here you are crawling along.... Come on!"

"Well, I'm coming, I'm coming," someone called in a quavering voice; and from behind the cottage, on the right, there appeared a short, stout, lame man. He wore a fairly clean cloth coat, with his arm in one sleeve only; a tall pointed cap, pushed down over his eyebrows, gave his round, plump face a sly and mocking expression. His little, yellow eyes fairly darted about, a restrained, forced smile never left his thin lips, while his thin, long nose thrust itself forward impudently, like a rudder. "I'm coming, my friend," he continued, hobbling toward the tavern; "why are you calling me? Who is waiting?"

"Why am I calling you?" repeated the man in the frieze coat. "What a queer one you are, Blinkard; you are called to the tavern, and you ask 'What for?' And the people who are waiting for you are all good men: Yashka the Turk, and Wild Squire and the contractor from Zhizdra. Yashka and the contractor have made a bet: the stake is a demijohn of beer—I mean as to who will outdo the other, that is, sing better...see?"

"Is Yashka going to sing?" the man addressed as Blinkard asked with interest. "And you are not fibbing, Loony?"

"I am not fibbing," answered Loony with dignity. "It's you who tell lies. Of course, he'll sing, if he has got a bet on, Blinkard, you ninny, you cheat, you!"

"Let's go in, stupid," said Blinkard.

"Well, give me a kiss at least, my soul," jabbered Loony, opening his arms wide.

"Look at the softy," responded Blinkard contemptuously, pushing him away with his elbow, and both of them, stooping, entered the low doorway.

The conversation I had overheard aroused my curiosity intensely. More than once I had heard rumors that Yashka the Turk was the best singer in the neighborhood and suddenly here was a chance to hear him in competition with another master. I quickened my pace and entered the establishment.

In all probability not many of my readers have had the opportunity of looking into country taverns, but we huntsmen, where don't we land? Their arrangement is very simple. They usually consist of a dark entry and a room with a proper stove so that it isn't sooty, divided in two by a partition, behind which no customer is allowed.

There is a wide oak table against this partition and right above is a large opening that runs lengthwise. On this table or counter liquor is sold. Sealed bottles of various sizes stand on the shelves, opposite the opening. In the front part of the room, which is left to the customers, there are benches, two or three empty barrels, a corner table. Country taverns are for the most part rather dark, and you will hardly ever see on their timbered walls the brightly colored cheap prints that are found in most peasant homes.

When I entered The Cheerful Nook, a fairly large company was already assembled there.

Behind the counter, in his usual place, almost filling up the aperture in the partition, stood Nikolay Ivanych in a gay print shirt, a lazy smile on his fat face; with his plump white hands he was pouring out two glasses of liquor for the friends who had just come in, Blinkard and Loony; behind him, in the corner near the window, his sharp-eyed wife was seen. In the middle of the room stood Yashka the Turk, a thin, well-built youth of twenty-three dressed in a long-skirted caftan of blue nankeen. He had the appearance of a factory hand, a dashing fellow, though apparently he could not boast of robust health. His hollow cheeks, his large restless gray eyes, his straight nose with delicate nostrils, his sloping, white forehead with the fair curls brushed back, his full-lipped, but beautiful, expressive mouth—his whole countenance betrayed an impressionable, passionate nature. He was greatly agitated: he blinked, his breathing was irregular, his hands trembled as with fever—and he really was in a fever, the troubling, sudden fever that is so well-known to all who have to speak or sing in public.

Near him stood a man of about forty with broad shoulders and broad cheekbones, a low forehead, narrow Tartar eyes, a short, flat nose, a square chin and shining black hair as stiff as bristles. The expression of his swarthy, leaden-hued face, especially of his pale lips, might have been called almost ferocious, had it not been so composed and thoughtful. He scarcely stirred and only slowly looked about him, like an ox from under its yoke. He wore some sort of threadbare jacket with smooth brass buttons; an old black silk kerchief was wrapped around his huge neck. He was called Wild Squire.

Directly opposite him, on a bench under the icons, sat Yashka's competitor, the contractor from Zhizdra: a short, thickset man, pockmarked and curly-haired, with a snub nose, small lively brown eyes and a short scanty beard. He cast lively glances about him, and, with his hands tucked under him, kept nonchalantly jigging his legs and tapping with his feet, which were shod in fashionable top-boots with an edging. He wore a new coat of gray cloth with a plush collar, in sharp contrast with his scarlet shirt, which was buttoned close around the throat. A peasant in a tight, shabby jacket with a huge hole on the shoulder sat at the table in the opposite corner to the right of the door. The sunlight was pouring through the dusty panes of two tiny windows in a thin yellowish stream and apparently could not overcome the habitual darkness of the room: all the objects were lighted up scantily, in spots, as it were. On the other hand, it was almost cool in the room, and the sensation of closeness and heat slipped from my shoulders like a load as soon as I crossed the threshold.

My arrival, I could see, at first somewhat disconcerted Nikolay Ivanych's customers; but noticing that he bowed to me as to an acquaintance, they were reassured and paid no further attention to me. I ordered a beer and sat in the corner, near the peasant in the torn jacket.

"Now then!" suddenly cried Loony, tossing off his glass at one gulp and accompanying his exclamation with the strange waving of the arms, without which he seemed unable to utter a word. "What are we waiting for? If we are to begin, let's begin, eh, Yasha?"

"Let's begin, let's begin," Nikolay Ivanych chimed in approvingly.

"Might as well begin," the contractor remarked coldly and smiling self-confidently; "I'm ready."

"And so am I," brought out Yakov excitedly.

"Well, begin, lads, begin," Blinkard squeaked. But in spite of all the unanimous protestations, no one began; the contractor did not even rise from the bench; it was as though all were waiting for something.

"Begin," broke in Wild Squire sullenly and sharply.

Yakov started. The contractor rose, tugged his belt and cleared his throat.

"But who is to begin?" he inquired in a slightly altered voice, turning to Wild Squire, who continued to stand motionlessly in the middle of the room, his heavy legs wide apart and his powerful arms thrust into the pockets of his trousers almost to the elbow.

"You, you, contractor," jabbered Loony, "you, brother."

Wild Squire looked at him askance, Loony blushed faintly, stared at the ceiling in confusion, twitched his shoulders and fell silent.

"Draw lots," said Wild Squire with deliberate emphasis, "and let the beer be placed on the counter."

Nikolay Ivanych bent down, picked up the demijohn from the floor with a grunt and set it on the counter.

Wild Squire glanced at Yakov, and said: "Well!"

Yakov dug into his pockets, produced a groat and marked it with his teeth. The contractor pulled from under the skirt of his caftan a new leather purse, unhurriedly untied the string and shaking out a quantity of small change into his palm, selected a brand new groat. Loony held out his worn cap, with its brown visor dangling; Yakov dropped his coin into it, the contractor his.

"You draw one out," said Wild Squire, turning to Blinkard.

Blinkard smiled complacently, took the cap in both hands and began to shake it.

Instantly a profound silence fell: the groats jingled faintly, clinking against each other. I looked around attentively: all faces expressed intense expectation; Wild Squire himself screwed up his eyes; even my neighbor, the peasant in the ragged jacket, craned his neck inquisitively. Blinkard put his hand into the cap and drew out the contractor's groat. Everyone heaved a sigh. Yakov blushed and the contractor passed his hand over his hair.

"There, I said that you should begin!" exclaimed Loony, "didn't I?"

"Come, come, don't squawk," remarked Wild Squire contemptuously. "Begin," he continued, nodding to the contractor.

"What song shall I sing?" asked the contractor, beginning to be flustered.

"Anything you please," answered Blinkard. "Sing whatever enters your head."

"Of course, anything you please," added Nikolay Ivanych, slowly folding his arms across his chest; "it's not for us to give you orders about that. Sing what you like, only sing well, and afterwards we'll decide in all fairness."

"In all fairness, to be sure," put in Loony and licked the rim of his empty glass.

"Let me clear my throat a bit, brother," said the contractor, fingering the collar of his caftan.

"Come, come, no dawdling—begin!" declared Wild Squire and dropped his eyes.

The contractor considered a while, shook his head and stepped forward. Yakov riveted his eyes on him. . . .

But before I commence the description of the contest itself, I believe it will not be amiss to say a few words about each of the characters in my tale. The lives of some of them were already known to me when I met them in The Cheerful Nook; I collected some information about the others later on.

Let us begin with Loony. The man's real name is Yevgraf Ivanov; but no one throughout the neighborhood called him anything but Loony, and he even referred to himself by that nickname: so well did it fit him. And indeed, nothing could have been better suited to his insignificant, perpetually agitated features. He was an unmarried house-serf who had gone on a permanent spree and had long since been given up by his own masters, and who, although having no employment and not earning a groat, nevertheless managed to get drunk every day at other people's expense. He had a multitude of acquaintances who treated him to liquor and tea, without knowing why they did so, for, far from being entertaining in company, he annoyed everyone with his meaningless gabble, his insufferable importunities, his feverish gestures and incessant, unnatural guffawing. He could neither sing nor dance; he had never in his life said a single clever or even sensible thing; he gabbled and told lies at random—a regular Loony.

And yet not a single drinking bout within a radius of sixty miles took place without his lanky figure turning up among the guests—people had become used to him and tolerant of his presence as an unavoidable evil. True, he was treated contemptuously, but Wild Squire was the only one who knew how to check his absurd outbursts.

Blinkard bore no resemblance to Loony. His nickname suited him to a T, though he did not blink his eyes any more than other people; it is well known that the Russian folk are past masters in giving nicknames. In spite of my efforts to ferret out more details about this man's past, there yet remained for me—as probably for many others—obscure passages in his life story, passages, as the bookish put it, veiled in darkness. All I found out was that he had once been a coachman to a childless old lady; that he had run away with the team entrusted to his care; that he had disappeared for a whole year, but that, apparently learning by experience the drawbacks and miseries of a roving existence, he had of his own accord returned home, now lame, and had flung himself at his mistress's feet. In the course of several years he had atoned for his offense by exemplary conduct. Gradually getting in her good graces, he ended by gaining her complete confidence, became her steward, and on her death, it turned out that he had received his freedom, no one knew how. Thereupon he had himself admitted to the burgher class, began to rent melon patches from his neighbors, waxed rich and was now in clover. He was something of a man of the world, a shrewd fellow, neither malicious nor kind, but rather calculating, who knew how to feather his nest; he understood people and knew how to take advantage of them. He was cautious and at the same time enterprising, like a fox; he was as garrulous as an old woman, but never gave himself away, while making everybody blurt out his secrets; he never played the simpleton, though, as so many crafty fellows of his ilk do. Besides, it would have been difficult for him to do so: I have never seen keener and more penetrating eyes than his tiny, sly "peepers." They never simply looked but always pried into or spied out. Blinkard sometimes pondered for weeks together over some apparently simple enterprise, then again he would suddenly plunge into a desperately bold venture in which he was sure, so it seemed, to lose his shirt. Yet, surprisingly enough, everything would go smoothly, and the affair would turn out to be a success. He was lucky and he believed in his luck and in omens generally. He was inclined to be very superstitious. He was not liked, because he cared nothing for anyone, but he was respected. His family consisted of one son, on whom he doted, and who, brought up by such a father, was likely to go far. "Young Blinkard takes after his father," old men were already whispering as they sat on their earthen benches, chatting on summer evenings; everyone knew what that meant without another word.

There is no need of saying much about Yakov the Turk, and the contractor. Yakov who owed his nickname to the fact that he descended from a captive Turkish woman, was a born artist in every sense of the word and by trade a scooper in a paper mill. As for the contractor, I knew nothing of his history; he struck me as a lively and astute townsman. But Wild Squire is worth describing in greater detail.

The first impression this man produced on you was of uncouth, massive, irresistible strength. He was clumsily built, "knocked together," as they say among us, but there was an air about him, and strange to say, his bearlike form was not without a certain peculiar grace, which was due perhaps to his complete confidence in his own power. It was hard to decide at first blush what the social background of this Hercules was; he did not look like either a house-serf or a burgher or an impoverished landowner fallen upon evil days, a huntsman or a brawler; he was, indeed, unique. No one knew whence he had dropped into our district; it was rumored that he came of a family of peasant freeholders, and he had presumably been in government service somewhere, but nothing positive was known about that, and from whom was one to find out? Certainly not from the man himself; there never was a more taciturn and sullen individual. Nor was anyone certain what he lived on: he plied no trade, paid no visits, associated with hardly anyone, yet he was not without money, little enough, it is true, but money nevertheless. His demeanor was not exactly unassuming—there was nothing unassuming about him—but unruffled; he lived as though he noticed no one around him and had no need of anyone at all.

Wild Squire (such was the nickname bestowed upon him; his real name was Perevlesov) enjoyed enormous prestige throughout the district; he was obeyed promptly and eagerly, although he not only had no right whatever to order anyone about, but himself laid no claim to obedience on the part of the people with whom he came into casual contact. He spoke, they obeyed: strength will always assert itself. He drank a little, had nothing to do with women and was passionately fond of singing. There was much that was puzzling about this man; vast forces seemed to repose sullenly within him, aware, as it were, that once roused and allowed free play, they were bound to destroy both themselves and everything they touched; and unless I am much mistaken, some such outburst had already occurred in this man's life, and, taught by experience and having narrowly escaped from ruin, he now was keeping himself strictly in hand. What particularly struck me in him was a mixture of inborn, native ferocity and of native nobility—a combination I have not met in anyone else.

So then, the contractor stepped forward and half-closing his eyes, began to sing in a high falsetto. His voice was rather pleasant and sweet, but somewhat husky; he played with it and spun it like a top, executing trills and roulades up and down the scale and constantly returning to the high notes, which he held and drew out with special care; then he would pause and suddenly again take up the melody with a certain dash and daring. Some of his translations were rather bold, some rather comical; they would have afforded great satisfaction to a connoisseur and made a German indignant. He was a Russian *tenore di grazia*, a *ténor léger*. He was singing a gay ballad, the words of which, insofar as I could make them out among all the embellishments, ejaculations and added consonants, ran as follows:

>I will plow, young Lassie,
>A small patch of earth;
>I will plant, young Lassie,
>A small scarlet bloom.

He sang; all listened to him with keen attention. He evidently felt that he was dealing with connoisseurs, and therefore was doing his best. And really people in our part of the country are good judges of singing and not for nothing is the village of Sergievskoe, on the Orel highway, renowned all over Russia for its sweet and harmonious singing.

For a long time the contractor sang without arousing too much enthusiasm in his audience. He lacked the support of a chorus. Finally, at one particular successful modulation, which made even Wild Squire smile, Loony could no longer control himself and shouted with delight. This roused everyone. Loony and Blinkard began to join in, humming in an undertone, and then shouting: "That's it! Go to it, you rascal! Go to it, keep it up, you devil! Draw it out further! Split it finer, you dog, you! May Herod blast your soul!" and so on. Nikolay Ivanych behind his counter shook his head approvingly. At last Loony started to stamp and shift his feet and twitch his shoulders—and Yakov's eyes blazed like coals of fire and he shook all over like a leaf and smiled spasmodically. Wild Squire alone did not change countenance or budge from where he stood, but his gaze, fastened on the contractor, grew somewhat softer, though the expression of his lips remained contemptuous. Encouraged by these signs of universal approval, the contractor burst into a whirlwind of song, and began to turn out such flourishes, to make such clicking and drumming sounds with his tongue, to work his throat so frantically, that when at last, exhausted, pale and bathed in hot perspiration, he flung his whole body back and uttered the final dying note, he was hailed by a general shout exploding frenziedly. Loony fell upon his neck and began to strangle him with his long, bony arms; color came into Nikolay Ivanych's fat face and he seemed to have grown younger; Yakov shouted like a madman: "Capital, capital!" Even my neighbor, the peasant in the torn jacket, could not contain himself, and striking the table with his fist, exclaimed: "Aha! Well done, devil take it, well done!" and he resolutely spat to one side.

"Well, brother, that was a treat!" shouted Loony, without releasing the exhausted contractor from his embrace, "that certainly was a treat! You have won the bet, brother, you surely have! Congratulations—the beer is yours! Yashka is far behind you. Take it from me: far behind you . . . take my word for it." And again he pressed the contractor to his breast.

"There, let go of him, let go, you confounded. . ." began Blinkard, annoyed; "let him sit down on the bench; he's tired, can't you see? What a blockhead you are, brother, what a blockhead! Why do you stick to him like a leech?"

"Well, let him sit down, and I'll drink his health," said Loony and stepped up to the bar. "At your expense, brother," he added, addressing the contractor.

The latter nodded in assent, sat down on a bench, pulled a towel out of his cap and started to mop his face, while Loony, grunting, downed his glass with greedy haste and, in the manner of sots, assumed a sad and careworn expression.

"You sing well, brother, very well," Nikolay Ivanych remarked affably. "And now it's your turn, Yasha; mind now, keep a stout heart. We shall see who is the better man, we shall see . . . The contractor sings well, though, by God."

"Very well," observed Nikolay Ivanych's wife and looked at Yakov with a smile.

"Very well, ha!" my neighbor repeated in an undertone.

"Ah, a wild Polekha!" Loony suddenly bawled, and stepping up to the peasant with the hole in the shoulder of his jacket, he pointed his finger at him, began to prance about and went off into a quavering guffaw. "Polekha! Polekha! Ha! Caveman! What has brought you here, caveman?" he shouted through his laughter.

The poor peasant was put out of countenance and was about to get up and leave in a hurry, when suddenly Wild Squire's iron voice rang out:

"What kind of insufferable animal is this?" he demanded, gnashing his teeth.

"I wasn't saying anything," mumbled Loony, "I wasn't . . . I only . . ."

"All right, then, shut up!" snapped Wild Squire. "Yakov, begin!"

Yakov clutched his throat with his hands.

"Well, brother," he said, "I mean . . . that is . . . H'm, I don't know, really, that is . . ."

"Come, enough of that, don't be scared," said Wild Squire. "For shame! Why do you wriggle? Sing as God prompts you."

And Wild Squire dropped his eyes and looked expectant.

Yakov was silent for a while, glanced round and covered his face with his hands. All stared at him intently, especially the contractor, whose countenance showed a slight uneasiness half concealed by his habitual expression of self-confidence and the flush of success. He sat leaning against the wall and again tucked both his hands under him, but no longer swung his legs. When at length Yakov uncovered his face, it was as pale as a dead man's, and his eyes barely glimmered through his lowered lashes. He drew a deep sigh and began to sing.

At first his voice was weak and trembling and seemed to come not from his chest, but from a distant point, as though it had been wafted accidentally into the room. This tremulous, resonant note affected all of us strangely; we looked at each other, and Nikolay Ivanych's wife drew herself up. The first note was followed by another, a firmer and more prolonged, but still obviously tremulous sound, like that of a string when suddenly at the touch of a strong finger it vibrates with a last, rapidly dying quiver. The second note was followed by a third, and, gradually growing warmer and broadening out, the melody swelled mournfully. "More than one road led through the fields," he sang, and our hearts were filled with sweetness and awe.

I confess, I have rarely heard such a voice: it was slightly dissonant and it rang as though it were cracked; one's first impression was that there was something morbid about it; but it had genuine, profound passion and youth, and vigor and tenderness and a kind of ravishingly heedless sadness. A Russian soul, truthful and fiery, sounded and breathed in that voice, and fairly gripped our hearts, gripped its Russian chords. The song swelled and flowed on. Yakov was clearly yielding to a kind of intoxication; he was no longer timid, he surrendered himself wholly to his rapture; his voice no longer trembled, but quivered with that scarcely perceptible inward vibration of passion which pierces the very soul of the listener like an arrow, and it steadily grew stronger, firmer, ampler.

I remember once at dusk, on a flat sandy beach, when the tide was low and the sea was thundering ponderously and menacingly in the distance, I saw a large white seagull. It was motionless, its silky breast exposed to the crimson glow of the sunset, and only now and then did it slowly spread its long wings to the familiar sea, to the low purple sun. I recalled the bird as I listened to Yakov. He sang utterly oblivious of his rival and of all of us, but evidently buoyed up by our silent, passionate sympathy, as a courageous swimmer is by the waves. He sang, and every sound of his voice breathed something that was our own, something that was immeasurably vast, as though the familiar steppes were unrolling before us, stretching out into infinity. I felt the tears seething within me and rising to my eyes. Muffled, suppressed sobs suddenly startled me. I looked around—the tavernkeeper's wife was crying, her bosom pressed against the window. Yakov darted a quick glance at her and there was an outburst of even sweeter singing. Nikolay Ivanych dropped his eyes; Blinkard turned aside; Loony completely melted, stood with his mouth stupidly agape; the peasant from Polesye was sobbing softly in the corner shaking his head and whispering bitterly; a heavy tear slowly rolled down Wild Squire's iron visage from under his knitted eyebrows; the contractor raised his clenched fist to his forehead and did not stir. I do not know how the general tension would have resolved itself had not Yakov suddenly come to a stop on a high, extraordinarily tenuous note, as though his voice had snapped. No one cried out, or even stirred; all seemed to be waiting to see if he would go on singing. But he opened his eyes, as though surprised at our silence, looked round with an inquiring glance, and saw that victory was his.

"Yasha," said Wild Squire, placing his hand on his shoulder—and broke off.

We all stood as if stunned. The contractor quietly rose and stepped up to Yakov. "You . . . your . . . you've won . . ." he brought out at last with an effort, and rushed from the room.

His abrupt, brusque movement broke the spell, as it were; all suddenly fell into noisy, jolly talk. Loony jumped up, and began to babble and wave his arms like a windmill; Blinkard limped up to Yakov and they started to kiss each other; Nikolay Ivanych rose and solemnly declared the company would be served another demijohn of beer, this one on his house. Wild Squire laughed a good-natured sort of laugh, of which I did not think he was capable; the humble peasant in his corner, as he wiped his eyes, cheeks, nose and beard with both his sleeves, kept repeating: "It was first-rate, by God, first-rate, damn my soul, but it was first-rate!" Nikolay Ivanych's wife, all flushed, hastily got up and left. Yakov was enjoying his victory like a child; his whole face was transformed;

his eyes fairly shone with happiness. They dragged him to the bar; he called the tearful peasant over, and sent the tavernkeeper's little son to find the contractor, which, however he failed to do, and the feast began. "You will sing to us again, you will sing to us till evening," Loony repeated, raising his hands high.

I took one more look at Yakov and left. I did not want to stay. I was afraid to spoil my impression. But the heat was as unbearable as before. It seemed to be hanging right over the earth like a thick, heavy pall; in the dark-blue sky tiny luminous dots seemed to whirl through the fine, almost black dust. Everything was still; there was something hopeless in this profound silence of prostrate nature, as though it had been flattened out by a crushing weight. I made my way to a hayloft and lay down on the freshly cut grass that was already nearly dry. For a long time I could not doze off; for a long time Yakov's irresistible voice rang in my ears ... At last, the heat and the fatigue asserted themselves and I became dead to the world.

When I woke up, it was already dark. The hay strewn round about exhaled a strong fragrance and had grown somewhat damp; between the slender rods supporting the half-covered roof pale stars were faintly twinkling. I went outside. The sunset had long since died away, and its last traces showed as a faint luminosity on the skyline, but through the freshness of the night one still felt warmth in the atmosphere, which had only recently been heated by the sun, and the breast still thirsted for a draught of cool air. There was no breeze, nor were there any clouds; the sky was clear and transparently dark, softly glimmering with numberless but barely visible stars. Lights gleamed about the village; from the brightly lit tavern hard by came a discordant hubbub, in the midst of which I thought that I recognized Yakov's voice. From time to time there were outbursts of violent laughter.

I stepped up to the window and pressed my face against the pane. I beheld a cheerless, though colorful and lively sight: all were drunk, Yakov first and foremost. His chest bare, he sat on a bench, humming some dancing tune of the streets in a husky voice, and lazily fingering and plucking the strings of a guitar. His moist hair hung in tufts over his face, which was now ghastly pale. In the center of the room Loony, completely "unscrewed" and without his caftan, was leaping about in front of the peasant in the torn jacket; the little peasant, on his part, was trying to stamp and scrape his feet which he could scarcely control, and, smiling sheepishly into his disheveled beard, from time to time flourished one arm as if to say: "What does it matter!" Nothing could be more comical than his face; no matter how much he tried to raise his eyebrows, his lids were so heavy with fatigue that they refused to obey him and continued to conceal his scarcely visible, bleary, yet sugary eyes. He was in the charming state of a man who is half-seas over, when every passer-by, as soon as he looks him in the face is sure to say: "You've been going it, brother, going it!" Blinkard, in a corner, as red as a lobster, his nostrils dilated, was laughing spitefully; Nikolay Ivanych alone, as befits a true tavernkeeper, preserved his invariable composure. The room was crowded with new customers, but I did not see Wild Squire among them.

I turned aside and with rapid steps began to descend the hill on which Kolotovka lies. At the foot of the hill stretches a broad plain; flooded with billows of evening mist, it seemed more immense than ever and appeared to merge with the darkened sky. I was proceeding with long strides down the road skirting the ravine, when suddenly from some point far away on the plain came a boy's ringing voice: "Antropka. Antropka-a-a!" he bawled in obstinately tearful desperation, drawing out the last syllable lingeringly.

He would pause for a few instants and then resume his shouting. His voice carried far on the still air that seemed to be dozing. Thirty times at least he had shouted the name, Antropka, when suddenly from the opposite end of the meadow, as from another world, came a scarcely audible response:

"Wha-a-at?"

The first boy shouted back at once with gleeful malice:

"Come here, you devil you, you forest fiend!"

"What for?" asked the other, after a long pause.

"Because daddy wants to spa-ank you!" the first boy shouted back quickly.

The second voice remained silent, and the first boy fell to calling Antropka again.

I still kept hearing his cries, growing fainter and less frequent, when it had become completely dark and I was skirting the edge of the wood which surrounds my little village and which is a distance of some three miles from Kolotovka. I still seemed to hear the call "Antropka-a!" in the air filled with the shadows of night.

(Translated by Constance Garnett)

ENGLISH

William Blake
(1757-1827)
from *Songs of Innocence*
Introduction

Piping down the valleys wild,
   Piping songs of pleasant glee,
On a cloud I saw a child,
   And he laughing said to me:

"Pipe a song about a Lamb!"
   So I piped with merry cheer.
"Piper, pipe that song again;"
   So I piped: he wept to hear.

"Drop thy pipe, thy happy pipe;
   Sing thy songs of happy cheer:"
So I sung the same again,
   While he wept with joy to hear.

"Piper, sit thee down and write
   In a book, that all may read."
So he vanished from my sight,
   And I plucked a hollow reed,

And I made a rural pen,
   And I stained the water clear,
And I wrote my happy songs
   Every child may joy to hear.

The Divine Image

To Mercy, Pity, Peace, and Love
   All pray in their distress;
And to these virtues of delight
   Return their thankfulness.

For Mercy, Pity, Peace, and Love
   Is God, our father dear;
And Mercy, Pity, Peace, and Love
   Is Man, his child and care.

For Mercy has a human heart,
    Pity a human face;
And Love, the human form divine,
    And Peace, the human dress.

Then every man, of every clime,
    That prays in his distress,
Prays to the human form divine,
    Love, Mercy, Pity, Peace.

And all must love the human form,
    In heathen, Turk, or Jew;
Where Mercy, Love, and Pity dwell
    There God is dwelling too.

from *Songs of Experience*
A Poison Tree

I was angry with my friend:
I told my wrath, my wrath did end.
I was angry with my foe:
I told it not, my wrath did grow.

And I watered it in fears,
Night and morning with my tears;
And I sunned it with smiles,
And with soft deceitful wiles.

And it grew both day and night
Till it bore an apple bright;
And my foe beheld it shine,
And he knew that it was mine,

And into my garden stole
When the night had veiled the pole:
In the morning glad I see
My foe outstretched beneath the tree.

London

I wander through each chartered street,
Near where the chartered Thames does flow,
And mark in every face I meet
Marks of weakness, marks of woe.

In every cry of every man,
In every infant's cry of fear,
In every voice, in every ban,
The mind-forged manacles I hear.

How the chimney-sweeper's cry
Every blackening church appals;
And the hapless soldier's sigh
Runs in blood down palace walls.

But most through midnight streets I hear
How the youthful harlot's curse
Blasts the new-born infant's tear,
And blights with plagues the marriage hearse.

Robert Burns
(1759-1796)
Ye Flowery Banks

Ye flowery banks o' bonnie Doon,
    How can ye blume sae fair?
How can ye chant, ye little birds,
    And I sae fu' o' care?

Thou'll break my heart, thou bonnie bird,
    That sings upon the bough;
Thou minds me o' the happy days,
    When my fause luve was true.

Thou'll break my heart, thou bonnie bird,
    That sings beside thy mate;
For sae I sat, and sae I sang,
    And wist na o' my fate.

Aft hae I roved by bonnie Doon,
    To see the woodbine twine,
And ilka bird sang o' its luve,
    And sae did I o' mine.

Wi' lightsome heart I pu'd a rose
   Frae aff its thorny tree;
But my fause luver staw my rose,
   And left the thorn wi' me.

Wi' lightsome heart I pu'd a rose
   Upon a morn in June;
And sae I flourished on the morn,
   And sae was pu'd ere noon.

Afton Water

Flow gently, sweet Afton, among thy green braes,
Flow gently, I'll sing thee a song in thy praise;
My Mary's asleep by thy murmuring stream,
Flow gently, sweet Afton, disturb not her dream.

Thou stock-dove whose echo resounds through the glen,
Ye wild whistling blackbirds in yon thorny den,
Thou green-crested lapwing, thy screaming forbear,
I charge you disturb not my slumbering fair.

How lofty, sweet Afton, thy neighboring hills,
Far marked with the courses of clear winding rills;
There daily I wander as noon rises high,
My flocks and my Mary's sweet cot in my eye.

How pleasant thy banks and green valleys below,
Where wild in the woodlands the primroses blow;
There oft as mild evening weeps over the lea,
The sweet-scented birk shades my Mary and me.

Thy crystal stream, Afton, how lovely it glides,
And winds by the cot where my Mary resides;
How wanton thy waters her snowy feet lave,
As gathering sweet flowerets she stems thy clear wave.

Flow gently, sweet Afton, among thy green braes,
Flow gently, sweet river, the theme of my lays;
My Mary's asleep by thy murmuring stream,
Flow gently, sweet Afton, disturb not her dream.

A Red, Red Rose

O, my luv is like a red, red rose,
   That's newly sprung in June:
O, my luv is like the melodie
   That's sweetly played in tune.

As fair art thou, my bonie lass,
   So deep in luve am I;
And I will luve thee still, my dear,
   Till a' the seas gang dry:

Till a' the seas gang dry, my dear,
   And the rocks melt wi' the sun;
And I will luve thee still, my dear,
   While the sands o' life shall run.

And fare thee weel, my only luve!
   And fare thee weel awhile!
And I will come again, my luve,
   Tho' it were ten thousand mile!

William Wordsworth
(1770-1850)

Composed Upon Westminster Bridge
September 3, 1802

Earth has not anything to show more fair:
Dull would he be of soul who could pass by
A sight so touching in its majesty:
This City now doth, like a garment, wear
The beauty of the morning; silent, bare,
Ships, towers, domes, theatres, and temples lie
Open unto the fields, and to the sky;
All bright and glittering in the smokeless air.
Never did sun more beautifully steep
In his first splendor, valley, rock, or hill;
Ne'er saw I, never felt, a calm so deep!
The river glideth at his own sweet will:
Dear God! the very houses seem asleep;
And all that mighty heart is lying still!

"My Heart Leaps Up When I Behold"

My heart leaps up when I behold
   A rainbow in the sky:
So was it when my life began;
So is it now I am a man:
So be it when I shall grow old,
   Or let me die!
The Child is father of the Man;
And I could wish my days to be
Bound each to each by natural piety.

"I Wandered Lonely as a Cloud"

I wandered lonely as a cloud
That floats on high o'er vales and hills,
When all at once I saw a crowd,
A host, of golden daffodils;
Beside the lake, beneath the trees,
Fluttering and dancing in the breeze.

Continuous as the stars that shine
And twinkle on the milky way,
They stretched in never-ending line
Along the margin of a bay:
Ten thousand saw I at a glance,
Tossing their heads in sprightly dance.

The waves beside them danced; but they
Out-did the sparkling waves in glee:
A poet could not but be gay,
In such a jocund company:
I gazed—and gazed—but little thought
What wealth the show to me had brought:

For oft, when on my couch I lie
In vacant or in pensive mood,
They flash upon that inward eye
Which is the bliss of solitude;
And then my heart with pleasure fills,
And dances with the daffodils.

JOSEPH MALLORD WILLIAM TURNER: *The Dogana and Santa Maria Della Salute, Venice*, GIVEN IN MEMORY OF GOVERNOR ALVAN T. FULLER BY THE FULLER FOUNDATION, NATIONAL GALLERY OF ART, WASHINGTON, D.C.

"It Is a Beauteous Evening, Calm and Free"

It is a beauteous evening, calm and free,
The holy time is quiet as a Nun
Breathless with adoration; the broad sun
Is sinking down in its tranquillity;
The gentleness of heaven broods o'er the Sea:
Listen! the mighty Being is awake,
And doth with his eternal motion make
A sound like thunder—everlastingly.
Dear Child! dear Girl! that walkest with me here,
If thou appear untouched by solemn thought,
Thy nature is not therefore less divine:
Thou liest in Abraham's bosom all the year;
And worshipp'st at the Temple's inner shrine,
God being with thee when we know it not.

Samuel Taylor Coleridge
(1772-1834)
Kubla Khan: or, a Vision in a Dream
A Fragment

In Xanadu did Kubla Khan
A stately pleasure-dome decree:
Where Alph, the sacred river, ran
Through caverns measureless to man
  Down to a sunless sea.
So twice five miles of fertile ground
With walls and towers were girdled round:
And there were gardens bright with sinuous rills,
Where blossomed many an incense-bearing tree;
And here were forests ancient as the hills,
Enfolding sunny spots of greenery.

But oh! that deep romantic chasm which slanted
Down the green hill athwart a cedarn cover!
A savage place! as holy and enchanted
As e'er beneath a waning moon was haunted
By woman wailing for her demon-lover!
And from this chasm, with ceaseless turmoil seething,
As if this earth in fast thick pants were breathing,
A mighty fountain momently was forced:
Amid whose swift half-intermitted burst
Huge fragments vaulted like rebounding hail,
Or chaffy grain beneath the thresher's flail:
And 'mid these dancing rocks at once and ever
It flung up momently the sacred river.
Five miles meandering with a mazy motion
Through wood and dale the sacred river ran,
Then reached the caverns measureless to man,
And sank in tumult to a lifeless ocean:
And 'mid this tumult Kubla heard from far
Ancestral voices prophesying war!

  The shadow of the dome of pleasure
  Floated midway on the waves;
  Where was heard the mingled measure
  From the fountain and the caves.
It was a miracle of rare device,
A sunny pleasure-dome with caves of ice!
  A damsel with a dulcimer
  In a vision once I saw:
  It was an Abyssinian maid,
  And on her dulcimer she played,
  Singing of Mount Abora.
  Could I revive within me
  Her symphony and song,
  To such a deep delight 'twould win me,

That with music loud and long,
I would build that dome in air,
That sunny dome! those caves of ice!
And all who heard should see them there,
And all should cry, Beware! Beware!
His flashing eyes, his floating hair!
Weave a circle round him thrice,
And close your eyes with holy dread,
For he on honey-dew hath fed,
And drunk the milk of Paradise.

The Eolian Harp
COMPOSED AT CLEVEDON, SOMERSETSHIRE

My pensive Sara! thy soft cheek reclined
Thus on mine arm, most soothing sweet it is
To sit beside our cot, our cot o'ergrown
With white-flowered jasmin, and the broad-leaved myrtle
(Meet emblems they of innocence and love!)
And watch the clouds, that late were rich with light,
Slow saddening round, and mark the star of eve
Serenely brilliant (such should wisdom be)
Shine opposite! How exquisite the scents
Snatched from yon bean-field! and the world *so* hushed!
The stilly murmur of the distant sea
Tells us of silence.

      And that simplest lute,
Placed length-ways in the clasping casement, hark!
How by the desultory breeze caressed,
Like some coy maid half yielding to her lover,
It pours such sweet upbraiding, as must needs
Tempt to repeat the wrong! And now, its strings
Boldlier swept, the long sequacious notes
Over delicious surges sink and rise,
Such a soft floating witchery of sound
As twilight elfins make, when they at eve
Voyage on gentle gales from fairy-land,
Where melodies round honey-dropping flowers,
Footless and wild, like birds of paradise,
Nor pause, nor perch, hovering on untamed wing!
O! the one life within us and abroad,
Which meets all motion and becomes its soul,

A light in sound, a sound-like power in light,
Rhythm in all thought, and joyance every where—
Methinks, it should have been impossible
Not to love all things in a world so filled;
Where the breeze warbles, and the mute still air
Is music slumbering on her instrument.

   And thus, my love! as on the midway slope
Of yonder hill I stretch my limbs at noon,
Whilst through my half-closed eye-lids I behold
The sunbeams dance, like diamonds, on the main,
And tranquil muse upon tranquillity;
Full many a thought uncalled and undetained,
And many idle flitting phantasies,
Traverse my indolent and passive brain,
As wild and various as the random gales
That swell and flutter on this subject lute!

   And what if all of animated nature
Be but organic harps diversely framed,
That tremble into thought, as o'er them sweeps
Plastic and vast, one intellectual breeze,
At once the soul of each, and God of all?
   But thy more serious eye a mild reproof
Darts, O belovèd woman! nor such thoughts
Dim and unhallowed dost thou not reject,
And biddest me walk humbly with my God.
Meek daughter in the family of Christ!
Well hast thou said and holily dispraised
These shapings of the unregenerate mind;
Bubbles that glitter as they rise and break
On vain philosophy's aye-babbling spring.
For never guiltless may I speak of him,
The Incomprehensible! save when with awe
I praise him, and with faith that inly feels;
Who with his saving mercies healèd me,
A sinful and most miserable man,
Wildered and dark, and gave me to possess
Peace, and this cot, and thee, heart-honored maid!

George Gordon, Lord Byron
(1788-1824)
from *Don Juan*

Probably no story, not even that of Faust, *has so caught the fancy of writers and operatic composers as has that of* Don Juan. *Playwrights from Tirso de Molina (in his* Trickster of Seville) *to George Bernard Shaw (in* Man and Superman) *and such composers as Gluck and Mozart* (Don Giovanni) *have used the story of the handsome nobleman of Seville who caps his numerous seductions with blasphemy and whose soul is ultimately snatched to Hell.*

But Byron's Don Juan *(pronounced* Joó an), *apart from its hero's name and birthplace, has little in common with any of the others. Even in his romances, Byron's hero is more often the pursued than the pursuer. After an early amorous misadventure in Spain, he is sent by his mother on a trip designed to strengthen his morals. But a storm at sea (one of the descriptive highlights of the poem) lands him on an island in the Aegean, where he is cared for by a lovely young girl named Haidée. She is the daughter of a wealthy privateer and slave trader, Lambro, who is away on his piratical business. Haidée, who has known no other men but her father and the servants, falls in love with Don Juan. But Lambro, whose death at sea has been rumored, returns unexpectedly, with consequences that are related in the episode included here. In further adventures, Haidée's father has Don Juan sold as a slave in Constantinople; later Juan finds his way to Russia, where the Empress Catherine admires him greatly; and then he is sent on a mission to England. The story of his amorous exploits there is left unfinished.*

However well Byron tells a romantic story, his plot is mostly a thread on which he hangs a great amount of wit and mockery—innumerable digressions, abrupt shifts of mood, barbs directed both at individual contemporaries (Southey, Wordsworth, and many others) and at the social, political, and moral conventions of his time—all in all, the most telling satire written in the romantic period.

Canto the Fourth
The Death of Haidée

I

Nothing so difficult as a beginning
   In poesy, unless, perhaps the end;
For oftentimes when Pegasus seems winning
   The race, he sprains a wing, and down we tend,
Like Lucifer when hurled from heaven for sinning;
   Our sin the same, and hard as his to mend,
Being pride, which leads the mind to soar too far,
Till our own weakness shows us what we are.

II

But Time, which brings all beings to their level,
   And sharp Adversity, will teach at last
Man,—and, as we would hope,—perhaps the devil,
   That neither of their intellects are vast;

While youth's hot wishes in our red veins revel,
   We know not this—the blood flows on too fast:
But as the torrent widens towards the ocean,
We ponder deeply on each past emotion.

III

As boy, I thought myself a clever fellow,
   And wished that others held the same opinion;
They took it up when my days grew more mellow,
   And other minds acknowledged my dominion:
Now my sere fancy "falls into the yellow
   Leaf," and Imagination droops her pinion,
And the sad truth which hovers o'er my desk
Turns what was once romantic to burlesque.

IV

And if I laugh at any mortal thing,
   'Tis that I may not weep; and if I weep,
'Tis that our nature cannot always bring
   Itself to apathy, for we must steep
Our hearts first in the depths of Lethe's spring,
   Ere what we least wish to behold will sleep:
Thetis baptized her mortal son in Styx;
A mortal mother would on Lethe fix.

V

Some have accused me of a strange design
   Against the creed and morals of the land,
And trace it in this poem every line;
   I don't pretend that I quite understand
My own meaning when I would be *very* fine;
   But the fact is that I have nothing planned,
Unless it were to be a moment merry,
A novel word in my vocabulary.

VI

To the kind reader of our sober clime
   This way of writing will appear exotic;
Pulci was sire of the half-serious rhyme,
   Who sang when chivalry was more Quixotic,
And revelled in the fancies of the time,
   True knights, chaste dames, huge giants, kings despotic:
But all these, save the last, being obsolete,
I chose a modern subject as more meet.

VII

How I have treated it, I do not know;
   Perhaps no better than *they* have treated me,
Who have imputed such designs as show
   Not what they saw, but what they wished to see;
But if it gives them pleasure, be it so,
   This is a liberal age, and thoughts are free:
Meantime Apollo plucks me by the ear,
And tells me to resume my story here.

VIII

Young Juan and his lady-love were left
   To their own hearts' most sweet society;
Even Time the pitiless in sorrow cleft
   With his rude scythe such gentle bosoms; he
Sighed to behold them of their hours bereft,
   Though foe to love; and yet they could not be
Meant to grow old, but die in happy spring,
Before one charm or hope had taken wing.

IX

Their faces were not made for wrinkles, their
   Pure blood to stagnate, their great hearts to fail!
The blank gray was not made to blast their hair,
   But like the climes that know nor snow nor hail,
They were all summer; lightning might assail
   And shiver them to ashes, but to trail
A long and snake-like life of dull decay
Was not for them—they had too little clay.

X

They were alone once more; for them to be
   Thus was another Eden; they were never
Weary, unless when separate: the tree
   Cut from its forest root of years—the river
Dammed from its fountain—the child from the knee
   And breast maternal weaned at once forever,—
Would wither less than these two torn apart:
Alas! there is no instinct like the human heart—

XI

The heart—which may be broken: happy they!
   Thrice fortunate! who of that fragile mold,
The precious porcelain of human clay,
   Break with the first fall: they can ne'er behold

The long year linked with heavy day on day,
    And all which must be borne, and never told;
While life's strange principle will often lie
Deepest in those who long the most to die.

XII

"Whom the gods love die young" was said of yore,
    And many deaths do they escape by this
The death of friends, and that which slays even more—
    The death of friendship, love, youth, all that is,
Except mere breath; and since the silent shore
    Awaits at last even those who longest miss
The old archer's shafts, perhaps the early grave
Which men weep over may be meant to save!

XIII

Haidée and Juan thought not of the dead—
    The heavens, and earth, and air seemed made for them:
They found no fault with Time, save that he fled;
    They saw not in themselves aught to condemn;
Each was the other's mirror, and but read
    Joy sparkling in their dark eyes like a gem,
And knew such brightness was but the reflection
Of their exchanging glances of affection.

XIV

The gentle pressure, and the thrilling touch,
    The least glance better understood than words,
Which still said all, and ne'er could say too much;
    A language, too, but like to that of birds,
Known but to them, at least appearing such
    As but to lovers a true sense affords;
Sweet playful phrases, which would seem absurd
To those who have ceased to hear such, or ne'er heard—

XV

All these were theirs, for they were children still,
    And children still they should have ever been;
They were not made in the real world to fill
    A busy character in the dull scene,
But like two beings born from out a rill,
    A nymph and her beloved, all unseen
To pass their lives in fountains and on flowers,
And never know the weight of human hours.

XVI

Moons changing had rolled on, and changeless found
   Those their bright rise had lighted to such joys
As rarely they beheld throughout their round;
   And these were not of the vain kind which cloys,
For theirs were buoyant spirits, never bound
   By the mere senses; and that which destroys
Most love, possession, unto them appeared
A thing which each endearment more endeared.

XVII

Oh beautiful! and rare as beautiful!
   But theirs was love in which the mind delights
To lose itself, when the old world grows dull,
   And we are sick of its hack sounds and sights,
Intrigues, adventures of the common school,
   Its petty passions, marriages, and flights,
Where Hymen's torch but brands one strumpet more,
Whose husband only knows her not a whore.

XVIII

Hard words; harsh truth; a truth which many know.
   Enough.—The faithful and the fairy pair,
Who never found a single hour too slow,
   What was it made them thus exempt from care?
Young innate feelings all have felt below,
   Which perish in the rest, but in them were
Inherent—what we mortals call romantic,
And always envy, though we deem it frantic.

XIX

This is in others a factitious state,
   An opium dream of too much youth and reading,
But was in them their nature or their fate
   No novels e'er had set their young hearts bleeding,
For Haidée's knowledge was by no means great,
   And Juan was a boy of saintly breeding;
So that there was no reason for their loves
More than for those of nightingales or doves.

XX

They gazed upon the sunset; 'tis an hour
   Dear unto all, but dearest to *their* eyes,
For it had made them what they were: the power
   Of love had first o'erwhelmed them from such skies,

When happiness had been their only dower,
    And twilight saw them linked in passion's ties;
Charmed with each other, all things charmed that brought
The past still welcome as the present thought.

XXI

I know not why, but in that hour tonight,
    Even as they gazed, a sudden tremor came,
And swept, as 'twere, across their hearts' delight,
    Like the wind o'er a harp-string, or a flame,
When one is shook in sound, and one in sight:
    And thus some boding flashed through either frame,
And called from Juan's breast a faint low sigh,
While one new tear arose in Haidée's eye.

XXII

That large black prophet eye seemed to dilate
    And follow far the disappearing sun,
As if their last day of a happy date
    With his broad, bright, and dropping orb were gone;
Juan gazed on her as to ask his fate—
    He felt a grief, but knowing cause for none,
His glance inquired of hers for some excuse
For feelings causeless, or at least abstruse.

XXIII

She turned to him, and smiled, but in that sort
    Which makes not others smile; then turned aside:
Whatever feeling shook her, it seemed short,
    And mastered by her wisdom or her pride;
When Juan spoke, too—it might be in sport—
    Of this their mutual feeling, she replied—
"If it should be so,—but—it cannot be—
Or I at least shall not survive to see."

XXIV

Juan would question further, but she pressed
    His lips to hers, and silenced him with this,
And then dismissed the omen from her breast,
    Defying augury with that fond kiss;
And no doubt of all methods 'tis the best:
    Some people prefer wine—'tis not amiss;
I have tried both; so those who would a part take
May choose between the headache and the heartache.

XXV

One of the two according to your choice,
   Woman or wine, you'll have to undergo;
Both maladies are taxes on our joys:
   But which to choose, I really hardly know;
And if I had to give a casting voice,
   For both sides I could many reasons show,
And then decide, without great wrong to either,
It were much better to have both than neither.

XXVI

Juan and Haidée gazed upon each other
   With swimming looks of speechless tenderness,
Which mixed all feelings—friend, child, lover, brother—
   All that the best can mingle and express
When two pure hearts are poured in one another,
   And love too much, and yet cannot love less;
But almost sanctify the sweet excess
By the immortal wish and power to bless.

XXVII

Mixed in each other's arms, and heart in heart,
   Why did they not then die?—they had lived too long
Should an hour come to bid them breathe apart;
   Years could but bring them cruel things or wrong;
The world was not for them, nor the world's art
   For beings passionate as Sappho's song;
Love was born *with* them, *in* them, so intense,
It was their very spirit—not a sense.

XXVIII

They should have lived together deep in woods,
   Unseen as sings the nightingale; they were
Unfit to mix in these thick solitudes
   Called social, haunts of Hate, and Vice, and Care;
How lonely every freeborn creature broods!
   The sweetest song-birds nestle in a pair;
The eagle soars alone; the gull and crow
Flock o'er their carrion, just like men below.

XXIX

Now pillowed cheek to cheek, in loving sleep,
   Haidée and Juan their siesta took,
A gentle slumber, but it was not deep,
   For ever and anon a something shook

Juan, and shuddering o'er his frame would creep;
  And Haidée's sweet lips murmured like a brook
A wordless music, and her face so fair
Stirred with her dream, as rose-leaves with the air;

XXX

Or as the stirring of a deep clear stream
  Within an Alpine hollow, when the wind
Walks o'er it, was she shaken by the dream,
  The mystical usurper of the mind—
O'erpowering us to be whate'er may seem
  Good to the soul which we no more can bind:
Strange state of being! (for 'tis still to be),
Senseless to feel, and with sealed eyes to see.

XXXI

She dreamed of being alone on the seashore,
  Chained to a rock; she knew not how, but stir
She could not from the spot, and the loud roar
  Grew, and each wave rose roughly, threatening her;
And o'er her upper lip they seemed to pour,
  Until she sobbed for breath, and soon they were
Foaming o'er her lone head, so fierce and high—
Each broke to drown her, yet she could not die.

XXXII

Anon—she was released, and then she strayed
  O'er the sharp shingles with her bleeding feet,
And stumbled almost every step she made;
  And something rolled before her in a sheet,
Which she must still pursue howe'er afraid:
  'Twas white and indistinct, nor stopped to meet
Her glance nor grasp, for still she gazed and grasped,
And ran, but it escaped her as she clasped.

XXXIII

The dream changed:—in a cave she stood, its walls
  Were hung with marble icicles; the work
Of ages on its water-fretted halls,
  Where waves might wash, and seals might breed and lurk;
Her hair was dripping, and the very balls
  Of her black eyes seemed turned to tears, and mirk
The sharp rocks looked below each drop they caught,
Which froze to marble as it fell,—she thought.

XXXIV

And wet, and cold, and lifeless at her feet,
   Pale as the foam that frothed on his dead brow,
Which she essayed in vain to clear, (how sweet
   Were once her cares, how idle seemed they now!),
Lay Juan, nor could aught renew the beat
   Of his quenched heart; and the sea dirges low
Rang in her sad ears like a mermaid's song,
And that brief dream appeared a life too long.

XXXV

And gazing on the dead, she thought his face
   Faded, or altered into something new—
Like to her father's features, till each trace
   More like and like to Lambro's aspect grew—
With all his keen worn look and Grecian grace;
   And starting, she awoke, and what to view?
Oh! Powers of Heaven! what dark eye meets she there
'Tis—'tis her father's—fixed upon the pair!

XXXVI

Then shrieking, she arose, and shrieking fell,
   With joy and sorrow, hope and fear, to see
Him whom she deemed a habitant where dwell
   The ocean-buried, risen from death, to be
Perchance the death of one she loved too well;
   Dear as her father had been to Haidée,
It was a moment of that awful kind—
I have seen such—but must not call to mind.

XXXVII

Up Juan sprang to Haidée's bitter shriek,
   And caught her falling, and from off the wall
Snatched down his sabre, in hot haste to wreak
   Vengeance on him who was the cause of all:
Then Lambro who till now forebore to speak,
   Smiled scornfully, and said, "Within my call,
A thousand scimitars await the word;
Put up, young man, put up your silly sword."

XXXVIII

And Haidée clung around him; "Juan, 'tis—
   'Tis Lambro—'tis my father! Kneel with me—
He will forgive us—yes—it must be—yes.
   Oh! dearest father, in this agony

Of pleasure and of pain—even while I kiss
   Thy garment's hem with transport, can it be
That doubt should mingle with my filial joy?
Deal with me as thou wilt, but spare this boy."

XXXIX

High and inscrutable the old man stood,
   Calm in his voice, and calm within his eye—
Not always signs with him of calmest mood:
   He looked upon her, but gave no reply;
Then turned to Juan, in whose cheek the blood
   Oft came and went, as there resolved to die;
In arms, at least, he stood, in act to spring
On the first foe whom Lambro's call might bring.

XL

"Young man, your sword"; so Lambro once more said:
   Juan replied, "Not while this arm is free."
The old man's cheek grew pale, but not with dread,
   And drawing from his belt a pistol, he
Replied, "Your blood be then on your own head."
   Then looked close at the flint, as if to see
'Twas fresh—for he had lately used the lock—
And next proceeded quietly to cock.

XLI

It has a strange quick jar upon the ear,
   That cocking of a pistol, when you know
A moment more will bring the sight to bear
   Upon your person, twelve yards off, or so;
A gentlemanly distance, not too near,
   If you have got a former friend for foe;
But after being fired at once or twice,
The ear becomes more Irish, and less nice.

XLII

Lambro presented, and one instant more
   Had stopped this Canto, and Don Juan's breath,
When Haidée threw herself her boy before;
   Stern as her sire: "On me," she cried, "let death
Descend—the fault is mine; this fatal shore
   He found—but sought not. I have pledged my faith;
I love him—I will die with him: I knew
Your nature's firmness—know your daughter's too."

XLIII

A minute past, and she had been all tears,
   And tenderness, and infancy; but now
She stood as one who championed human fears—
   Pale, statue-like, and stern, she wooed the blow;
And tall beyond her sex, and their compeers,
   She drew up to her height, as if to show
A fairer mark; and with a fixed eye scanned
Her father's face—but never stopped his hand.

XLIV

He gazed on her, and she on him; 'twas strange
   How like they looked! the expression was the same;
Serenely savage, with a little change
   In the large dark eye's mutual-darted flame;
For she, too, was as one who could avenge,
   If cause should be—a lioness, though tame;
Her father's blood before her father's face
Boiled up, and proved her truly of his race.

XLV

I said they were alike, their features and
   Their stature, differing but in sex and years:
Even to the delicacy of their hand
   There was resemblance, such as true blood wears;
And now to see them, thus divided, stand
   In fixed ferocity, when joyous tears,
And sweet sensations, should have welcomed both,
Shows what the passions are in their full growth.

XLVI

The father paused a moment, then withdrew
   His weapon, and replaced it; but stood still,
And looking on her, as to look her through,
   "Not I," he said, "have sought this stranger's ill;
Not *I* have made this desolation: few
   Would bear such outrage, and forbear to kill;
But I must do my duty—how thou hast
Done thine, the present vouches for the past.

XLVII

"Let him disarm; or, by my father's head,
   His own shall roll before you like a ball!"
He raised his whistle as the word he said,
   And blew; another answered to the call,

And rushing in disorderly, though led,
   And armed from boot to turban, one and all,
Some twenty of his train came, rank on rank;
He gave the word, "Arrest or slay the Frank."

XLVIII

Then, with a sudden movement, he withdrew
   His daughter; while compressed within his clasp,
'Twixt her and Juan interposed the crew;
   In vain she struggled in her father's grasp—
His arms were like a serpent's coil: then flew
   Upon their prey, as darts an angry asp,
The file of pirates: save the foremost, who
Had fallen, with his right shoulder half cut through.

XLIX

The second had his cheek laid open; but
   The third, a wary, cool old sworder, took
The blows upon his cutlass, and then put
   His own well in; so well, ere you could look,
His man was floored, and helpless at his foot,
   With the blood running like a little brook
From two smart sabre gashes, deep and red—
One on the arm, the other on the head.

L

And then they bound him where he fell, and bore
   Juan from the apartment: with a sign
Old Lambro bade them take him to the shore,
   Where lay some ships which were to sail at nine.
They laid him in a boat, and plied the oar
   Until they reached some galliots, placed in line;
On board of one of these and under hatches,
They stowed him, with strict orders to the watches.

LI

The world is full of strange vicissitudes,
   And here was one exceedingly unpleasant:
A gentleman so rich in the world's goods,
   Handsome and young, enjoying all the present,
Just at the very time when he least broods,
   On such a thing, is suddenly to sea sent,
Wounded and chained, so that he cannot move,
And all because a lady fell in love.

LII

Here I must leave him, for I grow pathetic,
    Moved by the Chinese nymph of tears, green tea!
Than whom Cassandra was not more prophetic;
    For if my pure libations exceed three,
I feel my heart become so sympathetic,
    That I must have recourse to black Bohea.
'Tis pity wine should be so deleterious,
For tea and coffee leave us much more serious,

LIII

Unless when qualified with thee, Cogniac!
    Sweet Naïad of the Phlegethontic rill!
Ah! why the liver wilt thou thus attack,
    And make, like other nymphs, thy lovers ill?
I would take refuge in weak punch, but *rack*
    (In each sense of the word), whene'er I fill
My mild and midnight beakers to the brim,
Wakes me next morning with its synonym.

LIV

I leave Don Juan for the present, safe—
    Not sound, poor fellow, but severely wounded;
Yet could his corporal pangs amount to half
    Of those with which his Haidée's bosom bounded!
She was not one to weep, and rave, and chafe,
    And then give way, subdued because surrounded;
Her mother was a Moorish maid from Fez,
Where all is Eden, or a wilderness.

LV

There the large olive rains its amber store
    In marble fonts; there grain, and flour, and fruit,
Gush from the earth until the land runs o'er;
    But there, too, many a poison-tree has root,
And midnight listens to the lion's roar,
    And long, long deserts scorch the camel's foot,
Or heaving whelm the helpless caravan;
And as the soil is, so the heart of man.

LVI

Afric is all the sun's, and as her earth
    Her human clay is kindled; full of power
For good or evil, burning from its birth,
    The Moorish blood partakes the planet's hour,

And like the soil beneath it will bring forth:
   Beauty and love were Haidée's mother's dower;
But her large dark eye showed deep Passion's force,
Though sleeping like a lion near a source.

LVII

Her daughter, tempered with a milder ray,
   Like summer clouds all silvery, smooth, and fair,
Till slowly charged with thunder they display
   Terror to earth, and tempest to the air,
Had held till now her soft and milky way,
   But overwrought with passion and despair,
The fire burst forth from her Numidian veins,
Even as the Simoom sweeps the blasted plains.

LVIII

The last sight which she saw was Juan's gore
   And he himself o'ermastered and cut down;
His blood was running on the very floor
   Where late he trod, her beautiful, her own;
Thus much she viewed an instant and no more,—
   Her struggles ceased with one convulsive groan;
On her sire's arm, which until now scarce held
Her writhing, fell she like a cedar felled.

LIX

A vein had burst, and her sweet lips' pure dyes
   Were dabbled with the deep blood which ran o'er;
And her head drooped, as when the lily lies
   O'ercharged with rain: her summoned handmaids bore
Their lady to her couch with gushing eyes;
   Of herbs and cordials they produced their store,
But she defied all means they could employ,
Like one life could not hold, nor death destroy.

LX

Days lay she in that state unchanged, though chill—
   With nothing livid, still her lips were red;
She had no pulse, but death seemed absent still;
   No hideous sign proclaimed her surely dead;
Corruption came not in each mind to kill
   All hope; to look upon her sweet face bred
New thoughts of life, for it seemed full of soul—
She had so much, earth could not claim the whole.

LXI

The ruling passion, such as marble shows
   When exquisitely chiselled, still lay there,
But fixed as marble's unchanged aspect throws
   O'er the fair Venus, but forever fair;
O'er the Laocoön's all eternal throes,
   And ever-dying Gladiator's air,
Their energy like life forms all their fame,
Yet looks not life, for they are still the same.

LXII

She woke at length, but not as sleepers wake.
   Rather the dead, for life seemed something new,
A strange sensation which she must partake
   Perforce, since whatsoever met her view
Struck not on memory, though a heavy ache
   Lay at her heart, whose earliest beat still true
Brought back the sense of pain without the cause,
For, for a while, the furies made a pause.

LXIII

She looked on many a face with vacant eye,
   On many a token without knowing what;
She saw them watch her without asking why,
   And recked not who around her pillow sat;
Not speechless, though she spoke not; not a sigh
   Relieved her thoughts; dull silence and quick chat
Were tried in vain by those who served; she gave
No sign, save breath, of having left the grave.

LXIV

Her handmaids tended, but she heeded not;
   Her father watched, she turned her eyes away;
She recognized no being, and no spot,
   However dear or cherished in their day;
They changed from room to room—but all forgot—
   Gentle, but without memory she lay;
At length those eyes, which they would fain be weaning
Back to old thoughts, waxed full of fearful meaning.

LXV

And then a slave bethought her of a harp;
   The harper came, and tuned his instrument;
At the first notes, irregular and sharp,
   On him her flashing eyes a moment bent,

Then to the wall she turned as if to warp
    Her thoughts from sorrow through her heart resent;
And he began a long low island song
Of ancient days, ere tyranny grew strong.

LXVI

Anon her thin wan fingers beat the wall
    In time to his old tune; he changed the theme,
And sung of love; the fierce name struck through all
    Her recollection; on her flashed the dream
Of what she was, and is, if ye could call
    To be so being; in a gushing stream
The tears rushed forth from her o'erclouded brain,
Like mountain mists at length dissolved in rain.

LXVII

Short solace, vain relief!—thought came too quick,
    And whirled her brain to madness; she arose
As one who ne'er had dwelt among the sick,
    And flew at all she met, as on her foes;
But no one ever heard her speak or shriek,
    Although her paroxysm drew towards its close;—
Hers was a frenzy which disdained to rave,
Even when they smote her, in the hope to save.

LXVIII

Yet she betrayed at times a gleam of sense;
    Nothing could make her meet her father's face,
Though on all other things with looks intense
    She gazed, but none she ever could retrace;
Food she refused, and raiment; no pretence
    Availed for either; neither change of place,
Nor time, nor skill, nor remedy, could give her
Senses to sleep—the power seemed gone forever.

LXIX

Twelve days and nights she withered thus; at last,
    Without a groan, or sigh, or glance, to show
A parting pang, the spirit from her passed:
    And they who watched her nearest could not know
The very instant, till the change that cast
    Her sweet face into shadow, dull and slow,
Glazed o'er her eyes—the beautiful, the black—
Oh! to possess such luster—and then lack!

JOHN SINGLETON COPLEY: *Watson and the Shark*, FERDINAND LAMMOT BELIN FUND, NATIONAL GALLERY OF ART, WASHINGTON, D. C.

LXX

She died, but not alone; she held within
   A second principle of life, which might
Have dawned a fair and sinless child of sin;
   But closed its little being without light,
And went down to the grave unborn, wherein
   Blossom and bough lie withered with one blight;
In vain the dews of Heaven descend above
The bleeding flower and blasted fruit of love.

LXXI

Thus lived—thus died she; never more on her
   Shall sorrow light, or shame. She was not made
Through years or moons the inner weight to bear,
   Which colder hearts endure till they are laid
By age in earth: her days and pleasures were
   Brief, but delightful—such as had not staid
Long with her destiny; but she sleeps well
By the sea-shore, whereon she loved to dwell.

LXXII

That isle is now all desolate and bare,
   Its dwellings down, its tenants passed away;
None but her own and father's grave is there,
   And nothing outward tells of human clay;
Ye could not know where lies a thing so fair,
   No stone is there to show, no tongue to say,
What was; no dirge, except the hollow sea's,
Mourns o'er the beauty of the Cyclades.

LXXIII

But many a Greek maid in a loving song
   Sighs o'er her name; and many an islander
With her sire's story makes the night less long;
   Valor was his, and beauty dwelt with her:
If she loved rashly, her life paid for wrong—
   A heavy price must all pay who thus err,
In some shape; let none think to fly the danger,
For soon or late love is his own avenger.

Stanzas for Music

There's not a joy the world can give like that it takes away,
When the glow of early thought declines in feeling's dull decay;
'Tis not on youth's smooth cheek the blush alone, which fades so fast,
But the tender bloom of heart is gone, ere youth itself be past.

Then the few whose spirits float above the wreck of happiness
Are driven o'er the shoals of guilt or ocean of excess:
The magnet of their course is gone, or only points in vain
The shore to which their shivered sail shall never stretch again.

Then the mortal coldness of the soul like death itself comes down;
It cannot feel for others' woes, it dare not dream its own;
That heavy chill has frozen o'er the fountain of our tears,
And though the eye may sparkle still, 'tis where the ice appears.

Though wit may flash from fluent lips, and mirth distract the breast,
Through midnight hours that yield no more their former hope of rest;
'Tis but as ivy-leaves around the ruined turret wreath,
All green and wildly fresh without, but worn and gray beneath.

Oh could I feel as I have felt,—or be what I have been,
Or weep as I could once have wept o'er many a vanished scene;
As springs in deserts found seem sweet, all brackish though they be,
So, midst the withered waste of life, those tears would flow to me.

She Walks in Beauty
from *Hebrew Melodies*

I

She walks in beauty, like the night
  Of cloudless climes and starry skies;
And all that's best of dark and bright
  Meet in her aspect and her eyes:
Thus mellowed to that tender light
  Which heaven to gaudy day denies.

II

One shade the more, one ray the less,
  Had half impaired the nameless grace
Which waves in every raven tress,
  Or softly lightens o'er her face;

Where thoughts serenely sweet express
   How pure, how dear their dwelling-place.

III

And on that cheek, and o'er that brow,
   So soft, so calm, yet eloquent,
The smiles that win, the tints that glow,
   But tell of days in goodness spent,
A mind at peace with all below,
   A heart whose love is innocent!

Percy Bysshe Shelley
(1792-1822)
Ode to the West Wind

I

O, wild West Wind, thou breath of Autumn's being,
Thou, from whose unseen presence the leaves dead
Are driven, like ghosts from an enchanter fleeing,

Yellow, and black, and pale, and hectic red,
Pestilence-stricken multitudes: O, thou,
Who chariotest to their dark wintry bed

The wingèd seeds, where they lie cold and low,
Each like a corpse within its grave, until
Thine azure sister of the spring shall blow

Her clarion o'er the dreaming earth, and fill
(Driving sweet buds like flocks to feed in air)
With living hues and odors plain and hill:

Wild Spirit, which art moving every where;
Destroyer and preserver; hear, O, hear!

II

Thou on whose stream, 'mid the steep sky's commotion,
Loose clouds like earth's decaying leaves are shed,
Shook from the tangled boughs of Heaven and Ocean,

Angels of rain and lightning: there are spread
On the blue surface of thine airy surge,
Like the bright hair uplifted from the head

Of some fierce Mænad, even from the dim verge
Of the horizon to the zenith's height
The locks of the approaching storm. Thou dirge

Of the dying year, to which this closing night
Will be the dome of a vast sepulchre,
Vaulted with all thy congregated might

Of vapors, from whose solid atmosphere
Black rain, and fire, and hail will burst: O, hear!

III

Thou who didst waken from his summer dreams
The blue Mediterranean, where he lay,
Lulled by the coil of his crystalline streams,

Beside a pumice isle in Baiæ's bay,
And saw in sleep old palaces and towers
Quivering within the wave's intenser day,

All overgrown with azure moss and flowers
So sweet, the sense faints picturing them! Thou
For whose path the Atlantic's level powers

Cleave themselves into chasms, while far below
The sea-blooms and the oozy woods which wear

The sapless foliage of the ocean, know

Thy voice, and suddenly grow grey with
    fear,
And tremble and despoil themselves: O,
    hear!

                IV

If I were a dead leaf thou mightest bear;
If I were a swift cloud to fly with thee;
A wave to pant beneath thy power, and
    share

The impulse of thy strength, only less free
Than thou, O, uncontrollable! If even
I were as in my boyhood, and could be

The comrade of thy wanderings over
    heaven,
As then, when to outstrip thy skiey speed
Scarce seemed a vision; I would ne'er have
    striven

As thus with thee in prayer in my sore
    need,
Oh! lift me as a wave, a leaf, a cloud!
I fall upon the thorns of life! I bleed!

A heavy weight of hours has chained and
    bowed
One too like thee: tameless, and swift, and
    proud.

                V

Make me thy lyre, even as the forest is:
What if my leaves are falling like its own!
The tumult of thy mighty harmonies

Will take from both a deep, autumnal
    tone,
Sweet though in sadness. Be thou, spirit
    fierce,
My spirit! Be thou me, impetuous one!

Drive my dead thoughts over the universe

Like withered leaves to quicken a new
    birth!
And, by the incantation of this verse,

Scatter, as from an unextinguished hearth
Ashes and sparks, my words among mankind!
Be through my lips to unawakened earth

The trumpet of a prophecy! O, wind,
If Winter comes, can Spring be far behind?

              Mutability

                I

The flower that smiles to-day
    Tomorrow dies;
All that we wish to stay
    Tempts and then flies.
What is this world's delight?
Lightning that mocks the night,
    Brief even as bright.

                II

Virtue, how frail it is!
    Friendship how rare!
Love, how it sells poor bliss
    For proud despair!
But we, though soon they fall,
Survive their joy, and all
    Which ours we call.

                III

Whilst skies are blue and bright,
    Whilst flowers are gay,
Whilst eyes that change ere night
    Make glad the day;
Whilst yet the calm hours creep,
    Dream thou—and from thy sleep
    Then wake to weep.

Ozymandias

I met a traveller from an antique land
Who said: Two vast and trunkless legs of
    stone
Stand in the desert. Near them, on the
    sand,
Half sunk, a shattered visage lies, whose
    frown,
And wrinkled lip, and sneer of cold com-
    mand,
Tell that its sculptor well those passions
    read
Which yet survive, stamped on these life-
    less things,
The hand that mocked them and the heart
    that fed:
And on the pedestal these words appear:
"My name is Ozymandias, king of kings:
Look on my works, ye Mighty, and de-
    spair!"
Nothing beside remains. Round the decay
Of that colossal wreck, boundless and bare
The lone and level sands stretch far away.

John Keats
(1795-1821)
La Belle Dame Sans Mercy

Ah, what can ail thee, wretched wight,
    Alone and palely loitering;
The sedge is withered from the lake,
    And no birds sing.

Ah, what can ail thee, wretched wight,
    So haggard and so woe-begone?
The squirrel's granary is full,
    And the harvest's done.

I see a lily on thy brow,
    With anguish moist and fever dew;
And on thy cheek a fading rose
    Fast withereth too.

I met a Lady in the meads
    Full beautiful, a fairy's child;
Her hair was long, her foot was light,
    And her eyes were wild.

I set her on my pacing steed,
    And nothing else saw all day long;
For sideways would she lean, and sing
    A fairy's song.

I made a garland for her head,
    And bracelets too, and fragrant zone;
She looked at me as she did love,
    And made sweet moan.

She found me roots of relish sweet,
    And honey wild, and manna dew;
And sure in language strange she said,
    "I love thee true."

She took me to her elfin grot,
    And there she gazed and sighèd deep,
And there I shut her wild sad eyes—
    So kissed to sleep.

And there we slumbered on the moss,
    And there I dreamed, ah woe betide,
The latest dream I ever dreamed
    On the cold hill side.

I saw pale kings, and princes too,
    Pale warriors, death-pale were they all;
Who cried—"La belle Dame sans mercy
    Hath thee in thrall!"

I saw their starved lips in the gloom
    With horrid warning gapèd wide,
And I awoke, and found me here
    On the cold hill side.

And this is why I sojourn here
    Alone and palely loitering,
Though the sedge is withered from the
    lake,
    And no birds sing.

Ode to a Nightingale

My heart aches, and a drowsy numbness pains
   My sense, as though of hemlock I had drunk,
Or emptied some dull opiate to the drains
   One minute past, and Lethe-wards had sunk:
'Tis not through envy of thy happy lot,
   But being too happy in thy happiness,—
      That thou, light-wingèd Dryad of the trees,
         In some melodious plot
   Of beechen green, and shadows numberless,
      Singest of summer in full-throated ease.

O for a draught of vintage! that hath been
   Cooled a long age in the deep-delvèd earth,
Tasting of Flora and the country green,
   Dance, and Provençal song, and sunburnt mirth!
O for a beaker full of the warm South,
   Full of the true, the blushful Hippocrene,
      With beaded bubbles winking at the brim,
         And purple-stainèd mouth;
   That I might drink, and leave the world unseen,
      And with thee fade away into the forest dim:

Fade far away, dissolve, and quite forget
   What thou among the leaves hast never known,
The weariness, the fever, and the fret
   Here, where men sit and hear each other groan;
Where palsy shakes a few, sad, last grey hairs,
   Where youth grows pale, and spectre-thin, and dies;
      Where but to think is to be full of sorrow
         And leaden-eyed despairs,
   Where Beauty cannot keep her lustrous eyes,
      Or new Love pine at them beyond to-morrow.

Away! away! for I will fly to thee,
   Not charioted by Bacchus and his pards,
But on the viewless wings of Poesy,
   Though the dull brain perplexes and retards:
Already with thee! tender is the night,
   And haply the Queen-Moon is on her throne,
      Clustered around by all her starry Fays;
         But here there is no light,
   Save what from heaven is with the breezes blown
      Through verdurous glooms and winding mossy ways.

I cannot see what flowers are at my feet,
   Nor what soft incense hangs upon the boughs,
But, in embalmèd darkness, guess each sweet
   Wherewith the seasonable month endows
The grass, the thicket, and the fruit tree wild;
   White hawthorn, and the pastoral eglantine;
      Fast fading violets covered up in leaves;
         And mid-May's eldest child,
    The coming musk rose, full of dewy wine,
      The murmurous haunt of flies on summer eves.

Darkling I listen; and, for many a time
   I have been half in love with easeful Death,
Called him soft names in many a musèd rhyme,
   To take into the air my quiet breath;
Now more than ever seems it rich to die,
   To cease upon the midnight with no pain,
      While thou art pouring forth thy soul abroad
         In such an ecstasy!
    Still wouldst thou sing, and I have ears in vain—
      To thy high requiem become a sod.

Thou wast not born for death, immortal Bird!
   No hungry generations tread thee down;
The voice I hear this passing night was heard
   In ancient days by emperor and clown:
Perhaps the self-same song that found a path
    Through the sad heart of Ruth, when, sick for home,
      She stood in tears amid the alien corn;
         The same that oft-times hath
    Charmed magic casements, opening on the foam
      Of perilous seas, in faery lands forlorn.

Forlorn! the very word is like a bell
   To toll me back from thee to my sole self!
Adieu! the fancy cannot cheat so well
   As she is famed to do, deceiving elf.
Adieu! adieu! thy plaintive anthem fades
    Past the near meadows, over the still stream,
      Up the hillside; and now 'tis buried deep
         In the next valley glades:
    Was it a vision, or a waking dream?
      Fled is that music:—Do I wake or sleep?

PARTHENON FRIEZE, THE TRUSTEES OF THE BRITISH MUSEUM

Ode on a Grecian Urn

Thou still unravished bride of quietness,
   Thou foster-child of silence and slow time,
Sylvan historian, who canst thus express
   A flowery tale more sweetly than our rhyme:
What leaf-fringed legend haunts about thy shape
   Of deities or mortals, or of both,
      In Tempe or the dales of Arcady?
   What men or gods are these? What maidens loth?
What mad pursuit? What struggle to escape?
   What pipes and timbrels? What wild ecstasy?

Heard melodies are sweet, but those unheard
   Are sweeter; therefore, ye soft pipes, play on;
Not to the sensual ear, but, more endeared,
   Pipe to the spirit ditties of no tone:
Fair youth, beneath the trees, thou canst not leave
   Thy song, nor ever can those trees be bare;
      Bold Lover, never, never canst thou kiss,
Though winning near the goal—yet, do not grieve;
   She cannot fade, though thou hast not thy bliss,
      For ever wilt thou love, and she be fair!

Ah, happy, happy boughs! that cannot shed
   Your leaves, nor ever bid the Spring adieu;
And, happy melodist, unwearièd,
   For ever piping songs for ever new;
More happy love! more happy, happy love!
   For ever warm and still to be enjoyed,
      For ever panting, and for ever young;
All breathing human passion far above,
   That leaves a heart high-sorrowful and cloyed,
      A burning forehead, and a parching tongue.

Who are these coming to the sacrifice?
   To what green altar, O mysterious priest,
Lead'st thou that heifer lowing at the skies,
   And all her silken flanks with garlands dressed?
What little town by river or sea-shore,
   Or mountain-built with peaceful citadel,
      Is emptied of its folk, this pious morn?
And, little town, thy streets for evermore
   Will silent be; and not a soul to tell
      Why thou art desolate, can e'er return.

O Attic shape! Fair attitude! with brede
   Of marble men and maidens overwrought,
With forest branches and the trodden weed;
   Thou, silent form, dost tease us out of thought
As doth eternity: Cold Pastoral!
   When old age shall this generation waste,
      Thou shalt remain, in midst of other woe
Than ours, a friend to man, to whom thou say'st,
   "Beauty is truth, truth beauty,"—that is all
      Ye know on earth, and all ye need to know.

[*"The Last Sonnet"*]
WRITTEN ON A BLANK PAGE IN
SHAKESPEARE'S POEMS, FACING
"A LOVER'S COMPLAINT"

Bright star, would I were steadfast as thou art—
   Not in lone splendor hung aloft the night
And watching, with eternal lids apart,
   Like nature's patient, sleepless Eremite,
The moving waters at their priest-like task
   Of pure ablution round earth's human shores,
Or gazing on the new soft-fallen mask
   Of snow upon the mountains and the moors—
No—yet still steadfast, still unchangeable,
   Pillowed upon my fair love's ripening breast,
To feel for ever its soft fall and swell,
   Awake for ever in a sweet unrest,
Still, still to hear her tender-taken breath,
And so live ever—or else swoon to death.

Alfred, Lord Tennyson
(1809-1892)
Mariana

"Mariana in the moated grange."
Measure for Measure

With blackest moss the flower-plots
   Were thickly crusted, one and all;
The rusted nails fell from the knots
   That held the pear to the gable-wall.
The broken sheds look'd sad and strange:
   Unlifted was the clinking latch;
   Weeded and worn the ancient thatch
Upon the lonely moated grange.
     She only said, "My life is dreary,
       He cometh not," she said;
     She said, "I am aweary, aweary,
       I would that I were dead!"

Her tears fell with the dews at even;
   Her tears fell ere the dews were dried;
She could not look on the sweet heaven,
   Either at morn or eventide.
After the flitting of the bats,
   When thickest dark did trance the sky,
   She drew her casement-curtain by,
And glanced athwart the glooming flats.
     She only said, "The night is dreary,
       He cometh not," she said;
     She said, "I am aweary, aweary,
       I would that I were dead!"

Upon the middle of the night,
   Waking she heard the night-fowl crow;
The cock sung out an hour ere light;
   From the dark fen the oxen's low
Came to her; without hope of change,
   In sleep she seem'd to walk forlorn,
   Till cold winds woke the gray-eyed morn
About the lonely moated grange.
     She only said, "The day is dreary,
       He cometh not," she said;
     She said, "I am aweary, aweary,
       I would that I were dead!"

About a stone-cast from the wall
   A sluice with blacken'd waters slept,
And o'er it many, round and small,
   The cluster'd marish-mosses crept.
Hard by a poplar shook alway,
   All silver-green with gnarled bark:
   For leagues no other tree did mark
The level waste, the rounding gray.
     She only said, "My life is dreary,
       He cometh not," she said;
     She said, "I am aweary, aweary,
       I would that I were dead!"

And ever when the moon was low,
   And the shrill winds were up and away,
In the white curtain, to and fro,
   She saw the gusty shadow sway.
But when the moon was very low,
   And wild winds bound within their cell,
   The shadow of the poplar fell
Upon her bed, across her brow.
     She only said, "The night is dreary,
       He cometh not," she said;
     She said, "I am aweary, aweary,
       I would that I were dead!"

All day within the dreamy house,
   The doors upon their hinges creak'd;
The blue fly sung in the pane; the mouse
   Behind the mouldering wainscot shriek'd,
Or from the crevice peer'd about.
   Old faces glimmer'd thro' the doors,
   Old footsteps trod the upper floors,
Old voices called her from without.
     She only said, "My life is dreary,
       He cometh not," she said;
     She said, "I am aweary, aweary,
       I would that I were dead!"

The sparrow's chirrup on the roof,
   The slow clock ticking, and the sound
Which to the wooing wind aloof
   The poplar made, did all confound
Her sense; but most she loathed the hour
   When the thick-moted sunbeam lay

Athwart the chambers, and the day
Was sloping toward his western bower.
Then she said, "I am very dreary,
He will not come," she said;
She wept, "I am aweary, aweary,
O God, that I were dead!"

Ulysses

It little profits that an idle king,
By this still hearth, among these barren crags,
Match'd with an aged wife, I mete and dole
Unequal laws unto a savage race,
That hoard, and sleep, and feed, and know not
  me.
I cannot rest from travel; I will drink
Life to the lees. All times I have enjoy'd
Greatly, have suffer'd greatly, both with those
That loved me, and alone; on shore, and when
Thro' scudding drifts the rainy Hyades
Vext the dim sea. I am become a name;
For always roaming with a hungry heart
Much have I seen and known,—cities of men
And manners, climates, councils, governments,
Myself not least, but honor'd of them all,—
And drunk delight of battle with my peers,
Far on the ringing plains of windy Troy.
I am a part of all that I have met;
Yet all experience is an arch wherethro'
Gleams that untravell'd world whose margin
  fades
For ever and for ever when I move.
How dull it is to pause, to make an end,
To rust unburnish'd, not to shine in use!
As tho' to breathe were life! Life piled on life
Were all too little, and of one to me
Little remains; but every hour is saved
From that eternal silence, something more,
A bringer of new things; and vile it were
For some three suns to store and hoard myself,
And this gray spirit yearning in desire
To follow knowledge like a sinking star,
Beyond the utmost bound of human thought.

This is my son, mine own Telemachus,
To whom I leave the sceptre and the isle,—
Well-loved of me, discerning to fulfil
This labor, by slow prudence to make mild
A rugged people, and thro' soft degrees
Subdue them to the useful and the good.
Most blameless is he, centered in the sphere
Of common duties, decent not to fail
In offices of tenderness, and pay
Meet adoration to my household gods,
When I am gone. He works his work, I mine.

   There lies the port; the vessel puffs her sail;
There gloom the dark, broad seas. My mariners,
Souls that have toil'd, and wrought, and thought with me,—
That ever with a frolic welcome took
The thunder and the sunshine, and opposed
Free hearts, free foreheads,—you and I are old;
Old age hath yet his honor and his toil.
Death closes all; but something ere the end,
Some work of noble note, may yet be done,
Not unbecoming men that strove with Gods.
The lights begin to twinkle from the rocks;
The long day wanes; the slow moon climbs; the deep
Moans round with many voices. Come, my friends,
'Tis not too late to seek a newer world.
Push off, and sitting well in order smite
The sounding furrows; for my purpose holds
To sail beyond the sunset, and the baths
Of all the western stars, until I die.
It may be that the gulfs will wash us down;
It may be we shall touch the Happy Isles,
And see the great Achilles, whom we knew.
Tho' much is taken, much abides; and tho'
We are not now that strength which in old days
Moved earth and heaven, that which we are, we are,—
One equal temper of heroic hearts,
Made weak by time and fate, but strong in will
To strive, to seek, to find, and not to yield.

Songs from *The Princess*

Sweet and Low

Sweet and low, sweet and low,
   Wind of the western sea,
Low, low, breathe and blow,
   Wind of the western sea!
Over the rolling waters go,
Come from the dying moon, and blow,
   Blow him again to me;
While my little one, while my pretty one sleeps.

Sleep and rest, sleep and rest,
   Father will come to thee soon;
Rest, rest, on mother's breast,
   Father will come to thee soon;
Father will come to his babe in the nest,
Silver sails all out of the west
   Under the silver moon;
Sleep, my little one, sleep, my pretty one, sleep.

The Splendor Falls on Castle Walls

The splendor falls on castle walls
   And snowy summits old in story;
The long light shakes across the lakes,
   And the wild cataract leaps in glory.
Blow, bugle, blow, set the wild echoes flying,
Blow, bugle; answer, echoes, dying, dying,
   dying.

O, hark, O, hear! how thin and clear,
   And thinner, clearer, farther going!
O, sweet and far from cliff and scar
   The horns of Elfland faintly blowing!
Blow, let us hear the purple glens replying,
Blow, bugle; answer, echoes, dying, dying,
   dying.

O love, they die in yon rich sky,
   They faint on hill or field or river;
Our echoes roll from soul to soul,
   And grow for ever and for ever.
Blow, bugle, blow, set the wild echoes flying,
And answer, echoes, answer, dying, dying,
   dying.

Tears, Idle Tears

Tears, idle tears, I know not what they
　　mean,
Tears from the depth of some divine despair
Rise in the heart, and gather to the eyes,
In looking on the happy autumn-fields,
And thinking of the days that are no more.

　　Fresh as the first beam glittering on a sail,
That brings our friends up from the under-
　　world,
Sad as the last which reddens over one
That sinks with all we love below the verge;
So sad, so fresh, the days that are no more.

　　Ah, sad and strange as in dark summer
　　　　dawns
The earliest pipe of half-awaken'd
　　　　birds
To dying ears, when unto dying eyes
The casement slowly grows a glimmering
　　　　square;
So sad, so strange, the days that are no
　　more.

　　Dear as remember'd kisses after death,
And sweet as those by hopeless fancy feign'd
On lips that are for others; deep as love,
Deep as first love, and wild with all regret;
O Death in Life, the days that are no more!

Now Sleeps the Crimson Petal

　　Now sleeps the crimson petal, now the white;
Nor waves the cypress in the palace walk;
Nor winks the gold fin in the porphyry font.
The fire-fly wakens; waken thou with me.

　　Now droops the milkwhite peacock like a
　　　ghost,
And like a ghost she glimmers on to me.

　　Now lies the Earth all Danaë to the stars,
And all thy heart lies open unto me.

Now slides the silent meteor on, and leaves
A shining furrow, as thy thoughts in me.

Now folds the lily all her sweetness up,
And slips into the bosom of the lake.
So fold thyself, my dearest, thou, and slip
Into my bosom and be lost in me.

Robert Browning
(1812-1889)
My Last Duchess
FERRARA

That's my last Duchess painted on the wall,
Looking as if she were alive. I call
That piece a wonder, now: Frà Pandolf's
    hands
Worked busily a day, and there she stands.
Will 't please you sit and look at her? I said
"Frà Pandolf" by design, for never read
Strangers like you that pictured countenance,
The depth and passion of its earnest glance,
But to myself they turned (since none puts by
The curtain I have drawn for you, but I)
And seemed as they would ask me, if they
    durst
How such a glance came there; so, not the
    first
Are you to turn and ask thus. Sir, 'twas not
Her husband's presence only, called that spot
Of joy into the Duchess' cheek: perhaps
Frà Pandolf chanced to say "Her mantle laps
Over my lady's wrist too much," or "Paint
Must never hope to reproduce the faint
Half-flush that dies along her throat"; such
    stuff
Was courtesy, she thought, and cause enough
For calling up that spot of joy. She had
A heart—how shall I say?—too soon made
    glad,

Too easily impressed; she liked whate'er
She looked on, and her looks went everywhere.
Sir, 'twas all one! My favor at her breast,
The dropping of the daylight in the West,
The bough of cherries some officious fool
Broke in the orchard for her, the white mule
She rode with round the terrace—all and
    each
Would draw from her alike the approving
    speech,
Or blush, at least. She thanked men,—good!
    but thanked
Somehow—I know not how—as if she
    ranked
My gift of a nine-hundred-years-old name
With anybody's gift. Who'd stoop to blame
This sort of trifling? Even had you skill
In speech—(which I have not)—to make
    your will
Quite clear to such an one, and say, "Just this
Or that in you disgusts me; here you miss,
Or there exceed the mark"—and if she let
Herself be lessoned so, nor plainly set
Her wits to yours, forsooth, and made excuse,
—E'en then would be some stooping; and I
    choose
Never to stoop. Oh sir, she smiled, no doubt,
Whene'er I passed her; but who passed with-
    out
Much the same smile? This grew; I gave com-
    mands;
Then all smiles stopped together. There she
    stands
As if alive. Will't please you rise? We'll meet
The company below, then. I repeat,
The Count your master's known munificence
Is ample warrant that no just pretence
Of mine for dowry will be disallowed;
Though his fair daughter's self, as I avowed
At starting, is my object. Nay, we'll go
Together down, sir! Notice Neptune, though,
Taming a sea-horse, thought a rarity,
Which Claus of Innsbruck cast in bronze for
    me!

The Bishop Orders His Tomb at Saint Praxed's Church
ROME, 15—

Vanity, saith the preacher, vanity!
Draw round my bed: is Anselm keeping back?
Nephews—sons mine . . . ah God, I know
    not! Well—
She, men would have to be your mother once,
Old Gandolf envied me, so fair she was!
What's done is done, and she is dead beside,
Dead long ago, and I am Bishop since,
And as she died so must we die ourselves,
And thence ye may perceive the world's a
    dream.
Life, how and what is it? As here I lie
In this state-chamber, dying by degrees,
Hours and long hours in the dead night, I ask
"Do I live, am I dead?" Peace, peace seems all.
Saint Praxed's ever was the church for peace;
And so, about this tomb of mine. I fought
With tooth and nail to save my niche, ye know:
—Old Gandolf cozened me, despite my care;
Shrewd was that snatch from out the corner
    South
He graced his carrion with, God curse the
    same!
Yet still my niche is not so cramped but thence
One sees the pulpit o' the epistle-side,
And somewhat of the choir, those silent seats,
And up into the aery dome where live
The angels, and a sunbeam's sure to lurk:
And I shall fill my slab of basalt there,
And 'neath my tabernacle take my rest,
With those nine columns round me, two and
    two,
The odd one at my feet where Anselm stands:
Peach-blossom marble all, the rare, the ripe
As fresh-poured red wine of a mighty pulse.
—Old Gandolf with his paltry onion-stone,
Put me where I may look at him! True peach,
Rosy and flawless: how I earned the prize!
Draw close: that conflagration of my church
—What then? So much was saved if aught
    were missed!

My sons, ye would not be my death? Go dig
The white-grape vineyard where the oil-press
    stood,
Drop water gently till the surface sink,
And if ye find . . . Ah God, I know not, I ! . . .
Bedded in store of rotten fig-leaves soft,
And corded up in a tight olive-frail,
Some lump, ah God, of *lapis lazuli*,
Big as a Jew's head cut off at the nape,
Blue as a vein o'er the Madonna's breast . . .
Sons, all have I bequeathed you, villas, all,
That brave Frascati villa with its bath,
So, let the blue lump poise between my knees,
Like God the Father's globe on both his hands
Ye worship in the Jesu Church so gay,
For Gandolf shall not choose but see and burst!
Swift as a weaver's shuttle fleet our years:
Man goeth to the grave, and where is he?
Did I say basalt for my slab, sons? Black—
'Twas ever antique-black I meant! How else
Shall ye contrast my frieze to come beneath?
The bas-relief in bronze ye promised me,
Those Pans and Nymphs ye wot of, and per-
    chance
Some tripod, thyrsus, with a vase or so,
The Saviour at his sermon on the mount,
Saint Praxed in a glory, and one Pan
Ready to twitch the Nymph's last garment off,
And Moses with the tables . . . but I know
Ye mark me not! What do they whisper thee,
Child of my bowels, Anselm? Ah, ye hope
To revel down my villas while I gasp
Bricked o'er with beggar's mouldy travertine
Which Gandolf from his tomb-top chuckles
    at!
Nay, boys, ye love me—all of jasper, then!
'Tis jasper ye stand pledged to, lest I grieve.
My bath must needs be left behind, alas!
One block, pure green as a pistachio-nut,
There's plenty jasper somewhere in the
    world—
And have I not Saint Praxed's ear to pray
Horses for ye, and brown Greek manuscripts,
And mistresses with great smooth marbly
    limbs?

—That's if ye carve my epitaph aright,
Choice Latin, picked phrase, Tully's every
    word,
No gaudy ware like Gandolf's second line—
Tully, my masters? Ulpian serves his need!
And then how I shall lie through centuries,
And hear the blessed mutter of the mass,
And see God made and eaten all day long,
And feel the steady candle-flame, and taste
Good strong thick stupefying incense-smoke!
For as I lie here, hours of the dead night,
Dying in state and by such slow degrees,
I fold my arms as if they clasped a crook,
And stretch my feet forth straight as stone can
    point,
And let the bedclothes, for a mortcloth, drop
Into great laps and folds of sculptor's-work:
And as yon tapers dwindle, and strange
    thoughts
Grow, with a certain humming in my ears,
About the life before I lived this life,
And this life too, popes, cardinals and priests,
Saint Praxed at his sermon on the mount,
Your tall pale mother with her talking eyes,
And new-found agate urns as fresh as day,
And marble's language, Latin pure, discreet,
—Aha, ELUCESCEBAT quoth our friend?
No Tully, said I, Ulpian at the best!
Evil and brief hath been my pilgrimage.
All *lapis,* all, sons! Else I give the Pope
My villas! Will ye ever eat my heart?
Ever your eyes were as a lizard's quick,
They glitter like your mother's for my soul,
Or ye would heighten my impoverished frieze,
Piece out its starved design, and fill my vase
With grapes, and add a vizor and a Term,
And to the tripod ye would tie a lynx
That in his struggle throws the thyrsus down,
To comfort me on my entablature
Whereon I am to lie till I must ask
"Do I live, am I dead?" There, leave me, there!
For ye have stabbed me with ingratitude
To death—ye wish it—God, ye wish it!
    Stone—
Gritstone, a-crumble! Clammy squares which sweat

As if the corpse they keep were oozing
    through—
And no more *lapis* to delight the world!
Well, go! I bless ye. Fewer tapers there,
But in a row: and, going, turn your backs
—Ay, like departing altar-ministrants,
And leave me in my church, the church for
    peace,
That I may watch at leisure if he leers—
Old Gandolf—at me, from his onion-stone,
As still he envied me, so fair she was!

Fra Lippo Lippi

I am poor brother Lippo, by your leave!
You need not clap your torches to my face.
Zooks, what's to blame? you think you see a
    monk!
What, 'tis past midnight, and you go the
    rounds,
And here you catch me at an alley's end
Where sportive ladies leave their doors ajar?
The Carmine's my cloister: hunt it up,
Do,—harry out, if you must show your zeal,
Whatever rat, there, haps on his wrong hole,
And nip each softling of a wee white mouse,
Weke, weke, that's crept to keep him company!
Aha, you know your betters! Then, you'll take
Your hand away that's fiddling on my throat,
And please to know me likewise. Who am I?
Why, one, sir, who is lodging with a friend
Three streets off—he's a certain . . . how d'ye
    call?
Master—a . . . Cosimo of the Medici,
I' the house that caps the corner. Boh! you
    were best!
Remember and tell me, the day you're hanged,
How you affected such a gullet's-gripe!
But you, sir, it concerns you that your knaves
Pick up a manner nor discredit you:
Zooks, are we pilchards, that they sweep the
    streets
And count fair prize what comes into their net?
He's Judas to a tittle, that man is!

Just such a face! Why, sir, you make amends.
Lord, I'm not angry! Bid your hangdogs go
Drink out this quarter-florin to the health
Of the munificent House that harbors me
(And many more beside, lads! more beside!)
And all's come square again. I'd like his face—
His, elbowing on his comrade in the door
With the pike and lantern,—for the slave
    that holds
John Baptist's head a-dangle by the hair
With one hand ("Look you, now," as who
    should say)
And his weapon in the other, yet unwiped!
It's not your chance to have a bit of chalk,
A wood-coal or the like? or you should see!
Yes, I'm the painter, since you style me so.
What, brother Lippo's doings, up and down,
You know them and they take you? like enough!
I saw the proper twinkle in your eye—
'Tell you, I liked your looks at very first.
Let's sit and set things straight now, hip to
    haunch.
Here's spring come, and the nights one makes
    up bands
To roam the town and sing out carnival,
And I've been three weeks shut within my
    mew,
A-painting for the great man, saints and saints
And saints again. I could not paint all night—
Ouf! I leaned out of window for fresh air.
There came a hurry of feet and little feet,
A sweep of lute-strings, laughs, and whifts of
    song,—
Flower o' the broom,
Take away love, and our earth is a tomb!
Flower o' the quince,
I let Lisa go, and what good in life since?
Flower o' the thyme—and so on. Round they
    went.
Scarce had they turned the corner when a titter
Like the skipping of rabbits by moonlight,—
    three slim shapes,
And a face that looked up . . . zooks, sir, flesh
    and blood,
That's all I'm made of! Into shreds it went,
Curtain and counterpane and coverlet,

All the bed-furniture—a dozen knots,
There was a ladder! Down I let myself,
Hands and feet, scrambling somehow, and so
    dropped,
And after them. I came up with the fun
Hard by Saint Laurence, hail fellow, well
    met,—
Flower o' the rose,
If I've been merry, what matter who knows?
And so as I was stealing back again
To get to bed and have a bit of sleep
Ere I rise up to-morrow and go work
On Jerome knocking at his poor old breast
With his great round stone to subdue the
    flesh,
You snap me of the sudden. Ah, I see!
Though your eye twinkles still, you shake your
    head—
Mine's shaved—a monk, you say—the sting's
    in that!
If Master Cosimo announced himself,
Mum's the word naturally; but a monk!
Come, what am I a beast for? tell us, now!
I was a baby when my mother died
And father died and left me in the street.
I starved there, God knows how, a year or two
On fig-skins, melon-parings, rinds and shucks,
Refuse and rubbish. One fine frosty day,
My stomach being empty as your hat,
The wind doubled me up and down I went.
Old Aunt Lapaccia trussed me with one
    hand,
(Its fellow was a stinger as I knew)
And so along the wall, over the bridge,
By the straight cut to the convent. Six words
    there,
While I stood munching my first bread that
    month:
"So, boy, you're minded," quoth the good fat
    father
Wiping his own mouth, 'twas refection-time,—
"To quit this very miserable world?
Will you renounce" . . . "the mouthful of
    bread?" thought I;
By no means! Brief, they made a monk of
    me;

I did renounce the world, its pride and greed,
Palace, farm, villa, shop and banking-house,
Trash, such as these poor devils of Medici
Have given their hearts to—all at eight years
    old.
Well, sir, I found in time, you may be sure,
'Twas not for nothing—the good bellyful,
The warm serge and the rope that goes all
    round,
And day-long blessed idleness beside!
"Let's see what the urchin's fit for"—that came
    next.
Not overmuch their way, I must confess.
Such a to-do! They tried me with their books:
Lord, they'd have taught me Latin in pure
    waste!
Flower o' the clove,
All the Latin I construe is, "amo" I love!
But, mind you, when a boy starves in the streets
Eight years together, as my fortune was,
Watching folk's faces to know who will fling
The bit of half-stripped grape-bunch he desires,
And who will curse or kick him for his pains,—
Which gentleman processional and fine,
Holding a candle to the Sacrament,
Will wink and let him lift a plate and catch
The droppings of the wax to sell again,
Or holla for the Eight and have him
    whipped,—
How say I?—nay, which dog bites, which lets
    drop
His bone from the heap of offal in the street,—
Why, soul and sense of him grow sharp alike,
He learns the look of things, and none the less
For admonition from the hunger-pinch.
I had a store of such remarks, be sure,
Which, after I found leisure, turned to use.
I drew men's faces on my copy-books,
Scrawled them within the antiphonary's
    marge,
Joined legs and arms to the long music-notes,
Found eyes and nose and chin for A's and B's,
And made a string of pictures of the world
Betwixt the ins and outs of verb and noun,
On the wall, the bench, the door. The monks
    looked black.

"Nay," quoth the prior, "turn him out, d' ye
    say?
In no wise. Lose a crow and catch a lark.
What if at last we get our man of parts.
We Carmelites, like those Camaldolese
And Preaching Friars, to do our church up
    fine
And put the front on it that ought to be!"
And hereupon he bade me daub away.
Thank you! my head being crammed, the walls
    a blank,
Never was such prompt disemburdening.
First, every sort of monk, the black and white,
I drew them, fat and lean: then, folk at church,
From good old gossips waiting to confess
Their cribs of barrel-droppings, candle-
    ends,—
To the breathless fellow at the altar-foot,
Fresh from his murder, safe and sitting there
With the little children round him in a row
Of admiration, half for his beard and half
For that white anger of his victim's son
Shaking a fist at him with one fierce arm,
Signing himself with the other because of
    Christ
(Whose sad face on the cross sees only this
After the passion of a thousand years)
Till some poor girl, her apron o'er her head,
(Which the intense eyes looked through) came
    at eve
On tiptoe, said a word, dropped in a loaf,
Her pair of earrings and a bunch of flowers
(The brute took growling), prayed, and so was
    gone.
I painted all, then cried " 'Tis ask and have;
Choose, for more's ready!"—laid the ladder
    flat,
And showed my covered bit of cloister-wall.
The monks closed in a circle and praised loud
Till checked, taught what to see and not to see,
Being simple bodies,—"That's the very man!
Look at the boy who stoops to pat the dog!
That woman's like the Prior's niece who comes
To care about his asthma: it's the life!"
But there my triumph's straw-fire flared and
    funked;

FRA FILIPPO LIPPI: *Madonna and Child*, SAMUEL H. KRESS COLLECTION, NATIONAL GALLERY OF ART, WASHINGTON, D. C.

Their betters took their turn to see and say:
The Prior and the learned pulled a face
And stopped all that in no time. "How? what's
　　here?
Quite from the mark of painting, bless us all!
Faces, arms, legs and bodies like the true
As much as pea and pea! it's devil's-game!
Your business is not to catch men with show,
With homage to the perishable clay,
But lift them over it, ignore it all,
Make them forget there's such a thing as flesh.
Your business is to paint the souls of men—
Man's soul, and it's a fire, smoke . . . no, it's
　　not . . .
It's vapor done up like a new-born babe—
(In that shape when you die it leaves your
　　mouth)
It's . . . well, what matters talking, it's the
　　soul!
Give us no more of body than shows soul!
Here's Giotto, with his Saint a-praising God,
That sets us praising,—why not stop with
　　him?
Why put all thoughts of praise out of our head
With wonder at lines, colors, and what not?
Paint the soul, never mind the legs and arms!
Rub all out, try at it a second time.
Oh, that white smallish female with the breasts,
She's just my niece . . . Herodias, I would
　　say,—
Who went and danced and got men's heads cut
　　off!
Have it all out!" Now, is this sense, I ask?
A fine way to paint soul, by painting body
So ill, the eye can't stop there, must go further
And can't fare worse! Thus, yellow does for
　　white
When what you put for yellow's simply black,
And any sort of meaning looks intense
When all beside itself means and looks naught.
Why can't a painter lift each foot in turn,
Left foot and right foot, go a double step,
Make his flesh liker and his soul more like,
Both in their order? Take the prettiest face,
The Prior's niece . . . patron-saint—is it so
　　pretty

You can't discover if it means hope, fear,
Sorrow or joy? won't beauty go with these?
Suppose I've made her eyes all right and blue,
Can't I take breath and try to add life's flash,
And then add soul and heighten them three-
    fold?
Or say there's beauty with no soul at all—
(I never saw it—put the case the same—)
If you get simple beauty and naught else,
You get about the best thing God invents:
That's somewhat: and you'll find the soul you
    have missed,
Within yourself, when you return him thanks.
"Rub all out!" Well, well, there's my life, in
    short,
And so the thing has gone on ever since.
I'm grown a man no doubt, I've broken
    bounds:
You should not take a fellow eight years old
And make him swear to never kiss the girls.
I'm my own master, paint now as I please—
Having a friend, you see, in the Corner-house!
Lord, it's fast holding by the rings in front—
Those great rings serve more purposes than just
To plant a flag in, or tie up a horse!
And yet the old schooling sticks, the old grave
    eyes
Are peeping o'er my shoulder as I work,
The heads shake still—"It's art's decline, my
    son!
You're not of the true painters, great and old;
Brother Angelico's the man, you'll find;
Brother Lorenzo stands his single peer;
Fag on at flesh, you'll never make the third!"
Flower o' the pine,
You keep your mistr . . . manners, and I'll stick
    to mine!
I'm not the third, then: bless us, they must
    know!
Don't you think they're the likeliest to know,
They with their Latin? So, I swallow my rage,
Clench my teeth, suck my lips in tight, and
    paint
To please them—sometimes do and sometimes
    don't;
For, doing most, there's pretty sure to come

A turn, some warm eve finds me at my saints—
A laugh, a cry, the business of the world—
(*Flower o' the peach,
Death for us all, and his own life for each!*)
And my whole soul revolves, the cup runs over,
The world and life's too big to pass for a dream,
And I do these wild things in sheer despite,
And play the fooleries you catch me at,
In pure rage! The old mill-horse, out at grass
After hard years, throws up his stiff heels so,
Although the miller does not preach to him
The only good of grass is to make chaff.
What would men have? Do they like grass or
    no—
May they or mayn't they? all I want's the thing
Settled forever one way. As it is,
You tell too many lies and hurt yourself:
You don't like what you only like too much,
You do like what, if given you at your word,
You find abundantly detestable.
For me, I think I speak as I was taught;
I always see the garden and God there
A-making man's wife: and, my lesson learned,
The value and significance of flesh,
I can't unlearn ten minutes afterwards.

   You understand me: I'm a beast, I know.
But see, now—why, I see as certainly
As that the morning-star's about to shine,
What will hap some day. We've a youngster
    here
Comes to our convent, studies what I do,
Slouches and stares and lets no atom drop:
His name is Guidi—he'll not mind the
    monks—
They call him Hulking Tom, he lets them
    talk—
He picks my practice up—he'll paint apace,
I hope so—though I never live so long,
I know what's sure to follow. You be judge!
You speak no Latin more than I, belike;
However, you're my man, you've seen the world
—The beauty and the wonder and the power,
The shapes of things, their colors, lights and
    shades,
Changes, surprises,—and God made it all!

—For what? Do you feel thankful, ay or no,
For this fair town's face, yonder river's line,
The mountain round it and the sky above,
Much more the figures of man, woman, child,
These are the frame to? What's it all about?
To be passed over, despised? or dwelt upon,
Wondered at? oh, this last of course!—you
    say.
But why not do as well as say,—paint these
Just as they are, careless what comes of it?
God's works—paint any one, and count it
    crime
To let a truth slip. Don't object, "His works
Are here already; nature is complete:
Suppose you reproduce her—(which you
    can't)
There's no advantage! you must beat her,
    then."
For, don't you mark? we're made so that we
    love
First when we see them painted, things we
    have passed
Perhaps a hundred times nor cared to see;
And so they are better, painted—better to us,
Which is the same thing. Art was given for
    that;
God uses us to help each other so,
Lending our minds out. Have you noticed,
    now,
Your cullion's hanging face? A bit of chalk,
And trust me but you should, though! How
    much more,
If I drew higher things with the same truth!
That were to take the Prior's pulpit-place,
Interpret God to all of you! Oh, oh,
It makes me mad to see what men shall do
And we in our graves! This world's no blot for
    us,
Nor blank; it means intensely, and means good:
To find its meaning is my meat and drink.
"Ay, but you don't so instigate to prayer!"
Strikes in the Prior: "when your meaning's
    plain
It does not say to folk—remember matins,
Or, mind you fast next Friday!" Why, for this

What need of art at all? A skull and bones,
Two bits of stick nailed crosswise, or, what's
    best,
A bell to chime the hour with, does as well.
I painted a Saint Laurence six months since
At Prato, splashed the fresco in fine style:
"How looks my painting, now the scaffold's
    down?"
I ask a brother: "Hugely," he returns—
"Already not one phiz of your three slaves
Who turn the Deacon off his toasted side,
But's scratched and prodded to our heart's content,
The pious people have so eased their own
With coming to say prayers there in a rage:
We get on fast to see the bricks beneath.
Expect another job this time next year,
For pity and religion grow i' the crowd—
Your painting serves its purpose!" Hang the
    fools!

Meeting at Night

I

The gray sea and the long black land;
And the yellow half-moon large and low;
And the startled little waves that leap
In fiery ringlets from their sleep,
As I gain the cove with pushing prow,
And quench its speed i' the slushy sand.

II

Then a mile of warm sea-scented beach;
Three fields to cross till a farm appears;
A tap at the pane, the quick sharp scratch
And blue spurt of a lighted match,
And a voice less loud, thro' its joys and fears,
Than the two hearts beating each to each!

Matthew Arnold
(1822-1888)
The Forsaken Merman

Come, dear children, let us away;
Down and away below!
Now my brothers call from the bay,
Now the great winds shoreward blow,
Now the salt tides seaward flow;
Now the wild white horses play,
Champ and chafe and toss in the spray.
Children dear, let us away!
This way, this way!

Call her once before you go—
Call once yet!
In a voice that she will know:
'Margaret! Margaret!'
Children's voices should be dear
(Call once more) to a mother's ear;
Children's voices, wild with pain—
Surely she will come again!
Call her once and come away;
This way, this way!
'Mother dear, we cannot stay!
The wild white horses foam and fret.'
Margaret! Margaret!

Come, dear children, come away down;
Call no more!
One last look at the white-wall'd town,
And the little grey church on the windy shore,
Then come down!
She will not come though you call all day;
Come away, come away!

Children dear, was it yesterday
We heard the sweet bells over the bay?
In the caverns where we lay,
Through the surf and through the swell,
The far-off sound of a silver bell?
Sand-strewn caverns, cool and deep,
Where the winds are all asleep;
Where the spent lights quiver and gleam,
Where the salt weed sways in the stream,
Where the sea-beasts, ranged all round,
Feed in the ooze of their pasture-ground;
Where the sea-snakes coil and twine,
Dry their mail and bask in the brine;
Where great whales come sailing by,
Sail and sail, with unshut eye,
Round the world for ever and aye?
When did music come this way?
Children dear, was it yesterday?

Children dear, was it yesterday
(Call yet once) that she went away?
Once she sate with you and me,
On a red gold throne in the heart of the sea,
And the youngest sate on her knee.
She comb'd its bright hair, and she tended it well,
When down swung the sound of a far-off bell.
She sigh'd, she look'd up through the clear green sea;
She said: 'I must go, for my kinsfolk pray
In the little grey church on the shore to-day.
'Twill be Easter-time in the world—ah me!
And I lose my poor soul, Merman, here with thee.'
I said: 'Go up, dear heart, through the waves;
Say thy prayer, and come back to the kind sea-caves.'
She smiled, she went up through the surf in the bay.
Children dear, was it yesterday?

Children dear, were we long alone?
'The sea grows stormy, the little ones moan;
Long prayers,' I said, 'in the world they say;
Come!' I said; and we rose through the surf in the bay.
We went up the beach, by the sandy down
Where the sea-stocks bloom, to the white-wall'd town;

Through the narrow paved streets, where all was still,

To the little grey church on the windy hill.
From the church came a murmur of folk at
    their prayers,
But we stood without in the cold blowing airs.
We climb'd on the graves, on the stones worn
    with rains,
And we gazed up the aisle through the small
    leaded panes.
She sate by the pillar; we saw her clear;
'Margaret, hist! come quick, we are here!
Dear heart,' I said, 'we are long alone;
The sea grows stormy, the little ones moan.'
But, ah, she gave me never a look,
For her eyes were seal'd to the holy book!
Loud prays the priest; shut stands the door.
Come away, children, call no more!
Come away, come down, call no more!

    Down, down, down!
Down to the depths of the sea!
She sits at her wheel in the humming town,
Singing most joyfully.
Hark what she sings: 'O joy, O joy,
For the humming street, and the child with its
    toy!
For the priest, and the bell, and the holy
    well;
For the wheel where I spun,
And the blessed light of the sun!'
And so she sings her fill,
Singing most joyfully,
Till the spindle drops from her hand,
And the whizzing wheel stands still.
She steals to the window, and looks at the sand,
And over the sand at the sea;
And her eyes are set in a stare;
And anon there breaks a sigh,
And anon there drops a tear,
From a sorrow-clouded eye,
And a heart sorrow-laden,
A long, long sigh;
For the cold strange eyes of a little Mermaiden
And the gleam of her golden hair.

    Come away, away children;
Come children, come down!

The hoarse wind blows coldly;
Lights shine in the town.
She will start from her slumber
When gusts shake the door;
She will hear the winds howling,
Will hear the waves roar.
We shall see, while above us
The waves roar and whirl,
A ceiling of amber,
A pavement of pearl.
Singing: 'Here came a mortal,
But faithless was she!
And alone dwell for ever
The kings of the sea.'

But, children, at midnight,
When soft the winds blow,
When clear falls the moonlight,
When spring-tides are low;
When sweet airs come seaward
From heaths starr'd with broom,
And high rocks throw mildly
On the blanch'd sands a gloom;
Up the still, glistening beaches,
Up the creeks we will hie,
Over banks of bright seaweed
The ebb-tide leaves dry.
We will gaze, from the sand-hills,
At the white, sleeping town;
At the church on the hill-side—
And then come back down.
Singing: 'There dwells a loved one,
But cruel is she!
She left lonely for ever
The kings of the sea.'

Dover Beach

The sea is calm to-night.
The tide is full, the moon lies fair
Upon the straits;—on the French coast the
    light
Gleams and is gone; the cliffs of England
    stand,

Glimmering and vast, out in the tranquil
   bay.
Come to the window, sweet is the night-air!
Only, from the long line of spray
Where the sea meets the moon-blanch'd land,
Listen! you hear the grating roar
Of pebbles which the waves draw back, and
   fling,
At their return, up the high strand,
Begin, and cease, and then again begin,
With tremulous cadence slow, and bring
The eternal note of sadness in.

Sophocles long ago
Heard it on the Ægæan, and it brought
Into his mind the turbid ebb and flow
Of human misery; we
Find also in the sound a thought,
Hearing it by this distant northern sea.

The Sea of Faith
Was once, too, at the full, and round earth's
   shore
Lay like the folds of a bright girdle furl'd.
But now I only hear
Its melancholy, long, withdrawing roar,
Retreating, to the breath
Of the night-wind, down the vast edges drear
And naked shingles of the world.

Ah, love, let us be true
To one another! for the world, which seems
To lie before us like a land of dreams,
So various, so beautiful, so new,
Hath really neither joy, nor love, nor light,
Nor certitude, nor peace, nor help for pain;
And we are here as on a darkling plain
Swept with confused alarms of struggle and
   flight,
Where ignorant armies clash by night.

Dante Gabriel Rossetti
(1828-1882)
19. Silent Noon

Your hands lie open in the long fresh grass,—
   The finger-points look through like rosy
      blooms:
   Your eyes smile peace. The pasture gleams
      and glooms
'Neath billowing skies that scatter and amass.
All round our nest, far as the eye can pass,
   Are golden kingcup-fields with silver edge
   Where the cow-parsley skirts the hawthorn-
      hedge.
'Tis visible silence, still as the hour-glass.

Deep in the sun-searched growths the dragon-
   fly
Hangs like a blue thread loosened from the
   sky:—
   So this wing'd hour is dropt to us from
      above.
Oh! clasp we to our hearts, for deathless
   dower,
This close-companioned inarticulate hour
When twofold silence was the song of love.

Christina Rossetti
(1830-1894)
A Birthday

My heart is like a singing bird
Whose nest is in a watered shoot:
My heart is like an apple tree
Whose boughs are bent with thickset fruit;
My heart is like a rainbow shell
That paddles in a halcyon[1] sea;
My heart is gladder than all these
Because my love is come to me.

---

[1] *Halcyon:* tranquil.

Raise me a dais of silk and down;
Hang it with vair[2] and purple dyes;
Carve it in doves and pomegranates,
And peacocks with a hundred eyes;
Work it in gold and silver grapes,
In leaves and silver fleur-de-lys;
Because the birthday of my life
Is come, my love is come to me.

Algernon Charles Swinburne
(1837-1909)
The Garden of Proserpine

Here, where the world is quiet;
   Here, where all trouble seems
Dead winds' and spent waves' riot
   In doubtful dreams of dreams;
I watch the green field growing
For reaping folk and sowing,
For harvest-time and mowing,
   A sleepy world of streams.

I am tired of tears and laughter,
   And men that laugh and weep;
Of what may come hereafter
   For men that sow to reap:
I am weary of days and hours,
Blown buds of barren flowers,
Desires and dreams and powers
   And everything but sleep.

Here life has death for neighbour,
   And far from eye or ear
Wan waves and wet winds labour,
   Weak ships and spirits steer;
They drive adrift, and whither
They wot not who make thither;
But no such winds blow hither,
   And no such things grow here.

No growth of moor or coppice,
   No heather-flower or vine,
But bloomless buds of poppies,
   Green grapes of Proserpine,
Pale beds of blowing rushes
Where no leaf blooms or blushes
Save this whereout she crushes
   For dead men deadly wine.

Pale, without name or number,
   In fruitless fields of corn,
They bow themselves and slumber
   All night till light is born;
And like a soul belated,
In hell and heaven unmated,
By cloud and mist abated
   Comes out of darkness morn.

Though one were strong as seven,
   He too with death shall dwell,
Nor wake with wings in heaven,
   Nor weep for pains in hell;
Though one were fair as roses,
His beauty clouds and closes;
And well though love reposes,
   In the end it is not well.

Pale, beyond porch and portal,
   Crowned with calm leaves, she stands
Who gathers all things mortal
   With cold immortal hands;
Her languid lips are sweeter
Than love's who fears to greet her
To men that mix and meet her
   From many times and lands.

She waits for each and other,
   She waits for all men born;
Forgets the earth her mother,
   The life of fruits and corn;
And spring and seed and swallow
Take wing for her and follow
Where summer song rings hollow
   And flowers are put to scorn.

---

[2]*Vair:* squirrel fur.

There go the loves that wither,
    The old loves with wearier wings;
And all dead years draw thither,
    And all disastrous things;
Dead dreams of days forsaken,
Blind buds that snows have shaken,
Wild leaves that winds have taken,
    Red strays of ruined springs.

We are not sure of sorrow,
    And joy was never sure;
To-day will die to-morrow;
    Time stoops to no man's lure;
And love, grown faint and fretful,
With lips but half regretful
Sighs, and with eyes forgetful
    Weeps that no loves endure.

From too much love of living,
    From hope and fear set free,
We thank with brief thanksgiving
    Whatever gods may be
That no life lives for ever;
That dead men rise up never;
That even the weariest river
    Winds somewhere safe to sea.

Then star nor sun shall waken,
    Nor any change of light:
Nor sound of waters shaken,
    Nor any sound or sight:
Nor wintry leaves nor vernal,
Nor days nor things diurnal;
Only the sleep eternal
    In an eternal night.

When the Hounds of Spring
Chorus from *Atalanta in Calydon*

When the hounds of spring are on winter's traces,
    The mother of months in meadow or plain
Fills the shadows and windy places
    With lisp of leaves and ripple of rain;
And the brown bright nightingale amorous
Is half assuaged for Itylus,
For the Thracian ships and the foreign faces,
    The tongueless vigil and all the pain.

Come with bows bent and with emptying of
    quivers,
    Maiden most perfect, lady of light,
With a noise of winds and many rivers,
    With a clamor of waters, and with might;
Bind on thy sandals, O thou most fleet,
Over the splendor and speed of thy feet;
For the faint east quickens, the wan west shivers,
    Round the feet of the day and the feet of the
        night.

Where shall we find her, how shall we sing to her,
　　Fold our hands round her knees, and cling?
O that man's heart were as fire and could spring to
　　　her,
　　Fire, or the strength of the streams that spring!
For the stars and the winds are unto her
As raiment, as songs of the harp player;
For the risen stars and the fallen cling to her,
　　And the southwest wind and the west wind sing.

For winter's rains and ruins are over,
　　And all the season of snows and sins;
The days dividing lover and lover,
　　The light that loses, the night that wins;
And time remembered is grief forgotten,
And frosts are slain and flowers begotten,
And in green underwood and cover
　　Blossom by blossom the spring begins.

The full streams feed on flower of rushes,
　　Ripe grasses trammel a traveling foot,
The faint fresh flame of the young year flushes
　　From leaf to flower and flower to fruit;
And fruit and leaf are as gold and fire,
And the oat is heard above the lyre,
And the hoofèd heel of a satyr crushes
　　The chestnut husk at the chestnut root.

And Pan by noon and Bacchus by night,
　　Fleeter of foot than the fleet-foot kid,
Follows with dancing and fills with delight
　　The Maenad and the Bassarid;
And soft as lips that laugh and hide,
The laughing leaves of the trees divide,
And screen from seeing and leave in sight
　　The god pursuing, the maiden hid.

The ivy falls with the Bacchanal's hair
　　Over her eyebrows hiding her eyes;
The wild vine slipping down leaves bare
　　Her bright breast shortening into sighs;
The wild vine slips with the weight of its leaves,
But the berried ivy catches and cleaves
To the limbs that glitter, the feet that scare
　　The wolf that follows, the fawn that flies.

Thomas Hardy
(1840-1928)

The Oxen

Christmas Eve, and twelve of the clock.
   "Now they are all on their knees,"
An elder said as we sat in a flock
   By the embers in hearthside ease.

We pictured the meek mild creatures where
   They dwelt in their strawy pen,
Nor did it occur to one of us there
   To doubt they were kneeling then.

So fair a fancy few would weave
   In these years! Yet, I feel,
If someone said on Christmas Eve,
   "Come; see the oxen kneel,

"In the lonely barton by yonder coomb
   Our childhood used to know,"
I should go with him in the gloom,
   Hoping it might be so.

In Time of "The Breaking of Nations"

I
Only a man harrowing clods
   In a slow silent walk
With an old horse that stumbles and nods
   Half asleep as they stalk.

II
Only thin smoke without flame
   From the heaps of couch-grass;
Yet this will go onward the same
   Though Dynasties pass.

III
Yonder a maid and her wight
   Come whispering by:
War's annals will cloud into night
   Ere their story die.

The Darkling Thrush

I leant upon a coppice gate
   When Frost was spectre-gray,
And Winter's dregs made desolate
   The weakening eye of day.
The tangled bine-stems scored the sky
   Like strings of broken lyres,
And all mankind that haunted nigh
   Had sought their household fires.

The land's sharp features seemed to be
   The Century's corpse outleant,
His crypt the cloudy canopy,
   The wind his death-lament.
The ancient pulse of germ and birth
   Was shrunken hard and dry,
And every spirit upon earth
   Seemed fervourless as I.

At once a voice arose among
   The bleak twigs overhead
In a full-hearted evensong
   Of joy illimited;
An aged thrush, frail, gaunt, and small,
   In blast-beruffled plume,
Had chosen thus to fling his soul
   Upon the growing gloom.

So little cause for carolings
   Of such ecstatic sound
Was written on terrestrial things
   Afar or nigh around,
That I could think there trembled through
   His happy good-night air
Some blessed Hope, whereof he knew
   And I was unaware.

Gerard Manley Hopkins
(1844-1889)

God's Grandeur

The world is charged with the grandeur of
   God.
  It will flame out, like shining from shook
    foil;
  It gathers to a greatness, like the ooze of oil
Crushed. Why do men then now not reck his
   rod?
Generations have trod, have trod, have trod;
  And all is seared with trade; bleared,
    smeared with toil;
  And wears man's smudge and shares man's
    smell: the soil
Is bare now, nor can foot feel, being shod.

And for all this, nature is never spent;
  There lives the dearest freshness deep down
    things;
  And though the last lights off the black West
    went
  Oh, morning, at the brown brink eastward,
    springs—
Because the Holy Ghost over the bent
  World broods with warm breast and with
    ah! bright wings.

The Windhover:
TO CHRIST OUR LORD

I caught this morning morning's minion, king-
  dom of daylight's dauphin, dapple-dawn-
    drawn Falcon, in his riding
  Of the rolling level underneath him steady
    air, and striding
High there, how he rung upon the rein of a
    wimpling wing
In his ecstasy! then off, off forth on swing,
  As a skate's heel sweeps smooth on a bow-
    bend: the hurl and gliding
  Rebuffed the big wind. My heart in hiding

Stirred for a bird,—the achieve of, the mastery of the thing!

Brute beauty and valour and act, oh, air, pride, plume, here
  Buckle! AND the fire that breaks from thee then, a billion
Times told lovelier, more dangerous, O my chevalier!

Pied Beauty

Glory be to God for dappled things—
  For skies of couple-colour as a brinded cow;
    For rose-moles all in stipple upon trout that swim;
Fresh-firecoal chestnut-falls; finches' wings;
  Landscape plotted and pieced—fold, fallow, and plough;
    And áll trádes, their gear and tackle and trim.

All things counter, original, spare, strange;
  Whatever is fickle, freckled (who knows how?)
    With swift, slow; sweet, sour; adazzle, dim;
He fathers-forth whose beauty is past change:
    Praise him.

Spring and Fall

TO A YOUNG CHILD

Márgarét, are you gríeving
Over Goldengrove unleaving?
Leáves, líke the things of man, you
With your fresh thoughts care for, can you?
Áh! ás the heart grows older
It will come to such sights colder
By and by, nor spare a sigh
Though worlds of wanwood leafmeal lie;
And yet you wíll weep and know why.
Now no matter, child, the name:
Sórrow's springs áre the same.

Nor mouth had, no nor mind, expressed
What heart heard of, ghost guessed:
It ís the blight man was born for,
It is Margaret you mourn for.

A. E. Housman
(1859-1936)

To an Athlete Dying Young

The time you won your town the race
We chaired you through the market-place;
Man and boy stood cheering by,
And home we brought you shoulder-high.

To-day, the road all runners come,
Shoulder-high we bring you home,
And set you at your threshold down,
Townsman of a stiller town.

Smart lad, to slip betimes away
From fields where glory does not stay
And early though the laurel grows
It withers quicker than the rose.

Eyes the shady night has shut
Cannot see the record cut,
And silence sounds no worse than cheers
After earth has stopped the ears:

Now you will not swell the rout
Of lads that wore their honours out,
Runners whom renown outran
And the name died before the man.

So set, before its echoes fade,
The fleet foot on the sill of shade,
And hold to the low lintel up
The still-defended challenge-cup.

And round that early-laurelled head
Will flock to gaze the strengthless dead,
And find unwithered on its curls
The garland briefer than a girl's.

Loveliest of Trees, the Cherry Now

Loveliest of trees, the cherry now
Is hung with bloom along the bough,
And stands about the woodland ride
Wearing white for Eastertide.

Now, of my threescore years and ten,
Twenty will not come again,
And take from seventy springs a score,
It only leaves me fifty more.

And since to look at things in bloom
Fifty springs are little room,
About the woodlands I will go
To see the cherry hung with snow.

AMERICAN

Philip Freneau
(1752-1832)
The Wild Honeysuckle

Fair flower, that dost so comely grow,
Hid in this silent, dull retreat,
Untouched thy honied blossoms blow,
Unseen thy little branches greet;
   No roving foot shall crush thee here,
   No busy hand provoke a tear.

By Nature's self in white arrayed,
She bade thee shun the vulgar eye,
And planted here the guardian shade,
And sent soft waters murmuring by;
   Thus quietly thy summer goes,
   Thy days declining to repose.

Smit with those charms, that must decay,
I grieve to see your future doom;
They died—nor were those flowers more gay,
The flowers that did in Eden bloom:
   Unpitying frosts, and Autumn's power
   Shall leave no vestige of this flower.

From morning suns and evening dews
At first thy little being came:
If nothing once, you nothing lose,
For when you die you are the same;
   The space between, is but an hour,
   The frail duration of a flower.

William Cullen Bryant
(1794-1878)
To a Waterfowl

   Whither, midst falling dew,
While glow the heavens with the last steps of day,
Far through their rosy depths dost thou pursue
   Thy solitary way?

   Vainly the fowler's eye
Might mark thy distant flight to do thee wrong,
As, darkly seen against the crimson sky,
   Thy figure floats along.

   Seek'st thou the plashy brink
Of weedy lake or marge of river wide,
Or where the rocking billows rise and sink
   On the chafed ocean-side?

   There is a Power whose care
Teaches thy way along that pathless coast—

The desert and illimitable air,—
    Lone wandering, but not lost.

    All day thy wings have fanned,
At that far height, the cold thin atmosphere,
Yet stoop not, weary, to the welcome land,
    Though the dark night is near.

    And soon that toil shall end:
Soon shalt thou find a summer home, and rest,
And scream among thy fellows; reeds shall bend,
    Soon, o'er thy sheltered nest.

    Thou'rt gone, the abyss of heaven
Hath swallowed up thy form; yet, on my heart
Deeply has sunk the lesson thou hast given,
    And shall not soon depart.

    He who, from zone to zone,
Guides through the boundless sky thy certain flight,
In the long way, that I must tread alone,
    Will lead my steps aright.

Ralph Waldo Emerson
(1803-1882)
The Rhodora:
On Being Asked, Whence Is the Flower?

In May, when sea-winds pierced our solitudes,
I found the fresh Rhodora in the woods,
Spreading its leafless blooms in a damp nook,
To please the desert and the sluggish brook.
The purple petals, fallen in the pool,
Made the black water with their beauty gay;
Here might the redbird come his plumes to cool,
And court the flower that cheapens his array.
Rhodora! if the sages ask thee why
This charm is wasted on the earth and sky,
Tell them, dear, that if eyes were made for seeing,
Then Beauty is its own excuse for being:
Why thou wert there, O rival of the rose!
I never thought to ask, I never knew:
But, in my simple ignorance, suppose
The self-same Power that brought me there
    brought you.

Days

Daughters of Time, the hypocritic Days,
Muffled and dumb like barefoot dervishes,
And marching single in an endless file,
Bring diadems and fagots in their hands.
To each they offer gifts after his will,
Bread, kingdoms, stars, and sky that holds
    them all.
I, in my pleachèd garden, watched the pomp,
Forgot my morning wishes, hastily
Took a few herbs and apples, and the Day
Turned and departed silent. I, too late,
Under her solemn fillet saw the scorn.

Henry Wadsworth Longfellow
(1807-1882)
Hymn to the Night

I heard the trailing garments of the Night
    Sweep through her marble halls!
I saw her sable skirts all fringed with light
    From the celestial walls!

I felt her presence, by its spell of might,
    Stoop o'er me from above;
The calm, majestic presence of the Night,
    As of the one I love.

I heard the sounds of sorrow and delight,
    The manifold, soft chimes,
That fill the haunted chambers of the Night,
    Like some old poet's rhymes.

From the cool cisterns of the midnight air
    My spirit drank repose;
The fountain of perpetual peace flows
      there,—
    From those deep cisterns flows.

O holy Night! from thee I learn to bear
    What man has borne before!
Thou layest thy finger on the lips of Care,
    And they complain no more.

from *Divina Commedia*

I

Oft have I seen at some cathedral door
A laborer, pausing in the dust and heat,
Lay down his burden, and with reverent feet
Enter, and cross himself, and on the floor
Kneel to repeat his paternoster o'er;
Far off the noises of the world retreat;
The loud vociferations of the street
Become an undistinguishable roar.
So, as I enter here from day to day,
And leave my burden at this minster gate,
Kneeling in prayer, and not ashamed to pray,
The tumult of the time disconsolate
To inarticulate murmurs dies away,
While the eternal ages watch and wait.

II

How strange the sculptures that adorn these
    towers!
This crowd of statues, in whose folded sleeves
Birds build their nests; while canopied with
    leaves
Parvis and portal bloom like trellised bowers,
And the vast minster seems a cross of flowers!
But fiends and dragons on the gargoyled
    eaves
Watch the dead Christ between the living
    thieves,
And, underneath, the traitor Judas lowers!
Ah! from what agonies of heart and brain,
What exultations trampling on despair,
What tenderness, what tears, what hate of
    wrong,
What passionate outcry of a soul in pain,
Uprose this poem of the earth and air,
This mediaeval miracle of song!

Michelangelo Buonarroti
(1475-1564)
Dante

What should be said of him cannot be said;
   By too great splendor is his name attended;
   To blame is easier those who him offended,
Than reach the faintest glory round him shed.
This man descended to the doomed and dead
   For our instruction; then to God ascended;
   Heaven opened wide to him its portals splendid,
Who from his country's, closed against him, fled.
Ungrateful land! To its own prejudice
   Nurse of his fortunes; and this showeth well
     That the most perfect most of grief shall see.
Among a thousand proofs let one suffice,
   That as his exile hath no parallel,
     Ne'er walked the earth a greater man than he.

               (Translated by H.W. Longfellow)

Edgar Allan Poe
(1809-1849)

To Helen

Helen, thy beauty is to me
   Like those Nicéan barks of yore,
That gently, o'er a perfumed sea,
   The weary, way-worn wanderer bore
   To his own native shore.

On desperate seas long wont to roam,
   Thy hyacinth hair, thy classic face,
Thy Naiad airs have brought me home
   To the glory that was Greece,
   And the grandeur that was Rome.

Lo! in yon brilliant window-niche
   How statue-like I see thee stand,
The agate lamp within thy hand!
   Ah, Psyche, from the regions which
   Are Holy-Land!

Ulalume

The skies they were ashen and sober;
   The leaves they were crispèd and sere—
   The leaves they were withering and sere;
It was night in the lonesome October
   Of my most immemorial year;
It was hard by the dim lake of Auber,
   In the misty mid region of Weir—
It was down by the dank tarn of Auber,
   In the ghoul-haunted woodland of Weir.

Here once, through an alley Titanic,
   Of cypress, I roamed with my soul—
   Of cypress, with Psyche, my Soul.
These were days when my heart was volcanic
   As the scoriac rivers that roll—
   As the lavas that restlessly roll
Their sulphurous currents down Yaanek

In the ultimate climes of the pole—
   That groan as they roll down Mount Yaanek
     In the realms of the boreal pole.

Our talk had been serious and sober,
     But our thoughts they were palsied and
         sere—
     Our memories were treacherous and
         sere—
For we knew not the month was October,
     And we marked not the night of the year—
     (Ah, night of all nights in the year!)
We noted not the dim lake of Auber—
     (Though once we have journeyed down
         here)—
Remembered not the dank tarn of Auber,
     Nor the ghoul-haunted woodland of Weir.

And now, as the night was senescent
     And star-dials pointed to morn—
     As the star-dials hinted of morn—
At the end of our path a liquescent
     And nebulous lustre was born,
Out of which a miraculous crescent
     Arose with a duplicate horn—
Astarte's bediamonded crescent
     Distinct with its duplicate horn.

And I said—"She is warmer than Dian:
     She rolls through an ether of sighs—
     She revels in a region of sighs:
She has seen that the tears are not dry on
     These cheeks, where the worm never dies
And has come past the stars of the Lion
     To point us the path to the skies—
     To the Lethean peace of the skies—
Come up, in despite of the Lion,
     To shine on us with her bright eyes—
Come up through the lair of the Lion,
     With love in her luminous eyes."

But Psyche, uplifting her finger,
     Said—"Sadly this star I mistrust—
     Her pallor I strangely mistrust:—
Oh, hasten!—oh, let us not linger!
     Oh, fly!—let us fly!—for we must."

In terror she spoke, letting sink her
     Wings until they trailed in the dust—
In agony sobbed, letting sink her
     Plumes till they trailed in the dust—
     Till they sorrowfully trailed in the dust.

I replied—"This is nothing but dreaming:
     Let us on by this tremulous light!
     Let us bathe in this crystalline light!
Its Sibyllic splendor is beaming
     With Hope and in Beauty to-night:—
See!—it flickers up the sky through the
     night!
Ah, we safely may trust to its gleaming,
     And be sure it will lead us aright—
We safely may trust to a gleaming
     That cannot but guide us aright,
     Since it flickers up to Heaven through the
     night."

Thus I pacified Psyche and kissed her,
     And tempted her out of her gloom—
     And conquered her scruples and gloom;
And we passed to the end of the vista,
     But were stopped by the door of a tomb—
     By the door of a legended tomb;
And I said—"What is written, sweet sister,
     On the door of this legended tomb?"
She replied—"Ulalume—Ulalume—
     'Tis the vault of thy lost Ulalume!"

Then my heart it grew ashen and sober
     As the leaves that were crispèd and sere—
     As the leaves that were withering and sere,
And I cried—"It was surely October
     On *this* very night of last year
     That I journeyed—I journeyed down
         here—
     That I brought a dread burden down
         here—
     On this night of all nights in the year,
     Ah, what demon has tempted me here?
Well I know, now, this dim lake of Auber—
     This misty mid region of Weir—
Well I know, now, this dank tarn of Auber,
     This ghoul-haunted woodland of Weir."

Israfel

In Heaven a spirit doth dwell
   "Whose heart-strings are a lute";
None sing so wildly well
As the angel Israfel,
And the giddy stars (so legends tell)
Ceasing their hymns, attend the spell
  Of his voice, all mute.

Tottering above
  In her highest noon,
  The enamoured moon
Blushes with love,
  While, to listen, the red levin
  (With the rapid Pleiads, even,
  Which were seven,)
  Pauses in Heaven.

And they say (the starry choir
  And the other listening things)
That Israfeli's fire
Is owing to that lyre
  By which he sits and sings—
The trembling living wire
Of those unusual strings.

But the skies that angel trod,
  Where deep thoughts are a duty—
Where Love's a grown-up God—
  Where the Houri glances are
Imbued with all the beauty
  Which we worship in a star.

Therefore, thou art not wrong,
  Israfeli, who despisest
An unimpassioned song;
To thee the laurels belong,
  Best bard, because the wisest!
Merrily live, and long!

The ecstasies above
  With thy burning measures suit—
Thy grief, thy joy, thy hate, thy love,
  With the fervour of thy lute—
  Well may the stars be mute!

Yes, Heaven is thine; but this
  Is a world of sweets and sours;
  Our flowers are merely—flowers,
And the shadow of thy perfect bliss
  Is the sunshine of ours.

If I could dwell
Where Israfel
  Hath dwelt, and he where I,
He might not sing so wildly well
  A mortal melody,
While a bolder note than this might swell
  From my lyre within the sky.

Walt Whitman
(1819-1892)
When I Heard the Learn'd Astronomer
(1865, 1867)

When I heard the learn'd astronomer;
When the proofs, the figures, were ranged in columns before me;
When I was shown the charts and the diagrams, to add, divide, and measure them:
When I, sitting, heard the astronomer, where he lectured with much applause in the lecture-room,

How soon, unaccountable, I became tired and sick;
Till rising and gliding out, I wander'd off by myself,
In the mystical moist night-air, and from time to time,
Look'd up in perfect silence at the stars.

There Was a Child Went Forth

There was a child went forth every day,
And the first object he look'd upon, that object he became,
And that object became part of him for the day or a certain part of the day,
Or for many years or stretching cycles of years.

The early lilacs became part of this child,
And grass and white and red morning-glories, and white and red clover, and the song of the phoebe-bird,
And the Third-month lambs and the sow's pink-faint litter, and the mare's foal and the cow's calf,
And the noisy brood of the barnyard or by the mire of the pond-side,
And the fish suspending themselves so curiously below there, and the beautiful curious liquid,
And the water-plants with their graceful flat heads, all became part of him.

The field-sprouts of Fourth-month and Fifth-month became part of him,
Winter-grain sprouts and those of the light-yellow corn, and the esculent roots of the garden,
And the apple-trees cover'd with blossoms and the fruit afterward, and wood-berries, and the commonest weeds by the road,
And the old drunkard staggering home from the outhouse of the tavern whence he had lately risen,
And the schoolmistress that pass'd on her way to the school,
And the friendly boys that pass'd, and the quarrelsome boys,
And the tidy and fresh-cheek'd girls, and the barefoot Negro boy and girl,
And all the changes of city and country wherever he went.
His own parents, he that had father'd him and she that had conceiv'd him in her womb and birth'd him,
They gave this child more of themselves than that,
They gave him afterward every day, they became part of him.

The mother at home quietly placing the dishes on the supper-table,
The mother with mild words, clean her cap and gown, a wholesome odor falling off her person and clothes as she walks by,
The father, strong, self-sufficient, manly, mean, anger'd, unjust,
The blow, the quick loud word, the tight bargain, the crafty lure,
The family usages, the language, the company, the furniture, the yearning and swelling heart,

JOHN CONSTABLE: *The Hay-Wain*. REPRODUCED BY COURTESY OF THE TRUSTEES, THE NATIONAL GALLERY, LONDON

Affection that will not be gainsay'd, the sense of what is real, the thought if after all
    it should prove unreal,
The doubts of day-time and the doubts of night-time, the curious whether and
    how,
Whether that which appears so is so, or is it all flashes and specks?
Men and women crowding fast in the streets, if they are not flashes and specks what
    are they?
The streets themselves and the façades of houses, and goods in the windows,
Vehicles, teams, the heavy-plank'd wharves, the huge crossing at the ferries,
The village on the highland seen from afar at sunset, the river between,
Shadows, aureola and mist, the light falling on roofs and gables of white or brown
    two miles off,
The schooner near by sleepily dropping down the tide, the little boat slack-tow'd
    astern,
The hurrying tumbling waves, quick-broken crests, slapping,
That strata of color'd clouds, the long bar of maroon-tint away solitary by itself,
    the spread of purity it lies motionless in,
The horizon's edge, the flying sea-crow, the fragrance of salt marsh and shore mud,
These became part of that child who went forth every day, and who now goes, and
    will always go forth every day.

Emily Dickinson
(1830-1886)

To Hear an Oriole Sing

To hear an oriole sing
May be a common thing,
Or only a divine.

It is not of the bird
Who sings the same, unheard,
As unto crowd.

The fashion of the ear
Attireth that it hear
In dun or fair.

So whether it be rune,
Or whether it be none,
Is of within;

The "tune is in the tree,"
The sceptic showeth me;
"No, sir! In thee!"

There's a Certain Slant of Light

There's a certain slant of light,
On winter afternoons,
That oppresses, like the weight
Of cathedral tunes.

Heavenly hurt it gives us;
We can find no scar,
But internal difference
Where the meanings are.

None may teach it anything,
'T is the seal, despair,—
An imperial affliction
Sent us of the air.

When it comes, the landscape listens,
Shadows hold their breath;
When it goes, 't is like the distance
On the look of death.

JEAN-BAPTIST CAMILLE COROT: *Interrupted Reading*, POTTER PALMER COLLECTION, THE ART INSTITUTE OF CHICAGO

There Is No Frigate like a Book

There is no frigate like a book
    To take us lands away,
Nor any coursers like a page
    Of prancing poetry.
This traverse may the poorest take
    Without oppress of toll;
How frugal is the chariot
    That bears the human soul!

Sidney Lanier
(1842-1881)
Evening Song

Look off, dear Love, across the sallow sands,
    And mark yon meeting of the sun and sea,
How long they kiss in sight of all the lands.
    Ah! longer, longer, we.

Now in the sea's red vintage melts the sun,
    As Egypt's pearl dissolved in rosy wine,
And Cleopatra night drinks all. 'Tis done,
    Love, lay thine hand in mine.

Come forth, sweet stars, and comfort heaven's heart;
    Glimmer, ye waves, round else-unlighted sands.
O night, divorce our sun and sky apart,
    Never our lips, our hands.

A Ballad of Trees and the Master[1]

Into the woods my Master went,
Clean forspent, forspent.
Into the woods my Master came,
Forspent with death and shame.
But the olives they were not blind to Him,
The little gray leaves were kind to Him:
The thorn-tree had a mind to Him
When into the woods he came.

Out of the woods my Master went,
And He was well content.
Out of the woods my Master came,
Content with death and shame.
When Death and Shame would woo Him last,
From under the trees they drew Him last:
'Twas on a tree they slew Him—last
When out of the woods he came.

---

[1] This lyric has been beautifully set to music by the American composer George W. Chadwick.

Edgar Allan Poe
(1809-1849)
The Masque of the Red Death

The "Red Death" had long devastated the country. No pestilence had ever been so fatal, or so hideous. Blood was its avatar and its seal—the redness and the horror of blood. There were sharp pains, and sudden dizziness, and then profuse bleeding at the pores, with dissolution. The scarlet stains upon the body, and especially upon the face, of the victim were the pest ban which shut him out from the aid and from the sympathy of his fellow-men. And the whole seizure, progress, and termination of the disease were the incidents of half an hour.

But the Prince Prospero was happy and dauntless and sagacious. When his dominions were half depopulated, he summoned to his presence a thousand hale and light-hearted friends from among the knights and dames of his court, and with these retired to the deep seclusion of one of his castellated abbeys. This was an extensive and magnificent structure, the creation of the Prince's own eccentric yet august taste. A strong and lofty wall girdled it in. This wall had gates of iron. The courtiers, having entered, brought furnaces and massy hammers, and welded the bolts. They resolved to leave means neither of ingress or egress to the sudden impulses of despair or of frenzy from within. The abbey was amply provisioned. With such precautions the courtiers might bid defiance to contagion. The external world could take care of itself. In the meantime it was folly to grieve, or to think. The Prince had provided all the appliances of pleasure. There were buffoons, there were improvisatori, there were ballet-dancers, there were musicians, there was Beauty, there was wine. All these and security were within. Without was the "Red Death."

It was toward the close of the fifth or sixth month of his seclusion, and while the pestilence raged most furiously abroad, that the Prince Prospero entertained his thousand friends at a masked ball of the most unusual magnificence.

It was a voluptuous scene, that masquerade. But first let me tell of the rooms in which it was held. There were seven—an imperial suite. In many palaces, however, such suites form a long and straight vista, while the folding-doors slide back nearly to the walls on either hand, so that the view of the whole extent is scarcely impeded. Here the case was very different, as might have been expected from the prince's love of the bizarre. The apartments were so irregularly disposed that the vision embraced but little more than one at a time. There was a sharp turn at every twenty or thirty yards, and at each turn a novel effect. To the right and left, in the middle of each wall, a tall and narrow Gothic window looked out upon a closed corridor which pursued the windings of the suite. These windows were of stained glass whose color varied in accordance with the prevailing hue of the decorations of the chamber into which it opened. That at the eastern extremity was hung, for example, in blue—and vividly blue were its windows. The second chamber was purple in its ornaments and tapestries, and here the panes were purple. The third was green throughout, and so were the casements. The fourth was furnished and lighted with orange—the fifth with white—the sixth with violet. The seventh apartment was closely shrouded in black velvet tapestries that hung all over the ceiling and down the walls, falling in heavy folds upon a carpet of the same material and hue. But in this chamber only, the color of the windows failed to correspond with the decorations. The panes here were scarlet—a deep blood-color. Now in no one of the seven apartments was there any lamp or candelabrum, amid the profusion of golden ornaments that lay scattered to and fro or depended from the roof. There was no light of any kind emanating from lamp or candle within the suite of chambers. But in the corridors that followed the suite there stood, opposite to each window, a heavy tripod, bearing a brazier of fire, that projected its rays through the tinted glass and so glaringly illumined the room. And thus were produced a multitude of gaudy and fantastic appearances. But in the western or black chamber the effect of the fire-light that streamed upon the dark hangings through the blood-tinted panes was ghastly in the extreme, and produced so wild a look upon the countenances of those who entered, that there were few of the company bold enough to set foot within its precincts at all.

It was in this apartment, also, that there stood against the western wall a gigantic clock of ebony. Its pendulum swung to and fro with a dull, heavy, monotonous clang; and, when the minute-hand made the circuit of the face, and the hour was to be stricken, there came from the brazen lungs of the clock a sound which was clear and loud and deep and exceedingly musical, but of so peculiar a note and emphasis that, at each lapse of an hour, the musicians of the orchestra were constrained to pause, momentarily, in their performance, to hearken to the sound; and thus the waltzers perforce ceased their evolutions; and there was a brief disconcert of the whole gay company; and, while the chimes of the clock yet rang, it was observed that the giddiest grew pale, and the more aged and sedate passed their hands over their brows as if in confused reverie or meditation. But when the echoes had fully ceased, a light laughter at once pervaded the assembly; the musicians looked at each other and smiled as if at their own nervousness and folly, and made whispering vows, each to the other, that the next chiming of the clock should produce in them no similar emotion; and then, after the lapse of sixty minutes (which embrace three thousand and six hundred seconds of the Time that flies), there came yet another chiming of the clock, and then were the same disconcert and tremulousness and meditation as before.

But, in spite of these things, it was a gay and magnificent revel. The tastes of the prince were peculiar. He had a fine eye for colors and effects. He disregarded the *decora* of mere fashion. His plans were bold and fiery, and his conceptions glowed with barbaric lustre. There are some who would have thought him mad. His followers felt that he was not. It was necessary to hear and see and touch him to be *sure* that he was not.

He had directed, in great part, the moveable embellishments of the seven chambers, upon occasion of this great *fête;* and it was his own guiding taste which had given character to the masqueraders. Be sure they were grotesque. There were much glare and glitter and piquancy and phantasm—much of what has been since seen in *Hernani*. There were arabesque figures with unsuited limbs and appointments. There were delirious fancies such as the madman fashions. There was much of the beautiful, much of the wanton, much of the bizarre, something of the terrible, and not a little of that which might have excited disgust. To and fro in the seven chambers there stalked, in fact, a multitude of dreams. And these—the dreams—writhed in and about, taking hue from the rooms, and causing the wild music of the orchestra to seem as the echo of their steps. And, anon, there strikes the ebony clock which stands in the hall of the velvet. And then, for a moment, all is still, and all is silent save the voice of the clock. The dreams are stiff-frozen as they stand. But the echoes of the chime die away—they have endured but an instant—and a light, half-subdued laughter floats after them as they depart. And now again the music swells, and the dreams live, and writhe to and fro more merrily than ever, taking hue from the many tinted windows through which stream the rays from the tripods. But to the chamber which lies most westwardly of the seven there are now none of the maskers who venture; for the night is waning away; and there flows a ruddier light through the blood-colored panes; and the blackness of the sable drapery appalls; and, to him whose foot falls upon the sable carpet, there comes from the near clock of ebony a muffled peal more solemnly emphatic than any which reaches *their* ears who indulge in the more remote gayeties of the other apartments.

But these other apartments were densely crowded, and in them beat feverishly the heart of life. And the revel went whirlingly on, until at length there commenced the sounding of midnight upon the clock. And then the music ceased, as I have told; and the evolutions of the waltzers were quieted; and there was an uneasy cessation of all things as before. But now there were twelve strokes to be sounded by the bell of the clock; and thus it happened, perhaps, that more of thought crept, with more of time, into the meditations of the thoughtful among those who reveled. And thus too it happened, perhaps, that before the last echoes of the last chime had utterly sunk into silence, there were many individuals in the crowd who had found leisure to become aware of the presence of a masked figure which had arrested the attention of no single individual before. And the rumor of this new presence having spread itself whisperingly around, there arose at length from the whole company a buzz, or murmur, expressive of disapprobation and surprise—then, finally, of terror, of horror, and of disgust.

In an assembly of phantasms such as I have painted, it may well be supposed that no ordinary appearance could have excited such sensation. In truth the masquerade license of the night was nearly unlimited; but the figure in question had out-Heroded Herod, and gone beyond the bounds of even the prince's indefinite decorum. There are chords in the hearts of the most reckless which cannot be touched without emotion. Even with the utterly lost, to whom life and death are equally jests, there are matters of which no jests can be made. The whole company, indeed, seemed now deeply to feel that in the costume and bearing of the stranger neither wit nor propriety existed. The figure was tall and gaunt, and shrouded from head to foot in the habiliments of the grave. The mask which concealed the visage was made so nearly to resemble the countenance of a stiffened corpse that the closest scrutiny must have had difficulty in detecting the cheat. And yet all this might have been endured, if not approved, by the mad revelers around. But the mummer had gone so far as to assume the type of the Red Death. His vesture was dabbled in *blood*—and his broad brow, with all the features of the face, was besprinkled with the scarlet horror.

When the eyes of Prince Prospero fell upon this spectral image (which with a slow and solemn movement, as if more fully to sustain its *rôle,* stalked to and fro among the waltzers) he was seen to be convulsed, in the first moment, with a strong shudder either of terror or distaste; but, in the next, his brow reddened with rage.

"Who dares?" he demanded hoarsely of the courtiers who stood near him—"who dares insult us with this blasphemous mockery? Seize him and unmask him—that we may know whom we have to hang at sunrise from the battlements!"

It was in the eastern or blue chamber in which stood the Prince Prospero as he uttered these words. They rang throughout the seven rooms loudly and clearly—for the prince was a bold and robust man, and the music had become hushed at the waving of his hand.

It was in the blue room where stood the prince, with a group of pale courtiers by his side. At first, as he spoke, there was a slight rushing movement of this group in the direction of the intruder, who at the moment was also near at hand, and now, with deliberate and stately step, made closer approach to the speaker. But from a certain nameless awe with which the mad assumption of the mummer had inspired the whole party, there were found none who put forth hand to seize him; so that, unimpeded, he passed within a yard of the prince's person; and, while the vast assembly, as if with one impulse, shrank from the centres of the rooms to the walls, he made his way uninterruptedly, but with the same solemn and measured step which had distinguished him from the first, through the blue chamber to the purple—through the purple to the green—through the green to the orange—through this again to the white—and even thence to the violet, ere a decided movement had been made to arrest him. It was then, however, that the Prince Prospero, maddening with rage and the shame of his own momentary cowardice, rushed hurriedly through the six chambers, while none followed him on account of a deadly terror that had seized upon all. He bore aloft a drawn dagger, and had approached, in rapid impetuosity, to within three or four feet of the retreating figure, when the latter, having attained the extremity of the velvet apartment, turned suddenly and confronted his pursuer. There was a sharp cry—and the dagger dropped gleaming upon the sable carpet, upon which, instantly afterwards, fell prostrate in death the Prince Prospero. Then, summoning the wild courage of despair, a throng of the revelers at once threw themselves into the black apartment, and, seizing the mummer, whose tall figure stood erect and motionless within the shadow of the ebony clock, gasped in unutterable horror at finding the grave cerements and corpselike mask, which they handled with so violent a rudeness, untenanted by any tangible form.

And now was acknowledged the presence of the Red Death. He had come like a thief in the night. And one by one dropped the revelers in the blood-bedewed halls of their revel, and died each in the despairing posture of his fall. And the life of the ebony clock went out with that of the last of the gay. And the flames of the tripods expired. And Darkness and Decay and the Red Death held illimitable dominion over all.

Nathaniel Hawthorne
(1804-1864)
The Wedding Knell

There is a certain church in the city of New York which I have always regarded with peculiar interest, on account of a marriage there solemnized, under very singular circumstances, in my grandmother's girlhood. That venerable lady chanced to be a spectator of the scene, and ever after made it her favorite narrative. Whether the edifice now standing on the same site be the identical one to which she referred, I am not antiquarian enough to know; nor would it be worth while to correct myself, perhaps, of an agreeable error, by reading the date of its erection on the tablet over the door. It is a stately church, surrounded by an inclosure of the loveliest green, within which appear urns, pillars, obelisks, and other forms of monumental marble, the tributes of private affection, or more splendid memorials of historic dust. With such a place, though the tumult of the city rolls beneath its tower, one would be willing to connect some legendary interest.

The marriage might be considered as the result of an early engagement, though there had been two intermediate weddings on the lady's part, and forty years of celibacy on that of the gentleman. At sixty-five, Mr. Ellenwood was a shy, but not quite a secluded man; selfish, like all men who brood over their own hearts, yet manifesting on rare occasions a vein of generous sentiment; a scholar throughout life, though always an indolent one, because his studies had no definite object, either of public advantage or personal ambition; a gentleman, high bred and fastidiously delicate, yet sometimes requiring a considerable relaxation, in his behalf, of the common rules of society. In truth, there were so many anomalies in his character, and though shrinking with diseased sensibility from public notice, it had been his fatality so often to become the topic of the day, by some wild eccentricity of conduct, that people searched his lineage for an hereditary taint of insanity. But there was no need of this. His caprices had their origin in a mind that lacked the support of an engrossing purpose, and in feelings that preyed upon themselves for want of other food. If he were mad, it was the consequence, and not the cause, of an aimless and abortive life.

The widow was as complete a contrast to her third bridegroom, in everything but age, as can well be conceived. Compelled to relinquish her first engagement, she had been united to a man of twice her own years, to whom she became an exemplary wife, and by whose death she was left in possession of a splendid fortune. A southern gentleman, considerably younger than herself, succeeded to her hand, and carried her to Charleston, where, after many uncomfortable years, she found herself again a widow. It would have been singular, if any uncommon delicacy of feeling had survived through such a life as Mrs. Dabney's; it could not but be crushed and killed by her early disappointment, the cold duty of her first marriage, the dislocation of the heart's principles, consequent on a second union, and the unkindness of her southern husband, which had inevitably driven her to connect the idea of his death with that of her comfort. To be brief, she was that wisest, but unloveliest, variety of woman, a philosopher, bearing troubles of the heart with equanimity, dispensing with all that should have been her happiness, and making the best of what remained. Sage in most matters, the widow was perhaps the more amiable for the one frailty that made her ridiculous. Being childless, she could not remain beautiful by proxy, in the person of a daughter; she therefore refused to grow old and ugly, on any consideration; she struggled with Time, and held fast her roses in spite of him, till the venerable thief appeared to have relinquished the spoil, as not worth the trouble of acquiring it.

The approaching marriage of this woman of the world with such an unworldly man as Mr. Ellenwood was announced soon after Mrs. Dabney's return to her native city. Superficial observers, and deeper ones, seemed to concur in supposing that the lady must have borne no inactive part in arranging the affair; there were considerations of expediency which she would be far more likely to appreciate than Mr. Ellenwood; and there was just the specious phantom of sentiment and romance in this late union of two early lovers which sometimes makes a fool of a woman who has lost her true feelings among the accidents of life. All the wonder was, how the gentleman, with his lack of worldly wisdom and agonizing consciousness of ridicule, could have been induced to take a measure at once so prudent and so laughable. But while people talked the wedding-day arrived. The ceremony was to be solemnized according to the Episcopalian forms, and in open church, with a degree of publicity that attracted many spectators, who occupied the front seats of the galleries, and the pews near the altar and along the broad aisle. It had been arranged, or possibly it was the custom of the day, that the parties should proceed separately to church. By some accident the bridegroom was a little less punctual than the widow and her bridal attendants; with whose arrival, after this tedious, but necessary preface, the action of our tale may be said to commence.

The clumsy wheels of several old-fashioned coaches were heard, and the gentlemen and ladies composing the bridal party came through the church door with the sudden and gladsome effect of a burst of sunshine. The whole group, except the principal figure, was made up of youth and gayety. As they streamed up the broad aisle, while the pews and pillars seemed to brighten on either side, their steps were as buoyant as if they mistook the church for a ball-room, and were ready to dance hand in hand to the altar. So brilliant was the spectacle that few took notice of a singular phenomenon that had marked its entrance. At the moment when the bride's foot touched the threshold the bell swung heavily in the tower above her, and sent forth its deepest knell. The vibrations died away and returned with prolonged solemnity, as she entered the body of the church.

"Good heavens! what an omen," whispered a young lady to her lover.

"On my honor," replied the gentleman, "I believe the bell has the good taste to toll of its own accord. What has she to do with weddings? If you, dearest Julia, were approaching the altar the bell would ring out its merriest peal. It has only a funeral knell for her."

The bride and most of her company had been too much occupied with the bustle of entrance to hear the first boding stroke of the bell, or at least to reflect on the singularity of such a welcome to the altar. They therefore continued to advance with undiminished gayety. The gorgeous dresses of the time, the crimson velvet coats, the gold-laced hats, the hoop petticoats, the silk, satin, brocade, and embroidery, the buckles, canes, and swords, all displayed to the best advantage on persons suited to such finery, made the group appear more like a bright-colored picture than anything real. But by what perversity of taste had the artist represented his principal figure as so wrinkled and decayed, while yet he had decked her out in the brightest splendor of attire, as if the loveliest maiden had suddenly withered into age, and become a moral to the beautiful around her! On they went, however, and had glittered along about a third of the aisle, when another stroke of the bell seemed to fill the church with a visible gloom, dimming and obscuring the bright pageant, till it shone forth again as from a mist.

This time the party wavered, stopped, and huddled closer together, while a slight scream was heard from some of the ladies, and a confused whispering among the gentlemen. Thus tossing to and fro, they might have been fancifully compared to a splendid bunch of flowers, suddenly shaken by a puff of wind, which threatened to scatter the leaves of an old, brown, withered rose, on the same stalk with two dewy buds,—such being the emblem of the widow between her fair young bridemaids. But her heroism was admirable. She had started with an irrepressible shudder, as if the stroke of the bell had fallen directly on her heart; then, recovering herself, while her attendants were yet in dismay, she took the lead, and paced calmly up the aisle. The bell continued to swing, strike, and vibrate, with the same doleful regularity as when a corpse is on its way to the tomb.

"My young friends here have their nerves a little shaken," said the widow, with a smile, to the clergyman at the altar. "But so many weddings have been ushered in with the merriest peal of the bells, and yet turned out unhappily, that I shall hope for better fortune under such different auspices."

"Madam," answered the rector, in great perplexity, "this strange occurrence brings to my mind a marriage sermon of the famous Bishop Taylor, wherein he mingles so many thoughts of mortality and future woe, that, to speak somewhat after his own rich style, he seems to hang the bridal chamber in black, and cut the wedding garment out of a coffin pall. And it has been the custom of divers nations to infuse something of sadness into their marriage ceremonies, so to keep death in mind while contracting that engagement which is life's chiefest business. Thus we may draw a sad but profitable moral from this funeral knell."

But, though the clergyman might have given his moral even a keener point, he did not fail to dispatch an attendant to inquire into the mystery, and stop those sounds, so dismally appropriate to such a marriage. A brief space elapsed, during which the silence was broken only by whispers, and a few suppressed titterings, among the wedding party and the spectators, who, after the first shock, were disposed to draw an ill-natured merriment from the affair. The young have less charity for aged follies than the old for those of youth. The widow's glance was observed to wander, for an instant, towards a window of the church, as if searching for the timeworn marble that she had dedicated to her first husband; then her eyelids dropped over their faded orbs, and her thoughts were drawn irresistibly to another grave. Two buried men, with a voice at her ear, and a cry afar off, were calling her to lie down beside them. Perhaps, with momentary truth of feeling, she thought how much happier had been her fate, if, after years of bliss, the bell were now tolling for her funeral, and she were followed to the grave by the old affection of her earliest lover, long her husband. But why had she returned to him, when their cold hearts shrank from each other's embrace?

Still the death-bell tolled so mournfully, that the sunshine seemed to fade in the air. A whisper, communicated from those who stood nearest the windows, now spread through the church; a hearse, with a train of several coaches, was creeping along the street, conveying some dead man to the churchyard, while the bride awaited a living one at the altar. Immediately after, the footsteps of the bridegroom and his friends were heard at the door. The widow looked down the aisle, and clinched the arm of one of her bridemaids in her bony hand with such unconscious violence, that the fair girl trembled.

"You frighten me, my dear madam!" cried she. "For Heaven's sake, what is the matter?"

"Nothing, my dear, nothing," said the widow; then, whispering close to her ear, "There is a foolish fancy that I cannot get rid of. I am expecting my bridegroom to come into the church, with my first two husbands for groomsmen!"

"Look, look!" screamed the bridemaid. "What is here? The funeral!"

As she spoke, a dark procession paced

into the church. First came an old man and woman, like chief mourners at a funeral, attired from head to foot in the deepest black, all but their pale features and hoary hair; he leaning on a staff, and supporting her decrepit form with his nerveless arm. Behind appeared another, and another pair, as aged, as black, and mournful as the first. As they drew near, the widow recognized in every face some trait of former friends, long forgotten, but now returning, as if from their old graves, to warn her to prepare a shroud; or, with purpose almost as unwelcome, to exhibit their wrinkles and infirmity, and claim her as their companion by the tokens of her own decay. Many a merry night had she danced with them, in youth. And now, in joyless age, she felt that some withered partner should request her hand, and all unite, in a dance of death, to the music of the funeral bell.

While these aged mourners were passing up the aisle, it was observed that, from pew to pew, the spectators shuddered with irrepressible awe, as some object, hitherto concealed by the intervening figures, came full in sight. Many turned away their faces; others kept a fixed and rigid stare; and a young girl giggled hysterically, and fainted with the laughter on her lips. When the spectral procession approached the altar, each couple separated, and slowly diverged, till, in the centre, appeared a form, that had been worthily ushered in with all this gloomy pomp, the death knell, and the funeral. It was the bridegroom in his shroud!

No garb but that of the grave could have befitted such a deathlike aspect; the eyes, indeed, had the wild gleam of a sepulchral lamp; all else was fixed in the stern calmness which old men wear in the coffin. The corpse stood motionless, but addressed the widow in accents that seemed to melt into the clang of the bell, which fell heavily on the air while he spoke.

"Come, my bride!" said those pale lips, "the hearse is ready. The sexton stands waiting for us at the door of the tomb. Let us be married; and then to our coffins!"

How shall the widow's horror be represented? It gave her the ghastliness of a dead man's bride. Her youthful friends stood apart, shuddering at the mourners, the shrouded bridegroom, and herself; the whole scene expressed, by the strongest imagery, the vain struggle of the gilded vanities of this world, when opposed to age, infirmity, sorrow, and death. The awe-struck silence was first broken by the clergyman.

"Mr. Ellenwood," said he, soothingly, yet with somewhat of authority, "you are not well. Your mind has been agitated by the unusual circumstances in which you are placed. The ceremony must be deferred. As an old friend, let me entreat you to return home."

"Home! yes, but not without my bride," answered he, in the same hollow accents. "You deem this mockery; perhaps madness. Had I bedizened my aged and broken frame with scarlet and embroidery—had I forced my withered lips to smile at my dead heart—that might have been mockery, or madness. But now, let young and old declare, which of us has come hither without a wedding garment, the bridegroom or the bride!"

He stepped forward at a ghostly pace, and stood beside the widow, contrasting the awful simplicity of his shroud with the glare and glitter in which she had arrayed herself for this unhappy scene. None, that beheld them, could deny the terrible strength of the moral which his disordered intellect had contrived to draw.

"Cruel! cruel!" groaned the heart-stricken bride.

"Cruel!" repeated he; then, losing his deathlike composure in a wild bitterness:

"Heaven judge which of us has been cruel to the other! In youth you deprived me of my happiness, my hopes, my aims; you took away all the substance of my life, and made it a dream without reality enough even to grieve at—with only a pervading gloom, through which I walked wearily, and cared not whither. But after forty years, when I have built my tomb, and would not give up the thought of resting there—no, not for such a life as we once pictured—you call me to the altar. At your summons I am here. But other husbands have enjoyed your youth, your beauty, your warmth of heart, and all that could be termed your life. What is there for me but your decay and death? And therefore I have bidden these funeral friends, and bespoken the sexton's deepest knell, and am come, in my shroud, to wed you, as with a burial service, that we may join our hands at the door of the sepulchre, and enter it together."

It was not frenzy; it was not merely the drunkenness of strong emotion, in a heart unused to it, that now wrought upon the bride. The stern lesson of the day had done its work; her worldliness was gone. She seized the bridegroom's hand.

"Yes!" cried she. "Let us wed, even at the door of the sepulchre! My life is gone in vanity and emptiness. But at its close there is one true feeling. It has made me what I was in youth; it makes me worthy of you. Time is no more for both of us. Let us wed for Eternity!"

With a long and deep regard, the bridegroom looked into her eyes, while a tear was gathering in his own. How strange that gush of human feeling from the frozen bosom of a corpse! He wiped away the tears even with his shroud.

"Beloved of my youth," said he, "I have been wild. The despair of my whole lifetime had returned at once, and maddened me. Forgive; and be forgiven. Yes; it is evening with us now; and we have realized none of our morning dreams of happiness. But let us join our hands before the altar, as lovers whom adverse circumstances have separated through life, yet who meet again as they are leaving it, and find their earthly affection changed into something holy as religion. And what is Time, to the married of Eternity?"

Amid the tears of many, and a swell of exalted sentiment, in those who felt aright, was solemnized the union of two immortal souls. The train of withered mourners, the hoary bridegroom in his shroud, the pale features of the aged bride, and the deathbell tolling through the whole, till its deep voice overpowered the marriage words, all marked the funeral of earthly hopes. But as the ceremony proceeded, the organ, as if stirred by the sympathies of this impressive scene, poured forth an anthem, first mingling with the dismal knell, then rising to a loftier strain, till the soul looked down upon its woe. And when the awful rite was finished, and with cold hand in cold hand, the Married of Eternity withdrew, the organ's peal of solemn triumph drowned the Wedding Knell.

REALISM AND IMPRESSIONISM

EDOUARD MANET: *Gare Saint-Lazare*, NATIONAL GALLERY OF ART, WASHINGTON, D. C., GIFT OF HORACE HAVEMEYER IN MEMORY OF HIS MOTHER LOUISINE W. HAVEMEYER

REALISM AND IMPRESSIONISM

From the middle of the nineteenth century on, the romantic spirit that had so strongly influenced the arts of the late eighteenth and early nineteenth centuries was challenged and altered by several artistic reactions. We will emphasize two early phases of these reactions, realism and impressionism. Here again, the student of the arts must be aware that elements of romanticism, realism, and other *isms* can be found in almost every period of art; the matter of emphasis is what makes the difference. For instance, naturalism grew out of realistic approaches to the arts, becoming the extreme form of realism. Impressionism leads to such movements as symbolism and imagism. The first two terms, realism and impressionism, will be treated more completely when we discuss the literature of the time.

The Changing Nineteenth Century

The world of the latter half of the nineteenth century experienced change as never before. Not only were machines displacing men in many areas of production; but the thirst for power that motivated many of the imperialistic tendencies of the larger nations, such as France, Belgium, Britain, and Germany, in their search for more raw materials to convert to products, and the desires of these and other nations to acquire and accomplish "all they could while they could," seemed to point out the inconsistency of the earlier romantic emphasis on the individual and the transcendent beauty of nature. Production and possession became the key words of the day, or so it seemed to most. And the great Civil War in America as well as her late nineteenth-century expansionist policies did much to question the reality of man's rights.

In many areas unemployment bred in the common man a particularly sharp discontent with his lot. Marxian thought urged the working classes to unite and oppose the exploitative tactics of their masters; in theory, they were to share in common property and so eliminate the class struggles that come from acquisition of property. Also, Darwin's *Origin of the Species* had a sharp impact on Christian theology, and it took a couple of decades for science and religion to begin to find a ground for compromise.

The rocking of traditional viewpoints tended to force men to look more closely at their world in order to understand it. Surely man, as a thinking animal, should be able to know his destiny, or at least have a voice in it. This understanding must arise from an intelligent, scientific study of the environment in which man finds himself. Comte laid the groundwork for social science with his empirical approach to the study of mankind, which was designed to provide a basis for predicting behavior, and for creating some means of controlling it. These ideas were, of course, reflected in late nineteenth-century and early twentieth-century literature.

Realism in Literature

Realism is best described as a reaction against romanticism. Where romanticism looks for the idealized, realism seeks out the actuality of experience. Romanticism may extol the noble savage, but realism simply describes the common, everyday man in direct terms. Romanticism selects and glorifies; realism selects and bares the truth of existence as the writer sees it. Characterization is important in realistic literature. Exploring the inner self provides a means for arriving at truth.

A great deal of realistic literature is aimed at social reform. In works by writers such as Twain, Ibsen, Shaw, and James, the realistic influence is evident in their adherence to detail, their direct handling of realities of life, and their attempts to present the problems they see in man's relationships with self, others, and the universe.

Impressionism in Literature

Impressionism is a very personal artistic style of writing. The impressionist tries to present the atmosphere or mood of a particular event at a specific moment in time and from an original vantage point. Sensory detail is important in creating this total atmosphere; symbols open the mind to varied images. In fact, impressionism moves toward symbolism and imagism in its intellectual and emotional impact.

Late nineteenth-century symbolic writers were much intrigued by earlier metaphysical poetry; intellectual complexity, as exemplified in writers such as Donne, had great appeal to poets who wanted to avoid the reportorial starkness of realism. To writers like Mallarmé, symbolism became an all-important vehicle for artistic expression. The use of recurring and indefinite symbolic patterns helped these writers create a mood or experience. Not only was the subconscious to be awakened by a work, but the work was to have an aesthetic impact similar to that of a finely wrought piece of music. Form and content should constitute an intellectually suggestive whole.

Both realism and impressionism are forerunners, then, of subsequent literary trends such as naturalism, imagism, and symbolism. An interesting point to the student of the arts is that these and other trends have found proponents in modern literature to such an extent that modern literature defies tight classification.

Henrik Ibsen
(1828-1906)
The Master Builder

Characters

HALVARD SOLNESS, *Master Builder*
ALINE SOLNESS, *his wife*
DOCTOR HERDAL
KNUT BROVIK, *formerly an architect, now in Solness' employment*
RAGNAR BROVIK, *his son, a draftsman*
KAIA FOSLI, *his niece, a bookkeeper*
MISS HILDA WANGEL
Some Women
A crowd in the street

The action takes place in and about the house of HALVARD SOLNESS.

ACT ONE

A plainly-furnished workroom in the house of HALVARD SOLNESS. *Folding doors on the left lead into the hall. On the right is the door leading to the inner rooms of the house. At the back is an open door into the draftsmen's office. In front, on the left, a desk with books, papers, and writing materials. Farther back than the folding doors, a stove. In the right-hand corner, a sofa, a table, and one or two chairs. On the table a water-bottle and glass. A mailer table, with a rocking-chair and armchair, in front on the right. Lighted lamps with shades on the table in the draftsmen's office, on the table in the corner, and on the desk.*

In the draftsmen's office sit KNUT BROVIK *and his son* RAGNAR, *occupied with plans and calculations. At the desk in the outer office stands* KAIA FOSLI, *writing in the ledger.* KNUT BROVIK *is a spare old man with white hair and beard. He wears a rather threadbare but well-brushed black coat, spectacles, and a somewhat discolored white neckscarf.* RAGNAR BROVIK *is a well-dressed, light-haired man in his thirties, with a slight stoop.* KAIA FOSLI *is a slightly-built girl, a little over twenty, carefully dressed, and delicate-looking. She has a green shade over her eyes.—All three go on working for some time in silence.*

BROVIK (*rises suddenly, as if in distress, from the table; breathes heavily and laboriously as he comes forward into the doorway*). No, I can't bear it much longer!

KAIA (*going up to him*). You are feeling very ill this evening, aren't you, uncle?

BROVIK. Oh, I seem to get worse every day.

RAGNAR (*has risen and advances*). You ought to go home, father. Try to get a little sleep—

BROVIK (*impatiently*). Go to bed I suppose? Would you have me stifled outright?

KAIA. Then take a little walk.

RAGNAR. Yes, do. I will come with you.

BROVIK (*with warmth*). I will not go till he comes! I am determined to have it out this evening with—(*In a tone of suppressed bitterness.*)—with him—with the chief.

KAIA (*anxiously*). Oh, no, uncle—do wait a while before doing *that!*

RAGNAR. Yes, better wait, father!

BROVIK (*draws his breath laboriously*). Ha—ha—! *I* haven't much time for waiting.

KAIA (*listening*). Hush! I hear him on the stairs.

(*All three go back to their work. A short silence.*)

(HALVARD SOLNESS *comes in through the hall door. He is a man no longer young, but healthy and vigorous, with close-cut curly hair, dark moustache, and dark, thick eyebrows. He wears a grayish-green buttoned jacket with an upstanding collar and broad lapels. On his head he wears a soft gray felt hat, and he has one or two light portfolios under his arm.*)

SOLNESS (*near the door, points towards the draftsmen's office, and asks in a whisper*). Are they gone?

KAIA (*softly, shaking her head*). No.

(*She takes the shade off her eyes.* SOLNESS *crosses the room, throws his hat on a chair, places the portfolios on the table by the sofa, and approaches the desk again.* KAIA *goes on writing without intermission, but seems nervous and uneasy.*)

SOLNESS (*aloud*). What is that you are entering, Miss Fosli?

KAIA (*starts*). Oh, it is only something that—

SOLNESS. Let me look at it, Miss Fosli. (*Bends over her, pretends to be looking into the ledger, and whispers.*) Kaia!

KAIA (*softly, still writing*). Well?

SOLNESS. Why do you always take that shade off when I come?

KAIA (*as before*). I look so ugly with it on.

SOLNESS (*smiling*). Then you don't like to look ugly, Kaia?

KAIA (*half glancing up at him*). Not for all the world. Not in *your* eyes.

SOLNESS (*strokes her hair gently*). Poor, poor little Kaia—

KAIA (*bending her head*). Hush—they can hear you!

(SOLNESS *strolls across the room to the right, turns and pauses at the door of the draftsmen's office.*)

SOLNESS. Has anyone been here for me?

RAGNAR (*rising*). Yes, the young couple who want a villa built, out at Lövstrand.

SOLNESS (*growling*). Oh, *those* two! *They* must wait. I am not quite clear about the plans yet.

RAGNAR (*advancing, with some hesitation*). They were very anxious to have the drawings at once.

SOLNESS (*as before*). Yes, of course—so they all are.

BROVIK (*looks up*). They say they are longing so to get into a house of their own.

SOLNESS. Yes, yes—we know all *that!* And so they are content to take whatever is offered them. They get a—a roof over their heads—an address—but nothing to call a home. No, thank you! In that case, let them apply to somebody else. Tell them *that*, the next time they call.

BROVIK (*pushes his glasses up on his forehead and looks in astonishment at him*). To somebody else? Are you prepared to give up the commission?

SOLNESS (*impatiently*). Yes, yes, yes, devil take it! If that is to be the way of it—. Rather that, than build away at random. (*Vehemently.*) Besides, I know very little about these people as yet.

BROVIK. The people are safe enough. Ragnar knows them. He is a friend of the family. Perfectly safe people.

SOLNESS. Oh, safe—safe enough! That is not at all what I mean. Good lord—don't *you* understand me either? (*Angrily.*) I won't have anything to do with these strangers. They may apply to whom they please, so far as I am concerned.

BROVIK (*rising*). Do you really mean that?

SOLNESS (*sulkily*). Yes, I do.—For once in a way.

(*He comes forward.* BROVIK *exchanges a glance with* RAGNAR, *who makes a warning gesture. Then* BROVIK *comes into the front room.*)

BROVIK. May I have a few words with you?

SOLNESS. Certainly.

BROVIK (*to* KAIA). Just go in there for a moment, Kaia.

KAIA (*uneasily*). Oh, but uncle—

BROVIK. Do as I say, child. And shut the door after you.

(KAIA *goes reluctantly into the draftsmen's office, glances anxiously and imploringly at* SOLNESS, *and shuts the door.*)

BROVIK (*lowering his voice a little*). I don't want the poor children to know how ill I am.

SOLNESS. Yes, you have been looking very poorly of late.

BROVIK. It will soon be all over with me. My strength is ebbing—from day to day.

SOLNESS. Won't you sit down?

BROVIK. Thanks—may I?

SOLNESS (*placing the armchair more conveniently*). Here—take this chair.—And now?

BROVIK (*has seated himself with difficulty*). Well, you see, it's about Ragnar. That is what weighs most upon me. What is to become of him?

SOLNESS. Of course your son will stay with me as long as ever he likes.

BROVIK. But that is just what he does not like. He feels that he cannot stay here any longer.

SOLNESS. Why, I should say he was very well off here. But if he wants more money, I should not mind—

BROVIK. No, no! It is not that. (*Impatiently.*) But sooner or later he, too, must have a chance of doing something on his own account.

SOLNESS (*without looking at him*). Do you think that Ragnar has quite talent enough to stand alone?

BROVIK. No, that is just the heart-breaking part of it—I have begun to have my doubts about the boy. For you have never said so much as—as one encouraging word about him. And yet I cannot but think there must be something in him—he *can't* be without talent.

SOLNESS. Well, but he has learnt nothing—nothing thoroughly, I mean. Except, of course, to draw.

BROVIK (*looks at him with covert hatred and says hoarsely*). *You* had learned little enough of the business when you were in my employment. But that did not prevent you from setting to work—(*Breathing with difficulty.*)—and pushing your way up, and taking the wind out of my sails—mine, and so many other people's.

SOLNESS. Yes, you see—circumstances favored me.

BROVIK. You are right there. Everything favored you. But then how can you have the heart to let me go to my grave—without having seen what Ragnar is fit for? And of course I am anxious to see them married, too—before I go.

SOLNESS (*sharply*). Is it she who wishes it?

BROVIK. Not Kaia so much as Ragnar—he talks about it every day. (*Appealingly.*) You must—you *must* help him to get some independent work now! I *must* see something that the lad has done. Do you hear?

SOLNESS (*peevishly*). Hang it, man, you can't expect me to drag commissions down from the moon for him!

BROVIK. He has the chance of a capital commission at this very moment. A big bit of work.

SOLNESS (*uneasily, startled*). Has he?

BROVIK. If *you* would give your consent.

SOLNESS. What sort of work do you mean?

BROVIK (*with some hesitation*). He can have the building of that villa out at Lövstrand.

SOLNESS. *That!* Why, I am going to build that myself.

BROVIK. Oh, *you* don't much care about doing it.

SOLNESS (*flaring up*). Don't care! I! Who dares to say that?

BROVIK. You said so yourself just now.

SOLNESS. Oh, never mind what I *say*.—Would they give Ragnar the building of that villa?

BROVIK. Yes. You see, he knows the family. And then—just for the fun of the thing—he has made drawings and estimates and so forth—

SOLNESS. Are they pleased with the drawings? The people who will have to live in the house?

BROVIK. Yes. If you would only look through them and approve of them—

SOLNESS. Then they would let Ragnar build their home for them?

BROVIK. They were immensely pleased with his idea. They thought it exceedingly original, they said.

SOLNESS. Oho! Original! Not the old-fashioned stuff that *I* am in the habit of turning out!

BROVIK. It seemed to them *different*.

SOLNESS (*with suppressed irritation*). So it was to see Ragnar that they came here—while I was out!

BROVIK. They came to call upon you—and at the same time to ask whether you would mind retiring—

SOLNESS (*angrily*). Retire? I?

BROVIK. In case you thought that Ragnar's drawings—

SOLNESS. I! Retire in favor of your son!

BROVIK. Retire from the agreement, they meant.

SOLNESS. Oh, it comes to the same thing. (*Laughs angrily.*) So that is it, is it? Halvard Solness is to see about retiring now! To make room for younger men! For the very youngest, perhaps! He must make room! Room! Room!

BROVIK. Why, good heavens! there is surely room for more than one single man—

SOLNESS. Oh, there's not so *very* much room to spare either. But, be that as it may—I will never retire! I will never give way to anybody! Never of my own free will. Never in this world will I do *that!*

BROVIK (*rises with difficulty*). Then I am to pass out of life without any certainty? Without a gleam of happiness? Without any faith or trust in Ragnar? Without having seen a single piece of work of his doing? Is that to be the way of it?

SOLNESS (*turns half aside and mutters*). H'm—don't ask more just now.

BROVIK. I must have an answer to this one question. Am I to pass out of life in such utter poverty?

SOLNESS (*seems to struggle with himself; finally he says in a low but firm voice*). You must pass out of life as best you can.

BROVIK. Then be it so. (*He goes up the room.*)

SOLNESS (*following him, half in desperation*). Don't you understand that I *cannot* help it? I am what I am, and I cannot change my nature!

BROVIK. No, no; I suppose you can't. (*reels and supports himself against the sofa-table.*) May I have a glass of water?

SOLNESS. By all means. (*Fills a glass and hands it to him.*)

BROVIK. Thanks.

(*Drinks and puts the glass down again.*
SOLNESS *goes up and opens the door of the draftsmen's office.*)

SOLNESS. Ragnar—you must come and take your father home.

(RAGNAR *rises quickly. He and* KAIA *come into the workroom.*)

RAGNAR. What is the matter, father?

BROVIK. Give me your arm. Now let us go.

RAGNAR. Very well. You had better put your things on too, Kaia.

SOLNESS. Miss Fosli must stay—just for a moment. There is a letter I want written.

BROVIK (*looks at* SOLNESS). Good-night. Sleep well—if you can.

SOLNESS. Good-night.

(BROVIK *and* RAGNAR *go out by the hall door:* KAIA *goes to the desk.* SOLNESS *stands with bent head, to the right, by the armchair.*)

KAIA (*dubiously*). Is there any letter—?

SOLNESS (*curtly*). No, of course not. (*Looks sternly at her.*) Kaia!

KAIA (*anxiously, in a low voice*). Yes!

SOLNESS (*Points imperatively to a spot on the floor*). Come here! At once!

KAIA (*hesitatingly*). Yes.

SOLNESS (*as before*). Nearer!

KAIA (*obeying*). What do you want with me?

SOLNESS (*looks at her for a while*). Is it you I have to thank for all this?

KAIA. No, no, don't think that!

SOLNESS. But confess now—you want to get married!

KAIA (*softly*). Ragnar and I have been engaged for four or five years, and so—

SOLNESS. And so you think it time there were an end of it. Isn't that so?

KAIA. Ragnar and Uncle say I *must*. So I suppose I shall have to give in.

SOLNESS (*more gently*). Kaia, don't you really care a little bit for Ragnar, too?

KAIA. I cared very much for Ragnar once—before I came here to you.

SOLNESS. But you don't now? Not in the least?

KAIA (*passionately, clasping her hands and holding them out towards him*). Oh, you know very well there is only *one* person I care for now! One, and one only, in all the world! I shall never care for anyone else.

SOLNESS. Yes, you say that. And yet you go away from me—leave me alone here with everything on my hands.

KAIA. But could I not stay with you, even if Ragnar—?

SOLNESS (*repudiating the idea*). No, no, that is quite impossible. If Ragnar leaves me and starts work on his own account, then of course he will need you himself.

KAIA (*wringing her hands*). Oh, I feel as if I *could* not be separated from you! It's quite, quite impossible!

SOLNESS. Then be sure you get those foolish notions out of Ragnar's head. Marry him as much as you please—(*Alters his tone.*) I mean—don't let him throw up his good situation with me. For then I can keep *you* too, my dear Kaia.

KAIA. Oh, yes, how lovely that would be, if it could only be managed!

SOLNESS (*clasps her head with his two hands and whispers*). For I cannot get on without you, you see. I must have you with me every single day.

KAIA (*in nervous exaltation*). My God! My God!

SOLNESS (*kisses her hair*). Kaia—Kaia!

KAIA (*sinks down before him*). Oh, how good you are to me! How unspeakably good you are!

SOLNESS (*vehemently*). Get up! For goodness' sake get up! I think I hear someone!

(*He helps her to rise. She staggers over to the desk.*)

(MRS. SOLNESS *enters by the door on the right. She looks thin and wasted with grief, but shows traces of bygone beauty. Blond ringlets. Dressed with good taste, wholly in black. Speaks somewhat slowly and in a plaintive voice.*)

MRS. SOLNESS (*in the doorway*). Halvard!

SOLNESS (*turns*). Oh, are you there, my dear—?

MRS. SOLNESS (*with a glance at* KAIA). I am afraid I am disturbing you.

SOLNESS. Not in the least. Miss Fosli has only a short letter to write.

MRS. SOLNESS. Yes, so I see.

SOLNESS. What do you want with me, Aline?

MRS. SOLNESS. I merely wanted to tell you that Dr. Herdal is in the drawing-room. Won't you come and see him, Halvard?

SOLNESS (*looks suspiciously at her*). H'm—is the doctor so very anxious to talk to me?

MRS. SOLNESS. Well, not exactly anxious. He really came to see me; but he would like to say how-do-you-do to you at the same time.

SOLNESS (*laughs to himself*). Yes, I dare say. Well, you must ask him to wait a little.

MRS. SOLNESS. Then you will come in presently?

SOLNESS. Perhaps I will. Presently, presently, dear. In a little while.

MRS. SOLNESS (*glancing again at* KAIA). Well now, don't forget, Halvard.

(*Withdraws and closes the door behind her.*)

KAIA (*softly*). Oh, dear, oh, dear—I am sure Mrs. Solness thinks ill of me in some way!

SOLNESS. Oh, not in the least. Not more than usual, at any rate. But all the same, you had better go now, Kaia.

KAIA. Yes, yes, now I *must* go.

SOLNESS (*severely*). And mind you get that matter settled for me. Do you hear?

KAIA. Oh, if it only depended on *me*—

SOLNESS. I *will* have it settled, I say! And tomorrow too—not a day later!

KAIA (*terrified*). If there's nothing else for it, I am quite willing to break off the engagement.

SOLNESS (*angrily*). Break it off! Are you mad? Would you think of breaking it off?

KAIA (*distracted*). Yes, if necessary. For I *must*—I must stay here with you! I can't leave you! That is utterly—utterly impossible!

SOLNESS (*with a sudden outburst*). But deuce take it—how about Ragnar then! It's Ragnar that I—

KAIA (*looks at him with terrified eyes*). It is chiefly on Ragnar's account, that—that you—?

SOLNESS (*collecting himself*). No, no, of course not! You don't understand me either. (*Gently and softly.*) Of course it is *you* I want to keep—you above everything, Kaia. But for that very reason, you must prevent Ragnar, too, from throwing up his situation. There, there—now go home.

KAIA. Yes, yes—good-night, then.

SOLNESS. Good-night. (*As she is going.*) Oh, stop a moment! Are Ragnar's drawings in there?

KAIA. I did not see him take them with him.

SOLNESS. Then just go and find them for me. I might perhaps glance over them, after all.

KAIA (*happy*). Oh, yes, please do!

SOLNESS. For your sake, Kaia dear. Now, let me have them at once, please.

(KAIA *hurries into the draftsmen's office, searches anxiously in the table-drawer, finds a portfolio, and brings it with her.*)

KAIA. Here are all the drawings.

SOLNESS. Good. Put them down there on the table.

KAIA (*putting down the portfolio*). Goodnight, then. (*Beseechingly.*) And please, please think kindly of me.

SOLNESS. Oh, that I always do. Goodnight, my dear little Kaia. (*Glances to the right.*) Go, go now!

(MRS. SOLNESS *and* DR. HERDAL *enter by the door on the right. He is a stoutish, elderly man, with a round, good-humored face, clean-shaven, with thin, light hair, and gold spectacles.*)

MRS. SOLNESS (*still in the doorway*). Halvard, I cannot keep the doctor any longer.

SOLNESS. Well then, come in here.

MRS. SOLNESS (*to* KAIA, *who is turning down the desk-lamp*). Have you finished the letter already, Miss Fosli?

KAIA (*in confusion*). The letter—?

SOLNESS. Yes, it was quite a short one.

MRS. SOLNESS. It must have been very short.

SOLNESS. You may go now, Miss Fosli. And please come in good time tomorrow morning.

KAIA. I will be sure to. Good-night, Mrs. Solness. (*She goes out by the hall door.*)

MRS. SOLNESS. She must be quite an acquisition to you, Halvard, this Miss Fosli.

SOLNESS. Yes, indeed. She is useful in all sorts of ways.

Mrs. Solness. So it seems.

Dr. Herdal. Is she good at bookkeeping too?

Solness. Well—of course she has had a good deal of practice during these two years. And then she is so nice and willing to do whatever one asks of her.

Mrs. Solness. Yes, that must be very delightful—

Solness. It is. Especially when one is not too much accustomed to that sort of thing.

Mrs. Solness (*in a tone of gentle remonstrance*). Can *you* say that, Halvard?

Solness. Oh, no, no, my dear Aline; I beg your pardon.

Mrs. Solness. There's no one occasion. —Well then, Doctor, you will come back later on and have a cup of tea with us?

Dr. Herdal. I have only that one patient to see, and then I'll come back.

Mrs. Solness. Thank you.

(*She goes out by the door on the right.*)

Solness. Are you in a hurry, Doctor?

Dr. Herdal. No, not at all.

Solness. May I have a little chat with you?

Dr. Herdal. With the greatest of pleasure.

Solness. Then let us sit down. (*He motions the* Doctor *to take the rocking-chair and sits down himself in the armchair. Looks searchingly at him.*) Tell me—did you notice anything odd about Aline?

Dr. Herdal. Do you mean just now, when she was here?

Solness. Yes, in her manner to me. Did you notice anything?

Dr. Herdal (*smiling*). Well, I admit —one couldn't well avoid noticing that your wife—h'm—

Solness. Well?

Dr. Herdal.—that your wife is not particularly fond of this Miss Fosli.

Solness. Is that all? I have noticed that myself.

Dr. Herdal. And I must say I am scarcely surprised at it.

Solness. At what?

Dr. Herdal. That she should not exactly approve of your seeing so much of another woman, all day and every day.

Solness. No, no, I suppose you are right there—and Aline too. But it's impossible to make any change.

Dr. Herdal. Could you not engage a clerk?

Solness. The first man that came to hand? No, thank you—that would never do for me.

Dr. Herdal. But now, if your wife—? Suppose, with her delicate health, all this tries her too much?

Solness. Even then—I might almost say—it can make no difference. I *must* keep Kaia Fosli. No one else could fill her place.

Dr. Herdal. No one else?

Solness (*curtly*). No, no one.

Dr. Herdal (*drawing his chair closer*). Now listen to me, my dear Mr. Solness. May I ask you a question, quite between ourselves?

Solness. By all means.

Dr. Herdal. Women, you see—in certain matters, they have a deucedly keen intuition—

Solness. They have, indeed. There is not the least doubt of that. But—?

Dr. Herdal. Well, tell me now—if your wife can't endure this Kaia Fosli—?

Solness. Well, what then?

Dr. Herdal.—may she not have just—just the least little bit of reason for this instinctive dislike?

Solness (*looks at him and rises*). Oho!

Dr. Herdal. Now don't be offended —but *hasn't* she?

Solness (*with curt decision*). No.

Dr. Herdal. No reason of any sort?

Solness. No other reason than her own suspicious nature.

DR. HERDAL. I know you have known a good many women in your time.

SOLNESS. Yes, I have.

DR. HERDAL. And have been a good deal taken with some of them, too.

SOLNESS. Oh, yes, I don't deny it.

DR. HERDAL. But as regards Miss Fosli, then? There is nothing of that sort in the case?

SOLNESS. No; nothing at all—on *my* side.

DR. HERDAL. But on her side?

SOLNESS. I don't think you have any right to ask that question, Doctor.

DR. HERDAL. Well, you know, we were discussing your wife's intuition.

SOLNESS. So we were. And for that matter—(*Lowers his voice.*)—Aline's intuition, as you call it—in a certain sense, it has not been so far astray.

DR. HERDAL. Aha! there we have it!

SOLNESS (*sits down*). Doctor Herdal—I am going to tell you a strange story—if you care to listen to it.

DR. HERDAL. I like listening to strange stories.

SOLNESS. Very well then, I dare say you recollect that I took Knut Brovik and his son into my employment—after the old man's business had gone to the dogs.

DR. HERDAL. Yes, so I have understood.

SOLNESS. You see, they really are clever fellows, these two. Each of them has talent in his own way. But then the son took it into his head to get engaged; and the next thing, of course, was that he wanted to get married—and begin to build on his own account. That is the way with all these young people.

DR. HERDAL (*laughing*). Yes, they have a bad habit of wanting to marry.

SOLNESS. Just so. But of course that did not suit *my* plans; for I needed Ragnar myself—and the old man too. He is exceedingly good at calculating bearing-strains and cubic contents—and all that sort of devilry, you know.

DR. HERDAL. Oh, yes, no doubt that's indispensable.

SOLNESS. Yes, it is. But Ragnar was absolutely bent on setting to work for himself. He would hear of nothing else.

DR. HERDAL. But he has stayed with you all the same.

SOLNESS. Yes, I'll tell you how that came about. One day this girl, Kaia Fosli, came to see them on some errand or other. She had never been here before. And when I saw how utterly infatuated they were with each other, the thought occurred to me: if I could only get her into the office here, then perhaps Ragnar too would stay where he is.

DR. HERDAL. That was not at all a bad idea.

SOLNESS. Yes, but at the time I did not breathe a word of what was in my mind. I merely stood and looked at her—and kept on wishing intently that I could have her here. Then I talked to her a little, in a friendly way—about one thing and another. And then she went away.

DR. HERDAL. Well?

SOLNESS. Well then, next day, pretty late in the evening, when old Brovik and Ragnar had gone home, she came here again, and behaved as if I had made an arrangement with her.

DR. HERDAL. An arrangement? What about?

SOLNESS. About the very thing my mind had been fixed on. But I hadn't said one single word about it.

DR. HERDAL. That was most extraordinary.

SOLNESS. Yes, was it not? And now she wanted to know what she was to do here—whether she could begin the very next morning, and so forth.

DR. HERDAL. Don't you think she did it in order to be with her sweetheart?

SOLNESS. That was what occurred to me at first. But no, that was not it. She seemed to drift quite away from *him*—when once she had come here to me.

DR. HERDAL. She drifted over to you, then?

SOLNESS. Yes, entirely. If I happen to look at her when her back is turned, I can tell that she feels it. She quivers and trembles the moment I come near her. What do you think of *that?*

DR. HERDAL. H'm—that's not very hard to explain.

SOLNESS. Well, but what about the other thing? That she believed I had said to her what I had only wished and willed—silently—inwardly—to myself? What do you say to *that?* Can you explain that, Dr. Herdal?

DR. HERDAL. No, I won't undertake to do that.

SOLNESS. I felt sure you would not; and so I have never cared to talk about it till now.—But it's a cursed nuisance to me in the long run, you understand. Here have I got to go on day after day pretending—. And it's a shame to treat her so, too, poor girl. (*Vehemently.*) But I *cannot* do anything else. For if *she* runs away from me—then Ragnar will be off too.

DR. HERDAL. And you have not told your wife the rights of the story?

SOLNESS. No.

DR. HERDAL. Then why on earth don't you?

SOLNESS (*looks fixedly at him and says in a low voice*). Because I seem to find a sort of—of salutary self-torture in allowing Aline to do me an injustice.

DR. HERDAL (*shakes his head*). I don't in the least understand what you mean.

SOLNESS. Well, you see—it is like paying off a little bit of a huge, immeasurable debt—

DR. HERDAL. To your wife?

SOLNESS. Yes; and that always helps to relieve one's mind a little. One can breathe more freely for a while, you understand.

DR. HERDAL. No, goodness knows, I don't understand at all—

SOLNESS (*breaking off, rises again*). Well, well, well—then we won't talk any more about it. (*He saunters across the room, returns, and stops beside the table. Looks at the* DOCTOR *with a sly smile.*) I suppose you think you have drawn me out nicely now, Doctor?

DR. HERDAL (*with some irritation*). Drawn you out? Again I have not the faintest notion what you mean, Mr. Solness.

SOLNESS. Oh, come, out with it; I have seen it quite clearly, you know.

DR. HERDAL. *What* have you seen?

SOLNESS (*in a low voice, slowly*). That you have been quietly keeping an eye upon me.

DR. HERDAL. That *I* have! And why in all the world should I do *that?*

SOLNESS. Because you think that I—(*Passionately.*) Well, devil take it—you think the same of me as Aline does.

DR. HERDAL. And what does *she* think about you?

SOLNESS (*having recovered his self-control*). She has begun to think that I am—that I am—ill.

DR. HERDAL. Ill! *You!* She has never hinted such a thing to me. Why, what can she think is the matter with you?

SOLNESS (*leans over the back of the chair and whispers*). Aline has made up her mind that I am mad. *That* is what she thinks.

DR. HERDAL (*rising*). Why, my dear good fellow—!

SOLNESS. Yes, on my soul she does! I tell you it is so. And she has got you to think the same! Oh, I can assure you, Doctor, I see it in your face as clearly as possible. You don't take me in so easily, I can tell you.

DR. HERDAL (*looks at him in amazement*). Never, Mr. Solness—never has such a thought entered my mind.

SOLNESS (*with an incredulous smile*). Really? Has it not?

DR. HERDAL. No, never! Nor your wife's mind either, I am convinced. I could almost swear to that.

SOLNESS. Well, I wouldn't advise you to. For, in a certain sense, you see, perhaps—perhaps she is not so far wrong in thinking something of the kind.

DR. HERDAL. Come now, I really must say—

SOLNESS (*interrupting, with a sweep of his hand*). Well, well, my dear Doctor—don't let us discuss this any further. We had better agree to differ. (*Changes to a tone of quiet amusement.*) But look here now, Doctor—h'm—

DR. HERDAL. Well?

SOLNESS. Since you don't believe that I am—ill—and crazy—and mad, and so forth—

DR. HERDAL. What then?

SOLNESS. Then I dare say you fancy that I am an extremely happy man.

DR. HERDAL. Is *that* mere fancy?

SOLNESS (*laughs*). No, no—of course not! Heaven forbid! Only think—to be Solness the master builder! Halvard Solness! What could be more delightful?

DR. HERDAL. Yes, I must say it seems to me you have had the luck on your side to an astounding degree.

SOLNESS (*suppresses a gloomy smile*). So I have. I can't complain on *that* score.

DR. HERDAL. First of all that grim old robbers' castle was burnt down for you. And *that* was certainly a great piece of luck.

SOLNESS (*seriously*). It was the home of Aline's family. Remember that.

DR. HERDAL. Yes, it must have been a great grief to *her*.

SOLNESS. She has not got over it to this day—not in all these twelve or thirteen years.

DR. HERDAL. Ah, but what followed must have been the worst blow for her.

SOLNESS. The one thing with the other.

DR. HERDAL. But you—yourself—*you* rose upon the ruins. You began as a poor boy from a country village—and now you are at the head of your profession. Ah, yes, Mr. Solness, you have undoubtedly had the luck on your side.

SOLNESS (*looking at him with embarrassment*). Yes, but that is just what makes me so horribly afraid.

DR. HERDAL. Afraid? Because you have the luck on your side!

SOLNESS. It terrifies me—terrifies me every hour of the day. For sooner or later the luck must turn, you see.

DR. HERDAL. Oh, nonsense! What should make the luck turn?

SOLNESS (*with firm assurance*). The younger generation.

DR. HERDAL. Pooh! The younger generation! You are not laid on the shelf yet, I should hope. Oh, no—your position here is probably firmer now than it has ever been.

SOLNESS. The luck *will* turn. I know it—I feel the day approaching. Someone or other will take it into his head to say: Give *me* a chance! And then all the rest will come clamoring after him, and shake their fists at me and shout: Make room—make room—make room! Yes, just you see, Doctor—presently the younger generation will come knocking at my door—

DR. HERDAL (*laughing*). Well, and what if they do?

SOLNESS. What if they do? Then there's an end of Halvard Solness.

(*There is a knock at the door on the left.*)

SOLNESS (*starts*). What's that? Didn't you hear something?

DR. HERDAL. Someone is knocking at the door.

SOLNESS (*loudly*). Come in.

(HILDA WANGEL *enters by the hall door. She is of middle height, supple and delicately built; somewhat sunburnt. Dressed in a tourist costume with skirt caught up for walking, a sailor's collar open at the throat, and a small sailor hat on her head. Knapsack on back, plaid shawl in strap, and alpenstock.*)

HILDA (*goes straight up to* SOLNESS, *her eyes sparkling with happiness*). Good-evening!

SOLNESS (*looks doubtfully at her*). Good-evening—

HILDA (*laughs*). I almost believe you don't recognize me!

SOLNESS. No—I must admit that—just for the moment—

DR. HERDAL (*approaching*). But *I* recognize you, my dear young lady—

HILDA (*pleased*). Oh, is it you that—

DR. HERDAL. Of course it is. (*To* SOLNESS.) We met at one of the mountain stations this summer. (*To* HILDA.) What became of the other ladies?

HILDA. Oh, *they* went westward.

DR. HERDAL. They didn't much like all the fun we used to have in the evenings.

HILDA. No, I believe they didn't.

DR. HERDAL (*holds up his finger at her*). And I am afraid it can't be denied that you flirted a little with us.

HILDA. Well, that was better fun than to sit there knitting stockings with all those old women.

DR. HERDAL (*laughs*). There I entirely agree with you!

SOLNESS. Have you come to town this evening?

HILDA. Yes, I have just arrived.

DR. HERDAL. Quite alone, Miss Wangel?

HILDA. Oh, yes!

SOLNESS. Wangel? Is your name Wangel?

HILDA (*looks in amused surprise at him*). Yes, of course it is.

SOLNESS. Then you must be a daughter of the district doctor up at Lysanger?

HILDA (*as before*). Yes, who else's daughter should I be?

SOLNESS. Oh, then I suppose we met up there, that summer when I was building a tower on the old church.

HILDA (*more seriously*). Yes, of course it was then we met.

SOLNESS. Well, that is a long time ago.

HILDA (*looks hard at him*). It is exactly the ten years.

SOLNESS. You must have been a mere child then, I should think.

HILDA (*carelessly*). Well, I was twelve or thirteen.

DR. HERDAL. Is this the first time you have ever been up to town, Miss Wangel?

HILDA. Yes, it is indeed.

SOLNESS. And don't you know anyone here?

HILDA. Nobody but you. And of course, your wife.

SOLNESS. So you know *her*, too?

HILDA. Only a little. We spent a few days together at the sanatorium.

SOLNESS. Ah, up there?

HILDA. She said I might come and pay her a visit if ever I came up to town. (*Smiles.*) Not that that was necessary.

SOLNESS. Odd that she should never have mentioned it.

(HILDA *puts her stick down by the stove, takes off the knapsack and lays it and the plaid on the sofa.* DR. HERDAL *offers to help her.* SOLNESS *stands and gazes at her.*)

HILDA (*going towards him*). Well, now I must ask you to let me stay the night here.

SOLNESS. I am sure there will be no difficulty about that.

HILDA. For I have no other clothes than those I stand in, except a change of linen in my knapsack. And that has to go to the wash, for it's very dirty.

SOLNESS. Oh, yes, that can be managed. Now, I'll just let my wife know—

DR. HERDAL. Meanwhile I will go and see my patient.

SOLNESS. Yes, do; and come again later on.

DR. HERDAL (*playfully, with a glance at* HILDA). Oh, that I will, you may be very certain! (*Laughs*) So your prediction has come true, Mr. Solness!

SOLNESS. How so?

DR. HERDAL. The younger generation *did* come knocking at your door.

SOLNESS (*cheerfully*). Yes, but in a very different way from what I meant.

DR. HERDAL. Very different, yes. That's undeniable.

(*He goes out by the hall door.* SOLNESS *opens the door on the right and speaks into the side room.*)

SOLNESS. Aline! Will you come in here, please. Here is a friend of yours—Miss Wangel.

MRS. SOLNESS (*appears in the doorway*). Who do you say it is? (*Sees* HILDA.) Oh, is it *you*, Miss Wangel? (*Goes up to her and offers her hand.*) So you have come to town after all.

SOLNESS. Miss Wangel has this moment arrived; and she would like to stay the night here.

MRS. SOLNESS. Here with us? Oh, yes, certainly.

SOLNESS. Till she can get her things a little in order, you know.

MRS. SOLNESS. I will do the best I can for you. It's no more than my duty. I suppose your trunk is coming on later?

HILDA. I *have* no trunk.

MRS. SOLNESS. Well, it will be all right, I dare say. In the meantime, you must excuse my leaving you here with my husband, until I can get a room made a little comfortable for you.

SOLNESS. Can we not give her one of the nurseries? They are all ready as it is.

MRS. SOLNESS. Oh, yes. There we have room and to spare. (*To* HILDA.) Sit down now, and rest a little.

(*She goes out to the right.* HILDA, *with her hands behind her back, strolls about the room and looks at various objects.* SOLNESS *stands in front, beside the table, also with his hands behind his back, and follows her with his eyes.*)

HILDA (*stops and looks at him*). Have you several nurseries?

SOLNESS. There are three nurseries in the house.

HILDA. That's a lot. Then I suppose you have a great many children?

SOLNESS. No. We have no child. But now *you* can be the child here, for the time being.

HILDA. For tonight, yes. I shall not cry. I mean to sleep as sound as a stone.

SOLNESS. Yes, you must be very tired, I should think.

HILDA. Oh, no! But all the same— It's so delicious to lie and dream.

SOLNESS. Do you dream much of nights?

HILDA. Oh, yes! Almost always.

SOLNESS. What do you dream about most?

HILDA. I shan't tell you tonight. Another time perhaps.

(*She again strolls about the room, stops at the desk, and turns over the books and papers a little.*)

SOLNESS (*approaching*). Are you searching for anything?

HILDA. No, I am merely looking at all these things. (*Turns.*) Perhaps I mustn't?

SOLNESS. Oh, by all means.

HILDA. Is it *you* that write in this great ledger?

SOLNESS. No, it's my bookkeeper.

HILDA. Is it a woman?

SOLNESS (*smiles*). Yes.

HILDA. One you employ here, in your office?

SOLNESS. Yes.

HILDA. Is she married?
SOLNESS. No, she is single.
HILDA. Oh, indeed!
SOLNESS. But I believe she is soon going to be married.
HILDA. That's a good thing for *her*.
SOLNESS. But not such a good thing for *me*. For then I shall have nobody to help me.
HILDA. Can't you get hold of someone else who will do just as well?
SOLNESS. Perhaps *you* would stay here and—and write in the ledger?
HILDA (*measures him with a glance*). Yes, I dare say! No, thank you—nothing of that sort for *me*.

(*She again strolls across the room and sits down in the rocking-chair. SOLNESS too goes to the table.*)

HILDA (*continuing*). For there must surely be plenty of other things to be done here. (*Looks smilingly at him.*) Don't you think so, too?
SOLNESS. Of course. First of all, I suppose, you want to make a round of the shops, and get yourself up in the height of fashion.
HILDA (*amused*). No, I think I shall let *that* alone!
SOLNESS. Indeed?
HILDA. For you must know I have run through all my money.
SOLNESS (*laughs*). Neither trunk nor money, then!
HILDA. Neither one nor the other. But never mind—it doesn't matter now.
SOLNESS. Come now, I like you for *that*.
HILDA. Only for *that?*
SOLNESS. For that among other things. (*Sits in the armchair.*) Is your father alive still?
HILDA. Yes, father's alive.
SOLNESS. Perhaps you are thinking of studying here?
HILDA. No, that hadn't occurred to me.

SOLNESS. But I suppose you will be staying for some time?
HILDA. That must depend upon circumstances.

(*She sits awhile rocking herself and looking at him, half seriously, half with a suppressed smile. Then she takes off her hat and puts it on the table in front of her.*)

HILDA. Mr. Solness!
SOLNESS. Well?
HILDA. Have you a very bad memory?
SOLNESS. A bad memory? No, not that I am aware of.
HILDA. Then have you nothing to say to me about what happened up there?
SOLNESS (*in momentary surprise*). Up at Lysanger? (*Indifferently.*) Why, it was nothing much to talk about, it seems to me.
HILDA (*looks reproachfully at him*). How can you sit there and say such things?
SOLNESS. Well, then, *you* talk to *me* about it.
HILDA. When the tower was finished, we had grand doings in the town.
SOLNESS. Yes, I shall not easily forget that day.
HILDA (*smiles*). Will you not? That comes well from *you*.
SOLNESS. Comes well?
HILDA. There was music in the churchyard—and many, many hundreds of people. We schoolgirls were dressed in white; and we all carried flags.
SOLNESS. Ah, yes, those flags—I can tell you I remember *them!*
HILDA. Then you climbed right up the scaffolding, straight to the very top; and you had a great wreath with you; and you hung that wreath right away up on the weathervane.
SOLNESS (*curtly interrupting*). I always did that in those days. It is an old custom.
HILDA. It was so wonderfully thrilling to stand below and look up at you. Fancy,

if he should fall over! He—the master builder himself!

SOLNESS (*as if to divert her from the subject*). Yes, yes, yes, that might very well have happened, too. For one of those white-frocked little devils—she went on in such a way, and screamed up at me so—

HILDA (*sparkling with pleasure*). "Hurrah for Master Builder Solness!" Yes!

SOLNESS. —and waved and flourished with her flag, so that I—so that it almost made me giddy to look at it.

HILDA (*in a lower voice, seriously*). That little devil—that was *I*.

SOLNESS (*fixes his eyes steadily upon her*). I am sure of that now. It *must* have been you.

HILDA (*lively again*). Oh, it was so gloriously thrilling! I could not have believed there was a builder in the whole world that could build such a tremendously high tower. And then, that you yourself should stand at the very top of it, as large as life! And that you should not be the least bit dizzy! It was *that* above everything that made one—made one dizzy to think of.

SOLNESS. How could you be so certain that I was not—?

HILDA (*scouting the idea*). No, indeed! Oh, no! I knew that instinctively. For if you had been, you could never have stood up there and sung.

SOLNESS (*looks at her in astonishment*). Sung? Did *I* sing?

HILDA. Yes, I should think you did.

SOLNESS (*shakes his head*). I have never sung a note in my life.

HILDA. Yes, indeed, you sang then. It sounded like harps in the air.

SOLNESS (*thoughtfully*). This is very strange—all this.

HILDA (*is silent awhile, looks at him and says in a low voice*). But then—it was after that—that the *real* thing happened.

SOLNESS. The real thing?

HILDA (*sparkling with vivacity*). Yes, I surely don't need to remind you of *that?*

SOLNESS. Oh, yes, do remind me a little of *that,* too.

HILDA. Don't you remember that a great dinner was given in your honor at the Club?

SOLNESS. Yes, to be sure. It must have been the same afternoon, for I left the place next morning.

HILDA. And from the Club you were invited to come round to our house to supper.

SOLNESS. Quite right, Miss Wangel. It is wonderful how all these trifles have impressed themselves on your mind.

HILDA. Trifles! I like that! Perhaps it was a trifle, too, that I was *alone* in the room when you came in?

SOLNESS. *Were* you alone?

HILDA (*without answering him*). You didn't call me a little devil *then?*

SOLNESS. No, I suppose I did not.

HILDA. You said I was lovely in my white dress, and that I looked like a little princess.

SOLNESS. I have no doubt you did, Miss Wangel.—And besides—I was feeling so buoyant and free that day—

HILDA. And then you said that when I grew up I should be *your* princess.

SOLNESS (*laughing a little*). Dear, dear—did I say *that* too?

HILDA. Yes, you did. And when I asked how long I should have to wait, you said that you would come again in ten years—like a troll—and carry me off—to Spain or some such place. And you promised you would buy me a kingdom there.

SOLNESS (*as before*). Yes, after a good dinner one doesn't haggle about the halfpence. But did I really *say* all that?

HILDA (*laughs to herself*). Yes. And you told me, too, what the kingdom was to be called.

SOLNESS. Well, what was it?

HILDA. It was to be called the kingdom of Orangia, you said.

SOLNESS. Well, that was an appetizing name.

HILDA. No, I didn't like it a bit; for it seemed as though you wanted to make game of me.

SOLNESS. I am sure *that* cannot have been my intention.

HILDA. No, I should hope not—considering what you did next—

SOLNESS. What in the world did I do next?

HILDA. Well, that's the finishing touch, if you have forgotten *that* too. I should have thought no one could help remembering such a thing as that.

SOLNESS. Yes, yes, just give me a hint, and then perhaps— Well?

HILDA (*looks fixedly at him*). You came and kissed me, Mr. Solness.

SOLNESS (*open-mouthed, rising from his chair*). I did!

HILDA. Yes, indeed you did. You took me in both your arms, and bent my head back, and kissed me—many times.

SOLNESS. Now really, my dear Miss Wangel—!

HILDA (*rises*). You surely cannot mean to deny it?

SOLNESS. Yes, I do. I deny it altogether!

HILDA (*looks scornfully at him*). Oh, indeed!

> (*She turns and goes slowly close up to the stove, where she remains standing motionless, her face averted from him, her hands behind her back. Short pause.*)

SOLNESS (*goes cautiously up behind her*). Miss Wangel—!

HILDA (*is silent and does not move*).

SOLNESS. Don't stand there like a statue. You must have dreamt all this. (*Lays his hand on her arm.*) Now just listen—

HILDA (*makes an impatient movement with her arm*).

SOLNESS (*as a thought flashes upon him*). Or—! Wait a moment! There is something under all this, you may depend!

HILDA (*does not move*).

SOLNESS (*in a low voice, but with emphasis*). I must have *thought* all that. I must have *wished* it—have *willed* it—have *longed* to do it. And then— May not that be the explanation?

HILDA (*is still silent*).

SOLNESS (*impatiently*). Oh, very well, deuce take it all—then I *did* do it, I suppose.

HILDA (*turns her head a little, but without looking at him*). Then you admit it now?

SOLNESS. Yes—whatever you like.

HILDA. You came and put your arms round me?

SOLNESS. Oh, yes!

HILDA. And bent my head back?

SOLNESS. Very far back.

HILDA. And kissed me?

SOLNESS. Yes, I did.

HILDA. Many times?

SOLNESS. As many as ever you like.

HILDA (*turns quickly towards him and has once more the sparkling expression of gladness in her eyes*). Well, you see, I got it out of you at last!

SOLNESS (*with a slight smile*). Yes—just think of my forgetting such a thing as that.

HILDA (*again a little sulky, retreats from him*). Oh, you have kissed so many people in your time, I suppose.

SOLNESS. No, you mustn't think *that* of me. (HILDA *seats herself in the armchair.* SOLNESS *stands and leans against the rocking-chair. Looks observantly at her.*) Miss Wangel!

HILDA. Yes!

SOLNESS. How *was* it now? What came of all this—between us two?

HILDA. Why, nothing more came of it. You know that quite well. For then the other guests came in, and then—bah!

SOLNESS. Quite so! The others came in. To think of my forgetting *that* too!

HILDA. Oh, you haven't really forgotten anything: you are only a little ashamed of it all. I am sure one doesn't forget things of that kind.

SOLNESS. No, one would suppose not.

HILDA (*lively again, looks at him*). Perhaps you have even forgotten what day it was?

SOLNESS. What day—?

HILDA. Yes, on what day did you hang the wreath on the tower? Well? Tell me at once!

SOLNESS. H'm—I confess I have forgotten the particular day. I only know it was ten years ago. Sometime in the autumn.

HILDA (*nods her head slowly several times*). It was ten years ago—on the nineteenth of September.

SOLNESS. Yes, it must have been about that time. Fancy your remembering that too! (*Stops.*) But wait a moment—! Yes—it's the nineteenth of September today.

HILDA. Yes, it is; and the ten years are gone. And you didn't come—as you had promised me.

SOLNESS. Promised you? Threatened, I suppose you mean?

HILDA. I don't think there was any sort of threat in *that*.

SOLNESS. Well, then a little bit of fun.

HILDA. Was *that* all you wanted? To make fun of me?

SOLNESS. Well, or to have a little joke with you. Upon my soul, I don't recollect. But it must have been something of that kind; for you were a mere child then.

HILDA. Oh, perhaps I wasn't quite such a child either. Not such a mere chit as you imagine.

SOLNESS (*looks searchingly at her.*) Did you really and seriously expect me to come again?

HILDA (*conceals a half-teasing smile*). Yes, indeed! I did expect *that* of you.

SOLNESS. That I should come back to your home, and take you away with me?

HILDA. Just like a troll—yes.

SOLNESS. And make a princess of you?

HILDA. That's what you promised.

SOLNESS. And give you a kingdom as well?

HILDA (*looks up at the ceiling*). Why not? Of course it need not have been an actual, everyday sort of kingdom.

SOLNESS. But something else just as good?

HILDA. Yes, at least as good. (*Looks at him a moment.*) I thought, if you could build the highest church-towers in the world, you could surely manage to raise a kingdom of one sort or another as well.

SOLNESS (*shakes his head*). I can't quite make you out, Miss Wangel.

HILDA. Can you not? To me it seems all so simple.

SOLNESS. No, I can't make up my mind whether you mean all you say, or are simply having a joke with me.

HILDA (*smiles*). Making fun of you, perhaps? I, too?

SOLNESS. Yes, exactly. Making fun—of both of us. (*Looks at her.*) Is it long since you found out that I was married?

HILDA. I have known it all along. Why do you ask me *that?*

SOLNESS (*lightly*). Oh, well, it just occurred to me. (*Looks earnestly at her and says in a low voice.*) What have you come for?

HILDA. I want my kingdom. The time is up.

SOLNESS (*laughs involuntarily*). What a girl you are!

HILDA (*gayly*). Out with my kingdom, Mr. Solness! (*Raps with her fingers.*) The kingdom on the table!

SOLNESS (*pushing the rocking-chair nearer and sitting down*). Now, seriously speaking—what have you come for? What do you really want to do here?

HILDA. Oh, first of all, I want to go round and look at all the things that you have built.

SOLNESS. That will give you plenty of exercise.

HILDA. Yes, I know you have built a tremendous lot.

SOLNESS. I have indeed—especially of late years.

HILDA. Many church-towers among the rest? Immensely high ones?

SOLNESS. No. I build no more church-towers now. Nor churches either.

HILDA. What *do* you build then?

SOLNESS. Homes for human beings.

HILDA (*reflectively*). Couldn't you build a little—a little bit of a church-tower over these homes as well?

SOLNESS (*starting*). What do you mean by *that?*

HILDA. I mean—something that points—points up into the free air. With the vane at a dizzy height.

SOLNESS (*pondering a little*). Strange that you should say *that*—for that is just what I am most anxious to do.

HILDA (*impatiently*). Why don't you do it, then?

SOLNESS (*shakes his head*). No, the people will not have it.

HILDA. Fancy their not wanting it!

SOLNESS (*more lightly*). But now I am building a new home for myself—just opposite here.

HILDA. For yourself?

SOLNESS. Yes. It is almost finished. And on that there is a tower.

HILDA. A high tower?

SOLNESS. Yes.

HILDA. Very high?

SOLNESS. No doubt people will say it is *too* high—too high for a dwelling-house.

HILDA. I'll go out and look at that tower the first thing tomorrow morning.

SOLNESS (*sits resting his cheek on his hand and gazes at her*). Tell me, Miss Wangel—what is your name? Your Christian name, I mean?

HILDA. Why, Hilda, of course.

SOLNESS (*as before*). Hilda? Indeed?

HILDA. Don't you remember *that?* You called me Hilda yourself—that day when you misbehaved.

SOLNESS. Did I really?

HILDA. But then you said "*little* Hilda"; and I didn't like that.

SOLNESS. Oh, you didn't like that, Miss Hilda?

HILDA. No, not at such a time as that. But—"Princess Hilda"—that will sound very well, I think.

SOLNESS. Very well indeed. Princess Hilda of—of—what was to be the name of the kingdom?

HILDA. Pooh! I won't have anything to do with *that* stupid kingdom. I have set my heart upon quite a different one!

SOLNESS (*has leaned back in the chair, still gazing at her*). Isn't it strange—? The more I think of it now, the more it seems to me as though I had gone about all these years torturing myself with—h'm—

HILDA. With what?

SOLNESS. With the effort to recover something—some experience, which I seemed to have forgotten. But I never had the least inkling of what it could be.

HILDA. You should have tied a knot in your pocket-handkerchief, Mr. Solness.

SOLNESS. In that case, I should simply have had to go racking my brains to discover what the knot could mean.

HILDA. Oh, yes, I suppose there are trolls of *that* kind in the world, too.

SOLNESS (*rises slowly*). What a good thing

it is that *you* have come to me now.

HILDA (*looks deeply into his eyes*). *Is* it a good thing!

SOLNESS. For I have been so lonely here. I have been gazing so helplessly at it all. (*In a lower voice*) I must tell you—I have begun to be so afraid—so terribly afraid of the younger generation.

HILDA (*with a little snort of contempt*). Pooh—is the younger generation a thing to be afraid of?

SOLNESS. It is indeed. And that is why I have locked and barred myself in. (*Mysteriously.*) I tell you the younger generation will one day come and thunder at my door! They will break in upon me!

HILDA. Then I should say you ought to go out and open the door to the younger generation.

SOLNESS. Open the door?

HILDA. Yes. Let them come in to you on friendly terms, as it were.

SOLNESS. No, no, no! The younger generation—it means retribution, you see. It comes, as if under a new banner, heralding the turn of fortune.

HILDA (*rises, looks at him, and says with a quivering twitch of her lips*). Can *I* be of any use to you, Mr. Solness?

SOLNESS. Yes, you can indeed! For you, too, come—under a new banner, it seems to me. Youth marshaled against youth—!

(DR. HERDAL *comes in by the hall door.*)

DR. HERDAL. What—you and Miss Wangel here still?

SOLNESS. Yes. We have had no end of things to talk about.

HILDA. Both old and new.

DR. HERDAL. Have you really?

HILDA. Oh, it has been the greatest fun! For Mr. Solness—he has such a miraculous memory. All the least little details he remembers instantly.

(MRS. SOLNESS *enters by the door on the right.*)

MRS. SOLNESS. Well, Miss Wangel, your room is quite ready for you now.

HILDA. Oh, how kind you are to me!

SOLNESS (*to* MRS. SOLNESS). The nursery?

MRS. SOLNESS. Yes, the middle one. But first let us go in to supper.

SOLNESS (*nods to* HILDA). Hilda shall sleep in the nursery, she shall.

MRS. SOLNESS (*looks at him*). Hilda?

SOLNESS. Yes, Miss Wangel's name is Hilda. I knew her when she was a child.

MRS. SOLNESS. Did you really, Halvard? Well, shall we go? Supper is on the table.

(*She takes* DR. HERDAL'*s arm and goes out with him to the right.* HILDA *has meanwhile been collecting her traveling things.*)

HILDA (*softly and rapidly to* SOLNESS). Is it true, what you said? *Can* I be of use to you?

SOLNESS (*takes the things from her*). *You* are the very being I have needed most.

HILDA (*looks at him with happy, wondering eyes and clasps her hands*). But then, great heavens—!

SOLNESS (*eagerly*). What—?

HILDA. Then I *have* my kingdom!

SOLNESS (*involuntarily*). Hilda—!

HILDA (*again with the quivering twitch of her lips*). Almost—I was going to say.

(*She goes out to the right;* SOLNESS *follows her.*)

CURTAIN

ACT TWO

A prettily furnished small drawing-room in SOLNESS'*s house. In the back, a glass door leading out to the veranda and garden. The right-hand corner is cut off transversely by a large bay-window, in which are flower-stands. The left-hand* corner is similarly cut off by a transverse wall, in which is a small door papered like the wall. On each side, an ordinary door. In front, on the right, a console table with a large mirror over it. Well-filled stands of plants and flowers. In front, on the left, a sofa with a table and chairs. Farther back, a bookcase. Well forward in the room, before the bay-window, a small table and some chairs. It is early in the day.

SOLNESS *sits by the little table with* RAGNAR BROVIK'S *portfolio open in front of him. He is turning the drawings over and closely examining some of them.* MRS. SOLNESS *moves about noiselessly with a small watering-pot, attending to her flowers. She is dressed in black as before. Her hat, cloak, and parasol lie on a chair near the mirror. Unobserved by her,* SOLNESS *now and again follows her with his eyes. Neither of them speaks.*

(KAIA FOSLI *enters quietly by the door on the left.*)

SOLNESS (*turns his head and says in an offhand tone of indifference*). Well, is that you?

KAIA. I merely wished to let you know that I have come.

SOLNESS. Yes, yes, that's all right. Hasn't Ragnar come too?

KAIA. No, not yet. He had to wait a little while to see the doctor. But he is coming presently to hear—

SOLNESS. How is the old man today?

KAIA. Not well. He begs you to excuse him; he is obliged to keep his bed today.

SOLNESS. Why, of course; by all means let him rest. But now, get to your work.

KAIA. Yes. (*Pauses at the door.*) Do you wish to speak to Ragnar when he comes?

SOLNESS. No—I don't know that I have anything particular to say to him.

(KAIA *goes out again to the left.* SOLNESS *remains, turning over the drawings.*)

MRS. SOLNESS (*over beside the plants*). I wonder if *he* isn't going to die now, as well?

SOLNESS (*looks up at her*). As well as who?

MRS. SOLNESS (*without answering*). Yes, yes—depend upon it, Halvard, old Brovik is going to die too. You'll see that he will.

SOLNESS. My dear Aline, shouldn't you go out for a little walk?

MRS. SOLNESS. Yes, I suppose I ought to.

(*She continues to attend to the flowers.*)

SOLNESS (*bending over the drawings*). Is she still asleep?

MRS. SOLNESS (*looking at him*). Is it Miss Wangel you are sitting there thinking about?

SOLNESS (*indifferently*). I just happened to recollect her.

MRS. SOLNESS. Miss Wangel was up long ago.

SOLNESS. Oh, was she?

MRS. SOLNESS. When I went in to see her, she was busy putting her things in order.

(*She goes in front of the mirror and slowly begins to put on her hat.*)

SOLNESS (*after a short pause*). So we have found a use for one of our nurseries after all, Aline.

MRS. SOLNESS. Yes, we have.

SOLNESS. That seems to me better than to have them all standing empty.

MRS. SOLNESS. That emptiness is dreadful; you are right there.

SOLNESS (*closes the portfolio, rises, and approaches her*). You will find that we shall get on far better after this, Aline. Things will be more comfortable. Life will be easier—especially for *you.*

MRS. SOLNESS (*looks at him*). After this?

SOLNESS. Yes, believe me, Aline—

MRS. SOLNESS. Do you mean—because *she* has come here?

SOLNESS (*checking himself*). I mean, of course—when once we have moved into the new house.

MRS. SOLNESS (*takes her cloak*). Ah, do you

think so, Halvard? Will it be better then?

SOLNESS. I can't think otherwise. And surely you think so too?

MRS. SOLNESS. I think nothing at all about the new house.

SOLNESS (*cast down*). It's hard for me to hear you say that; for you know it is mainly for your sake that I have built it. (*He offers to help her on with her cloak.*)

MRS. SOLNESS (*evades him*). The fact is, you do far too much for my sake.

SOLNESS (*with a certain vehemence*). No, no, you really mustn't say that, Aline! I cannot bear to hear you say such things!

MRS. SOLNESS. Very well, then I won't say it, Halvard.

SOLNESS. But I stick to what *I* said. You'll see that things will be easier for you in the new place.

MRS. SOLNESS. Oh, heavens—easier for me—!

SOLNESS (*eagerly*). Yes, indeed they will! You may be quite sure of that! For you see—there will be so very, very much *there* that will remind you of your own home—

MRS. SOLNESS. The home that used to be father's and mother's—and that was burnt to the ground—

SOLNESS (*in a low voice*). Yes, yes, my poor Aline. That was a terrible blow for you.

MRS. SOLNESS (*breaking out in lamentation*). You may build as much as ever you like, Halvard—you can never build up again a real home for *me!*

SOLNESS (*crosses the room*). Well, in Heaven's name, let us talk no more about it then.

MRS. SOLNESS. We are not in the habit of talking about it. For you always put the thought away from you—

SOLNESS (*stops suddenly and looks at her*). Do I? And why should I do *that?* Put the thought away from me?

MRS. SOLNESS. Oh, yes, Halvard, I understand you very well. You are so anxious to spare me—and to find excuses for me too—as much as ever you can.

SOLNESS (*with astonishment in his eyes*). You! Is it *you*—yourself, that you are talking about, Aline?

MRS. SOLNESS. Yes, who else should it be but myself?

SOLNESS (*involuntarily to himself*). *That* too!

MRS. SOLNESS. As for the old house, I wouldn't mind so much about that. When once misfortune was in the air—why—

SOLNESS. Ah, you are right there. Misfortune will have its way—as the saying goes.

MRS. SOLNESS. But it's what came of the fire—the dreadful thing that followed—! *That* is the thing! That, that, that!

SOLNESS (*vehemently*). Don't think about *that*, Aline!

MRS. SOLNESS. Ah, that is exactly what I cannot help thinking about. And now, at last, I must speak about it, too; for I don't seem able to bear it any longer. And then never to be able to forgive myself—

SOLNESS (*exclaiming*). Yourself—!

MRS. SOLNESS. Yes, for I had duties on both sides—both towards you and towards the little ones. I ought to have hardened myself—not to have let the horror take such hold upon me—nor the grief for the burning of my home. (*Wrings her hands.*) Oh, Halvard, if I had only had the strength!

SOLNESS (*softly, much moved, comes closer*). Aline—you must promise me never to think these thoughts any more.—Promise me that, dear!

MRS. SOLNESS. Oh, promise, promise! One can promise anything.

SOLNESS (*clenches his hands and crosses the room*). Oh, but this is hopeless, hopeless! Never a ray of sunlight! Not so much as a gleam of brightness to light up our home!

MRS. SOLNESS. This is no home, Halvard.

SOLNESS. Oh, no, you may well say that. (*Gloomily.*) And God knows whether you are not right in saying that it will be no better for us in the new house, either.

MRS. SOLNESS. It will never be any better. Just as empty—just as desolate—there as here.

SOLNESS (*vehemently*). Why in all the world have we built it then? Can you tell me that?

MRS. SOLNESS. No; you must answer that question for yourself.

SOLNESS (*glances suspiciously at her*). What do you mean by *that*, Aline?

MRS. SOLNESS. What do I mean?

SOLNESS. Yes, in the devil's name! You said it so strangely—as if you had some hidden meaning in it.

MRS. SOLNESS. No, indeed, I assure you—

SOLNESS (*comes closer*). Oh, come now—I know what I know. I have both my eyes and my ears about me, Aline—you may depend upon that!

MRS. SOLNESS. Why, what are you talking about? What is it?

SOLNESS (*places himself in front of her*). Do you mean to say you don't find a kind of lurking, hidden meaning in the most innocent word I happen to say?

MRS. SOLNESS. *I*, do you say? *I* do that?

SOLNESS (*laughs*). Ho-ho-ho! It's natural enough, Aline! When you have a sick man on your hands—

MRS. SOLNESS (*anxiously*). Sick? Are you ill, Halvard?

SOLNESS (*violently*). A half-mad man then! A crazy man! Call me what you will.

MRS. SOLNESS (*feels blindly for a chair and sits down*). Halvard—for God's sake—

SOLNESS. But you are wrong, both you and the Doctor. I am not in the state you imagine.

(*He walks up and down the room.* MRS. SOLNESS *follows him anxiously with her eyes. Finally he goes up to her.*)

SOLNESS (*calmly*). In reality there is nothing whatever the matter with me.

MRS. SOLNESS. No, there isn't, is there? But then what is it that troubles you so?

SOLNESS. Why *this*, that I often feel ready to sink under this terrible burden of debt—

MRS. SOLNESS. Debt, do you say? But you owe no one anything, Halvard!

SOLNESS (*softly, with emotion*). I owe a boundless debt to you—to you—to you, Aline.

MRS. SOLNESS (*rises slowly*). What is behind all this? You may just as well tell me at once.

SOLNESS. But there *is* nothing behind it! I have never done you any wrong—not wittingly and willfully, at any rate. And yet—and yet it seems as though a crushing debt rested upon me and weighed me down.

MRS. SOLNESS. A debt to me?

SOLNESS. Chiefly to you.

MRS. SOLNESS. Then you are—ill after all, Halvard.

SOLNESS (*gloomily*). I suppose I must be—or not far from it. (*Looks towards the door to the right, which is opened at this moment.*) Ah! now it grows lighter.

(HILDA WANGEL *comes in. She has made some alteration in her dress and let down her skirt.*)

HILDA. Good morning, Mr. Solness!

SOLNESS (*nods*). Slept well?

HILDA. Quite deliciously! Like a child in a cradle. Oh—I lay and stretched myself like—like a princess!

SOLNESS (*smiles a little*). You were thoroughly comfortable then?

HILDA. I should think so.

SOLNESS. And no doubt you dreamed, too.

HILDA. Yes, I did. But *that* was horrid.

SOLNESS. Was it?

HILDA. Yes, for I dreamed I was falling over a frightfully high, sheer precipice. Do you never have that kind of dream?

SOLNESS. Oh, yes—now and then—

HILDA. It's tremendously thrilling—when you fall and fall—

SOLNESS. It seems to make one's blood run cold.

HILDA. Do you draw your legs up under you while you are falling?

SOLNESS. Yes, as high as ever I can.

HILDA. So do I.

MRS. SOLNESS (*takes her parasol*). I must go into town now, Halvard. (*To* HILDA.) And I'll try to get one or two things that you may require.

HILDA (*making a motion to throw her arms round her neck*). Oh, you dear, sweet Mrs. Solness! You are really much too kind to me! Frightfully kind—

MRS. SOLNESS (*deprecatingly, freeing herself*). Oh, not at all. It's only my duty, so I am very glad to do it.

HILDA (*offended, pouts*). But really, I think I am quite fit to be seen in the streets—now that I've put my dress to rights. Or do you think I am not?

MRS. SOLNESS. To tell you the truth, I think people would stare at you a little.

HILDA (*contemptuously*). Pooh! Is that all? That only amuses me.

SOLNESS (*with suppressed ill-humor*). Yes, but people might take it into their heads that *you* were mad too, you see.

HILDA. Mad? Are there so many mad people here in town, then?

SOLNESS (*points to his own forehead*). Here you see *one* at all events.

HILDA. You—Mr. Solness!

MRS. SOLNESS. Oh, don't talk like that, my dear Halvard!

SOLNESS. Have you not noticed *that* yet?

HILDA. No, I certainly have not. (*Reflects and laughs a little.*) And yet—perhaps in one single thing.

SOLNESS. Ah, do you hear *that*, Aline?

MRS. SOLNESS. What is that one single thing, Miss Wangel?

HILDA. No, I won't say.

SOLNESS. Oh, yes, do!

HILDA. No, thank you—I am not so mad as that.

MRS. SOLNESS. When you and Miss Wangel are alone, I dare say she will tell you, Halvard.

SOLNESS. Ah—you think she will?

MRS. SOLNESS. Oh, yes, certainly. For you have known her so well in the past. Ever since she was a child—you tell me.

(*She goes out by the door on the left.*)

HILDA (*after a little while*). Does your wife dislike me very much?

SOLNESS. Did you think you noticed anything of the kind?

HILDA. Did you not notice it yourself?

SOLNESS (*evasively*). Aline has become exceedingly shy with strangers of late years.

HILDA. Has she really?

SOLNESS. But if only you could get to know her thoroughly—! Ah, she is so good—so kind—so excellent a creature—

HILDA (*impatiently*). But if she is all that—what made her say that about her duty?

SOLNESS. Her duty?

HILDA. She said that she would go out and buy something for me, because it was her *duty*. Oh, I can't bear that ugly, horrid word!

SOLNESS. Why not?

HILDA. It sounds so cold, and sharp, and stinging. Duty—duty—duty. Don't you think so, too? Doesn't it seem to sting you?

SOLNESS. H'm—haven't thought much about it.

HILDA. Yes, it does. And if she is so good—as you say she is—why should she talk in that way?

SOLNESS. But, good Lord, what would you have had her say, then?

HILDA. She might have said she would do it because she had taken a tremendous fancy to me. She might have said something like that—something really warm and cordial, you understand.

SOLNESS (*looks at her*). Is that how you would like to have it?

HILDA. Yes, precisely. (*She wanders about the room, stops at the bookcase and looks at the books.*) What a lot of books you have.

SOLNESS. Yes, I have got together a good many.

HILDA. Do you read them all, too?

SOLNESS. I used to try to. Do you read much?

HILDA. No, never! I have given it up. For it all seems so irrelevant.

SOLNESS. That is just my feeling.

(HILDA *wanders about a little, stops at the small table, opens the portfolio, and turns over the contents.*)

HILDA. Are all these drawings yours?

SOLNESS. No, they are drawn by a young man whom I employ to help me.

HILDA. Someone you have taught?

SOLNESS. Oh, yes, no doubt he has learnt something from *me*, too.

HILDA (*sits down*). Then I suppose he is very clever. (*Looks at a drawing.*) Isn't he?

SOLNESS. Oh, he might be worse. For *my* purpose—

HILDA. Oh, yes—I'm sure he is frightfully clever.

SOLNESS. Do you think you can see that in the drawings?

HILDA. Pooh—these scrawlings! But if he has been learning from *you*—

SOLNESS. Oh, so far as that goes—there are plenty of people here that have learnt from *me*, and have come to little enough for all that.

HILDA (*looks at him and shakes her head*). No, I can't for the life of me understand how you can be so stupid.

SOLNESS. Stupid? Do you think I am so very stupid?

HILDA. Yes, I do indeed. If you are content to go about here teaching all these people—

SOLNESS (*with a slight start*). Well, and why not?

HILDA (*rises, half serious, half laughing*). No indeed, Mr. Solness! What can be the good of that? No one but *you* should be allowed to build. You should stand quite alone—do it all yourself. Now you know it.

SOLNESS (*involuntarily*). Hilda—

HILDA. Well!

SOLNESS. How in the world did *that* come into your head?

HILDA. Do you think I am so very far wrong then?

SOLNESS. No, that's not what I mean. But now I'll tell you something.

HILDA. Well?

SOLNESS. I keep on—incessantly—in silence and alone—brooding on that very thought.

HILDA. Yes, that seems to me perfectly natural.

SOLNESS (*looks somewhat searchingly at her*). Perhaps you have noticed it already?

HILDA. No, indeed I haven't.

SOLNESS. But just now—when you said you thought I was—off my balance? In one thing, you said—

HILDA. Oh, I was thinking of something quite different.

SOLNESS. What was it?

HILDA. I am not going to tell you.

SOLNESS (*crosses the room*). Well, well—as you please. (*Stops at the bay-window.*) Come here, and I will show you something.

HILDA (*approaching*). What is it?

SOLNESS. Do you see—over there in the garden—?

HILDA. Yes?

SOLNESS (*points*). Right above the great quarry—?

HILDA. That new house, you mean?
SOLNESS. The one that is being built, yes. Almost finished.
HILDA. It seems to have a very high tower.
SOLNESS. The scaffolding is still up.
HILDA. Is that your new house?
SOLNESS. Yes.
HILDA. The house you are soon going to move into?
SOLNESS. Yes.
HILDA (*looks at him*). Are there nurseries in *that* house, too?
SOLNESS. Three, as there are here.
HILDA. And no child.
SOLNESS. And there never will be one.
HILDA (*with a half-smile*). Well, isn't it just as I said—?
SOLNESS. That—?
HILDA. That you *are* a little—a little mad after all.
SOLNESS. Was that what you were thinking of?
HILDA. Yes, of all the empty nurseries I slept in.
SOLNESS (*lowers his voice*). We *have* had children—Aline and I.
HILDA (*looks eagerly at him*). Have you—?
SOLNESS. Two little boys. They were of the same age.
HILDA. Twins, then.
SOLNESS. Yes, twins. It's eleven or twelve years ago now.
HILDA (*cautiously*). And so both of them—? You have lost both the twins, then?
SOLNESS (*with quiet emotion*). We kept them only about three weeks. Or scarcely so much. (*Bursts forth.*) Oh, Hilda, I can't tell you what a good thing it is for me that you have come! For now at last I have someone I can talk to!
HILDA. Can you not talk to—*her*, too?
SOLNESS. Not about this. Not as I want to talk and must talk. (*Gloomily*). And not about so many other things, either.

HILDA (*in a subdued voice*). Was that all you meant when you said you needed me?
SOLNESS. That was mainly what I meant—at all events, yesterday. For today I am not so sure—(*Breaking off.*) Come here and let us sit down, Hilda. Sit there on the sofa—so that you can look into the garden. (HILDA *seats herself in the corner of the sofa.* SOLNESS *brings a chair closer.*) Should you like to hear about it?
HILDA. Yes, I shall love to sit and listen to you.
SOLNESS (*sits down*). Then I will tell you all about it.
HILDA. Now I can see both the garden and you, Mr. Solness. So now, tell away! Begin!
SOLNESS (*points towards the bay-window*). Out there on the rising ground—where you see the new house—
HILDA. Yes?
SOLNESS. Aline and I lived there in the first years of our married life. There was an old house up there that had belonged to her mother; and we inherited it, and the whole of the great garden with it.
HILDA. Was there a tower on *that* house, too?
SOLNESS. No, nothing of the kind. From the outside it looked like a great, dark, ugly wooden box; but all the same, it was snug and comfortable enough inside.
HILDA. Then did you pull down the ramshackle old place?
SOLNESS. No, it was burnt down.
HILDA. The whole of it?
SOLNESS. Yes.
HILDA. Was that a great misfortune for you?
SOLNESS. That depends on how you look at it. As a builder, the fire was the making of me—
HILDA. Well, but—?
SOLNESS. It was just after the birth of the two little boys—

HILDA. The poor little twins, yes.

SOLNESS. They came into the world healthy and bonny. And they were growing too—you could see the difference from day to day.

HILDA. Little children do grow quickly at first.

SOLNESS. It was the prettiest sight in the world to see Aline lying with the two of them in her arms.—But then came the night of the fire—

HILDA (*excitedly*). What happened? Do tell me! Was anyone burnt?

SOLNESS. No, not that. Everyone got safe and sound out of the house—

HILDA. Well, and what then—?

SOLNESS. The fright had shaken Aline terribly. The alarm—the escape—the break-neck hurry—and then the ice-cold night air—for they had to be carried out just as they lay—both she and the little ones.

HILDA. Was it too much for them?

SOLNESS. Oh, no, *they* stood it well enough. But Aline fell into a fever, and it affected her milk. She would insist on nursing them herself; because it was her duty, she said. And both our little boys, they—(*clenching his hands*)—they—oh!

HILDA. They did not get over *that?*

SOLNESS. No, *that* they did not get over. *That* was how we lost them.

HILDA. It must have been terribly hard for you.

SOLNESS. Hard enough for me; but ten times harder for Aline. (*Clenching his hands in suppressed fury.*) Oh, that such things should be allowed to happen here in the world! (*Shortly and firmly.*) From the day I lost them I had no heart for building churches.

HILDA. Did you not like the church-tower in our town?

SOLNESS. I didn't like it. I know how free and happy I felt when that tower was finished.

HILDA. *I* know that, too.

SOLNESS. And now I shall never—never build anything of that sort again! Neither churches nor church-towers.

HILDA (*nods slowly*). Nothing but houses for people to live in.

SOLNESS. Homes for human beings, Hilda.

HILDA. But homes with high towers and pinnacles upon them.

SOLNESS. If possible. (*Adopts a lighter tone.*) But, as I said before, that fire was the making of me—as a builder, I mean.

HILDA. Why don't you call yourself an architect, like the others?

SOLNESS. I have not been systematically enough taught for that. Most of what I know I have found out for myself.

HILDA. But you succeeded all the same.

SOLNESS. Yes, thanks to the fire. I laid out almost the whole of the garden in villa lots; and *there* I was able to build after my own heart. So I came to the front with a rush.

HILDA (*looks keenly at him*). You must surely be a very happy man, as matters stand with you.

SOLNESS (*gloomily*). Happy? Do *you* say that, too—like all the rest of them?

HILDA. Yes, I should say you must be. If you could only cease thinking about the two little children—

SOLNESS (*slowly*). The two little children—they are not so easy to forget, Hilda.

HILDA (*somewhat uncertainly*). Do you still feel their loss so much—after all these years?

SOLNESS (*looks fixedly at her, without replying*). A happy man you said—

HILDA. Well, now, aren't you happy—in other respects?

SOLNESS (*continues to look at her*). When I told you all this about the fire—h'm—

HILDA. Well?

SOLNESS. Was there not one special

thought that you—that you seized upon?

HILDA (*reflects in vain*). No. What thought should *that* be?

SOLNESS (*with subdued emphasis*). It was simply and solely by that fire that I was enabled to build homes for human beings. Cozy, comfortable, bright homes, where father and mother and the whole troop of children can live in safety and gladness, feeling what a happy thing it is to be alive in the world—and most of all to belong to each other—in great things and in small.

HILDA (*ardently*). Well, and is it not a great happiness for you to be able to build such beautiful homes?

SOLNESS. The price, Hilda! The terrible price I had to pay for the opportunity!

HILDA. But can you *never* get over that?

SOLNESS. No. That I might build homes for others, I had to forego—to forego for all time—the home that might have been my own. I mean a home for a troop of children—and for father and mother, too.

HILDA (*cautiously*). But *need* you have done that? For all time, you say?

SOLNESS (*nods slowly*). *That* was the price of this happiness that people talk about. (*Breathes heavily.*) This happiness—h'm—this happiness was not to be bought any cheaper, Hilda.

HILDA (*as before*). But may it not come right even yet?

SOLNESS. Never in this world—never. That is another consequence of the fire—and of Aline's illness afterwards.

HILDA (*looks at him with an indefinable expression*). And yet you build all these nurseries?

SOLNESS (*seriously*). Have you never noticed, Hilda, how the impossible—how it seems to beckon and cry aloud to one?

HILDA (*reflecting*). The impossible? (*With animation.*) Yes, indeed! Is that how *you* feel too?

SOLNESS. Yes, I do.

HILDA. Then there must be—a little of the troll in you too.

SOLNESS. Why of the troll?

HILDA. What would *you* call it, then?

SOLNESS (*rises*). Well, well, perhaps you are right. (*Vehemently.*) But how can I help turning into a troll, when this is how it always goes with me in everything—in everything!

HILDA. How do you mean?

SOLNESS (*speaking low, with inward emotion*). Mark what I say to you, Hilda. All that I have succeeded in doing, building, creating—all the beauty, security, cheerful comfort—aye, and magnificence too—(*Clenches his hands.*) Oh, is it not terrible even to think of—!

HILDA. *What* is so terrible?

SOLNESS. That all this I have to make up for, to pay for—not in money, but in human happiness. And not with my own happiness only, but with other people's too. Yes, yes, do you see *that*, Hilda? That is the price which my position as an artist has cost me—and others. And every single day I have to look on while the price is paid for me anew. Over again, and over again—and over again forever!

HILDA (*rises and looks steadily at him*). Now I can see that you are thinking of—of *her*.

SOLNESS. Yes, mainly of Aline. For Aline—*she*, too, had her vocation in life, just as much as I had mine. (*His voice quivers.*) But her vocation has had to be stunted, and crushed, and shattered—in order that mine might force its way to—to a sort of great victory. For you must know that Aline—she, too, had a talent for building.

HILDA. She! For building?

SOLNESS (*shakes his head*). Not houses and towers, and spires—not such things as I work away at—

HILDA. Well, but *what* then?

SOLNESS (*softly, with emotion*). For building up the souls of little children, Hilda. For building up children's souls in perfect balance, and in noble and beautiful forms. For enabling them to soar up into erect and full-grown human souls. *That* was Aline's talent. And there it all lies now—unused and unusable forever—of no earthly service to anyone—just like the ruins left by a fire.

HILDA. Yes, but even if this were so—?

SOLNESS. It is so! It is so! I know it!

HILDA. Well, but in any case it is not *your* fault.

SOLNESS (*fixes his eyes on her, and nods slowly*). Ah, *that* is the great, the terrible question. *That* is the doubt that is gnawing me—night and day.

HILDA. That?

SOLNESS. Yes. Suppose the fault *was* mine—in a certain sense.

HILDA. Your fault! The fire!

SOLNESS. All of it; the whole thing. And yet, perhaps—I may not have had anything to do with it.

HILDA (*looks at him with a troubled expression*). Oh, Mr. Solness—if you can talk like that, I am afraid you must be—ill, after all.

SOLNESS. H'm—I don't think I shall ever be of quite sound mind on that point.

(RAGNAR BROVIK *cautiously opens the little door in the left-hand corner.* HILDA *comes forward.*)

RAGNAR (*when he sees* HILDA). Oh, I beg pardon, Mr. Solness—

(*He makes a movement to withdraw.*)

SOLNESS. No, no, don't go. Let us get it over.

RAGNAR. Oh, yes—if only we could.

SOLNESS. I hear your father is no better.

RAGNAR. Father is fast growing weaker—and therefore I beg and implore you to write a few kind words for me on one of the plans! Something for father to read before he—

SOLNESS (*vehemently*). I won't hear anything more about those drawings of yours!

RAGNAR. Have you looked at them?

SOLNESS. Yes—I have.

RAGNAR. And they are good for nothing? And *I* am good for nothing, too?

SOLNESS (*evasively*). Stay here with me, Ragnar. You shall have everything your own way. And then you can marry Kaia, and live at your ease—and happily too, who knows? Only don't think of building on your own account.

RAGNAR. Well, well, then I must go home and tell father what you say—I promised I would.—*Is* this what I am to tell father—before he dies?

SOLNESS (*with a groan*). Oh, tell him—tell him what you will, for me. Best to say nothing at all to him! (*With a sudden outburst.*) I *cannot* do anything else, Ragnar!

RAGNAR. May I have the drawings to take with me?

SOLNESS. Yes, take them—take them by all means! They are lying there on the table.

RAGNAR (*goes to the table*). Thanks.

HILDA (*puts her hand on the portfolio*). No, no; leave them here.

SOLNESS. Why?

HILDA. Because I want to look at them, too.

SOLNESS. But you *have* been— (*To* RAGNAR.) Well, leave them here, then.

RAGNAR. Very well.

SOLNESS. And go home at once to your father.

RAGNAR. Yes, I suppose I must.

SOLNESS (*as if in desperation*). Ragnar—you *must* not ask me to do what is beyond my power! Do you hear, Ragnar? You *must* not!

RAGNAR. No, no. I beg your pardon—

(*He bows and goes out by the corner door.*

(HILDA *goes over and sits down on a chair near the mirror.*)

HILDA (*looks angrily at* SOLNESS). That was a very ugly thing to do.

SOLNESS. Do *you* think so, too?

HILDA. Yes, it was horribly ugly—and hard and bad and cruel as well.

SOLNESS. Oh, you don't understand my position.

HILDA. No matter—I say you ought not to be like that.

SOLNESS. You said yourself, only just now, that no one but *I* ought to be allowed to build.

HILDA. *I* may say such things—but *you* must not.

SOLNESS. I most of all, surely, who have paid so dear for my position.

HILDA. Oh, yes—with what you call domestic comfort—and that sort of thing.

SOLNESS. And with my peace of soul into the bargain.

HILDA (*rising*). Peace of soul! (*With feeling.*) Yes, yes, you are right in that! Poor Mr. Solness—you fancy that—

SOLNESS (*with a quiet, chuckling laugh*). Just sit down again, Hilda, and I'll tell you something funny.

HILDA (*sits down; with intent interest*). Well?

SOLNESS. It sounds such a ludicrous little thing; for, you see, the whole story turns upon nothing but a crack in a chimney.

HILDA. No more than that?

SOLNESS. No, not to begin with.

(*He moves a chair nearer to* HILDA *and sits down.*)

HILDA (*impatiently, taps on her knee*). Well, now for the crack in the chimney!

SOLNESS. I had noticed the split in the flue long, long before the fire. Every time I went up into the attic, I looked to see if it was still there.

HILDA. And it *was?*

SOLNESS. Yes; for no one else knew about it.

HILDA. And you said nothing?

SOLNESS. Nothing.

HILDA. And did not think of repairing the flue either?

SOLNESS. Oh, yes, I thought about it—but never got any further. Every time I intended to set to work, it seemed just as if a hand held me back. Not today, I thought—tomorrow; and nothing ever came of it.

HILDA. But why did you keep putting it off like that?

SOLNESS. Because I was revolving something in my mind. (*Slowly, and in a low voice.*) Through that little black crack in the chimney, I might, perhaps, force my way upwards—as a builder.

HILDA (*looking straight in front of her*). That must have been thrilling.

SOLNESS. Almost irresistible—quite irresistible. For at that time it appeared to me a perfectly simple and straightforward matter. I would have had it happen in the wintertime—a little before midday. I was to be out driving Aline in the sleigh. The servants at home would have made huge fires in the stoves.

HILDA. For, of course, it was to be bitterly cold that day?

SOLNESS. Rather biting, yes—and they would want Aline to find it thoroughly snug and warm when she came home.

HILDA. I suppose she is very chilly by nature?

SOLNESS. She *is*. And as we drove home, we were to see the smoke.

HILDA. Only the smoke?

SOLNESS. The smoke first. But when we came up to the garden gate, the whole of the old timberbox was to be a rolling mass of flames.—That is how I wanted it to be, you see.

HILDA. Oh, why, *why* couldn't it have happened so!

SOLNESS. You may well say that, Hilda.

HILDA. Well, but now listen, Mr. Solness. Are you perfectly certain that the fire was caused by that little crack in the chimney?

SOLNESS. No, on the contrary—I am perfectly certain that the crack in the chimney had nothing whatever to do with the fire.

HILDA. What!

SOLNESS. It has been clearly ascertained that the fire broke out in a clothes-cupboard—in a totally different part of the house.

HILDA. Then what is all this nonsense you are talking about the crack in the chimney!

SOLNESS. May I go on talking to you a little, Hilda?

HILDA. Yes, if you'll only talk sensibly—

SOLNESS. I will try to.

(*He moves his chair nearer.*)

HILDA. Out with it, then, Mr. Solness.

SOLNESS (*confidentially*). Don't you agree with me, Hilda, that there exist special, chosen people who have been endowed with the power and faculty of *desiring* a thing, *craving* for a thing, *willing* a thing—so persistently and so—so inexorably—that at last it *has* to happen? Don't you believe that?

HILDA (*with an indefinable expression in her eyes*). If that is so, we shall see, one of these days, whether *I* am one of the chosen.

SOLNESS. It is not oneself *alone* that can do such great things. Oh, no—the helpers and the servers—they must do their part too, if it is to be of any good. But they never come of themselves. One has to call upon them very persistently—inwardly, you understand.

HILDA. What are these helpers and servers?

SOLNESS. Oh, we can talk about that some other time. For the present, let us keep to this business of the fire.

HILDA. Don't you think that fire would have happened all the same—even without your wishing for it?

SOLNESS. If the house had been old Knut Brovik's, it would never have burnt down so conveniently for *him*. I am sure of that; for he does not know how to call for the helpers—no, nor for the servers, either. (*Rises in unrest.*) So you see, Hilda—it is my fault, after all, that the lives of the two little boys had to be sacrificed. And do you think it is not my fault, too, that Aline has never been the woman she should and might have been—and that she most longed to be?

HILDA. Yes, but if it is all the work of those helpers and servers—?

SOLNESS. Who called for the helpers and servers? It was I! And they came and obeyed my will. (*In increasing excitement.*) That is what people call having the luck on your side; but I must tell you what this sort of luck feels like! It feels like a great raw place here on my breast. And the helpers and servers keep on flaying pieces of skin off other people in order to close *my* sore!—But still the sore is not healed —never, never! Oh, if you knew how it can sometimes gnaw and burn!

HILDA (*looks attentively at him*). You are ill, Mr. Solness. Very ill, I almost think.

SOLNESS. Say *mad;* for that is what you mean.

HILDA. No, I don't think there is much amiss with your intellect.

SOLNESS. With *what* then? Out with it!

HILDA. I wonder whether you were not sent into the world with a sickly conscience.

SOLNESS. A sickly conscience? What devilry is that?

HILDA. I mean that your conscience is feeble—too delicately built, as it were—hasn't strength to take a grip of things—to lift and bear what is heavy.

SOLNESS (*growls*). H'm! May I ask, then, what sort of a conscience one ought to have?

HILDA. I should like *your* conscience to be—to be thoroughly robust.

SOLNESS. Indeed? Robust, eh? Is your own conscience robust, may I ask?

HILDA. Yes, I think it is. I have never noticed that it wasn't.

SOLNESS. It has not been put very severely to the test, I should think.

HILDA (*with a quivering of the lips*). Oh, it was no such simple matter to leave father—I am so awfully fond of him.

SOLNESS. Dear me! for a month or two—

HILDA. I think I shall never go home again.

SOLNESS. Never? Then why did you leave him?

HILDA (*half-seriously, half-banteringly*). Have you forgotten again that the ten years are up?

SOLNESS. Oh, nonsense. Was anything wrong at home? Eh?

HILDA (*quite seriously*). It was this impulse within me that urged and goaded me to come—and lured and drew me on, as well.

SOLNESS (*eagerly*). There we have it! There we have it, Hilda! There is a troll in you too, as in me. For it's the troll in one, you see—it is *that* that calls to the powers outside us. And then you *must* give in—whether you will or no.

HILDA. I almost think you are right, Mr. Solness.

SOLNESS (*walks about the room*). Oh, there are devils innumerable abroad in the world, Hilda, that one never *sees!*

HILDA. Devils, too?

SOLNESS (*stops*). Good devils and bad devils; light-haired devils and black-haired devils. If only you could always tell whether it is the light or dark ones that have got hold of you! (*Paces about.*) Ho-ho! Then it would be simple enough!

HILDA (*follows him with her eyes*). Or if one had a really vigorous, radiantly healthy conscience—so that one *dared* to do what one *would*.

SOLNESS (*stops beside the console table*). I believe, now, that most people are just as puny creatures as I am in that respect.

HILDA. I shouldn't wonder.

SOLNESS (*leaning against the table*). In the sagas— Have you read any of the old sagas?

HILDA. Oh, yes! When I used to read books, I—

SOLNESS. In the sagas you read about vikings, who sailed to foreign lands, and plundered and burned and killed men—

HILDA. And carried off women—

SOLNESS. —and kept them in captivity—

HILDA. —took them home in their ships—

SOLNESS. —and behaved to them like —like the very worst of trolls.

HILDA (*looks straight before her, with a half-veiled look*). I think *that* must have been thrilling.

SOLNESS (*with a short, deep laugh*). To carry off women, eh?

HILDA. To *be* carried off.

SOLNESS (*looks at her a moment*). Oh, indeed.

HILDA (*as if breaking the thread of the conversation*). But what made you speak of these vikings, Mr. Solness?

SOLNESS. Why, *those* fellows must have had robust consciences, if you like! When they got home again, they could eat and drink, and be as happy as children. And the women, too! They often would not leave them on any account. Can you understand that, Hilda?

HILDA. Those women I can understand exceedingly well.

SOLNESS. Oho! Perhaps you could do the same yourself?

HILDA. Why not?

SOLNESS. Live—of your own free will—with a ruffian like that?

HILDA. If it was a ruffian I had come to love—

SOLNESS. *Could* you come to love a man like that?

HILDA. Good heavens, you know very well one can't choose whom one is going to love.

SOLNESS (*looks meditatively at her*). Oh, no, I suppose it is the troll within one that's responsible for that.

HILDA (*half-laughing*). And all those blessèd devils, that *you* know so well—both the light-haired and the dark-haired ones.

SOLNESS (*quietly and warmly*). Then I hope with all my heart that the devils will choose carefully for you, Hilda.

HILDA. For me they *have* chosen already—once and for all.

SOLNESS (*looks earnestly at her*). Hilda—you are like a wild bird of the woods.

HILDA. Far from it. I don't hide myself away under the bushes.

SOLNESS. No, no. There is rather something of the bird of prey in you.

HILDA. That is nearer it—perhaps. (*Very vehemently.*) And why not a bird of prey? Why should not *I* go a-hunting—I, as well as the rest? Carry off the prey I want—if only I can get my claws into it, and do with it as I will.

SOLNESS. Hilda—do you know what you are?

HILDA. Yes, I suppose I am a strange sort of bird.

SOLNESS. No. You are like a dawning day. When I look at you—I seem to be looking towards the sunrise.

HILDA. Tell me, Mr. Solness—are you certain that you have never called me to you? Inwardly, you know?

SOLNESS (*softly and slowly*). I almost think I must have.

HILDA. What did you want with me?

SOLNESS. You are the younger generation, Hilda.

HILDA (*smiles*). That younger generation that you are so afraid of?

SOLNESS (*nods slowly*). And which, in my heart, I yearn towards so deeply.

(HILDA *rises, goes to the little table, and fetches* RAGNAR BROVIK'*s portfolio.*)

HILDA (*holds out the portfolio to him*). We were talking of these drawings—

SOLNESS (*shortly, waving them away*). Put those things away! I have seen enough of them.

HILDA. Yes, but you have to write your approval on them.

SOLNESS. Write my approval on them? Never!

HILDA. But the poor old man is lying at death's door! Can't you give him and his son this pleasure before they are parted? And perhaps he might get the commission to carry them out, too.

SOLNESS. Yes, that is just what he would get. He has made sure of that—has my fine gentleman!

HILDA. Then, good heavens—if that is so—can't you tell the least little bit of a lie for once in a way?

SOLNESS. A lie? (*Raging.*) Hilda—take those devil's drawings out of my sight!

HILDA (*draws the portfolio a little nearer to herself*). Well, well, well—don't bite me.—You talk of trolls—but I think you go on like a troll yourself. (*Looks around.*) Where do you keep your pen and ink?

SOLNESS. There is nothing of the sort in here.

HILDA (*goes towards the door*). But in the office where that young lady is—

SOLNESS. Stay where you are, Hilda!—I ought to tell a lie, you say. Oh, yes, for the sake of his old father I might well do that—for in my time I have crushed him, trodden him under foot—

HILDA. Him, too?

SOLNESS. I needed room for myself. But this Ragnar—he must on no account be allowed to come to the front.

HILDA. Poor fellow, there is surely no fear of that. If he has nothing in him—

SOLNESS (*comes closer, looks at her, and whispers*). If Ragnar Brovik gets his chance, he will strike me to the earth. Crush me—as I crushed his father.

HILDA. Crush you? Has he the ability for that?

SOLNESS. Yes, you may depend upon it *he* has the ability! He is the younger generation that stands ready to knock at my door—to make an end of Halvard Solness.

HILDA (*looks at him with quiet reproach*). And yet you would bar him out. Fie, Mr. Solness!

SOLNESS. The fight I have been fighting has cost heart's blood enough.—And I am afraid, too, that the helpers and servers will not obey me any longer.

HILDA. Then you must go ahead without them. There is nothing else for it.

SOLNESS. It is hopeless, Hilda. The luck is bound to turn. A little sooner or a little later. Retribution is inexorable.

HILDA (*in distress, putting her hands over her ears*). Don't talk like that! Do you want to kill me? To take from me what is more than my life?

SOLNESS. And what is that?

HILDA. The longing to see you great. To see you, with a wreath in your hand, high, high up on a church-tower. (*Calm again.*) Come, out with your pencil now. You must have a pencil about you.

SOLNESS (*takes out his pocketbook*). I have one here.

HILDA (*lays the portfolio on the sofa-table*). Very well. Now let us two sit down here, Mr. Solness. (SOLNESS *seats himself at the table.* HILDA *stands behind him, leaning over the back of the chair.*) And now we will write on the drawings. We must write very, very nicely and cordially—for this horrid Ruar—or whatever his name is.

SOLNESS (*writes a few words, turns his head, and looks at her*). Tell me one thing, Hilda.

HILDA. Yes!

SOLNESS. If you have been waiting for me all these ten years—

HILDA. What then?

SOLNESS. Why have you never written to me? Then I could have answered you.

HILDA (*hastily*). No, no, no! That was just what I did not want.

SOLNESS. Why not?

HILDA. I was afraid the whole thing might fall to pieces.—But we were going to write on the drawings, Mr. Solness.

SOLNESS. So we were.

HILDA (*bends forward and looks over his shoulder while he writes*). Mind now, kindly and cordially! Oh, how I hate—how I hate this Ruald—

SOLNESS (*writing*). Have you never really cared for anyone, Hilda?

HILDA (*harshly*). What do you say?

SOLNESS. Have you never cared for anyone?

HILDA. For anyone else, I suppose you mean?

SOLNESS (*looks up at her*). For anyone else, yes. Have you never? In all these ten years? Never?

HILDA. Oh, yes, now and then. When I was perfectly furious with you for not coming.

SOLNESS. Then you did take an interest in other people, too?

HILDA. A little bit—for a week or so. Good heavens, Mr. Solness, you surely know how such things come about.

SOLNESS. Hilda—what is it you have come for?

HILDA. Don't waste time talking. The poor old man might go and die in the meantime.

SOLNESS. Answer me, Hilda. What do you want of me?

HILDA. I want my kingdom.

SOLNESS. H'm—
(He gives a rapid glance towards the door on the left and then goes on writing on the drawings. At the same moment MRS. SOLNESS *enters; she has some packages in her hand.)*

MRS. SOLNESS. Here are a few things I have got for you, Miss Wangel. The large parcels will be sent later on.

HILDA. Oh, how very, very kind of you!

MRS. SOLNESS. Only my simple duty. Nothing more than that.

SOLNESS (*reading over what he has written*). Aline!

MRS. SOLNESS. Yes?

SOLNESS. Did you notice whether the—the bookkeeper was out there?

MRS. SOLNESS. Yes, of course, *she* was there.

SOLNESS (*puts the drawings in the portfolio*). H'm—

MRS. SOLNESS. She was standing at the desk, as she always is—when *I* go through the room.

SOLNESS (*rises*). Then I'll give this to her and tell her that—

HILDA (*takes the portfolio from him*). Oh, no, let me have the pleasure of doing that! (*Goes to the door but turns.*) What is her name?

SOLNESS. Her name is Miss Fosli.

HILDA. Pooh, that sounds so cold! Her Christian name, I mean.

SOLNESS. Kaia—I believe.

HILDA (*opens the door and calls out*). Kaia, come in here! Make haste! Mr. Solness wants to speak to you.

(KAIA FOSLI *appears at the door.*)

KAIA (*looking at him in alarm*). Here I am—

HILDA (*handing her the portfolio*). See here, Kaia! You can take this home; Mr. Solness has written on them now.

KAIA. Oh, at last!

SOLNESS. Give them to the old man as soon as you can.

KAIA. I will go straight home with them.

SOLNESS. Yes, do. Now Ragnar will have a chance of building for himself.

KAIA. Oh, may he come and thank you for all—?

SOLNESS (*harshly*). I won't have any thanks! Tell him *that* from me.

KAIA. Yes, I will—

SOLNESS. And tell him at the same time that henceforward I do not require his services—nor yours either.

KAIA (*softly and quiveringly*). Not mine either?

SOLNESS. You will have other things to think of now and to attend to; and that is a very good thing for you. Well, go home with the drawings now, Miss Fosli. At once! Do you hear?

KAIA (*as before*). Yes, Mr. Solness.

(*She goes out.*)

MRS. SOLNESS. Heavens! What deceitful eyes she has.

SOLNESS. She? That poor little creature?

MRS. SOLNESS. Oh—I can see what I can see, Halvard.—Are you really dismissing them?

SOLNESS. Yes.

MRS. SOLNESS. Her as well?

SOLNESS. Was not that what you wished?

MRS. SOLNESS. But how can you get on without *her*—? Oh well, no doubt you have someone else in reserve, Halvard.

HILDA (*playfully*). Well, *I* for one am not the person to stand at that desk.

SOLNESS. Never mind, never mind—it will be all right, Aline. Now all you have to do is to think about moving into our new home—as quickly as you can. This evening we will hang up the wreath —(*Turns to* HILDA.)—right on the very pinnacle of the tower. What do you say to *that,* Miss Hilda?

HILDA (*looks at him with sparkling eyes*). It will be splendid to see you so high up once more.

SOLNESS. Me!

MRS. SOLNESS. For Heaven's sake, Miss Wangel, don't imagine such a thing! My husband!—when he always gets so dizzy!

HILDA. *He* gets dizzy! No, I know quite well he does not!

MRS. SOLNESS. Oh, yes, indeed he does.

HILDA. But I have seen him with my own eyes right up at the top of a high church-tower!

MRS. SOLNESS. Yes, I hear people talk of that; but it is utterly impossible—

SOLNESS (*vehemently*). Impossible—impossible, yes! But there I stood all the same!

MRS. SOLNESS. Oh, how can you say so, Halvard? Why, you can't even bear to go out on the second-story balcony here. You have always been like that.

SOLNESS. You may perhaps see something different this evening.

MRS. SOLNESS (*in alarm*). No, no, no! Please God I shall never see that. I will write at once to the doctor—and I am sure he won't let you do it.

SOLNESS. Why, Aline—!

MRS. SOLNESS. Oh, you know you're ill, Halvard. This *proves* it! Oh, God—Oh, God!

(*She goes hastily out to the right.*)

HILDA (*looks intently at him*). Is it so, or is it not?

SOLNESS. That I turn dizzy?

HILDA. That my master builder *dares* not—*cannot*—climb as high as he builds?

SOLNESS. Is that the way you look at it?

HILDA. Yes.

SOLNESS. I believe there is scarcely a corner in me that is safe from you.

HILDA (*looks towards the bay-window*). Up there, then. Right up there—

SOLNESS (*approaches her*). You might have the topmost room in the tower, Hilda—there you might live like a princess.

HILDA (*indefinably, between earnest and jest*). Yes, that is what you promised me.

SOLNESS. *Did* I really?

HILDA. Fie, Mr. Solness! You said I should be a princess and that you would give me a kingdom. And then you went and—Well!

SOLNESS (*cautiously*). Are you quite certain that this is not a dream—a fancy, that has fixed itself in your mind?

HILDA (*sharply*). Do you mean that you did not do it?

SOLNESS. I scarcely know myself. (*More softly.*) But now I know *so much* for certain, that I—

HILDA. That you—? Say it at once!

SOLNESS.—that I *ought* to have done it.

HILDA (*exclaims with animation*). Don't tell me *you* can ever be dizzy!

SOLNESS. This evening, then, we will hang up the wreath—Princess Hilda.

HILDA (*with a bitter curve of the lips*). Over your new home, yes.

SOLNESS. Over the new house, which will never be a *home* for *me*.

(*He goes out through the garden door.*)

HILDA (*looks straight in front of her with a faraway expression and whispers to herself. The only words audible are*)—frightfully thrilling—

CURTAIN

ACT THREE

The large, broad veranda of SOLNESS'S *dwellinghouse. Part of the house, with outer door leading to the veranda, is seen to the left. A railing along the veranda to the right. At the back, from the end of the veranda, a flight of steps leads down to the garden below. Tall old trees in the garden spread their branches over the veranda and towards the house. Far to the right, in among the trees, a glimpse is caught of the lower part of the new villa, with scaffolding round so much as is seen of the tower. In the background the garden is bounded by an old wooden fence. Outside the fence, a street with low, tumbledown cottages.*

Evening sky with sunlit clouds.

On the veranda, a garden bench stands along the wall of the house, and in front of the bench a long table. On the other side of the table, an armchair and some stools. All the furniture is of wickerwork.

MRS. SOLNESS, *wrapped in a large white crape shawl, sits resting in the armchair and gazes over to the right. Shortly after,* HILDA WANGEL *comes up the flight of steps from the garden. She is dressed as in the last act and wears her hat. She has in her bodice a little nosegay of small common flowers.*

MRS. SOLNESS (*turning her head a little*). Have you been round the garden, Miss Wangel?

HILDA. Yes, I have been taking a look at it.

MRS. SOLNESS. And found some flowers too, I see.

HILDA. Yes, indeed! There are such heaps of them in among the bushes.

MRS. SOLNESS. Are there really? Still? You see I scarcely ever go there.

HILDA (*closer*). What! Don't you take a run down into the garden every day, then?

MRS. SOLNESS (*with a faint smile*). I don't "run" anywhere, nowadays.

HILDA. Well, but do you not go down now and then to look at all the lovely things there?

MRS. SOLNESS. It has all become so strange to me. I am almost afraid to see it again.

HILDA. Your own garden!

MRS. SOLNESS. I don't feel that it is *mine* any longer.

HILDA. What do you mean—?

MRS. SOLNESS. No, no, it is not—not as it was in my mother's and father's time. They have taken away so much—so much of the garden, Miss Wangel. Fancy—they have parceled it out—and built houses for strangers—people that I don't know. And *they* can sit and look in upon me from their windows.

HILDA (*with a bright expression*). Mrs. Solness!

MRS. SOLNESS. Yes!

HILDA. May I stay here with you a little?

MRS. SOLNESS. Yes, by all means, if you care to.

(HILDA *moves a stool close to the armchair and sits down.*)

HILDA. Ah—here one can sit and sun oneself like a cat.

MRS. SOLNESS (*lays her hand softly on* HILDA's *neck*). It is nice of you to be willing to sit with me. I thought you wanted to go in to my husband.

HILDA. What should I want with him?

MRS. SOLNESS. To help him, I thought.

HILDA. No, thank you. And besides, he is not in. He is over there with his workmen. But he looked so fierce that I did not dare to talk to him.

MRS. SOLNESS. He is so kind and gentle in reality.

HILDA. He!

MRS. SOLNESS. You do not really know him yet, Miss Wangel.

HILDA (*looks affectionately at her*). Are you pleased at the thought of moving over to the new house?

MRS. SOLNESS. I *ought* to be pleased; for it is what Halvard wants—

HILDA. Oh, not just on that account, surely.

MRS. SOLNESS. Yes, yes, Miss Wangel; for it is only my duty to submit myself to *him*. But very often it is dreadfully difficult to force one's mind to obedience.

HILDA. Yes, that must be difficult indeed.

MRS. SOLNESS. I can tell you it is—when one has so many faults as I have—

HILDA. When one has gone through so much trouble as you have—

MRS. SOLNESS. How do you know about that?

HILDA. Your husband told me.

MRS. SOLNESS. To me he very seldom mentions these things.—Yes, I can tell you I have gone through more than enough trouble in my life, Miss Wangel.

HILDA (*looks sympathetically at her and nods slowly*). Poor Mrs. Solness. First of all there was the fire—

MRS. SOLNESS (*with a sigh*). Yes, everything that was *mine* was burnt.

HILDA. And then came what was worse.

MRS. SOLNESS (*looking inquiringly at her*). Worse?

HILDA. The worst of all.

MRS. SOLNESS. What do you mean?

HILDA (*softly*). You lost the two little boys.

MRS. SOLNESS. Oh, yes, the boys. But, you see, *that* was a thing apart. That was a dispensation of Providence; and in such things one can only bow in submission—yes, and be thankful, too.

HILDA. Then you are so?

MRS. SOLNESS. Not always, I am sorry to say. I know well enough that it is my duty—but all the same I *cannot*.

HILDA. No, no, I think that is only natural.

MRS. SOLNESS. And often and often I have to remind myself that it was a righteous punishment for me—

HILDA. Why?

MRS. SOLNESS. Because I had not fortitude enough in misfortune.

HILDA. But I don't see that—

MRS. SOLNESS. Oh, no, no, Miss Wangel—do not talk to me any more about the two little boys. We ought to feel nothing but joy in thinking of *them;* for they are so happy—so happy now. No, it is the *small* losses in life that cut one to the heart—the loss of all that other people look upon as almost nothing.

HILDA (*lays her arms on* MRS. SOLNESS'S *knees and looks up at her affectionately*). Dear Mrs. Solness—tell me what things you mean!

MRS. SOLNESS. As I say, only little things. All the old portraits were burnt on the walls. And all the old silk dresses were burnt, that had belonged to the family for generations and generations. And all mother's and grandmother's lace—that was burnt, too. And only think—the jewels, too! (*Sadly.*) And then all the dolls.

HILDA. The dolls?

MRS. SOLNESS (*choking with tears*). I had nine lovely dolls.

HILDA. And *they* were burnt too?

MRS. SOLNESS. All of them. Oh, it was hard—so hard for me.

HILDA. Had you put by all these dolls, then? Ever since you were little?

MRS. SOLNESS. I had not put them by. The dolls and I had gone on living together.

HILDA. After you were grown up?

MRS. SOLNESS. Yes, long after that.

HILDA. After you were married, too?

MRS. SOLNESS. Oh, yes, indeed. So long as he did not see it—But they were all burnt up, poor things. No one thought of saving *them*. Oh, it is so miserable to think of. You mustn't laugh at me, Miss Wangel.

HILDA. I am not laughing in the least.

MRS. SOLNESS. For you see, in a certain sense, there was life in them, too. I carried them under my heart—like little unborn children.

(DR. HERDAL, *with his hat in his hand, comes out through the door and observes* MRS. SOLNESS *and* HILDA.)

DR. HERDAL. Well, Mrs. Solness, so you are sitting out here catching cold?

MRS. SOLNESS. I find it so pleasant and warm here today.

Dr. Herdal. Yes, yes. But is there anything going on here? I got a note from you.

Mrs. Solness (*rises*). Yes, there is something I must talk to you about.

Dr. Herdal. Very well; then perhaps we had better go in. (*To* Hilda.) Still in your mountaineering dress, Miss Wangel?

Hilda (*gaily, rising*). Yes—in full uniform! But today I am not going climbing and breaking my neck. We two will stop quietly below and look on, Doctor.

Dr. Herdal. What are we to look on at?

Mrs. Solness (*softly, in alarm, to* Hilda). Hush, hush—for God's sake! He is coming! Try to get that idea out of his head. And let us be friends, Miss Wangel. Don't you think we can?

Hilda (*throws her arms impetuously round* Mrs. Solness's *neck*). Oh, if we only could!

Mrs. Solness (*gently disengages herself*). There, there, there! There he comes, Doctor. Let me have a word with you.

Dr. Herdal. Is it about *him*?

Mrs. Solness. Yes, to be sure it's about him. Do come in.

(*She and the* Doctor *enter the house. Next moment* Solness *comes up from the garden by the flight of steps. A serious look comes over* Hilda's *face.*)

Solness (*glances at the house door, which is closed cautiously from within*). Have you noticed, Hilda, that as soon as I come, she goes?

Hilda. I have noticed that as soon as you come, you *make* her go.

Solness. Perhaps so. But I cannot help it. (*Looks observantly at her.*) Are you cold, Hilda? I think you look cold.

Hilda. I have just come out of a tomb.

Solness. What do you mean by *that*?

Hilda. That I have got chilled through and through, Mr. Solness.

Solness (*slowly*). I believe I understand—.

Hilda. What brings you up here just now?

Solness. I caught sight of you from over there.

Hilda. But then you must have seen her too?

Solness. I knew she would go at once if I came.

Hilda. Is it very painful for you that she should avoid you in this way?

Solness. In one sense, it's a relief as well.

Hilda. Not to have her before your eyes?

Solness. Yes.

Hilda. Not to be always seeing how heavily the loss of the little boys weighs upon her?

Solness. Yes. Chiefly that.

(Hilda *drifts across the veranda with her hands behind her back, stops at the railing, and looks out over the garden.*)

Solness (*after a short pause*). Did you have a long talk with her?

(Hilda *stands motionless and does not answer.*)

Solness. Did you have a long talk, I asked?

(Hilda *is silent as before.*)

Solness. What was she talking about, Hilda?

(Hilda *continues silent.*)

Solness. Poor Aline! I suppose it was about the little boys. (*A nervous shudder runs through* Hilda; *then she nods hurriedly once or twice.*) She will never get over it—never in this world. (*Approaches her.*) Now you are standing there again like a statue; just as you stood last night.

Hilda (*turns and looks at him, with great serious eyes*). I am going away.

Solness. Going away!

Hilda. Yes.

Solness. But I won't allow you to!

Hilda. What am I to do *here* now?

Solness. Simply to *be* here, Hilda!

Hilda (*measures him with a look*). Oh,

thank you. You know it wouldn't end *there*.

SOLNESS (*heedlessly*). So much the better!

HILDA (*vehemently*). I *cannot* do any harm to one whom I know! I can't take away anything that belongs to her.

SOLNESS. Who wants you to do that?

HILDA (*continuing*). A stranger, yes! for that is quite a different thing! A person I have never set eyes on. But one that I have come into close contact with—! Oh, no! Oh, no! Ugh!

SOLNESS. Yes, but I never proposed you should.

HILDA. Oh, Mr. Solness, you know quite well what the end of it would be. And that is why I am going away.

SOLNESS. And what is to become of *me* when you are gone? What shall I have to live for *then?*—After that?

HILDA (*with the indefinable look in her eyes*). It is surely not so hard for *you*. You have your duties to her. Live for those duties.

SOLNESS. Too late. These powers—these—these—

HILDA.—devils—

SOLNESS. Yes, these devils! And the troll within me as well—they have drawn all the lifeblood out of her. (*Laughs in desperation.*) They did it for my *happiness!* Yes, yes! (*Sadly.*) And now she is dead—for my sake. And I am chained alive to a dead woman. (*In wild anguish.*) I—I who cannot live without joy in life!

(HILDA *moves round the table and seats herself on the bench with her elbows on the table and her head supported by her hands.*)

HILDA (*sits and looks at him awhile*). What will you build next?

SOLNESS (*shakes his head*). I don't believe I shall build much more.

HILDA. Not those cozy, happy homes for mother and father and for the troop of children?

SOLNESS. I wonder whether there will be any use for such homes in the coming time.

HILDA. Poor Mr. Solness! And you have gone all these ten years—and staked your whole life—on that alone.

SOLNESS. Yes, you may well say so, Hilda.

HILDA (*with an outburst*). Oh, it all seems to me so foolish—so foolish!

SOLNESS. All what?

HILDA. Not to be able to grasp at your own happiness—at your own life! Merely because someone you know happens to stand in the way!

SOLNESS. One whom you have no right to set aside.

HILDA. I wonder whether one really has *not* the right! And yet, and yet—Oh! if one could only sleep the whole thing away!

(*She lays her arms flat down on the table, rests the left side of her head on her hands, and shuts her eyes.*)

SOLNESS (*turns the armchair and sits down at the table*). Had *you* a cozy, happy home—up there with your father, Hilda?

HILDA (*without stirring, answers as if half asleep*). I had only a cage.

SOLNESS. And you are determined not to go back to it?

HILDA (*as before*). The wild bird never wants to go into the cage.

SOLNESS. Rather range through the free air—

HILDA (*still as before*). The bird of prey loves to range—

SOLNESS (*lets his eyes rest on her*). If only one had the viking-spirit in life—

HILDA (*in her usual voice; opens her eyes but does not move*). And the other thing? Say what *that* was!

SOLNESS. A robust conscience.

(HILDA *sits erect on the bench, with animation. Her eyes have once more the sparkling expression of gladness.*)

HILDA (*nods to him*). *I* know what you are going to build next!

SOLNESS. Then you know more than I do, Hilda.

HILDA. Yes, builders are such stupid people.

SOLNESS. What is it to be then?

HILDA (*nods again*). The castle.

SOLNESS. What castle?

HILDA. My castle, of course.

SOLNESS. Do you want a castle now?

HILDA. Don't you owe me a kingdom, I should like to know?

SOLNESS. You say I do.

HILDA. Well—you admit you owe me this kingdom. And you can't have a kingdom without a royal castle, I should think!

SOLNESS (*more and more animated*). Yes, they usually go together.

HILDA. Good! Then build it for me! This moment!

SOLNESS (*laughing*). Must you have that on the instant, too?

HILDA. Yes, to be sure! For the ten years are up now, and I am not going to wait any longer. So—out with the castle, Mr. Solness!

SOLNESS. It's no light matter to owe *you* anything, Hilda.

HILDA. You should have thought of that before. It is too late now. So—(*Tapping the table.*)—the castle on the table! It is *my* castle! I will have it *at once!*

SOLNESS (*more seriously, leans over towards her, with his arms on the table*). What sort of castle have you imagined, Hilda?

(*Her expression becomes more and more veiled. She seems gazing inwards at herself.*)

HILDA (*slowly*). My castle shall stand on a height—on a very great height—with a clear outlook on all sides, so that I can see far—far around.

SOLNESS. And no doubt it is to have a high tower!

HILDA. A tremendously high tower. And at the very top of the tower there shall be a balcony. And I will stand out upon it—

SOLNESS (*involuntarily clutches at his forehead*). How can you like to stand at such a dizzy height—?

HILDA. Yes, I will! Right up there will I stand and look down on the other people—on those that are building churches, and homes for mother and father and the troop of children. And *you* may come up and look on at it, too.

SOLNESS (*in a low tone*). Is the builder to be allowed to come up beside the princess?

HILDA. If the builder *will*.

SOLNESS (*more softly*). Then I think the builder will come.

HILDA (*nods*). The builder—he will come.

SOLNESS. But he will never be able to build any more. Poor builder!

HILDA (*animated*). Oh, yes, he will! We two will set to work together. And then we will build the loveliest—the very loveliest—thing in all the world.

SOLNESS (*intently*). Hilda—tell me what that is!

HILDA (*looks smilingly at him, shakes her head a little, pouts, and speaks as if to a child*). Builders—they are such very—very stupid people.

SOLNESS. Yes, no doubt they are stupid. But now tell me what it is—the loveliest thing in the world—that we two are to build together.

HILDA (*is silent a little while, then says with an indefinable expression in her eyes*). Castles in the air.

SOLNESS. Castles in the air?

HILDA (*nods*). Castles in the air, yes! Do you know what sort of thing a castle in the air is?

SOLNESS. It is the loveliest thing in the world, you say.

HILDA (*rises with vehemence and makes a gesture of repulsion with her hand*). Yes, to be sure it is! Castles in the air—they are so easy to take refuge in. And so easy to build, too—(*Looks scornfully at him.*)—especially for the builders who have a—a dizzy conscience.

SOLNESS. (*rises*). After this day we two will build together, Hilda.

HILDA (*with a half-dubious smile*). A *real* castle in the air?

SOLNESS. Yes. One with a firm foundation under it.

(RAGNAR BROVIK *comes out from the house. He is carrying a large, green wreath with flowers and silk ribbons.*)

HILDA (*with an outburst of pleasure*). The wreath! Oh, that will be glorious!

SOLNESS (*in surprise*). Have *you* brought the wreath, Ragnar?

RAGNAR. I promised the foreman I would.

SOLNESS (*relieved*). Ah, then I suppose your father is better?

RAGNAR. No.

SOLNESS. Was he not cheered by what I wrote?

RAGNAR. It came too late.

SOLNESS. Too late!

RAGNAR. When she came with it he was unconscious. He had had a stroke.

SOLNESS. Why, then, you must go home to him! You must attend to your father!

RAGNAR. He does not need me any more.

SOLNESS. But surely you ought to be with him.

RAGNAR. *She* is sitting by his bed.

SOLNESS (*rather uncertainly*). Kaia?

RAGNAR (*looking darkly at him*). Yes—Kaia.

SOLNESS. Go home, Ragnar—both to him and to her. Give *me* the wreath.

RAGNAR (*suppresses a mocking smile*). You don't mean that you yourself—?

SOLNESS. I will take it down to them myself. (*Takes the wreath from him.*) And now you go home; we don't require you today.

RAGNAR. I know you do not require me any more; but today I shall remain.

SOLNESS. Well, remain then, since you are bent upon it.

HILDA (*at the railing*). Mr. Solness, I will stand here and look on at you.

SOLNESS. At me!

HILDA. It will be fearfully thrilling.

SOLNESS (*in a low tone*). We will talk about that presently, Hilda.

(*He goes down the flight of steps with the wreath and away through the garden.*)

HILDA (*looks after him, then turns to* RAGNAR). I think you might at least have thanked him.

RAGNAR. Thanked him? Ought I to have thanked *him?*

HILDA. Yes, of course you ought!

RAGNAR. I think it is rather *you* I ought to thank.

HILDA. How can you say such a thing?

RAGNAR (*without answering her*). But I advise you to take care, Miss Wangel! For you don't know *him* rightly yet.

HILDA (*ardently*). Oh, no one knows him as I do!

RAGNAR (*laughs in exasperation*). Thank him, when he has held me down year after year! When he made father disbelieve in me—made me disbelieve in myself! And all merely that he might—!

HILDA (*as if divining something*). That he might—? Tell me at once!

RAGNAR. That he might keep her with him.

HILDA (*with a start towards him*). The girl at the desk?

RAGNAR. Yes.

HILDA (*threateningly, clenching her hands*). That is not true! You are telling falsehoods about him!

RAGNAR. I would not believe it either until today—when she said so herself.

HILDA (*as if beside herself*). *What* did she say? I *will* know! At once! at once!

RAGNAR. She said that he had taken possession of her mind—her whole mind—centered all her thoughts upon himself alone. She says that she can never leave him—that she will remain here, where *he* is—

HILDA (*with flashing eyes*). She will not be allowed to!

RAGNAR (*as if feeling his way*). Who will not allow her?

HILDA (*rapidly*). *He* will not either!

RAGNAR. Oh, no—I understand the whole thing now. After this, she would merely be—in the way.

HILDA. You understand nothing—since you can talk like that! No, *I* will tell you why he kept hold of her.

RAGNAR. Well then, why?

HILDA. In order to keep hold of you.

RAGNAR. Has he told you so?

HILDA. No, but it *is* so. It *must* be so! (*Wildly.*) I will—I *will* have it so!

RAGNAR. And at the very moment when *you* came—he let her go.

HILDA. It was *you—you* that he let go! What do you suppose he cares about strange women like her?

RAGNAR (*reflects*). Is it possible that all this time he has been afraid of me?

HILDA. He afraid! I would not be so conceited if I were you.

RAGNAR. Oh, he must have seen long ago that I had something in me, too. Besides—cowardly—that is just what he is, you see.

HILDA. He! Oh, yes, I am likely to believe *that!*

RAGNAR. In a certain sense he *is* cowardly—he, the great master builder. He is not afraid of robbing others of their life's happiness—as he has done both for my father and for me. But when it comes to climbing up a paltry bit of scaffolding—he will do anything rather than *that.*

HILDA. Oh, you should just have seen him high, high up—at the dizzy height where I once saw him.

RAGNAR. Did you see that?

HILDA. Yes, indeed I did. How free and great he looked as he stood and fastened the wreath to the church vane!

RAGNAR. I know that he ventured that, *once* in his life—one solitary time. It is a legend among us younger men. But no power on earth would induce him to do it again.

HILDA. Today he will do it again!

RAGNAR (*scornfully*). Yes, I dare say!

HILDA. We shall see it!

RAGNAR. That neither you nor I will see.

HILDA (*with uncontrollable vehemence*). I *will* see it! I *will* and I *must* see it!

RAGNAR. But he will not do it. He simply dare not do it. For you see he cannot get over this infirmity—master builder though he be.

(MRS. SOLNESS *comes from the house on to the veranda.*)

MRS. SOLNESS (*looks around*). Isn't he here? Where has he gone to?

RAGNAR. Mr. Solness is down with the men.

HILDA. He took the wreath with him.

MRS. SOLNESS (*terrified*). Took the wreath with him! Oh, God! oh, God! Brovik—you must go down to him! Get him to come back here!

RAGNAR. Shall I say you want to speak to him, Mrs. Solness?

MRS. SOLNESS. Oh, yes, do!—No, no—don't say that *I* want anything! You can say that somebody is here, and that he must come at once.

RAGNAR. Good. I will do so, Mrs. Solness.

(*He goes down the flight of steps and away through the garden.*)

MRS. SOLNESS. Oh, Miss Wangel, you can't think how anxious I feel about him.

HILDA. Is there anything in this to be so terribly frightened about?

MRS. SOLNESS. Oh, yes; surely you can understand. Just think, if he were really to do it! If he should take it into his head to climb up the scaffolding!

HILDA (*eagerly*). Do you think he will?

MRS. SOLNESS. Oh, one can never tell what he might take into his head. I am afraid there is nothing he mightn't think of doing.

HILDA. Aha! Perhaps you too think that he is—well—?

MRS. SOLNESS. Oh, I don't know what to think about him now. The doctor has been telling me all sorts of things; and putting it all together with several things I have heard him say—

(DR. HERDAL *looks out at the door.*)

DR. HERDAL. Isn't he coming soon?

MRS. SOLNESS. Yes, I think so. I have sent for him at any rate.

DR. HERDAL (*advancing*). I am afraid you will have to go in, my dear lady—

MRS. SOLNESS. Oh, no! Oh, no! I shall stay out here and wait for Halvard.

DR. HERDAL. But some ladies have just come to call on you—

MRS. SOLNESS. Good heavens, *that* too! And just at this moment!

DR. HERDAL. They say they positively must see the ceremony.

MRS. SOLNESS. Well, well, I suppose I must go to them after all. It is my duty.

HILDA. Can't you ask the ladies to go away?

MRS. SOLNESS. No, that would never do. Now that they are here, it is my duty to see them. But you stay out here in the meantime—and receive him when he comes.

DR. HERDAL. And try to occupy his attention as long as possible—

MRS. SOLNESS. Yes, do, dear Miss Wangel. Keep as firm hold of him as ever you can.

HILDA. Would it not be best for you to do that?

MRS. SOLNESS. Yes; God knows that is my duty. But when one has duties in so many directions—

DR. HERDAL (*looks towards the garden*). There he is coming.

MRS. SOLNESS. And I have to go in!

DR. HERDAL (*to* HILDA). Don't say anything about *my* being here.

HILDA. Oh, no! I dare say I shall find something else to talk to Mr. Solness about.

MRS. SOLNESS. And be sure you keep firm hold of him. I believe *you* can do it best.

(MRS. SOLNESS *and* DR. HERDAL *go into the house.* HILDA *remains standing on the veranda.* SOLNESS *comes from the garden, up the flight of steps.*)

SOLNESS. Somebody wants me, I hear.

HILDA. Yes; it is I, Mr. Solness.

SOLNESS. Oh, is it you, Hilda? I was afraid it might be Aline or the Doctor.

HILDA. You are very easily frightened, it seems!

SOLNESS. Do you think so?

HILDA. Yes; people say that you are afraid to climb about—on the scaffoldings, you know.

SOLNESS. Well, that is quite a special thing.

HILDA. Then it is true that you are afraid to do it?

SOLNESS. Yes, I am.

HILDA. Afraid of falling down and killing yourself?

SOLNESS. No, not of that.

HILDA. Of what, then?

SOLNESS. I am afraid of retribution, Hilda.

HILDA. Of retribution? (*Shakes her head.*) I don't understand that.

SOLNESS. Sit down, and I will tell you something.

HILDA. Yes, do! At once!

(*She sits on a stool by the railing and looks expectantly at him.*)

SOLNESS (*throws his hat on the table*). You know that I began by building churches.

HILDA (*nods*). I know that well.

SOLNESS. For, you see, I came as a boy from a pious home in the country; and so it seemed to me that this church-building was the noblest task I could set myself.

HILDA. Yes, yes.

SOLNESS. And I venture to say that I built those poor little churches with such honest and warm and heartfelt devotion that—that—

HILDA. That—? Well?

SOLNESS. Well, that I think that he ought to have been pleased with me.

HILDA. *He?* What *he?*

SOLNESS. He who was to have the churches, of course! He to whose honor and glory they were dedicated.

HILDA. Oh, indeed! But are you certain, then, that—he was not—pleased with you?

SOLNESS (*scornfully*). *He* pleased with *me!* How can you talk so, Hilda? He who gave the troll in me leave to lord it just as it pleased. He who bade them be at hand to serve me, both day and night—all these—all these—

HILDA. Devils—

SOLNESS. Yes, of both kinds. Oh, no, he made me feel clearly enough that he was not pleased with me. (*Mysteriously.*) You see, that was really the reason why he made the old house burn down.

HILDA. Was that why?

SOLNESS. Yes, don't you understand? He wanted to give me the chance of becoming an accomplished master in my own sphere—so that I might build all the more glorious churches for him. At first I did not understand what he was driving at; but all of a sudden it flashed upon me.

HILDA. When was that?

SOLNESS. It was when I was building the church-tower up at Lysanger.

HILDA. I thought so.

SOLNESS. For you see, Hilda—up there, amidst those new surroundings, I used to go about musing and pondering within myself. Then I saw plainly why he had taken my little children from me. It was that I should have nothing else to attach myself to, no such thing as love and happiness, you understand. I was to be only a master builder—nothing else. And all my life long I was to go on building for him. (*Laughs.*) But I can tell you nothing came of *that!*

HILDA. What did you do, then?

SOLNESS. First of all, I searched and tried my own heart—

HILDA. And then?

SOLNESS. Then I did the *impossible*—I no less than *he.*

HILDA. The impossible?

SOLNESS. I had never before been able to climb up to a great, free height. But that day I did it.

HILDA (*leaping up*). Yes, yes, you did!

SOLNESS. And when I stood there, high over everything, and was hanging the wreath over the vane, I said to him: Hear me now, thou Mighty One! From this day forward I will be a free builder—I too, in my sphere—just as thou in thine. I will never more build churches for thee—only homes for human beings.

HILDA (*with great sparkling eyes*). *That* was the song that I heard through the air!

SOLNESS. But afterwards his turn came.

HILDA. What do you mean by *that?*

SOLNESS (*looks despondently at her*). Building homes for human beings—is not worth a rap, Hilda.

HILDA. Do you say *that* now?

SOLNESS. Yes, for now I see it. Men have no use for these homes of theirs—to be happy in. And I should not have had any use for such a home, if I had had one. (*With a quiet, bitter laugh.*) See, that is the upshot of the whole affair, however far back I look. Nothing really built; nor anything sacrificed for the chance of building. Nothing, nothing! the whole is nothing!

HILDA. Then you will never build anything more?

SOLNESS (*with animation*). On the contrary, I am just going to begin!

HILDA. What, then? What will you build? Tell me at once!

SOLNESS. I believe there is only one possible dwelling-place for human happiness—and that is what I am going to build now.

HILDA (*looks fixedly at him*). Mr. Solness—you mean our castles in the air.

SOLNESS. The castles in the air—yes.

HILDA. I am afraid you would turn dizzy before we got halfway up.

SOLNESS. Not if I can mount hand in hand with you, Hilda.

HILDA (*with an expression of suppressed resentment*). Only with me? Will there be no others of the party?

SOLNESS. Who else should there be?

HILDA. Oh—that girl—that Kaia at the desk. Poor thing—don't you want to take her with you too?

SOLNESS. Oho! Was it about her that Aline was talking to you?

HILDA. Is it so—or is it not?

SOLNESS (*vehemently*). I will not answer such a question. You must believe in me, wholly and entirely!

HILDA. All these ten years I have believed in you so utterly—so utterly.

SOLNESS. You must go on believing in me!

HILDA. Then let me see you stand free and high up!

SOLNESS (*sadly*). Oh, Hilda—it is not every day that I can do that.

HILDA (*passionately*). I will have you do it! I will have it! (*Imploringly.*) Just once more, Mr. Solness! Do the *impossible* once again!

SOLNESS (*stands and looks deep into her eyes*). If I try it, Hilda, I will stand up there and talk to him as I did that time before.

HILDA (*in rising excitement*). What will you say to him?

SOLNESS. I will say to him: Hear me, Mighty Lord—thou may'st judge me as seems best to thee. But hereafter I will build nothing but the loveliest thing in the world—

HILDA (*carried away*). Yes—yes—yes!

SOLNESS.—build it together with a princess, whom I love—

HILDA. Yes, tell him that! Tell him that!

SOLNESS. Yes. And then I will say to him: Now I shall go down and throw my arms round her and kiss her—

HILDA.—many times! Say that!

SOLNESS.—many, many times, I will say.

HILDA. And then—?

SOLNESS. Then I will wave my hat—and come down to the earth—and do as I said to him.

HILDA (*with outstreched arms*). Now I see you again as I did when there was song in the air!

SOLNESS (*looks at her with his head bowed*). How have you become what you are, Hilda?

HILDA. How have you made me what I am?

SOLNESS (*shortly and firmly*). The princess shall have her castle.

HILDA (*jubilant, clapping her hands*). Oh, Mr. Solness—! My lovely, lovely castle. Our castle in the air!

SOLNESS. On a firm foundation.

>   (*In the street a crowd of people has assembled, vaguely seen through the trees. Music of wind-instruments is heard far away behind the new house.*)

(MRS. SOLNESS, *with a fur collar round her neck.*

Doctor Herdal *with her white shawl on his arm, and some women come out on the veranda.* Ragnar Brovik *comes at the same time up from the garden.*)

Mrs. Solness (*to* Ragnar). Are we to have music, too?

Ragnar. Yes. It's the band of the Masons' Union. (*To* Solness.) The foreman asked me to tell you that he is ready now to go up with the wreath.

Solness (*takes his hat*). Good. I will go down to him myself.

Mrs. Solness (*anxiously*). What have you to do down there, Halvard?

Solness (*curtly*). I must be down below with the men.

Mrs. Solness. Yes, down below—only down below.

Solness. That is where I always stand—on everyday occasions.

(*He goes down the flight of steps and away through the garden.*)

Mrs. Solness (*calls after him over the railing*). But do beg the man to be careful when he goes up! Promise me that, Halvard!

Dr. Herdal (*to* Mrs. Solness). Don't you see that I was right? He has given up all thought of that folly.

Mrs. Solness. Oh, what a relief! Twice workmen have fallen, and each time they were killed on the spot. (*Turns to* Hilda.) Thank you, Miss Wangel, for having kept such a firm hold upon him. I should never have been able to manage him.

Dr. Herdal (*playfully*). Yes, yes, Miss Wangel, you know how to keep firm hold on a man, when you give your mind to it.

(Mrs. Solness *and* Dr. Herdal *go up to the women, who are standing nearer to the steps and looking over the garden.* Hilda *remains standing beside the railing in the foreground.* Ragnar *goes up to her.*)

Ragnar (*with suppressed laughter, half whispering*). Miss Wangel—do you see all those young fellows down in the street?

Hilda. Yes.

Ragnar. They are my fellow students, come to look at the master.

Hilda. What do they want to look at *him* for?

Ragnar. They want to see how he daren't climb to the top of his own house.

Hilda. Oh, *that* is what those boys want, is it?

Ragnar. (*spitefully and scornfully*). He has kept us down so long—now we are going to see *him* keep quietly down below himself.

Hilda. You will not see that—not this time.

Ragnar (*smiles*). Indeed! Then where shall we see him?

Hilda. High—high up by the vane! That is where you will see him!

Ragnar (*laughs*). Him! Oh, yes, I dare say!

Hilda. His *will* is to reach the top—so at the top you shall see him.

Ragnar. His *will*, yes; that I can easily believe. But he simply *cannot* do it. His head would swim round long, long before he got halfway. he would have to crawl down again on his hands and knees.

Dr. Herdal (*points across*). Look! There goes the foreman up the ladders.

Mrs. Solness. And of course he has the wreath to carry too. Oh, I do hope he will be careful!

Ragnar (*stares incredulously and shouts*). Why, but it's—

Hilda (*breaking out in jubilation*). It is the master builder himself.

Mrs. Solness (*screams with terror*). Yes, it is Halvard! Oh, my great God—! Halvard! Halvard!

Dr. Herdal. Hush! Don't shout to him!

Mrs. Solness (*half beside herself*). I must go to him! I must get him to come down again!

Dr. Herdal (*holds her*). Don't move, any of you! Not a sound!

Hilda (*immovable, follows* Solness *with her eyes*). He climbs and climbs. Higher and higher! Higher and higher! Look! Just look!

Ragnar (*breathless*). He *must* turn now. He can't possibly help it.

Hilda. He climbs and climbs. He will soon be at the top now.

Mrs. Solness. Oh, I shall die of terror. I cannot bear to see it.

Dr. Herdal. Then don't look up at him.

Hilda. There he is standing on the topmost planks. Right at the top!

Dr. Herdal. Nobody must move! Do you hear?

Hilda (*exulting with quiet intensity*). At last! At last! Now I see him great and free again!

Ragnar (*almost voiceless*). But this is im—

Hilda. So I have seen him all through these ten years. How secure he stands! Frightfully thrilling all the same. Look at him! Now he is hanging the wreath round the vane!

Ragnar. I feel as if I were looking at something utterly impossible.

Hilda. Yes, it is the *impossible* that he is doing now! (*With the indefinable expression in her eyes.*) Can you see anyone else up there with him?

Ragnar. There is no one else.

Hilda. Yes, there is one he is striving with.

Ragnar. You are mistaken.

Hilda. Then do you hear no song in the air, either?

Ragnar. It must be the wind in the tree-tops.

Hilda. *I* hear a song—a mighty song! (*Shouts in wild jubilation and glee.*) Look, look! Now he is waving his hat! He is waving it to us down here! Oh, wave, wave back to him! For now it is finished! (*Snatches the white shawl from the* Doctor, *waves it, and shouts up to* Solness.) Hurrah for Master Builder Solness!

Dr. Herdal. Stop! Stop! For God's sake—!

(*The women on the veranda wave their pocket-handkerchiefs, and the shouts of "Hurrah" are taken up in the street below. Then they are suddenly silenced, and the crowd bursts out into a shriek of horror. A human body, with planks and fragments of wood, is vaguely perceived crashing down behind the trees.*)

Mrs. Solness *and the* Women (*at the same time*). He is falling! He is falling!

(Mrs. Solness *totters, falls backwards, swooning, and is caught, amid cries and confusion, by the women. The crowd in the street breaks down the fence and storms into the garden. At the same time* Dr. Herdal, *too, rushes down thither. A short pause.*)

Hilda (*stares fixedly upwards and says, as if petrified*). My Master Builder.

Ragnar (*supports himself, trembling, against the railing*). He must be dashed to pieces—killed on the spot.

One of the Women (*while* Mrs. Solness *is carried into the house*). Run down for the doctor—

Ragnar. I can't stir a foot—

Another Woman. Then call to someone!

Ragnar (*tries to call out*). How is it? Is he alive?

A Voice (*below, in the garden*). Mr. Solness is dead!

Other Voices (*nearer*). The head is all crushed.—He fell right into the quarry.

Hilda (*turns to* Ragnar *and says quietly*). I can't see him up there now.

Ragnar. This is terrible. So, after all, he could not do it.

Hilda (*as if in quiet spellbound triumph*). But he mounted right to the top. And I heard harps in the air. (*Waves her shawl in the air and shrieks with wild intensity.*) *My—my* Master Builder!

CURTAIN

Leo Tolstoy
(1828-1910)
Three Deaths: A Tale

I

It was autumn. Two vehicles were going along the highway at a quick trot. In the first sat two women: a lady, thin and pale, and a maidservant, plump and rosy and shining. The maid's short dry hair escaped from under her faded bonnet and her red hand in its torn glove kept pushing it back by fits and starts; her full bosom, covered by a woolen shawl, breathed health, her quick black eyes now watched the fields as they glided past the window, now glanced timidly at her mistress, and now restlessly scanned the corners of the carriage. In front of her nose dangled her mistress's bonnet, pinned to the luggage carrier, on her lap lay a puppy, her feet were raised on the boxes standing on the floor and just audibly tapped against them to the creaking of the coach-springs and the clatter of the window panes.

Having folded her hands on her knees and closed her eyes, the lady swayed feebly against the pillows placed at her back, and, frowning slightly, coughed inwardly. On her head she had a white nightcap, and a blue kerchief was tied around her delicate white throat. A straight line receding under the cap parted her light brown, extremely flat, pomaded hair, and there was something dry and deathly about the whiteness of the skin of that wide parting. Her features were delicate and handsome, but her skin was flabby and rather sallow, though there was a hectic flush on her cheeks. Her lips were dry and restless, her scanty eyelashes had no curl in them, and her cloth traveling coat fell in straight folds over a sunken breast. Though her eyes were closed her face bore an expression of weariness, irritation, and habitual suffering.

A footman, leaning on the arms of his seat, was dozing on the box. The mail-coach driver, shouting lustily, urged on his four big sweating horses, occasionally turning to the other driver who called to him from the calèche behind. The broad parallel tracks of the tires spread themselves evenly and fast on the muddy, chalky surface of the road. The sky was gray and cold and a damp mist was settling on the fields and road. It was stuffy in the coach and there was a smell of Eau-de-Cologne and dust. The invalid drew back her head and slowly opened her beautiful dark eyes, which were large and brilliant.

"Again," she said, nervously pushing away with her beautiful thin hand an end of her maid's cloak which had lightly touched her foot, and her mouth twitched painfully. Matryosha gathered up her cloak with both hands, rose on her strong legs, and seated herself further away, while her fresh face grew scarlet. The lady, leaning with both hands on the seat, also tried to raise herself so as to sit up higher, but her strength failed her. Her mouth twisted, and her whole face became distorted by a look of impotent malevolence and irony. "You might at least help me! . . . No, don't bother! I can do it myself, only don't put your bags or anything behind me, for goodness' sake! . . . No, better not touch me since you don't know how to!" The lady closed her eyes and then, again quickly raising her eyelids, glared at the maid. Matryosha, looking at her, bit her red nether lip. A deep sigh rose from the invalid's chest and turned into a cough before it was completed. She turned away, puckered her face, and clutched her chest with both hands. When the coughing fit was over she once more closed her eyes and continued to sit motionless. The carriage and calèche entered a village. Matryosha stretched out her thick hand from under her shawl and crossed herself.

"What is it?" asked her mistress.

"A post-station, madam."

"I am asking why you crossed yourself."

"There's a church, madam."

The invalid turned to the window and began slowly to cross herself, looking with large wide-open eyes at the big village church her carriage was passing.

The carriage and calèche both stopped at the post-station and the invalid's husband and a doctor stepped out of the calèche and went up to the coach.

"How are you feeling?" asked the doctor, taking her pulse.

"Well, my dear, how are you—not tired?" asked the husband in French. "Wouldn't you like to get out?"

Matryosha, gathering up the bundles, squeezed herself into a corner so as not to interfere with their conversation.

"Nothing much, just the same," replied the invalid. "I won't get out."

Her husband after standing there a while went into the station-house, and Matryosha, too, jumped out of the carriage and ran on tiptoe across the mud and in at the gate.

"If I feel ill, it's no reason for you not to have lunch," said the sick woman with a slight smile to the doctor, who was standing at her window.

"None of them has any thought for me," she added to herself as soon as the doctor, having slowly walked away from her, ran quickly up the steps to the station-house. "They are well, so they don't care. Oh, my God!"

"Well, Eduard Ivanovich?" said the husband, rubbing his hands as he met the doctor with a merry smile. "I have ordered the lunch-basket to be brought in. What do you think about it?"

"A capital idea," replied the doctor.

"Well, how is she?" asked the husband with a sigh, lowering his voice and lifting his eyebrows.

"As I told you: it is impossible for her to reach Italy—God grant that she sets even as far as Moscow, especially in this weather."

"But what are we to do? Oh, my God, my God!" and the husband hid his eyes with his hand. "Bring it here!" he said to the man who had brought in the lunch-basket.

"She ought to have stayed at home," said the doctor, shrugging his shoulders.

"But what could I do?" rejoined the husband. "You know I used every possible means to get her to stay. I spoke of the expense, of our children whom we had to leave behind, and of my business affairs, but she would not listen to anything. She is making plans for life abroad as if she were in good health. To tell her of her condition would be to kill her."

"But she is killed already—you must know that, Vasili Dmitrich. A person can't live without lungs, and new lungs won't grow. It is sad and hard, but what is to be done? My business and yours is to see that her end is made as peaceful as possible. It's a priest who is needed for that."

"Oh, my God! Think of my condition, having to remind her about her will. Come what may I can't tell her that, you know how good she is . . ."

"Still, try to persuade her to wait till the roads are fit for sleighing," said the doctor, shaking his head significantly, "or something bad may happen on the journey."

"Aksyusha, hello Aksyusha!" yelled the stationmaster's daughter, throwing her jacket over her head and stamping her feet on the muddy back porch. "Come and let's have a look at the Shirkin lady: they say she is being taken abroad for a chest trouble, and I've never seen what consumptive people look like!"

She jumped onto the threshold, and seizing one another by the hand the two girls ran out of the gate. Checking their pace, they passed by the coach and looked in at the open window. The invalid turned her head towards them but, noticing their curiosity, frowned and turned away.

"Dearie me!" said the stationmaster's daughter, quickly turning her head away. "What a wonderful beauty she must have been, and see what she's like now! It's dreadful. Did you see, did you, Aksyusha?"

"Yes, how thin!" Aksyusha agreed. "Let's go and look again, as if we were going to the well. See, she has turned away, and I hadn't seen her yet. What a pity, Masha!"

"Yes, and what mud!" said Masha, and they both ran through the gate.

"Evidently I look frightful," thought the invalid. "If only I could get abroad quicker, quicker. I should soon recover there."

"Well, my dear, how are you?" said her husband, approaching her and still chewing.

"Always the same question," thought the invalid, "and he himself is eating."

"So-so," she murmured through her closed teeth.

"You know, my dear, I'm afraid you'll get worse traveling in this weather, and Eduard Ivanovich says so too. Don't you think we'd better turn back?"

She remained angrily silent.

"The weather will perhaps improve and the roads be fit for sleighing; you will get better meanwhile, and we will all go together."

"Excuse me. If I had not listened to you for so long, I should now at least have reached Berlin, and have been quite well."

"What could be done, my angel? You know it was impossible. But now if you stayed another month you would get nicely better, I should have finished my business, and we could take the children with us."

"The children are well, but I am not."

"But do understand, my dear, that if in this weather you should get worse on the road.... At least you would be at home."

"What of being at home?... To die at home?" answered the invalid, flaring up. But the word "die" evidently frightened her, and she looked imploringly and questioningly at her husband. He hung his head and was silent. The invalid's mouth suddenly widened like a child's, and tears rolled down her cheeks. Her husband hid his face in his handkerchief and stepped silently away from the carriage.

"No, I will go on," said the invalid, and lifting her eyes to the sky she folded her hands and began whispering incoherent words: "Oh, my God, what is it for?" she said, and her tears flowed faster. She prayed long and fervently, but her chest ached and felt as tight as before; the sky, the fields, and the road were just as gray and gloomy, and the autumnal mist fell, neither thickening nor lifting, and settled on the muddy road, the roofs, the carriage, and the sheepskin coats of the drivers, who, talking in their strong merry voices, were greasing the wheels and harnessing the horses.

II

The carriage was ready but the driver still loitered. He had gone into the drivers' room at the station. It was hot, stuffy, and dark there, with an oppressive smell of baking bread, cabbage, sheepskin garments, and humanity. Several drivers were sitting in the room, and a cook was busy at the oven, on the top of which lay a sick man wrapped in sheepskins.

"Uncle Fyodor! I say, Uncle Fyodor!" said the young driver, entering the room in his sheepskin coat with a whip stuck in his belt, and addressing the sick man.

"What do you want Fyodor for, lazybones?" asked one of the drivers. "There's your carriage waiting for you."

"I want to ask for his boots; mine are quite worn out," answered the young fellow, tossing back his hair and straightening the mittens tucked in his belt. "Is he asleep? I say, Uncle Fyodor!" he repeated, walking over to the oven.

"What is it?" answered a weak voice, and a lean face with a red beard looked down from the oven, while a broad, emaciated, pale, and hairy hand pulled up the coat over the dirty shirt covering his angular shoulder.

"Give me a drink, lad. . . . What is it you want?"

The lad handed him up a dipper with water.

"Well, you see, Fyodor," he said, stepping from foot to foot, "I expect you don't need your new boots now; won't you let me have them? I don't suppose you'll go about anymore."

The sick man, lowering his weary head to the shiny dipper and immersing his sparse drooping mustache in the turbid water, drank feebly but eagerly. His matted beard was dirty, and his sunken clouded eyes had difficulty in looking up at the lad's face. Having finished drinking he tried to lift his hand to wipe his wet lips, but he could not do so, and rubbed them on the sleeve of his coat instead. Silently, and breathing heavily through his nose, he looked straight into the lad's eyes, collecting his strength.

"But perhaps you have promised them to someone else?" asked the lad. "If so, it's all right. The worst of it is, it's wet outside and I have to go about my work, so I said to myself: 'Suppose I ask Fyodor for his boots; I expect he doesn't need them.' If you need them yourself—just say so."

Something began to rumble and gurgle in the sick man's chest; he doubled up and began to choke with an abortive cough in his throat.

"Need them indeed!" the cook snapped out unexpectedly so as to be heard by the whole room. "He hasn't come down from the oven for more than a month! Hear how he's choking—it makes me ache inside just to hear him. What does he want with boots? They won't bury him in new boots. And it was time long ago—God forgive me the sin! See how he chokes. He ought to be taken into the other room or somewhere. They say there are hospitals in the town. Is it right that he should take up the whole corner?—there's no more to be said. I've no room at all, and yet they expect cleanliness."

"Hullo, Sergey! Come along and take your place, the gentlefolk are waiting!" shouted the drivers' overseer, looking in at the door.

Sergey was about to go without waiting for a reply, but the sick man, while coughing, let him understand by a look that he wanted to give him an answer.

"Take my boots, Sergey," he said when he had mastered the cough and rested a moment. "But listen. . . . Buy a stone for me when I die," he added hoarsely.

"Thank you, uncle. Then I'll take them, and I'll buy a stone for sure."

"There, lads, you heard that?" the sick man managed to utter, and then bent double again and began to choke.

"All right, we heard," said one of the drivers. "Go and take your seat, Sergey, there's the overseer running back. The Shirkin lady is ill, you know."

Sergey quickly pulled off his unduly big, dilapidated boots and threw them under a bench. Uncle Fyodor's new boots just fitted him, and having put them on he went to the carriage with his eyes fixed on his feet.

"What fine boots! Let me grease them," said a driver, who held some axle-grease in his hand, as Sergey climbed onto the box and gathered up the reins. "Did he give them to you for nothing?"

"Why, are you envious?" Sergey replied, rising and wrapping the skirts of his coat under his legs. "Off with you! Gee up, my beauties!" he shouted to the horses, flourishing the whip, and the carriage and calèche with their occupants, portmanteaux, and trunks rolled rapidly along the wet road and disappeared in the gray autumnal mist.

The sick driver was left on the top of the oven in the stuffy room and, unable to relieve himself by coughing, turned with an effort onto his other side and became silent.

Till late in the evening people came in and out of the room and dined there. The sick man made no sound. When night came, the cook climbed up onto the oven and reached over his legs to get down her sheepskin coat.

"Don't be cross with me, Nastasya," said the sick man. "I shall soon leave your corner empty."

"All right, all right, never mind," muttered Nastasya. "But what is it that hurts you? Tell me uncle."

"My whole inside has wasted away. God knows what it is!"

"I suppose your throat hurts when you cough?"

"Everything hurts. My death has come—that's how it is. Oh, oh, oh!" moaned the sick man.

"Cover up your feet like this," said Nastasya, drawing his coat over him as she climbed down from the oven.

A night-light burned dimly in the room. Nastasya and some ten drivers slept on the floor or on the benches, loudly snoring. The sick man groaned feebly, coughed, and turned about on the oven. Toward morning he grew quite still.

"I had a queer dream last night," said Nastasya next morning, stretching herself in the dim light. "I dreamt Uncle Fyodor got down from the oven and went out to chop wood. 'Come, Nastasya,' he says, 'I'll help you!' and I say, 'How can you chop wood now?' but he just seizes the ax and begins chopping quickly, quickly, so that the chips fly all about. 'Why,' I say, 'haven't you been ill?' 'No,' he says, 'I am well,' and he swings the ax so that I was quite frightened. I gave a cry and woke up. I wonder whether he is dead! Uncle Fyodor! I say, Uncle Fyodor!"

Fyodor did not answer.

"True enough, he may have died. I'll go and see," said one of the drivers, waking up.

The lean hand covered with reddish hair that hung down from the oven was pale and cold.

"I'll go and tell the stationmaster," said the driver. "I think he is dead."

Fyodor had no relatives: he was from some distant place. They buried him next day in the new cemetery beyond the wood, and Nastasya went on for days telling everybody of her dream, and of having been the first to discover that Uncle Fyodor was dead.

III

Spring had come. Rivulets of water

hurried down the wet streets of the city, gurgling between lumps of frozen manure; the colors of the people's clothes as they moved along the streets looked vivid and their voices sounded shrill. Behind the garden fences the buds on the trees were swelling and their branches were just audibly swaying in the fresh breeze. Everywhere transparent drops were forming and falling.... The sparrows chirped, and fluttered awkwardly with their little wings. On the sunny side of the street, on the fences, houses, and trees, everything was in motion and sparkling. There was joy and youth everywhere in the sky, on the earth, and in the hearts of men.

In one of the chief streets fresh straw had been strewn on the road before a large, important house, where the invalid who had been in a hurry to go abroad lay dying.

At the closed door of her room stood the invalid's husband and an elderly woman. On the sofa a priest sat with bowed head, holding something wrapped in his stole. In a corner of the room the sick woman's old mother lay on an invalid chair weeping bitterly: beside her stood one maidservant holding a clean handkerchief, waiting for her to ask for it; while another was rubbing her temples with something and blowing under the old lady's cap onto her gray head.

"Well, may Christ aid you, dear friend," the husband said to the elderly woman who stood near him at the door. "She has such confidence in you and you know so well how to talk to her, so persuade her as well as you can, my dear—go to her." He was about to open the door, but her cousin stopped him, pressing her handkerchief several times to her eyes and giving her head a shake.

"Well, I don't think I look as if I had been crying now," said she and, opening the door herself, went in.

The husband was in great agitation and seemed quite distracted. He walked towards the old woman, but while still several steps from her turned back, walked about the room, and went up to the priest. The priest looked at him, raised his eyebrows to heaven, and sighed: his thick, grayish beard also rose as he sighed and then came down again.

"My God, my God!" said the husband.

"What is to be done?" said the priest with a sigh, and again his eyebrows and beard rose and fell.

"And her mother is here!" said the husband almost in despair. "She won't be able to bear it. You see, loving her as she does ... I don't know! If you would only try to comfort her, Father, and persuade her to go away."

The priest got up and went to the old woman.

"It is true, no one can appreciate a mother's heart," he said—"but God is merciful."

The old woman's face suddenly twitched all over, and she began to hiccup hysterically.

"God is merciful," the priest continued when she grew a little calmer. "Let me tell you of a patient in my parish who was much worse than Marya Dmitrievna, and a simple tradesman cured her in a short time with various herbs. That tradesman is even now in Moscow. I told Vasily Dmitrich—we might try him.... It would at any rate comfort the invalid. To God all is possible."

"No, she will not live," said the old woman. "God is taking her instead of me," and the hysterical hiccuping grew so violent that she fainted.

The sick woman's husband hid his face in his hands and ran out of the room.

In the passage the first person he met

was his six-year-old son, who was running full speed after his younger sister.

"Won't you order the children to be taken to their mamma?" asked the nurse.

"No, she doesn't want to see them—it would upset her."

The boy stopped a moment, looked intently into his father's face, then gave a kick and ran on, shouting merrily.

"She pretends to be the black horse, Papa!" he shouted, pointing to his sister.

Meanwhile in the other room the cousin sat down beside the invalid, and tried by skillful conversation to prepare her for the thought of death. The doctor was mixing a draught at another window.

The patient, in a white dressing gown, sat up in bed supported all round by pillows, and looked at her cousin in silence.

"Ah, my dear friend," she said, unexpectedly interrupting her, "don't prepare me! Don't treat me like a child. I am a Christian. I know it all. I know I have not long to live, and know that if my husband had listened to me sooner I should now have been in Italy and perhaps—no, certainly—should have been well. Everybody told him so. But what is to be done? Evidently this is God's wish. We have all sinned heavily. I know that, but I trust in God's mercy everybody will be forgiven, probably all will be forgiven. I try to understand myself. I have many sins to answer for, dear friend, but then how much I have had to suffer! I try to bear my sufferings patiently..."

"Then shall I call the priest, my dear? You will feel still more comfortable after receiving communion," said her cousin.

The sick woman bent her head in assent.

"God forgive me, sinner that I am!" she whispered.

The cousin went out and signaled with her eyes to the priest.

"She is an angel!" she said to the husband, with tears in her eyes. The husband burst into tears; the priest went into the next room; the invalid's mother was still unconscious, and all was silent there. Five minutes later he came out again, and after taking off his stole, straightened out his hair.

"Thank God she is calmer now," he said, "and wishes to see you."

The cousin and the husband went into the sickroom. The invalid was silently weeping, gazing at an icon.

"I congratulate[1] you, my dear," said her husband.

"Thank you! How well I feel now, what inexpressible sweetness I feel!" said the sick woman, and a soft smile played on her thin lips. "How merciful God is! Is He not? Merciful and all powerful!" and again she looked at the icon with eager entreaty and her eyes full of tears.

Then suddenly, as if she remembered something, she beckoned to her husband to come closer.

"You never want to do what I ask..." she said in a feeble and dissatisfied voice.

The husband, craning his neck, listened to her humbly.

"What is it, my dear?"

"How many times have I not said that these doctors don't know anything; there are simple women who can heal, and who do cure. The priest told me...there is also a tradesman...Send!"

"For whom, my dear?"

"O God, you don't want to understand anything!"... And the sick woman's face puckered and she closed her eyes.

The doctor came up and took her hand. Her pulse was beating more and more feebly. He glanced at the husband. The invalid noticed that gesture and looked round in affright. The cousin turned away

---

[1] It was customary in Russia to congratulate people who had received communion.—Translator

and began to cry.

"Don't cry, don't torture yourself and me," said the patient. "Don't take from me the last of my tranquillity."

"You are an angel," said the cousin, kissing her hand.

"No, kiss me here! Only dead people are kissed on the hand. My God, my God!"

That same evening the patient was a corpse, and the body lay in a coffin in the music room of the large house. A deacon sat alone in that big room reading the psalms of David through his nose in a monotonous voice. A bright light from the wax candles in their tall silver candlesticks fell on the pale brow of the dead woman, on her heavy wax-like hands, on the stiff folds of the pall which brought out in awesome relief the knees and the toes. The deacon without understanding the words read on monotonously, and in the quiet room the words sounded strangely and died away. Now and then from a distant room came the sounds of children's voices and the patter of their feet.

"Thou hidest thy face, they are troubled," said the psalter. "Thou takest away their breath, they die and return to their dust. Thou sendest forth thy spirit, they are created: and thou renewest the face of the earth. The glory of the Lord shall endure for ever."

The dead woman's face looked stern and majestic. Neither in the clear cold brow nor in the firmly closed lips was there any movement. She seemed all attention. But had she even now understood those solemn words?

IV

A month later a stone chapel was being erected over the grave of the deceased woman. Over the driver's tomb there was still no stone, and only the light green grass sprouted on the mound which served as the only token of the past existence of a man.

"It will be a sin, Sergey," said the cook at the station-house one day, "if you don't buy a stone for Fyodor. You kept saying, 'It's winter, it's winter!' but why don't you keep your word now? You know I witnessed it. He has already come back once to ask you to do it; if you don't buy him one, he'll come again and choke you."

"But why? I'm not backing out of it," replied Sergey. "I'll buy a stone as I said I would, and give a ruble and a half for it. I haven't forgotten it, but it has to be fetched. When I happen to be in town I'll buy one."

"You might as well put up a cross—you ought to—else it's really wrong," interposed an old driver. "You know you are wearing his boots."

"Where can I get a cross? I can't cut one out of a log."

"What do you mean, can't cut one out of a log? You take an ax and go into the forest early, and you can cut one there. Cut down a young ash or something like that, and you can make a cross of it...you may have to treat the forester to vodka; but one can't afford to treat him for every trifle. There now, the other day I broke my splinter-bar and went and cut a new one, and nobody said a word."

Early in the morning, as soon as it was daybreak, Sergey took an ax and went into the wood.

A cold white cover of dew, which was still falling untouched by the sun, lay on everything. The east was imperceptibly growing brighter, reflecting its pale light on the vault of heaven still veiled by a covering of clouds. Not a blade of grass below, nor a leaf on the topmost branches of the trees, stirred. Only occasionally a sound of wings amid the brushwood, or a rustling on the ground, broke the silence of the forest. Suddenly a strange sound, foreign to Nature, resounded and died away at the outskirts of the forest. Again the sound was heard, and was rhythmically repeated at the foot of the trunk of one of the motionless trees. A tree-top began to tremble in an unwonted manner, its juicy leaves whispered something, and the robin who had been sitting on one of its branches fluttered twice from place to place with a whistle, and, jerking its tail, perched on another tree.

The ax at the bottom gave off a more and more muffled sound, sappy white chips were scattered on the dewy grass and a slight creaking was heard above the sound of the blows. The tree, shuddering in its whole body, bent down and quickly rose again, vibrating with fear in its roots. For an instant all was still, but the tree bent again, a crashing sound came from the trunk, and with its branches breaking and its boughs hanging down it fell with its crown on the damp earth.

The sounds of the ax and of the footsteps were silenced. The robin whistled and flitted higher. A twig which it brushed with its wings shook a little and then with all its foliage grew still like the rest. The trees flaunted the beauty of their motionless branches still more joyously in the newly cleared space.

The first sunbeams, piercing the translucent cloud, shone out and spread over earth and sky. The mist began to quiver like waves in the hollows, the dew sparkled and played on the verdure, the transparent cloudlets grew whiter, and hurriedly dispersed over the deepening azure vault of the sky. The birds stirred in the thicket and, as though bewildered, twittered joyfully about something; the sappy leaves whispered gladly and peacefully on the treetops, and the branches of those that were living began to rustle slowly and majestically over the dead and prostrate tree.

Mark Twain
(1835-1910)
from *The Innocents Abroad*

Samuel Langhorne Clemens, according to Parrington, was "an authentic American," and his writing showed it. His boyhood in Mississippi and his years in the West provided him with much of his material for both novels and short stories. Twain was also a favorite on the lecture circuits; he traveled widely both in America and abroad.

This excerpt from The Innocents Abroad *was written after Twain had traveled in Europe and the Holy Land. Determined not to become rapturous about things European, as so many American travelers have done simply because it is expected of them, Twain depicts with ironical humor the color and detail of the world he sees.*

In this connection I wish to say one word about Michael Angelo Buonarotti. I used to worship the mighty genius of Michael Angelo—that man who was great in poetry, painting, sculpture, architecture—great in every thing he undertook. But I do not want Michael Angelo for breakfast—for luncheon—for dinner—for tea—for supper—for between meals. I like a change, occasionally. In Genoa, he designed everything; in Milan he or his pupils designed everything; he designed the Like of Como; in Padua, Verona, Venice, Bologna, who did we ever hear of, from guides, but Michael Angelo? In Florence, he painted everything, designed everything, nearly, and what he did not design he used to sit on a favourite stone and look at, and they showed us the stone. In Pisa he designed everything but the old shot-tower, and they would have attributed that to him if it had not been so awfully out of perpendicular. He designed the piers of Leghorn and the custom house regulations of Civita Vecchia. But, here—here it is frightful. He designed St. Peter's; he designed the

WINSLOW HOMER: *Breezing Up*, GIFT OF THE W. L. AND MAY T. MELLON FOUNDATION, NATIONAL GALLERY OF ART, WASHINGTON, D. C.

Pantheon, the uniform of the pope's soldiers, the Tiber, the Vatican, the Coliseum, the Capitol, the Tarpeian Rock, the Barberini Palace, St. John Lateran, the Campagna, the Appian Way, the Seven Hills, the Baths of Caracalla, the Claudian Aqueduct, the Cloaca Maxima—the eternal bore designed the Eternal City, and unless all men and books do lie, he painted everything in it! Dan said the other day to the guide, "Enough, enough! Say no more! Lump the whole thing! say that the Creator made Italy from the designs of Michael Angelo!"

I never felt so fervently thankful, so soothed, so tranquil, so filled with the blessed peace, as I did yesterday when I learned that Michael Angelo was dead.

But we have taken it out on this guide. He has marched us through miles of pictures and sculpture in the vast corridors of the Vatican; and through miles of pictures and sculpture in twenty other places; he has shown us the great picture in the Sistine Chapel, and frescoes enough to fresco the heavens—pretty much all done by Michael Angelo. So with him we have played that game which has vanquished so many guides for us—imbecility and idiotic questions. These creatures never suspect—they have no idea of sarcasm.

He shows us a figure and says: "Statuo brunzo." (Bronze statue)

We look at it indifferently and the doctor asks: "By Michael Angelo?"

"No—not know who."

Then he shows us the ancient Roman Forum. The doctor asks: "Michael Angelo?"

A stare from the guide. "No—thousan' year before he is born."

Then an Egyptian obelisk. Again: "Michael Angelo?"

"Oh, *mon dieu*, genteelmen! Zis is *two*

thousan' year before he is born!"

He grows so tired of that unceasing question sometimes, that he dreads to show us anything at all. He has tried all the ways he can think of to make us comprehend that Michael Angelo is only responsible for the creation of *part* of the world, but somehow he has not succeeded yet. Relief for overtasked eyes and brain from study and sightseeing is necessary, or we shall become idiotic sure enough. Therefore this guide must continue to suffer. If he does not enjoy it, so much the worse for him. We do.

In this place I may as well jot down a chapter concerning those necessary obstructions, European guides. Many a man has wished in his heart he could do without his guide; but knowing he could not, has wished he could get some amusement out of him as a remuneration for the affliction of his society. We accomplished this latter matter, and if our experience can be made useful to others they are welcome to it.

Guides know about enough English to tangle everything up so that a man can make neither head or tail of it. They know their story by heart—the history of every statue, painting, cathedral, or other wonder they show you. They know it and tell it as a parrot would—and if you interrupt, and throw them off the track, they have to go back and begin over again. All their lives long, they are employed in showing strange things to foreigners and listening to their bursts of admiration. It is human nature to take delight in exciting admiration. It is what prompts children to say "smart" things, and do absurd ones, and in other ways "show off" when company is present. It is what makes gossips turn out in rain and storm to go and be the first to tell a startling bit of news. Think, then, what a passion it becomes with a guide, whose privilege it is, every day, to show to strangers wonders that throw them into perfect ecstasies of admiration! He gets so that he could not by any possibility live in a soberer atmosphere. After we discovered this, we *never* went into ecstasies any more—we never admired anything—we never showed any but impassible faces and stupid indifference in the presence of the sublimest wonders a guide had to display. We had found their weak point. We have made good use of it ever since. We have made some of those people angry at times, but we have never lost our own serenity.

The doctor asks the questions, generally, because he can keep his countenance, and look more like an inspired idiot, and throw more imbecility into the tone of his voice than any man that lives. It comes natural to him.

The guides in Genoa are delighted to secure an American party, because Americans so much wonder, and deal so much in sentiment and emotion before any relic of Columbus. Our guide there was full of animation—full of impatience. He said:

"Come wis me, genteelmen!—come! I show you ze letter writing by Christopher Colombo!—write it himself!—write it wis his own hand!—come!"

He took us to the municipal palace. After much impressive fumbling of keys and opening of locks, the stained and aged document was spread before us. The guide's eyes sparkled. He danced about us and tapped the parchment with his finger.

"What I tell you, genteelmen! Is it not so? See! handwriting Christopher Colombo!—write it himself!"

We simulated indifference. The doctor examined the document very deliberately, during a painful pause. —Then he said without any show of interest:

"Ah—what—what did you say was the name of the party who wrote this?"

"Christopher Colombo! ze great Christopher Colombo!"

Another deliberate examination.

"Ah—did he write it himself, or—or how?"

"He write it himself!—Christopher Colombo! he's own handwriting, write by himself!"

Then the doctor laid the document down and said:

"Why, I have seen boys in America only fourteen years old that could write better than that."

"But zis is ze great Christo——"

"I don't care who it is! It's the worst writing I ever saw. Now you mustn't think you can impose on us because we are strangers. We won't put up with that sort of treatment. If you have got any specimens of penmanship of real merit, we shall be glad to inspect them—but if you haven't, let us not procrastinate here."

We moved on. The guide was considerably shaken up, but he made one more venture. He had something which he thought would overcome us. He said:

"Ah, genteelmen, you come vis me! I show you beautiful, O, magnificent bust Christopher Colombo!—splendid, grand, magnificent!"

He brought us before the beautiful bust—for it *was* beautiful—and sprung back and struck an attitude:

"Ah, look genteelmen!—beautiful, grand—bust Christopher Colombo! —beautiful bust, beautiful pedestal!"

The doctor put up his eye-glass—procured for such occasions:

"Ah—what did you say this gentleman's name was?"

"Christopher Colombo!—ze great Christopher Colombo!"

"Christopher Colombo—the *great* Christopher Colombo. Well what did *he* do?"

"Discover America!—discover America, Oh, ze devil!"

"Discover America. No—that statement will hardly wash. We are just from America ourselves. We heard nothing about it. Christopher Colombo—pleasant name—is—is he dead?"

"Oh, corpo di Baccho! —three hundred year!"

"What did he die of?"

"I do not know!—I cannot tell."

"Small-pox, think?"

"I do not know, genteelmen!—I do not know what he die of."

"Measles, likely?"

"May be—may be—I do *not* know—I think he die of somethings."

"Parents living?"

"Im-posseeble!"

"Ah—which is the bust and which is the pedestal?"

"Santa Maria!—*zis* ze bust!—*zis* ze pedestal!"

"Ah, I see, I see—happy combination—very happy combination, indeed. Is—is this the first time this gentleman was ever on a bust?"

That joke was lost on the defendant—guides cannot master the subtleties of the foreign joke.

We have made it interesting for this Roman guide. Yesterday we spent three or four hours in the Vatican, again, that wonderful world of curiosities. We came very near expressing interest, sometimes—even admiration—it was very hard to keep from it. We succeeded though. The guide was bewildered—nonplussed. He walked his legs off, nearly, hunting up extraordinary things, and exhausted all his ingenuity on us, but it was a failure; we never showed any interest in anything. He had reserved what he considered his greatest wonder till the last—a royal Egyptian mummy, the best preserved in the world, perhaps. He took us there. He felt so sure, this time, that some of his old enthusiasm came back to him:

"See, genteelmen!—Mummy! Mummy!"

The eye-glass came up as calmly, as deliberately as ever.

"Ah—what did I understand you to say this genteelman's name was?"

"Name?—he got no name!—Mummy! 'Gyptian mummy!"

"Yes, yes. Born here?"

"No! *'Gyptian* mummy!"

"Ah, just so. Frenchman, I presume?"

"No!—*not* Frenchman, not Roman! —born in Egypta!"

"Born in Egypt. Never heard of Egypt before. Foreign locality, likely. Mummy—mummy. How calm he is—how self possessed. Is, ah—is he dead?"

"Oh, *sacrè bleu*, been dead for three thousan' year!"

The doctor turned on him savagely:

"Here, now, what do you mean by such conduct as this. Playing us for Chinamen because we are strangers and trying to learn! Trying to impose your vile second hand carcases on *us*!—thunder and lightning, I've a notion to—to—if you've got a nice *fresh* corpse, fetch him out!—or by George we'll brain you!"

We make it exceedingly interesting for this Frenchman. However, he has paid us back, partly, without knowing it. He came to the hotel this morning to ask if we were up, and he endeavoured as well as he could to describe us, so that the landlord would know which persons he meant. He finished with the casual remark that we were lunatics. The observation was so innocent and so honest that it amounted to a very good thing for a guide to say.

Stéphane Mallarmé
(1842-1898)
Afternoon of a Faun

I would immortalize these nymphs: so bright
Their sunlit coloring, so airy light,
It floats like drowsy down. Loved I a dream?
My doubts, born of oblivious darkness, seem
A subtle tracery of branches grown
The tree's true self—proving that I have known,
Thinking it love, the blushing of a rose.
But think. These nymphs, their loveliness . . . suppose
They bodied forth your senses' fabulous thirst?
Illusion! which the blue eyes of the first,
As cold and chaste as is the weeping spring,
Beget: the other, sighing, passioning,
Is she the wind, warm in your fleece at noon?
No; through this quiet, when a weary swoon
Crushes and chokes the latest faint essay
Of morning, cool against the encroaching day,
There is no murmuring water, save the gush
Of my clear fluted notes; and in the hush
Blows never a wind, save that which through my reed
Puffs out before the rain of notes can speed

Upon the air, with that calm breath of art
That mounts the unwrinkled zenith visibly,
Where inspiration seeks its native sky.
You fringes of a calm Sicilian lake,
The sun's own mirror which I love to take,
Silent beneath your starry flowers, tell
How here I cut the hollow rushes, well
Tamed by my skill, when on the glaucous gold
Of distant lawns about their fountain cold
A living whiteness stirs like a lazy wave;
And at the first slow notes my panpipes gave
These flocking swans, these naiads, rather, fly
Or dive. Noon burns inert and tawny dry,
Nor marks how clean that Hymen slipped away
From me who seek in song the real A.
Wake, then, to the first ardor and the sight,
O lonely faun, of the old fierce white light,
With, lilies, one of you for innocence.
Other than their lips' delicate pretense,
The light caress that quiets treacherous lovers,
My breast, I know not how to tell, discovers
The bitten print of some immortal's kiss.

But hush! a mystery so great as this
I dare not tell, save to my double reed,
Which, sharer of my every joy and need,
Dreams down its cadenced monologues that we
Falsely confuse the beauties that we see
With the bright palpable shapes our song creates:
My flute, as loud as passion modulates,
Purges the common dream of flank and breast
Seen through closed eyes and inwardly caressed,
Of every empty and monotonous line.
Bloom then, O Syrinx, in thy flight malign,
A reed once more beside our trysting-lake.
Proud of my music, let me often make
A song of goddesses and see their rape
Profanely done on many a painted shape.
So when the grape's transparent juice I drain,
I quell regret for pleasures past and feign
A new real grape. For holding towards the sky
The empty skin, I blow it tight and lie
Dream-drunk till evening, eyeing it.
                                            Tell o'er
Remembered joys and plump the grape once more.
Between the reeds I saw their bodies gleam

Who cool no mortal fever in the stream
Crying to the woods the rage of their desires
And their bright hair went down in jeweled fire
Where crystal broke and dazzled shudderingly.
I check my swift pursuit: for see where lie,
Bruised, being twins in love, by languor sweet,
Two sleeping girls, clasped at my very feet.
I seize and run with them, nor part the pair,
Breaking this covert of frail petals, where
Roses drink scent of the sun and our light play
'Mid tumbled flowers shall match the death of day.
I love that virginal fury—ah, the wild
Thrill when a maiden body shrinks, defiled,
Shuddering like arctic light, from lips that sear
Its nakedness . . . the flesh in secret fear!
Contagiously through my linked pair it flies
Where innocence in either, struggling, dies,
Wet with fond tears or some less piteous dew.
Gay in the conquest of these fears, I grew
So rash that I must needs the sheaf divide
Of ruffled kisses heaven itself had tied.
For as I leaned to stifle in the hair
Of one my passionate laughter (taking care
With a stretched finger, that her innocence
Might stain with her companion's kindling sense
To touch the younger little one, who lay
Child-like unblushing) my ungrateful prey
Slips from me, freed by passion's sudden death
Nor heeds the frenzy of my sobbing breath.
Let it pass! others of their hair shall twist
A rope to drag me to those joys I missed.
See how the ripe pomegranates bursting red
To quench the thirst of the mumbling bees have bled;
So too our blood, kindled by some chance fire,
Flows for the swarming legions of desire.
At evening, when the woodland green turns gold
And ashen gray, 'mid the quenched leaves, behold!
Red Etna glows, by Venus visited,
Walking the lava with her snowy tread
Whene'er the flames in thunderous slumber die.
I hold the goddess!
              Ah, sure penalty!
But the unthinking soul and body swoon
At last beneath the heavy hush of noon.
Forgetful let me lie where summer's drouth

Sifts fine the sand and then with gaping mouth
Dream planet-struck by the grape's round wine-red star.

Nymphs, I shall see the shade that now you are.

(Translated by Aldous Huxley)

GEORGES SEURAT: *Sunday Afternoon on the Island of La Grande Jatte,* THE ART INSTITUTE OF CHICAGO

Paul Verlaine
(1844-1896)
Song of Autumn

The sobbing strains
Of violins
By autumn borne
On my heart fall
With bruising dull,
Grey and forlorn.

All stifling, still
And pale until
The hour looms.
As mem'ries dawn
Of days long gone
My tears find room.

Now I am gone
By ill breeze borne
Without reprieve,
Now here, now there.
The fate I share
Of withered leaf.

(Translated by Irene Osmond Spears)

Thou Hast Wounded Me, Lord

Thou hast wounded me, Lord, with thy love,
And the wound is vibrating here still.
Thou hast wounded me, Lord, with thy love.

O my Lord, now thy fear has struck home,
And the burning is thundering still.
O my Lord, now thy fear has struck home.

O my Lord, I have learned all is vile,
And thy glory's installed in my heart.
O my Lord, I have learned all is vile.

Drown my soul in the floods of thy wine.
Found my life on thy table's own bread
Drown my soul in the floods of thy wine.

Take my blood that I never have shed

And my flesh all unworthy of pain.
Take my blood that I never have shed.

Take my forehead that's stained with its blush
To repose thy adorable feet.
Take my forehead that's stained with its blush.

Take my hands that have never known work,
For live coals and exquisite incense,
Take my hands that have never known work.

Take my heart that beat only in vain,
Palpitating at Calvary's thorns.
Take my heart that beat only in vain.

Take my frivolous, wandering feet,
To approach at the cry of thy grace;
Take my frivolous wandering feet.

Take my voice, gloomy sound full of lies
For reproaches of Penitence mild.
Take my voice, gloomy sound full of lies.

Take my eyes, luminaries of wrong
To extinguish in weeping in prayer.
Take my eyes, luminaries of wrong.

Alas, God of off'ring and grace,
What a well of ingratitude's mine'
Alas, God of off'ring and grace.

God of terror and sanctity pure,
Alas, dark abyss of my crime;
God of terror and sanctity pure.

Thou, God of peace, joy, and content
All misgivings, all ignorance mine;
Thou, God of peace, joy, and content.

Thou understand'st all I have said—
That of all creatures I am most poor;
Thou understand'st all I have said.

But all that I have, Lord, is thine.

(Translated by Irene Osmond Spears)

Oscar Wilde
(1854-1900)
Preface to *The Picture of Dorian Gray*

The artist is the creator of beautiful things.

To reveal art and conceal the artist is art's aim.

The critic is he who can translate into another manner or a new material his impression of beautiful things.

The highest, as the lowest, form of criticism is a mode of autobiography.

Those who find ugly meanings in beautiful things are corrupt without being charming. This is a fault.

Those who find beautiful meanings in beautiful things are cultivated. For these there is hope.

They are the elect to whom beautiful things mean only Beauty.

There is no such thing as a moral or an immoral book. Books are well written, or badly written. That is all.

The nineteenth-century dislike of Realism is the rage of Caliban seeing his own face in a glass.

The nineteenth-century dislike of Romanticism is the rage of Caliban not seeing his own face in a glass.

The moral life of man forms part of the subject-matter of the artist, but the morality of art consists in the perfect use of an imperfect medium. No artist desires to prove anything. Even things that are true can be proved.

No artist has ethical sympathies. An ethical sympathy in an artist is an unpardonable mannerism of style.

No artist is ever morbid. The artist can express everything.

Thought and language are to the artist instruments of an art.

Vice and virtue are to the artist materials for an art.

From the point of view of form, the type of all the arts is the art of the musician. From the point of view of feeling, the actor's craft is the type.

All art is at once surface and symbol.

Those who go beneath the surface do so at their peril.

Those who read the symbol do so at their peril.

It is the spectator, and not life, that art really mirrors.

Diversity of opinion about a work of art shows that the work is new, complex and vital.

When critics disagree the artist is in accord with himself.

We can forgive a man for making a useful thing as long as he does not admire it. The only excuse for making a useless thing is that one admires it intensely.

All art is quite useless.

George Bernard Shaw
(1856-1950)
Shaw on Music

One of the finest playwrights of his age, Shaw was also a great essayist and critic. His music criticism, written largely for newspapers, has endured even though many of the performers and performances he reviewed are now forgotten. Shaw's unusual musical insight and sharp wit are largely responsible for the continued popularity of his articles about music.

His Gentleness

In the ardent regions where all the rest are excited and vehement, Mozart alone is completely self-possessed: where they are clutching their bars with a grip of iron and forging them with Cyclopean blows, his gentleness of touch never deserts him: he is considerate, economical, practical under the same pressure of inspiration that throws your Titan into convulsions. This is the secret of his unpopularity with Titan fanciers. We all in our native barbarism have a relish for the strenuous: your tenor whose B flat is like the bursting of a boiler always brings down the house, even when the note brutally effaces the song; and the composer who can artistically express in music a transport of vigor and passion of the more muscular kind, such as the finale to the Seventh Symphony, the *Walkürenritt,* or the Hailstone chorus, not to mention the orgies of Raff, Liszt, and Berlioz, is always a hero with the intemperate in music, who are so numerous nowadays that we may confidently expect to see some day a British Minister of the Fine Arts introducing a local Option Bill applied to concert rooms.

With Mozart you are safe from inebriety. Hurry, excitement, eagerness, loss of consideration, are to him purely comic or vicious states of mind: he gives us Monostatos and the Queen of Night on the stage, but not in his chamber music. Now it happens that I have, deep in my nature, which is quite as deep as the average rainfall in England, a frightful contempt for your Queens of Night and Titans and their like. The true Parnassian air acts on these people like oxygen on a mouse: it first excites them, and then kills them. Give me the artist who breathes it like a native, and goes about his work in it as quietly as a common man goes about his ordinary business. Mozart did so; and that is why I like him. Even if I did not, I should pretend to; for a taste for his music is a mark of caste among musicians, and should be worn, like a tall hat, by the amateur who wishes to pass for a true Brahmin.

19 April 1893

Mozart, Beethoven, and Grieg

Do you know that noble fantasia in C minor, in which Mozart shewed what Beethoven was to do with the pianoforte sonata, just as in Das Veilchen he showed what Schubert was to do with the song? Imagine my feelings when Madame Backer Gröndahl, instead of playing this fantasia (which she would have done beautifully), set Madame Haas to play it, and then sat down beside her and struck up "an original part for a second piano," in which every interpolation was an impertinence and every addition a blemish. Shocked and pained as every one who knew and loved the fantasia must have been, there was a certain grim ironic interest in the fact that the man who has had the unspeakable presumption to offer us his improvements on Mozart is the infinitesimal Grieg. The world reproaches Mozart for his inspired variation on Handel's "The people that walked in darkness." I do not know what the world will now say to Grieg; but if ever he plays that "original second part" himself to an audience equipped with adequate musical culture, I sincerely advise him to ascertain beforehand that no brickbats or other loose and suitably heavy articles have been left carelessly about the room.

7 March 1890

The Beethoven Centenary, 1927

A hundred years ago a crusty old bachelor of fifty-seven, so deaf that he could not hear his own music played by a full orchestra, yet still able to hear thunder, shook his fist at the roaring heavens for the last time, and died as he had lived, challenging God and defying the universe. He was Defiance Incarnate: he could not even meet a Grand Duke and his court in the street without jamming his hat tight down on his head and striding through the very middle of them. He had the manners of a disobliging steamroller (most steamrollers are abjectly obliging and conciliatory); and he was rather less particular about his dress than a scarecrow: in fact he was once arrested as a tramp because the police refused to believe that such a tatterdemalion could be a famous composer, much less a temple of the most turbulent spirit that ever found expression in pure sound. It was indeed a mighty spirit; but if I had written the mightiest, which would mean mightier than the spirit of Handel, Beethoven himself would have rebuked me; and what mortal man could pretend to a spirit mightier than Bach's? But that Beethoven's spirit was the most turbulent is beyond all question. The impetuous fury of his strength, which he could quite easily contain and control, but often would not, and the uproariousness of his fun, go beyond anything of the kind to be found in the works of other composers. Greenhorns write of syncopation now as if it were a new way of giving the utmost impetus to a musical measure; but the rowdiest jazz sounds like The Maiden's Prayer after Beethoven's third Leonora overture; and certainly no negro corobbery that I ever heard could inspire the blackest dancer with such *diable au corps* as the last movement of the Seventh Symphony. And no other composer has ever melted his hearers into complete sentimentality by the tender beauty of his music, and then suddenly turned on them and mocked them with derisive trumpet blasts for being such fools. Nobody but Beethoven could govern Beethoven; and when, as happened when the fit was on him, he deliberately refused to govern himself, he was ungovernable.

It was this turbulence, this deliberate disorder, this mockery, this reckless and triumphant disregard of conventional manners, that set Beethoven apart from the musical geniuses of the ceremonious seventeenth and eighteenth centuries. He was a giant wave in that storm of the human spirit which produced the French Revolution. He called no man master. Mozart, his greatest predecessor in his own department, had from his childhood been washed, combed, spendidly dressed, and beautifully behaved in the presence of royal personages and peers. His childish outburst at the Pompadour, "Who is this woman who does not kiss me? The Queen kisses me," would be incredible of Beethoven, who was still an unlicked cub even when he had grown into a very grizzly bear. Mozart had the refinement of convention and society as well as the refinement of nature and of the solitudes of the soul. Mozart and Gluck are refined as the court of Louis XIV was refined: Haydn is refined as the most cultivated country gentlemen of his day were refined: compared to them socially Beethoven was an obstreperous Bohemian: a man of the people. Haydn, so superior to envy that he declared his junior, Mozart, to be the greatest composer that ever lived, could not stand Beethoven: Mozart, more farseeing, listened to his playing, and said "You will hear of him someday"; but the two would never have hit it off together had Mozart lived long enough to try. Beethoven had a moral horror of Mozart, who in Don Giovanni had thrown a halo of enchantment round an aristocratic blackguard, and then, with the unscrupulous moral versatility of a born dramatist, turned round to cast a halo of divinity round Sarastro, setting his words to the only music yet written that would not sound out of place in the mouth of God.

Beethoven was no dramatist: moral versatility was to him revolting cynicism. Mozart was still to him the master of masters (this is not an empty eulogistic superlative: it means literally that Mozart is a composer's composer much more than he has ever been a really popular composer); but he was a court flunkey in breeches whilst Beethoven was a Sansculotte; and Haydn also was a flunkey in the old livery: the Revolution stood between them as it stood between the eighteenth and nineteenth centuries. But to Beethoven Mozart was worse than Haydn because he trifled with morality by setting vice to music as magically as virtue. The Puritan who is in every true Sansculotte rose up against him in Beethoven, though Mozart had shewn him all the possibilities of nineteenth-century music. So Beethoven cast back for a hero to Handel, another crusty old bachelor of his own kidney, who despised Mozart's hero Gluck, though the pastoral symphony in The Messiah is the nearest thing in music to the scenes in which Gluck, in his Orfeo, opened to us the plains of Heaven.

Thanks to broadcasting, millions of musical novices will hear the music of Beethoven this anniversary year for the first time with their expectations raised to an extraordinary pitch by hundreds of newspaper articles piling up all the conventional eulogies that are applied indiscriminately to all the great composers. And like his contemporaries they will be puzzled by getting from him not merely a music that they did not expect, but often an orchestral hurlyburly that they may not recognize as what they call music at all, though they can appreciate Gluck and Haydn and Mozart quite well. The explanation is simple enough. The music of the eighteenth century is all dance music. A dance is a symmetrical pattern of steps that are pleasant to move to; and its music is a symmetrical pattern of sound that is pleasant to listen to even when you are not dancing to it. Consequently the sound patterns, though they begin by being as simple as chessboards, get lengthened and elaborated and enriched with harmonies until they are more like Persian carpets; and the composers who design these patterns no longer expect people to dance to them. Only a whirling Dervish could dance a Mozart symphony: indeed, I have reduced two young and practised dancers to exhaustion by making them dance a Mozart overture. The very names of the dances are dropped: instead of suites consisting of sarabands, pavanes, gavottes, and jigs, the designs are presented as sonatas and symphonies consisting of sections called simply movements, and labelled according to their speed (in Italian) as allegros, adagios, scherzos, and prestos. But all the time, from Bach's preludes to Mozart's Jupiter Symphony, the music makes a symmetrical sound pattern, and gives us the dancer's pleasure always as the form and foundation of the piece.

Music, however, can do more than make beautiful sound patterns. It can express emotion. You can look at a Persian carpet and listen to a Bach prelude with a delicious admiration that goes no further than itself; but you cannot listen to the overture to Don Giovanni without being thrown into a complicated mood which prepares you for a tragedy of some terrible doom overshadowing an exquisite but Satanic gaiety. If you listen to the last movement of Mozart's Jupiter Symphony, you hear that it is as much a riotous corobbery as the last movement of Beethoven's Seventh Symphony: it is an orgy of ranting drumming tow-row-row, made poignant by an opening strain of strange and painful beauty which is woven through the pattern all through. And yet the movement is a masterpiece of pattern designing all the time.

Now what Beethoven did, and what

made some of his greatest contemporaries give him up as a madman with lucid intervals of clowning and bad taste, was that he used music altogether as a means of expressing moods, and completely threw over pattern designing as an end in itself. It is true that he used the old patterns all his life with dogged conservatism (another Sansculotte characteristic, by the way); but he imposed on them such an overwhelming charge of human energy and passion, including that highest passion which accompanies thought, and reduces the passion of the physical appetites to mere animalism, that he not only played Old Harry with their symmetry but often made it impossible to notice that there was any pattern at all beneath the storm of emotion. The Eroica Symphony begins by a pattern (borrowed from an overture which Mozart wrote when he was a boy), followed by a couple more very pretty patterns; but they are tremendously energized, and in the middle of the movement the patterns are torn up savagely; and Beethoven, from the point of view of the mere pattern musician, goes raving mad, hurling out terrible chords in which all the notes of the scale are sounded simultaneously, just because he feels like that, and wants you to feel like it.

And there you have the whole secret of Beethoven. He could design patterns with the best of them; he could write music whose beauty will last you all your life; he could take the driest sticks of themes and work them up so interestingly that you find something new in them at the hundredth hearing: in short, you can say of him all that you can say of the greatest pattern composers; but his diagnostic, the thing that marks him out from all the others, is his disturbing quality, his power of unsettling us and imposing his giant moods on us. Berlioz was very angry with an old French composer who expressed the discomfort Beethoven gave him by saying "*J'aime la musique qui me berce,*" "I like music that lulls me." Beethoven's is music that wakes you up; and the one mood in which you shrink from it is the mood in which you want to be let alone.

When you understand this you will advance beyond the eighteenth century and the old-fashioned dance band (jazz, by the way, is the old dance band Beethovenized), and understand not only Beethoven's music, but what is deepest in post-Beethoven music as well.

From the RADIO TIMES
18 March 1927

Androcles and The Lion *is a philosophical comedy which concerns the old story of the Christian who is saved in the Colosseum because he had previously pulled a thorn from a lion's paw. Some of the play is quite serious, but the general tone is set by the prologue given here.*

from *Androcles and The Lion*
Introduction from *G. B. Shaw*
Prologue

Overture: forest sounds, roaring of lions, Christian hymn faintly. A jungle path. A lion's roar, a melancholy suffering roar, comes from the jungle. It is repeated nearer. The lion limps from the jungle on three legs, holding up his right forepaw, in which a huge thorn sticks. He sits down and contemplates it. He licks it. He shakes it. He tries to extract it by scraping it along the ground, and hurts himself worse. He roars piteously. He licks it again. Tears drop from his eyes. He limps painfully off the path and lies down under the trees, exhausted with pain. Heaving a long sigh, like wind in a trombone, he goes to sleep.

Androcles and his wife Megaera come along the path. He is a small, thin, ridiculous little man who might be any age from thirty to fifty-five. He has sandy hair, watery compassionate blue eyes, sensitive nostrils, and a very presentable forehead; but his good points go no further: his arms and legs and back, though wiry of their kind, look shrivelled and starved. He carries a big bundle, is very poorly clad, and seems tired and hungry.

His wife is a rather handsome pampered slattern, well fed and in the prime of life. She has nothing to carry, and has a stout stick to help her along.

MEGAERA [*suddenly throwing down her stick*] I wont go another step.

ANDROCLES [*pleading wearily*] Oh, not again, dear. Whats the good of stopping every two miles and saying you wont go another step? We must get on to the next village before night. There are wild beasts in this wood: lions, they say.

MEGAERA. I dont believe a word of it. You are always threatening me with wild beasts to make me walk the very soul out of my body when I can hardly drag one foot before another. We havnt seen a single lion yet.

ANDROCLES. Well, dear, do you want to see one?

MEGAERA [*tearing the bundle from his back*] You cruel brute, you dont care how tired I am, or what becomes of me [*she throws the bundle on the ground*]: always thinking of yourself. Self! self! self! always yourself! [*She sits down on the bundle*].

ANDROCLES [*sitting down sadly on the ground with his elbows on his knees and his head in his hands*] We all have to think of ourselves occasionally, dear.

MEGAERA. A man ought to think of his wife sometimes.

ANDROCLES. He cant always help it, dear. You make me think of you a good deal. Not that I blame you.

MEGAERA. Blame me! I should think not indeed. Is it my fault that I'm married to you?

ANDROCLES. No, dear: that is my fault.

MEGAERA. Thats a nice thing to say to me. Arnt you happy with me?

ANDROCLES. I dont complain, my love.

MEGAERA. You ought to be ashamed of yourself.

ANDROCLES. I am, my dear.

MEGAERA. Youre not: you glory in it.

ANDROCLES. In what, darling?

MEGAERA. In everything. In making me a slave, and making yourself a laughing-stock. It's not fair. You get me the name of being a shrew with your meek ways, always talking as if butter wouldnt melt in your mouth. And just because I look a big strong woman, and because I'm goodhearted and a bit hasty, and because youre always driving me to do things I'm sorry for afterwards, people say "Poor man: what a life his wife leads him!" Oh, if they only knew! And you think I dont know. But I do, I do, [*screaming*] I do.

ANDROCLES. Yes, my dear: I know you do.

MEGAERA. Then why dont you treat me properly and be a good husband to me?

ANDROCLES. What can I do, my dear?

MEGAERA. What can you do! You can return to your duty, and come back to your home and your friends, and sacrifice to the gods as all respectable people do, instead of having us hunted out of house and home for being dirty disreputable blaspheming atheists.

ANDROCLES. I'm not an atheist, dear: I am a Christian.

MEGAERA. Well, isnt that the same thing, only ten times worse? Everybody knows that the Christians are the very lowest of the low.

ANDROCLES. Just like us, dear.

MEGAERA. Speak for yourself. Dont you dare to compare me to common people. My father owned his own public-house; and sorrowful was the day for me when you first came drinking in our bar.

ANDROCLES. I confess I was addicted to it, dear. But I gave it up when I became a Christian.

MEGAERA. Youd much better have remained a drunkard. I can forgive a man being addicted to drink: it's only natural; and I dont deny I like a drop myself sometimes. What I cant stand is your being addicted to Christianity. And whats worse again, your being addicted to animals. How is any woman to keep her house clean when you bring in every stray cat and lost cur and lame duck in the whole countryside? You took the bread out of my mouth to feed them: you know you did: dont attempt to deny it.

ANDROCLES. Only when they were hungry and you were getting too stout, dearie.

MEGAERA. Yes: insult me, do. [*Rising*] Oh! I wont bear it another moment. You used to sit and talk to those dumb brute beasts for hours, when you hadnt a word for me.

ANDROCLES. They never answered back, darling. [*He rises and again shoulders the bundle*].

MEGAERA. Well, if youre fonder of animals than of your own wife, you can live with them here in the jungle. Ive had enough of them and enough of you. I'm going back. I'm going home.

ANDROCLES [*barring the way back*] No, dearie: dont take on like that. We cant go back. Weve sold everything: we should starve; and I should be sent to Rome and thrown to the lions—

MEGAERA. Serve you right! I wish the lions joy of you. [*Screaming*] Are you going to get out of my way and let me go home?

ANDROCLES. No, dear—

MEGAERA. Then I'll make my way through the forest; and when I'm eaten by the wild beasts youll know what a wife youve lost. [*She dashes into the jungle and nearly falls over the sleeping lion*]. Oh! Oh! Andy! Andy! [*She totters back and collapses into the arms of Androcles, who, crushed by her weight, falls on his bundle*].

ANDROCLES [*extracting himself from beneath her and slapping her hands in great anxiety*] What is it, my precious, my pet? Whats the matter? [*He raises her head. Speechless with terror, she points in the direction of the sleeping lion. He steals cautiously towards the spot indicated by Megaera. She rises with an effort and totters after him*].

MEGAERA. No, Andy: youll be killed. Come back.

The lion utters a long snoring sigh. Androcles sees the lion, and recoils fainting into the arms of Megaera, who falls back on the bundle. They roll apart and lie staring in terror at one another. The lion is heard groaning heavily in the jungle.

ANDROCLES [*whispering*] Did you see? A lion.

MEGAERA [*despairing*] The gods have sent him to punish us because youre a Christian. Take me away, Andy. Save me.

ANDROCLES [*rising*] Meggy: theres one chance for you. Itll take him pretty nigh twenty minutes to eat me (I'm rather stringy and tough) and you can escape in less time than that.

MEGAERA. Oh, dont talk about eating. [*The lion rises with a great groan and limps towards them*]. Oh! [*She faints*].

ANDROCLES [*quaking, but keeping between the lion and Megaera*] Dont you come near my wife, do you hear? [*The lion groans. Androcles can hardly stand for trembling*]. Meggy: run. Run for your life. If I take my eye off him, it's all up. [*The lion holds up his wounded paw and flaps it piteously before Androcles*]. Oh, he's lame, poor old chap! He's got a thorn in his paw. A frightfully big thorn. [*Full of sympathy*]. Oh, poor old man! Did um get an awful thorn into um's tootsums wootsums? Has it made um to sick to eat a nice little Christian man for um's breakfast? Oh, a nice little Christian man will get um's thorn out for um; and then um shall eat

PAUL CÉZANNE: *La Gardanne*. THE METROPOLITAN MUSEUM OF ART, GIFT OF DR. AND MRS. FRANZ H. HIRSCHLAND, SUBJECT TO A LIFE ESTATE IN THE DONORS, 1957

the nice Christian man and the nice Christian man's nice big tender wifey pifey. [*The lion responds by moans of self-pity*]. Yes, yes, yes, yes, yes. Now, now [*taking the paw in his hand*], um is not to bite and not to scratch, not even if it hurts a very very little. Now make velvet paws. Thats right. [*He pulls gingerly at the thorn. The lion, with an angry yell of pain, jerks back his paw so abruptly that Androcles is thrown on his back*]. Steadeee! Oh, did the nasty cruel little Christian man hurt the sore paw? [*The lion moans assentingly but apologetically*]. Well, one more little pull and it will be all over. Just one little, little, leetle pull; and then um will live happily ever after. [*He gives the thorn another pull. The lion roars and snaps his jaws with a terrifying clash*]. Oh, mustnt frighten um's good kind doctor, um's affectionate nursey. That didnt hurt at all: not a bit. Just one more. Just to shew how the brave big lion can bear pain, not like the little crybaby Christian man. Oopsh! [*The thorn comes out. The lion yells with pain, and shakes his paw wildly*]. Thats it! [*Holding up the thorn*]. Now it's out. Now lick um's paw to take away the nasty inflammation. See? [*He licks his own hand. The lion nods intelligently and licks his paw industriously*]. Clever little liony-piony! Understands um's dear old friend Andy Wandy. [*The lion licks his face*]. Yes, kissums Andy Wandy. [*The lion, wagging his tail violently, rises on his hind legs, and embraces Androcles, who makes a wry face and cries*]. Velvet paws! Velvet paws! [*The lion draws in his claws*]. Thats right. [*He embraces the lion, who finally takes the end of his tail in one paw, places that tight around Androcles' waist, resting it on his hip. Androcles takes the other paw in his hand, stretches out his arm, and the two waltz rapturously round and round and finally away through the jungle*].

MEGAERA [*who has revived during the waltz*] Oh, you coward, you havnt danced with me for years; and now you go off dancing with a great brute beast that you havnt known for ten minutes and that wants to eat your own wife. Coward! Coward! Coward! [*She rushes off after them into the jungle*].

Anton Pavlovich Chekhov
(1860-1904)
In the Cart

They drove out of the town at half past eight in the morning.

The paved road was dry, a splendid April sun was shedding warmth, but there was still snow in the ditches and in the woods. Winter, evil, dark, long, had ended so recently; spring had arrived suddenly; but neither the warmth nor the languid, transparent woods, warmed by the breath of spring, nor the black flocks flying in the fields over huge puddles that were like lakes, nor this marvelous, immeasurably deep sky, into which it seemed that one would plunge with such joy, offered anything new and interesting to Marya Vasilyevna, who was sitting in the cart. She had been teaching school for thirteen years, and in the course of all those years she had gone to town for her salary countless times; and whether it was spring, as now, or a rainy autumn evening, or winter, it was all the same to her, and what she always, invariably, longed for was to reach her destination as soon as possible.

She felt as though she had been living in these parts for a long, long time, for a hundred years, and it seemed to her that she knew every stone, every tree on the road from the town to her school. Here was her past and her present, and she could imagine no other future than the school, the road to the town and back, and again the school and again the road.

She had lost the habit of thinking of the time before she had become a schoolmistress and had almost forgotten all about it. She had once had a father and a mother; they had lived in Moscow in a big apartment near the Red Gate, but all that remained in her memory of that part of her life was something vague and formless like a dream. Her father had died when she was ten years old, and her mother had died soon after. She had a brother, an officer; at first they used to write each other, then her brother had stopped answering her letters, he had lost the habit. Of her former belongings, all that remained was a photograph of her mother, but the dampness in the school had faded it, and now nothing could be seen on it but the hair and the eyebrows.

When they had gone a couple of miles, old Semyon, who was driving, turned round and said:

"They have nabbed an official in the town. They have sent him away. They say that he and some Germans killed Alexeyev, the mayor, in Moscow."

"Who told you that?"

"They read it in the papers, in Ivan Ionov's teahouse."

And again there was a long silence. Marya Vasilyevna thought of her school, of the examinations that were coming soon, and of the girl and the four boys whom she was sending up for them. And just as she was thinking about the examinations she was overtaken by a landowner named Hanov in a carriage with four horses, the very man who had acted as examiner in her school the previous year. As he drew alongside he recognized her and bowed.

"Good morning," he said. "Are you driving home, madam?"

This Hanov, a man of about forty, with a worn face and a lifeless expression, was beginning to age noticeably, but was still handsome and attractive to women. He lived alone on his large estate, was not in the service, and it was said of him that he did nothing at home but pace from one end of the room to the other, whistling, or play chess with his old footman. It was said, too, that he drank heavily. And indeed, at the examination the previous year the very papers he had brought with him smelt of scent and wine. On that occasion everything he wore was brand-new, and Marya Vasilyevna had found him very attractive and, sitting next to him, had felt embarrassed. She was used to seeing cold, hardheaded examiners at the school, but this one did not remember a single prayer, did not know what questions to ask, was exceedingly polite and considerate, and gave only the highest marks.

"I am on my way to visit Bakvist," he continued, addressing Marya Vasilyevna, "but I wonder if he is at home."

They turned off the highway onto a dirt road, Hanov leading the way and Semyon following. The team of four horses kept to the road, slowly pulling the heavy carriage through the mud. Semyon changed his course continually, leaving the road now and then to drive over a hillock, now to skirt a meadow, often jumping down from the cart and helping the horse. Marya Vasilyevna kept thinking about the school, and wondering whether the arithmetic problem at the examination would be hard or easy. And she was annoyed with the Zemstvo office, where she had found no one the previous day. What negligence! For the past two years she had been asking them to discharge the janitor, who did nothing, was rude to her, and cuffed the boys, but no one paid any attention to her. It was hard to find the chairman at the office and when you did find him, he would say with tears in his eyes that he had no time; the inspector visited the school once in three years and had no understanding of anything connected with it, since he had formerly been employed in the Finance Department and had obtained the post of school inspector through pull; the School Board met very rarely and no one knew where; the Trustee was a half literate peasant, the owner of a tannery, stupid, coarse, and a bosom friend of the janitor's—and heaven knows to whom she could turn with complaints and inquiries.

"He is really handsome," she thought, glancing at Hanov.

Meanwhile the road was growing worse and worse. They drove into the woods. Here there was no turning off the road, the ruts were deep, and water flowed and gurgled in them. Twigs struck them stingingly in the face.

"How's the road?" asked Hanov, and laughed.

The schoolmistress looked at him and could not understand why this odd fellow lived here. What could his money, his interesting appearance, his refinement get him in this Godforsaken place, with its mud, its boredom? Life granted him no privileges, and here, like Semyon, he was jogging slowly along over an abominable road and suffering the same discomforts. Why live here, when one had a chance to live in Petersburg or abroad? And it seemed as though it would be a simple matter for a rich man like him to turn this bad road into a good one so as to avoid having to endure this misery and seeing the despair written on the faces of his coachman and Semyon? But he merely laughed, and apparently it was all the same to him, and he asked nothing better of life. He was kind, gentle, naive; he had no grasp of this coarse life, he did not know it, any more than he had known the prayers at the examination. He presented nothing to the schools but globes, and sincerely regarded himself as a useful person and a prominent worker in the field of popular education. And who had need of his globes here?

"Hold on, Vasilyevna!" said Semyon.

The cart lurched violently and was about to turn over; something heavy fell on Marya Vasilyevna's feet—it was her purchases. There was a steep climb uphill over a clayey road; noisy rivulets were flowing in winding ditches; the water had gullied the road; and how could one drive here! The horses breathed heavily. Hanov got out of the carriage and walked at the edge of the road in his long coat. He was hot.

"How's the road?" he repeated, and laughed. "This is the way to smash your carriage?"

"But who tells you to go driving in such weather?" asked Semyon in a surly voice. "You ought to stay home."

"I'm bored at home, grandfather. I don't like staying home."

Next to old Semyon he seemed well-built and vigorous, but there was something barely perceptible in his gait which betrayed him as a weak creature, already blighted, approaching its end. And suddenly it seemed as though there were a whiff of liquor in the woods. Marya Vasilyevna felt frightened and was filled with pity for this man who was going to pieces without rhyme or reason, and it occurred to her that if she were his wife or his sister she would devote her whole life to his rescue. His wife! Life was so ordered that here he was living in his great house alone, while she was living in a Godforsaken village alone, and yet for some reason the mere thought that he and she might meet on an equal footing and become intimate seemed impossible, absurd. Fundamentally, life was so arranged and human relations were complicated so utterly beyond all understanding that when you thought about it you were terrified and your heart sank.

"And you can't understand," she thought, "why God gives good looks, friendliness, charming, melancholy eyes to weak, unhappy, useless people—why they are so attractive."

"Here we must turn off to the right," said Hanov, getting into his carriage. "Good-by! All good wishes!"

And again she thought of her pupils, of the examination, of the janitor, of the School Board; and when the wind brought her the sound of the receding carriage these thoughts mingled with others. She wanted to think of beautiful eyes, of love, of the happiness that would never be....

His wife? It is cold in the morning, there is no one to light the stove, the janitor has gone off somewhere; the children come in as soon as it is light, bringing in snow and mud and making a noise; it is all so uncomfortable, so unpleasant. Her quarters consist of one little room and a kitchen close by. Every day when school is over she has a headache and after dinner she has heartburn. She has to collect money from the children for firewood and to pay the janitor, and to turn it over to the Trustee, and then to implore him—that overfed, insolent peasant—for God's sake to send her firewood. And at night she dreams of examinations, peasants, snowdrifts. And this life has aged and coarsened her, making her homely, angular, and clumsy, as though they had poured lead into her. She is afraid of everything, and in the presence of a member of the Zemstvo Board or of the Trustee, she gets up and does not dare sit down again. And she uses obsequious expressions when she mentions any one of them. And no one likes her, and life is passing drearily, without warmth, without friendly sympathy, without interesting acquaintances. In her position how terrible it would be if she were to fall in love!

"Hold on, Vasilyevna!"

Another steep climb.

She had begun to teach school from necessity, without feeling called to it; and she had never thought of a call, of the need for enlightenment; and it always seemed to her that what was most important in her work was not the children, not enlightenment, but the examinations. And when did she have time to think of a call, of enlightenment? Teachers, impecunious physicians, doctors' assistants, for all their terribly hard work, do not even have the comfort of thinking that they are serving an ideal or the people, because their heads are always filled with thoughts of their daily bread, of firewood, of bad roads, of sickness. It is a hard, humdrum existence, and only stolid cart horses like Marya Vasilyevna can bear it a long time; lively, alert, impressionable people who talk about their calling and about serving the ideal are soon weary of it and give up the work.

Semyon kept on picking out the driest and shortest way, traveling now across a meadow, now behind the cottages, but in one place the peasants would not let them pass and in another the land belonged to the priest and so they could not cross it, in yet another Ivan Ionov had bought a plot from the landowner and had dug a ditch around it. They kept turning back.

They reached Nizhneye Gorodishche. Near the teahouse, on the dung-strewn, snowy ground, there stood wagons loaded with great bottles of oil of vitriol. There were a great many people in the teahouse, all drivers, and it smelled of vodka, tobacco, and sheepskins. The place was noisy with loud talk and the banging of the door which was provided with a pulley. In the shop next door someone was playing an accordion steadily. Marya Vasilyevna was sitting down, having tea, while at the next table some peasants were drinking vodka and beer, sweaty with the tea they had had and the bad air.

"Hey, Kuzma!" people kept shouting confusedly. "What's doing?" "The Lord bless us!" "Ivan Dementyich, that I can do for you!" "See here, friend!"

A little pockmarked peasant with a black beard, who was quite drunk, was suddenly taken aback by something and began using foul language.

"What are you cursing about, you there?" Semyon, who was sitting some way off, remarked angrily. "Don't you see the young lady?"

"The young lady!" someone jeered in another corner.

"The swine!"

"I didn't mean nothing—" The little peasant was embarrassed. "Excuse me. I pays my money and the young lady pays hers. How-de-do, ma'am?"

"How do you do?" answered the schoolmistress.

"And I thank you kindly."

Marya Vasilyevna drank her tea with pleasure, and she, too, began turning red like the peasants, and again she fell to thinking about firewood, about the janitor. . . .

"Wait, brother," came from the next table. "It's the school-ma'am from Vyazovye. I know; she's a good sort."

"She's all right!"

The door was banging continually, some coming in, others going out. Marya Vasilyevna went on sitting there, thinking of the same things all the time, while the accordion went on playing and playing behind the wall. There had been patches of sunlight on the floor, they shifted to the counter, then to the wall, and finally disappeared together; this meant that it was past midday. The peasants at the next table were getting ready to leave. The little peasant went up to Marya Vasilyevna somewhat unsteadily and shook hands with her; following his example, the others shook hands with her at parting, and filed out singly, and the door squeaked and slammed nine times.

"Vasilyevna, get ready," Semyon called to her.

They drove off. And again they went at a walking pace.

"A little while back they were building a school here at this Nizhneye Gorodishche," said Semyon, turning round. "There were wicked doings then!"

"Why, what happened?"

"They say the chairman pocketed a cool thousand, and the Trustee another thousand, and the teacher five hundred."

"The whole school only cost a thousand. It's wrong to slander people, grandfather. That's all nonsense."

"I don't know. I only repeat what folks say."

But it was clear that Semyon did not

believe the schoolmistress. The peasants did not believe her. They always thought she received too large a salary, twenty-one rubles a month (five would have been enough), and that she kept for herself the greater part of the money that she received for firewood and for the janitor's wages. The Trustee thought as the peasants did, and he himself made something on the firewood and received a salary from the peasants for acting as Trustee—without the knowledge of the authorities.

The woods, thank God, were behind them, and now it would be clear, level ground all the way to Vyazovye, and they had not far to go now. All they had to do was to cross the river and then the railway line, and then they would be at Vyazovye.

"Where are you going?" Marya Vasilyevna asked Semyon. "Take the road to the right across the bridge."

"Why, we can go this way just as well, it's not so deep."

"Mind you don't drown the horse."

"What?"

"Look; Hanov is driving to the bridge, too," said Marya Vasilyevna, seeing the four-horse team far away to the right. "I think it's he."

"It's him all right. So he didn't find Bakvist in. What a blockhead he is. Lord have mercy on us! He's driving over there, and what for? It's all of two miles nearer this way."

They reached the river. In summer it was a shallow stream, easily forded and usually dried up by August, but now, after the spring floods, it was a river forty feet wide, rapid, muddy, and cold; on the bank, and right up to the water, there were fresh wheel tracks, so it had been crossed there.

"Giddap!" shouted Semyon angrily and anxiously, tugging violently at the reins and flapping his elbows as a bird does its wings. "Giddap!"

The horse went into the water up to its belly and stopped, but at once went on again, straining its muscles, and Marya Vasilyevna felt a sharp chill at her feet.

"Giddap!" she shouted, too, standing up. "Giddap!"

They got to the bank.

"Nice mess, Lord have mercy on us!" muttered Semyon, setting the harness straight. "It's an affliction, this Zemstvo."

Her shoes and rubbers were full of water, the lower edge of her dress and of her coat and one sleeve were wet and dripping; the sugar and flour had got wet, and that was the worst of it, and Marya Vasilyevna only struck her hands together in despair and said:

"Oh, Semyon, Semyon! What a fellow you are, really!"

The barrier was down at the railway crossing. An express was coming from the station. Marya Vasilyevna stood at the crossing waiting for the train to pass, and shivering all over with cold. Vyazovye was in sight now, and the school with the green roof, and the church with its blazing crosses that reflected the setting sun; and the station windows were aflame, too, and a pink smoke rose from the engine. . . . And it seemed to her that everything was shivering with cold.

Here was the train; the windows, like the crosses on the church, reflected the blazing light; it hurt her eyes to look at them. On the platform of one of the first-class carriages a lady was standing, and Marya Vasilyevna glanced at her as she flashed by. Her mother! What a resemblance! Her mother had had just such luxuriant hair, just such a forehead and that way of holding her head. And with amazing distinctness, for the first time in thirteen years, she imagined vividly her mother, her father, her brother, their apartment in Moscow, the aquarium with the little fishes, everything down to the smallest detail; she suddenly heard the piano playing, her father's voice; she felt as then, young, good-looking, well-dressed, in a bright warm room among her own people. A feeling of joy and happiness suddenly overwhelmed her, she pressed her hands to her temples in ecstasy, and called softly, imploringly:

"Mama!"

And she began to cry, she did not know why. Just at that moment Hanov drove up with his team of four horses, and seeing him she imagined such happiness as had never been, and smiled and nodded to him as an equal and intimate, and it seemed to her that the sky, the windows, the trees, were glowing with her happiness, her triumph. No, her father and mother had never died, she had never been a schoolmistress, that had been a long, strange, oppressive dream, and now she had awakened....

"Vasilyevna, get in!"

And suddenly it all vanished. The barrier was slowly rising. Marya Vasilyevna, shivering and numb with cold, got into the cart. The carriage with the four horses crossed the railway track, Semyon followed. The guard at the crossing took off his cap.

"And this is Vyazovye. Here we are."

(Translated by Avrahm Yarmolinsky)

Maurice Maeterlinck
(1862-1949)
from *Pelléas and Mélisande*

The Belgian poet and playwright Maurice Maeterlinck strongly disliked the realism that dominated the European theater of his time. His neoromantic impulses led him toward the delicate nuances of mood, the shifting lights and shadows, the sense of impermanence and of the inexorable passing of time that characterized the art of the Impressionist painters and composers. Like his fellow Symbolists Mallarmé, Rimbaud, and others, Maeterlinck believed that an object or sound—a lost ring, the striking of a bell, a stagnant pool—can convey a mood or an emotion or even an idea more effectively than pages of dialogue.

Maeterlinck's two best-known plays are The Blue Bird *and* Pelléas and Mélisande. *Claude Debussy used the latter play, with almost no changes, as the libretto for his own* Pelléas and Mélisande, *which has become the most famous of impressionist-symbolist operas. Gabriel Fauré composed incidental music for the play.*

The story, the settings, and especially the symbols of Pelléas and Mélisande *are designed to evoke memories of fairy tales—castles by the sea, children lost in* the woods, Rapunzel's long hair, and so forth. The plot, though deliberately vague, is a variation of such celebrated stories as those of Lancelot and Gwenevere, Paolo and Francesca, and especially Tristram and Iseult: the ill-fated romance of a knight or prince and the beautiful wife of his superior, usually his king or his older brother or both.

In Pelléas and Mélisande *the widowed Prince Golaud, lost in a forest, comes upon a young princess, Mélisande, who is also lost and who has allowed her crown to fall into a fountain. Golaud takes her with him, marries her, and journeys with her in a phantom ship to his own castle. Here his younger half-brother Pelléas befriends her in her loneliness. Pelléas is with her when she loses another object in a fountain (the Fountain of the Blind)—this time the wedding ring Golaud has given her. Golaud is deeply troubled when he learns of the lost ring, and more disturbed when he comes upon Pelléas and Mélisande together near a tower of the castle.*

ACT III

SCENE I

[*One of the towers of the castle. A watchman's path passes under a window of the tower.*] MÉLISANDE (*at the window combing her unbound hair*):

    My long hair hangs down to the foot of the tower,
    My hair waits for you all the way down the tower.
        The livelong day!
        The livelong day!
    Saint Daniel and Saint Michael,
    Saint Michael and Saint Raphael,
        I was born on Sunday,
        On Sunday at noon!

        [*Enter* PELLÉAS *along the path.*]

PELLÉAS: Hola! hola! ho!

MÉLISANDE: Who's there?

PELLÉAS: Me, me and me again! ... What are you doing at the window, singing, singing like a bird that doesn't belong here.

MÉLISANDE: I am fixing my hair for the night.

PELLÉAS: Is that what I see on the wall? ... I thought that you had a light. ...

MÉLISANDE: I opened the window. It's too hot in the tower; it's beautiful tonight. . . .
PELLÉAS: There are innumerable stars; I have never seen so many as tonight; . . . but the moon is still on the sea. . . . Do not stay in the shadow, Mélisande, lean forward a little so that I can see your unbound hair.

[MÉLISANDE *leans out of the window.*]

MÉLISANDE: I look frightful like this.
PELLÉAS: Oh, Mélisande! . . . Oh! you are beautiful! . . . you are beautiful like that! . . . lean over! lean over! . . . let me come nearer to you. . . .
MÉLISANDE: I can't come any nearer . . . I'm leaning over as much as I can. . . .
PELLÉAS: I can't climb any higher . . . give me your hand at least tonight . . . before I go away . . . I'm leaving tomorrow. . . .
MÉLISANDE: No, no, no. . . .
PELLÉAS: Yes, yes; I'm going, I shall leave tomorrow . . . give me your hand, your hand, your little hand upon my lips. . . .
MÉLISANDE: I won't give you my hand if you are going away. . . .
PELLÉAS: Give, give, give. . . .
MÉLISANDE: You won't go? . . .
PELLÉAS: I'll stay, I'll stay.
MÉLISANDE: I see a rose in the shadows. . . .
PELLÉAS: Where? . . . I see only the branches of the willow overhanging the wall. . . .
MÉLISANDE: Lower down, lower down, in the garden; over there in the dark shrubbery.
PELLÉAS: It's not a rose. . . . I'll go and see in a moment but first give me your hand. . . .
MÉLISANDE: There, there. . . . I can't lean over any farther. . . .
PELLÉAS: My lips can't reach your hand. . . .
MÉLISANDE: I can't lean over any farther . . . I am almost falling. . . .—Oh! oh! my hair is falling from the tower! . . .

[*Her hair suddenly falls down as she leans over and covers* PELLÉAS.]

PELLÉAS: Oh! oh! what's this? . . . Your hair, your hair is falling down on me! . . . All your hair, Mélisande, all your hair is falling from the tower! ... I'm holding it in my hands, I'm holding it in my mouth.... I'm holding it in my arms, and I'm putting it around my neck.... I shall not open my hands again tonight.

MÉLISANDE: Let me go! let me go! ... You're going to make me fall! ...

PELLÉAS: No, no, no; ... I've never seen hair like yours, Mélisande! ... Look, look, look, it comes from above and covers me to my very heart.... It covers me more, even to my knees. ... It's soft, it's as soft as if it fell from heaven! ... I can no longer see the sky through your hair. See, see, my hands no longer can hold it. It even reaches to the branches of the willow tree.... It's living like a bird in my hands ... and it loves me, it loves me a thousand times more than you do! ...

MÉLISANDE: Let me go ... let me go ... someone might come....

PELLÉAS: No, no, no; I will not let you go tonight.... You are my prisoner tonight; all night, all night....

MÉLISANDE: Pelléas! Pelléas! ...

PELLÉAS: You shall not go away any more.... I am tying it, I am tying it to the branches of the willow—your hair. You'll never get away ... you'll never get away.... Look, look, I'm kissing your hair.... I no longer am suffering in the tangles of your hair. Do you hear my kisses all along your hair? They climb up along your hair. Each one must carry some to you. See, see, I can open my hands.... See, my hands are open, yet you cannot leave me....

[*Some doves come out of the tower and fly about them in the night.*]

MÉLISANDE: Oh! oh! you've hurt me.... What's that, Pelléas?—What's flying around me?

PELLÉAS: It is the doves coming out of the tower.... I have frightened them; they are flying away....

MÉLISANDE: They are my doves, Pelléas.—Let's go away, leave me; they may never return....

PELLÉAS: Why should they never return?

MÉLISANDE: They'll be lost in the darkness.... Let me go.... Let me lift my head.... I hear the sound of footsteps.... Let me go!—It's

Golaud! . . . I think it's Golaud! . . . He's heard us. . . .
PELLÉAS: Wait! Wait! . . . Your hair is tangled in the branches. . . . It got caught in the dark. Wait, wait! . . . It's dark. . . .

[*Enter* GOLAUD *by the watchman's path.*]

GOLAUD: What are you doing here?
PELLÉAS: What am I doing here? . . . I. . . .
GOLAUD: What children you are. . . . Mélisande, do not lean that way out of the window, you will fall. . . . Don't you know that it is late?—It is almost midnight.—Don't play that way in the darkness.—You are both children. . . . (*Laughing nervously.*) What children! . . . What children! . . .

[*He goes out with* PELLÉAS.]

His suspicions aroused, Golaud warns Pelléas to "play no more children's games" with Mélisande. Knowing the hopelessness of their love, Pelléas makes plans to go away. King Arkël, half-blind old grandfather of the two princes, senses Mélisande's deep sadness and tells her of his pity. Pelléas and Mélisande meet for a moment of farewell that ends in a passionate embrace. Golaud sees them and kills Pelléas with his sword; then he follows Mélisande as she tries to run away. As the final act begins, Mélisande is lying ill in her bedchamber in the castle.

ACT V

SCENE I

[*A bedchamber in the castle.* ARKËL, GOLAUD, *and the* DOCTOR *are discovered in a corner of the room.* MÉLISANDE *lies upon a bed.*]

DOCTOR: She couldn't die from this little wound; it wouldn't kill a bird. . . . So you haven't killed her, my good lord; don't grieve this way. . . . Then, too, it has not been decreed that we shall not save her. . . .
ARKËL: No, no, it seems to me that we are too silent, in spite of ourselves, in her room. . . . That is not a good sign. . . . Look how she sleeps . . . slowly, slowly. . . . It's as though her soul were frozen for all eternity. . . .
GOLAUD: I have killed without provocation! Wouldn't that make the very stones cry out? . . . They were kissing each other like little chil-

dren.... They were brother and sister.... And I, I suddenly!... I did it in spite of myself, you see... I did it in spite of myself....

DOCTOR: Look, I think she is awakening....

MÉLISANDE: Open the window... open the window....

ARKËL: Do you wish me to open this one, Mélisande?

MÉLISANDE: No, no, the large window... so that I can see....

ARKËL: Isn't the sea air too cold tonight?

DOCTOR: Go ahead....

MÉLISANDE: Thank you.... Is the sun setting?

ARKËL: Yes, the sun is sinking in the sea; it is late.—How do you feel, Mélisande?

MÉLISANDE: Very well.—Why do you ask that? I have never felt better.—It seems to me, however, that I know something....

ARKËL: What are you saying?—I don't understand you.

MÉLISANDE: I don't understand all that I say any longer, you see.... I don't know what I am saying.... I don't know what I know.... I no longer say what I want to....

ARKËL: Oh, yes, indeed.... I'm so happy to hear you talk this way; you have been a little delirious these last few days, and we no longer understood you.... But now all that's over....

MÉLISANDE: I don't know....—Are you all alone in the room, grandfather?

ARKËL: No, there is also the doctor who cured you....

MÉLISANDE: Ah....

ARKËL: And then there is someone else....

MÉLISANDE: Who?

ARKËL: It is... you mustn't be frightened... he doesn't wish you the least harm, you may be sure.... If you're afraid, he will go away... he is very unhappy....

MÉLISANDE: Who is it?

ARKËL: It is... it is your husband... it is Golaud....

MÉLISANDE: Is Golaud here? Why doesn't he come near me?

GOLAUD (*dragging himself toward the bed*): Mélisande . . . Mélisande. . . .

MÉLISANDE: Is that you, Golaud? I hardly recognized. . . . It's because the evening sun is in my eyes. . . . Why are you gazing at the walls? You have grown thin and old. . . . Is it long since we last saw each other?

GOLAUD: (*to* ARKËL *and the* DOCTOR): Will you go away a moment, my poor friends. . . . I'll leave the door wide open. . . . Only a moment. . . . I should like to tell her something; without it I could never die in peace. . . . Will you?—You may return immediately. . . . Don't refuse me this . . . I'm a miserable man.

[ARKËL *and the* DOCTOR *go out.*]

Mélisande, do you pity me as I pity you? . . . Mélisande? . . . Do you forgive me, Mélisande? . . .

MÉLISANDE: Yes, yes, I forgive you. . . . What is there to forgive?

GOLAUD: I have done you so much wrong, Mélisande. . . . I cannot tell you the wrong I have done you. . . . But I see it, I see it so clearly today . . . since the first day. . . . And it's all my fault, all that's happened, all that's going to happen. . . . If I could explain, you would see it as I see it! . . . I see everything, I see everything! . . . But I love you so much! . . . I love you so much! . . . But now someone is going to die. . . . I am going to die. . . . And I should like to know . . . I should like to ask you. . . . You'll not be angry with me? . . . The truth must be told a man about to die. . . . He must know the truth, otherwise he couldn't sleep in peace. . . . Do you swear to tell me the truth?

MÉLISANDE: Yes.

GOLAUD: Did you love Pelléas?

MÉLISANDE: Why, yes, I loved him. Where is he?

GOLAUD: You don't understand me?—Don't you want to understand me?—It seems to me . . . it seems to me. . . . Well then, here: I'm asking you if you loved him with a forbidden love. . . . Have you . . . have you both sinned? Say it, say it, yes, yes, yes.

MÉLISANDE: No, no, we haven't sinned.—Why do you ask that?

GOLAUD: Mélisande! . . . for God's sake, tell me the truth!
MÉLISANDE: Haven't I told you the truth?
GOLAUD: Don't continue to lie this way, at the point of death!
MÉLISANDE: Who is going to die?—Am I?
GOLAUD: You, you! and I, I too, after you! . . . And we must have the truth. . . . We must at last know the truth, do you hear! . . . Tell me everything! Tell me everything! I forgive you everything! . . .
MÉLISANDE: Why am I going to die?—I didn't know it. . . .
GOLAUD: Now you know it! . . . It is time! it is time! . . . Quickly! quickly! . . . The truth! the truth! . . .
MÉLISANDE: The truth . . . the truth. . . .
GOLAUD: Where are you?—Mélisande!—Where are you?—This is not natural! Mélisande! Where are you? (*Seeing* ARKËL *and the* DOCTOR *at the door of the chamber.*) Yes, yes, you can return. . . . I know nothing; it's useless. . . . She's already too far away from us. . . . I shall never know! . . . I'm going to die here like a blind man! . . .
ARKËL: What have you done? You are going to kill her. . . .
GOLAUD: I already have killed her. . . .
ARKËL: Mélisande. . . .
MÉLISANDE: Is that you, grandfather?
ARKËL: Yes, my daughter. . . . What do you want me to do?
MÉLISANDE: Is the winter really coming?
ARKËL: Why do you ask that?
MÉLISANDE: Because it's cold and there are no more leaves. . . .
ARKËL: Are you cold?—Do you want the windows closed?
MÉLISANDE: No, no . . . until the sun is at the bottom of the sea.—It goes down slowly. . . . Does that mean that winter's coming?
ARKËL: Yes.—Don't you like winter?
MÉLISANDE: Oh! no. . . . I'm afraid of the cold—Ah! I'm afraid of extreme cold. . . .
ARKËL: Are you feeling better?

MÉLISANDE: Yes, yes, I no longer have all those worries....

ARKËL: Do you want to see your child?

MÉLISANDE: What child?

ARKËL: Your baby, your little girl....

MÉLISANDE: Where is she?

ARKËL: Here....

MÉLISANDE: It is strange.... I can't lift my arms to take her....

ARKËL: That is because you still are very weak.... I'll hold her myself; see....

MÉLISANDE: She doesn't laugh.... She's tiny.... She's going to cry too.... I'm sorry for her....

[*The room is filled, little by little, by maidservants of the castle, who range themselves in silence along the walls and wait.*]

GOLAUD (*suddenly rising*): What is the matter?—Why are all these women coming here?

DOCTOR: They are the maidservants....

ARKËL: Who called them?

DOCTOR: I didn't....

GOLAUD: Why have you come here?—Nobody asked you.... What are you coming here to do?—What is it?—Answer!...

[*The servants do not reply.*]

ARKËL: Don't speak so loudly.... She's going to sleep; she has closed her eyes....

GOLAUD: It isn't—?...

DOCTOR: No, no, see, she still breathes....

ARKËL: Her eyes are full of tears.—Now her soul is weeping.... Why does she reach her arms out that way?—What does she want?

DOCTOR: Toward the child, no doubt. It's a mother's struggle against death....

GOLAUD: Right away?—Right away?—You must tell me, speak! speak!

DOCTOR: Perhaps....

GOLAUD: At once?... Oh! oh! I must tell her....—Mélisande! Mélisande!... Leave me alone! leave me alone with her!...

ARKËL: No, no, do not come near.... Do not trouble her.... Do not speak to her any more.... You don't know what the soul—

GOLAUD: It is not my fault, it is not my fault!

ARKËL: Hark... hark.... We must speak low

now.—Don't trouble her any more.... The human soul is very silent.... The human soul likes to go away alone.... It suffers so timidly. ... But the pity of it, Golaud... the pity of everything we see!... Oh! oh! oh!...

[*At this moment all the servants suddenly fall on their knees at the end of the room.*]

ARKËL: What's the matter?

DOCTOR (*approaching the bed and feeling the body*): They are right....

[*A long silence.*]

ARKËL: I saw nothing.—Are you sure?...

DOCTOR: Yes, yes.

ARKËL: I heard nothing.... So quickly, so quickly.... All of a sudden.... She goes away without saying a thing....

GOLAUD: (*sobbing*): Oh! oh!...

ARKËL: Don't stay here, Golaud.... Now she needs silence.... Come, come.... It's terrible, but it's not your fault.... She was a little creature, so peaceful, so timid, so silent.... She was a poor little creature, mysterious like everyone else.... She lies there as if she were the big sister of her baby.... Come, the child must not stay here in this room.... It must live now in her place.... It's the poor little one's turn....

[*They go out silently.*]

THE END

TWENTIETH CENTURY

WASSILY KANDINSKY: *La flèche*, KUNSTMUSEUM, BASEL

TWENTIETH CENTURY

The twentieth century is a period of such extremes in literature, as in all the other arts, that it defies attempts at ready classification. Part of this diversity comes from a world in which modernization and invention preclude tomorrow's ever appearing quite the same as today. Obviously this has been true in the past as well but in no other age has change—physical, psychological, social, and otherwise—occurred with such bewildering speed. And no other age has had the capacity, if it so wills, to change the face of the earth in a matter of minutes.

World Impact

Now, as never before, social problems, altering philosophies, and even new art movements that in an earlier age would have affected a single country and perhaps its neighbors can have an impact on the world in general. World War I, for instance, was an all-encompassing conflict that had its effect, economically if not militarily, not only on the Western European and American countries involved but on the rest of the world. World War II, of course, was even greater in its impact. Whether it be wars, depressions, political maneuverings, or social problems, their force has helped shape modern art in its attempts to report, to reform, or to escape.

Prose

Prose fiction, whether realistic, naturalistic, or late-romantic, had a fairly strong identity in the first decades of the twentieth century. The novel, the great literary form of the later nineteenth century, continued to be one of the favorite vehicles of expression. Representing prose fiction in this anthology are a number of short stories, which were (and continue to be) produced in quantity and often at a high level of artistic excellence by novelists as well as specialists in short fiction.

Moving from the nineteenth-century "tale" to the modern psychological and often symbolic "slice of life" experience, the short story has achieved an audience more extensive than that of poetry. The popularity of journals has encouraged the development of the short story, and vice versa. As is demonstrated by the selections in the earlier sections of this text (those by Poe, Hawthorne, Tolstoy and Chekhov, for instance), as well as by those that follow, the short story can be predominantly romantic or symbolic or realistic or whatever, depending on the attitude and intentions of the author.

Poetry

Vitality of movement and freedom of form give much modern poetry a powerful impact, especially when it concerns sociological and psychological issues. After World War I many schools and movements of poetic art manifested themselves in reaction to the world the artists confronted. Symbolists such as Yeats, Valery, and Pound attempted to evaluate change and cope with reality by intensely personal, emotional responses as they sought to redefine that reality. A modern realism, on the other hand, asserts itself in such poets as Sandburg, Jeffers, and Roethke.

Another significant occurrence in modern poetry has been a diminishing of the reading audience, in proportionate terms, and the placing of greater demands on that audience. In the modern period the reading audience has become quite select, for the allusions, intricacies, and semiprivate symbolisms of a T. S. Eliot or a Dylan Thomas often require a degree of artistic sophistication if one is to understand and appreciate them.

What does all this hold for the future? One can only guess. Writers in all ages seem to swing from the romantic, individual-centered mode of expression to the classical, society-centered. But more than ever today, both tendencies exist side by side. Twentieth-century literature fluctuates with the vagaries of the international milieu: it reflects hope, disillusionment, a romantic longing for the past, and a realism that has lost some of its earlier naturalistic tendencies. There is no precise label to affix to the modern writer; one can only attempt to place him in some sort of historical perspective and to evaluate him from that standpoint. The modern period reflects the constantly dynamic movement of an age that has loosed a Pandora's box of psychological analysis and technology, skepticism and hope, and is now trying to understand the consequences.

HENRI MATISSE: *Back*, LOS ANGELES COUNTY MUSEUM

William Butler Yeats
(1865-1939)
The Lake Isle of Innisfree

I will arise and go now, and go to Innisfree,
And a small cabin build there, of clay and wattles made:
Nine bean-rows will I have there, a hive for the honey-bee,
And live alone in the bee-loud glade.

And I shall have some peace there, for peace comes dropping slow,
Dropping from the veils of the morning to where the cricket sings;
There midnight's all a glimmer, and noon a purple glow,
And evening full of linnet's wings.

I will arise and go now, for always night and day
I hear lake water lapping with low sounds by the shore;
While I stand on the roadway, or on the pavements grey,
I hear it in the deep heart's core.

The Wild Swans at Coole

The trees are in their autumn beauty,
The woodland paths are dry,
Under the October twilight the water
Mirrors a still sky;
Upon the brimming water among the stones
Are nine and fifty swans.

The nineteenth Autumn has come upon me
Since I first made my count;
I saw, before I had well finished,
All suddenly mount
And scatter, wheeling, in great broken rings
Upon their clamorous wings.

I have looked upon those brilliant creatures,
And now my heart is sore.
All's changed since I, hearing at twilight,
The first time on this shore,
The bell-beat of their wings above my head,
Trod with a lighter tread.

Unwearied still, lover by lover,
They paddle in the cold,
Companionable streams or climb the air;
Their hearts have not grown old;
Passion or conquest, wander where they will,
Attend upon them still.

But now they drift on the still water
Mysterious, beautiful;
Among what rushes will they build,
By what lake's edge or pool
Delight men's eyes, when I awake some day
To find they have flown away?

When You Are Old

When you are old and grey and full of sleep,
And nodding by the fire, take down this book,
And slowly read, and dream of the soft look
Your eyes had once, and of their shadows deep;

How many loved your moments of glad grace,
And loved your beauty with love false or true,
But one man loved the pilgrim soul in you,
And loved the sorrows of your changing face;

And bending down beside the glowing bars,
Murmur, a little sadly, how Love fled
And paced upon the mountains overhead
And hid his face amid a crowd of stars.

Edwin Arlington Robinson
(1869-1935)
Luke Havergal

Go to the western gate, Luke Havergal,
There where the vines cling crimson on the wall,
And in the twilight wait for what will come.
The leaves will whisper there of her, and some,
Like flying words, will strike you as they fall;
But go, and if you listen, she will call.
Go to the western gate, Luke Havergal—
Luke Havergal.

No, there is not a dawn in eastern skies
To rift the fiery night that's in your eyes;
But there, where western glooms are gathering,
The dark will end the dark, if anything:
God slays himself with every leaf that flies,
And hell is more than half of paradise.
No, there is not a dawn in eastern skies—
In eastern skies.

Out of a grave I come to tell you this,
Out of a grave I come to quench the kiss
That flames upon your forehead with a glow
That blinds you to the way that you must go.
Yes, there is yet one way to where she is,
Bitter, but one that faith may never miss.
Out of a grave I come to tell you this—
To tell you this.

There is the western gate, Luke Havergal,
There are the crimson leaves upon the wall.
Go, for the winds are tearing them away,—
Nor think to riddle the dead words they say,
Nor any more to feel them as they fall;
But go, and if you trust her she will call.
There is the western gate, Luke Havergal—
Luke Havergal.

Paul Valéry
(1871-1945)
The Graveyard by the Sea

This quiet roof, where dove-sails saunter by,
Between the pines, the tombs, throbs visibly.
Impartial noon patterns the sea in flame—
That sea forever starting and re-starting.
When thought has had its hour, oh how rewarding
Are the long vistas of celestial calm!

What grace of light, what pure toil goes to form
The manifold diamond of the elusive foam!
What peace I feel begotten at that source!
When sunlight rests upon a profound sea,
Time's air is sparkling, dream is certainty—
Pure artifice both of an eternal Cause.

Sure treasure, simple shrine to intelligence,
Palpable calm, visible reticence,
Proud-lidded water, Eye wherein there wells
Under a film of fire such depth of sleep—
O silence! . . . Mansion in my soul, you slope
Of gold, roof of a myriad golden tiles.

Temple of time, within a brief sigh bounded,
To this rare height inured I climb, surrounded
By the horizons of a sea-girt eye.
And, like my supreme offering to the gods,
That peaceful coruscation only breeds
A loftier indifference on the sky.

Even as a fruit's absorbed in the enjoying,
Even as within the mouth its body dying
Changes into delight through dissolution,
So to my melted soul the heavens declare
All bounds transfigured into a boundless air,
And I breathe now my future's emanation.

Beautiful heaven, true heaven, look how I change!
After such arrogance, after so much strange
Idleness—strange, yet full of potency—
I am all open to these shining spaces;
Over the homes of the dead my shadow passes,
Ghosting along—a ghost subduing me.

My soul laid bare to your midsummer fire,
O just, impartial light whom I admire,
Whose arms are merciless, you have I stayed
And give back, pure, to your original place.
Look at yourself . . . But to give light implies
No less a somber moiety of shade.

Oh, for myself alone, mine, deep within
At the heart's quick, the poem's fount, between
The void and its pure issue, I beseech
The intimations of my secret power.
O bitter, dark, and echoing reservoir
Speaking of depths always beyond my reach.

But know you—feigning prisoner of the boughs,
Gulf which eats up their slender prison-bars,
Secret which dazzles though mine eyes are closed—

What body drags me to its lingering end,
What mind draws *it* to this bone-peopled ground?
A star broods there on all that I have lost.

Closed, hallowed, full of insubstantial fire,
Morsel of earth to heaven's light given o'er—
This plot, ruled by its flambeaux, pleases me—
A place all gold, stone, and dark wood, where shudders
So much marble above so many shadows:
And on my tombs, asleep, the faithful sea.

Keep off the idolaters, bright watch-dog, while—
A solitary with the shepherd's smile—
I pasture long my sheep, my mysteries,
My snow-white flock of undisturbéd graves!
Drive far away from here the careful doves,
The vain daydreams, the angels' questioning eyes!

Now present here, the future takes its time.
The brittle insect scrapes at the dry loam;
All is burnt up, used up, drawn up in air
To some ineffably rarefied solution . . .
Life is enlarged, drunk with annihilation,
And bitterness is sweet, and the spirit clear.

The dead lie easy, hidden in earth where they
Are warmed and have their mysteries burnt away.
Motionless noon, noon aloft in the blue
Broods on itself—a self-sufficient theme.
O rounded dome and perfect diadem,
I am what's changing secretly in you.

I am the only medium for your fears.
My penitence, my doubts, my baulked desires—
These are the flaw within your diamond pride . . .
But in their heavy night, cumbered with marble,
Under the roots of trees a shadow people
Has slowly now come over to your side.

To an impervious nothingness they're thinned,
For the red clay has swallowed the white kind;
Into the flowers that gift of life has passed.
Where are the dead?—their homely turns of speech,
The personal grace, the soul informing each?
Grubs thread their way where tears were once composed.

The bird-sharp cries of girls whom love is teasing,
The eyes, the teeth, the eyelids moistly closing,
The pretty breast that gambles with the flame,
The crimson blood shining when lips are yielded,
The last gift, and the fingers that would shield it—
All go to earth, go back into the game.

And you, great soul, is there yet hope in you
To find some dream without the lying hue
That gold or wave offers to fleshly eyes?
Will you be singing still when you're thin air?
All perishes. A thing of flesh and pore
Am I. Divine impatience also dies.

Lean immortality, all crêpe and gold,
Laurelled consoler frightening to behold,
Death is a womb, a mother's breast, you feign—
The fine illusion, oh the pious trick!
Who does not know them, and is not made sick—
That empty skull, that everlasting grin?

Ancestors deep down there, O derelict heads
Whom such a weight of spaded earth o'erspreads,
Who *are* the earth, in whom our steps are lost,
The real flesh-eater, worm unanswerable
Is not for you that sleep under the table:
Life is his meat, and I am still his host.

"Love," shall we call him? "Hatred of self," maybe?
His secret tooth is so intimate with me
That any name would suit him well enough,
Enough that he can see, will, daydream, touch—
My flesh delights him, even upon my couch
I live but as a morsel of his life.

Zeno, Zeno, cruel philosopher Zeno,
Have you then pierced me with your feathered arrow
That hums and flies, yet does not fly! The sounding
Shaft gives me life, the arrow kills. Oh, sun!—
Oh, what a tortoise-shadow to outrun
My soul, Achilles' giant stride left standing!

No, no! Arise! The future years unfold.
Shatter, O body, meditation's mould!
And, O my breast, drink in the wind's reviving!
A freshness, exhalation of the sea,
Restores my soul . . . Salt-breathing potency!
Let's run at the waves and be hurled back to living!

Yes, mighty sea with such wild frenzies gifted
(The panther skin and the rent chlamys), sifted
All over with sun-images that glisten,
Creature supreme, drunk on your own blue flesh,
Who in a tumult like the deepest hush
Bite at your sequin-glittering tail—yes, listen!

The wind is rising! . . . We must try to live!
The huge air opens and shuts my book: the wave
Dares to explode out of the rocks in reeking
Spray. Fly away, my sun-bewildered pages!
Break, waves! Break up with your rejoicing surges
This quiet roof where sails like doves were pecking.

Robert Frost
(1874-1963)
Acquainted with the Night

I have been one acquainted with the night.
I have walked out in rain—and back in rain.
I have outwalked the furthest city light.

I have looked down the saddest city lane.
I have passed by the watchman on his beat
And dropped my eyes, unwilling to explain.

I have stood still and stopped the sound of feet
When far away an interrupted cry
Came over houses from another street,

But not to call me back or say good-by;
And further still at an unearthly height
One luminary clock against the sky

Proclaimed the time was neither wrong nor right.
I have been one acquainted with the night.

Tree at My Window

Tree at my window, window tree,
My sash is lowered when night comes on;
But let there never be curtain drawn
Between you and me.

Vague dream-head lifted out of the ground,
And thing next most diffuse to cloud,
Not all your light tongues talking aloud
Could be profound.

But, tree, I have seen you taken and tossed,
And if you have seen me when I slept,
You have seen me when I was taken and swept
And all but lost.

That day she put our heads together,
Fate had her imagination about her,
Your head so much concerned with outer,
Mine with inner, weather.

The Onset

Always the same, when on a fated night
At last the gathered snow lets down as white
As may be in dark woods, and with a song
It shall not make again all winter long
Of hissing on the yet uncovered ground,
I almost stumble looking up and round,
As one who overtaken by the end
Gives up his errand, and lets death descend
Upon him where he is, with nothing done
To evil, no important triumph won,
More than if life had never been begun.

Yet all the precedent is on my side:
I know that winter death has never tried
The earth but it has failed: the snow may heap
In long storms an undrifted four feet deep
As measured against maple, birch, and oak,
It cannot check the peeper's silver croak;

And I shall see the snow all go downhill
In water of a slender April rill
That flashes tail through last year's withered brake
And dead weeds, like a disappearing snake.
Nothing will be left white but here a birch,
And there a clump of houses with a church.

The Tuft of Flowers

I went to turn the grass once after one
Who mowed it in the dew before the sun.

The dew was gone that made his blade so keen
Before I came to view the leveled scene.

I looked for him behind an isle of trees;
I listened for his whetstone on the breeze.

But he had gone his way, the grass all mown,
And I must be, as he had been—alone,

"As all must be," I said within my heart,
"Whether they work together or apart."

But as I said it, swift there passed me by
On noiseless wing a bewildered butterfly,

Seeking with memories grown dim o'er night
Some resting flower of yesterday's delight.

And once I marked his flight go round and round,
As where some flower lay withering on the ground.

And then he flew as far as eye could see,
And then on tremulous wing came back to me.

I thought of questions that have no reply,
And would have turned to toss the grass to dry;

But he turned first, and led my eye to look
At a tall tuft of flowers beside a brook,

A leaping tongue of bloom the scythe had spared
Beside a reedy brook the scythe had bared.

The mower in the dew had loved them thus,
By leaving them to flourish, not for us,

Nor yet to draw one thought of ours to him,
But from sheer morning gladness at the brim.

The butterfly and I had lit upon,
Nevertheless, a message from the dawn,

That made me hear the wakening birds around,
And hear his long scythe whispering to the ground,

And feel a spirit kindred to my own;
So that henceforth I worked no more alone;

But glad with him, I worked as with his aid,
And weary, sought at noon with him the shade;

And dreaming, as it were, held brotherly speech
With one whose thought I had not hoped to reach.

"Men work together," I told him from the heart,
"Whether they work together or apart."

Rainer Maria Rilke
(1875-1926)
Autumn Day

Lord, it is time. The summer was too long.
Lay now thy shadow over the sundials,
and on the meadows let the winds blow strong.

Bid the last fruit to ripen on the vine;
allow them still two friendly southern days
to bring them to perfection and to force
the final sweetness in the heavy wine.

Who has no house now will not build him one.
Who is alone now will be long alone,

will waken, read, and write long letters
and through the barren pathways up and down
restlessly wander when dead leaves are blown.

Autumn

The leaves fall, fall as if from far away,
like withered things from gardens deep in sky;
they fall with gestures of renunciation.

And through the night the heavy earth falls too,
down from the stars, into the loneliness.

And we all fall. This hand must fall.
Look everywhere: it is the lot of all.

Yet there is one who holds us as we fall
eternally in his hands' tenderness.

The Panther
Jardin des Plantes, Paris

His sight from ever gazing through the bars
has grown so blunt that it sees nothing more.
It seems to him that thousands of bars are
before him, and behind them nothing merely.

The easy motion of his supple stride,
which turns about the very smallest circle,
is like a dance of strength about a center
in which a mighty will stands stupefied.

Only sometimes when the pupil's film
soundlessly opens . . . then one image fills
and glides through the quiet tension of the limbs
into the heart and ceases and is still.

(Translated by C. F. MacIntyre)

GIORGIO DE CHIRICO: *The Child's Brain*, NATIONALMUSEUM, STOCKHOLM

Thomas Mann
(1875-1955)
Little Lizzy

There are marriages which the imagination, even the most practiced literary one, cannot conceive. You must just accept them, as you do in the theater when you see the ancient and doddering married to the beautiful and gay, as the given premises on which the farce is mechanically built up.

Yes, the wife of Jacoby the lawyer was lovely and young, a woman of unusual charm. Some years—shall we say thirty years?—ago, she had been christened with the names of Anna, Margarete, Rosa, Amalie; but the name she went by was always Amra, composed of the initials of her four real ones; it suited to perfection her somewhat exotic personality. Her soft, heavy hair, which she wore parted on one side and brushed straight back above her ears from the narrow temples, had only the darkness of the glossy chestnut; but her skin displayed the dull, dark sallowness of the south and clothed a form which southern suns must have ripened. Her slow, voluptuous indolent presence suggested the harem; each sensuous, lazy movement of her body strengthened the impression that with her the head was entirely subordinate to the heart. She needed only to have looked at you once, with her artless brown eyes, lifting her brows in the pathetically narrow forehead, horizontally, in a quaint way she had, for you to be certain of that. But she herself was not so simple as not to know it too. Quite simply, she avoided exposing herself, she spoke seldom and little—and what is there to say against a woman who is both beautiful and silent? Yes, the word "simple" is probably the last which should be applied to her. Her glance was artless; but also it had a kind of luxurious cunning—you could see that she was not dull, also that she might be a mischief-maker. In profile her nose was rather too thick; but her full, large mouth was utterly lovely, if also lacking in any expression save sensuality.

This disturbing phenomenon was the wife of Jacoby the lawyer, a man of forty. Whoever looked at him was bound to be amazed at the fact. He was stout, Jacoby the lawyer; but stout is not the word, he was a perfect colossus of a man! His legs, in their columnar clumsiness and the slate-gray trousers he always wore, reminded one of an elephant's. His round, fat-upholstered back was that of a bear; and over the vast round of his belly his funny little gray jacket was held by a single button strained so tight that when it was unbuttoned the jacket came wide open with a pop. Scarcely anything which could be called a neck united this huge torso with the little head atop. The head had narrow watery eyes, a squabby nose, and a wee mouth between cheeks drooping with fullness. The upper lip and the round head were covered with harsh, scanty, light-colored bristles that showed the naked skin, as on an overfed dog. There was no doubt that Jacoby's fatness was not of a healthy kind. His gigantic body, tall as well as stout, was not muscular, but flabby. The blood would sometimes rush to his puffy face, then ebb away leaving it of a yellowish pallor; the mouth would be drawn and sour.

Jacoby's practice was a limited one; but he was well-to-do, partly from his wife's side; and the childless pair lived in a comfortable apartment in the Kaiserstrasse and entertained a good deal. This must have been Frau Amra's taste, for it is unthinkable that the lawyer could have cared for it; he participated with an enthusiasm of a peculiarly painful kind. This fat man's character was the oddest in the world. No human being could have been politer, more accommodating, more complaisant than he. But you unconsciously knew that this over-obligingness was somehow forced, that its true source was an inward insecurity and cowardice—the impression it gave was not very pleasant. A man who despises himself is a very ugly sight; worse still when vanity combines with his cowardice to make him wish to please. This was the case, I should say, with Jacoby: his obsequiousness was almost crawling, it went beyond the bounds of personal decency. He was quite capable of saying to a lady as he escorted her to table: "My dear lady, I am a disgusting creature, but will you do me the honor?" No humor would be mingled with the remark; it was simply cloying, bitter, self-tortured—in a word, disgusting, as he said.

The following once actually happened: the lawyer was taking a walk, and a clumsy porter with a hand-cart ran over his foot. Too late the man stopped his cart and turned round—whereupon Jacoby, quite pale and dazed, his cheeks shaking up and down, took off his hat and stuttered: "I b-beg your pardon." A thing like that is infuriating. But this extraordinary colossus seemed perpetually to suffer from a plague of conscience. When he took a walk with his wife on the Lerchenberg, the Corso of the little city, he would roll his eyes round at Amra, walking with her wonderful elastic gait at his side, and bow so anxiously, diligently, and zealously in all directions that he seemed to be begging pardon of all the lieutenants they met for being in unworthy possession of such a beautiful wife. His mouth had a pathetically ingratiating expression, as though he wanted to disarm their scorn.

I have already hinted that the reason why Amra married Jacoby is unfathomable. As for him, he was in love with her; ardently, as people of his physical make-up seldom are, and with such anxious humility as fitted the rest of his character. Sometimes, late in the evening, he would enter their large sleeping-chamber with its high windows and flowered hangings—softly, so softly that there was no sound, only the slow shaking of floor and furniture. He would come up to Amra's massive bed, where she already lay, kneel down, and with infinite caution take her hand. She would lift her brows in a level line, in the quaint way she had, and look at her husband, abject before her in the dim light, with a look of malice and sensuality combined. With his puffy, trembling hands he would softly stroke back the sleeve and press his tragic fat face into the soft brown flesh of her wrist, where little blue veins stood out. And he would speak to her, in a shaking, half-smothered voice, as a sensible man in everyday life never speaks:

"Amra, my dear Amra! I am not disturbing you? You were not asleep yet? Dear God! I have been thinking all day how beautiful you are and how much I love you. I beg you to listen, for it is so very hard to express what I feel: I love you so much that sometimes my heart contracts and I do not know where to turn. I love you beyond my strength. You do not understand that, I know; but you believe it, and you must say, just one single time, that you are a little grateful to me. For, you see, such a love as mine to you is precious, it has its value in this life of ours. And that you will never betray or deceive me, even if you cannot love me, just out of gratitude for this love. I have come to you to beg you, as seriously, as fervently as I can . . ." Here the lawyer's speech would be dissolved in sobs, in low, bitter weeping, as he knelt. Amra would feel moved; she would stroke her husband's bristles and say over and over, in the soothing, contemptuous singsong one uses to a dog who comes to lick one's feet: "Yes, yes, good doggy, good doggy!"

And this behavior of Amra's was certainly not that of a moral woman. For to relieve my mind of the truth which I have so far withheld, she did already deceive her husband; she betrayed him for the embraces of a gentleman named Alfred Läutner, a gifted young musician, who at twenty-seven had made himself a small reputation with amusing little compositions. He was a slim young chap with a provocative face, a flowing blond mane, and a sunny smile in his eyes, of which he was quite aware. He belonged to the present-day race of small artists, who do not demand the utmost of themselves, whose first requirement is to be jolly and happy, who employ their pleasing little talents to heighten their personal charms. It pleases them to play in society the rôle of the naïve genius. Consciously childlike, entirely unmoral and unscrupulous, merry and self-satisfied as they are, and healthy enough to enjoy even their disorders, they are agreeable even in their vanity, so long as that has not been wounded. But woe to these wretched little poseurs when serious misfortune befalls them, with which there is no coquetting, and when they can no longer be pleasant in their own eyes. They will not know how to be wretched decently and in order, they do not know how to attack the problem of suffering. They will be destroyed. All that is a story in itself. But Herr Alfred Läutner wrote pretty things, mostly waltzes and mazurkas. They would have been rather too gay and popular to be considered music as I understand it, if each of them had not contained a passage of some originality, a modulation, a harmonic phrasing, some sort of bold effect that betrayed wit and invention, which was evidently the point of the whole and which made it interesting to genuine musicians. Often these two single measures would have a strange plaintive, melancholy tone which would come out abruptly in the midst of a piece of dance-music and as suddenly be gone.

Amra Jacoby was on fire with guilty passion for this young man, and as for him he had not enough moral fibre to resist her seductions. They met here, they met there, and for some years an immoral relation had subsisted between them, known to the whole town, who laughed at it behind the lawyer's back. But what did he think? Amra was not sensitive enough to betray herself on account of a guilty conscience, so we must take it as certain that, however the lawyer's heart, he could cherish no definite suspicions.

Spring had come, rejoicing all hearts; and Amra conceived the most charming idea.

"Christian," said she—Jacoby's name was Christian—"let us give a party, a beer party to celebrate the new beer—of course quite simple, but let's have a lot of people."

"Certainly," said the lawyer, "but could we not have it a little later?"

To which Amra made no reply, having passed on to the consideration of details.

"It will be so large that we cannot have it here, we must hire a place, some sort of outdoor restaurant where there is plenty of room and fresh air. You see that, of course. The place I am thinking of is Wendelin's big hall at the foot of the Lerchenberg. The hall is independent of the restaurant and brewery, connected by a passage only. We can decorate it for the occasion and set up long tables, drink our bocks, and dance—we must have music and even perhaps some sort of entertainment. There is a little stage, as I happen to know, that makes it very suitable. It will be a very original party and no end to fun."

The lawyer's face had gone a pale yellow as she spoke, and the corners of his mouth went down. He said:

"My dear Amra! How delightful it will be! I can leave it all to you, you are so clever. Make any arrangements you like."

And Amra made her arrangements. She took counsel of various ladies and gentlemen, she went in person to hire the hall, she even formed a committee of people who were invited or who volunteered to co-operate in the entertainment. These were exclusively men, except for the wife of Herr Hildebrandt, an actor at the Hoftheater, who was herself a singer. Then there was Herr Hildebrandt, an Assessor Witznagel, a young painter, Alfred Läutner the musician, and some students brought in by Herr Witznagel, who were to do Negro dances.

A week after Amra had made her plan, this committee met in Amra's drawing-room in the Kaiserstrasse—a small, crowded, overheated room, with a heavy carpet, a sofa with quantities of cushions, a fan table, English leather chairs, and a splay-legged mahogany table with a velvet cover, upon which rested several large illustrated morocco-bound volumes. There was a fireplace too, with a small fire still burning, and on the marble chimney-top were plates of dainty sandwiches, glasses, and two decanters of sherry. Amra reclined in one corner of the sofa under the fan palm, with her legs crossed. She had the beauty of a warm summer night. A thin blouse of light-colored silk covered her bosom, but her skirt was of heavy dark stuff embroidered with large flowers. Sometimes she put up one hand to brush back the chestnut hair from her narrow forehead. Frau Hildebrandt sat beside her on the sofa; she had red hair and wore riding clothes. Opposite the two all the gentlemen formed a semicircle—among them Jacoby himself, in the lowest chair he could find. He looked unutterably wretched, kept drawing a long breath and swallowing as though struggling against increasing nausea. Herr Alfred Läutner was in tennis clothes—he would not take a chair, but leaned decoratively against the chimney-piece, saying merrily that he could not sit still so long.

Herr Hildebrandt talked sonorously about English songs. He was a most respectable gentleman, in a black suit, with a Roman head and an assured manner—in short a proper actor for a court theater, cultured, knowledgeable, and with enlightened tastes. He liked to hold forth in condemnation of Ibsen, Zola, and Tolstoi, all of whom had the same objectionable aims. But today he was benignly interested in the small affair under discussion.

"Do you know that priceless song 'That's Maria'?" he asked. "Perhaps it is a little racy—but very effective. And then" so-and-so—he suggested other songs, upon which they came to an agreement and Frau Hildebrandt said that she would sing them. The young painter, who had sloping shoulders and a very blond beard, was to give a burlesque conjuring turn. Herr Hildebrandt offered to impersonate various famous characters. In short, everything was developing nicely, the programme was apparently arranged, when Assessor Witznagel, who had command of fluent gesture and a good many duelling scars, suddenly took the word.

"All very well, ladies and gentlemen, it looks like being most amusing. But if I may say so, it still lacks something; it wants some kind of high spot, a climax as it were, something a bit startling, perhaps, to round the thing off. I leave it to you, I have nothing particular in mind, I only think..."

"That is true enough!" Alfred Läutner's tenor voice came from the chimney-piece where he leaned. "Witznagel is right. We need a climax. Let us put our heads together!" He settled his red belt and looked engagingly about him.

"Well, if we do not consider the famous characters as the high spot," said Herr Hildebrandt. Everybody agreed with the Assessor. Something piquant was wanted for the principal number. Even Jacoby nodded, and murmured: "Yes, yes, something jolly and striking...." They all reflected.

At the end of a minute's pause, which was broken only by stifled exclamations, an extraordinary thing happened. Amra was sitting reclined among the cushions, gnawing as busily as a mouse at the pointed nail of her little finger. She had a very odd look on her face: a vacant, almost an irresponsible smile, which betrayed a sensuality both tormented and cruel. Her eyes, very bright and wide, turned slowly to the chimney-piece, where for a second they met the musician's. Then suddenly she jerked her whole body to one side as she sat, in the direction of her husband. With both hands in her lap she stared into his face with an avid and clinging gaze, her own growing visibly paler, and said in her rich, slow voice:

"Christian, suppose you come on at the end as a *chanteuse*, in a red satin baby frock, and do a dance."

The effect of these few words was tremendous. The young painter essayed to laugh good-humoredly; Herr Hildebrandt, stony-faced, brushed a crumb from his sleeve; his wife colored up, a rare thing for her; the students coughed and used their handkerchiefs loudly; and Herr Assessor Witznagel simply left the field and got himself a sandwich. The lawyer sat huddled on his little chair, yellow in the face, with a terrified smile. He looked all around the circle, and stammered:

"But, by God ... I—I—I am not up to—not that I—I beg pardon, but..."

Alfred Läutner had lost his insouciant expression; he even seemed to have reddened a little, and he thrust out his neck to peer searchingly into Amra's face. He looked puzzled and upset.

But she, Amra, holding the same persuasive pose, went on with the same impressiveness:

"And you must sing, too, Christian, a song which Herr Läutner shall compose, and he can accompany you on the piano. We could not have a better or more effective climax."

There was a pause, an oppressive pause. Then this extraordinary thing happened, that Herr Läutner, as it were seized upon and carried away by his excitement, took a step forward and his voice fairly trembled with enthusiasm as he said:

"Herr Jacoby, that is a priceless idea, and I am more than ready to compose something. You must have a dance and song, anything else is unthinkable as a wind-up to our affair. You will see, it will be the best thing I have ever written or ever shall write. In a red satin baby frock. Oh, your wife is an artist, only an artist could have hit upon the idea! Do say yes, I beg of you. I will do my part, you will see, it will be an achievement."

Here the circle broke up and the meeting became lively. Out of politeness, or out of malice, the company began to storm the lawyer with entreaties—Frau Hildebrandt went so far as to say, quite loudly, in her Brünnhilde voice:

"Herr Jacoby, after all, you are such a jolly and entertaining man!"

But the lawyer had pulled himself together and spoke, a little yellow, but with a strong effort at resolution:

"But listen to me, ladies and gentlemen—what can I say to you? It isn't my line, believe me. I have no comic gift, and besides... in short, no, it is quite impossible, alas!"

He stuck obstinately to his refusal, and Amra no longer insisted, but sat still with her absent look. Herr Läutner was silent too, staring in deep abstraction at a pattern in the rug. Herr Hildebrandt changed the subject, and presently the committee meeting broke up without coming to a final decision about the "climax."

On the evening of the same day Amra had gone to bed and was lying there with her eyes wide open; her husband came lumbering into the bedroom, drew a chair up beside the bed, dropped into it, and said, in a low, hesitating voice:

"Listen, Amra; to be quite frank, I am feeling very disturbed. I refused them today—I did not mean to be offensive—goodness knows I did not mean that. Or do you seriously feel that—I beg you to tell me."

Amra was silent for a moment, while her brows rose slowly. Then she shrugged her shoulders and said:

"I do not know, my dear friend, how to answer you. You behaved in a way I should not have expected from you. You were unfriendly, you refused to support our enterprise in a way which they flatteringly considered to be indispensable to it. To put it mildly, you disappointed everybody and upset the whole company with your rude lack of compliance. Whereas it was your duty as host—"

The lawyer hung his head and sighed heavily. He said:

"Believe me, Amra, I had no intention to be disobliging. I do not like to offend anybody; if I have behaved badly I am ready to make amends. It is only a joke, after all, an innocent little dressing-up—why not? I will not upset the whole affair, I am ready to . . ."

The following afternoon Amra went out again to "make preparations." She drove to Number 78 Holzstrasse and went up to the second storey, where she had an appointment. And when she lay relaxed by the expression of her love she pressed her lover's head passionately to her breast and whispered:

"Write it for four hands. We will accompany him together while he sings and dances. I will see to the costume myself."

And an extraordinary shiver, a suppressed and spasmodic burst of laughter went through the limbs of both.

For anyone who wants to give a large party out of doors Herr Wendlin's place on the slope of the Lerchenberg is to be recommended. You enter it from the pretty suburban street through a tall trellised gateway and pass into the parklike garden, in the center of which stands a large hall, connected only by a narrow passage with restaurant, kitchen, and brewery. It is a large, brightly painted wooden hall, in an amusing mixture of Chinese and Renaissance styles. It has folding doors which stand open in good weather to admit the woodland air, and it will hold a great many people.

On this evening as the carriages rolled up they were greeted from afar by the gleam of colored lights. The whole gateway, the trees, and the hall itself were set thick with lanterns, while the interior made an entrancing sight. Heavy garlands were draped across the ceiling and studded with paper lanterns. Hosts of electric lights hung among the decorations of the walls, which consisted of pine boughs, flags, and artificial flowers; the whole hall was brilliantly lighted. The stage had foliage plants grouped on either side, and a red curtain with a painted design of a presiding genius hovering in the air. A long row of decorated tables ran almost the whole length of the hall. And at these tables the guests of Attorney Jacoby were doing themselves well on cold roast veal and bock beer. There were certainly more than a hundred and fifty people: officers, lawyers, business men, artists, upper officials, with their wives and daughters. They were quite simply dressed, in black coats and light spring toilettes, for this was a jolly, informal occasion. The gentlemen carried their mugs in person to the big casks against one of the walls; the spacious, festive, brightly lighted room was filled with a heavy sweetish atmosphere of evergreen boughs, flowers, beer, food, and human beings; and there was a clatter and buzz of laughter and talk—the loud, simple talk and the high, good-natured, unrestrained, carefree laughter of the sort of people there assembled.

The attorney sat shapeless and helpless at one end of the table, near the stage. He drank little and now and then addressed a labored remark to his neighbor, Frau Regierungsrat Havermann. He breathed offensively, the corners of his mouth hung down, he stared fixedly with his bulging watery eyes into the lively scene, with a sort of melancholy remoteness, as though there resided in all this noisy merriment something inexpressibly painful and perplexing.

Large fruit tarts were now being handed round for the company to cut from; they drank sweet wine with these, and the time for the speeches arrived. Herr Hildebrandt celebrated the new brew in a speech almost entirely composed of classical quotations, even Greek. Herr Witznagel, with florid gestures and ingenious turns of phrase, toasted the ladies, taking a handful of flowers from the nearest vase and comparing each flower to some feminine charm. Amra Jacoby, who sat opposite him in a pale-yellow silk frock, he called "a lovelier sister of the Maréchal Niel."

Then she nodded meaningfully to her husband, brushing back her hair from her forehead; whereupon the fat man arose and almost ruined the whole atmosphere by stammering a few words with painful effort, smiling a repulsive smile. Some half-hearted bravos rewarded him, then there was an oppressive pause, after which jollity resumed its sway. All smoking, all a little elevated by drink, they rose from table and with their own hands and a great deal of noise removed the tables from the hall to make way for the dancing.

It was after eleven and high spirits reigned supreme. Some of the guests streamed out into the brightly lighted garden to get the fresh air; others stood about the hall in groups, smoking, chatting, drawing beer from the kegs, and drinking it standing. Then a loud trumpet call sounded from the stage, summoning everybody to the entertainment. The band arrived and took its place before the curtains; rows of chairs were put in place and red programmes distributed on them; the gentlemen ranged themselves along the walls. There was an expectant hush.

The band played a noisy overture, and the curtains parted to reveal a row of Negroes horrifying to behold in their barbaric costumes and their blood-red lips, gnashing their teeth and emitting savage yells.

Certainly the entertainment was the crowning success of Amra's party. As it went on, the applause grew more and more enthusiastic. Frau Hildebrandt came on in a powdered wig, pounded with a shepherdess' crook on the floor and sang—in too large a voice—"That's Maria!" A conjuror in a dress coat covered with orders performed the most amazing feats; Herr Hildebrandt impersonated Goethe, Bismarck, and Napoleon in an amazingly lifelike manner; and a newspaper editor, Dr. Wiesensprung, improvised a humorous lecture which had as its theme bock beer and its social significance. And now the suspense reached its height, for it was time for the last, the mysterious number which appeared on the programme framed in a laurel wreath and was entitled: *"Little Lizzy.* Song and Dance. Music by Alfred Läutner."

A movement swept through the hall, and people's eyes met as the band sat down at their instruments and Alfred Läutner came from the doorway where he had been lounging with a cigarette between his pouting lips to take his place beside Amra Jacoby at the piano, which stood in the center of the stage in front of the curtains. Herr Läutner's face was flushed and he turned over his manuscript score nervously; Amra for her part was rather pale. She leaned one arm on the back of her chair and looked loweringly at the audience. The bell rang, the pianist played a few bars of an insignificant accompaniment, the curtains parted, little Lizzy appeared.

The whole audience stiffened with amazement as that tragic and bedizened bulk shambled with a sort of bear-dance into view. It was Jacoby. A wide, shapeless garment of crimson satin, without folds, fell to his feet; it was cut out above to make a repulsive display of the fat neck, stippled with white powder. The sleeves consisted merely of a shoulder puff, but the flabby arms were covered by long lemon-colored gloves; on the head perched a high blond wig with a swaying green feather. And under the wig was a face, a puffy, pasty, unhappy, and desperately mirthful face, with cheeks that shook pathetically up and down and little red-rimmed eyes that strained in anguish towards the floor and saw nothing else at all. The fat man hoisted himself with effort from one leg to the other, while with his hands he either held up his skirts or else weakly raised his index fingers—these two gestures he had and knew no others. In a choked and gasping voice he sang, to the accompaniment of the piano.

The lamentable figure exhaled more than ever a cold breath of anguish. It killed every light-hearted enjoyment and lay like an oppressive weight upon the assembled audience. Horror was in the depths of all these spellbound eyes, gazing at this pair at the piano and at that husband there. The monstrous, unspeakable scandal lasted five long minutes.

Then came a moment which none of those present will forget as long as they live. Let us picture to ourselves what happened in that frightful and frightfully involved little instant of time.

You know of course the absurd little jingle called "Lizzy." And you remember the lines:

> *I can polka until I am dizzy,*
> *I can waltz with the best and beyond,*
> *I'm the popular pet, little Lizzy,*
> *Who makes all the menfolks so fond—*

which form the trivial and unlovely refrain to three longish stanzas. Alfred Läutner had composed a new setting to the verses I have quoted, and it was, as he had said it would be, his masterpiece. He had, that is, brought to its highest pitch his little artifice of introducing into a fairly vulgar and humorous piece of hackwork a sudden phrase of genuine creative art. The melody, in C-sharp major, had been in the first bars rather pretty and perfectly banal. At the beginning of the refrain the rhythm became livelier and dissonances occurred, which by means of the constant accentuation of a B-natural made one expect a transition into F-sharp major. These dissonances went on developing until the word "beyond"; and after the "I'm the" a culmination into F-sharp major should have followed. Instead of which the most surprising thing happened. That is, through a harsh turn, by means of an inspiration which was almost a stroke of genius, the key changed to F-major, and this little interlude which followed, with the use of both pedals on the long-drawn-out first syllable of the word "Lizzy," was indescribably, almost gruesomely effective. It was a complete surprise, an abrupt assault on the nerves, it shivered down the back, it was a miracle, a revelation, it was like a curtain suddenly torn away to reveal something nude.

And on the F-major chord Attorney Jacoby stopped dancing. He stood still, he stood as though rooted to the stage with his two forefingers lifted, one a little lower than the other. The word "Lizzy" stuck in his throat, he was dumb; almost at the same time the accompaniment broke sharp off, and the incredible, absurd, and ghastly figure stood there frozen, with his head thrust forward like a steer's, staring with inflamed eyes straight before him. He stared into the brightly lighted, decorated, crowded hall, in which, like an exhalation from all these people, the scandal hung and thickened into visibility. He stared at all these upturned faces, foreshortened and distorted by the lighting, into these hundreds of pairs of eyes all directed with the same knowing expression upon himself and the two at the piano. In a frightful stillness, unbroken by the smallest sound, his gaze traveled slowly and uneasily from the pair to the audience, from the audience to the pair, while his eyes widened more and more. Then knowledge seemed to flash across his face, like a sudden rush of blood, making it red as the frock he wore, only to give way to a waxen yellow pallor—and the fat man collapsed, making the platform creak beneath his weight.

For another moment the stillness reigned. Then there came shrieks, hubbub ensued, a few gentlemen took heart to spring upon the platform, among them a young doctor—and the curtains were drawn together.

Amra Jacoby and Alfred Läutner still sat at the piano. They had turned a little away from each other, and he, with his head bent, seemed to be listening to the echo of his F-major chord, while she, with her birdlike brain, had not yet grasped the situation, but gazed round her with vacant face.

The young doctor came back presently. He was a little Jewish gentleman with a serious face and a small pointed beard. Some people surrounded him at the door with questions—to which he replied with a shrug of the shoulders and the words:

"All over."

Willa Cather
(1876-1947)
Paul's Case

It was Paul's afternoon to appear before the faculty of the Pittsburgh High School to account for his various misdemeanors. He had been suspended a week ago, and his father had called at the Principal's office and confessed his perplexity about his son. Paul entered the faculty room suave and smiling. His clothes were a trifle outgrown, and the tan velvet on the collar of his open overcoat was frayed and worn; but for all that there was something of the dandy about him, and he wore an opal pin in his neatly knotted black four-in-hand, and a red carnation in his buttonhole. This latter adornment the faculty somehow felt was not properly significant of the contrite spirit befitting a boy under the ban of suspension.

Paul was tall for his age and very thin, with high, cramped shoulders and a narrow chest. His eyes were remarkable for a certain hysterical brilliancy, and he continually used them in a conscious, theatrical sort of way, peculiarly offensive in a boy. The pupils were abnormally large, as though he were addicted to belladonna, but there was a glassy glitter about them which that drug does not produce.

When questioned by the Principal as to why he was there, Paul stated, politely enough, that he wanted to come back to school. This was a lie, but Paul was quite accustomed to lying; found it, indeed, indispensable for overcoming friction. His teachers were asked to state their respective charges against him, which they did with such a rancor and aggrievedness as evinced that this was not a usual case. Disorder and impertinence were among the offences named, yet each of his instructors felt that it was scarcely possible to put into words the real cause of the trouble, which lay in a sort of hysterically defiant manner of the boy's; in the contempt which they all knew he felt for them, and which he seemingly made not the least effort to conceal. Once, when he had been making a synopsis of a paragraph at the blackboard, his English teacher had stepped to his side and attempted to guide his hand. Paul had started back with a shudder and thrust his hands violently behind him. The astonished woman could scarcely have been more hurt and embarrassed had he struck at her. The insult was so involuntary and definitely personal as to be unforgettable. In one way and another, he had made all his teachers, men and women alike, conscious of the same feeling of physical aversion. In one class he habitually sat with his hand shading his eyes; in another he always looked out of the window during the recitation; in another he made a running commentary on the lecture, with humorous intent.

His teachers felt this afternoon that his whole attitude was symbolized by his shrug and his flippantly red carnation flower, and they fell upon him without mercy, his English teacher leading the pack. He stood through it smiling, his pale lips parted over his white teeth. (His lips were continually twitching, and he had a habit of raising his eyebrows that was contemptuous and irritating to the last degree.) Older boys than Paul had broken down and shed tears under that ordeal, but his set smile did not once desert him, and his only sign of discomfort was the nervous trembling of the fingers that toyed with the buttons of his overcoat, and an occasional jerking of the other hand which held his hat. Paul was always smiling, always glancing about him, seeming to feel that people might be watching him and trying to detect something. This conscious expression, since it was as far as possible from boyish mirthfulness, was usually attributed to insolence or "smartness."

As the inquisition proceeded, one of his instructors repeated an impertinent remark of the boy's, and the Principal asked him whether he thought that a courteous speech to make to a woman. Paul shrugged his shoulders slightly and his eyebrows twitched.

"I don't know," he replied. "I didn't mean to be polite or impolite, either. I guess it's a sort of way I have of saying things regardless."

The Principal asked him whether he didn't think that a way it would be well to get rid of. Paul grinned and said he guessed so. When he was told that he could go, he bowed gracefully and went out. His bow was like a repetition of the scandalous red carnation.

His teachers were in despair, and his drawing master voiced the feeling of them all when he declared there was something about the boy which none of them understood. He added: "I don't really believe that smile of his comes altogether from insolence; there's something sort of haunted about it. The boy is not strong, for one thing. There is something wrong about the fellow."

The drawing master had come to realize that, in looking at Paul, one saw only his white teeth and the forced animation of his eyes. One warm afternoon the boy had gone to sleep at his drawing-board, and his master had noted with amazement what a white blue-veined face it was; drawn and wrinkled like an old man's about the eyes, the lips twitching even in his sleep.

His teachers left the building dissatisfied and unhappy; humiliated to have felt so vindictive toward a mere boy, to have uttered this feeling in cutting terms, and to have set each other on, as it were, in the gruesome game of intemperate reproach. One of them remembered having seen a miserable street cat set at bay by a ring of tormentors.

As for Paul, he ran down the hill whistling the Soldier's Chorus from *Faust*, looking wildly behind him now and then to see whether some of his teachers were not there to witness his lightheartedness. As it was now late in the afternoon and Paul was on duty that evening as usher at Carnegie Hall, he decided that he would not go home to supper.

When he reached the concert hall the doors were not yet open. It was chilly outside, and he decided to go up into the picture gallery—always deserted at this hour—where there were some of Raffelli's gay studies of Paris streets and an airy blue Venetian scene or two that always exhilarated him. He was delighted to find no one in the gallery but the old guard, who sat in the corner, a newspaper on his knee, a black patch over one eye and the other closed. Paul possessed himself of the place and walked confidently up and down, whistling under his breath. After a while he sat down before a blue Rico and lost himself. When he bethought him to look at his watch, it was after seven o'clock, and he rose with a start and ran downstairs, making a face at Augustus Caesar, peering out from a castroom, and an evil gesture at the Venus of Milo as he passed her on the stairway.

When Paul reached the ushers' dressing-room half a dozen boys were there already, and he began excitedly to tumble into his uniform. It was one of the few that at all approached fitting, and Paul thought it very becoming—though he knew the tight, straight coat accentuated his narrow chest, about which he was exceedingly sensitive. He was always excited when he dressed, twanging all over to the tuning of the strings and the preliminary flourishes of the horns in the music room; but tonight he seemed quite beside himself, and he teased and plagued the boys until, telling him that he was crazy, they put him down on the floor and sat on him.

Somewhat calmed by his suppression, Paul dashed out to the front of the house to seat the early comers. He was a model usher. Gracious and smiling he ran up and down the aisles. Nothing was too much trouble for him; he carried messages and brought programs as though it were his greatest pleasure in life, and all the people in his section thought him a charming boy, feeling that he remembered and admired them. As the house filled, he grew more and more vivacious and animated, and the color came to his cheeks and lips. It was very much as though this were a great reception and Paul were the host. Just as the musicians came to take their places, his English teacher arrived with checks for the seats which a prominent manufacturer had taken for the season. She betrayed some embarrassment when she handed Paul the tickets, and a *hauteur* which subsequently made her feel very foolish. Paul was startled for a moment, and had the feeling of wanting to put her out; what business had she here among all these fine people and gay colors? He looked her over and decided that she was not appropriately dressed and must be a fool to sit downstairs in such togs. The tickets had probably been sent her out of kindness, he reflected, as he put down a seat for her, and she had about as much right to sit there as he had.

When the symphony began Paul sank into one of the rear seats with a long sigh of relief, and lost himself as he had done before the Rico. It was not that symphonies, as such, meant anything in particular to Paul, but the first sigh of the instruments seemed to free some hilarious spirit within him; something that struggled there like the Genius in the bottle found by the Arab fisherman. He felt a sudden zest of life; the lights danced before his eyes and the concert hall blazed into unimaginable splendor. When the soprano soloist came on, Paul forgot even the nastiness of his teacher's being there, and gave himself up to the peculiar intoxication such personages always had for him. The soloist chanced to be a German woman, by no means in her first youth, and the mother of many children; but she wore a satin gown and a tiara, and she had that indefinable air of achievement, that world-shine upon her, which always blinded Paul to any possible defects.

After a concert was over, Paul was often irritable and wretched until he got to sleep—and tonight he was even more than usually restless. He had the feeling of not being able to let down; of its being impossible to give up this delicious excitement which was the only thing that could be called living at all. During the last number he withdrew and, after hastily changing his clothes in the dressing-room, slipped out to the side door where the singer's carriage stood. Here he began pacing rapidly up and down the walk, waiting to see her come out.

Over yonder the Schenley, in its vacant stretch, loomed big and square through the fine rain, the windows of its twelve stories glowing like those of a lighted cardboard house under a Christmas tree. All the actors and singers of any importance stayed there when they were in the city, and a number of the big manufacturers of the place lived there in the winter. Paul had often hung about the hotel, watching the people go in and out, longing to enter and leave school masters and dull care behind him forever.

At last the singer came out, accompanied by the conductor, who helped her into her carriage and closed the door with a cordial *auf wiedersehen*—which set Paul to wondering whether she were not an old sweetheart of his. Paul followed the carriage over to the hotel, walking so rapidly as not to be far from the entrance when the singer alighted and disappeared behind the swinging glass doors which were opened by a negro in a tall hat and a long coat. In the moment that the door was ajar, it seemed to Paul that he, too, entered. He seemed to feel himself go after her up the steps, into the warm, lighted building, into an exotic, a tropical world of shiny, glistening surfaces and basking ease. He reflected upon the mysterious dishes that were brought into the dining-room, the green bottles in buckets of ice, as he had seen them in the supper party pictures of the Sunday supplement. A quick gust of wind brought the rain down with sudden vehemence, and Paul was startled to find that he was still outside in the slush of the gravel driveway; that his boots were letting in the water and his scanty overcoat was clinging wet about him; that the lights in front of the concert hall were out, and that the rain was driving in sheets between him and the orange glow of the windows above him. There it was, what he wanted—tangibly before him like the fairy world of a Christmas pantomime; as the rain beat in his face, Paul wondered whether he were destined always to shiver in the black night outside, looking up at it.

He turned and walked reluctantly toward the car tracks. The end had to come some time; his father in his night clothes at the top of the stairs, explanations that did not explain, hastily improvised fictions that were forever tripping him up, his upstairs room and its horrible yellow wallpaper, the creaking bureau with the greasy plush collar-box, and over his painted wooden bed the pictures of George Washington and John Calvin, and the framed motto, "Feed my Lambs," which had been worked in red worsted by his mother, whom Paul could not remember.

Half an hour later Paul alighted from the Negley Avenue car and went down one of the side streets off the main thoroughfare. It was a highly respectable street, where all the houses were exactly alike, and where businessmen of moderate means begot and reared large families of children, all of whom went to Sabbath school and learned the shorter catechism, and were interested in arithmetic; all of whom were as exactly alike as their homes, and of a piece with the monotony in which they lived. Paul never went up Cordelia Street without a shudder of loathing. His home was next the house of the Cumberland minister. He approached it tonight with the nerveless sense of defeat, the hopeless feeling of sinking back forever into ugliness and commonness that he had always had when he came home. The moment he turned into Cordelia Street he felt the waters close above his head. After each of these orgies of living, he experienced all the physical depression which follows a debauch; the loathing of respectable beds, of common food, of a house permeated by kitchen odours; a shuddering repulsion for the flavourless, colourless mass of everyday existence; a morbid desire for cool things and soft lights and fresh flowers.

The nearer he approached the house, the more absolutely unequal Paul felt to the sight of it all; his ugly sleeping chamber; the cold bath-room with the grimy zinc tub, the cracked mirror, the dripping spigots; his father, at the top of the stairs, his hairy legs sticking out from his night-shirt, his feet thrust into carpet slippers. He was so much later than usual that there would certainly be inquiries and reproaches. Paul stopped short before the door. He felt that he could not be accosted by his father tonight; that he could not toss again on that miserable bed. He would not go in. He would tell his father that he had no car fare, and it was raining so hard he had gone home with one of the boys and stayed all night.

Meanwhile, he was wet and cold. He went around to the back of the house and tried one of the basement windows, found it open, raised it cautiously, and scrambled down the cellar wall to the floor. There he stood, holding his breath, terrified by the noise he had made; but the floor above him was silent, and there was no creak on the stairs. He found a soap-box, and carried it over to the soft ring of light that streamed from the furnace door, and sat down. He was horribly afraid of rats, so he did not try to sleep, but sat looking distrustfully at the dark, still terrified lest he might have awakened his father. In such reactions, after one of the experiences which made days and nights out of the dreary blanks of the calendar, when his senses were deadened, Paul's head was always singularly clear. Suppose his father had heard him getting in at the window and had come down and shot him for a burglar? Then, again, suppose his father had come down, pistol in hand, and he had cried out in time to save himself, and his father had been horrified to think how nearly he had killed him? Then, again, suppose a day should come when his father would remember that night, and wish there had been no warning cry to stay his hand? With this supposition Paul entertained himself until daybreak.

The following Sunday was fine; the sodden November chill was broken by the last flash of autumnal summer. In the morning Paul had to go to church and Sabbath-school, as always. On seasonable Sunday afternoons the burghers of Cordelia Street usually sat out on their front "stoops," and talked to their neighbors on the next stoop, or called to those across the street in neighborly fashion. The men sat placidly on gay cushions placed upon the steps that led down to the sidewalk, while the women, in their Sunday "waists," sat in rockers on the cramped porches, pretending to be greatly at their ease. The children played in the streets; there were so many of them that the place resembled the recreation grounds of a kindergarten. The men on the steps—all in their sleeves, their vests unbuttoned—sat with their legs well apart, their stomachs comfortably protuding, and talked of the prices of things, or told anecdotes of the sagacity of their various chiefs and overlords. They occasionally looked over the multitude of squabbling children, listened affectionately to their high-pitched, nasal voices, smiling to see their own proclivities reproduced in their offspring, and interspersed their legends of the iron kings with remarks about their sons' progress at school, their grades in arithmetic, and the amounts they had saved in their toy banks.

On this last Sunday of November, Paul sat all the afternoon on the lowest step of his "stoop," staring into the street, while his sisters, in their rockers, were talking to the minister's daughters next door about how many shirtwaists they had made in the last week, and how many waffles some one had eaten at the last church supper. When the weather was warm, and his father was in a particularly jovial frame of mind, the girls made lemonade, which was always brought out in a red glass pitcher, ornamented with forget-me-nots in blue enamel. This the girls thought very fine, and the neighbors joked about the suspicious colour of the pitcher.

Today Paul's father, on the top step, was talking to a young man who shifted a restless baby from knee to knee. He happened to be the young man who was daily held up to Paul as a model, and after whom it was his father's dearest hope that he would pattern. This young man was of a ruddy complexion, with a compressed, red mouth, and faded, near-sighted eyes, over which he wore thick spectacles, with gold bows that curved about his ears. He was clerk to one of the magnates of a great steel corporation, and was looked upon in Cordelia Street as a young man with a future. There was a story that, some five years ago—he was now barely twenty-six—he had been a trifle "dissipated," but in order to curb his appetites and save the loss of time and strength that a sowing of wild oats might have entailed, he had taken his chief's advice, oft reiterated to his employes, and at twenty-one had married the first woman whom he could persuade to share his fortunes. She happened to be an angular schoolmistress, much older than he, who also wore thick glasses, and who had now borne him four children, all near-sighted, like herself.

The young man was relating how his chief, now cruising in the Mediterranean, kept in touch with all the details of the business, arranging his office hours on his yacht just as though he were at home, and "knocking off work enough to keep two stenographers busy." His father told, in turn, the plan his corporation was considering, of putting in an electric railway plant at Cairo. Paul snapped his teeth; he had an awful apprehension that they might spoil it all before he got there. Yet he rather liked to hear these legends of the iron kings, that were told and retold on Sundays and holidays; these stories of palaces in Venice, yachts on the Mediterranean, and high play at Monte Carlo appealed to his fancy, and he was interested in the triumphs of cash boys who had become famous, though he had no mind for the cash-boy stage.

After supper was over, and he had helped to dry the dishes, Paul nervously asked his father whether he could go to George's to get some help in his geometry, and still more nervously asked for car fare. This latter request he had to repeat, as his father, on principle, did not like to hear requests for money, whether much or little. He asked Paul whether he could not go to some boy who lived nearer, and told him that he ought not to leave his school work until Sunday; but he gave him the dime. He was not a poor man, but he had a worthy ambition to come up in the world. His only reason for allowing Paul to usher was that he thought a boy ought to be earning a little.

Paul bounded upstairs, scrubbed the greasy odor of the dish-water from his hands with the ill-smelling soap he hated, and then shook over his fingers a few drops of violet water from the bottle he kept hidden in his drawer. He left the house with his geometry conspicuously under his arm, and the moment he got out of Cordelia Street and boarded a downtown car, he shook off the lethargy of two deadening days, and began to live again.

The leading juvenile of the permanent stock company which played at one of the downtown theatres was an acquaintance of Paul's, and the boy had been invited to drop in at the Sunday night rehearsals whenever he could. For more than a year Paul had spent every available moment loitering about Charley Edwards's dressing-room. He had won a place among Edwards's following not only because the young actor, who could not afford to employ a dresser, often found him useful, but because he recognized in Paul something akin to what churchmen term "vocation."

It was at the theatre and at Carnegie Hall that Paul really lived; the rest was but a sleep and a forgetting. This was Paul's fairy tale, and it had for him all the allurement of a secret love. The moment he inhaled the gassy, painty, dusty odor behind the scenes, he breathed like a prisoner set free, and felt within him the possibility of doing or saying splendid, brilliant things. The moment the cracked orchestra beat out the overture from *Martha,* or jerked at the serenade from *Rigoletto,* all stupid and ugly things slid from him, and his senses were deliciously, yet delicately fired.

Perhaps it was because, in Paul's world, the natural nearly always wore the guise of ugliness, that a certain element of artificiality seemed to him necessary in beauty. Perhaps it was because his experience of life elsewhere was so full of Sabbath-school picnics, petty economies, wholesome advice as to how to succeed in life, and the unescapable odors of cooking, that he found this existence so alluring, these smartly clad men and women so attractive, that he was so moved by these starry apple orchards that bloomed perennially under the limelight.

It would be difficult to put it strongly enough how convincingly the stage entrance of that theatre was for Paul the actual portal of Romance. Certainly none of the company ever suspected it, least of all Charley Edwards. It was very like the old stories that used to float about London of fabulously rich Jews, who had subterranean halls, with palms, and fountains, and soft lamps and richly apparelled women who never saw the disenchanting light of London day. So, in the midst of that smoke-palled city, enamoured of figures and grimy toil, Paul had his secret temple, his wishing-carpet, his bit of blue-and-white Mediterranean shore bathed in perpetual sunshine.

Several of Paul's teachers had a theory that his imagination had been perverted by garish fiction; but the truth was, he scarcely ever read at all. The books at home were not such as would either tempt or corrupt a youthful mind, and as for reading the novels that some of his friends urged upon him—well, he got what he wanted much more quickly from music; any sort of music, from an orchestra to a barrel organ. He needed only the spark, the indescribable thrill that made his imagination master of his senses, and he could make plots and pictures enough of his own. It was equally true that he was not stage-struck—not, at any rate, in the usual acceptation of that expression. He had no desire to become an actor, any more than he had to become a musician. He felt no necessity to do any of these things; what he wanted was to see, to be in the atmosphere, float on the wave of it, to be carried out, blue league after blue league, away from everything.

After a night behind the scenes, Paul found the school-room more than ever repulsive; the hard floors and naked walls; the prosy men who never wore frock coats, or violets in their buttonholes; the women with their dull gowns, shrill voices, and pitiful seriousness about prepositions that govern the dative. He could not bear to have the other pupils think, for a moment, that he took these people seriously; he must convey to them that he considered it all trivial, and was there only by way of a joke, anyway. He had autographed pictures of all the members of the stock company, which he showed his classmates, telling them the most incredible stories of his familiarity with these people, of his acquaintance with the soloists who came to Carnegie Hall, his suppers with them and the flowers he sent them. When these stories lost their effect, and his audience grew listless, he would bid all the boys good-bye, announcing that he was going to travel for a while, going to Naples, to California, to Egypt. Then, next Monday, he would slip back, conscious and nervously smiling; his sister was ill, and he would have to defer his voyage until spring.

Matters went steadily worse with Paul at school. In the itch to let his instructors know how heartily he despised them, and how thoroughly he was appreciated elsewhere, he mentioned once or twice that he had no time to fool with theorems, adding—with a twitch of the eyebrows and a touch of that nervous bravado which so perplexed them—that he was helping the people down at the stock company; they were old friends of his.

The upshot of the matter was that the Principal went to Paul's father, and Paul was taken out of school and put to work. The manager at Carnegie Hall was told to get another usher in his stead; the doorkeeper at the theatre was warned not to admit him to the house; and Charley Edwards remorsefully promised the boy's father not to see him again.

The members of the stock company were vastly amused when some of Paul's stories reached them—especially the women. They were hardworking women, most of them supporting indolent husbands or brothers, and they laughed rather bitterly at having stirred the boy to such fervid and florid inventions. They agreed with the faculty and with his father, that Paul's was a bad case.

The east-bound train was ploughing through a January snow-storm; the dull dawn was beginning to show gray when the engine whistled a mile out of Newark. Paul started up from the seat where he had lain curled in uneasy slumber, rubbed the breath-misted window glass with his hand, and peered out. The snow was whirling in curling eddies above the white bottom lands, and the drifts lay already deep in the fields and along the fences, while here and there the long dead grass and dried weed stalks protruded black above it. Lights shone from the scattered houses, and a gang of laborers who stood beside the track waved their lanterns.

Paul had slept very little, and he felt grimy and uncomfortable. He had made the all-night journey in a day coach because he was afraid if he took a Pullman he might be seen by some Pittsburgh businessman who had noticed him in Denny & Carson's office. When the whistle woke him, he clutched quickly at his breast pocket, glancing about him with an uncertain smile. But the little, clay-bespattered Italians were still sleeping, the slatternly women across the aisle were in open-mouthed oblivion, and even the crumby, crying babies were for the nonce stilled. Paul settled back to struggle with his impatience as best he could.

When he arrived at the Jersey City Station, he hurried through his breakfast, manifestly ill at ease and keeping a sharp eye about him. After he reached the Twenty-third Street Station, he consulted a cabman, and had himself driven to a men's furnishing establishment which was just opening for the day. He spent upward of two hours there, buying with endless reconsidering and great care. His new street suit he put on in the fitting-room; the frock coat and dress clothes he had bundled into the cab with his new shirts. Then he drove to a hatter's and a shoe house. His next errand was at Tiffany's, where he selected silver-mounted brushes and a scarfpin. He would not wait to have his silver marked, he said. Lastly, he stopped at a trunk shop on Broadway, and had his purchases packed into various traveling bags.

It was a little after one o'clock when he drove up to the Waldorf, and, after settling with the cabman, went into the office. He registered from Washington, said his mother and father had been abroad, and that he had come down to await the arrival of their steamer. He told his story plausibly and had no trouble, since he offered to pay for them in advance, in engaging his rooms: a sleeping-room, sitting-room and bath.

Not once, but a hundred times Paul had planned this entry into New York. He had gone over every detail of it with Charley Edwards, and in his scrapbook at home there were pages of description about New York hotels, cut from the Sunday papers.

When he was shown to his sitting-room on the eighth floor, he saw at a glance that everything was as it should be; there was but one detail in his mental picture that the place did not realize, so he rang for the bell boy and sent him down for flowers. He moved about nervously until the boy returned, putting away his new linen and fingering it delightedly as he did so. When the flowers came, he put them hastily into the water, and then tumbled into a hot bath. Presently he came out of his white bath-room, resplendent in his new silk underwear, and playing with the tassels of his red robe. The snow was whirling so fiercely outside his windows that he could scarcely see across the street; but within, the air was deliciously soft and fragrant. He put the violets and jonquils on the

GRANT WOOD: *American Gothic*, THE ART INSTITUTE OF CHICAGO

taboret beside the couch, and threw himself down with a long sigh, covering himself with a Roman blanket. He was thoroughly tired; he had been in such haste, he had stood up to such a strain, covered so much ground in the last twenty-four hours, that he wanted to think how it had all come about. Lulled by the sound of the wind, the warm air, and the cool fragrance of the flowers, he sank into deep, drowsy retrospection.

It had been wonderfully simple; when they had shut him out of the theatre and concert hall, when they had taken away his bone, the whole thing was virtually determined. The rest was a mere matter of opportunity. The only thing that at all surprised him was his own courage—for he realized well enough that he had always been tormented by fear, a sort of apprehensive dread that, of late years, as the meshes of the lies he had told closed about him, had been pulling the muscles of his body tighter and tighter. Until now, he could not remember a time when he had not been dreading something. Even when he was a little boy, it was always there—behind him, or before, or on either side. There had always been the shadowed corner, the dark place into which he dared not look, but from which something seemed always to be watching him—and Paul had done things that were not pretty to watch, he knew.

But now he had a curious sense of relief, as though he had at last thrown down the gauntlet to the thing in the corner.

Yet it was but a day since he had been sulking in the traces; but yesterday afternoon that he had been sent to the bank with Denny & Carson's deposit as usual—but this time he was instructed to leave the book to be balanced. There was above two thousand dollars in checks, and nearly a thousand in the bank notes which he had taken from the book and quietly transferred to his pocket. At the bank he had made out a new deposit slip. His nerves had been steady enough to permit of his returning to the office, where he had finished his work and asked for a full day's holiday tomorrow, Saturday, giving a perfectly reasonable pretext. The bank book, he knew, would not be returned before Monday or Tuesday, and his father would be out of town for the next week. From the time he slipped the bank notes into his pocket until he boarded the night train for New York, he had not known a moment's hesitation.

How astonishingly easy it had all been; here he was, the thing done; and this time there would be no awakening, no figure at the top of the stairs. He watched the snow flakes whirling by his window until he fell asleep. When he awoke, it was four o'clock in the afternoon. He bounded up with a start; one of his precious days gone already! He spent nearly an hour in dressing, watching every stage of his toilet carefully in the mirror. Everything was quite perfect; he was exactly the kind of boy he had always wanted to be.

When he went downstairs, Paul took a carriage and drove up Fifth Avenue toward the Park. The snow had somewhat abated; carriages and tradesmen's wagons were hurrying soundlessly to and fro in the winter twilight; boys in woollen mufflers were shovelling off the doorsteps; the avenue stages made fine spots of color against the white street. Here and there on the corners were stands, with whole flower gardens blooming behind glass windows, against which the snow flakes stuck and melted; violets, roses, carnations, lilies of the valley—somehow vastly more lovely and alluring that they blossomed thus unnaturally in the snow. The Park itself was a wonderful stage winter-piece.

When he returned, the pause of the twilight had ceased, and the tune of the streets had changed. The snow was falling faster, lights streamed from the hotels that reared their many stories fearlessly up into the storm, defying the raging Atlantic winds. A long, black stream of carriages poured down the avenue, intersected here and there by other streams, tending horizontally. There were a score of cabs about the entrance of his hotel, and his driver had to wait. Boys in livery were running in and out of the awning stretched across the sidewalk, up and down the red velvet carpet laid from the door to the street. Above, about, within it all, was the rumble and roar, the hurry and toss of thousands of human beings as hot for pleasure as himself, and on every side of him towered the glaring affirmation of the omnipotence of wealth.

The boy set his teeth and drew his shoulders together in a spasm of realization; the plot of all dramas, the text of all romances, the nerve-stuff of all sensations were whirling about him like the snow flakes. He burnt like a faggot in a tempest.

When Paul came down to dinner, the music of the orchestra floated up the elevator shaft to greet him. As he stepped into the thronged corridor, he sank back into one of the chairs against the wall to get his breath. The lights, the chatter, the perfumes, the bewildering medley of color—he had, for a moment, the feeling of not being able to stand it. But only for a moment; these were his own people, he told himself. He went slowly about the corridors through the writing-rooms, smoking-rooms, reception-rooms, as though he were exploring the chambers of an enchanted palace, built and peopled for him alone.

When he reached the dining-room he sat down at a table near a window. The flowers, the white linen, the many-colored wine glasses, the gay toilettes of the women, the low popping of corks, the undulating repetitions of the *Blue Danube* from the orchestra, all flooded Paul's dream with bewildering radiance. When the roseate tinge of his champagne was added—that cold, precious bubbling stuff that creamed and foamed in his glass—Paul wondered that there were honest men in the world at all. This was what all the world was fighting for, he reflected; this was what all the struggle was about. He doubted the reality of his past. Had he ever known a place called Cordelia Street, a place where fagged-looking businessmen boarded the early car? Mere rivets in a machine they seemed to Paul,—sickening men, with combings of children's hair always hanging to their coats, and the smell of cooking in their clothes. Cordelia Street—Ah, that belonged to another time and country! Had he not always been thus, had he not sat here night after night, from as far back as he could remember, looking pensively over just such shimmering textures, and slowly twirling the stem of a glass like this one between his thumb and middle finger? He rather thought he had.

He was not in the least abashed or lonely. He had no especial desire to meet or to know any of these people; all he demanded was the right to look on and conjecture, to watch the pageant. The mere stage properties were all he contended for. Nor was he lonely later in the evening, in his loge at the Opera. He was entirely rid of his nervous misgivings, of his forced aggressiveness, of the imperative desire to show himself different from his surroundings. He felt now that his surroundings explained him. Nobody questioned his purple; he had only to wear it passively. He had only to glance down at his dress coat to reassure himself that here it would be impossible for any one to humiliate him.

He found it hard to leave his beautiful sitting-room to go to bed that night, and sat long watching the raging storm from his turret window. When he went to sleep, it was with the lights turned on in his bedroom, partly because of his old timidity, and partly so that, if he should wake in the night, there would be no wretched moment of doubt, no horrible suspicion of yellow wall-paper, or of Washington and Calvin above his bed.

On Sunday morning the city was practically snow-bound. Paul breakfasted late, and in the afternoon he fell in with a wild San Francisco boy, a freshman at Yale, who said he had run down for a "little flyer" over Sunday. The young man offered to show Paul the night side of the town, and the two boys went off together after dinner, not returning to the hotel until seven o'clock the next morning. They had started out in the confiding warmth of a champagne friendship, but their parting in the elevator was singularly cool. The freshman pulled himself together to make his train and Paul went to bed. He awoke at two o'clock in the afternoon, very thirsty and dizzy, and rang for ice-water, coffee, and the Pittsburgh papers.

On the part of the hotel management, Paul excited no suspicion. There was this to be said for him, that he wore his spoils with dignity and in no way made himself conspicuous. His chief greediness lay in his ears and eyes, and his excesses were not offensive ones. His dearest pleasures were the gray winter twilights in his sitting-room, his quiet enjoyment of his flowers, his clothes, his wide divan, his cigarette and his sense of power. He could not remember a time when he had felt so at peace with himself. The mere release from the necessity of petty lying, lying every day and every day, restored his self-respect. He had never lied for pleasure, even at school; but to make himself noticed and admired, to assert his difference from other Cordelia Street boys; and he felt a good deal more manly, more honest, even, now that he had no need for boastful pretensions, now that he could, as his actor friends used to say, "dress the part." It was characteristic that remorse did not occur to him. His golden days went by without a shadow, and he made each as perfect as he could.

On the eighth day after his arrival in New York, he found the whole affair exploited in the Pittsburgh papers, exploited with a wealth of detail which indicated that local news of a sensational nature was at a low ebb. The firm of Denny & Carson announced that the boy's father had refunded the full amount of his theft, and that they had no intention of prosecuting. The Cumberland minister had been interviewed, and expressed his hope of yet reclaiming the motherless lad, and Paul's Sabbath-school teacher declared that she would spare no effort to that end. The rumor had reached Pittsburgh that the boy had been seen in a New York hotel, and his father had gone East to find him and bring him home.

Paul had just come in to dress for dinner; he sank into a chair, weak in the knees, and clasped his head in his hands. It was to be worse than jail, even; the tepid waters of Cordelia Street were to close over him finally and forever. The gray monotony stretched before him in hopeless, unrelieved years; Sabbath school, Young People's Meeting, the yellow-papered room, the damp dish-towels; it all rushed back upon him with sickening vividness. He had the old feeling that the orchestra had suddenly stopped, the sinking sensation that the play was over. The sweat broke out on his face, and he sprang to his feet, looked about him with his white, conscious smile, and winked at himself in the mirror. With something of the childish belief in miracles with which he had so often gone to class, all his lessons unlearned, Paul dressed and dashed whistling down the corridor to the elevator.

He had no sooner entered the dining-room and caught the measure of the music than his remembrance was lightened by his old elastic power of claiming the moment, mounting with it, and finding it all sufficient. The glare and glitter about him, the mere scenic accessories had again, and for the last time, their old potency. He would show himself that he was game, he would finish the thing splendidly. He doubted, more than ever, the existence of Cordelia Street, and for the first time he drank his wine recklessly. Was he not, after all, one of these fortunate beings? Was he not still himself, and in his own place? He drummed a nervous accompaniment to the music and looked about him, telling himself over and over that it had paid.

He reflected drowsily, to the swell of the violin and the chill sweetness of his wine, that he might have done it more wisely. He might have caught an outbound steamer and been well out of their clutches by now. But the other side of the world had seemed too far away and too uncertain then; he could not have waited for it; his need had been too sharp. If he had to choose over again, he would do the same thing tomorrow. He looked affectionately about the dining-room, now gilded with a soft mist. Ah, it had paid, indeed!

Paul was awakened next morning by a painful throbbing in his head and feet. He had thrown himself across the bed without undressing, and had slept with his shoes on. His limbs and hands were lead-heavy, and his tongue and throat were parched. There came upon him one of those fateful attacks of clear-headedness that never occurred except when he was physically exhausted and his nerves hung loose. He lay still and closed his eyes and let the tide of realities wash over him.

His father was in New York; "stopping at some joint or other," he told himself. The memory of successive summers on the front stoop fell upon him like a weight of black water. He had not a hundred dollars left; and he knew now, more than ever, that money was everything, the wall that stood between all he loathed and all he wanted. The thing was winding itself up; he had thought of that on his first glorious day in New York, and had even provided a way to snap the thread. It lay on his dressing table now; he had got it out last night when he came blindly up from dinner,—but the shiny metal hurt his eyes, and he disliked the look of it, anyway.

He rose and moved about with a painful effort, succumbing now and again to attacks of nausea. It was the old depression exaggerated; all the world had become Cordelia Street. Yet somehow he was not afraid of anything, was absolutely calm; perhaps because he had looked into the dark corner at last, and knew. It was bad enough, what he saw there; but somehow not so bad as his long fear of it had been. He saw everything clearly now. He had a feeling that he had made the best of it, that he had lived the sort of life he was meant to live, and for half an hour he sat staring at the revolver. But he told himself that was not the way, so he went downstairs and took a cab to the ferry.

When Paul arrived at Newark, he got off the train and took another cab, directing the driver to follow the Pennsylvania tracks out of town. The snow lay heavy on the roadways and had drifted deep in the open fields. Only here and there the dead grass or dried weed stalks projected, singularly black, above it. Once well into the country, Paul dismissed the carriage and walked, floundering along the tracks, his mind a medley of irrelevant things. He seemed to hold in his brain an actual picture of everything he had seen that morning. He remembered every feature of both his drivers, the toothless old woman from whom he had bought the red flowers in his coat, the agent from whom he had got his ticket, and all of his fellow-passengers on the ferry. His mind, unable to cope with vital matters near at hand, worked feverishly and deftly at sorting and grouping these images. They made for him a part of the ugliness of the world, of the ache in his head, and the bitter burning on his tongue. He stopped and put a handful of snow into his mouth as he walked, but that, too, seemed hot. When he reached a little hillside, where the tracks ran through a cut some twenty feet below him, he stopped and sat down.

The carnations in his coat were drooping with the cold, he noticed; all their red glory over. It occurred to him that all the flowers he had seen in the show windows that first night must have gone the same way, long before this. It was only one splendid breath they had, in spite of their brave mockery at the winter outside the glass. It was a losing game in the end, it seemed, this revolt against the homilies by which the world is run. Paul took one of the blossoms carefully from his coat and scooped a little hole in the snow, where he covered it up. Then he dozed a while, from his weak condition, seeming insensible to the cold.

The sound of an approaching train woke him, and he started to his feet, remembering only his resolution, and afraid lest he should be too late. He stood watching the approaching locomotive, his teeth chattering, his lips drawn away from them in a frightened smile; once or twice he glanced nervously sidewise, as though he were afraid of being watched. When the right moment came, he jumped. As he fell, the folly of his haste occurred to him with merciless clearness, the vastness of what he had left undone. There flashed through his brain, clearer than ever before, the blue of Adriatic water, the yellow of Algerian sands.

He felt something strike his chest,—his body was being thrown swiftly through the air, on and on, immeasurably far and fast, while his limbs gently relaxed. Then, because the picture-making mechanism was crushed, the disturbing visions flashed into black, and Paul dropped back into the immense design of things.

Hermann Hesse
(1877-1962)
Within and Without

There was once a man by the name of Frederick; he devoted himself to intellectual pursuits and had a wide range of knowledge. But not all knowledge was the same to him, nor was any thought as good as any other: he loved a certain type of thinking, and disdained and abominated the others. What he loved and revered was logic—that so admirable method—and, in general, what he called "science."

"Twice two is four," he used to say. "This I believe; and man must do his thinking on the basis of this truth."

He was not unaware, to be sure, that there were other sorts of thinking and knowledge; but they were not "science," and he held a low opinion of them. Although a freethinker, he was not intolerant of religion. Religion was founded on a tacit agreement among scientists. For several centuries their science had embraced nearly everything that existed on earth and was worth knowing, with the exception of one single province: the human soul. It had become a sort of custom, as time went on, to leave this to religion, and to tolerate its speculations on the soul, though without taking them seriously. Thus Frederick too was tolerant toward religion; but everything he recognized as superstition was profoundly odious and repugnant to him. Alien, uncultured, and retarded peoples might occupy themselves with it; in remote antiquity there might have been mystical or magical thinking; but since the birth of science and logic there was no longer any sense in making use of these outmoded and dubious tools.

So he said and so he thought; and when traces of superstition came to his attention he became angry and felt as if he had been touched by something hostile.

It angered him most of all, however, if he found such traces among his own sort, among educated men who were conversant with the principles of scientific thinking. And nothing was more painful and intolerable to him than that scandalous notion which lately he had sometimes heard expressed and discussed even by men of great culture—that absurd idea that "scientific thinking" was possibly not a supreme, timeless, eternal, foreordained, and unassailable mode of thought, but merely one of many, a transient way of thinking, not impervious to change and downfall. This irreverent, destructive, poisonous notion was abroad—even Frederick could not deny it; it had cropped up here and there as a result of the distress throughout the world brought about by war, revolution, and hunger, like a warning, like a white hand's ghostly writing on a white wall.

The more Frederick suffered from the fact that this idea existed and could so deeply distress him, the more passionately he assailed it and those whom he suspected of secretly believing in it. So far only a very few from among the truly educated had openly and frankly professed their belief in this new doctrine, a doctrine that seemed destined, should it gain in circulation and power, to destroy all spiritual values on earth and call forth chaos. Well, matters had not reached that point yet, and the scattered individuals who openly embraced the idea were still so few in number that they could be considered oddities and crotchety, peculiar fellows. But a drop of the poison, an emanation of that idea, could be perceived first on this side, then on that. Among the people and the half-educated no end of new doctrines could be found anyway, esoteric doctrines, sects, and discipleships; the world was full of them; everywhere one could scent out superstition, mysticism, spiritualistic cults, and other mysterious forces, which it was really necessary to combat, but to which science, as if from a private feeling of weakness, had for the present given free rein.

One day Frederick went to the house of one of his friends, with whom he had often studied. It so happened that he had not seen this friend for some time. While he was climbing the stairs of the house he tried to recall when and where it was that he had last been in his friend's company; but much as he could pride himself on his good memory for other things he could not remember. Because of this he fell imperceptibly into a certain vexation and ill humor, from which, as he stood before his friend's door, he was obliged forcibly to free himself.

Hardly had he greeted Erwin, his friend, when he noticed on his genial countenance a certain, as it were forbearing, smile, which it seemed to him he had never seen there before. And hardly had he seen this smile, which despite its friendliness he at once felt to be somehow mocking or hostile, when he immediately remembered what he had just been searching his memory for in vain—his last previous meeting with Erwin. He remembered that they had parted then without having quarreled, to be sure, but yet with a sense of inner discord and dissatisfaction, because Erwin, as it had seemed to him, had given far too little support to his attacks at that time on the realm of superstition.

It was strange. How could he have forgotten that entirely? And now he also knew that this was his only reason for not having sought out his friend for so long, merely this dissatisfaction, and that he had known this all the time, although he had invented for himself a host of other excuses for his repeated postponement of this visit.

Now they confronted one another; and it seemed to Frederick as if the little rift of that day had meantime tremendously widened. He felt that in this moment something was lacking between him and Erwin that had always been there before, an aura of solidarity, of spontaneous understanding—indeed, even of affection. Instead of these there was a vacuum. They greeted each other; spoke of the weather, their acquaintances, their health; and—God knows why!—with every word Frederick had the disquieting sensation that he was not quite understanding his friend, that his friend did not really know him, that his words were missing their mark, that they could find no common ground for a real conversation. Moreover Erwin still had that friendly smile on his face, which Frederick was beginning almost to hate.

During a pause in the laborious conversation Frederick looked about the studio he knew so well and saw, pinned loosely on the wall, a sheet of paper. This sight moved him strangely and awakened ancient memories; for he recalled that, long ago in their student years, this had been a habit of Erwin's, a way he sometimes chose of keeping a thinker's saying or a poet's verse fresh in his mind. He stood up and went to the wall to read the paper.

There, in Erwin's beautiful script, he read the words: "Nothing is without, nothing is within; for what is without is within."

Blanching, he stood motionless for a moment. There it was! There he stood face to face with what he feared! At another time he would have let this leaf of paper pass, would have tolerated it charitably as a whim, as a harmless foible to which anyone was entitled, perhaps as a trifling sentimentality calling for indulgence. But now it was different. He felt that these words had not been set down for the sake of a fleeting poetic mood; it was not a vagary that Erwin had returned after so many years to a practice of his youth. What stood written here, as an avowal of his friend's concern at the moment, was mysticism! Erwin was unfaithful!

Slowly he turned to face him, whose smile was again radiant.

"Explain this to me!" he demanded.

Erwin nodded, brimming with friendliness.

"Haven't you ever read this saying?"

"Certainly!" Frederick cried. "Of course I know it. It's mysticism, it's Gnosticism. It may be poetic, but—well, anyway, explain the saying to me, and why's it's hanging on your wall!"

"Gladly," Erwin said. "The saying is a first introduction to an epistemology that I've been going into lately, and which has already brought me much happiness."

Frederick restrained his temper. He asked, "A new epistemology? Is there such a thing? And what is it called?"

"Oh," Erwin answered, "it's only new to me. It's already very old and venerable. It's called magic."

The word had been uttered. Profoundly astonished and startled by so candid a confession, Frederick, with a shudder, felt that he was confronted eye to eye with the arch-enemy, in the person of his friend. He did not know whether he was nearer rage or tears; the bitter feeling of irreparable loss possessed him. For a long time he remained silent.

Then, with a pretended decision in his voice, he began, "So now you want to become a magician?"

"Yes," Erwin replied unhesitatingly.

"A sort of sorcerer's apprentice, eh?"

"Certainly."

A clock could be heard ticking in the adjoining room, it was so quiet.

Then Frederick said, "This means, you know, that you are abandoning all fellowship with serious science, and hence all fellowship with me."

"I hope that is not so," Erwin answered. "But if that's the way it has to be, what else can I do?"

"What else can you do?" Frederick burst out. "Why, break, break once and for all with this childishness, this wretched and contemptible belief in magic! That's what else you can do, if you want to keep my respect."

Erwin smiled a little, although he too no longer seemed cheerful.

"You speak as if," he said, so gently that through his quiet words Frederick's angry voice still seemed to be echoing about the room, "you speak as if that lay within my will, as if I had a choice, Frederick. That is not the case. I have no choice. It was not I that chose magic: magic chose me."

Frederick sighed deeply. "Then goodby," he said wearily, and stood up, without offering to shake hands.

"Not like that!" Erwin cried out. "No you must not go from me like that. Pretend that one of us is lying on his deathbed—and that is so!—and that we must say farewell."

"But which of us, Erwin, is dying?"

"Today it is probably I, my friend. Whoever wishes to be born anew must be prepared to die."

Once more Frederick went up to the sheet of paper and read the saying about within and without.

"Very well," he said finally. "You are right, it won't do any good to part in anger. I'll do what you wish; I'll pretend that one of us is dying. Before I go I want to make a last request of you."

"I'm glad," Erwin said. "Tell me, what kindness can I show you on our leavetaking?"

"I repeat my first question, and this is also my request: explain this saying to me, as well as you can."

Erwin reflected a moment and then spoke:

"Nothing is without, nothing is within. You know the religious meaning of this: God is everywhere. He is in the spirit, and also in nature. All is divine, because God is all. Formerly this was called pantheism. Then the philosophic meaning: we are used to divorcing the within from the without in our thinking, but this is not necessary. Our spirit is capable of withdrawing behind the limits we have set for it, into the beyond. Beyond the pair of antitheses of which our world consists a new and different knowledge begins.... But, my dear friend, I must confess to you—since my thinking has changed there are no longer any unambiguous words and sayings for me: every word has tens and hundreds of meanings. And here what you fear begins—magic."

Frederick wrinkled his brow and was about to interrupt, but Erwin looked at him disarmingly and continued, speaking more distinctly, "Let me give you an example. Take something of mine along with you, any object, and examine it a little from time to time. Soon the principle of the within and the without will reveal one of its many means to you."

He glanced about the room, took a small clay figurine from a wall shelf, and gave it to Frederick, saying:

"*Take this with you as my parting gift. When this thing that I am now placing in your hands ceases to be outside you and is within you, come to me again! But if it remains outside you, the way it is now, forever, then this parting of yours from me shall also be forever!"*

Frederick wanted to say a great deal more; but Erwin took his hand, pressed it, and bade him farewell with an expression that permitted no further conversation.

Frederick left; descended the stairs (how prodigiously long ago he had climbed them!); went through the streets to his home, the little earthen figure in his hand, perplexed and sick of heart. In front of his house he stopped, shook the fist fiercely for a moment in which he was clutching the figurine, and felt a great urge to smash the ridiculous thing to the ground. He did not do so; he bit his lip and entered the house. Never before had he been so agitated, so tormented by conflicting emotions.

He looked for a place for his friend's gift, and put the figure on top of a bookcase. For the time being it stayed there.

Occasionally, as the days went by, he looked at it, brooding on it and on its origins, and pondering the meaning that this foolish thing was to have for him. It was a small figure of a man or a god or an idol, with two faces, like the Roman god Janus, modeled rather crudely of clay and covered with a burnt and somewhat cracked glaze. The little image looked coarse and insignificant; certainly it was not Roman or Greek workmanship; more likely it was the work of some backward, primitive race in Africa or the South Seas. The two faces, which were exactly alike, bore an apathetic, indolent faintly grinning smile—it was downright ugly the way the little gnome squandered his stupid smile.

Frederick could not get used to the figure. It was totally unpleasant and offensive to him, it got in his way, it disturbed him. The very next day he took it down and put it on the stove, and a few days later moved it to a cupboard. Again and again it got in the path of his vision, as if it were forcing itself upon him; it laughed at him coldly and dull-wittedly, put on airs, demanded attention. After a few weeks he put it in the anteroom, between the photographs of Italy and the trivial little souvenirs which no one ever looked at. Now at least he saw the idol only when he was entering or leaving, and then he passed it quickly, without examining it more closely. But here too the thing still bothered him, though he did not admit this to himself.

With this shard, this two-faced monstrosity, vexation and torment had entered his life.

One day, months later, he returned from a short trip—he undertook such excursions now from time to time, as if something were driving him restlessly about; he entered his house, went through the anteroom, was greeted by the maid, and read the letters waiting for him. But he was ill at ease, as if he had forgotten something important; no book tempted him, no chair was comfortable. He began to rack his mind—what was the cause of this? Had he neglected something important? eaten something unsettling? In reflecting it occurred to him that this disturbing feeling had come over him as he had entered the apartment. He returned to the anteroom and involuntarily his first glance sought the clay figure.

A strange fright went through him when he did not see the idol. It had disappeared. It was missing. Had it walked away on its little crockery legs? Flown away? By magic?

Frederick pulled himself together, and smiled at his nervousness. Then he began quietly to search the whole room. When he found nothing he called the maid. She came, was embarrassed, and admitted at once that she had dropped the thing while cleaning up.

"Where is it?"

It was not there any more. It had seemed so solid, that little thing; she had often had it in her hands; and yet it had shattered to a hundred little pieces and splinters, and could not be fixed. She had taken the fragments to a glazier, who had simply laughed at her; and then she had thrown them away.

Frederick dismissed the maid. He smiled. That was perfectly all right with him. He did not feel bad about the idol, God knows. The abomination was gone; now he would have peace. If only he had knocked the thing to pieces that very first day! What he had suffered in all this time! How sluggishly, strangely, craftily, evilly, satanically that idol had smiled at him! Well, now that it was gone he could admit it to himself: he had feared it, truly and sincerely feared it, this earthen god. Was it not the emblem and symbol of everything that was repugnant and intolerable to him, everything that he had recognized all along as pernicious, inimical, and worthy of suppression—an emblem of all superstitions, all darkness, all coercion of conscience and spirit? Did it not represent that ghastly power that one sometimes felt raging in the bowels of the earth, that distant earthquake, that approaching extinction of culture, that looming chaos? Had not this contemptible figure robbed him of his best friend—nay, not merely robbed, but made of the friend an enemy? Well, now the thing was gone. Vanished. Smashed to pieces. Done for. It was good so; it was much better than if he had destroyed it himself.

So he thought, or said. And he went about his affairs as before.

But it was like a curse. Now, just when he had got more or less used to that ridiculous figure, just when the sight of it in its usual place on the anteroom table had gradually become a bit familiar and unimportant to him, now its absence began to torment him! Yes, he missed it every time he went through that room; all he could see there was the empty spot where it had formerly stood, and emptiness emanated from the spot and filled the room with strangeness.

Bad days and worse nights began for Frederick. He could no longer go through the anteroom without thinking of the idol with the two faces, missing it, and feeling that his thoughts were tethered to it. This became an agonizing compulsion for him. And it was not by any means simply on the occasions when he went through that room that he was gripped by this compulsion—ah, no. Just as emptiness and desolation radiated from the now empty spot on the anteroom table, so this compulsive idea radiated within him, gradually crowded all else aside, rankling and filling him with emptiness and strangeness.

Again and again he pictured the figure with utmost distinctness, just to make it clear to himself how preposterous it was to grieve its loss. He could see it in all its stupid ugliness and barbarity, with its vacuous yet crafty smile, with its two faces—indeed, as if under duress, full of hatred and with his mouth drawn awry, he found himself attempting to reproduce that smile. The question pestered him whether the two faces were really exactly alike. Had not one of them, perhaps only because of a little roughness or a crack in the glaze, had a somewhat different expression? Something quizzical? Something sphinxlike? And how peculiar the color of that glaze had been! Green, and blue, and gray, but also red, were in it—a glaze that he now kept finding often in other objects, in a window's reflection of the sun or in the mirrorings of a wet pavement.

He brooded a great deal on this glaze,

at night too. It also struck him what a strange, foreign, ill-sounding, unfamiliar, almost malignant word "glaze" was. He analyzed the word, and once he even reversed the order of its letters. Then it read "ezalg." Now where the devil did this word get its sound from? He knew this word "ezalg," certainly he knew it; moreover, it was an unfriendly and bad word, a word with ugly and disturbing connotations. For a long while he tormented himself with this question. Finally he hit upon it: "ezalg" reminded him of a book that he had bought and read many years ago on a trip, and that had dismayed, plagued, and yet secretly fascinated him; it had been entitled *Princess Ezalka*. It was like a curse: everything connected with the figurine —the glaze, the blue, the green, the smile—signified hostility, tormenting and poisoning him. And how very peculiarly *he*, Erwin, his erstwhile friend, had smiled as he had given the idol into his hand! How very peculiarly, how very significantly, how very hostily.

Frederick resisted manfully—and on many days not without success—the compulsive trend of his thoughts. He sensed the danger clearly: he did not want to go insane! No, it were better to die. Reason was necessary, life was not. And it occurred to him that perhaps *this* was magic, that Erwin, with the aid of that figure, had in some way enchanted him, and that he should fall as a sacrifice, as the defender of reason and science against these dismal powers. But if this were so, if he could even conceive of that as possible, then there *was* such a thing as magic, then there *was* sorcery. No, it were better to die!

A doctor recommended walks and baths; and sometimes, in search of amusement, he spent an evening at an inn. But it helped very little. He cursed Erwin; he cursed himself.

One night, as he often did now, he retired early and lay restlessly awake in bed, unable to sleep. He felt unwell and uneasy. He wanted to meditate; he wanted to find solace, wanted to speak sentences of some sort to himself, good sentences, comforting, reassuring ones, something with the straightforward serenity and lucidity of the sentence, "Twice two is four." Nothing came to mind; but, in a state almost of lightheadedness, he mumbled sounds and syllables to himself. Gradually words formed on his lips, and several times, without being sensible of its meaning, he said the same short sentence to himself, which had somehow taken form in him. He muttered it to himself, as if it might stupefy him, as if he might grope his way along it, as along a parapet, to the sleep that eluded him on the narrow, narrow path that skirted the abyss.

But suddenly, when he spoke somewhat louder, the words he was mumbling penetrated his consciousness. He knew them: they were, "Yes, now you are within me!" And instantly he knew. He knew what they meant—that they referred to the clay idol and that now, in this gray night hour, he had accurately and exactly fulfilled the prophecy Erwin had made on that unearthly day, that now the figure, which he had held contemptuously in his fingers then, was no longer outside him but within him! "For what is without is within."

Bounding up in a leap, he felt as if transfused with ice and fire. The world reeled about him, the planets stared at him insanely. He threw on some clothes, put on the light, left his house and ran in the middle of the night to Erwin's. There he saw a light burning in the studio window he knew so well; the door to the house was unlocked: everything seemed to be awaiting him. He rushed up the stairs. He walked unsteadily into Erwin's study, supported himself with trembling hands on the table. Erwin sat by the lamp, in its

ANDREW NEWELL WYETH: *Ground Hog Day*, PHOTOGRAPH BY A. J. WYATT, STAFF PHOTOGRAPHER, PHILADELPHIA MUSEUM OF ART. PURCHASED: ADELE HAAS TURNER AND BEATRICE PASTORIUS TURNER MEMORIAL FUND AND CONTRIBUTIONS FROM MRS. JOHN WINTERSTEEN AND A FRIEND OF THE MUSEUM

gentle light, contemplative, smiling.

Graciously Erwin arose. "You have come. That is good."

"Have you been expecting me?" Frederick whispered.

"I have been expecting you, as you know, from the moment you left here, taking my little gift with you. Has what I said then happened?"

"It has happened," Frederick said. "The idol is within me. I can't bear it any longer."

"Can I help you?" Erwin asked.

"I don't know. Do as you will. Tell me more of your magic! Tell me how the idol can get out of me again."

Erwin placed his hand on his friend's shoulder. He led him to an armchair and pressed him down in it. Then he spoke cordially to Frederick, smiling in an almost brotherly tone of voice:

"The idol will come out of you again. Have trust in me. Have trust in yourself. You have learned to believe in it. Now learn to love it! It is within you, but it is still dead, it is still a phantom to you. Awaken it, speak to it, question it! For it is you yourself! Do not hate it any longer, do not fear it, do not torment it—how you have tormented this poor idol, who was yet you yourself! How you have tormented yourself!"

"Is this the way to magic?" Frederick asked. He sat deep in the chair, as if he had grown older, and his voice was low.

"This is the way," Erwin replied, "and perhaps you have already taken the most difficult step. You have found by experience: the without can become the within. You have been beyond the pair of antitheses. It seemed hell to you; learn, my friend, it is heaven! For it is heaven that awaits you. Behold, this is magic: to interchange the without and the within, not by compulsion, not in anguish, as you have done it, but freely, voluntarily. Summon up the past, summon up the future: both are in you! Until today you have been the slave of the within. Learn to be its master. That is magic."

(Translated by T. K. Brown, III)

John Masefield
(1878-1967)
On Growing Old

Be with me, Beauty, for the fire is dying;
My dog and I are old, too old for roving.
Man, whose young passion sets the spindrift flying,
Is soon too lame to march, too cold for loving.
I take the book and gather to the fire,
Turning old yellow leaves; minute by minute
The clock ticks to my heart. A withered wire
Moves a thin ghost of music in the spinet.
I cannot sail your seas, I cannot wander

Your cornland, nor your hill-land, nor your valleys
Ever again, nor share the battle yonder
Where the young knight the broken squadron rallies.
Only stay quiet while my mind remembers
The beauty of fire from the beauty of embers.

Beauty, have pity! for the strong have power,
The rich their wealth, the beautiful their grace,
Summer of man its sunlight and its flower.
Spring-time of man all April in a face.
Only, as in the jostling in the Strand,
Where the mob thrusts or loiters or is loud,
The beggar with the saucer in his hand
Asks only a penny from the passing crowd,
So, from this glittering world with all its fashion,
Its fire, and play of men, its stir, its march,
Let me have wisdom, Beauty, wisdom and passion,
Bread to the soul, rain when the summers parch.
Give me but these, and though the darkness close
Even the night will blossom as the rose.

Carl Sandburg
(1878-1967)
Fog

The fog comes
on little cat feet.
It sits looking
over the harbor and city
on silent haunches
and then moves on.

Nocturne in a Deserted Brickyard

Stuff of the moon
Runs on the lapping sand
Out to the longest shadows.
Under the curving willows,
And round the creep of the wave line,
Fluxions of yellow and dusk on the waters
Make a wide dreaming pansy of an old pond in the night.

Jazz Fantasia

Drum on your drums, batter on your banjos, sob on the long cool winding saxophones. Go to it, O jazzmen.

Sling your knuckles on the bottoms of the happy tin pans, let your trombones ooze, and go husha-husha-hush with the slippery sandpaper.

Moan like an autumn wind high in the lonesome treetops, moan soft like you wanted somebody terrible, cry like a racing car slipping away from a motor-cycle-cop, bang-bang! you jazzmen, bang altogether drums, traps, banjos, horns, tin cans—make two people fight on the top of a stairway and scratch each other's eyes in a clinch tumbling down the stairs.

Can the rough stuff . . . Now a Mississippi steamboat pushes up the night river with a hoo-hoo-hoo-oo . . . and the green lanterns calling to the high soft stars . . . a red moon rides on the humps of the low river hills . . . Go to it, O jazzmen.

Wind Song

Long ago I learned how to sleep,
In an old apple orchard where the wind swept by
    counting its money and throwing it away,
In a wind-gaunt orchard where the limbs forked out
    and listened or never listened at all,
In a passel of trees where the branches trapped the
    wind into whistling, "Who, who are you?"
I slept with my head in an elbow on a summer
    afternoon and there I took a sleep lesson.
There I went away saying: I know why they sleep,
    I know how they trap the tricky winds.
Long ago I learned how to listen to the singing wind
    and how to forget and how to hear the deep
    whine,
Slapping and lapsing under the day blue and the
    night stars:

    Who, who are you?

    Who can ever forget
    listening to the wind go by
    counting its money
    and throwing it away?

Wallace Stevens
(1879-1955)
Peter Quince at the Clavier

The "perfect little tale" of Susanna and the elders is told in one of the Apocryphal books of the Old Testament. Because she repulsed two lustful elders, they obtained her condemnation to death on a false charge. But the prophet Daniel proved her to be innocent and obtained a reversal of the sentence, whereupon the elders were put to death. Here the poet has Peter Quince think of her story as he plays the clavier, an early keyboard instrument.

I

Just as my fingers on these keys
Make music, so the self-same sounds
On my spirit make a music, too.

Music is feeling, then, not sound;
And thus it is that what I feel,
Here in this room, desiring you,

Thinking of your blue-shadowed silk,
Is music. It is like the strain
Waked in the elders by Susanna:

Of a green evening, clear and warm,
She bathed in her still garden, while
The red-eyed elders, watching, felt

The basses of their beings throb
In witching chords, and their thin blood
Pulse pizzicati of Hosanna.

II

In the green water, clear and warm,
Susanna lay,
She searched
The touch of springs,

And found
Concealed imaginings.
She sighed,
For so much melody.

Upon the bank, she stood
In the cool
Of spent emotions.
She felt, among the leaves,
The dew
Of old devotions.

She walked upon the grass,
Still quavering.
The winds were like her maids
On timid feet,
Fetching her woven scarves,
Yet wavering.

A breath upon her hand
Muted the night.
She turned—
A cymbal crashed,
And roaring horns.

III

Soon, with a noise like tambourines,
Came her attendant Byzantines.

They wondered why Susanna cried
Against the elders by her side;

And as they whispered, the refrain
Was like a willow swept by rain.

Anon, their lamps' uplifted flame
Revealed Susanna and her shame.

And then, the simpering Byzantines
Fled, with a noise like tambourines.

IV

Beauty is momentary in the mind—
The fitful tracing of a portal;
But in the flesh it is immortal.

The body dies; the body's beauty lives.
So evenings die, in their green going,
A wave, interminably flowing.
So gardens die, their meek breath scenting
The cowl of Winter, done repenting.
So maidens die, to the auroral
Celebration of a maiden's choral.

Susanna's music touched the bawdy strings
Of those white elders; but, escaping,
Left only Death's ironic scraping.
Now, in its immortality, it plays
On the clear viol of her memory,
And makes a constant sacrament of praise.

E. M. Forster
(1879-1970)
The Road from Colonus

When he was nearly ninety, Sophocles wrote Oedipus at Colonus. *In this lyrical drama the old Theban King is self-blinded and self-exiled because of the sins he unknowingly committed long before. Now he has found his way, with the help of his daughter Antigone, to a sacred shrine at Colonus, near Athens. He is befriended by Theseus, king of Athens; but when Oedipus' sons and brother-in-law try to lure him back to Thebes for their own political purposes, he wrathfully sends them away. Then he hears sounds of thunder that he recognizes as signs of his approaching death. Proudly, convinced at last that his life has been blameless, he leads the others to the palace where he is to be buried. There death (or translation?) comes to him in mysterious splendor. . . . There are interesting relationships between Sophocles' drama and the short story that follows.*

For no very intelligible reason, Mr. Lucas had hurried ahead of his party. He was perhaps reaching the age at which independence becomes valuable, because it is so soon to be lost. Tired of attention and consideration, he liked breaking away from the younger members, to ride by himself, and to dismount unassisted. Perhaps he also relished that more subtle pleasure of being kept waiting for lunch, and of telling the others on their arrival that it was of no consequence.

So, with childish impatience, he battered the animal's sides with his heels, and made the muleteer bang it with a thick stick and prick it with a sharp one, and jolted down the hill sides through clumps of flowering shrubs and stretches of anemones and asphodel, till he heard the sound of running water, and came in sight of the group of plane trees where they were to have their meal.

Even in England those trees would have been remarkable, so huge were they, so interlaced, so magnificently clothed in quivering green. And here in Greece they were unique, the one cool spot in that hard brilliant landscape, already scorched by the heat of an April sun. In their midst was hidden a tiny Khan or country inn, a frail mud building with a broad wooden balcony in which sat an old woman spinning, while a small brown pig, eating orange peel, stood beside her. On the wet earth below squatted two children, playing some primeval game with their fingers; and their mother, none too clean either, was messing with some rice inside. As Mrs. Forman would have said, it was all very Greek, and the fastidious Mr. Lucas felt thankful that they were bringing their food with them, and should eat it in the open air.

Still, he was glad to be there—the muleteer had helped him off—and glad that Mrs. Forman was not there to forestall his opinions—glad even that he should not see Ethel for quite half an hour. Ethel was his youngest daughter, still unmarried. She was unselfish and affectionate, and it was generally understood that she was to devote her life to her father, and be the comfort of his old age. Mrs. Forman always referred to her as Antigone, and Mr. Lucas tried to settle down to the role of Oedipus, which seemed the only one that public opinion allowed him.

He had this in common with Oedipus, that he was growing old. Even to himself it had become obvious. He had lost interest in other people's affairs, and seldom attended when they spoke to him. He was fond of talking himself but often forgot what he was going to say, and even when he succeeded, it seldom seemed worth the effort. His phrases and gestures had become stiff and set, his anecdotes, once so successful, fell flat, his silence was as meaningless as his speech. Yet he had led a healthy, active life, had worked steadily, made money, educated his children. There was nothing and no one to blame: he was simply growing old.

At the present moment, here he was in Greece, and one of the dreams of his life was realized. Forty years ago he had caught the fever of Hellenism, and all his life he had felt that could he but visit that land, he would not have lived in vain. But Athens had been dusty, Delphi wet, Thermopylae flat, and he had listened with amazement and cynicism to the rapturous explanations of his companions. Greece was like England: it was a man who was growing old, and it made no difference whether that man looked at the Thames or the Eurore. It was his last hope of contradicting that logic of experience, and it was failing.

Yet Greece had done something for him, though he did not know it. It had made him discontented, and there are stirrings of life in discontent. He knew that he was not the victim of continual ill-luck. Something great was wrong, and he was pitted against no mediocre or accidental enemy. For the last month a strange desire had possessed him to die fighting.

"Greece is the land for young people," he said to himself as he stood under the plane trees, "but I will enter into it, I will possess it. Leaves shall be green again, water shall be sweet, the sky shall be blue. They were forty years ago, and I will win them back. I do mind being old, and I will pretend no longer."

He took two steps forward, and immediately cold waters were gurgling over his ankle.

"Where does the water come from?" he asked himself. "I do not even know that." He remembered that all the hill sides were dry; yet here the road was suddenly covered with flowing streams.

He stopped still in amazement, saying: "Water out of a tree—out of a hollow tree? I never saw nor thought of that before."

For the enormous plane that leant towards the Khan was hollow—it had been burnt out for charcoal—and from its living trunk there gushed an impetuous spring, coating the bark with fern and moss, and flowing over the mule track to create fertile meadows beyond. The simple country folk had paid to beauty and mystery such tribute as they could, for in the rind of the tree a shrine was cut, holding a lamp and a little picture of the Virgin, inheritor of the Naiad's and Dryad's joint abode.

"I never saw anything so marvellous before," said Mr. Lucas. "I could even step inside the trunk and see where the water comes from."

For a moment he hesitated to violate the shrine. Then he remembered with a smile his own thought—"the place shall be mine; I will enter it and possess it"—and leapt almost aggressively on to a stone within.

The water pressed up steadily and noiselessly from the hollow roots and hidden crevices of the plane, forming a wonderful amber pool ere it spilt over the lip of bark on to the earth outside. Mr. Lucas tasted it and it was sweet, and when he looked up the black funnel of the trunk he saw sky which was blue, and some leaves which were green; and he remembered, without smiling, another of his thoughts.

Others had been before him—indeed he had a curious sense of companionship. Little votive offerings to the presiding power were fastened on to the bark—tiny arms and legs and eyes in tiny, grotesque models of the brain or the heart—all tokens of some recovery of strength or wisdom or love. There was no such thing as the solitude of nature, for the sorrows and joys of humanity had pressed even into the bosom of a tree. He spread out his arms and steadied himself against the soft charred wood, and then slowly leant back, till his body was resting on the trunk behind. His eyes closed, and he had the strange feeling of one who is moving, yet at peace—the feeling of the swimmer, who, after long struggling with chopping seas, finds that after all the tide will sweep him to his goal.

So he lay motionless, conscious only of the stream below his feet, and that all things were a stream, in which he was moving.

He was aroused at last by a shock—the shock of an arrival perhaps, for when he opened his eyes, something unimagined, undefinable, had passed over all things, and made them intelligible and good.

There was meaning in the stoop of the old woman over her work, and in the quick motions of the little pig, and in her diminishing globe of wool. A young man came singing over the streams on a mule, and there was beauty in his pose and sincerity in his greeting. The sun made no accidental patterns upon the spreading roots of the trees, and there was intention in the nodding clumps of asphodel, and in the music of the water. To Mr. Lucas, who, in a brief space of time, had discovered not only Greece, but England and all the world and life, there seemed nothing ludicrous in the desire to hang within the tree another votive offering—a little model of an entire man.

"Why, here's papa, playing at being a Merlin."

All unnoticed they had arrived—Ethel, Mrs. Forman, Mr. Graham, and the English-speaking dragoman. Mr. Lucas peered out at them suspiciously. They had suddenly become unfamiliar, and all that they did seemed strained and coarse.

"Allow me to give you a hand," said Mr. Graham, a young man who was always polite to his elders.

Mr. Lucas felt annoyed. "Thank you, I can manage perfectly well by myself," he replied. His foot slipped as he stepped out of the tree, and went into the spring.

"Oh papa, my papa!" said Ethel, "what are you doing? Thank goodness I have got a change for you on the mule."

She tended him carefully, giving him clean socks and dry boots, and then sat him down on the rug beside the lunch basket, while she went with the others to explore the grove.

They came back in ecstasies, in which Mr. Lucas tried to join. But he found them intolerable. Their enthusiasm was superficial, commonplace, and spasmodic. They had no perception of the coherent beauty that was flowering around them. He tried at least to explain his feelings, and what he said was:

"I am altogether pleased with the appearance of this place. It impresses me very favourably. The trees are fine, remarkably fine for Greece, and there is something very poetic in the spring of clear running water. The people too seem kindly and civil. It is decidedly an attractive place."

Mrs. Forman upbraided him for his tepid praise.

"Oh, it is a place in a thousand!" she cried. "I could live and die here! I really would stop if I had not to be back at Athens! It reminds me of the Colonus of Sophocles."

"Well, I must stop," said Ethel. "I positively must."

"Yes, do! You and your father! Antigone and Oedipus. Of course you must stop at Colonus."

Mr. Lucas was almost breathless with excitement. When he stood within the tree, he had believed that his happiness would be independent of locality. But these few minutes' conversation had undeceived him. He no longer trusted himself to journey through the world, for old thoughts, old wearinesses might be waiting to rejoin him as soon as he left the shade of the planes, and the music of the virgin water. To sleep in the Khan with the gracious, kind-eyed country people, to watch the bats flit about within the globe of shade, and see the moon turn the golden patterns into silver—one such night would place him beyond relapse, and confirm him for ever in the kingdom he had regained. But all his lips could say was: "I should be willing to put in a night here."

"You mean a week, papa! It would be sacrilege to put in less."

"A week then, a week," said his lips, irritated at being corrected, while his heart was leaping with joy. All through lunch he spoke to them no more, but watched the place he should know so well, and the people who would so soon be his companions and friends. The inmates of the Khan only consisted of an old woman, a middle-aged woman, a young man and two children, and to none of them had he spoken, yet he loved them as he loved everything that moved or breathed or existed beneath the benedictory shade of the planes.

"En route!" said the shrill voice of Mrs. Forman. "Ethel! Mr. Graham! The best of things must end."

"To-night," thought Mr. Lucas, "they will light the little lamp by the shrine. And when we all sit together on the balcony, perhaps they will tell me which offerings they put up."

"I beg your pardon, Mr. Lucas," said Graham, "but they want to fold up the rug you are sitting on."

Mr. Lucas got up, saying to himself: "Ethel shall go to bed first, and then I will try to tell them about my offering too—for it is a thing I must do. I think they will understand if I am left with them alone."

Ethel touched him on the cheek. "Papa! I've called you three times. All the mules are here."

"Mules? What mules?"

"Our mules. We're all waiting. Oh, Mr. Graham, do help my father on."

"I don't know what you're talking about, Ethel."

"My dearest papa, we must start. You know we have to get to Olympia to-night."

Mr. Lucas in pompous, confident tones replied: "I always did wish, Ethel, that you had a better head for plans. You know perfectly well that we are putting in a week here. It is your own suggestion."

Ethel was startled into impoliteness. "What a perfectly ridiculous idea. You must have known I was joking. Of course I meant I wished we could."

"Ah! if we could only do what we wished!" sighed Mrs. Forman, already seated on her mule.

"Surely," Ethel continued in calmer tones, "you didn't think I meant it."

"Most certainly I did. I have made all plans on the supposition that we are stopping here, and it will be extremely inconvenient, indeed, impossible for me to start."

He delivered this remark with an air of great conviction, and Mrs. Forman and Mr. Graham had to turn away to hide their smiles.

"I am sorry I spoke so carelessly; it was wrong of me. But, you know, we can't break up our party, and even one night here would make us miss the boat at Patras."

Mrs. Forman, in an aside, called Mr. Graham's attention to the excellent way in which Ethel managed her father.

"I don't mind about the Patras boat. You said that we should stop here, and we are stopping."

It seemed as if the inhabitants of the Khan had divined in some mysterious way that the altercation touched them. The old woman stopped her spinning, while the young man and the two children stood behind Mr. Lucas, as if supporting him.

Neither arguments nor entreaties moved him. He said little, but he was absolutely determined, because for the first time he saw his daily life aright. What need had he to return to England? Who would miss him? His friends were dead or cold. Ethel loved him in a way, but, as was right, she had other interests. His other children he seldom saw. He had only one other relative, his sister Julia, whom he both feared and hated. It was no effort to struggle. He would be a fool as well as a coward if he stirred from the place which brought him happiness and peace.

At last Ethel, to humour him, and not disinclined to air her modern Greek, went into the Khan with the astonished dragoman to look at the rooms. The woman inside received them with loud welcomes, and the young man, when no one was looking, began to lead Mr. Lucas' mule to the stable.

"Drop it, you brigand!" shouted Graham, who always declared that foreigners understand English if they choose. He was right, for the man obeyed, and they all stood waiting for Ethel's return.

She emerged at last, with close-gathered skirts, followed by the dragoman bearing the little pig, which he had bought at a bargain.

"My dear papa, I will do all I can for you, but stop in that Khan—no."

"Are there—fleas?" asked Mrs. Forman.

Ethel intimated that "fleas" was not the word.

"Well, I am afraid that settles it," said Mrs. Forman, "I know how particular Mr. Lucas is."

"It does not settle it," said Mr. Lucas. "Ethel, you go on, I do not want you. I don't know why I ever consulted you. I shall stop here alone."

"That is absolute nonsense," said Ethel, losing her temper. "How can you be left alone at your age? How would you get your meals or your bath? All your letters are waiting for you at Patras. You'll miss the boat. That means missing the London operas, and upsetting all your engagements for the month. And as if you could travel by yourself!"

"They might knife you," was Mr. Graham's contribution.

The Greeks said nothing; but whenever Mr. Lucas looked their way, they beckoned him towards the Khan. The children would even have drawn him by the coat, and the old woman on the balcony stopped her almost completed spinning, and fixed him with mysterious appealing eyes. As he fought, the issue assumed gigantic proportions, and he believed that he was not merely stopping because he had regained youth or seen beauty or found happiness, but because in that place and with those people a supreme event was awaiting him which would transfigure the face of the world. The moment was so tremendous that he abandoned words and arguments as useless, and rested on the strength of his mighty unrevealed allies: silent men, murmuring water, and whispering trees. For the whole place called with one voice, articulate to him, and his garrulous opponents became every minute more meaningless and absurd. Soon they would be tired and go chattering away into the sun, leaving him to the cool grove and the moonlight and the destiny he foresaw.

Mrs. Forman and the dragoman had indeed already started, amid the piercing screams of the little pig, and the struggle might have gone on indefinitely if Ethel had not called in Mr. Graham.

"Can you help me?" she whispered. "He is absolutely unmanageable."

"I'm no good at arguing—but if I could help you in any other way—" and he looked down complacently at his well-made figure.

Ethel hesitated. Then she said: "Help me in any way you can. After all, it is for his good that we do it."

"Then have his mule led up behind him."

So when Mr. Lucas thought he had gained the day, he suddenly felt himself lifted off the ground, and sat sideways on the saddle, and at the same time the mule started off at a trot. He said nothing, for he had nothing to say, and even his face showed little emotion as he felt the shade pass and heard the sound of the water cease. Mr. Graham was running at his side, hat in hand, apologizing.

"I know I had no business to do it, and I do beg your pardon awfully. But I do hope that some day you too will feel that I was—damn!"

A stone had caught him in the middle of the back. It was thrown by the little boy, who was pursuing them along the mule track. He was followed by his sister, also throwing stones.

Ethel screamed to the dragoman, who was some way ahead with Mrs. Forman, but before he could rejoin them, another adversary appeared. It was the young Greek, who had cut them off in front, and now dashed down at Mr. Lucas' bridle. Fortunately, Graham was an expert boxer, and it did not take him a moment to beat down the youth's feeble defence, and to send him sprawling with a bleeding mouth into the asphodel. By this time the dragoman had arrived, the children, alarmed at the fate of their brother, had desisted, and the rescue party, if such it was to be considered, retired in disorder to the trees.

"Little devils!" said Graham, laughing with triumph. "That's the modern Greek all over. Your father meant money if he stopped, and they consider we were taking it out of their pocket."

"Oh, they are terrible—simple savages! I don't know how I shall ever thank you. You've saved my father."

"I only hope you didn't think me brutal."

"No," replied Ethel with a little sigh. "I admire strength."

Meanwhile the cavalcade reformed, and Mr. Lucas, who, as Mrs. Forman said, bore his disappointment wonderfully well, was put comfortably on to his mule. They hurried up the opposite hillside, fearful of another attack, and it was not until they had left the eventful place far behind that Ethel found an opportunity to speak to her father and ask his pardon for the way she had treated him.

"You seemed so different, dear father, and you quite frightened me. Now I feel that you are your old self again."

He did not answer, and she concluded

that he was not unnaturally offended at her behaviour.

By one of those curious tricks of mountain scenery, the place they had left an hour before suddenly reappeared far below them. The Khan was hidden under the green dome, but in the open there still stood three figures, and through the pure air rose up a faint cry of defiance or farewell.

Mr. Lucas stopped irresolutely, and let the reins fall from his hand.

"Come, father dear," said Ethel gently.

He obeyed, and in another moment a spur of the hill hid the dangerous scene for ever.

II

It was breakfast time, but the gas was alight, owing to the fog. Mr. Lucas was in the middle of an account of a bad night he had spent. Ethel, who was to be married in a few weeks, had her arms on the table, listening.

"First the door bell rang, then you came back from the theatre. Then the dog started, and after the dog the cat. And at three in the morning a young hooligan passed by singing. Oh yes: then there was the water gurgling in the pipe above my head."

"I think that was only the bath water running away," said Ethel, looking rather worn.

"Well, there's nothing I dislike more than running water. It's perfectly impossible to sleep in the house. I shall give it up. I shall give notice next quarter. I shall tell the landlord plainly, 'The reason I am giving up the house is this: it is perfectly impossible to sleep in it.' If he says—says—well, what has he got to say?"

"Some more toast, father?"

"Thank you, my dear." He took it, and there was an interval of peace.

But he soon recommenced. "I'm not going to submit to the practising next door as tamely as they think. I wrote and told them so—didn't I?"

"Yes," said Ethel, who had taken care that the letter should not reach. "I have seen the governess, and she has promised to arrange it differently. And Aunt Julia hates noise. It is sure to be all right."

Her aunt, being the only unattached member of the family, was coming to keep house for her father when she left him. The reference was not a happy one, and Mr. Lucas commenced a series of half articulate sighs, which was only stopped by the arrival of the post.

"Oh, what a parcel!" cried Ethel. "For me! What can it be! Greek stamps. This is most exciting!"

It proved to be some asphodel bulbs sent by Mrs. Forman from Athens for planting in the conservatory.

"Doesn't it bring it all back! You remember the asphodels, father. And all wrapped up in Greek newspapers. I wonder if I can read them still. I used to be able to, you know."

She rattled on, hoping to conceal the laughter of children next door—a favourite source of querulousness at breakfast time.

"Listen to me! 'A rural disaster.' Oh, I've hit on something sad. But never mind. 'Last Tuesday at Platansite, in the province of Messenia, a shocking tragedy occurred. A large tree'—aren't I getting on well?—'blew down in the night and'—wait a minute—oh dear! 'crushed to death the five occupants of the little Khan there, who had apparently been sitting on the balcony. The bodies of Maria Rhomaides, the aged proprietress, and of her daughter, aged forty-six, were easily recognizable, whereas that of her grandson'—oh, the rest is really too horrid; I wish I had never tried it, and what's more I feel to have heard the name Platansite before. We didn't stop there, did we, in the spring?"

"We had lunch," said Mr. Lucas, with a faint expression of trouble on his vacant face. "Perhaps it was where the dragoman bought the pig."

"Of course," said Ethel in a nervous voice. "Where the dragoman bought the little pig. How terrible!"

"Very terrible!" said her father, whose attention was wandering to the noisy children next door. Ethel suddenly started to her feet with genuine interest.

"Good gracious!" she exclaimed. "This is an old paper. It happened not lately but in April—the night of Tuesday the eighteenth—and we-we must have been there in the afternoon."

"So we were," said Mr. Lucas. She put her hand to her heart, scarcely able to speak.

"Father, dear father, I must say it: you wanted to stop there. All those people, those poor half-savage people, tried to keep you, and they're dead. The whole place, it says, is in ruins, and even the stream has changed its course. Father, dear, if it had not been for me, and if Arthur had not helped me, you must have been killed."

Mr. Lucas waved his hand irritably. "It is not a bit of good speaking to the governess, I shall write to the landlord and say, 'The reason I am giving up the house is this: the dog barks, the children next door are intolerable, and I cannot stand the noise of running water.'"

Ethel did not check his babbling. She was aghast at the narrowness of the escape, and for a long time kept silence. At last she said: "Such a marvellous deliverance does make one believe in Providence."

Mr. Lucas, who was still composing his letter to the landlord, did not reply.

Juan Ramón Jiménez
(1881-1958)
Platero and I

I
Platero

Platero is a small donkey, a soft, hairy donkey: so soft to the touch that he might be said to be made of cotton, with no bones. Only the jet mirrors of his eyes are hard like two black crystal scarabs.

I turn him loose, and he goes to the meadow, and, with his nose, he gently caresses the little flowers of rose and blue and gold.... I call him softly, "Platero?" and he comes to me at a gay little trot that is like laughter of a vague, idyllic, tinkling sound.

He eats whatever I give him. He likes mandarin oranges, amber-hued muscatel grapes, purple figs tipped with crystalline drops of honey.

He is as loving and tender as a child, but strong and sturdy as a rock. When on Sundays I ride him through the lanes in the outskirts of the town, slow-moving countrymen, dressed in their Sunday clean, watch him a while, speculatively:

"He is like steel," they say.

Steel, yes. Steel and moon silver at the same time.

. . .

X
Angelus

Look, Platero, how roses are falling everywhere: blue roses, pink ones, white ones, roses with no color. One might say that the sky is dissolving in roses. See how my forehead, my shoulders, my hands, are covered with roses.... What shall I do with so many roses?

Do you perhaps know where all this tender flora comes from, for I myself do not know its source, which each day softens the landscape and leaves it sweetly rosy, white, and blue—more roses, more roses—like a painting by Fra Angelico, he who used to paint glory on his knees?

It might be thought that roses are being thrown down from the seven heavens of Paradise. As in a warm and vaguely colored snowfall, the roses fall on tower, on roof, on trees. Look: everything harsh turns delicate with their adornment. Roses, roses, roses. . . .

It seems, Platero, while the Angelus rings, that this life of ours loses its everyday strength and that another force within, more high-minded, more constant and pure, makes everything—as though fed from a reservoir of grace—rise to the stars, which are already shining among the roses. . . . More roses. . . . Your eyes, which you cannot see, Platero, and which you raise humbly to the sky, are two beautiful roses.

. . .

XIX
Landscape in Scarlet

The hilltop. The setting sun lies pierced by his own crystal spears, bleeding purple and crimson from every vein. Before his splendor the green pine grove is dulled, turns vaguely red; and from the flushed transparent grass and small flowers a penetrating and luminous essence emanates.

I stop entranced in the twilight. Platero, his black eyes turned to scarlet by the sunset, walks softly to a pool of crimson, violet, rose-colored waters; gently he sinks his mouth in these mirrors, which again become liquid at his touch, and there is a profuse passing of dark waters up his huge throat.

I know this place well; but the moment has changed it and made it portentous. At any moment an unearthly adventure may befall us, an abandoned castle may loom before us. . . . Evening prolongs itself beyond itself, and the hour, imbued with the spirit of eternity, is infinite, peaceful, beyond sounding.

"Come, Platero."

. . .

XXIV
Don José, the Curate

Now, Platero, he goes forth, very holy and full of honeyed words. But the one that in reality is always angelic is his she-ass; she is a lady.

I think you saw him in his orchard one day, wearing sailor's breeches and broad-brimmed hat, throwing curses and rocks at the urchins that were stealing his oranges. A thousand times on Fridays you have seen poor Baltasar, his houseboy, dragging his rupture, which looks like a circus balloon, along the roads, coming to town to sell his miserable brooms or to pray with the poor for the dead relatives of the rich. . . .

Never have I heard a man utter worse profanity nor raise higher heaven with his oaths. It is true that he no doubt knows—at least, so he says in his five o'clock mass—where and how things are up there. . . . The tree, the clod, the water, the wind, the chestnut bloom—all this, so graceful, so fresh, so pure, so bright, seems to be for him an example of disorder, hardness, coldness, violence, ruin. By the end of each day the rocks in his orchard lie in a different place, having been hurled in furious hostility against birds and washerwomen, children and flowers.

At vespers everything changes. Don José's silence is heard in the silence of the countryside. He dons his habit, cloak, and low-crown hat, and, almost without seeing, enters the dark town on his slow she-ass, like a carnival image on a skeleton. . . .

. . .

XLIV
Lullaby

The charcoal-burner's little daughter, as pretty and dirty as a coin, with eyes of burnished black and full lips that seem about to burst with the red blood behind the grime, is at the cabin door, sitting on a tile, rocking her baby brother to sleep.

The vibrant break of Maytime is everywhere, ardent and clear as an inner sunlight. In the bright peacefulness the boiling of the pot in the open fire is heard, with the lowing of cattle from the pasture and the mirth of the sea wind in the tangled branches of the eucalyptus trees.

Feelingly, sweetly, the charcoal-burner's daughter sings:

> "Sleep, little one, sleep
> To please the good shepherdess...."

A pause. The wind in the treetops....

> "Sleep, my little one, dream
> While the little mother sings...."

The wind.... Platero, who is walking gently among the pines, approaches, little by little.... Then he lies down on the hard earth, and, soothed by the monotonous lullaby of the singer, he falls asleep, like a child.

• • •

LXXXIX
Antonia

The brook was so full that the yellow lilies, hardy gold band of its banks in summer, were drowning in isolated dispersal, bestowing their beauty petal by petal on the swift current.

Where would Antoñilla, in that Sunday dress of hers, be able to cross it? The stones that we tried sank in the mud. The girl walked up along the bank as far as the poplar hedge to see whether she could cross there. She could not.... Then in a gallant gesture I offered her Platero.

As I addressed her, Antoñilla blushed all over, her blushes burning the freckles that modestly framed her gray eyes. Then suddenly she burst into laughter and leaned against a tree.... Finally she made up her mind. She threw her pink woolen shawl on the grass, took a running start, and, nimble as a greyhound, landed on Platero, letting her legs hang on each side, hard legs whose unsuspected ripeness was encircled by the red and white stripes of her coarse stockings.

Platero pondered a moment, and, in a sure leap, he reached the opposite bank. Then, as Antoñilla, between whose bashfulness and me the brook now lay, spurred him with her heels, he went trotting across the plain, accompanied by the gold and silver laughter of the jolting, dark-skinned girl.

There was a fragrance of lilies, of rain, of love. Like a crown of thorny roses, the line that Shakespeare gave Cleopatra to speak rounded out my thought:

"O happy horse, to bear the weight of Antony!"

"Platero!" I called out discordantly, feeling outraged and angry....

CIII
The Old Fountain

Always white above the evergreen pine grove; rose or blue, though white, in the dawn; gold or mauve, though white, at dusk; green or sky-blue, though white, at night; the old fountain, Platero, beside which you have so often seen me standing for so long, holds in itself, like a key or a tomb, all the elegy of the world; that is, the sense of real life.

In it I have seen the Parthenon, the Pyramids, all the cathedrals. Every time a mausoleum, a fountain, a portico has kept me awake with the insistence of its beauty, its image has become confused in my daydreams with the image of the old fountain.

From it I went to all other beauties. From them all I returned to it. So completely is it in its place, such a harmonious simplicity makes it immortal, color and light are so entirely its own, that one might almost take from it, bodily, the complete wealth of life. Böcklin painted it above Greece; Fray Luis translated it; Beethoven brimmed it with happy tears; Michelangelo gave it to Rodin.

The fountain is the cradle and the wedding feast; the song and the sonnet; reality and gladness; death.

There it is dead tonight, Platero, like marble flesh amid the murmuring green; dead, yet distilling for my soul the drink of my eternity.

(Translated by Eloïse Roach)

James Joyce
(1882-1941)
Clay
from *Dubliners*

The matron had given her leave to go out as soon as the women's tea was over and Maria looked forward to her evening out. The kitchen was spick and span: the cook said you could see yourself in the big copper boilers. The fire was nice and bright and one of the side-tables were four very big barmbracks. These barmbracks seemed uncut; but if you went closer you would see that they had been cut into long thick even slices and were ready to be handed round at tea. Maria had cut them herself.

Maria was a very, very small person indeed but she had a very long nose and a very long chin. She talked a little through her nose, always soothingly: *"Yes, my dear,"* and *"No, my dear."* She was always sent for when the women quarreled over their tubs and always succeeded in making peace. One day the matron had said to her:

"Maria, you are a veritable peacemaker!"

And the submatron and two of the Board ladies had heard the compliment. And Ginger Mooney was always saying what she wouldn't do to the dummy who had charge of the irons if it wasn't for Maria. Everyone was fond of Maria.

The women would have their tea at six o'clock and she would be able to get away before seven. From Ballsbridge to the Pillar, twenty minutes; from the Pillar to Drumcondra, twenty minutes; and twenty minutes to buy the things. She would be there before eight. She took out her purse with the silver clasps and read again the words *A Present from Belfast*. She was very fond of that purse because Joe had brought it to her five years before when he and Alphy had gone to Belfast on a Whit-Monday trip. In the purse were two half-crowns and some coppers. She would have five shillings clear after paying tram fare. What a nice evening they would have, all the children singing! Only she hoped Joe wouldn't come in drunk. He was so different when he took any drink.

Often he had wanted her to go and live with them; but she would have felt herself in the way (though Joe's wife was ever so nice to her) and she had become accustomed to the life of the laundry. Joe was a good fellow. She had nursed him and Alphy too; and Joe used often say:

"Mamma is mamma but Maria is my proper mother."

After the break-up at home the boys had got her that position in the *Dublin by Lamplight* laundry, and she liked it. She used to have such a bad opinion of Protestants but now she thought they were very nice people, a little quiet and serious, but still very nice people to live with. Then she had her plants in the conservatory and she liked looking after them. She had lovely ferns and wax-plants and, whenever anyone came to visit her, she always gave the visitor one or two slips from her conservatory. There was one thing she didn't like and that was the tracts on the walls; but the matron was such a nice person to deal with, so genteel.

When the cook told her everything was ready she went into the women's room and began to pull the big bell. In a few minutes the women began to come in by twos and threes, wiping their steaming hands in their petticoats and pulling down the sleeves of their blouses over their red steaming arms. They settled down before their huge mugs which the cooks and the dummy filled up with hot tea, already mixed with milk and sugar in huge tin cans. Maria superintended the distribution of the barmbrack and saw that every woman got her four slices. There was a great deal of laughing and joking during the meal. Lizzie Fleming said Maria was sure to get the ring and, though Fleming had said that for so many Hallow Eves, Maria had to laugh and say she didn't want any ring or man either; and when she laughed her gray-green eyes sparkled with disappointed shyness and the tip of her nose nearly met the tip of her chin. Then Ginger Mooney lifted up her mug of tea and proposed Maria's health while all the other women clattered with their mugs on the table, and said she was sorry she hadn't a sup of porter to drink it in. And Maria laughed again till the tip of her nose nearly met the tip of her chin and till the minute body nearly shook itself asunder because she knew that Mooney meant well though, of course, she had the notions of a common woman.

But wasn't Maria glad when the women had finished their tea and the cook and the dummy had begun to clear away the tea-things! She went into her little bedroom and, remembering that the next morning was a mass morning, changed the hand of the alarm from seven to six. Then she took off her working skirt and her house-boots and laid her best skirt out on the bed and her tiny dress-boots beside the foot of the bed. She changed her blouse too and, as she stood before the mirror, she thought of how she used to dress for mass on Sunday morning when she was a young girl; and she looked with quaint affection at the diminutive body which she had so often adorned. In spite of its years she found it a nice tidy little body.

When she got outside the streets were shining with rain and she was glad of her old brown waterproof. The tram was full and she had to sit on a little stool at the end of the car, facing all the people, with her toes barely touching the floor. She arranged in her mind all she was going to do and thought how much better it was to be independent and to have your own money in your pocket. She hoped they would have a nice evening. She was sure they would but she could not help thinking what a pity it was Alphy and Joe were not speaking. They were always falling out now but when they were boys together they used to be the best of friends: but such was life.

She got out of her tram at the Pillar and ferreted her way quickly among the crowds. She went into Downes's cake-shop but the shop was so full of people that it was a long time before she could get herself attended to. She bought a dozen of mixed penny cakes, and at last came out of the shop laden with a big bag. Then she thought what else would she buy: she wanted to buy something really nice. They would be sure to have plenty of apples and nuts. It was hard to know what to buy and all she could think of was cake. She decided to buy some plumcake but

Downes's plumcake had not enough almond icing on top of it so she went over to a shop in Henry Street. Here she was a long time in suiting herself and the stylish young lady behind the counter, who was evidently a little annoyed by her, asked her was it wedding-cake she wanted to buy. That made Maria blush and smile at the young lady; but the young lady took it all very seriously and finally cut a thick slice of plumcake, parceled it up and said:

"Two-and-four, please."

She thought she would have to stand in the Drumcondra tram because none of the young men seemed to notice her but an elderly gentleman made room for her. He was a stout gentleman and he wore a brown hard hat; he had a square red face and a grayish mustache. Maria thought he was a colonel-looking gentleman and she reflected how much more polite he was than the young men who simply stared straight before them. The gentleman began to chat with her about Hallow Eve and the rainy weather. He supposed the bag was full of good things for the little ones and said it was only right that the youngsters should enjoy themselves while they were young. Maria agreed with him and favored him with demure nods and hems. He was very nice with her, and when she was getting out at the Canal Bridge she thanked him and bowed, and he bowed to her and raised his hat and smiled agreeably; and while she was going up along the terrace, bending her tiny head under the rain, she thought how easy it was to know a gentleman even when he has a drop taken.

Everybody said: *"O, here's Maria!"* when she came to Joe's house. Joe was there, having come home from business, and all the children had their Sunday dresses on. There were two big girls in from next door and games were going on. Maria gave the bag of cakes to the eldest boy, Alphy, to divide and Mrs. Donnelly said it was good of her to bring such a big bag of cakes and made all the children say:

"Thanks, Maria."

But Maria said she had brought something special for papa and mamma, something they would be sure to like and she began to look for her plumcake. She tried Downes's bag and then in the pockets of her waterproof and then on the hallstand but nowhere could she find it. Then she asked all the children had any of them eaten it—by mistake, of course—but the children all said no and looked as if they did not like to eat cake if they were to be accused of stealing. Everybody had a solution for the mystery and Mrs. Donnelly said it was plain that Maria had left it behind her in the tram. Maria, remembering how confused the gentleman with the grayish mustache had made her, colored with shame and vexation and disappointment. At the thought of the failure of her little surprise and the two and fourpence she had thrown away for nothing she nearly cried outright.

But Joe said it didn't matter and made her sit down by the fire. He was very nice with her. He told her all that went on in his office, repeating for her a smart answer he had made to the manager. Maria did not understand why Joe laughed so much over the answer he had made but she said that the manager must have been a very overbearing person to deal with. Joe said he wasn't so bad when you knew how to take him, that he was a decent sort so long as you didn't rub him the wrong way. Mrs. Donnelly played the piano for the children and they danced and sang. Then the two next-door girls handed round the nuts. Nobody could find the nutcrackers and Joe was nearly getting cross over it and asked how did they expect Maria to crack nuts without a nutcracker. But Maria said she didn't like nuts and they weren't to bother about her. Then Joe asked would she take a bottle of stout and Mrs. Donnelly said there was port wine too in the house if she would prefer that. Maria said she would rather they didn't ask her to take anything: but Joe insisted.

So Maria let him have his way and they sat by the fire talking over old times and Maria thought she would put in a good word for Alphy. But Joe cried that God might strike him stone dead if ever he spoke a word to his brother again and Maria said she was sorry she had mentioned the matter. Mrs. Donnelly told her husband it was a great shame for him to speak that way of his own flesh and blood but Joe said Alphy was no brother of his and there was nearly being a row on the head of it. But Joe said he would not lose his temper on account of the night it was and asked his wife to open some more stout. The two next-door girls had arranged some Hallow Eve games and soon everything was merry again. Maria was delighted to see the children so merry and Joe and his wife in such good spirits. The next-door girls put some saucers on the table and then led the children up to the table, blindfold. One got the prayer-book and the other three got water; and when the next-door girls got the ring Mrs. Donnelly shook her finger at the blushing girls as much as to say: *O, I know all about it!* They insisted then on blindfolding Maria and leading her up to the table to see what she would get; and, while they were putting on the bandage, Maria laughed and laughed again till the tip of her nose nearly met the tip of her chin.

They led her up to the table amid laughing and joking and she put her hand out in the air as she was told to do. She moved her hand about here and there in the air and descended on one of the saucers. She felt a soft wet substance with her fingers and was surprised that nobody spoke or took off her bandage. There was a pause for a few seconds; and then a great deal of scuffling and whispering. Somebody said something about the garden, and at last Mrs. Donnelly said something very cross to one of the next-door girls and told her to throw it out at once: that was no play. Maria understood that it was wrong that time and so she had to do it over again: and this time she got the prayer-book.

After that Mrs. Donnelly played Miss McCloud's Reel for the children and Joe made Maria take a glass of wine. Soon they were all quite merry again and Mrs. Donnelly said Maria would enter a convent before the year was out because she got the prayer-book. Maria had never seen Joe so nice to her as he was that night, so full of pleasant talk and reminiscences. She said they were all very good to her.

At last the children grew tired and sleepy and Joe asked Maria would she not sing some little song before she went, one of the old songs. Mrs. Donnelly said: *"Do, please, Maria!"* and so Maria had to get up and stand beside the piano. Mrs. Donnelly bade the children be quiet and listen to Maria's song. Then she played the prelude and said *"Now, Maria!"* and Maria, blushing very much, began to sing in a tiny quavering voice. She sang *I Dreamt that I Dwelt*, and when she came to the second verse she sang again:

> *I dreamt that I dwelt in marble halls*
> *With vassals and serfs at my side*
> *And of all who assembled within those walls*
> *That I was the hope and the pride.*

> *I had riches too great to count, could boast*
> *Of a high ancestral name,*
> *But I also dreamt, which pleased me most,*
> *That you loved me still the same.*

But no one tried to show her her mistake; and when she had ended her song Joe was very much moved. He said that there was no time like the long ago and no music for him like poor old Balfe, whatever other people might say; and his eyes filled up so much with tears that he could not find what he was looking for and in the end he had to ask his wife to tell him where the corkscrew was.

Nikos Kazantzakis
(1883-1957)
from *The Odyssey: A Modern Sequel*

Kazantzakis, most famous of modern Greek writers, is known in America primarily for his novels, including The Last Temptation of Christ, The Greek Passion, *and especially* Zorba the Greek. *But his masterpiece is a vast epic poem,* The Odyssey: A Modern Sequel. *In this work he takes his cue from Dante's* Inferno, *Canto 26, and Tennyson's "Ulysses" (both included in the present volume) and continues the story of Ulysses or Odysseus after he has returned to his island home of Ithaca and reestablished himself as ruler. Kazantzakis gives his hero even greater breadth of character than did Homer: he makes him a man both of violence and of gentleness, a destroyer and a builder of cities, a sensualist and an ascetic, a near-savage and a philosopher. Kazantzakis takes his hero through a series of adventures that lead him to Sparta, Crete (Kazantzakis' native land), Egypt, South Africa, and the Antarctic, always in search of a self-knowledge and an enlightened concept of God that will ultimately set him free.*

Kazantzakis' translator, Kimon Friar, aptly describes the Greek poet's style. He says that the reader of the new Odyssey, *probably expecting an ordered, controlled poem in the "classical" tradition, will "fall headlong into an adjectival cataract of rich epithets, a gothic profusion of metaphors and similes, of allegorical and symbolistic characters and episodes, of fables and legends that seem to digress and never to return. He will be confronted, in short, not only with a work which is not 'classical,' but which, in fact, is anti-classical, anti-Hellenistic, and most definitely romantic and baroque."*

The excerpts that follow, from Book I, pick up Odysseus' story from that point in Homer's Book XXII at which Odysseus and his son Telemachus have disposed of the obnoxious suitors for his wife Penelope's hand.

Book I

And when in his wide courtyards Odysseus had cut down
the insolent youths, he hung on high his sated bow
and strode to the warm bath to cleanse his bloodstained body.
Two slaves prepared his bath, but when they saw their lord
they shrieked with terror, for his loins and belly steamed
and thick black blood dripped down from both his murderous palms;
their copper jugs rolled clanging on the marble tiles.
The wandering man smiled gently in his thorny beard
and with his eyebrows signed the frightened girls to go.
For hours he washed himself in the warm water, his veins
spread out like rivers in his body, his loins cooled,

HENRI MATISSE. *Bathers*, THE ROYAL MUSEUM OF FINE ARTS, J. RUMP COLLECTION, COPENHAGEN

and his great mind was in the waters cleansed and calmed.
Then softly sweet with aromatic oils he smoothed
his long coarse hair, his body hardened by black brine,
till youthfulness awoke his wintry flesh with flowers.
On golden-studded nails in fragrant shadows flashed
row upon row the robes his faithful wife had woven,
adorned with hurrying winds and gods and swift triremes,
and stretching out a sunburnt hand, he quickly chose
the one most flaming, flung it flat across his back,
and steaming still, shot back the bolt and crossed the threshold.
His slaves in shade were dazzled till the huge smoked beams
of his ancestral home flashed with reflected light,
and as she waited by the throne in pallid, speechless dread,
Penelope turned to look, and her knees shook with fright:
"That's not the man I've awaited year on year, O Gods,
this forty-footed dragon that stalks my quaking house!"
But the mind-archer quickly sensed the obscure dread
of his poor wife and to his swelling breast replied:
"O heart, she who for years has waited you to force
her bolted knees and join you in rejoicing cries,
she is that one you've longed for, battling the far seas,
the cruel gods and deep voices of your deathless mind."
He spoke, but still his heart leapt not in his wild chest,
still in his nostrils steamed the blood of newly slain;
he saw his wife still tangled in their naked forms,
and as he watched her sideways, his eyes glazed, almost
in slaughter's seething wrath he might have pierced her through.
Swiftly he passed and mutely stood on his wide sill;
the burning sun in splendor sank and filled all nooks
and every vaulted cell with rose and azure shade.
Athena's altar in the court still smoked, replete,
while in the long arcades in cool night air there swung
the new-hung slaves, their eyes and swollen tongues protruding.
His own eyes calmly gazed in the starry eyes of night,
who from the mountains with her curly flocks descended,
till all his murderous work and whir of arrows sank
within his heart in peace, distilled like mist or dream,
and his wild tiger heart in darkness licked its lips.
After the joy of bathing, his mind grew serene,
nor did he once glance backward toward the splattered blood,
nor in its cunning coils once scheme for ways to save
his dreadful head from dangers that besieged it now.
Thus in this holy hour Odysseus basked in peace,
on his ancestral threshold standing, bathed and shorn of care.

. . .

And you, in the quiet of night, you felt, O harsh sea-battler,
the tumult of the insolent crowd, the flaming torches,
and as you stretched your neck to listen, your heart flared:
"Even my isle moves under my feet like the angry seas,
and here I thought to find firm earth, to plant deep roots!
The armature of earth is rent, the hull gapes open;
the mob roars to my left, the archons crowd my right;
how heavy the cargo grows; I'll heave to, and unballast!"
He spoke, then with great strides sped to his central court,
his ears, lips, temples quivering like a slender hound,
and as he groped his body stealthily, he seized
his wide, two-bladed sword, in many slaughters steeped,
and all at once his heart grew whole again and calm.
From the high roofs his slaves discerned the seething mob,
unloosed their locks and filled their rooms with lamentation;
the queen took courage, rushed to where her husband stood
and mutely flung her arms about his ruthless knees,
but he commanded all to lock themselves in the high towers,
then bellowed for his son till all the palace rang.

. . .

Father and son unbarred the outer gate and sped
stealthily down the road, treading the earth like leopards.
It was a sweet spring night, in blue-black heavens hung
the dewy stars enwrapped in a soft down, and trembled
like early almond flowers swung by evening breezes.

. . .

Somewhere high up in heaven's gorges, in the wind's blast,
the stars like molting pure-white flowers in darkness fell;
low on the grass, like constellations, houses gleamed;
lamps stood in doorways suddenly to watch with stealth
the two night prowlers plunging headlong from the palace.
But doors were bolted quickly, clanging in the strange hush;
old women spat thrice past their breasts to ward off evil;
and black dogs thrust their tails between their thighs, and whined.
The stooped house-wrecker in his brine-black heart drank in
the uncivil poisoned welcome of his shameless people
and in his wrathful heart a lightning longing seized him
to fall on his isle ruthlessly and put to the sword
men, women, and gods, and on the flaming shores of dawn
scatter to the wide winds the ashes of his own homeland.
Such were the thoughts that whirled in his blood-lapping brain;

his son watched him askance and guessed with dread what thoughts
swirled in this ruthless stranger who so suddenly swooped,
flung into seething uproar palace, mother, and slaves,
then from his own long locks snatched off the royal crown.
Who was he? His own blood leapt not when he first saw
this grimy stranger crouched in rags, hunched on his threshold;
nor had his mother flung herself on his breast for haven
but in the women's quarter had crouched in speechless dread.
"Speak now with kindness to your loved subjects, father, repress
your rage like a great lord, consider that they too
possess a soul, are even a god, but know it not."
Thus spoke the son and looked straight in his father's eyes;
but as Odysseus neared the shore and breathed the sea,
his mind grew cool, and soon within his pulsing heart
a white gull soared from far-off seas and flapped its wings.

(Translated by Kimon Friar)

D. H. Lawrence
(1885-1930)
Piano

Softly, in the dusk, a woman is singing to me;
Taking me back down the vista of years, till I see
A child sitting under the piano, in the boom of
    the tingling strings
And pressing the small, poised feet of a mother
    who smiles as she sings.

In spite of myself, the insidious mastery of song
Betrays me back, till the heart of me weeps to be-
    long
To the old Sunday evenings at home, with winter
    outside
And hymns in the cozy parlor, the tinkling piano
    our guide.

So now it is vain for the singer to burst into clamor
With the great black piano appassionato. The
    glamor
Of childish days is upon me, my manhood is cast
Down in the flood of remembrance, I weep like a
    child for the past.

William Carlos Williams
(1883-1963)
Dawn

Ecstatic bird songs pound
the hollow vastness of the sky
with metallic clinkings—
beating color up into it
at a far edge,—beating it, beating it
with rising, triumphant ardor,—
stirring it into warmth,
quickening in it a spreading change,—
bursting wildly against it as
dividing the horizon, a heavy sun
lifts himself—is lifted—
bit by bit above the edge
of things,—runs free at last
out into the open—! lumbering
glorified in full release upward—
                         songs cease.

Elinor Wylie
(1885-1928)
Velvet Shoes

Let us walk in the white snow
  In a soundless space;
With footsteps quiet and slow,
  At a tranquil pace,
  Under veils of white lace.

I shall go shod in silk,
  And you in wool,
White as a white cow's milk,
  More beautiful
  Than the breast of a gull.

We shall walk through the still town
  In a windless peace;
We shall step upon white down,
  Upon silver fleece,
  Upon softer than these.

We shall walk in velvet shoes:
  Wherever we go
Silence will fall like dews
  On white silence below.
  We shall walk in the snow.

Castilian

Velasquez took a pliant knife
And scraped his palette clean;
He said, "I lead a dog's own life
Painting a king and queen."

He cleaned his palette with oil rags
And oakum from Seville wharves;
"I am sick of painting painted hags
And bad ambiguous dwarves.

"The sky is silver, the clouds are pearl,
Their locks are looped with rain.
I will not paint Maria's girl
For all the money in Spain."

He washed his face in water cold,
His hands in turpentine;
He squeezed out colour like coins of gold
And colour like drops of wine.

Each colour lay like a little pool
On the polished cedar wood;
Clear and pale and ivory-cool
Or dark as solitude.

He burnt the rags in the fireplace
And leaned from the window high;
He said, "I like that gentleman's face
Who wears his cap awry."

This is the gentleman, there he stands,
Castilian, sombre-caped,
With arrogant eyes, and narrow hands
Miraculously shaped.

Ezra Pound
(1885-   )

The River-Merchant's Wife: A Letter
(After Rihaku)

While my hair was still cut straight across my forehead
I played about the front gate, pulling flowers.
You came by on bamboo stilts, playing horse,
You walked about my seat, playing with blue plums.
And we went on living in the village of Chokan:
Two small people, without dislike or suspicion.

At fourteen I married My Lord you.
I never laughed, being bashful.
Lowering my head, I looked at the wall.
Called to, a thousand times, I never looked back.

At fifteen I stopped scowling,
I desired my dust to be mingled with yours
Forever and forever and forever.
Why should I climb the lookout?

At sixteen you departed,
You went into far Ku-to-yen, by the river of swirling eddies,
And you have been gone five months.
The monkeys make sorrowful noise overhead.
You dragged your feet when you went out.
By the gate now, the moss is grown, the different mosses,
Too deep to clear them away!
The leaves fall early this autumn, in wind.
The paired butterflies are already yellow with August
Over the grass in the West garden;
They hurt me. I grow older.
If you are coming down through the narrows of the river Kiang,
Please let me know beforehand,
And I will come out to meet you
      As far as Cho-fu-sa.

A Virginal

No, no! Go from me. I have left her lately.
I will not spoil my sheath with lesser brightness,
For my surrounding air has a new lightness;
Slight are her arms, yet they have bound me straitly
And left me cloaked as with a gauze of ether;

As with sweet leaves; as with a subtle clearness.
Oh, I have picked up magic in her nearness
To sheathe me half in half the things that sheathe her.

No, no! Go from me. I have still the flavor,
Soft as spring wind that's come from birchen bowers.
Green come the shoots, aye April in the branches,
As winter's wound with her sleight hand she staunches,
Hath of the trees a likeness of the savor:
As white their bark, so white this lady's hours.

Robinson Jeffers
(1887-1962)
Hurt Hawks

The broken pillar of the wing jags from the clotted shoulder,
The wing trails like a banner in defeat,
No more to use the sky forever but live with famine
And pain a few days: cat nor coyote
Will shorten the week of waiting for death, there is game without talons.

He stands under the oak-bush and waits
The lame feet of salvation; at night he remembers freedom
And flies in a dream, the dawns ruin it.
He is strong and pain is worse to the strong, incapacity is worse.
The curs of the day come and torment him
At distance, no one but death the redeemer will humble that head,
The intrepid readiness, the terrible eyes.
The wild God of the world is sometimes merciful to those
That ask mercy, not often to the arrogant.
You do not know him, you communal people, or you have forgotten him;
Intemperate and savage, the hawk remembers him;
Beautiful and wild, the hawks, and men that are dying remember him.

I'd sooner, except the penalties, kill a man than a hawk; but the great redtail
Had nothing left but unable misery
From the bone too shattered for mending, the wing that trailed under his talons when he moved.
We had fed him six weeks, I gave him freedom,
He wandered over the foreland hill and returned in the evening, asking for death,
Not like a beggar, still eyed with the old
Implacable arrogance. I gave him the lead gift in the twilight.
         What fell was relaxed,
Owl-downy, soft feminine feathers; but what
Soared: the fierce rush: the night-herons by the flooded river cried fear at its rising
Before it was quite unsheathed from reality.

Love the Wild Swan

"I hate my verses, every line, every word,
Oh pale and brittle pencils ever to try
One grass-blade's curve, or the throat of one bird
That clings to twig, ruffled against white sky.
Oh cracked and twilight mirrors ever to catch
One color, one glinting flash, of the splendor of things.
Unlucky hunter, Oh bullets of wax,
The lion beauty, the wild-swan wings, the storm of the wings."
—This wild swan of a world is no hunter's game.
Better bullets than yours would miss the white breast,
Better mirrors than yours would crack in the flame.
Does it matter whether you hate your . . . self? At least
Love your eyes that can see, your mind that can
Hear the music, the thunder of the wings. Love the wild swan.

Marianne Moore
(1887-   )
Poetry

I, too, dislike it: there are things that are important beyond all this
 fiddle.
 Reading it, however, with a perfect contempt for it, one discovers in
it, after all, a place for the genuine.
  Hands that can grasp, eyes
   that can dilate, hair that can rise
    if it must, these things are important not because a

high-sounding interpretation can be put upon them but because they
  are
 useful. When they become so derivative as to become unintelligible,
 the same thing may be said for all of us, that we do not admire what
  we cannot understand: the bat
   holding on upside down or in quest of something to

eat, elephants pushing, a wild horse taking a roll, a tireless wolf under
 a tree, the immovable critic twitching his skin like a horse that feels
   a flea, the base-
ball fan, the statistician—
  nor is it valid
   to discriminate against 'business documents and

school-books'; all these phenomena are important. One must make a
  distinction

however: when dragged into prominence by half poets, the result
  is not poetry,
nor till the poets among us can be
  'literalists of
    the imagination'—above
      insolence and triviality and can present

for inspection, imaginary gardens with real toads in them, shall we
    have
  it. In the meantime, if you demand on the one hand,
    the raw material of poetry in
      all its rawness and
        that which is on the other hand
          genuine, then you are interested in poetry.

T. S. Eliot
(1888-1965)
Journey of the Magi

"A cold coming we had of it,
Just the worst time of the year
For a journey, and such a long journey:
The ways deep and the weather sharp,
The very dead of winter."
And the camels galled, sore-footed, refractory,
Lying down in the melting snow.
There were times we regretted
The summer palaces on slopes, the terraces,
And the silken girls bringing sherbet.
Then the camel men cursing and grumbling
  And running away, and wanting their liquor and
    women,
And the night-fires going out, and the lack of shel-
    ters,
And the cities hostile and the towns unfriendly
And the villages dirty and charging high prices:
A hard time we had of it.
At the end we preferred to travel all night,
Sleeping in snatches,
With the voices singing in our ears, saying
That this was all folly.

Then at dawn we came down to temperate valley,
Wet, below the snow line, smelling of vegetation;
With a running stream and a water-mill beating the
    darkness,

And three trees on the low sky,
And an old white horse galloped away in the meadow.
Then we came to a tavern with vine-leaves over the
    lintel,
Six hands at an open door dicing for pieces of silver,
And feet kicking the empty wine-skins.
But there was no information, and so we continued
And arriving at evening, not a moment too soon
Finding the place; it was (you may say) satisfactory.

All this was a long time ago, I remember,
And I would do it again, but set down
This set down
This: were we led all that way for
Birth or Death? There was a Birth, certainly,
We had evidence and no doubt. I had seen birth and
    death,
But had thought they were different; this Birth was
Hard and bitter agony for us, like Death, our death.
We returned to our places, three Kingdoms,
But no longer at ease here, in the old dispensation,
With an alien people clutching their gods.
I should be glad of another death.

Sweeney among the Nightingales
ὤμοι πέπληγμαι καιρίαν πληγὴν ἔσω[1]

Apeneck Sweeney spreads his knees
Letting his arms hang down to laugh,
The zebra stripes along his jaw
Swelling to maculate giraffe.

The circles of the stormy moon
Slide westward toward the River Plate,
Death and the Raven drift above
And Sweeney guards the hornèd gate.

Gloomy Orion and the Dog
Are veiled; and hushed the shrunken seas;
The person in the Spanish cape
Tries to sit on Sweeney's knees

Slips and pulls the table cloth
Overturns a coffee-cup,

---

[1] Woe's me! I'm stricken a mortal blow within.—Aeschylus, *Agamemnon*, 1343.

Reorganized upon the floor
She yawns and draws a stocking up;

The silent man in mocha brown
Sprawls at the window-sill and gapes;
The waiter brings in oranges
Bananas figs and hothouse grapes;

The silent vertebrate in brown
Contracts and concentrates, withdraws;
Rachel *née* Rabinovitch
Tears at the grapes with murderous paws;

She and the lady in the cape
Are suspect, thought to be in league;
Therefore the man with heavy eyes
Declines the gambit, shows fatigue,

Leaves the room and reappears
Outside the window, leaning in,
Branches of wistaria
Circumscribe a golden grin;

The host with someone indistinct
Converses at the door apart,
The nightingales are singing near
The Convent of the Sacred Heart,

And sang within the bloody wood
When Agamemnon cried aloud,
And let their liquid siftings fall
To stain the stiff dishonored shroud.

Conrad Aiken
(1889-   )
Morning Song of Senlin

It is morning, Senlin says, and in the morning
When the light drips through the shutters like the dew,
I arise, I face the sunrise,
And do the things my fathers learned to do.
Stars in the purple dusk above the rooftops
Pale in a saffron mist and seem to die,
And I myself on a swiftly tilting planet
Stand before a glass and tie my tie.

Vine leaves tap my window,
Dew-drops sing to the garden stones,
The robin chirps in the chinaberry tree
Repeating three clear tones.

It is morning. I stand by the mirror
And tie my tie once more.
While waves far off in a pale rose twilight
Crash on a white sand shore.
I stand by a mirror and comb my hair:
How small and white my face!—
The green earth tilts through a sphere of air
And bathes in a flame of space.

There are houses hanging above the stars
And stars hung under a sea . . .
And a sun far off in a shell of silence
Dapples my walls for me . . .

It is morning, Senlin says, and in the morning
Should I not pause in the light to remember god?
Upright and firm I stand on a star unstable,
He is immense and lonely as a cloud.
I will dedicate this moment before my mirror
To him alone; for him I will comb my hair.
Accept these humble offerings, cloud of silence!
I will think of you as I descend the stair.

Vine leaves tap my window,
The snail-track shines on the stones,
Dew-drops flash from the chinaberry tree
Repeating two clear tones.

It is morning, I awake from a bed of silence,
Shining I rise from the starless waters of sleep.
The walls are about me still as in the evening,
I am the same, and the same name still I keep.

The earth revolves with me, yet makes no motion,
The stars pale silently in a coral sky.
In a whistling void I stand before my mirror,
Unconcerned, and tie my tie.

There are horses neighing on far-off hills
Tossing their long white manes,
And mountains flash in the rose-white dusk,

Their shoulders black with rains . . .
It is morning. I stand by the mirror
And surprise my soul once more;
The blue air rushes above my ceiling,
There are suns beneath my floor . . .

. . . It is morning, Senlin says, I ascend from darkness
And depart on the winds of space for I know not where,
My watch is wound, a key is in my pocket,
And the sky is darkened as I descend the stair.
There are shadows across the windows, clouds in heaven,
And a god among the stars; and I will go
Thinking of him as I might think of daybreak
And humming a tune I know . . .

Vine leaves tap at the window,
Dew-drops sing to the garden stones,
The robin chirps in the chinaberry tree
Repeating three clear tones.

At a Concert of Music

Be still, while the music rises about us; the deep enchantment
Towers, like a forest of singing leaves and birds,
Built, for an instant, by the heart's troubled beating,
Beyond all power of words.

And while you are listening, silent, I escape you;
And I run by a secret path through that dark wood
To another time, long past, and another woman,
And another mood.

Then, too, the music's cold algebra of enchantment
Wrought all about us a bird-voice-haunted grove;
Then, too, I escaped, as now, to an earlier moment,
And a brighter love.

Alas! Can I never have peace in the shining instant?
The hard bright crystal of being, in time and space?
Must I always touch, in the moment, an earlier moment,
And an earlier face?

Absolve me. I would adore you, had I the secret,
With all this music's power, for yourself alone;
I would try to answer, in the world's chaotic symphony,
Your one clear tone;

But alas, alas, being everything you are nothing—
The history of all my life is in your face;
And all I can know is an earlier, more haunted moment,
And a happier place.

Edna St. Vincent Millay
(1892-1950)
Euclid Alone Has Looked on Beauty Bare

Euclid alone has looked on Beauty bare.
Let all who prate of Beauty hold their peace,
And lay them prone upon the earth and cease
To ponder on themselves, the while they stare
At nothing, intricately drawn nowhere
In shapes of shifting lineage; let geese
Gabble and hiss, but heroes seek release
From dusty bondage into luminous air.

O blinding hour, O holy, terrible day
When first the shaft into his vision shone
Of light anatomized! Euclid alone
Has looked on Beauty bare. Fortunate they
Who, though once only and then but far away,
Have heard her massive sandal set on stone.

On Hearing a Symphony of Beethoven

Sweet sounds, oh, beautiful music, do not
    cease!
Reject me not into the world again.
With you alone is excellence and peace,
Mankind made plausible, his purpose plain.
Enchanted in your air benign and shrewd,
With limbs a-sprawl and empty faces pale,
The spiteful and the stingy and the rude
Sleep like the scullions in the fairy-tale.
This moment is the best the world can give:
The tranquil blossom on the tortured stem.
Reject me not, sweet sounds! oh, let me live,
Till Doom espy my towers and scatter them,
A city spell-bound under the aging sun.
Music my rampart, and my only eye.

Archibald MacLeish
(1892-   )
You, Andrew Marvell

And here face down beneath the sun
And here upon earth's noonward height
To feel the always coming on
The always rising of the night

To feel creep up the curving east
The earthly chill of dusk and slow
Upon those under lands the vast
And ever-climbing shadow grow

And strange at Ecbatan the trees
Take leaf by leaf the evening strange
The flooding dark about their knees
The mountains over Persia change

And now at Kermanshah the gate
Dark empty and the withered grass
And through the twilight now the late
Few travelers in the westward pass

And Baghdad darken and the bridge
Across the silent river gone

And through Arabia the edge
Of evening widen and steal on

And deepen on Palmyra's street
The wheel rut in the ruined stone
And Lebanon fade out and Crete
High through the clouds and overblown

And over Sicily the air
Still flashing with the landward gulls
And loom and slowly disappear
The sails above the shadowy hulls

And Spain go under and the shore
Of Africa and gilded sand
And evening vanish and no more
The low pale light across that land

Nor now the long light on the sea—

And here face downward in the sun
To feel how swift how secretly
The shadow of the night comes on . . .

Franz Kafka
(1883-1924)
A Hunger Artist

During these last decades the interest in professional fasting has markedly diminished. It used to pay very well to stage such great performances under one's own management, but today that is quite impossible. We live in a different world now. At one time the whole town took a lively interest in the hunger artist; from day to day of his fast the excitement mounted; everybody wanted to see him at least once a day; there were people who bought season tickets for the last few days and sat from morning till night in front of his small barred cage; even in the nighttime there were visiting hours, when the whole effect was heightened by torch flares; on fine days the cage was set out in the open air, and then it was the children's special treat to see the hunger artist; for their elders he was often just a joke that happened to be in fashion, but the children stood open-mouthed, holding each other's hands for greater security, marveling at him as he sat there pallid in black tights, with his ribs sticking out so prominently, not even on a seat but down among straw on the ground, sometimes giving a courteous nod, answering questions with a constrained smile, or perhaps stretching an arm through the bars so that one might feel how thin it was, and then again withdrawing deep into himself, paying no attention to anyone or anything, not even to the all-important striking of the clock that was the only piece of furniture in his cage, but merely staring into vacancy with half-shut eyes, now and then taking a sip from a tiny glass of water to moisten his lips.

Besides casual onlookers there were also relays of permanent watchers selected by the public, usually butchers, strangely enough, and it was their task to watch the hunger artist day and night, three of them at a time, in case he should have some secret recourse to nourishment. This was nothing but a formality, instituted to reassure the masses, for the initiates knew well enough that during his fast the artist would never in any circumstances, not even under forcible compulsion, swallow the smallest morsel of food; the honor of his profession forbade it. Not every watcher, of course, was capable of understanding this, there were often groups of night watchers who were very lax in carrying out their duties and deliberately huddled together in a retired corner to play cards with great absorption, obviously intending to give the hunger artist the chance of a little refreshment, which they supposed he could draw from some private hoard. Nothing annoyed the artist more than such watchers; they made him miserable; they made his fast seem unendurable; sometimes he mastered his feebleness sufficiently to sing during their watch for as long as he could keep going, to show them how unjust their suspicions were. But that was of little use; they only wondered at his cleverness in being able to fill his mouth even while singing. Much more to his taste were the watchers who sat close up to the bars, who were not content with the dim night lighting of the hall but focused him in the full glare of the electric pocket torch given them by the impresario. The harsh light did not trouble him at all. In any case he could never sleep properly, and he could always drowse a little, whatever the light, at any hour, even when the hall was thronged with noisy onlookers. He was quite happy at the prospect of spending a sleepless night with such watchers; he was ready to exchange jokes with them, to tell them stories out of his nomadic life, anything at all to keep them awake and demonstrate to them again that he had no eatables in his cage and that he was fasting as not one of them could fast. But his happiest moment was when the morning came and an enormous breakfast was brought them, at his expense, on which they flung themselves with the keen appetite of healthy men after a weary night of wakefulness. Of course there were people who argued that this breakfast was an unfair attempt to bribe the watchers, but that was going rather too far, and when they were invited to take on a night's vigil without a breakfast, merely for the sake of the cause, they made themselves scarce, although they stuck stubbornly to their suspicions.

Such suspicions, anyhow, were a necessary accompaniment to the profession of fasting. No one could possibly watch the hunger artist continuously, day and night, and so no one could produce first-hand evidence that the fast had really been rigorous and continuous; only the artist himself could know that; he was therefore bound to be the sole completely satisfied spectator of his own fast. Yet for other reasons he was never satisfied; it was not perhaps mere fasting that had brought him to such skeleton thinness that many people had regretfully to keep away from his exhibitions, because the sight of him was too much for them, perhaps it was dissatisfaction with himself that had worn him down. For he alone knew, what no other initiate knew, how easy it was to fast. It was the easiest thing in the world. He made no secret of this, yet people did not believe him; at the best they set him down as modest, most of them, however, thought he was out for publicity or else was some kind of cheat who found it easy to fast because he had discovered a way of making it easy, and then had the impudence to admit the fact, more or less. He had to put up with all that, and in the course of time had got used to it, but his inner dissatisfaction always rankled, and never yet, after any term of fasting—this must be granted to his credit—had he left the cage of his own free will. The longest period of fasting was fixed by his impresario at forty days, beyond that term he was not allowed to go, not even in great cities, and there was good reason for it, too. Experience had proved that for about forty days the interest of the public could be stimulated by a steadily increasing pressure of advertisement, but after that the town began to lose interest, sympathetic support began notably to fall off; there were of course local variations as between one town and another or one country and another, but as a general rule forty days marked the limit. So on the fortieth day the flower-bedecked cage was opened, enthusiastic spectators filled the hall, a military band played, two doctors entered the cage to measure the results of the fast, which were announced through a megaphone, and finally two young ladies appeared, blissful at having been selected for the honor, to help the hunger artist down the few steps leading to a small table on which was spread a carefully chosen invalid repast. And at this very moment the artist always turned stubborn. True, he would entrust his bony arms to the outstretched helping hands of the ladies bending over him, but stand up he would not. Why stop fasting at this particular moment, after forty days of it? He had held out for a long time, an illimitably long time; why stop now, when he was in his best fasting form, or rather, not yet quite in his best fasting form? Why should he be cheated of the fame he would get for fasting longer, for being not only the record hunger artist of all time, which presumably he was already, but for beating his own record by a performance beyond human imagination, since he felt that there were no limits to his capacity for fasting? His public pretended to admire him so much, why should it have so little patience with him; if he could endure fasting longer, why shouldn't the public endure it? Besides, he was tired, he was comfortable sitting in the straw, and now he was supposed to lift himself to his full height and go down to a meal the very thought of which gave him a nausea that only the presence of the ladies kept him from betraying, and even that with an effort. And he looked up into the eyes of the ladies who were apparently so friendly and in reality so cruel, and shook his head, which felt too heavy on its strengthless neck. But then there happened yet again what always happened. The impresario came forward, without a word—for the band made speech impossible—lifted his arms in the air above the artist, as if inviting Heaven to look down upon its creature here in the straw, this suffering martyr, which indeed he was, although in quite another sense; grasped him round the emaciated waist, with exaggerated caution, so that the frail condition he was in might be appreciated; and committed him to the care of the blenching ladies, not without secretly giving him a shaking so that his legs and body tottered and swayed. The artist now submitted completely; his head lolled on his breast as if it had landed there by chance; his body was hollowed out; his legs in a spasm of self-preservation clung close to each other at the knees, yet scraped on the ground as if it were not really solid ground, as if they were only trying to find solid ground; and the whole weight of his body, a featherweight after all, relapsed onto one of the ladies, who, looking round for help and panting a little—this post of honor was not at all what she had expected it to be—first stretched her neck as far as she could to keep her face at least free from contact with the artist, then finding this impossible, and her more fortunate companion not coming to her aid but merely holding extended on her own trembling hand the little bunch of knucklebones that was the artist's, to the great delight of the spectators burst into tears and had to be replaced by an attendant who had long been stationed in readiness. Then came the food, a little of which the impresario managed to get between the artist's lips, while he sat in a kind of half-fainting trance, to the accompaniment of cheerful patter designed to distract the public's attention from the artist's condition; after that, a toast was drunk to the public, supposedly prompted by a whisper from the artist in the impresario's ear; the band confirmed it with a mighty flourish, the spectators melted away, and no one had any cause to be dissatisfied with the proceedings, no one except the hunger artist himself, he only, as always.

So he lived for many years, with small regular intervals of recuperation, in visible glory, honored by the world, yet in spite of that troubled in spirit, and all the more troubled because no one would take his trouble seriously. What comfort could he possibly need? What more could he possibly wish for? And if some good-natured person, feeling sorry for him, tried to console him by pointing out that his melancholy was probably caused by fasting, it could happen, especially when he had been fasting for some time, that he reacted with an outburst of fury and to the general alarm began to shake the bars of his cage like a wild animal. Yet the impresario had a way of punishing these outbreaks which he rather enjoyed putting into operation. He would apologize publicly for the artist's behavior, which was only to be excused, he admitted, because of the irritability caused by fasting; a condition hardly to be understood by well-fed people; then by natural transition he went on to mention the artist's equally incomprehensible boast that he could fast for much longer than he was doing; he praised the high ambition, the good will, the great self-denial undoubtedly implicit in such a statement; and then quite simply countered it by bringing out photographs, which were also on sale to the public, showing the artist on the fortieth day of a fast lying in bed almost dead from exhaustion. This perversion of the truth, familiar to the artist though it was, always unnerved him afresh and proved too much for him. What was a consequence of the premature ending of his fast was here presented as the cause of it! To fight against this lack of understanding, against a whole world of non-understanding, was impossible. Time and again in good faith he stood by the bars listening to the impresario, but as soon as the photographs appeared he always let go and sank with a groan back on to his straw, and the reassured public could once more come close and gaze at him.

A few years later when the witnesses of such scenes called them to mind, they often failed to understand themselves at all. For meanwhile the aforementioned change in public interest had set in; it seemed to happen almost overnight; there may have been profound causes for it, but who was going to bother about that; at any rate the pampered hunger artist suddenly found himself deserted one fine day by the amusement seekers, who went streaming past him to other more favored attractions. For the last time the impresario hurried him over half Europe to discover whether the old interest might still survive here and there; all in vain; everywhere, as if by secret agreement, a positive revulsion from professional fasting was in evidence. Of course it could not really have sprung up so suddenly as all that, and many premonitory symptoms which had not been sufficiently remarked or suppressed during the rush and glitter of success now came retrospectively to mind, but it was now too late to take any countermeasures. Fasting would surely come into fashion again at some future date, yet that was no comfort for those living in the present. What, then, was the hunger artist to do? He had been applauded by thousands in his time and could hardly come down to showing himself in a street booth at village fairs, and as for adopting another profession, he was not only too old for that but too fanatically devoted to fasting. So he took leave of the impresario, his partner in an unparalleled career, and hired himself to a large circus; in order to spare his own feelings he avoided reading the conditions of his contract.

A large circus with its enormous traffic in replacing and recruiting men, animals and apparatus can always find a use for people at any time, even for a hunger artist, provided of course that he does not ask too much, and in this particular case anyhow it was not only the artist who was taken on but his famous and long-known name as well; indeed considering the peculiar nature of his performance, which was not impaired by advancing age, it could not be objected that here was an artist past his prime, no longer at the height of his professional skill, seeking a refuge in some quiet corner of a circus; on the contrary, the hunger artist averred that he could fast as well as ever, which was entirely credible; he even alleged that if he were allowed to fast as he liked, and this was at once promised him without more ado, he could astound the world by establishing a record never yet achieved, a statement which certainly provoked a smile among the other professionals, since it left out of account the change in public opinion, which the hunger artist in his zeal conveniently forgot.

He had not, however, actually lost his sense of the real situation and took it as a matter of course that he and his cage should be stationed, not in the middle of the ring as a main attraction, but outside, near the animal cages, on a site that was after all easily accessible. Large and gaily painted placards made a frame for the cage and announced what was to be seen inside it. When the public came thronging out in the intervals to see the animals, they could hardly avoid passing the hunger artist's cage and stopping there for a moment, perhaps they might even have stayed longer had not those pressing behind them in the narrow gangway, who did not understand why they should be held up on their way towards the excitements of the menagerie, made it impossible for anyone to stand gazing quietly for any length of time. And that was the reason why the hunger artist, who had of course been looking forward to these visiting hours as the main achievement of his life, began instead to shrink from them. At first he could hardly wait for the intervals; it was exhilarating to watch the crowds come streaming his way, until only too soon—not even the most obstinate self-deception, clung to almost consciously, could hold out against the fact—the conviction was borne in upon him that these people, most of them, to judge from their actions, again and again, without exception, were all on their way to the menagerie. And the first sight of them from the distance remained the best. For when they reached his cage he was at once deafened by the storm of shouting and abuse that arose from the two contending factions, which renewed themselves continuously, of those who wanted to stop and stare at him—he soon began to dislike them more than the others—not out of real interest but only out of obstinate self-assertiveness, and those who wanted to go straight on to the animals. When the first great rush was past, the stragglers came along, and these, whom nothing could have prevented from stopping to look at him as long as they had breath, raced past with long strides, hardly even glancing at him, in their haste to get to the menagerie in time. And all too rarely did it happen that he had a stroke of luck, when some father of a family fetched up before him with his children, pointed a finger at the hunger artist and explained at length what the phenomenon meant, telling stories of earlier years when he himself had watched similar but much more thrilling performances, and the children, still rather uncomprehending, since neither inside nor outside school had they been sufficiently prepared for this lesson—what did they care about fasting?—yet showed by the brightness of their intent eyes that new and better times might be coming. Perhaps, said the hunger artist to himself many a time, things would be a little better if his cage were set not quite so near the menagerie. That made it too easy for people to make their choice, to say nothing of what he suffered from the stench of the menagerie, the animals' restlessness by night, the carrying past of raw lumps of flesh for the beasts of prey, the roaring at feeding times, which depressed him continually. But he did not dare to lodge a complaint with the management; after all, he had the animals to thank for the troops of people who passed his cage, among whom there might always be one here and there to take an interest in him, and who could tell where they might seclude him if he called attention to his existence and thereby to the fact that, strictly speaking, he was only an impediment on the way to the menagerie.

A small impediment, to be sure, one that grew steadily less. People grew familiar with the strange idea that they could be expected, in times like these, to take an interest in a hunger artist, and with this familiarity the verdict went out against him. He might fast as much as he could, and he did so; but nothing could save him now, people passed him by. Just try to explain to anyone the art of fasting! Anyone who has no feeling for it cannot be made to understand it. The fine placards grew dirty and illegible, they were torn down; the little notice board telling the number of fast days achieved, which at first was changed carefully every day, had long stayed at the same figure, for after the first few weeks even this small task seemed pointless to the staff; and so the artist simply fasted on and on, as he had once dreamed of doing, and it was no trouble to him, just as he had always foretold, but no one counted the days, no one, not even the artist himself, knew what records he was already breaking, and his heart grew heavy. And when once in a time some leisurely passer-by stopped, made merry over the old figure on the board and spoke of swindling, that was in its way the stupidest lie ever invented by indifference and inborn malice, since it was not the hunger artist who was cheating; he was working honestly, but the world was cheating him of his reward.

Many more days went by, however, and

that too came to an end. An overseer's eye fell on the cage one day and he asked the attendants why this perfectly good stage should be left standing there unused with dirty straw inside it; nobody knew, until one man, helped out by the notice board, remembered about the hunger artist. They poked into the straw with sticks and found him in it. "Are you still fasting?" asked the overseer. "When on earth do you mean to stop?" "Forgive me, everybody," whispered the hunger artist; only the overseer, who had his ear to the bars, understood him. "Of course," said the overseer, and tapped his forehead with a finger to let the attendants know what state the man was in, "we forgive you." "I always wanted you to admire my fasting," said the hunger artist. "We do admire it," said the overseer, affably. "But you shouldn't admire it," said the hunger artist. "Well, then we don't admire it," said the overseer, "but why shouldn't we admire it?" "Because I have to fast, I can't help it," said the hunger artist. "What a fellow you are," said the overseer, "and why can't you help it?" "Because," said the hunger artist, lifting his head a little and speaking, with his lips pursed, as if for a kiss, right into the overseer's ear, so that no syllable might be lost, "because I couldn't find the food I liked. If I had found it, believe me, I should have made no fuss and stuffed myself like you or anyone else." These were his last words, but in his dimming eyes remained the firm though no longer proud persuasion that he was still continuing to fast.

"Well, clear this out now!" said the overseer, and they buried the hunger artist, straw and all. Into the cage they put a young panther. Even the most insensitive felt it refreshing to see this wild creature leaping around the cage that had so long been dreary. The panther was all right. The food he liked was brought him without hesitation by the attendants; he seemed not even to miss his freedom; his noble body, furnished almost to the bursting point with all that it needed, seemed to carry freedom around with it too; somewhere in his jaws it seemed to lurk; and the joy of life streamed with such ardent passion from his throat that for the onlookers it was not easy to stand the shock of it. But they braced themselves, crowded round the cage, and did not want ever to move away.

(Translated by Willa and Edwin Muir)

Gottfried Benn
(1886-1956)
Ah, the Distant Land

Ah, the distant land,
where the breaking heart
at rounded pebble
or reed-flats flown by dragonflies
makes murmur,
and the moon
with its cunning light
—half hoar, half white-tufted—
sets up so comfortably
the doubleground of night—

ah, the distant land,
where from the shimmer of lakes
the hills are warmed,
just think of Asolo, where Duse lies,
from Pittsburgh the "Duilio" took her home,
all the warships, even the English, had their flags at halfmast,
when it passed Gibraltar—

there soliloquies
without relationship to what's near,
self-consciousness,
early mechanisms,
totem fragments
in the gentle air—
some raisinbread in the coat—
so the days drift down,
till at the sky the bough stands,
on which the birds perch
after long flight.
    (Translated by Edgar Lohner and Cid Corman)

e. e. cummings
(1894-1962)
this is the garden

this is the garden: colours come and go,
frail azures fluttering from night's outer wing
strong silent greens serenely lingering,
absolute lights like baths of golden snow.
This is the garden: pursèd lips do blow
upon cool flutes within wide glooms, and sing
(of harps celestial to the quivering string)
invisible faces hauntingly and slow.

This is the garden. Time shall surely reap,
and on Death's blade lie many a flower curled,
in other lands where other songs be sung;
yet stand They here enraptured, as among
the slow deep trees perpetual of sleep
some silver-fingered fountain steals the world.

PABLO PICASSO: *Mandolin and Guitar*. THE SOLOMON R. GUGGENHEIM MUSEUM

Federico García Lorca
(1899-1936)
Lament for Ignacio Sanchez Mejias
1. *Cogida and Death*

At five in the afternoon.
It was exactly five in the afternoon.
A boy brought the white sheet
at five in the afternoon.
A frail of lime ready prepared
at five in the afternoon.
The rest was death, and death alone
at five in the afternoon.

The wind carried away the cottonwool
at five in the afternoon.
And the oxide scattered crystal and nickel
at five in the afternoon.
Now the dove and the leopard wrestle
at five in the afternoon.
And a thigh with a desolate horn
at five in the afternoon.
The bass-string struck up
at five in the afternoon.
Arsenic bells and smoke
at five in the afternoon.
Groups of silence in the corners
at five in the afternoon.
And the bull alone with a high heart!
At five in the afternoon.
When the sweat of snow was coming
at five in the afternoon,
when the bull ring was covered in iodine
at five in the afternoon.
death laid eggs in the wound
at five in the afternoon.
At five in the afternoon.
Exactly at five o'clock in the afternoon.

A coffin on wheels is his bed
at five in the afternoon.
Bones and flutes resound in his ears
at five in the afternoon.
Now the bull was bellowing through his forehead
at five in the afternoon.
The room was iridescent with agony

at five in the afternoon.
In the distance the gangrene now comes
at five in the afternoon.
Horn of the lily through green groins
at five in the afternoon.
The wounds were burning like suns
at five in the afternoon,
and the crowd was breaking the windows
at five in the afternoon.
At five in the afternoon.
Ah, that fatal five in the afternoon!
It was five by all the clocks!
It was five in the shade of the afternoon!

2. *The Spilled Blood*

I will not see it!

Tell the moon to come
for I do not want to see the blood
of Ignacio on the sand.

I will not see it!

The moon wide open.
Horse of still clouds,
and the grey bull ring of dreams
with willows in the barreras.

I will not see it!

Let my memory kindle!
Warn the jasmines
of such minute whiteness!

I will not see it!

The cow of the ancient world
passed her sad tongue
over a snout of blood
spilled on the sand,
and the bulls of Guisando,
partly death and partly stone,
bellowed like two centuries
sated with treading the earth.
No.
I do not want to see it!
I will not see it!

Ignacio goes up the tiers
with all his death on his shoulders.
He sought for the dawn
but the dawn was no more.
He seeks for his confident profile
and the dream bewilders him.
He sought for his beautiful body
and encountered his opened blood.
I will not see it!
I do not want to hear it spurt
each time with less strength:
that spurt that illuminates
the tiers of seats, and spills
over the corduroy and the leather
of a thirsty multitude.
Who shouts that I should come near!
Do not ask me to see it!

His eyes did not close
when he saw the horns near,
but the terrible mothers
lifted their heads.
And across the ranches,
an air of secret voices rose,
shouting to celestial bulls,
herdsmen of pale mist.
There was no prince in Seville
who could compare with him,
nor sword like his sword
nor heart so true.
Like a river of lions
was his marvellous strength,
and like a marble torso
his firm drawn moderation.
The air of Andalusian Rome
gilded his head
where his smile was a spikenard
of wit and intelligence.
What a great torero in the ring!
What a good peasant in the sierra!
How gentle with the sheaves!
How hard with the spurs!
How tender with the dew!
How dazzling in the fiesta!
How tremendous with the final
banderillas of darkness!

But now he sleeps without end.
Now the moss and the grass
open with sure fingers
the flower of his skull.
And now his blood comes out singing;
singing along marshes and meadows,
sliding on frozen horns,
faltering soulless in the mist,
stumbling over a thousand hoofs
like a long, dark, sad tongue,
to form a pool of agony
close to the starry Guadalquivir.
Oh, white wall of Spain!
Oh, black bull of sorrow!
Oh, hard blood of Ignacio!
Oh, nightingale of his veins!
No.
I will not see it!
No chalice can contain it,
no swallows can drink it,
no frost of light can cool it,
nor song nor deluge of white lilies,
no glass can cover it with silver.
No.
I will not see it!

3. *The Laid Out Body*

Stone is a forehead where dreams grieve
without curving waters and frozen cypresses.
Stone is a shoulder on which to bear Time
with trees formed of tears and ribbons and planets.

I have seen grey showers move towards the waves
raising their tender riddled arms,
to avoid being caught by the lying stone
which loosens their limbs without soaking the blood.

For stone gathers seed and clouds,
skeleton larks and wolves of penumbra:
but yields not sounds nor crystals nor fire,
only bull rings and bull rings and more bull rings without walls.

Now, Ignacio the well born lies on the stone.
All is finished. What is happening? Contemplate his face:
death has covered him with pale sulphur
and has placed on him the head of a dark minotaur.

All is finished. The rain penetrates his mouth.
The air, as if mad, leaves his sunken chest,
and Love, soaked through with tears of snow,
warms itself on the peak of the herd.

What are they saying? A stenching silence settles down.
We are here with a body laid out which fades away,
with a pure shape which had nightingales
and we see it being filled with depthless holes.

Who creases the shroud? What he says is not true!
Nobody sings here, nobody weeps in the corner,
nobody pricks the spurs, nor terrifies the serpent.
Here I want nothing else but the round eyes
to see this body without a chance of rest.

Here I want to see those men of hard voice.
Those that break horses and dominate rivers;
those men of sonorous skeleton who sing
with a mouth full of sun and flint.

Here I want to see them. Before the stone.
Before this body with broken reins.
I want to know from them the way out
for this captain strapped down by death.

I want them to show me a lament like a river
which will have sweet mists and deep shores,
to take the body of Ignacio where it loses itself
without hearing the double panting of the bulls.

Loses itself in the round bull ring of the moon
which feigns in its youth a sad quiet bull:
loses itself in the night without song of fishes
and in the white thicket of frozen smoke.

I don't want them to cover his face with handkerchiefs
that he may get used to the death he carries.
Go, Ignacio; feel not the hot bellowing.
Sleep, fly, rest: even the sea dies!

4. *Absent Soul*

The bull does not know you, nor the fig tree,
nor the horses, nor the ants in your own house.
The child and the afternoon do not know you
because you have died for ever.

The back of the stone does not know you,
nor the black satin in which you crumble.
Your silent memory does not know you
because you have died for ever.

The autumn will come with small white snails,
misty grapes and with clustered hills,
but no one will look into your eyes
because you have died for ever.

Because you have died for ever,
like all the dead of the Earth,
like all the dead who are forgotten
in a heap of lifeless dogs.

Nobody knows you. No. But I sing of you.
For posterity I sing of your profile and grace.
Of the signal maturity of your understanding.
Of your appetite for death and the taste of its mouth.
Of the sadness of your once valiant gaiety.

It will be a long time, if ever, before there is born
an Andalusian so true, so rich in adventure.
I sing of his elegance with words that groan,
and I remember a sad breeze through the olive trees.

(Translated by Stephen Spencer and J. L. Gili)

Ernest Hemingway
(1899-1961)
A Clean, Well-Lighted Place

It was late and every one had left the café except an old man who sat in the shadow the leaves of the tree made against the electric light. In the day time the street was dusty, but at night the dew settled the dust and the old man liked to sit late because he was deaf and now at night it was quiet and he felt the difference. The two waiters inside the café knew that the old man was a little drunk, and while he was a good client they knew that if he became too drunk he would leave without paying, so they kept watch on him.

"Last week he tried to commit suicide," one waiter said.
"Why?"
"He was in despair."
"What about?"
"Nothing."
"How do you know it was nothing?"
"He has plenty of money."

They sat together at a table that was close against the wall near the door of the café and looked at the terrace where the tables were all empty except where the old man sat in the shadow of the leaves of the tree that moved slightly in the wind. A girl and a soldier went by in the street. The street light shone on the brass number on his collar. The girl wore no head covering and hurried beside him.

"The guard will pick him up," one waiter said.

"What does it matter if he gets what he's after?"

"He had better get off the street now. The guard will get him. They went by five minutes ago."

The old man sitting in the shadow rapped on his saucer with his glass. The younger waiter went over to him.

"What do you want?"

The old man looked at him. "Another brandy," he said.

"You'll be drunk," the waiter said. The old man looked at him. The waiter went away.

"He'll stay all night," he said to his colleague. "I'm sleepy now. I never get into bed before three o'clock. He should have killed himself last week."

The waiter took the brandy bottle and another saucer from the counter inside the café and marched out to the old man's table. He put down the saucer and poured the glass full of brandy.

"You should have killed yourself last week," he said to the deaf man. The old man motioned with his finger. "A little more," he said. The waiter poured on into the glass so that the brandy slopped over and ran down the stem into the top saucer of the pile. "Thank you," the old man said. The waiter took the bottle back inside the café. He sat down at the table with his colleague again.

"He's drunk now," he said.

"He's drunk every night."

"What did he want to kill himself for?"

"How should I know."

"How did he do it?"

"He hung himself with a rope."

"Who cut him down?"

"His niece."

"Why did they do it?"

"Fear for his soul."

"How much money has he got?"

"He's got plenty."

"He must be eighty years old."

"Anyway I should say he was eighty."

"I wish he would go home. I never get to bed before three o'clock. What kind of hour is that to go to bed?"

"He stays up because he likes it."

"He's lonely. I'm not lonely. I have a wife waiting in bed for me."

"He had a wife once too."

"A wife would be no good to him now."

"You can't tell. He might be better with a wife."

"His niece looks after him."

"I know. You said she cut him down."

"I wouldn't want to be that old. An old man is a nasty thing."

"Not always. This old man is clean. He drinks without spilling. Even now, drunk. Look at him."

"I don't want to look at him. I wish he would go home. He has no regard for those who must work."

The old man looked from his glass across the square, then over at the waiters.

"Another brandy," he said, pointing to his glass. The waiter who was in a hurry came over.

"Finished," he said, speaking with that omission of syntax stupid people employ when talking to drunken people or foreigners. "No more tonight. Close now."

"Another," said the old man.

"No. Finished." The waiter wiped the edge of the table with a towel and shook his head.

The old man stood up, slowly counted the saucers, took a leather coin purse from his pocket and paid for the drinks, leaving half a peseta tip.

The waiter watched him go down the

street, a very old man walking unsteadily but with dignity.

"Why didn't you let him stay and drink?" the unhurried waiter asked. They were putting up the shutters. "It is not half-past two."

"I want to go home to bed."

"What is an hour?"

"More to me than to him."

"An hour is the same."

"You talk like an old man yourself. He can buy a bottle and drink at home."

"It's not the same."

"No, it is not," agreed the waiter with a wife. He did not wish to be unjust. He was only in a hurry.

"And you? You have no fear of going home before your usual hour?"

"Are you trying to insult me?"

"No, hombre, only to make a joke."

"No," the waiter who was in a hurry said, rising from pulling down the metal shutters. "I have confidence. I am all confidence."

"You have youth, confidence, and a job," the older waiter said. "You have everything."

"And what do you lack?"

"Everything but work."

"You have everything I have."

"No. I have never had confidence and I am not young."

"Come on. Stop talking nonsense and lock up."

"I am of those who like to stay late at the café," the older waiter said. "With all those who do not want to go to bed. With all those who need a light for the night."

"I want to go home and into bed."

"We are of two different kinds," the older waiter said. He was now dressed to go home. "It is not only a question of youth and confidence although those things are very beautiful. Each night I am reluctant to close up because there may be some one who needs the café."

"Hombre, there are bodegas open all night long."

"You do not understand. This is a clean and pleasant café. It is well lighted. The light is very good and also, now, there are shadows of the leaves."

"Good night," said the younger waiter.

"Good night," the other said. Turning off the electric light he continued the conversation with himself. It is the light of course but it is necessary that the place be clean and pleasant. You do not want music. Certainly you do not want music. Nor can you stand before the bar with dignity although that is all that is provided for these hours. What did he fear? It was not fear or dread. It was a nothing that he knew too well. It was all a nothing and a man was nothing too. It was only that and light was all it needed and a certain cleanness and order. Some lived in it and never felt it but he knew it all was nada y pues nada y pues nada. Our nada who art in nada, nada be thy name thy kingdom nada thy will be nada in nada as it is in nada. Give us this nada our daily nada and nada us our nada as we nada our nadas and nada us not into nada but deliver us from nada; pues nada. Hail nothing full of nothing, nothing is with thee. He smiled and stood before a bar with a shining steam pressure coffee machine.

"What's yours?" asked the barman.

"Nada."

"Otro loco mas," said the barman and turned away.

"A little cup," said the waiter.

The barman poured it for him.

"The light is very bright and pleasant but the bar is unpolished," the waiter said.

The barman looked at him but did not answer. It was too late at night for conversation.

"You want another copita?" the barman asked.

"No, thank you," said the waiter and went out. He disliked bars and bodegas. A clean, well-lighted café was a very different thing. Now, without thinking further, he would go home to his room. He would lie in the bed and finally, with daylight, he would go to sleep. After all, he said to himself, it is probably only insomnia. Many must have it.

Langston Hughes
(1902-1967)

Homesick Blues

De railroad bridge's
A sad song in de air.
De railroad bridge's
A sad song in de air.
Ever' time de trains pass
I wants to go somewhere.

I went down to de station;
Ma heart was in ma mouth.
Went down to de station;
Heart was in ma mouth.
Lookin' for a box car
To roll me to de South.

Homesick blues, Lawd,
'S a terrible thing to have.
Homesick blues is
A terrible thing to have.
To keep from cryin'
I opens ma mouth an' laughs.

Saturday Night

Play it once.
O, play it some more.
Charlie is a gambler
An' Sadie is a whore.
   A glass o' whiskey
   An' a glass o' gin:
   Strut, Mr. Charlie,
   Till de dawn comes in.
Pawn yo' gold watch
An' diamond ring.
Git a quart o' licker.
Let's shake dat thing!
   Skee-de-dad! De-dad!
   Doo-doo-doo!
   Won't be nothin' left
   When de worms git through.
   An' you's a long time
   Dead
   When you is
   Dead, too.
So beat dat drum, boy!
Shout dat song:
Shake 'em up an' shake 'em up
All night long.
   Hey! Hey!
   Ho . . . Hum!
   Do it, Mr. Charlie,
   Till de red dawn come.

W. H. Auden
(1907-   )
Musée des Beaux Arts

About suffering they were never wrong,
The Old Masters: how well they understood
Its human position; how it takes place
While someone else is eating or opening a window or
    just walking dully along;
How, when the aged are reverently, passionately waiting
For the miraculous birth, there must always be
Children who did not specially want it to happen, skating
On a pond at the edge of the wood:
They never forget
That even the dreadful martyrdom must run its course
Anyhow in a corner, some untidy spot
Where the dogs go on with their doggy life and the torturer's horse
Scratches its innocent behind on a tree.

In Brueghel's *Icarus*,[1] for instance: how everything turns away
Quite leisurely from the disaster; the plowman may
Have heard the splash, the forsaken cry,
But for him it was not an important failure; the sun shone
As it had to on the white legs disappearing into the green
Water; and the expensive delicate ship that must have seen
Something amazing, a boy falling out of the sky,
Had somewhere to get to and sailed calmly on.

Theodore Roethke
(1908-1963)
Elegy for Jane
My Student, Thrown by a Horse

I remember the neckcurls, limp and damp as tendrils;
And her quick look, a sidelong pickerel smile;
And how, once startled into talk, the light syllables leaped for her,
And she balanced in the delight of her thought,
A wren, happy, tail into the wind,
Her song trembling the twigs and small branches.
The shade sang with her;
The leaves, their whispers turned to kissing;
And the mold sang in the bleached valleys under the rose.

---

[1] Brueghel's *Icarus* hangs in the Musée des Beaux Arts—Museum of Fine Arts—in Brussels.

Oh, when she was sad, she cast herself down into such a pure depth,
Even a father could not find her:
Scraping her cheek against straw;
Stirring the clearest water.

My sparrow, you are not here,
Waiting like a fern, making a spiny shadow.
The sides of wet stones cannot console me,
Nor the moss, wound with the last light.

If only I could nudge you from this sleep,
My maimed darling, my skittery pigeon.
Over this damp grave I speak the words of my love:
I, with no rights in this matter,
Neither father nor lover.

I Knew a Woman

I knew a woman, lovely in her bones,
When small birds sighed, she would sigh back at them;
Ah, when she moved, she moved more ways than one:
The shapes a bright container can contain!
Of her choice virtues only gods should speak,
Or English poets who grew up on Greek
(I'd have them sing in chorus, cheek to cheek).

How well her wishes went! She stroked my chin,
She taught me Turn, and Counter-turn, and Stand;
She taught me Touch, that undulant white skin;
I nibbled meekly from her proffered hand;
She was the sickle; I, poor I, the rake,
Coming behind her for her pretty sake
(But what prodigious mowing we did make).

Love likes a gander, and adores a goose:
Her full lips pursed, the errant note to seize;
She played it quick, she played it light and loose;
My eyes, they dazzled at her flowing knees;
Her several parts could keep a pure repose,
Or one hip quiver with a mobile nose
(She moved in circles, and those circles moved).

Let seed be grass, and grass turn into hay:
I'm martyr to a motion not my own;
What's freedom for? To know eternity.
I swear she cast a shadow white as stone.
But who would count eternity in days?
These old bones live to learn her wanton ways:
(I measure time by how a body sways).

Stephen Spender
(1909-   )
I Think Continually of Those

I think continually of those who were truly great.
Who, from the womb, remembered the soul's history
Through corridors of light where the hours are suns,
Endless and singing. Whose lovely ambition
Was that their lips, still touched with fire,
Should tell of the spirit clothed from head to foot in song.
And who hoarded from the spring branches
The desires falling across their bodies like blossoms.

What is precious is never to forget
The delight of the blood drawn from ageless springs
Breaking through rocks in worlds before our earth;
Never to deny its pleasure in the simple morning light,
Nor its grave evening demand for love;
Never to allow gradually the traffic to smother
With noise and fog the flowering of the spirit.

Near the snow, near the sun, in the highest fields
See how these names are fêted by the waving grass,
And by the streamers of white cloud,
And whispers of wind in the listening sky;
The names of those who in their lives fought for life,
Who wore at their hearts the fire's center.
Born of the sun they traveled a short while towards the sun,
And left the vivid air signed with their honor.

Dylan Thomas
(1914-1953)
Do Not Go Gentle into That Good Night

Do not go gentle into that good night,
Old age should burn and rave at close of day;
Rage, rage against the dying of the light.

Though wise men at their end know dark is right,
Because their words had forked no lightning they
Do not go gentle into that good night.

Good men, the last wave by, crying how bright
Their frail deeds might have danced in a green bay,
Rage, rage against the dying of the light.

Wild men who caught and sang the sun in flight,
And learn, too late, they grieved it on its way,
Do not go gentle into that good night.

Grave men, near death, who see with blinding sight
Blind eyes could blaze like meteors and be gay,
Rage, rage against the dying of the light.

And you, my father, there on the sad height,
Curse, bless, me now with your fierce tears, I pray.
Do not go gentle into that good night.
Rage, rage against the dying of the light.

In My Craft or Sullen Art

In my craft or sullen art
Exercised in the still night
When only the moon rages
And the lovers lie abed
With all their griefs in their arms,
I labour by singing light
Not for ambition or bread
Or the strut and trade of charms
On the ivory stages
But for the common wages
Of their most secret heart.

Not for the proud man apart
From the raging moon I write
On these spindrift pages
Nor for the towering dead
With their nightingales and psalms
But for the lovers, their arms
Round the griefs of the ages,
Who pay no praise or wages
Nor heed my craft or art.

Fern Hill

Now as I was young and easy under the apple boughs
About the lilting house and happy as the grass was green,
    The night above the dingle starry,
      Time let me hail and climb
    Golden in the heydays of his eyes,

And honoured among wagons I was prince of the apple
          towns
And once below a time I lordly had the trees and leaves
      Trail with daisies and barley
    Down the rivers of the windfall light.

And as I was green and carefree, famous among the barns
About the happy yard and singing as the farm was home,
    In the sun that is young once only,
      Time let me play and be
    Golden in the mercy of his means,
And green and golden I was huntsman and herdsman, the
          calves
Sang to my horn, the foxes on the hills barked clear and cold,
      And the sabbath rang slowly
    In the pebbles of the holy streams.

All the sun long it was running, it was lovely, the hay
Fields high as the house, the tunes from the chimneys, it
          was air
    And playing, lovely and watery
      And fire green as grass.
    And nightly under the simple stars
As I rode to sleep the owls were bearing the farm away,
All the moon long I heard, blessed among stables, the night-
        jars
    Flying with the ricks, and the horses
      Flashing into the dark.

And then to awake, and the farm, like a wanderer white
With the dew, come back, the cock on his shoulder: it was all
    Shining, it was Adam and maiden,
      The sky gathered again
    And the sun grew round that very day.
So it must have been after the birth of the simple light
In the first, spinning place, the spellbound horses walking
      warm
    Out of the whinnying green stable
    On to the fields of praise.

And honoured among foxes and pheasants by the gay house
Under the new made clouds and happy as the heart was long,
    In the sun born over and over,
      I ran my heedless ways,
    My wishes raced through the house high hay

And nothing I cared, at my sky blue trades, that time allows
In all his tuneful turning so few and such morning songs
    Before the children green and golden
        Follow him out of grace,

Nothing I cared, in the lamb white days, that time would
        take me
Up to the swallow thronged loft by the shadow of my hand,
    In the moon that is always rising,
        Nor that riding to sleep
I should hear him fly with the high fields
And wake to the farm forever fled from the childless land.
Oh as I was young and easy in the mercy of his means,
        Time held me green and dying
    Though I sang in my chains like the sea.

Albert Camus
(1913-1960)
from *The Plague*

When next day, a few days before the date fixed for the opening of the gates, Dr. Rieux came home at noon, he was wondering if the telegram he was expecting had arrived. Though his days were no less strenuous than at the height of the epidemic, the prospect of imminent release had obliterated his fatigue. Hope had returned and with it a new zest for life. No man can live on the stretch all the time, with his energy and willpower strained to the breaking-point, and it is a joy to be braced for the struggle. If the telegram, too, that he awaited brought good news, Rieux would be able to make a fresh start. Indeed, he had a feeling that everyone in those days was making a fresh start.

He walked past the concierge's room in the hall. The new man, old Michel's successor, his face pressed to the window looking on the hall, gave him a smile. As he went up the stairs, the man's face, pale with exhaustion and privation, but smiling, hovered before his eyes.

Yes, he'd make a fresh start, once the period of "abstractions" was over, and with any luck—He was opening the door with these thoughts in his mind when he saw his mother coming down the hall to meet him. M. Tarrou, she told him, wasn't well. He had risen at the usual time, but did not feel up to going out and had returned to bed. Mme Rieux felt worried about him.

"Quite likely it's nothing serious," her son said.

Tarrou was lying on his back, his heavy head deeply indenting the pillow, the coverlet bulging above his massive chest. His head was aching and his temperature up. The symptoms weren't very definite, he told Rieux, but they might well be those of plague.

After examining him Rieux said: "No, there's nothing definite as yet."

But Tarrou also suffered from a raging thirst, and in the hallway the doctor told his mother that it might be plague.

"Oh!" she exclaimed. "Surely that's not

possible, not now!" And after a moment added: "Let's keep him here, Bernard."

Rieux pondered. "Strictly speaking, I've no right to do that," he said doubtfully. "Still, the gates will be opened quite soon. If you weren't here, I think I'd take it on myself."

"Bernard, let him stay, and let me stay too. You know, I've just had another inoculation."

The doctor pointed out that Tarrou, too, had had inoculations, though it was possible, tired as he was, he'd overlooked the last one or omitted to take the necessary precautions.

Rieux was going to the surgery as he spoke, and when he returned to the bedroom Tarrou noticed that he had a box of big ampoules containing serum.

"Ah, so it is that," he said.

"Not necessarily; but we mustn't run any risks."

Without replying Tarrou extended his arm and submitted to the prolonged injections he himself had so often administered to others.

"We'll judge better this evening." Rieux looked Tarrou in the eyes.

"But what about isolating me, Rieux?"

"It's by no means certain that you have plague."

Tarrou smiled with an effort.

"Well, it's the first time I've known you do the injection without ordering the patient off to the isolation ward."

Rieux looked away.

"You'll be better here. My mother and I will look after you."

Tarrou said nothing and the doctor, who was putting away the ampoules in the box, waited for him to speak before looking round. But still Tarrou said nothing, and finally Rieux went up to the bed. The sick man was gazing at him steadily, and though his face was drawn, the gray eyes were calm. Rieux smiled down on him.

"Now try to sleep. I'll be back soon."

As he was going out he heard Tarrou calling, and turned back. Tarrou's manner had an odd effect, as though he were at once trying to keep back what he had to say and forcing himself to say it.

"Rieux," he said at last, "you must tell me the whole truth. I count on that."

"I promise it."

Tarrou's heavy face relaxed in a brief smile.

"Thanks. I don't want to die, and I shall put up a fight. But if I lose the match, I want to make a good end of it."

Bending forward, Rieux pressed his shoulder.

"No. To become a saint, you need to live. So fight away!"

In the course of that day the weather, which after being very cold had grown slightly milder, broke in a series of violent hailstorms followed by rain. At sunset the sky cleared a little, and it was bitterly cold again. Rieux came home in the evening. His overcoat still on, he entered his friend's bedroom. Tarrou did not seem to have moved, but his set lips, drained white by fever, told of the effort he was keeping up.

"Well?" Rieux asked.

Tarrou raised his broad shoulders a little out of the bedclothes.

"Well," he said, "I'm losing the match."

The doctor bent over him. Ganglia had formed under the burning skin and there was a rumbling in his chest, like the sound of a hidden forge. The strange thing was that Tarrou showed symptoms of both varieties of plague at once.

Rieux straightened up and said the serum hadn't yet had time to take effect. An uprush of fever in his throat drowned the few words that Tarrou tried to utter.

After dinner Rieux and his mother took up their posts at the sick man's bedside. The night began with a struggle, and Rieux knew that this grim wrestling with the angel of plague was to last till dawn. In this struggle Tarrou's robust shoulders and chest were not his greatest assets; rather, the blood that had spurted under Rieux's needle and, in this blood, that something more vital than the soul, which no human skill can bring to light. The doctor's task could be only to watch his friend's struggle. As to what he was about to do, the stimulants to inject, the abscesses to stimulate—many months' repeated failures had taught him to appreciate such expedients at their true value. Indeed, the only way in which he might help was to provide opportunities for the beneficence of chance, which too often stays dormant unless roused to action. Luck was an ally he could not dispense with. For Rieux was confronted by an aspect of the plague that baffled him. Yet again it was doing all it could to confound the tactics used against it; it launched attacks in unexpected places and retreated from those where it seemed definitely lodged. Once more it was out to darken counsel.

Tarrou struggled without moving. Not once in the course of the night did he counter the enemy's attacks by restless agitation; only with all his stolid bulk, with silence, did he carry on the fight. Nor did he even try to speak, thus intimating, after his fashion, that he could no longer let his attention stray. Rieux could follow the vicissitudes of the struggle only in his friend's eyes, now open and now shut; in the eyelids, now more closely welded to the eyeball, now distended; and in his gaze fixed on some object in the room or brought back to the doctor and his mother. And each time it met the doctor's gaze, with a great effort Tarrou smiled.

At one moment there came a sound of hurrying footsteps in the street. They were in flight before a distant throbbing which gradually approached until the street was loud with the clamor of the downpour; another rain-squall was sweeping the town, mingled presently with hailstones that clattered on the sidewalk. Window awnings were flapping wildly. Rieux, whose attention had been diverted momentarily by the noises of the squall, looked again across the shadows at Tarrou's face, on which fell the light of a small bedside lamp. His mother was knitting, raising her eyes now and then from her work to gaze at the sick man. The doctor had done everything that could be done. When the squall had passed, the silence in the room grew denser, filled only by the silent turmoil of the unseen battle. His nerves overwrought by sleeplessness, the doctor fancied he could hear, on the edge of the silence, that faint eerie sibilance which had haunted his ears ever since the beginning of the epidemic. He made a sign to his mother, indicating she should go to bed. She shook her head, and her eyes grew brighter; then she examined carefully, at her needle-tips, a stitch of which she was unsure. Rieux got up, gave the sick man a drink, and sat down again.

Footsteps rang on the pavement, nearing, then receding; people were taking advantage of the lull to hurry home. For the first time the doctor realized that this night without the clang of ambulances and full of belated wayfarers, was just like a night of the past—a plague-free night. It was as if the pestilence, hounded away by cold, the street-lamps, and the crowd, had fled from the depths of the town and taken shelter in this warm room and was launching its last offensive at Tarrou's inert body. No longer did it thresh the air above the houses with its flail. But it was whistling softly in the stagnant air of the sickroom, and this it was that Rieux had been hearing since the long vigil began. And now it was for him to wait and watch until that strange sound ceased here too, and here as well the plague confessed defeat.

A little before dawn Rieux leaned toward his mother and whispered:

"You'd better have some rest now, as you'll have to relieve me at eight. Mind you take your drops before going to bed."

Mme Rieux rose, folded her knitting, and went to the bedside. Tarrou had had his eyes shut for some time. Sweat had plastered his hair on his stubborn forehead. Mme Rieux sighed, and he opened his eyes. He saw the gentle face bent over him and, athwart the surge of fever, that steadfast smile took form again. But at once the eyes closed. Left to himself, Rieux moved into the chair his mother had just left. The street was silent and no sound came from the sleeping town. The chill of daybreak was beginning to make itself felt.

The doctor dozed off, but very soon an early cart rattling down the street awaked him. Shivering a little, he looked at Tarrou and saw that a lull had come; he, too, was sleeping. The iron-shod wheels rumbled away into the distance. Darkness still was pressing on the window panes. When the doctor came beside the bed, Tarrou gazed at him with expressionless eyes, like a man still on the frontier of sleep.

"You slept, didn't you?" Rieux asked.

"Yes."

"Breathing better?"

"A bit. Does that mean anything?"

"No, Tarrou, it doesn't mean anything. You know as well as I that there's often a remission in the morning."

"Thanks." Tarrou nodded his approval. "Always tell me the exact truth."

Rieux was sitting on the side of the bed. Beside him he could feel the sick man's legs, stiff and hard as the limbs of an effigy on a tomb. Tarrou was breathing with more difficulty.

"The fever'll come back, won't it, Rieux?" he gasped.

"Yes. But at noon we shall know where we stand."

Tarrou shut his eyes; he seemed to be mustering up his strength. There was a look of utter weariness on his face. He was waiting for the fever to rise and already it was stirring somewhat in the depths of his being. When he opened his eyes, his gaze was misted. It brightened only when he saw Rieux bending over him, a tumbler in his hand.

"Drink."

Tarrou drank, then slowly lowered his head on to the pillow.

"It's a long business," he murmured.

Rieux clasped his arm, but Tarrou, whose head was averted, showed no reaction. Then suddenly, as if some inner dike had given way without warning, the fever surged back, dyeing his cheeks and forehead. Tarrou's eyes came back to the doctor, who, bending, again, gave him a look of affectionate encouragement. Tarrou tried to shape a smile, but it could not force its way through the set jaws and lips welded by dry saliva. In the rigid face only the eyes lived still, glowing with courage.

At seven Mme Rieux returned to the bedroom. The doctor went to the surgery to ring up the hospital and arrange for a substitute. He also decided to postpone his consultations; then lay down for some moments on the surgery couch. Five minutes later he went back to the bedroom. Tarrou's face was turned toward Mme Rieux, who was sitting close beside the bed, her hands folded on her lap; in the dim light of the room she seemed no more than a darker patch of shadow. Tarrou was gazing at her so intently that, putting a finger to her lips, Mme Rieux rose and switched off the bedside lamp. Behind the curtains the light was growing, and presently, when the sick man's face grew visible, Mme Rieux could see his eyes still intent on her. Bending above the bed, she smoothed out the bolster and, as she straightened up, laid her hand for a moment on his moist tangled hair. Then she heard a muffled voice, which seemed to come from very far away, murmur: "Thank you," and that all was well now. By the time she was back in her chair Tarrou had shut his eyes, and despite the sealed mouth, a faint smile seemed to hover on the wasted face.

At noon the fever reached its climax. A visceral cough racked the sick man's body and he now was spitting blood. The ganglia had ceased swelling, but they were still there, like lumps of iron embedded in the joints. Rieux decided that lancing them was impracticable. Now and then, in the intervals between bouts of fever and coughing fits, Tarrou still gazed at his friends. But soon his eyes opened less and less often and the glow that shone out from the ravaged face in the brief moments of recognition grew steadily fainter. The storm, lashing his body into convulsive movement, lit it up with ever rarer flashes, and in the heart of the tempest he was slowly drifting, derelict. And now Rieux had before him only a masklike face, inert from which the smile had gone forever. This human form, his friend's, lacerated by the spear-thrusts of the plague, consumed by searing superhuman fires, buffeted by all the raging winds of heaven, was foundering under his eyes in the dark flood of pestilence, and he could do nothing to avert the wreck. He could only stand, unavailing, on the shore, empty-handed and sick at heart, unarmed and helpless yet again under the onset of calamity. And thus, when the end came, the tears that blinded Rieux's eyes were tears of impotence; and he did not see Tarrou roll over, face to the wall, and die with a short, hollow groan as if somewhere within him an essential chord had snapped.

The next night was not one of struggle but of silence. In the tranquil death-chamber, beside the dead body now in everyday clothing—here, too, Rieux felt it brooding, that elemental peace which, when he was sitting many nights before the terrace high above the plague, had followed the brief foray at the gates. Then, already, it had brought to his mind the silence brooding over the beds in which he had let men die. There as here it was the same solemn pause, the lull that follows battle; it was the silence of defeat. But the silence now enveloping his dead friend, so dense, so much akin to the nocturnal silence of the streets and of the town was final, the last disastrous battle that ends a war and makes peace itself an ill beyond all remedy. The doctor could not tell if Tarrou had found peace, now that all was over, but for himself he had a feeling that no peace was possible to him henceforth, any more than there can be an armistice for a mother bereaved of her son or for a man who buries his friend.

The night was cold again, with frosty stars sparkling in a clear, wintry sky. And in the dimly lit room they felt the cold pressing itself to the windowpanes and heard the long, silvery suspiration of a polar night. Mme Rieux sat near the bed in her usual attitude, her right side lit up by the bedside lamp. In the center of the room, outside the little zone of light, Rieux sat, waiting. Now and then thoughts of his wife waylaid him, but he brushed them aside each time.

When the night began, the heels of passers-by had rung briskly in the frozen air.

"Have you attended to everything?" Mme Rieux had asked.

"Yes, I've telephoned."

Then they had resumed their silent vigil. From time to time Mme Rieux stole a glance at her son, and whenever he caught her doing this, he smiled. Out in the street the usual night-time sounds bridged the long silences. A good many cars were on the road again, though officially this was not yet permitted; they sped past with a long hiss of tires on the pavement, receded, and returned. Voices, distant calls, silence again, a clatter of horse hoofs, the squeal of streetcars rounding a curve, vague murmurs—then once more the quiet breathing of the night.

"Bernard?"

"Yes?"

"Not too tired?"

"No."

At that moment he knew what his mother was thinking, and that she loved him. But he knew, too, that to love someone means relatively little; or, rather, that love is never strong enough to find the words befitting it. Thus he and his mother would always love each other silently. And one day she—or he—would die, without ever, all their lives long, having gone farther than this by way of making their affection known. Thus, too, he had lived at Tarrou's side, and Tarrou had died this evening without their friendship's ever having had time to enter fully into the life of either. Tarrou had "lost the match," as he put it. But what had he, Rieux, won? No more than the experience of having known plague and remembering it, of having known friendship and remembering it, of knowing affection and being destined one day to remember it. So all a man could win in the conflict between plague and life was knowledge and memories. But Tarrou, perhaps, would have called that winning the match.

Another car passed, and Mme Rieux stirred slightly. Rieux smiled toward her. She assured him she wasn't tired and immediately added:

"You must go and have a good long rest in the mountains, over there."

"Yes, Mother."

Certainly he'd take a rest "over there." It, too, would be a pretext for memory. But if that was what it meant, winning the match—how hard it must be to live only with what one knows and what one remembers, cut off from what one hopes for! It was thus, most probably, that Tarrou had lived, and he realized the bleak sterility of a life without illusions. There can be peace without hope, and Tarrou, denying as he did the right to condemn anyone whomsoever—though he knew well that no one can help condemning and it befalls even the victim sometimes to turn executioner—Tarrou had lived a life riddled with contradictions and had never known hope's solace. Did that explain his aspiration toward saintliness, his quest of peace by service in the cause of others? Actually Rieux had no idea of the answer to that question, and it mattered little. The only picture of Tarrou he would always have would be the picture of a man who firmly gripped the steering-wheel of his car when driving, or else the picture of that stalwart body, now lying motionless. Knowing meant that: a living warmth, and a picture of death.

That, no doubt, explains Dr. Rieux's composure on receiving next morning the news of his wife's death. He was in the surgery. His mother came in, almost running, and handed him a telegram; then went back to the hall to give the telegraph-boy a tip. When she returned, her son was holding the telegram open in his hand. She looked at him, but his eyes were resolutely fixed on the window; it was flooded with the effulgence of the morning sun rising above the harbor.

"Bernard," she said gently.

The doctor turned and looked at her almost as if she were a stranger.

"The telegram?"

"Yes," he said, "that's it. A week ago."

Mme Rieux turned her face toward the window. Rieux kept silent for a while.

Then he told his mother not to cry, he'd been expecting it, but it was hard all the same. And he knew, in saying this, that this suffering was nothing new. For many months, and for the last two days, it was the selfsame suffering going on and on.

(Translated by Stuart Gilbert)

Joseph Langland
(1917-   )
Hunters in the Snow: Brueghel

Quail and rabbit hunters with tawny hounds,
Shadowless, out of late afternoon
Trudge toward the neutral evening of indeterminate form.
Done with their blood-annunciated day
Public dogs and all the passionless mongrels
Through deep snow
Trail their deliberate masters
Descending from the upper village home in lowering light.
Sooty lamps
Glow in the stone-carved kitchens.

This is the fabulous hour of shape and form
When Flemish children are gray-black-olive
And green-dark-brown
Scattered and skating figures
On the mill ice pond.

Moving in stillness
A hunched dame struggles with her bundled sticks,
Letting her evening's comfort cudgel her
While she, like jug or wheel, like a wagon cart
Walked by lazy oxen along the old snowlanes,
Creeps and crunches down the dusky street.
High in the fire-red dooryard
Half unhitched the sign of the Inn
Hangs in wind
Tipped to the pitch of the roof.
Near it anonymous parents and peasant girl,
Living like proverbs carved in the alehouse walls,
Gather the country evening into their arms
And lean to the glowing flames.

Now in the dimming distance fades
The other village; across the valley

PIETER BRUEGEL, *Hunters in the Snow*, COURTESY OF KUNSTHISORISCHEN MUSEUMS

Imperturbable Flemish cliffs and crags
Vaguely advance, close in, loom
Lost in nearness. Now
The night-black raven perched in branching boughs
Opens its early wing and slipping out
Above the gray-green valley
Weaves a net of slumber over the snow-capped homes.
And now the church, and then the walls and roofs
Of all the little houses are become
Close kin to shadow with small lantern eyes.
And now the bird of evening
With shadows streaming down from its gliding wings
Circles the neighboring hills
Of Hertogenbosch, Brabant.

Darkness stalks the hunters,
Slowly gliding down,
Falling in beating rings and soft diagonals.
Lodged in the vague vast valley the village sleeps.

Robert Lowell
(1917-   )
Falling Asleep over the Aeneid

An old man in Concord forgets to go to morning service. He falls asleep, while reading Vergil, and dreams that he is Aeneas at the funeral of Pallas, an Italian prince.

The sun is blue and scarlet on my page,
And *yuck-a, yuck-a, yuck-a, yuck-a,* rage
The yellowhammers mating. Yellow fire
Blankets the captives dancing on their pyre,
And the scorched lictor screams and drops his rod.
Trojans are singing to their drunken God,
Ares. Their helmets catch on fire. Their files
Clank by the body of my comrade—miles
Of filings! Now the scythe-wheeled chariot rolls
Before their lances long as vaulting poles,
And I stand up and heil the thousand men,
Who carry Pallas to the bird-priest. Then
The bird-priest groans, and as his birds foretold,
I greet the body, lip to lip. I hold
The sword that Dido used. It tries to speak,
A bird with Dido's sworded breast. Its beak

Clangs and ejaculates the Punic word
I hear the bird-priest chirping like a bird.
I groan a little. "Who am I, and why?"
It asks, a boy's face, though its arrow-eye
Is working from its socket. "Brother, try,
O Child of Aphrodite, try to die:
To die is life." His harlots hang his bed
With feathers of his long-tailed birds. His head
Is yawning like a person. The plumes blow;
The beard and eyebrows ruffle. Face of snow,
You are the flower that country girls have caught,
A wild bee-pillaged honey-suckle brought
To the returning bridegroom—the design
Has not yet left it, and the petals shine;
The earth, its mother, has, at last, no help:
It is itself. The broken-winded yelp
Of my Phoenician hounds, that fills the brush
With snapping twigs and flying, cannot flush
The ghost of Pallas. But I take his pall,
Stiff with its gold and purple, and recall
How Dido hugged it to her, while she toiled,
Laughing—her golden threads, a serpent coiled
In cypress. Now I lay it like a sheet;
It clinks and settles down upon his feet,
The careless yellow hair that seemed to burn
Beforehand. Left foot, right foot—as they turn,
More pyres are rising: armed horses, bronze,
And gagged Italians, who must file by ones
Across the bitter river, when my thumb
Tightens into their wind-pipes. The beaks drum;
Their headman's cow-horned death's-head bites its tongue,
And stiffens, as it eyes the hero slung
Inside his feathered hammock on the crossed
Staves of the eagles that we winged. Our cost
Is nothing to the lovers, whoring Mars
And Venus, father's lover. Now his car's
Plumage is ready, and my marshals fetch
His squire, Acoetes, white with age, to hitch
Aethon, the hero's charger, and its ears
Prick, and it steps and steps, and stately tears
Lather its teeth; and then the harlots bring
The hero's charms and baton—but the King,
Vain-glorious Turnus, carried off the rest.
"I was myself, but Ares thought it best
The way it happened." At the end of time
He sets his spear, as my descendants climb

The knees of Father Time, his beard of scalps,
His scythe, the arc of steel that crowns the Alps.
The elephants of Carthage hold those snows,
Turms of Numidian horse unsling their bows,
The flaming turkey-feathered arrows swarm
Beyond the Alps. "Pallas," I raise my arm
And shout, "Brother, eternal health. Farewell
Forever." Church is over, and its bell
Frightens the yellowhammers, as I wake
And watch the whitecaps wrinkle up the lake.
Mother's great-aunt, who died when I was eight,
Stands by our parlor sabre. "Boy, it's late.
Vergil must keep the Sabbath." Eighty years!
It all comes back. My Uncle Charles appears.
Blue-capped and bird-like. Phillips Brooks and Grant
Are frowning at his coffin, and my aunt,
Hearing his colored volunteers parade
Through Concord, laughs, and tells her English maid
To clip his yellow nostril hairs, and fold
His colors on him. . . . It is I, I hold
His sword to keep from falling, for the dust
On the stuffed birds is breathless, for the bust
Of young Augustus weighs on Vergil's shelf:
It scowls into my glasses at itself.

Lawrence Ferlinghetti
(1919-   )
Constantly Risking Absurdity
from *A Coney Island of the Mind*

    Constantly risking absurdity
                      and death
       whenever he performs
                    above the heads
                              of his audience
  the poet like an acrobat
                climbs on rime
                      to a high wire of his own making
and balancing on eyebeams
                      above a sea of faces
      paces his way
                  to the other side of day
     performing entrechats
                 and sleight-of-foot tricks

     and other high theatrics
                     and all without mistaking
   any thing
           for what it may not be

For he's the super realist
            who must perforce perceive
  taut truth
         before the taking of each stance or step
in his supposed advance
          toward that still higher perch
where Beauty stands and waits
         with gravity
               to start her death-defying leap

And he
   a little charleychaplin man
              who may or may not catch
  her fair eternal form
         spreadeagled in the empty air
  of existence

Yuvgeny Yevtushenko
(1932-   )
Babii Yar

No monument stands over Babii Yar.
A drop sheer as a crude gravestone.
I am afraid.
       Today I am as old in years
as all the Jewish people.
Now I seem to be
    a Jew.
Here I plod through ancient Egypt.
Here I perish crucified, on the cross,
and to this day I bear the scars of nails.
I seem to be
    Dreyfus.
The Philistine
      is both informer and judge.
I am behind bars.
      Beset on every side.

Hounded,
        spat on,
                slandered.
Squealing, dainty ladies in flounced Brussels lace
stick their parasols into my face.
I seem to be then
              a young boy in Byelostok.
Blood runs, spilling over the floors.
The bar-room rabble-rousers
give off a stench of vodka and onion.
A boot kicks me aside, helpless.
In vain I plead with these pogrom bullies.
While they jeer and shout,
                "Beat the Yids. Save Russia!"
some grain-marketeer beats up my mother.
O my Russian people!
           I know
                you
are international to the core.
But those with unclean hands
have often made a jingle of your purest name.
I know the goodness of my land.
How vile these antisemites—
              without a qualm
they pompously called themselves
"The Union of the Russian People"!
I seem to be
        Anne Frank
transparent
        as a branch in April.
And I love.
        And have no need of phrases.
My need
        is that we gaze into each other.
How little we can see
              or smell!
We are denied the leaves,
              we are denied the sky.
Yet we can do so much—
              tenderly
embrace each other in a dark room.
They're coming here?
              Be not afraid. Those are the booming
sounds of spring:
        spring is coming here.

Come then to me.
                    Quick, give me your lips.
Are they smashing down the door?
                                    No, it's the ice breaking . . .
The wild grasses rustle over Babii Yar.
The trees look ominous,
                        like judges.
Here all things scream silently,
                                and, baring my head,
slowly I feel myself
                    turning gray.
And I myself
            am one massive, soundless scream
above the thousand thousand buried here.
I am
    each old man
                here shot dead.
I am
    every child
            here shot dead.
Nothing in me
            shall ever forget!
The "Internationale," let it
                            thunder
when the last antisemite on earth
is buried forever.
In my blood there is no Jewish blood.
In their callous rage, all antisemites
must hate me now as a Jew.
For that reason
                I am a true Russian!

Andrey Voznesensky
(1933-   )
Parabolic Ballad

Fate-the-rocket describes a parabola
In darkness mostly, more rarely on a rainbow.

Fiery-haired Gauguin the painter lived
As a bohemian, though once he'd been a stockbroker.

To get into the royal Louvre
                    from Montmartre,
He turned a somersault through Java and Sumatra!
He rushed off, forgetting the craze for money,
The clucking wives, the stale air of Academies.
He conquered
                    the gravity of earth.
The augurs guffawed over their steins of beer:
"A straight line is shorter, a parbola steeper.
Isn't it better to copy the groves of paradise?"
And he sped away, a roaring rocket,
Though the wind ripped off coat-tails and ears.
And he landed in the Louvre, through no main entrance
But in a parabola
                    fiercely
                              smashing in the ceiling!
Bravely each man in his fashion seeks truth:
A worm crawling through a crack, man in a parabola.

There was a girl who lived in my quarter.
We attended school together, sent in our term papers.

Where had I gone?!
                    And the devil made off with me
In between the ponderous, ambiguous stars of Tbilisi!
Please forgive me this foolish parabola.
Those frail shivering shoulders in best evening black . . .
O how you rang out to me in the black Universe,
Direct and resilient—like the rod of an antenna!
But I was still flying,
                    getting my bearings to land
From your earthly, chilled, persistent summonses.
How hard it is for us to execute this parabola! . . .

Sweeping aside canons, prognoses, paragraphs,
Art, love and history speed along
A parabolic trajectory.

Galoshes sink in the Siberian spring . . .
Perhaps the straight line is shorter after all?

                    (Translated by George Reavey)

ROBERT RAUSCHENBERG: *Monogram*, NATIONALMUSEUM, STOCKHOLM

INDEX OF AUTHORS AND WORK TITLES

A

Acquainted with the Night 625
ADAMS, HENRY 203
Aeneid, from 103
AESCHYLUS 43
After a Quarrel 115
Afternoon of a Faun 584
Afton Water 438
Agamemnon, from 43
Agony and the Ecstasy, The, from 261
Ah, the Distant Land 700
AIKEN, CONRAD 692
ALIGHIERI, DANTE 163
Altar, The 283
ANACREON 36
Androcles and the Lion, from 594
Annunciation, The (Bible) 141
Antigone 46
ARCHILOCHUS 35
ARISTOTLE 87
ARNOLD, MATTHEW 492
Art 363
At a Concert of Music 692
Atalanta in Calydon, from 496
At the Grave of His Brother 115
AUDEN, W. H. 712
AUGUSTINE, SAINT 143
AURELIUS, MARCUS 127
Autumn 629
Autumn Day 628

B

Babii Yar 728
Ballad of Trees and the Master, A 513
BAUDELAIRE, CHARLES 365
BENN, GOTTFRIED 700
Beowulf, from 148
Bible, from 137

Birthday, A 494
Birth of Christ, The (Bible) 141
Bishop Orders His Tomb at Saint Praxed's Church, The 478
BLAKE, WILLIAM 436
BOCCACCIO, GIOVANNI 219
Bourgeois Gentleman, The, from 303
BROWNING, ROBERT 476
BRYANT, WILLIAM CULLEN 502
BUONARROTI, MICHELANGELO 506
BURNS, ROBERT 437
BYRON, GEORGE GORDON, LORD 444

C

CALDERÓN 284
CALLIMACHUS 41
CAMUS, ALBERT 717
Candide, from 337
Canterbury Tales, The, from 198
Canto the Fourth (Don Juan) 444
Castilian 684
Casting of the Perseus, The 239
CATHER, WILLA 639
CATULLUS 115
CELLINI, BENVENUTO 239
CERVANTES, MIGUEL DE 273
CHAUCER, GEOFFREY 198
CHEKHOV, ANTON PAVLOVICH 599
Chichibio and the Crane 226
Clay 675
Clean, Well-Lighted Place, A 708
COLERIDGE, SAMUEL TAYLOR 441
Complaint of a Lover Rebuked 247
Composed upon Westminster Bridge 439
Coney Island of the Mind, A, from 727
Confessions, from 143
Confessions, The, from 366
Constantly risking absurdity (A Coney Island of the Mind) 727
Corinna's Going a-Maying 343
Correspondences 365
Creation, The (Bible) 137
Crethis 41
CUMMINGS, E. E. 701

D

Dante 506

Darkling Thrush, The 498
Dawn 684
Days 504
Death of Socrates, The (Phaedo) 85
Decameron, from 219
Description of the Contrarious Passions in a Lover 247
DICKINSON, EMILY 511
Dies Irae 161
Divina Commedia, from 505
Divine Comedy, from 163
Divine Image (Songs of Innocence) 436
Djinns, The 360
Don Juan, from 444
DONNE, JOHN 280
Do Not Go Gentle into That Good Night 714
Don Quixote, from 273
Dover Beach 493
DRAYTON, MICHAEL 249
Dream Called Life, The (Life Is a Dream) 284
DRYDEN, JOHN 314
Du Bist wie eine Blume 359
Dubliners, from 675

E

Easter Wings 284
Elegy for Jane 712
ELIOT, T. S. 688
EMERSON, RALPH WALDO 503
EMPEDOCLES 40
Eolian Harp, The 442
ERASMUS, DESIDERIUS 216
Erl-King, The 420
Essay on Man, An, from 332
Euclid alone has looked on Beauty bare 693
Eugene Onegin, from 421
EURIPIDES 79
Evening Song 513

F

Falcon of Federigo, The 223
Falling Asleep over the Aeneid 725
Faust I, from 368
FERLINGHETTI, LAWRENCE 727
Fern Hill 715
Final Sonnet 235

First Olympian Ode 37
Flaming Heart or the Life of the Glorious Saint Teresa, The, from 271
Fog 662
Forsaken Merman, The 492
FORSTER, E. M. 665
Fortune Is a Woman (The Prince) 237
Fra Lippo Lippi 481
FRANCIS OF ASSISI, SAINT 159
FRENEAU, PHILIP 502
FROST, ROBERT 625

G

Garden of Proserpine, The 495
GAUTIER, THÉOPHILE 363
GIBBONS, ORLANDO 251
God's Grandeur 499
GOETHE, JOHANN WOLFGANG VON 368
Graveyard by the Sea, The 621
Gulliver's Travels, from 315

H

HARDY, THOMAS 498
HAWTHORNE, NATHANIEL 517
Hebrew Melodies, from 462
HEINE, HEINRICH 359
HEMINGWAY, ERNEST 708
Heraclitus 41
HERBERT, GEORGE 283
Her Golden Hair 234
HERRICK, ROBERT 343
He Sees Her Everywhere 235
Hesperus, the Bringer 36
HESSE, HERMANN 653
Holy Sonnets, from 282
HOMER 7
Homesick Blues 711
HOPKINS, GERARD MANLEY 499
HORACE 116
Housewifery 314
HOUSMAN, A. E. 501
HUGHES, LANGSTON 711
HUGO, VICTOR 360
Hunger Artist, A 694
Hunters in the Snow: Brueghel 723
Hurt Hawks 686

Hymn in Honour of Beauty, An, from   213
Hymn to God the Father, A   282
Hymn to the Night   504

I

IBSEN, HENRIK   526
If It Be Destined   233
I Knew a Woman   713
Iliad, The, from   7
Incantation, The   95
Inferno (Divine Comedy)   163
In Gratitude to Love   234
In My Craft or Sullen Art   715
Innocents Abroad, The, from   580
In the Cart   599
In Time of "The Breaking of Nations"   498
Introduction (Songs of Innocence)   436
In What Way Faith Should Be Kept by Princes (The Prince)   235
Israfel   508
I Think Continually of Those   714
It Is a Beauteous Evening, Calm and Free   441
I Wandered Lonely as a Cloud   439

J

Jazz Fantasia   663
JEFFERS, ROBINSON   686
JIMÉNEZ, JUAN RAMÓN   672
JOHN OF THE CROSS, SAINT   279
Journey of the Magi   688
JOYCE, JAMES   675

K

KAFKA, FRANZ   694
KAZANTZAKIS, NIKOS   679
KEATS, JOHN   465
Kubla Khan: or, A Vision in a Dream   441

L

La Belle Dame Sans Mercy   465
La Gioconda (The Renaissance)   251

Lake Isle of Innisfree, The 619
Lament for Ignacio Sanchez Mejias 703
LANGLAND, JOSEPH 723
LANIER, SIDNEY 513
Last Supper, The (*Bible*) 142
Last Sonnet, The 470
LAWRENCE, D. H. 683
Leave Me, O Love 248
Life Is a Dream, from 284
Little Flowers, from 159
Little Lizzy 631
London (*Songs of Experience*) 437
LONGFELLOW, HENRY WADSWORTH 504
LORCA, FEDERICO GARCÍA 703
Love Is Best 115
Love the Wild Swan 687
Loveliest of Trees, the Cherry Now 501
LOWELL, ROBERT 725
LUCRETIUS 99
Luke Havergal 620
Lycidas 285

M

MACHIAVELLI, NICCOLO 235
MACLEISH, ARCHIBALD 694
MAETERLINCK, MAURICE 605
MALLARMÉ, STÉPHANE 584
MANN, THOMAS 631
Mariana 471
MARVELL, ANDREW 301
MASEFIELD, JOHN 661
Masque of the Red Death, The 514
Master Builder, The 526
Medea, from 79
Meditation 280
Meditations, The, from 127
Meeting at Night 491
MEREZHKOVSKY, DMITRI 252
Messiah, The (*Bible*) 138
MILLAY, EDNA ST. VINCENT 693
MILTON, JOHN 285
MOLIÈRE 303
Monna Lisa Gioconda (*The Romance of Leonardo da Vinci*) 252
Mont-Saint-Michel and Chartres, from 203
MOORE, MARIANNE 687
Morning Song of Senlin 690
Mother, I Cannot Mind My Wheel 36

Musée des Beaux Arts 712
Mutability 464
My Heart Leaps Up When I Behold 439
My Last Duchess 476

N

Nature of Tragedy, The (On Tragedy) 87
Nocturne in a Deserted Brickyard 662
Now Sleeps the Crimson Petal (The Princess) 475

O

Obscure Night of the Soul, The 279
Ode on a Grecian Urn 469
Ode to a Nightingale 466
Ode to Aphrodite 35
Ode to the West Wind 463
Odyssey: A Modern Sequel, The, from 679
Odyssey, The, from 24
Of the Nature of Things, from 99
On Growing Old 661
On Hearing a Symphony of Beethoven 693
On Hearing of Laura's Death 234
On Lesbia 115
On Losing His Shield 35
Onset, The 626
On Tragedy, from 87
Orpheus and Eurydice 116
OVID 116
Oxen, The 498
Ozymandias 465

P

Panther, The 629
Parabolic Ballad 730
Paradise Lost, from 288
PATER, WALTER 251
Patient Griselda, The 227
Paul's Case 639
Pelléas and Mélisande, from 605
Peter Quince at the Clavier 664
PETRARCH 233
Phaedo, from 85
Piano 683

Picture of Dorian Gray, The, from 590
Pied Beauty 500
PINDAR 37
Plague, The, from 717
Plague of 1348, The 219
Platero and I, from 672
PLATO 85
PLINY THE YOUNGER 121
POE, EDGAR ALLAN 506, 514
Poetry 687
Poison Tree, A (Songs of Experience) 437
POPE, ALEXANDER 332
POUND, EZRA 685
Powers and Pleasures of Folly, The (The Praise of Folly) 216
Praise of Folly, The, from 216
Preface (The Picture of Dorian Gray) 590
Prince, The, from 235
Prioress's Tale, The (The Canterbury Tales) 198
Psalms (Bible) 139
PUSHKIN, ALEXANDER 421

R

Red, Red Rose, A 439
Rembrandt, from 344
Renaissance, The, from 251
Rhodora, The 503
RILKE, RAINER MARIA 628
River-Merchant's Wife: A Letter, The 685
Road from Colonus, The 665
ROBINSON, EDWIN ARLINGTON 620
ROETHKE, THEODORE 712
Romance of Leonardo da Vinci, The, from 252
Rome (The Innocents Abroad) 580
RONSARD, PIERRE DE 248
ROSSETTI, CHRISTINA 494
ROSSETTI, DANTE GABRIEL 494
ROUSSEAU, JEAN-JACQUES 366
RUSKIN, JOHN 201

S

Saint Mark's (The Stones of Venice) 201
SANDBURG, CARL 662
SAPPHO 35
Saturday Night 711

SCHMITT, GLADYS   344
Sculpturing of the David, The (The Agony and the Ecstasy)   261
SHAKESPEARE, WILLIAM   249
SHAW, GEORGE BERNARD   590
Shaw on Music   590
SHELLEY, PERCY BYSSHE   463
She Walks in Beauty (Hebrew Melodies)   462
SIDNEY, SIR PHILIP   248
Silent Noon   494
Silver Swan, The   251
Since There's No Help   249
Singers, The   425
Sir Gawain and the Green Knight, from   187
Sois Sage O Ma Douleur   365
Song for St. Cecilia's Day, A   314
Song (Go and catch a falling star)   281
Song (Sweetest love, I do not go)   281
Song of Autumn   588
Song of Roland, The, from   151
Songs from the Princess   474
Songs of Experience, from   437
Songs of Innocence, from   436
Sonnet 8 Music to Hear   249
Sonnet 55 Not Marble Nor the Gilded Monuments   250
Sonnet 18 Shall I Compare Thee   249
Sonnet 73 That Time of Year   250
Sonnet 30 When to the Sessions   250
Sonnet 15 Ye Tradeful Merchants   248
SOPHOCLES   46
SPENDER, STEPHEN   714
SPENSER, EDMUND   213, 248
Splendor Falls on Castle Walls, The (The Princess)   474
Spring and Fall   500
Stanzas for Music   462
STEVENS, WALLACE   664
STONE, IRVING   261
Stones of Venice, The, from   201
SURREY, HENRY HOWARD, EARL OF   247
Sweeney among the Nightingales   689
Sweet and Low (The Princess)   474
SWIFT, JONATHAN   315
SWINBURNE, ALGERNON CHARLES   495
Syndics, The (Rembrandt)   344

T

TAYLOR, EDWARD   314
Tears, Idle Tears (The Princess)   475

Te Deum 157
TENNYSON, ALFRED, LORD 471
TERESA OF AVILA, SAINT 271
THEOCRITUS 95
There Is No Frigate like a Book 513
There's a Certain Slant of Light 511
There Was a Child Went Forth 509
this is the garden 701
THOMAS, DYLAN 714
THOMAS OF CELANO 161
Thou Hast Wounded Me, Lord 588
Three Deaths: A Tale 572
To an Athlete Dying Young 501
To a Waterfowl 502
To Daffodils 343
To Hear an Oriole Sing 511
To Helen 506
To His Coy Mistress 301
TOLSTOY, LEO 572
To Marie 248
To Postumus 116
Tree at My Window 626
Tuft of Flowers, The 627
TURGENEV, IVAN 425
Tuscan Villa, The 121
TWAIN, MARK 580
Twofold Truth, A 40
Two Grenadiers, The 359

U

Ulalume 506
Ulysses 472

V

VALÉRY, PAUL 621
Velvet Shoes 684
VERLAINE, PAUL 588
Villas of Pliny the Younger, The, from 121
VIRGIL 103
Virginal, A 685
Virgin of Chartres, The (Mont-Saint-Michel and Chartres) 203
VOLTAIRE 337
Voyage to Brobdingnag, A (Gulliver's Travels) 315
VOZNESENSKY, ANDREY 730

W

Wedding Knell, The 517
When I Heard the Learn'd Astronomer 508
When I Reflect 233
When the Hounds of Spring 496
When You Are Old 620
WHITMAN, WALT 508
Who Is Sylvia 251
WILDE, OSCAR 590
Wild Honeysuckle, The 502
Wild Swans at Coole, The 619
WILLIAMS, WILLIAM CARLOS 684
Windhover, The 499
Wind Song 663
With How Sad Steps 248
Within and Without 653
WORDSWORTH, WILLIAM 439
Wounded Cupid, The 36
WYATT, SIR THOMAS 247
WYLIE, ELINOR 684

Y

YEATS, WILLIAM BUTLER 619
Ye Flowery Banks 437
YEVTUSHENKO, YUVGENY 728
You, Andrew Marvell 694